INEQUALITY IN LATIN AMERICA
Breaking with History?

WORLD BANK LATIN AMERICAN
AND CARIBBEAN STUDIES

INEQUALITY
IN LATIN AMERICA

Breaking with History?

David de Ferranti
Guillermo E. Perry
Francisco H. G. Ferreira
Michael Walton

THE WORLD BANK
Washington, D.C.

Library of Congress Cataloging-in-Publication Data

Inequality in Latin America : breaking with history? / David de Ferranti
    ... [et al.].
        p. cm.—(World Bank Latin American and Caribbean studies. Viewpoints)
    Includes bibliographical references and index.
    ISBN 0-8213-5665-8
    1. Equality—Latin America. 2. Equality—Caribbean Area. 3. Latin America—Social
    conditions—1982- 4. Caribbean Area—Social conditions—1945- 5. Latin
America—Economic conditions—1982- 6. Caribbean Area—Economic conditions—1945- I.
    De Ferranti, David M. II. Series.

HN110.5.Z9S646 2004
305'.09729—dc22   2003063203

Contents

Boxes

Chapter 7

Chapter 8

Chapter 9

Figures

Summary

Chapter 1

Chapter 2

Chapter 3

Chapter 9

Tables

Summary

Chapter 1

Chapter 2

Chapter 3

Chapter 4

Acknowledgments

INEQUALITY IN LATIN AMERICA: BREAKING WITH HISTORY? IS THE PRODUCT OF A COLLABORATIVE EFFORT that brought together a diverse team of professionals from both within and outside the World Bank. The report was prepared under the guidance of David de Ferranti and Guillermo Perry by a team led by Francisco H. G. Ferreira and Michael Walton. Team members included David Coady (Institute for Food Policy Research), Wendy Cunningham (World Bank), Leonardo Gasparini (Universidad Nacional de la Plata, Argentina), Joyce Jacobsen (Wesleyan University), Yasuhiko Matsuda (World Bank), James Robinson (University of California, Berkeley), Kenneth Sokoloff (University of California, Los Angeles) and Quentin Wodon (World Bank).

The preparation of the report benefited greatly from two meetings with the authors and a group of advisors, in Rio de Janeiro in August 2002 and in Washington DC in April 2003. The group of advisors comprised Barry Ames, Richard Bird, François Bourguignon, John DiNardo, Patrick Heller, James Mahoney, Lant Pritchett, Sergio Schmuckler, Judith Tendler, and André Urani. The report was also significantly influenced by commentary of the three principal reviewers: Martin Ravallion, Ana Revenga, and Michael Woolcock.

Initial findings of the work were presented at two meetings of the Network on Inequality and Poverty, a group that operates under the auspices of the Latin American and Caribbean Economics Association (LACEA), with the institutional involvement of the Inter-American Development Bank and the World Bank. These meetings, both held in June 2003, were organized, respectively, by Máximo Rossi in Costa Rica, on behalf of the whole network, and by Sebastián Galiani and Leonardo Gasparini in Argentina, on behalf of the Argentine Chapter of the Network. A preliminary conference edition of the report was released to the public in Mexico City in October 2003 and then discussed at a combined meeting of the Network on Inequality and Poverty and the World Bank's Annual Conference on Development, in Puebla, Mexico, as part of the annual LACEA meeting. Valuable commentary was provided by José Pablo Arellano, Raquel Fernández, Sebastián Galiani, Santiago Levy, Ricardo López-Murphy, Nora Lustig, José Antonio Ocampo, Ricardo Paes de Barros, and Miguel Székely, as well as by meeting participants.

While the writing of this report has been a collective effort, the principal authors for the various chapters are as follows:

- Summary: David de Ferranti, Francisco Ferreira, Guillermo Perry, and Michael Walton
- Chapter 1: Francisco Ferreira, Guillermo Perry, and Michael Walton
- Chapter 2: Leonardo Gasparini
- Chapter 3: Wendy Cunningham and Joyce Jacobsen
- Chapter 4: Kenneth Sokoloff and James Robinson
- Chapter 5: Yasuhiko Matsuda and Michael Walton
- Chapter 6: Francisco Ferreira
- Chapters 7 and 8: Michael Walton
- Chapter 9: David Coady, Francisco Ferreira, Guillermo Perry, and Quentin Wodon

This report would never have been completed without the excellent assistance of a number of individuals: Anna Crespo for chapters 1 and 3; Phillippe Leite for chapters 1 and 6; Jorge Balat, Matías Busso, Cecilia Calderón, Martín Cicowiez, Nicolás Epele, Federico Gutiérrez, Marcela Massini, Augusto Mercadier, Alejandro Támola, and Julieta Trías for chapter 2; Lucas Siga for chapter 3; Rodrigo Suescun and Mariana Fajardo for chapter 9; Mayuresh Kshetramade for chapter 6; Mary Fran Malone for chapter 5; Marcela Rubio Sánchez for chapters 7 and 8; and Kihoon Lee for assistance in provision of data sets.

The authors would also like to thank the many dedicated professionals within the World Bank who provided specific contributions or commentary. These included, in particular, Ana-María Arriagada, José María Caballero, Antonio Estache, Marianne Fay, Ariel Fiszbein, Vivien Foster, Daniel Kaufmann, Peter Lanjouw, Daniel Lederman, William Maloney, Andrew Mason, Ernesto May, Harry Patrinos, John Redwood, Luis Servén, and Mauricio Santamaría.

Finally, a number of background papers and notes were commissioned especially for this study. These papers are by Ângela Albernaz, Barry Ames, Richard Bird, Wendy Cunningham and Maurico Santamaría, Ariel Fiszbein and Sebastian Galiani, Marina Halac and Sergio Schmuckler, Patrick Heller and James Mahoney, Alberto Maldonado, Valéria Pero, and Judith Tendler. A preliminary version of this report and background papers can be downloaded at http://www.worldbank.org/laceconomist.

Summary

INEQUALITY IN LATIN AMERICA IS EXTENSIVE: THE COUNTRY IN THE REGION WITH THE LEAST income inequality is still more unequal than any Organization for Economic Cooperation and Development (OECD) or Eastern European country. Latin American inequality is also pervasive, characterizing every aspect of life, including access to education, health and public services; access to land and other assets; the functioning of credit and formal labor markets; and attainment of political voice and influence. Inequality is also resilient; in its modern form, high inequality is rooted in exclusionary institutions that have been perpetuated ever since colonial times and that have survived different political and economic regimes, from interventionist and import substitution strategies to more market-oriented policies. Significant racial and ethnic differences also continue to persist even today.

High inequality has major costs. It increases poverty and reduces the impact of economic development on poverty reduction. It is probably bad for aggregate economic growth, especially when associated with unequal access to credit and education, and with social tensions. A large majority of Latin Americans judge current levels of income inequality to be unfair. Inequality of opportunities is especially unacceptable. For all these reasons, Latin American countries must make an effort to break with their long history of inequality.

Can this be done? This report suggests that the answer is yes, if there is decisive action to tackle the range of mechanisms that reproduce inequality. First and foremost, there is a need to reduce inequality in access to productive assets. Equalizing access to quality education is central because of its influence on economic opportunities, social status, and political influence. However, more equal education will take decades to subsequently transform other inequalities. Also important is the achievement of more equal access to land, property rights, and other assets such as infrastructure.

Second, there is a need to make market institutions work better for everyone through deeper financial and product market, and more inclusive labor institutions that balance flexibility with protection for workers. In the macroeconomic domain, a concern with distribution reinforces the case for sound management, since crises tend to be highly regressive. Attaining this will require building institutions and rules to reduce the risk of crisis, and to make the distribution of losses less unequal when crises do occur.

Third, the state needs to strengthen its capacity to redistribute. For most countries in the region this will imply increasing their (low) tax efforts, and, over the longer term, making taxes more progressive through effective collection of personal income and property taxes. Increased taxes only make sense if they are used effectively. Despite some progress and the increased progressivity of social spending in the 1990s, much public expenditure remains highly regressive (for example subsidies to tertiary education and the "truncated" welfare state, especially with respect to pension payments). Redistributive transfers have a role to play precisely because asset-based strategies take time to implement. A particular area of promise is conditional cash transfers, which can have a significant impact on income redistribution today, while at the same time extending social protection against shocks to the poor and encouraging investment in the human capital of the poor. These and other instruments can provide the basis for a truly progressive social protection system in Latin America.

Given the deep historical, institutional roots of high inequality, progress on all these fronts will require decisive social action and political leadership. This implies making progress toward more inclusive political institutions, since inequalities in influence lie behind many of the mechanisms that reproduce overall inequality.

This is no easy task. But it may be more possible to accomplish today than in the past, given increased social demands for deeper democracies, more equal sharing of political influence, broader access to education and health, and greater recognition for Afro-descendents and indigenous groups. These demands are palpable across the region, and are partly a consequence of the globalization of information, economic opportunities, and human rights. There are promising examples of change underway, notably at subnational levels, with new alliances between progressive elites, public officials, middle classes, and the poor currently spurring the establishment of more inclusive and efficient institutions.

These are the main messages of this report, on which the rest of this summary section elaborates. Readers interested in the evidence and analysis that underpin these conclusions will have to immerse themselves in the entire, extensive text. We hope they will find it worth the effort.

Latin America suffers from extreme inequality—on many dimensions

Inequality is a pervasive feature of Latin American[1] societies in terms of differences in income, access to services, power and influence and, in many countries, treatment by police and justice systems.

According to household surveys, the richest 10 percent of individuals receive between 40 and 47 percent of total income in most Latin American societies, while the poorest 20 percent receive only 2–4 percent (see table 1). These differences are substantially higher than in OECD countries, Eastern Europe, and most of Asia. Moreover, the most distinctive attribute of Latin American income inequality is the unusually large concentration of income at the very top of the distribution. (Only some countries in Africa and the successor states of the former Soviet Union have comparable inequalities.) By way of comparison, the richest 10 percent in the United States receive 31 percent of total income, and in Italy they receive 27 percent. Even the most equal countries in Latin America (Costa Rica and Uruguay) have significantly higher levels of income inequality. Inequality in consumption—where it can be adequately measured—also appears to be higher in Latin American countries, although differences with other regions seem not to be as sharp as in the case of inequality of incomes.[2]

Inequalities with respect to education, health, water, sanitation, electricity, and telephony are also typically large and correlated with differences in income. For example, differences in average years of education between the top and bottom income quintiles ranged between 5 and 9 years for 31–40 and 51–60 year-olds across the region (figure 1). Standard surveys do not provide comparable material on inequalities of power or influence within a society, but a wealth of political, historical, and sociological information attests to both their salience and association with wealth.

TABLE 1

Indicators of inequality for selected Latin American countries, the United States, and Italy

	Gini coefficient	Share of top 10 percent in total income (percent)	Share of bottom 20 percent in total income (percent)	Ratio of incomes of 10th to 1st decile
Brazil (2001)	59.0	47.2	2.6	54.4
Guatemala (2000)	58.3	46.8	2.4	63.3
Colombia (1999)	57.6	46.5	2.7	57.8
Chile (2000)	57.1	47.0	3.4	40.6
Mexico (2000)	54.6	43.1	3.1	45.0
Argentina (2000)	52.2	38.9	3.1	39.1
Jamaica (1999)	52.0	40.1	3.4	36.5
Dominican Republic (1997)	49.7	38.6	4.0	28.4
Costa Rica (2000)	46.5	34.8	4.2	25.1
Uruguay (2000)	44.6	33.5	4.8	18.9
United States (1997)	40.8	30.5	5.2	16.9
Italy (1998)	36.0	27.4	6.0	14.4

Source: Statistical appendix and SDStats database.

FIGURE 1

Difference in average years of education between top and bottom quintiles, for people 31–40 and 51–60, in 2000

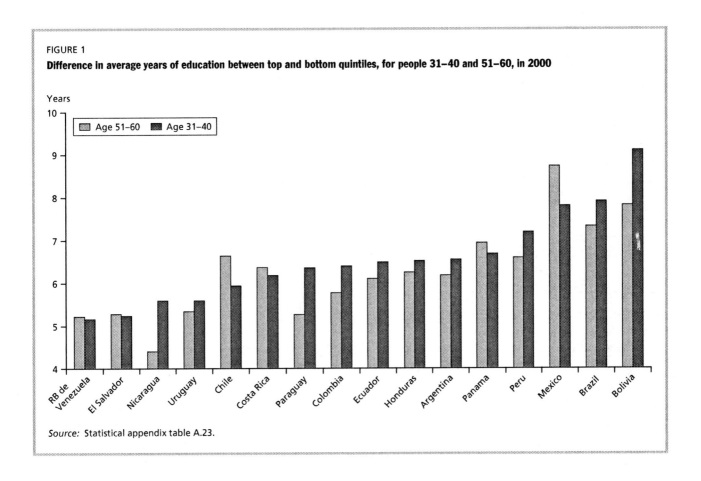

Source: Statistical appendix table A.23.

A further divide that cuts across all these dimensions is that of race and ethnicity, that affects all societies with a significant indigenous or Afro-descended population, as discussed further below.

Is inequality improving? During the last decade, diverse patterns have emerged with respect to income differences, with more countries experiencing a worsening than an improving trend. On balance, relatively equal countries experienced some worsening, with a dramatic deterioration for Argentina both before and during its economic crisis. At the other end of the scale, Brazil, historically the most unequal country in the region, experienced a modest but significant decline in income inequality (see figure 2). In previous decades, there was a trend toward reduced inequality in the 1970s and a more pronounced trend toward rising inequality during the crisis-ridden 1980s. However, the more striking fact for the long term is the resilience of high inequality in the face of diverse economic and political regimes.

With respect to services and human investment, the general tendency in the past decade was more positive. Most of the region experienced at least some equalization in terms of access to services and basic education status. However, in

one key area, that of access to college education, the dominant pattern was of widening differences between the rich and the poor as attendance rose faster for members of households at the top of the distribution. This is important for future income dynamics, in light of the high and rising premium placed on tertiary education in the labor market. The wave of democratization in the 1980s brought, at a basic level, some equalization in citizenship, and potentially in differences in power. However, inequalities in influence and in the application of the rule of law remained large in most of the region, even under democratic auspices.

High inequality hurts both poverty reduction and development

Most people would agree that some degree of inequality in a society is necessary to provide incentives for work and investment. However, the levels of inequality prevailing in Latin America are clearly costly for well-being. There are three broad reasons for concern. First, higher inequality, whether in income or other dimensions of well-being, means more poverty at any given point in time. High inequality also implies a lower dynamic impact on poverty

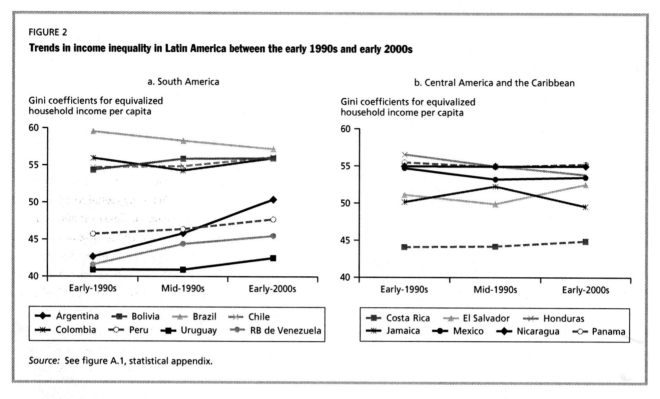

FIGURE 2

Trends in income inequality in Latin America between the early 1990s and early 2000s

a. South America

Gini coefficients for equivalized
household income per capita

b. Central America and the Caribbean

Gini coefficients for equivalized
household income per capita

Legend (South America): Argentina, Bolivia, Brazil, Chile, Colombia, Peru, Uruguay, RB de Venezuela

Legend (Central America and the Caribbean): Costa Rica, El Salvador, Honduras, Jamaica, Mexico, Nicaragua, Panama

Source: See figure A.1, statistical appendix.

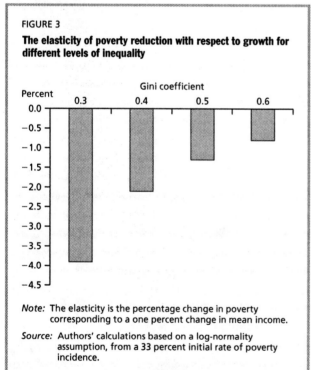

FIGURE 3

The elasticity of poverty reduction with respect to growth for different levels of inequality

Note: The elasticity is the percentage change in poverty corresponding to a one percent change in mean income.

Source: Authors' calculations based on a log-normality assumption, from a 33 percent initial rate of poverty incidence.

from development, unless significant redistribution takes place (figure 3 provides a numerical illustration of the relation between economic growth and income poverty reduction). For example, Brazil could reduce poverty to half in ten years with 3 percent growth and an improvement of 5 percent in the Gini coefficient (the most common measure of income inequality); it would take the country 30 years to achieve the same objective with 3 percent growth and no improvements in income distribution.

Second, inequality can slow the overall development process. In contrast to some earlier strands of development thought, most economists (and other social scientists) now see high inequality as a potential drag on development for a variety of reasons: unequal access to credit implies missing highly profitable investment opportunities for the economy as a whole; unequal educational opportunities limit the potential contribution to society of some of the most talented individuals; distributional conflicts are heightened, especially in the context of managing adverse shocks; crime and violence increase; and, under some conditions, the institutional underpinnings for growth become weaker, for example with respect to property rights.

Third, according to surveys from Latinobarómetro, the public opinion survey organization, high inequality is widely disliked: in almost all countries surveyed, some 80–90 percent of citizens consider prevailing levels of income inequality to be unfair or very unfair.

Inequality of opportunities is especially unacceptable in ethical terms—implying that individuals at birth face totally different life options—and is particularly harmful for the overall growth potential of societies. Although it is difficult to disentangle the effect of inequality of opportunities from the effect of other factors (such as differences in preferences and efforts) on the inequality of outcomes, some attempts indicate that they do indeed account for a significant fraction of inequality of income in countries such as Brazil (see chapter 1).

Latin America's inequality has deep historical roots and pervades contemporary institutions

The genesis of current structures of inequality lies in Latin America's colonial past, and in particular in the interactions between European colonists and subordinate populations. During the early colonial period, influences on inequality were reinforced by economic conditions and power differences. European settlement was initially concentrated in areas where natural resources—especially mining and sugar production—could be exploited with the use of unskilled labor. Labor was provided either by subjugated indigenous populations or imported African slaves. The colonists developed institutions—notably those related to labor management (including slavery), land use, and political control—that consolidated and perpetuated their influence and wealth. In the post-independence period, domestic elites continued to shape institutions and policies to maintain their privileged positions, for example in the areas of restricted suffrage, access to education, and land policy.

In those parts of the Americas where there was no economic potential for combining subordinate labor with valuable natural resources, the evolution of inequality was different. This is most clearly the case in North America, where immigrant smallholders (who were able to pursue settlement with lower mortality rates) successfully resisted attempts to impose authoritarian forms of government. (Nonetheless, the use of slavery in the American South was a story similar to that found in Latin American sugar-producing countries.) Similarly, in Costa Rica and the Southern Cone, the depth of social divisions was less than that found in the areas where indigenous and slave populations were concentrated. However, in the latter countries, a range of forces, including abundant land and high concentrations of power among elites, led to these societies pursuing paths that also fostered relatively high levels of inequality. The granting of suffrage and extension of education in Argentina and Chile, for example, substantially lagged behind that of

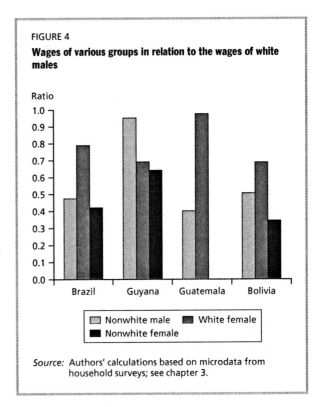

FIGURE 4

Wages of various groups in relation to the wages of white males

Source: Authors' calculations based on microdata from household surveys; see chapter 3.

the United States and Canada, but was ahead of countries such as Brazil, Peru, and Mexico.

Despite the immense political, social, and economic changes of the past century, these historically-formed sources of inequality persisted until the present time, albeit in shifting institutional forms. In countries with indigenous or Afro-descended populations, differences remain large: incomes of these groups are half that of their "white" counterparts in Bolivia, Brazil, and Guatemala. (See figure 4; Guyana is an exception, with relatively small differences between Afro- and Indian-descended groups.) These disparities in turn reflect differences in education and other assets of disadvantaged ethnic and racial groups. At the other end of the scale, elites have perpetuated their position through a variety of mechanisms, including in the realm of social relations. One example is the high propensity of people to choose marital partners with the same education (figure 5).

Of particular importance for the design of public action is the historical heritage in the capacities of the state. At the end of the 20th century, most Latin American states still conformed most closely to a model of patronage and clientelism that was embedded within a broader pattern of unequal societal relations, albeit with islands of high levels of technical competency. This pattern is associated with high degrees of inequality of influence, with disproportionate influence over the state by

FIGURE 5

Marital sorting and income inequality

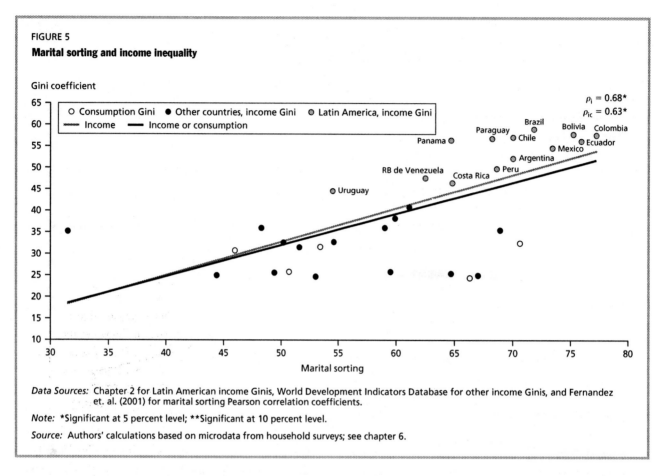

Data Sources: Chapter 2 for Latin American income Ginis, World Development Indicators Database for other income Ginis, and Fernandez et. al. (2001) for marital sorting Pearson correlation coefficients.

Note: *Significant at 5 percent level; **Significant at 10 percent level.

Source: Authors' calculations based on microdata from household surveys; see chapter 6.

wealthy individuals or corporations while poorer groups typically interact with the state through vertical relations of patronage, or are excluded. Few states have effected the transition to programmatic parties and autonomous bureaucracies that was a feature of institutional change in much of Europe and North America.[3] This is further reflected in the relatively weak capacity of Latin American states to deliver key public goods (especially macroeconomic stability, safe property rights, and citizenship) and a broad-based provisioning of services financed by taxes. Such failures in the provisioning of public goods and services are almost always disequalizing.

But a "break with history" is possible . . .

While this report emphasizes the influence of history and its contemporary reflection in institutional structures, it is *not* deterministic. Economic, political, and social analyses indicate the potential for change, and of political agency as a source of change, whether with regard to experiences within Latin America or comparisons with other societies. The speed of potential change varies across dimensions of inequality. It is intrinsically slow for education and, in part as a consequence,

is also likely to be slow for overall income inequality. However, change *can* be relatively fast in terms of patterns of service provision, for specific parts of the income distribution (including among the poorest), and, under some conditions, in reducing inequalities of power. In addition, precisely because change takes time, concerted, early action is of great importance. A range of economic policy levers that are key to making a difference are outlined below, followed by consideration of the underlying political and social changes that will be required to support and sustain shifts in economic policy.

. . . Through a range of economic policy levers

Guidance for economic policy choice is provided by an analysis of the correlates of high inequality in the region, drawing both on international comparisons and diagnoses within countries. This analysis indicates that there is no *single* economic reason for excess inequality in Latin America. In economic terms, high levels of inequality are reproduced via interactions among several influences: moderate levels of inequalities in education (exacerbated by low and unequal educational quality); high market returns on education, especially college education; high levels of concentration of land and other productive assets; unequal access to critical markets (particularly financial and labor markets); and weak redistribution through the state.[4] An economic strategy to reduce inequality needs to reflect these interactions. This in particular implies *complementary* actions in the following three areas: asset inequalities; the institutions that shape market access and returns; and use of the redistributive potential of the state. In some areas, policies to reduce inequality will support higher aggregate growth and even bring gains to all (or almost all). In other areas there will be tradeoffs, if not in aggregate growth then in reducing the privileges of those who currently benefit from inequality.

Broadening asset ownership: Redistribution with growth

Democratizing education

Education is the most important productive asset most people will ever own. Apart from its economic effects, education is intimately linked to sociocultural and political inequalities. More equal education has potentially multiple influences on more equal outcomes and practices. In addition, it has two important advantages as a strategy: its distribution can be improved without the need to redistribute it away from someone else, and improvements in its distribution (which go hand-in-hand with increases in overall mean levels of education) are good for efficiency and growth.

Although the importance of education is now largely accepted by governments, implementation has not always been easy. In particular, the recent "massification" of basic education appears to be associated with new forms of inequality, in particular those associated with high variance in quality (see figure 6), and with the fact that elites have the financial means to opt out of public systems.

Despite widespread experimentation, the magic bullet for raising educational quality has yet to be found. Furthermore, the key divide in terms of market returns is now the attainment of a college education. The increased value of higher education is driven by the skill-biased nature of technological change. But higher education remains largely the preserve of the children of the rich, with, as noted above, increases in inequality of enrollment in the past decade. In this context, an important element of a deeper education strategy could be the introduction of a civic drive, involving both the public and the business sector, to achieve

a significant jump in both coverage and quality across the public school system at both primary and, in particular, secondary levels.

While there is no specific institutional blueprint for this strategy, successful actions are likely to involve mechanisms to increase the accountability of teachers and schools. These may take the form of incentives for results (as is the case with Chile's school contests and vouchers), special funds to supplement school budgets (as with Brazil's FUNDEF program), or greater participation by local communities (as with El Salvador's EDUCO approach). Such supply-side measures can be complemented by demand-side incentives that encourage kids to stay in school, as with Oportunidades (previously Progresa) in Mexico and Bolsa Escola in Brazil. (These latter measures can also serve the purpose of broadening social protection systems to poorer groups, as discussed further below.) All these experiments will have to be accompanied by ongoing evaluation of which approaches have the highest impact on student learning, in order to guarantee an efficient use of education spending.

For tertiary education, the challenge is to increase the access of bright children from poor backgrounds. Part of the problem in this regard is low quality and lack of coverage at lower levels. However, there is also potential for tackling the credit and informational constraints that limit entry. Measures such as sharply expanding the availability of educational credit, targeted scholarships for students from poorest families, state exams, accreditation programs, and labor observatories would greatly facilitate the required expansion of tertiary education. In this context, higher cost recovery in public universities and performance-based budget support would be important complements.

In addition to such general measures, there is a need for action to deal with the exclusionary structures faced by historically subordinate groups. A case can be made for investing in the curricula and teachers to provide multicultural and multiracial education, including bilingual education in areas with a strong presence of indigenous people. At the tertiary level, there is a prima facie case for use of affirmative action programs, especially for such excluded groups such as Afro-descendents in Brazil. However, such programs can lead to backlash and stigmatization and need to be carefully discussed, designed, and monitored.

Although a push toward equalizing access to quality education is critical for the distribution of income in the long run, the effects of education will take time. Since children

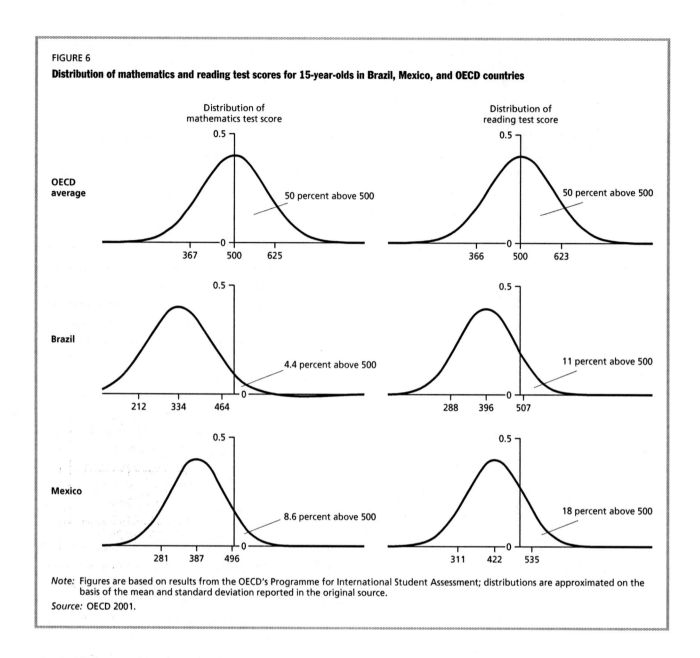

FIGURE 6

Distribution of mathematics and reading test scores for 15-year-olds in Brazil, Mexico, and OECD countries

Distribution of mathematics test score

Distribution of reading test score

OECD average

50 percent above 500

50 percent above 500

Brazil

4.4 percent above 500

11 percent above 500

Mexico

8.6 percent above 500

18 percent above 500

Note: Figures are based on results from the OECD's Programme for International Student Assessment; distributions are approximated on the basis of the mean and standard deviation reported in the original source.
Source: OECD 2001.

who benefit from better schooling now will enter the labor market in the future, it will take decades to transform the educational composition of the entire labor force. During the transition, tertiary expansion could even lead to increased inequality, if the high returns to tertiary level graduates persist. There is also uncertainty over what will happen to the pattern of returns on education over the long term. A comparison between Brazil and the United States (see chapter 6 and table 6.3) found that differences in the pattern of education in the labor force "explained" about a third of the difference in income inequality, with another third explained by differences in the pattern of returns on education. However,

a comparison between Chile and Italy found that differences in the structure of income were related more to differences in returns than to differences in the distribution of years of education. While these comparisons are only statistical exercises, they suggest that many factors influence the effect of education on income inequality.

The distribution of land and the security of property rights

Unequal distribution of land was historically a major source of both high levels of economic inequality and unequal political influence. With the enormous rise in urbanization and, in most countries, the disappearance of landed elites as a major source of political influence, rural landholdings are less important than in the past. However, rural land distribution still matters for an important, and relatively poor, minority in middle income countries, as well as for larger groups in the poorer countries in the region.

Latin America can be categorized as a region of extensive but incomplete land reform. Some past efforts succeeded in breaking up haciendas, but almost all failed to transform the position of poor peasants, because of shortcomings in design and the political context. When property rights became more insecure, landed elites often used other means to preserve their economic position, such as evicting tenants and securing subsidies on capital or outputs. In addition, newly reformed areas were not supported by the infrastructure and other economic services necessary to generate a vibrant small-scale sector.

There is scope for rural land reform, but its nature and degree depend on the country. Where property rights for land are generally recognized and legitimate (as in most of the Southern Cone, for example), coercive action would be undesirable and counterproductive. However, there are many countries that have regions of land settlement where rights are ill defined or illegitimate. In those cases, redistribution can potentially go hand-in-hand with a strengthening of property rights if the process is well managed. This is likely to involve a range of techniques, from repossession and redistribution of land owned by druglords to the changed use of land that is still in public hands. In Brazil and Colombia, processes of state purchase for redistribution and experiments in community and market-based land reform are ongoing. In terms of post-reform designs, indigenous groups sometimes prefer to maintain traditional collective forms of land management, with the issue being how to provide adequate access to credit and services in the context of these property and governance structures. In all areas, it is essential to complement small-scale production with infrastructure and other support services, to integrate new schemes within territorial strategies for development, and to provide the legal underpinnings for rental markets.

Issues of urban land and housing have increased in importance with urbanization. An important divide is that of the security of property rights, since poorer groups are more likely to suffer from lack of legal title. Experience from Peru indicates that it is possible to run large-scale titling programs, an approach that needs to be complemented by measures to make housing markets work better, provide local infrastructure, and ensure that local governments are responsive to poor urban dwellers.

In both rural and urban areas, strengthening property taxes is an important area for public action. Latin America's property taxes are low by international standards, even after controlling for incomes. Increased property taxation can both be a valuable source of revenue for local governments and provide incentives for more efficient land use.

Broadening the provision of infrastructure

Unequal access to public infrastructure is another important determinant of inequality dynamics. Recent cross-country work indicates that the more infrastructure a country has in place (including electric power, telecommunications, roads, and railways), the less unequal it is. Evidence suggests that this relationship is causal, and that the effects can be large over the long term (Calderón and Chong 2004). The sharp reduction in investments in infrastructure during the 1980s and 1990s in many countries in Latin America (see Calderón, Easterly and Servén 2003) is thus cause for concern from the perspective of both growth and equity. This trend has in turn led to a large and growing gap in terms of infrastructure between Latin America and both OECD and successful East Asian countries. The decline was driven by large declines in public spending on infrastructure, first during the debt crisis of the 1980s and then within a context of bullish expectations related to the potential of privatization in the 1990s. Although private provisioning did increase, it only fully compensated for public declines in the case of telecommunications.

Tackling inequalities in the future will require a judicious mix of public provisioning and privatization. The privatization process has become highly politically charged. In many areas, pure private provisioning is unlikely, especially in such areas as rural road networks and water supply. In these subsectors, public and private investments in infrastructure are complements, not substitutes. The issues here are analogous to the challenges of making any public service responsive to the needs of all citizens. In many areas, however, a case for privatization can still be made, including on grounds of equity.

Many public utilities have been part of clientelistic structures and have been both inequitable and inefficient. Privatization efforts can break through these barriers, but will only succeed if they are well designed and subject to strong, autonomous regulation. Evidence of past privatizations of utilities suggests that most tend to lead to more equal access and higher quality services, but price effects have varied from case to case depending on initial conditions and the quality of regulation. In addition, the process is key: in most cases, privatization processes have not been used to distribute ownership more broadly and, where transparency and competition have been weak, regressive wealth transfers and corruption have occurred. This is particularly the case in noncompetitive sectors, in which the establishment of sound regulatory structures alongside privatization is essential to achieving both efficient and equitable outcomes.

Developing deeper markets and more equitable institutions

Deeper markets

Promarket reforms are often accused of favoring the rich at the expense of the poor. While this tends to ignore the fact that most nonmarket institutions in Latin America were historically shaped to favor the rich, it is important to understand the distributional impacts of market reforms in light of their importance for the growth agenda. A survey of the literature finds no strong general pattern associated with the impact of structural reforms on inequality. On balance, market-based reforms have been associated with greater income inequality more often than not, but the effects are not large and often not statistically robust. The big picture is that inequality has been notably resilient to a range of policy experiments, from import-substituting industrialization to populist policies and market-oriented reforms.

More can be said when specific reforms are considered individually. Whenever fiscal reforms have led to price stabilization, the result has been a reduction of inequality. Furthermore, the effects of privatization on distribution have often been positive (see discussion above). However, many countries in the region experienced rising inequality in the wages of individual workers in the past decade or so,[5] which appears to have been mediated by an opening up of trade and foreign direct investment (De Ferranti and others 2003). Trade liberalization, in addition to the unequal distribution of education, has been associated with increased wage disparity because it has led to faster adoption of new techniques and production processes that are intensive in skilled labor. However, there is some evidence that this is a once-off effect,

with a recent leveling off in wage inequalities in the case of both Chile and Mexico, two of the most internationally integrated economies in the region.

The best response to such inequality-augmenting forces is not to avoid the use of markets, but to tackle the underlying sources of inequality. Doing so involves broadening and equalizing the asset base—notably in education and infrastructure—and reforming social protection systems to make them more inclusive. It is also important to extend and deepen the reach of markets. Part of the problem is that market access is very different for poorer households and informal sector workers than for the rich and established companies. Financial markets are of particular importance in this regard, both for improving equality of opportunities in productive investment and facilitating more equal access to assets such as land, housing, and education. Transparency, disclosure, good corporate governance, credit bureaus, and strong property rights for creditors and minority shareholders have proven to be important determinants of financial deepening, and thus of greater access to financial services. There are also a host of specific institutions, products, and collateral regulations that may increase access to credit by micro- and small-scale enterprises.

Inclusive and efficient labor markets

The labor market is the most important domain for income determination for most households. Labor market institutions can have a significant influence in this area, particularly with regard to the quality of work. Current labor market and social security institutions in Latin America (such as unions, minimum wage rules, and employment benefits) protect the interests of formal sector workers and largely exclude informal workers and most of the unemployed. In contrast with conditions in OECD countries, formal sector workers in Latin America seldom make up a majority of the working class, and are usually located in the middle or upper parts of the income distribution. In almost all countries, a majority of poor workers are employed (or self-employed) in the informal sector, where they are not protected by formal benefits, minimum wage rules, or unions. Organized workers sometimes effectively practice a form of "opportunity hoarding," or protection of their privileges, that can limit the scope for equitable reforms. Examples include efforts to protect favored public sector pensions in Brazil and the resistance of some teachers' unions to quality-enhancing reforms in basic education that could benefit all children.

There is a need to move toward a labor and social security framework that is both more inclusive and less distorting. Such a framework should seek, on the one hand, to extend basic labor rights and security protection to all workers while, on the other hand, increasing labor flexibility, especially in areas where groups have significant, entrenched privileges. This approach is consistent with an active role for unions within competitive environments.

Avoiding crises and regressive workouts from macroeconomic shocks

A notable finding of this report is the regressivity of financial crises. Crises are regressive because the wealthy and better informed move money out of their countries first, sometimes enjoying capital gains in terms of purchasing power at home. Crises are also regressive because of the fiscal costs of the resolution mechanisms that have been adopted to deal with recent banking problems in Latin America. During the 1980s and 1990s, public transfers to large depositors and bank shareholders, undertaken as crisis-resolution mechanisms (that is, bailouts), were in the range of 13–55 percent of gross domestic product (GDP). These transfers dwarfed poverty-targeted programs and were financed by a combination of higher taxes and lower public benefits and services. Since the incidence of overall tax systems is generally proportional (or possibly mildly progressive) and the marginal incidence of service expansion in the 1990s was typically progressive, these transfers were strongly regressive. It is unlikely that such large regressive transfers to large debtors and depositors—and even shareholders on occasion—were actually needed to avoid the collapse of banking systems.

Policies to reduce the likelihood and severity of crises are thus a necessary part of an agenda to reduce inequality. Latin American economies have remained excessively vulnerable to reversals of capital flows due to a combination of moderate to high public debt levels, excessive reliance on foreign and dollar-linked debt, low export and tax ratios, weak prudential regulation and supervision, and procyclical fiscal policies. The best course for macroeconomic policy in the region, from the point of view of reducing poverty and inequality, would most likely be one of increasing public sector savings and adopting "super-prudent" regulatory and supervisory practices in the financial system during good economic times, while at the same time increasing the level of openness of the economies, developing long-term domestic capital markets, improving debt management, and increasing tax ratios. Since the latter objectives will take time to achieve, it would also be desirable to generate cyclically adjusted public sector surpluses for a period of time in countries with high debt burdens, in order to reduce vulnerability to shocks and the likelihood of crisis.

A key element is the establishment of rules and institutions that would allow for the operation of countercyclical fiscal policies, by mitigating the political economy and informational problems that lay behind procyclical fiscal policies. In turn, this would overcome the procyclicality of social expenditures and avoid their reduction when they are most needed.

Pursuit of fiscal prudence on equity grounds may seem surprising to those who have long equated propoor governance with budget deficits. This view is consistent with the need for substantial amounts of public action—and public spending—to reduce poverty, inequality, and various sources of inefficiency across Latin America. However, financing for these expenditures should not be generated through larger fiscal deficits because doing so would increase the likelihood of inflation and balance-of-payment and banking crises, both of which have highly regressive resolutions. Instead, financing should come from other sources, including higher taxes and the redirection of existing spending, some of which is almost certainly wasteful and much of which is regressive.

Finally, since crises can never be avoided entirely, it is critical to have in place ex ante efficient and equitable crisis resolution mechanisms (especially with respect to potential financial problems) in order to avoid the wasteful and highly regressive transfers that have characterized the management of most banking crises in the past. These mechanisms should be complemented by safety nets that automatically kick in to protect the poor when crises do hit (De Ferranti and others 2000).

Using the redistributive power of the state

Raising taxes for an effective state

A healthy tax system is a vital ingredient for an effective state. Currently, most countries in Latin America have low tax-to-GDP ratios given their level of development (see figure 7). Some, notably Uruguay and to a lesser extent Chile and Costa Rica, have moderately high taxes and significant and somewhat redistributive public provisioning. Brazil stands out as a case in which a relatively high tax effort coincides with highly unequal public provisioning. While

FIGURE 7

Tax revenue in relation to GDP per capita

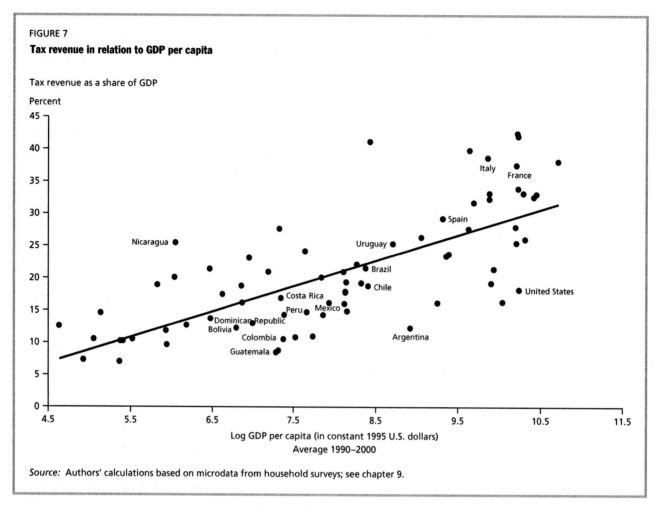

Tax revenue as a share of GDP

Source: Authors' calculations based on microdata from household surveys; see chapter 9.

methodological problems bedevil incidence analysis and little can be stated with confidence, a reasonable working assumption is that, given very low collections of personal income and property taxes, most tax regimes in the region are proportional or only mildly progressive or regressive. This situation implies that the poor, middle class, and rich pay roughly the same proportion of their incomes in taxes.

What kinds of changes in tax policy are desirable will depend on the initial position of a country. In poorer countries, often the greatest priority lies in developing a reasonably well-functioning tax administration in order to expand the resources available to the state. Where this has not yet been done, there is a case to be made for moving indirect tax systems in the direction of applying broad-based value-added taxes (VATs) that can combine strong revenue-generating capacities with reasonable levels of efficiency. In order to achieve modest levels of progressivity, a new VAT system should have a simple rate structure, possibly consisting of a few product exemptions (largely for food), a basic

rate for most other products, and a higher rate for luxury items. Excise taxes may be imposed on goods that carry high negative externalities, such as tobacco, alcohol, and motor vehicles. However, some excise taxes (such as those placed on kerosene and tobacco) are typically quite regressive, implying the need to balance equity with other objectives.

There is also an important long-term role for personal income and property taxes to play, since tax collections are very low in most Latin American countries in comparison to the OECD. Income tax structures need not have many rates to be progressive. Efforts to tax the rich a little more should focus largely on improving enforcement and closing loopholes and exemptions in order to reduce tax avoidance and evasion. This is also true for property taxes, which exist in many countries but generally raise almost no revenue, and which are critically important to financing local public services. Reform efforts should not focus on raising the rates of these taxes, but on eliminating exemptions and devising disclosure mechanisms to improve collection and enforcement.

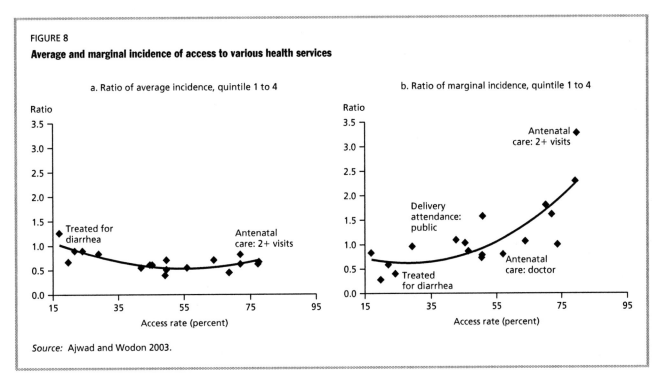

FIGURE 8

Average and marginal incidence of access to various health services

a. Ratio of average incidence, quintile 1 to 4

b. Ratio of marginal incidence, quintile 1 to 4

Source: Ajwad and Wodon 2003.

Providing services for all

Given the limits on redistribution from taxes, especially in the short term, the spending side of the equation is of fundamental importance. Evidence confirms what historical and political analyses often suggest: most public services reach the rich before they reach the poor. The average incidence of a large number of services remains regressive in most countries in Latin America. The good news, however, is that during the 1990s, the expansion of access to basic education and health was quite progressive. To a large extent, this is simply because expansions automatically brought in poorer people, since the rich already had access to such services. In many cases, however, this shift also resulted from deliberate, well-meaning, effective public action.

Given the weight of these basic services, the overall increase in social spending that took place in almost every country in the region in the 1990s (due to both increases in the ratio of social expenditures to GDP and growth) was in general progressive, in spite of the fact that an important chunk went to pension subsidies, which are usually highly regressive. Nonetheless, problems remain. There are still very large differences across programs with regard to their distributional impact. As noted above, the subsidized expansion of tertiary education enrollments has been disequalizing. This also seems to be true for any service for which the initial access rate is low. Figure 8 shows the

average and marginal incidence of health programs, and indicates how marginal incidence is more progressive for those programs that have initially high access rates. In infrastructure sectors with low coverage (such as telecommunications in most of the region and electricity in the poorest countries), expansions have also tended to favor richer groups first.

Latin American countries also have significant experience in the use of targeted delivery mechanisms. Some programs are highly successful in targeting the poor, but they tend to remain small. Indeed, there appears to be a tradeoff between effective targeting and the degree of coverage of programs among the poor (see figure 9 for examples from Brazil). Such a tradeoff may be partly due to administrative difficulties, but is also likely to be an outcome of interactions with political and economic institutions. Progressive policies generally need to be based on broad coalitions of support. Thus, targeted programs probably should be linked or "packaged" together with universal access programs that also benefit the middle class. The use of transfers to the poor that are conditional on children participating in general schooling and health systems is a good example (see below).

Finally, the historical pattern of social spending has been far from optimal in relation to the business cycle. Social spending per poor person is in fact highly procyclical almost everywhere in Latin America, which means that resources

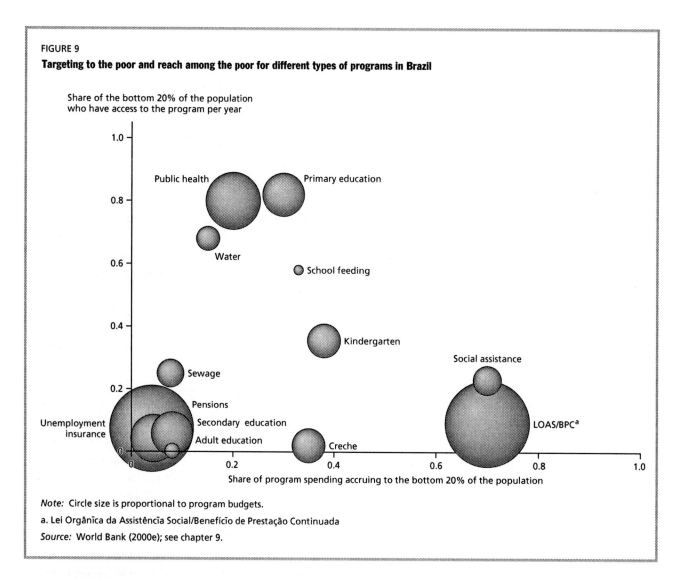

FIGURE 9

Targeting to the poor and reach among the poor for different types of programs in Brazil

Share of the bottom 20% of the population
who have access to the program per year

Note: Circle size is proportional to program budgets.

a. Lei Orgânĭca da Assistêncĭa Social/Benefícĭo de Prestação Continuada

Source: World Bank (2000e); see chapter 9.

are scarce exactly when they are most needed. This is not a pattern unique to this region, and it is easy to understand the political processes that may lead to this outcome. Yet the fact remains that it has high costs for overall economic activity, and especially for the poor. Hence the importance of adopting fiscal rules and institutions that would help overcome the procyclicality of fiscal policies in general, and of propoor social expenditures in particular.

Reforming and extending the truncated welfare state

Transfers have an important role to play in all societies in helping households manage risks—for example, those related to health, unemployment, and the failure of crops—and in redistributing resources to the poor. The case for redistributive transfers is heightened by the fact that the transition to more equal societies through broadening asset

ownership is likely to take time. Yet Latin America's historical evolution has led to the formation of what might be described as "truncated" welfare states that provide benefits only to formal workers. Such states tend to be highly unequal; for example, Mexican social security systems for public and private workers result in some of the most unequal programs in the country.

Many countries have been reforming their welfare states to make them more efficient and less burdensome. The concern here is to design instruments that make states more inclusive, while simultaneously minimizing efficiency costs. This is likely to involve a range of policies, depending on the area of vulnerability. For example, reaching poor senior citizens is best achieved through basic pensions financed by general revenues, as illustrated by Brazil's pension system for farmers. Dealing with unemployment risks is likely to involve a range of employment-related transfers—including unemployment insurance systems that already exist—and workfare programs targeted to poor, informal sector workers, such as Trabajar in Argentina (which was redesigned as Jefas y Jefes de Hogar during the recent economic crisis), A Trabajar in Peru, and Manos a la Obra in Colombia.

Particularly promising are cash transfer programs that are targeted toward certain groups on the basis of need and delivered only when recipients have taken a set of actions, which usually consist of investments in their own human capital. Evidence underscores the capacity of some of these programs (such as Oportunidades in Mexico, Bolsa Escola in Brazil, and the Red de Protección Social in Nicaragua) to reach the poor in an efficient manner and to have positive effects on their accumulation of human capital. In addition to effecting redistributive transfers, such programs also have potential as risk management instruments, and could become an effective part of a comprehensive and equitable social protection system. As mentioned above, coupling conditional cash transfers to the poor with overall expansions of basic education and health services makes eminent sense both from the point of view of efficiency (since otherwise the poor may not demand these services) and the political sustainability of targeted programs.

Policy reform must be underpinned by political and social change

The economic policies described above provide a potentially potent set of instruments to make Latin American societies substantially more equal, especially over the long run. But neither the design of policy nor its implementation is a purely technocratic affair. Analysis of history and current social and political conditions shows that redistributive and efficient economic policies are only likely to be chosen and effectively implemented if underpinned by supportive political and social conditions. To varying degrees most Latin American societies do not have such conditions today. Public action needs to foster shifts to a new political equilibrium.

From clientelistic and weak to effective and redistributive states

History bequeathed Latin America with unequal social relations and weak states, in degrees that vary across the region. This has been a fundamental source of the characteristic mix of underprovisioning of the public goods of macro stability, property rights, and citizenship, as well as low levels of

provisioning of broad-based services. Democratization was probably necessary for transformation, but has not been sufficient. Clientelistic relationships tend to continue under democratic auspices, especially when associated with unequal cultures across groups. This pattern is by no means unique to Latin America: the political machines of major U.S. cities also persisted for a significant part of the 20th century.

Both international and Latin American experiences underscore the potential for change. This is most likely to occur when there are both shifts in the opportunities for political influence (including via electoral competition) and strengthening of the capacities of poorer groups to articulate their interests and organize for effective action. These processes may take various forms. In the long run, frequently maligned political parties have a crucial role to play, provided they are formed along programmatic or policy lines rather than on a vertical, patronage-oriented basis. There are also important complementary relationships between programmatic demands and the development of autonomous bureaucracies. Chile is the best example in the region of a case in which the combination of programmatic parties and bureaucratic competency helped support important shifts to a more effective and redistributive state following the transition to democracy—with the result that progressive consequences flowed from the improved provisioning of key public goods and both broad-based and targeted services. Other national cases, including Brazil over the past decade, appear to be moving along this path.

Where programmatic parties are absent, change is often effected by outsiders, generally in the form of political entrepreneurs or movements that can be catalysts for breaking with history. However, such outsider-driven changes are only likely to be sustainable if they are embedded in formal institutions, especially those that create the capacity of lower and middle groups to articulate and organize for an effective, redistributive state. Important complements to—but not substitutes for—change from within or outside the prevailing system include measures to increase transparency, promote public debate, and strengthen public administrative capacities. These aspects both sustain societal pressure and increase the capacity for developing and maintaining a responsive government.

The subnational state has become an increasingly important arena of action for political change and economic policy, owing to the combination of political decentralization (including the introduction of elections for mayors) and devolution of responsibilities. In this context, a number of cases of major changes in performance of the state have occurred in just a few years, notably in Bogotá, Colombia, and Porto Alegre, Brazil. These cases show signs of a real shift toward a new political equilibrium, with large, redistributive improvements of services, reductions in patronage and corruption, and increases in tax efforts.

Confronting ethnic and racial divisions

History has also left some countries in Latin America with major divides between ethnic and racial groups, in particular indigenous and Afro-descended groups. (Although gender differences are still present, tangible progress appears to have been made in this area.) While this report could not deal with these issues in depth, tackling group-based divisions is clearly an important part of the overall agenda of reducing inequality in the region. As with the transition to democracy, most countries have made formal moves in this direction, for example by recognizing multiculturalism in national constitutions.

The real issues now lie in changing the social dynamics that perpetuate such group-based inequalities. One area for action, noted above, is bilingual and multicultural education. There are also rising demands in a range of other areas, including land rights and judicial and health practices. In the recent past, these demands have been forcefully articulated by indigenous movements, especially in the Andes, Mexico, and Central America. However, in many countries there is a related but distinct agenda around Afro-descended groups, as evidenced by growing public recognition of the issue in Brazil. In many cases movements representing indigenous and Afro-descended groups have an "outsider" quality. A challenge for the coming decade and beyond will be their inclusion within core political and social processes.

Alliances, open-minded elites, and economic dynamism

Latin American societies have the economic policy instruments to make, over time, major changes in their embedded patterns of inequality. Sound choices and the effective execution of these policies will only occur when they are associated with inclusive political and social structures, a process that may first require a shift in the political equilibrium. That this can happen at all is illustrated by developments both within and outside the region. The forging of alliances between poorer and middle groups, and with progressive elements of elites, will be essential. A key consequence of such alliances will be the equalizing of economic and political opportunity, including moving toward societies with more open elite structures. History suggests that this will be good for economic and societal dynamism, and certainly for equity.

Notes

1. General statements about Latin America throughout this report refer to *continental* Latin America, excluding Belize, French Guiana, and Suriname. Unfortunately, the authors are unable to make general statements regarding the Caribbean, since household surveys were available for only 3 of the 15 Caribbean countries: the Dominican Republic, Jamaica, and Trinidad and Tobago. However, results are reported for these three countries, and they are included in the regional averages presented. Nevertheless, there would be no statistical justification for making inferences for the Caribbean subregion as a whole, on the basis of a primary data analysis for those three nations.

2. Although higher volatility in income and consumption may overstate the degree of excess inequality that exists in Latin America (in comparison to other regions), the underreporting of capital income in household surveys, particularly in top deciles, may tend to understate it. For a detailed discussion of such measurement problems, see chapter 2.

3. There is, of course, wide variation within the region, with Chile probably closest to such a model.

4. Unequal social relations can exacerbate these influences—as in the example of marital sorting, which can cause household inequality to magnify individual inequality—and can also be sources of economic differences, for example by playing a key role in the processes that determine educational levels and market returns.

5. Nonetheless, rising wage inequality did not necessarily translate into rising household income inequality, for many reasons. For example, the increased participation of women in the labor marker at low wages can increase wage inequality without increasing household income inequality.

CHAPTER 1

Introduction: Motivation and Conceptual Framework

FOR AS LONG AS DATA ON LIVING STANDARDS HAVE BEEN AVAILABLE, LATIN AMERICA HAS BEEN one of the regions of the world with the greatest inequality.[1] With the possible exception of Sub-Saharan Africa, this is true with regard to almost every conceivable indicator, from income and consumption expenditures to measures of political influence and voice, and including most aspects of health and education.

Whereas the richest tenth of the population in the region earn 48 percent of total income, the poorest tenth earn only 1.6 percent. By contrast, in developed countries the top tenth receive 29 percent of total income, compared to 2.5 percent for the bottom tenth.[2] Gini coefficients tell a similar story: whereas they averaged 0.52 in Latin America in the 1990s, the averages for the OECD, Eastern Europe, and Asia during the same period were much lower: 0.34, 0.33 and 0.41, respectively.[3]

This trend implies that very high ratios of income accrue to the wealthiest segments of the population relative to the poorest. In Guatemala, the ratio of the top to the bottom tenth of the population was 58.6 in 2000. In Panama, it declined from 71.6 in 1991 to 53.5 in 2000. Even the lowest 10/1 ratio in the region in 2000—15.8 in Uruguay—is higher than most figures found in Europe. (For example, the closest comparison is a ratio of 11.2 in Italy.)

Such enormous differences in the incomes of citizens of the same country clearly imply correspondingly different degrees of access to the goods and services that people consume in order to satisfy their needs and wants. However, disparities extend much beyond private consumption. Following the terminology of Amartya Sen, there are profound differences in the freedom, or capability, of different individuals and groups to follow lives of their choosing—to do things that they have cause to value (Sen 1985a, 1992, 1999). Private resources and patterns of public provisioning affect such capabilities, while social and political arrangements affect the capacity to participate meaningfully in society, influence decision-making, or live without shame.

With respect to education, even though public systems exist in most countries in Latin America, the disparities of attainment are equally striking to those in income. In Mexico, the average person in the poorest fifth of the population has 3.5 years of schooling, as compared with 11.6 years for the average person in the richest fifth. These numbers are likely to underestimate actual educational differences because of marked differences in the quality of education. In many countries, educational attainment also differs among gender, ethnic, and racial groups. In most places, differences between men and women are becoming less marked with time and have even reversed for young cohorts, but severe disparities still exist among older people. In Bolivia, for instance, average years of schooling for persons age 61 or older are 4.1 for men and 2.4 for women.[4]

Health outcomes also vary dramatically along with income distribution, resulting in enormous impacts on life

Note: All tables and figures referred to in the text with the designation "A" can be found in the statistical appendix, p. 285.

opportunities and quality. In Brazil, children born to households in the poorest fifth of the population are three times as likely to die before they reach the age of five as are children born to households in the richest fifth. In Bolivia, this figure is more than four times as high among the poor, with children in the bottom fifth of the population experiencing under-five mortality rates of 146.5 per 1,000, which is as high as the South Asian average.

In fact, it is not an exaggeration to say that every aspect of life is affected by pervasive inequality. A Guatemalan family whose income places it in the bottom fifth of the income distribution has on average three children, whereas its counterpart in the top fifth has 1.9 children. In the former household, 4.5 people live in each room, compared to 1.6 in the latter. The former household has a 57 percent chance of being connected to water mains and a 49 percent probability of having access to electricity. The corresponding probabilities for the latter household are 92 and 93 percent, respectively.

In every conceivable way, the lives of these two families have very little in common. The very meaning of being a citizen of a country is almost certainly substantively different for the families. A poor Guatemalan household has at worst experienced violence and repression, and at best "low-density" citizenship and the "unrule" of law in recent decades.[5] Poor Guatemalan families are predominantly indigenous and have experienced centuries of exploitation and exclusion, with weak influence over local and national decision-making. The richest 20 percent of the population is more likely to be white and to have enjoyed at least some measure of normal citizenship. Although Guatemala is at the upper end of the inequality league in Latin America, and has particularly unequal and weak social and political institutions, the picture in most of the region is qualitatively similar. Worryingly, even in countries that were distinctly more egalitarian by Latin American standards (such as Argentina, Uruguay, and Venezuela), the recent trend has been one of growing inequality, at least in terms of income.

In this report, the World Bank seeks to do three things. First, *facts related to inequality will be presented*, to the extent allowed by the data. The authors build on an array of unit-level household survey data sets in order to construct an up-to-date picture of the distributions of income and other indicators of living standards across 20 countries in Latin America. For three-quarters of these countries, the pattern of change during the 1990s is examined. In so doing, the authors look at the levels of and trends in personal distributions (of income or other indicators), as well as at group-based differences, whether by race, ethnicity, or gender. In addition to private incomes, the authors consider goods and services provided publicly and the taxes levied to finance their provision.

Second, the authors *investigate the causes of Latin America's extreme inequality* by considering the historical roots and current processes that result in the reproduction of the problem. This takes us to questions of the social, cultural, and political sources of inequality that have interacted systematically with economic mechanisms.

The third and final objective of this report is to *consider some of the options available to policymakers in the region* for breaking with the long history of inequality that has characterized the countries studied. In so doing, the authors suggest policies and policy directions that can help reform economies and societies in such a way as to make them more equitable, without detracting from economic efficiency.

To prepare readers for the journey contained in the rest of this report, the remainder of this chapter is divided into two parts. The first poses the question "inequality of what?" and defines the realm of concern and conceptual framework. The second section considers the question "why should we care?"

1.1. A conceptual framework

The idea of inequality generally refers to a measure of dispersion in a distribution.[6] Most economic analysis is concerned with inequality in the distribution of some measure of individual well-being, with household income (or consumption expenditure) per capita being the most commonly used proxy. In light of the growing recognition that well-being has many dimensions besides income, inequalities are discussed with regard to other variables, such as education, health, safety, and access to services.[7] In addition, the report is not concerned only with economic welfare. Political power, or influence within a society, is also unequally distributed, and these "inequalities of agency" are powerfully intertwined with economic inequality.

One of the themes considered in this report is that differences in voice, influence, and power are both driven by economic differences and are a key element in ensuring the resilience and adaptability of such differences. While much of the focus will be on differences across the whole distribution, there is often particular interest in "horizontal" inequalities in all these dimensions between groups, for example between races, indigenous and nonindigenous groups, and men and women (discussed in particular in chapter 4).

In addition to looking at the distribution of outcomes (such as incomes, health indicators, or safety from crime), it is also possible to look at the distribution of assets and opportunities. Opportunities are crucial determinants of outcomes. In fact, a long-standing view among students of theories of social justice is that "equity" and "fairness" are more properly defined in terms of opportunities than outcomes, since the latter depend also on a range of variable human characteristics, including age, gender, talent, physical ability, social background, and preferences.

Sen (1992) argues that it is of great importance to distinguish between "achievement" and "the freedom to achieve" in assessing both the extent and normative significance of inequalities.[8] Among achievements, Sen emphasizes the doings and beings (or "functionings") that constitute well-being rather than the means with which to achieve well-being, such as incomes and resources. Such achievements can range from quite basic functionings, including "being well-nourished, avoiding escapable morbidity and premature mortality, etc. to more sophisticated ones, such as having self-respect, being able to participate in the life of the community and so on." The "capability set" represents the range of potential functionings that an individual can achieve, or the "overall freedom a person enjoys to pursue her well-being."

A core theme of this report is that the profound differences in capabilities among individuals and groups in Latin America are based on interactions between economic assets, economic opportunities, political forces, and sociocultural processes. One aspect of this line of thought concerns the moral assessment of which differences are fair. It is sometimes argued that differences in outcomes that may be morally offensive or "socially unjust" if they are caused by disparities in opportunities or life chances beyond the control of the individual may actually be much less objectionable if they are due instead to choices made in the level of effort—for example, studying or working hard rather than enjoying more leisure—or to differences in needs.[9]

In this context, it may be useful to draw a distinction in the way societies judge outcomes between the poor and other segments of the income distribution. It is probably possible to gain widespread consensus about valuing strongly any outcome that reduces the number of people living below a minimum income level (that is, below a socially accepted income poverty line) and that guarantees everyone's access to, say, basic education and health services and social security of a minimum quality. Governments around the world have already taken a strong stance on these issues by committing to the Millennium Development Goals as a guide to their own actions and the actions of international organizations. In many countries in the region, broad consultations have led to strong endorsements of these goals by political parties, nongovernmental organizations, the private sector, and other social actors.

It is probably harder to construct a similar consensus about valuing equality of *outcomes* across the entire distribution. However, it may be easier to instead form broad coalitions in favor of the concept of equality of *opportunities,* even if such a concept means different things to different people and is more difficult to operationalize (see below). In many chapters in this report (notably chapter 5), the authors stress the need to build effective coalitions that bring together the poor, the middle classes, and enlightened elites to support policies and programs oriented toward reductions of inequality and, in particular, of poverty. It might be easier to achieve such coalitions if objectives are defined in terms of two key outcomes, income poverty reduction and minimum access to basic services, as well as greater equality of opportunities for all.

In this report, the authors take the position that the distributions of both outcomes and opportunities matter and therefore provide information on both aspects, leaving the reader to make his or her own social judgments. In addition to the existence of different views on valuation, there is also a practical reason for adopting this approach. While an approach based on freedom to achieve, or capabilities, has important conceptual and ethical attractions, it also poses significant measurement challenges. Sen (1992) argues that using a capability-based approach to assess freedom to achieve has to rely heavily on measures of actual achievements.

The measurement challenge is illustrated by the application of a specific approach to the question of opportunities. This example follows Roemer (1998) in defining opportunities as the set of circumstances that affect people's outcomes, but that do not depend on their own efforts or decisions and are instead determined beyond their control. Even this apparently simple conceptual definition, however, turns out to be rather difficult to operationalize. Box 1.1 presents the results

BOX 1.1.

Measuring inequality of opportunities in Brazil

The *Pesquisa Nacional por Amostra de Domicílios* (PNAD) is Brazil's main household survey instrument. In 1996, it contained a set of supplemental questions on the parents of respondents, including their level of educational achievement and occupation when the respondents were 15 years old. Using this data, Bourguignon, Ferreira, and Menéndez (2003) seek to decompose total income inequality into both a component based on inequality in observed opportunities and a residual.

Roemer (1998) defines opportunities as the set of circumstances that lie beyond an individual's own control. The key question is delineating what is and is not beyond an individual's control. To provide the basis for this determination, Bourguignon, Ferreira, and Menéndez (2003) estimate an augmented Mincer earnings equation, regressing an individual's labor earnings on several variables: a constant, race, parental schooling (mean and difference between parents), the father's occupation, region where the individual was born, years of schooling (linear and squared), and a dummy if the individual had migrated at some point in his or her lifetime. These regressions are estimated separately for men and women. In both cases, the sample is restricted to workers aged 26–60 living in urban areas of Brazil.

The authors then classify the last two variables (education and migration) as efforts, on the assumption that they were at least in part under the individual's own control. The remaining variables are treated as circumstances. However, education and migration may also be influenced by circumstances (for example, parents affect the education of their children). To partly account for this, the authors regress education and migration on the vector of circumstances as well and use a Monte Carlo simulation

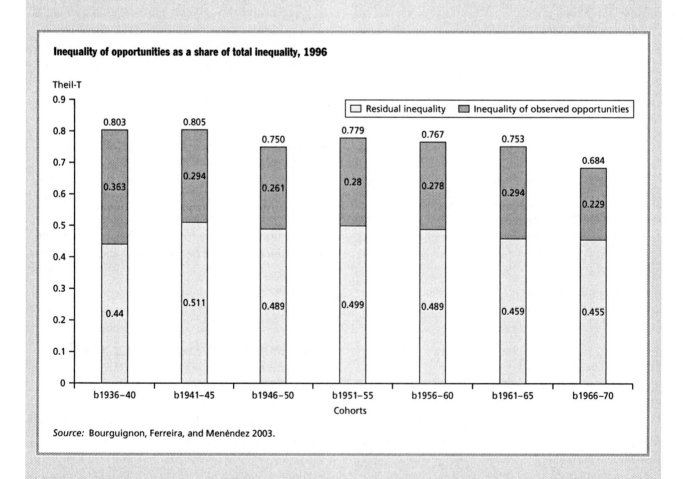

Inequality of opportunities as a share of total inequality, 1996

Source: Bourguignon, Ferreira, and Menéndez 2003.

procedure to correct for the attendant endogeneity bias. This effectively treats education and migration as being partly due to circumstance and partly to effort. They end up with a system that looks as follows:

$$\ln w_i = C_i \alpha + E_i \beta + u_i$$
$$E_i = C_i \delta + v_i$$

In this equation, w denotes earnings, C is a vector of observed circumstance variables, E is a vector of observed effort variables, and u and v are unobserved determinants that might in principle be either circumstance or efforts. The method used to estimate inequality of observed opportunities in this setup is to simulate the distribution of predicted earnings when each and every circumstance variable is assumed to be equal to a constant (for example, an average $\bar{c}$) in both equations of the system. The resulting inequality is clearly not due to any variance in observed circumstances. It must instead be due to effort made and to any unobserved circumstances, such as family wealth, which might be included in u and v. Inequality of observed opportunities—denoted by Θ—would, under the assumptions, correspond to the difference between observed income inequality and the simulated inequality when circumstances are equal for all:

$$\Theta = I(y) - I(y \mid C = \bar{c})$$

The authors test a variety of specifications and assumptions about the nature of the residual term v. They present results for earnings and household incomes per capita under various assumptions. The figure below presents the results of the preferred specification for the seven cohorts most active in the Brazilian labor market in 1996. The height of the bar is overall observed income inequality in household incomes per capita, as measured by the Theil-T index. The bottom part is residual inequality after observed circumstances are equalized. The upper part thus corresponds to one estimate of inequality of observed opportunities in Brazil in 1996.

Even though a number of important circumstances (such as family wealth and contacts, cultural history, or the quality of the school where a child is first placed) are not explicitly controlled for, inequality of opportunities still appears to be high in Brazil. According to this measure, it accounts for 36–45 percent of total inequality for the older cohorts and 33–39 percent for the younger ones. There is a slight but perceptible downward trend in the share of inequalities accounted for by opportunities, which seems closely connected to a reduction in the degree of intergenerational transmission of educational inequality.

of a 1996 study in Brazil, one attempt to empirically identify the share of inequality that is due to opportunities. The study highlights both the methodological difficulties and the potential insights inherent in focusing on the inequality of opportunities, which account for a considerable share of Brazil's high level of income inequality.

More generally in this report, the authors note that opportunities are highly correlated with the set of assets on which people can draw, as well as on the set of markets they can access and the institutions that surround them. For this reason, the report presents information on the distributions of individual assets and access to services and markets, and discusses the operation of a range of formal and informal institutions likely to affect people's opportunities. The authors list inequality measures for a wide range of outcomes and assets, including, among others, distributions of household per capita incomes; household per capita consumption expenditures; individual earnings; hourly wages; hours worked; access to various public services; years of schooling; and land owned and farmed.

The authors do not attempt to classify, for example, educational attainment as either an asset or an outcome because it clearly is both things. Education, like health, affects worker productivity and remuneration, and is thus a human capital asset. But, as Sen (2000) and others have forcefully argued, health and education are also of value in their own right, both as functionings and as determinants of capabilities. This is equally true of power and influence: political rights are valuable as such, and can thus be thought of as outcomes with intrinsic value. However, they are equally important as capabilities that influence the set of opportunities available to agents.

Opportunities, assets, and outcomes are also related in causal ways. This report clearly cannot attempt to provide

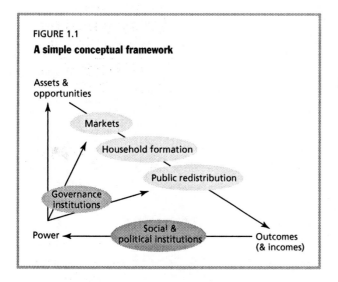

FIGURE 1.1

A simple conceptual framework

an exhaustive treatment of the determinants of inequality. After all, as just stated, even "simple" income inequality refers to dispersion in the distribution of all incomes. This distribution is determined within the general equilibrium of complex modern economies in which market imperfections, incomplete information, strategic interactions, and political processes simultaneously occur. Going beyond static economics, the institutions that mediate a number of these economic processes have long historical roots and reflect cultural patterns that are often deeply ingrained.

Pretense to an exhaustive discussion of the causes of inequality is thus a shortcut to failure. Instead, a very simple, general framework of the circular interaction between the distributions of assets and opportunities, incomes and other outcomes, and power and influence in society is schematically presented in figure 1.1. The (joint) distribution of assets and opportunities is depicted at the top. These assets include not only physical and financial wealth such as land or stocks, but also human capital endowments such as education. Individuals may inherit some of these, but others are produced during a person's lifetime. Education is of particular interest since it is, for most people, the main productive asset and is primarily acquired early in life.

People then make choices about the use of their assets in the specific markets in which they are remunerated. Financial savings generate interest or dividends in bonds or stock markets; land generates returns through rents or profits; and human capital is remunerated in labor markets. The combination of incomes arising from the remuneration of assets in these different markets combines to form individual incomes. Primary household incomes depend on how indi-

viduals match to form households and on decisions related to family size and composition.

Finally, secondary incomes are also affected by taxes and transfers, grouped together here under the category of public redistribution. There are obviously feedback loops in all these processes—notably from market processes—and this linear presentation should be treated as a way of organizing thinking, and not as a unidirectional view of causation. This part of the framework is obviously a highly stylized way of seeing economic influences on household per capita incomes. However, it is also one that is useful for the authors' attempts to understand just where along the chain of assets, markets, households, and governments Latin American countries generate so much more inequality than others. These economic processes will be further examined in chapter 6.

These economic processes do not take place in a vacuum. At every step of the way, they are mediated by social and political institutions that are very broadly understood to encompass the rules and norms of behavior in society, as well as more specific institutions that formally or informally regulate markets and affect governments.[10] This approach includes both the "macroinstitutional" arrangements in societies and the sociocultural processes that are products of interactions between different groups in a society, notably those that occur between dominant and subordinate groups. As sociologists such as Charles Tilly and Pierre Bourdieu have emphasized, the latter are essentially *relational,* and are deeply intertwined with both the organization of economic production and the structure of power. Social arrangements and sociocultural processes are the sources of large "inequalities in agency" of different groups, or differences in their capacity to shape and influence the conditions in which they live.[11] These political and social forces are discussed in chapter 5.

In turn, formal and informal institutions are neither immutable nor indifferent to economics. Income and wealth—or "economic power"—is closely linked to political power, influence, and voice. This report represents these latter aspects through the link between income and power and considers them to be mediated by political institutions and sociocultural processes. In figure 1.1, both the economic processes on the hypotenuse of the triangle and the social and political processes on the other sides of the triangle succinctly summarize broad traditions of economics, social science, and political economy in an extremely reduced form. The concepts underlying this figure are considered in more detail in chapters 5 and 6, while salient aspects of group-based differences (that is, those related to race, ethnicity, and gender) are discussed in chapter 3.

In addition, power can be used to shape economic realities in a number of different ways. Both historical and contemporary experiences vividly illustrate the linkages between power, asset accumulation, market functioning, and fiscal action. Despite the magic of the "invisible hand," markets themselves never really operate independently of regulatory institutions or the purposeful activity of different groups holding greater or lesser degrees of political and market power—a theme that Adam Smith himself forcefully emphasized.[12]

At the most basic level, the enforcement of law and order is necessary to secure the property rights of those who sell, as well as of those who buy. At a more sophisticated level, a number of markets (in particular some financial and "knowledge-intensive" markets) would be highly incomplete, or missing altogether, in the absence of regulatory and enforcement institutions that guarantee the rights of creditors, investors, or innovators. The use of power, or political agency, to effect change will therefore typically work through specific policy actions. A significant part of the report is concerned with the ways in which policies can influence inequality. In terms of economic policies, this can work through a number of the points summarized in the hypotenuse of the triangle in figure 1.1.

First, policy can affect the distribution of assets, either through direct redistribution (such as land reform or privatization processes), through taxation and subsidies (as in the direct provision of education and health services) or through regulations that facilitate access to information, credit, and insurance. The overall economic incentives with which agents are faced are influenced by political forces through mechanisms ranging from the design of taxes and subsidies to the enforcement of property rights and the general investment climate. In turn, economic incentives shape differential rates of accumulation, which then influence how asset distributions evolve. Some policy options referring to asset distributions are discussed in chapter 7.

Second, policy can influence how markets work. Even in the most minimalist view of governments (that is, in the tradition of Hobbes, Locke, and Nozick), room was always made for a "night-watchman" state. As commodities themselves and the markets in which they are traded become increasingly complex—moving, for example, from apples in a farmers' market to microenterprise credit or financial derivatives—the enforcement of property rights and the need to correct for informational and other market failures also grow. Financial regulators, inspectors of working conditions in labor markets, and antitrust investigators are examples of governance institutions through which political systems provide a framework for the activities of markets, which in turn shapes economic processes and outcomes. Of particular importance to Latin America are the interactions between policies and macroeconomic conditions. Some of the policy mechanisms available to increase equity through markets and other institutions are considered in chapter 8.

Third, governments inevitably affect the distribution of disposable household incomes through the need to finance their operations. Taxes serve to raise the revenue that supports the regulatory roles discussed above, but may also finance a number of redistributive services and transfers, whether in kind (such as through the provision of free education or health care) or in cash (such as in the form of unemployment insurance or various cash subsidies). Chapter 9 considers policy options in this realm.

By treating policies as emanating from a given social, cultural, and political context—which itself reflects a certain distribution of power and influence and underlying distributions of income and wealth—the authors acknowledge that policies are not designed in a vacuum. The usefulness of this contribution to the policy debate will be enhanced by the recognition that the context of a society places important constraints on what can be done and helps shape preferences about desirable outcomes. As figure 1.1 indicates, the policies arising from social and political institutions affect both the economic opportunities available to people and the market processes in which they engage.

Such "circular causality" between wealth, income, and power mediated through institutions evolves throughout time and history. The position of a country at a given point is powerfully shaped by the initial distributions of assets, as well as by the past history of institutions that exist today. A brief treatment of the historical roots of Latin American inequality is provided in chapter 4.

While acknowledging the importance of history and of existing social and political institutions is crucial in order to avoid policy-related mistakes, a fatalistic view of the world is both wrong and counterproductive. To propose policies without an understanding of history and the specific contexts in which they were developed often leads to failure.

However, this is not equivalent to the view that no policies should be suggested at all because they will emerge endogenously from historically predetermined institutions. Such a view fails to recognize the major role played by purposeful social and political action in achieving significant policy and institutional changes, and would ultimately result in fatalism and inaction.

A core theme of this report is that the circular causality that underpins the resilience of inequality can be altered by both economic forces and the social agency of different groups (see, in particular, chapter 5). The authors believe that the possibility exists for domestic policymakers to break with Latin America's long history of persistently high inequality by advancing equity-enhancing policies in the economic, social, and political realms. They also believe that chances of success are higher if policymakers are equipped with a deep historical understanding of the social and political norms and institutions that shape societies.

1.2. The consequences of high inequality

Before embarking on an entire volume on inequality, it may be worth pausing to ask a central question: "Why should we care?" The mission of the World Bank is to help countries eliminate poverty. However, poverty and inequality, although related, are very different phenomena. It is therefore legitimate to ask why the World Bank should be concerned with inequality. There are three key reasons, namely:

- The peoples and governments in World Bank client countries dislike inequality per se, both in terms of outcomes and opportunities.
- For a given level of mean income, greater inequality generally means greater poverty. Perhaps worse, for a given rate of growth in mean incomes, greater inequality usually implies a slower rate of poverty reduction.
- Evidence suggests that—in addition to reducing poverty more slowly for each percentage point in the growth rate of the economy—high inequality of opportunities and outcomes reduces the rate of growth itself. In cases of extreme inequality and significant negative influences of inequality on growth, the combination of these two effects may imply that high inequality countries find it difficult or even impossible to escape absolute poverty (see Ravallion 1997). There is also evidence that inequality is associated with a greater prevalence of conflict and violence and may impair an

economy's ability to respond effectively to macroeconomic shocks.

Each of these three issues is discussed in turn below.

Inequality is a bad thing in itself

Both in economics and in political philosophy, there is a common presumption that a unit increment in the income of a poor person should be valued more highly than the same increment accruing to a richer person. This normative view was initially associated with utilitarian thinkers dating back to Jeremy Bentham, who attributed it to the process whereby utilities increase with income or consumption, but at a decreasing rate. This property of "declining marginal utility" is consistent with a preference for equity, but it is not its sole source.

Beyond this consideration, there is also a generalized agreement among economists around social welfare functions that value greater increases of utility (and hence of incomes) among the poor than among the rich.[13] Other thinkers, such as John Rawls, have derived grounds for even stronger degrees of inequality aversion from different philosophical and ethical sources. However it is ethically motivated, the fact is that aversion to inequality or, conversely, a preference for equity, has been a dominant (although not consensual) view in political philosophy and the theories of social justice.

Recent evidence suggests that this view is not restricted to rarefied intellectual debate. Opinion surveys support the view that most Latin Americans are unhappy with the extent of inequality that exists in the region, which is consistent with what economists call "concave" social welfare functions. The results of a region-wide opinion survey conducted in 2001 by Latinobarómetro, a public opinion project based in Chile, indicate that on average, 89 percent of Latin Americans regard the income distribution in their countries to be unfair or very unfair. With the exception of Venezuela, no country had fewer than 80 percent of respondents answering affirmatively in those categories. Figure 1.2 reports results for the 17 countries for which they are available.

Such high levels of disapproval of income distribution are a cause for concern. They imply that the vast majority of the population believes that the way the national income is divided up is not just. Nor is it necessarily the case that such disapproval will go away with sustained growth. While relative differences in income often change little with growth, absolute income differences systematically increase.

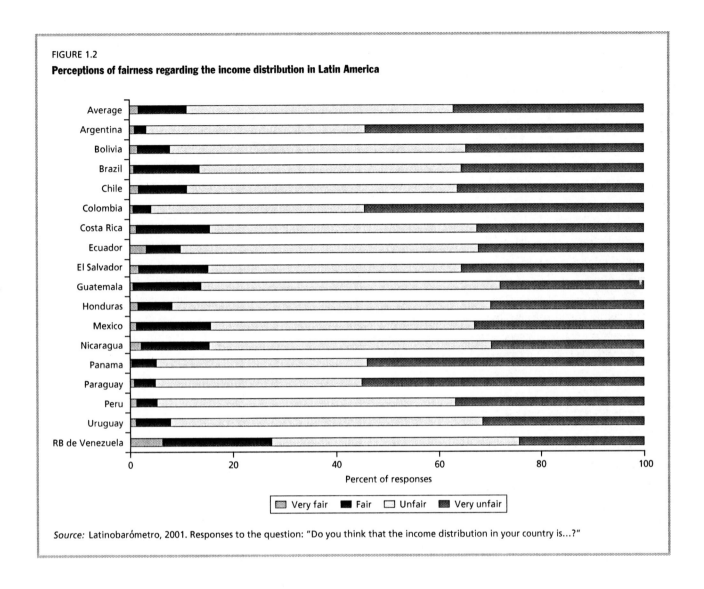

FIGURE 1.2

Perceptions of fairness regarding the income distribution in Latin America

Percent of responses

Very fair · Fair · Unfair · Very unfair

Source: Latinobarómetro, 2001. Responses to the question: "Do you think that the income distribution in your country is...?"

There is evidence that many people think about inequality in such absolute, rather then relative, terms.[14]

Moreover, it would not be surprising if this belief also implied a general lack of ownership of or belief in the entire set of institutions that are responsible for income distribution. Indeed, evidence from other opinion surveys indicates that the level of trust for institutions in Latin America is unusually low. The first reason the World Bank should care about inequality is thus a rather simple one: the Bank's clients do. Inequality makes people unhappy and reduces their faith in national institutions.

High inequality makes poverty reduction harder

The second reason governments and international institutions may care about inequality is that high levels are associated with high poverty levels. This is true in two different, although related, senses.

First, poverty will rise if the poverty line in a given society is below the mean of the income distribution, and if inequality increases in that distribution in a way that affects the poor without affecting the mean.[15] Figure 1.3 illustrates this point: if society moves from the less unequal distribution A to the more unequal distribution B, and both distributions have the same mean, then the incidence of poverty will rise from area C to area C + D.

This argument is based on theory. It is consistent with empirical observations of historical experiences of the relationships between distributional and poverty changes. On the basis of a sample of 114 episodes for 50 countries, Bourguignon (2002) confirms previous findings that higher

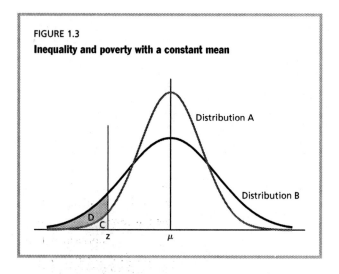

FIGURE 1.3

Inequality and poverty with a constant mean

growth elasticity of poverty reduction) becomes smaller in absolute value as initial inequality rises.

In other words, more unequal countries convert a percentage point of growth in mean household income into a smaller reduction in the incidence of poverty than do more egalitarian countries. Conversely, in order to obtain a 1 percent reduction in the number of people living in poverty, more unequal countries need to grow faster than do more egalitarian countries. Bourguignon (2002) analytically establishes this negative impact of inequality on the rate of poverty reduction for the case of lognormal distributions, which are the most common functional form approximations for empirical income distributions. At the same time, he also finds strong empirical support (under various alternative model specifications) for the negative relationship within his sample. Drawing on the same data set, figure 1.4 illustrates the basic result: after controlling for initial income levels, the growth elasticity of poverty reduction falls in

rates of economic growth are unambiguously associated with higher rates of poverty reduction.[16] However, he also finds that the impact of growth on poverty (that is, the negative

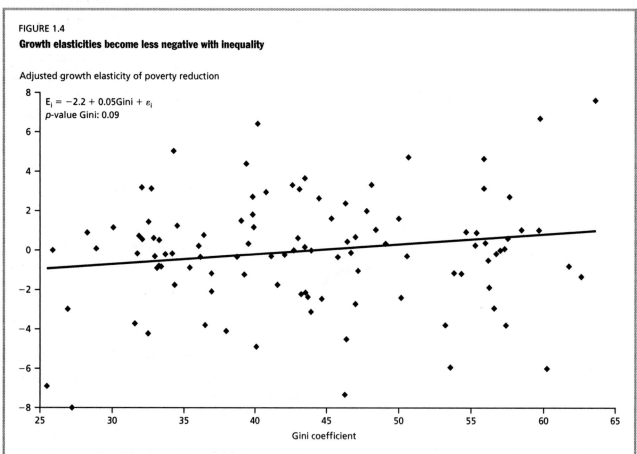

FIGURE 1.4

Growth elasticities become less negative with inequality

Adjusted growth elasticity of poverty reduction

$E_i = -2.2 + 0.05Gini + \varepsilon_i$
p-value Gini: 0.09

Gini coefficient

Note: This is a country scatterplot in which adjusted elasticity (E_i) is the residual from a simple regression of the empirical elasticity on initial mean household survey income.

Source: Bourguignon 2002, with sample truncated at empirical elasticity values of −8, +8.

absolute terms (that is, it becomes less negative, so that more growth is needed to reduce poverty) along with the Gini coefficient. The result is statistically significant at the 10 percent level.

Bourguignon (2002, p. 14) concludes that ". . . income redistribution plays essentially two roles in poverty reduction. A permanent redistribution of incomes reduces poverty instantaneously [through the effect described in figure 1.2]. But, in addition, it also contributes to a permanent increase in the elasticity of poverty reduction with respect to growth and therefore to *an acceleration of poverty reduction* for a given rate of economic growth." (Emphasis in the original; comment added.)

In a similar exercise, López (2003) corroborates the finding that the absolute value of the theoretical growth elasticity of poverty reduction (again under a lognormal assumption) declines with inequality and with the ratio of the poverty line to mean income. These results are reported in the first panel of table 1.1 below. The second panel of the table reveals that the magnitude of the direct (that is, instantaneous) effect of inequality on poverty also falls with initial inequality. In other words, the effect depicted in figure 1.2 of an inequality reduction on poverty is concave.

TABLE 1.1

Theoretical elasticities of poverty with respect to aggregate income growth

	Growth			
	Gini			
PL[a]	0.3	0.4	0.5	0.6
0.33	−3.9	−2.1	−1.3	−0.8
0.50	−2.8	−1.6	−1.0	−0.7
0.67	−2.0	−1.2	−0.8	−0.5
1.00	−1.2	−0.8	−0.5	−0.4
	Inequality			
	Gini			
PL[a]	0.3	0.4	0.5	0.6
0.33	5.2	3.3	2.4	2.0
0.50	2.5	1.7	1.3	1.2
0.67	1.2	0.9	0.8	0.8
1.00	0.2	0.2	0.3	0.4

[a]Poverty line as share of per capita GDP.
Source: López 2003.

Inequality impairs the development process itself

The third and final reason development practitioners should care about inequality is that there is evidence that it may have negative consequences for the overall process of development, including slowing down the rate of economic growth. In fact, it likely has an effect on a number of other development goals and processes—such as the capacity to resolve conflict without resorting to violence and the ability to manage aggregate shocks effectively. Effects on growth must therefore be considered along with other aspects contained in the broader category of the impact of inequality on the development process.

The first aspect to consider is economic growth. After all, as Robert Lucas famously wrote (Lucas 1988, p. 5), "Once one starts to think about [economic growth], it is hard to think about anything else." Whereas during the 1960s, 1970s, and 1980s, most of the thinking about economic growth ignored distributional considerations, in the last 10 years or so the distribution of income and wealth has returned to center stage of the concerns related to growth (Atkinson 1997). While there is as yet no consensus throughout the economics profession on this question, it is probably fair to say that the balance of academic opinion leans toward the view that high levels of inequality in incomes or in assets are causally related to lower rates of growth in mean incomes.

There are two main conceptual reasons why this might be the case. First, if credit or insurance markets are imperfect, people may depend on their initial wealth to undertake important investment decisions. If this indeed happens, a situation may in turn arise in which the poorest people in society are unable to invest in socially efficient (that is, profitable) projects, while richer individuals receive lower returns on the marginal dollar of their wealth. Credit market imperfections refer precisely to the reasons why intermediation might fail, preventing the rich from lending to the poor and enabling both groups to gain from higher returns. Economists refer to such a situation—in which both parties might be made better off without anyone losing out—as a Pareto inefficient allocation.

Why would credit markets fail in this way? Largely because lenders do not have all the information they might like to have about borrowers and because contracts may not be fully enforceable. Because enforcing credit contracts may be costly, interest rates may be higher for borrowers than for lenders. This difference may mean that poorer agents borrow too little. If some projects (such as a child's education) require minimum "lumpy" investments, the result may be aggregate underinvestment and an inefficient overall equilibrium (Galor and Zeira 1993).

Credit market imperfections may also manifest themselves through collateral requirements. If loan amounts increase with the collateral available to an agent, the poor will again be at a disadvantage. Some people may not be able to start projects with positive expected social returns—including investments in human and physical capital, land, and housing, —and the result will be inefficiency. Indeed, if there are "too many" such people, they may drive down the aggregate wage rate, with additional implications for the long-term steady-state of the economy (Banerjee and Newman, 1993). A third variant on this story is that those agents who need to borrow the most (that is, the poorest) are faced with such a large "debt overhang" that they have very little incentive to work on their projects. Lenders ration excessively large credit burdens because they may have a "moral hazard" effect on effort supply (Aghion and Bolton 1997). Similar arguments explain how the poor may be rationed out of insurance and other financial markets.

In sum, economists have modeled a variety of ways in which the combination of imperfect financial markets and unequal wealth distributions lead to outcomes which are not efficient in the "first best" sense. The specifics of financial markets may vary, but the essential issue is that inequality generates allocations through which the poor do not have the means to undertake projects that, if undertaken, would have high expected social returns. At the same time, the rich are left receiving lower marginal returns on their wealth. Further, income and wealth inequality, coupled with imperfect financial markets, will also limit the capacity of the poor to acquire assets such as human capital, land, and housing, which will in turn limit their future opportunities and the possibility of smoothing consumption in the presence of large shocks. Such indirect effects will also reduce overall growth and welfare.

The second conceptual reason that inequality may lead to lower growth involves questions of political economy. In societies with high degrees of concentration of power and wealth, elites may have more leeway to choose strategies that benefit themselves rather than middle- and lower-income groups. Within the economics literature, this has often been developed in terms of the links between the credit market failures (discussed above) that might be remedied through

effective public action. The private costs of education, for instance, can be considerably reduced (though never eliminated) through a variety of government actions, such as the provision of free public schooling or of good roads and public transportation by which students can reach schools. However, unequal societies in which political power is intertwined with wealth may be less likely to choose policies that reduce those inefficiencies than to allocate scarce resources to alternative uses. These can include private consumption of the rich (through lower taxes) or public spending on alternative programs that do not reach the poor (Bénabou 2000).

One study, inspired by a Latin American brand of political economy, characterizes the links between wealth inequality, income inequality, and political inequality as follows (Ferreira 2001). Wealth inequality means that some children attend good private schools, while others have no choice but to enroll in lower-quality public schools. Those who attend public schools enter the labor market with lower levels of human capital and thus command lower incomes. If decisions about public spending are influenced by incomes, the inequality in incomes that arises from large educational inequalities in turn leads to political outcomes in which a richer, better educated minority blocks the votes for more funding for public schools.

The authors shows that there are multiple equilibria at play in this system, with societies where initial wealth inequality is lower ending up being more egalitarian than those with higher initial levels of inequality. Furthermore, a change in political regime leading to less influence of income on political decisions (that is, a process of real democratization such as that discussed in chapter 5) could lead to equilibrium-switching in this model. The result would be a shift from a high-inequality, lower-welfare equilibrium to one that is dominant both in inequality and welfare terms.

The mechanisms whereby elites act in ways that do not serve the interests of all segments of the population may be more pervasive than can be captured in these economic models. A strand of thought in the political science and sociological literature that is relevant to parts of this report is that elites help form and perpetuate institutional structures that are characterized by governance, limited accountability, and high levels of corruption. Such "weak" institutional arrangements, rather than being symptomatic of immature institutional evolution, may be functional for the rich (Heller and Mahoney 2003). In addition, where institutions are weak, it is the poor who suffer most, since the rich can use their political power and financial influence to further their interests (Glaeser, Scheinkman, and Schleifer 2002). Such processes would have powerful adverse impacts on overall growth and other aspects of the development process.

Do the data support the hypothesis that high inequality is bad for growth and efficiency? Most studies do find a negative coefficient of initial inequality when this aspect is included as an explanatory variable in empirical growth models. In regressing the average growth rate during 1960–1985 on Gini coefficients for income and land around 1960, Alesina and Rodrik (1994) find statistically significant coefficients for both. Persson and Tabellini (1994) employ an alternative measure: using the share of income accruing to the middle fifth of the income distribution as a proxy for equality. The coefficient for that variable is statistically significant and positive, which is consistent with the Alesina and Rodrik results. Although Perotti (1996) uses a larger set of countries and tests additional specifications, the results remain significant.

More recently, this budding consensus has been challenged by Forbes (2000) based on analysis of a new data set known as the Deininger and Squire "high-quality" data set.[17] Forbes found a positive relationship between lagged inequality and growth. There are, however, a number of reasons why these findings, although important, remain a minority view in the economics profession. First, as the author herself points out, this study differs from the others in considering the effect of time-varying lagged inequality rather than some fixed, initial level of inequality. The interpretation thus has a more short-run effect. Second, questions have been raised both about the data set and the econometric technique employed (see Aghion, Caroli, and García-Peñalosa 1999).

Finally, other studies have continued to find significant negative coefficients for measures of wealth and asset inequality in growth regressions. For example, Birdsall and Londoño (1997) use a subset of the Deninger-Squire data set and conclude (p. 35) that "Initial inequalities in the distribution of land and human capital have a clear negative effect on economic growth, and the effects are almost twice as great for the poor as for the population as a whole." López (2003) uses a similar econometric approach as Forbes and the Deininger-Squire data. Taking into account the simultaneous nature of the determination of growth and inequality dynamics, he finds no sign of an effect of growth on inequality—in keeping with

work by Ravallion and Chen (1997) and Dollar and Kraay (2002a)—but rather statistically significant evidence that initial inequality reduces growth.

In addition, it seems that the harmful effects of high inequality on economic development are not restricted to economic efficiency and growth, important though these aspects are. A broader view of development includes more than output per capita, considering, for instance, a country's institutional ability to cope with economic and other aggregate shocks, such as a change in terms of trade or a key foreign interest rate. Rodrik (1999) suggests that countries suffering from more pervasive social divisions—whether ethnic and racial in nature or income- and class-based—seem not to adjust to large shocks as well as other, more egalitarian and cohesive societies. The implicit mechanism is that the institutions responsible for sharing the burdens of adjustment work less well in economies in which distributions are more unequal.

In order to understand the process of adjustment to the first oil-price shock of 1973, Rodrik (1999) regresses the difference between the per capita growth rate during 1975–1989 and the same rate during 1960–1975. He finds a significant negative coefficient on the dummy variable for Latin America, suggesting that the region suffered more from the shock (in terms of reduced ex-post growth) than did developed or East Asian countries. Interestingly, this effect disappears (that is, the coefficient becomes insignificant) when three specific aspects are controlled for: income inequality in the 1970s; land inequality; and the murder rate (the latter serves as a general proxy for the prevalence of violence or weakness in conflict resolution in a society).[18]

This result is interpreted as indicating that the prevalence of high inequality in Latin America (when compared to, for example, East Asia) was partly to blame for the region's poorer performance in adjusting to the severe terms-of-trade shocks of the 1970s. Institutions were not able to achieve closure on the incidence of the costs of adjustments. In the meantime, fiscal and current account deficits grew, planting the seeds for the ensuing debt crises of the 1980s. Chapter 8 discusses the continuing importance of crisis management and the links with inequality in Latin America.

The link between high inequality and weak institutions, which may appear tenuous at this stage and which is treated in a much reduced form in Rodrik (1999), is further explored in chapters 4 and 5. In those chapters, the theme emerges that Latin America is, in a range of areas, characterized by institutions that are weak and controlled by unequal power structures. Both these aspects tend to lead to sub-optimal levels of development and to perpetuate unequal gains from development that does occur.

Returning for a moment to the significance of the murder rate variable in Rodrik's specifications, it is important to note that the fact that it mimicked the effect of the omitted inequality variables in the growth regression is not a coincidence. Evidence across countries suggests that high inequality is significantly and positively associated with the prevalence of violence.[19] Fajnzylber, Lederman, and Loayza (2000) regress homicide rates (from the World Health Organization database) on income inequality (measured by the Gini coefficient) and a number of control variables in a panel data set of about 40 countries and 140–190 observations (depending on the specification). Results show that income inequality is always positive and strongly significant, and remains so even when educational inequality and income polarization are added as controls. Both social conflict and personal violence are associated with higher levels of inequality, especially when institutions of conflict management and the rule of law are weak.

Finally, it is worth noting that interaction occurs between possible effects of inequality on the growth rate and the adverse effects of inequality on poverty reduction. If inequality is sufficiently high, countries that would have good growth prospects with strong poverty-reducing potential at low levels of inequality will experience little or no growth or poverty reduction. Ravallion (1997) calculates that about one-fifth of observations in a data set for developing countries could fall into a category in which there would be no absolute poverty reduction.

The balance of the evidence is such that high levels of income and wealth inequality observed in Latin America have the following features. They:

- Are considered unfair by large majorities of the continent's population.
- Slow down the pace of poverty reduction in the region by lowering the growth elasticity of poverty reduction.
- Slow down economic growth and development itself.
- Possibly hamper the region's ability to manage economic volatility and worsen the quality of its macroeconomic responses to shocks, which are unfortunately all too frequent.
- Make violent crime more pervasive.

These are the main reasons why a better understanding of inequality is important. Most people and governments in the region regard Latin American levels of inequality as too high. They would like to reduce them in terms of both outcomes and opportunities. In addition, such a reduction would likely help policymakers become more effective in fighting poverty and promoting broader economic development.

An overview of the report

The remainder of the report is divided into three parts, one for each objective outlined above. **Part I** establishes basic facts about inequality in Latin America, to the extent allowed by the available data, in terms of both evidence on differences across individuals and households (chapter 2) and between groups, across ethnic, racial, and gender lines (chapter 3). **Part II** turns to the causes and determinants of high and persistent inequality in Latin America, from its historical origins (chapter 4), contemporary social and political influences (chapter 5), and economic forces for the reproduction of inequality (chapter 6). **Part III** considers what can be done in terms of specific policies in the domains of assets (chapter 7), market institutions (chapter 8), and the redistributive role of the state through taxation, services, and transfers (chapter 9).

Notes

1. General statements about Latin America throughout this report refer to *continental* Latin America, excluding Belize, French Guiana, and Suriname. Unfortunately, the authors are unable to make general statements regarding the Caribbean, since household surveys are available for only three Caribbean countries: the Dominican Republic, Jamaica, and Trinidad and Tobago. Nonetheless, results for these three countries are reported and included in the regional averages presented. However, there would be no statistical justification for making inferences for the Caribbean subregion as a whole on the basis of the primary data analysis for those three countries.

2. This refers to unweighted averages for the distribution of household per capita income in 1992, with estimates based on Bourguignon and Morrison 2002. See table A.18 in the statistical appendix.

3. The Gini coefficient is a standard measure of inequality in a distribution. It ranges from zero to one, and increases with inequality. A value of zero corresponds to perfect equality and a value of one corresponds to a distribution in which a single unit receives all of the income and the other units receive nothing.

4. These figures refer to the national 1999 survey. See table A.22 in the statistical appendix.

5. See O'Donnell 1999b for discussion of low-density citizenship and Méndez and others 1999 for the unequal reach of the rule of law in much of Latin America. The most recent and important symbolic change in Guatemala was the signing of the peace accords in 1996. However, major institutional weaknesses and patterns of social exclusion remain; see World Bank 2002b.

6. Most measures frequently used in the economics literature evaluate dispersion in ways that are consistent with certain desirable attributes, known as axioms of inequality measurement. For a discussion of measurement issues, see Cowell 1995 or 2000.

7. This report does not focus on full multivariate welfare analysis. For more on this subject, see Bourguignon and Chakravarty 2003.

8. Quotes in this paragraph are from Sen 1992, pp. 4–5 and p.150.

9. The literature on the theories of social justice is vast. See Sen 2000 for a recent survey.

10. See North 1990 for a classic treatment of institutions as norms and "rules of the game."

11. See Heller and Mahoney 2003 for a review, Tilly 1999 and Bourdieu 1990 for key examples, and Rao and Walton 2004 for a discussion of "inequality of agency" from a cultural perspective. A related strand of the economics literature on measurement of inequality concerns the development of the theory and measurement of polarization. This starts from the conceptual insight that individuals' evaluation of the salience of inequalities is linked to differences between the groups with which they *identify* relative to the groups from which they feel *alienated* (see Esteban and Ray 1994).

12. See Rothschild 2001 for a rich account of how Adam Smith and other enlightenment thinkers were greatly concerned with the abuse of unequal influence and the role of the purposive agency of different groups in shaping economic and social outcomes.

13. In technical jargon, this refers to the "concavity" of social welfare functions.

14. In experiments on attitudes toward inequality, Amiel and Cowell (1997) found that 40 percent of participants thought of inequality in terms of absolute, rather than relative, differences.

15. An increase in overall inequality could occur solely through increases in differences above the poverty line, for example shifts from the moderately rich to the very rich. This type of increase would not affect poverty, although it would be judged as a worsening in social welfare under most welfare functions.

16. That result was established for the same data set by Ravallion and Chen 1997.

17. Forbes also used a different econometric technique, applying the Arellano and Bond (1991) Generalized Method of Moments (GMM).

18. There are, of course, other factors that influence the effects of shocks on countries, such as the overall degree of openness, which tends to be associated with lower long-term impacts of adverse external shocks.

19. However, there is some evidence that the Caribbean is an exception to this pattern. Inequality levels are often lower in that subregion than they are on the continent, although crime rates can be rather high in particular countries due largely to the drug trade.

PART I

The Nature of Inequality
in Latin America

CHAPTER 2

Different Lives: Inequality in Latin America

THIS CHAPTER SUMMARIZES INFORMATION FOR LATIN AMERICA ON MANY DIMENSIONS OF inequality, a topic that by itself deserves a large book. The chapter highlights some of the main features of inequality in the region in order to help readers understand the level and structure of and trends related to this phenomenon and to set the stage for the following chapters of this report, in which determinants of inequality and redistributive public policies are analyzed.

The empirical counterpart of the concept of inequality is far from trivial. The most important issue is to identify the variables for which the measurement of inequality is informative with regard to social unfairness. This process involves both theoretical and empirical problems, which are discussed briefly in section 2.1.

Most of the statistics in this chapter are drawn from a sample of household surveys for 20 countries at three points during the period 1989–2001. These statistics and other results of the current study are periodically updated with new information on the Web site <www.depeco.econo.unlp.edu.ar/cedlas/wb>. Section 2.2 introduces the sample of household surveys, presents a large set of inequality measures for the distribution of household income (adjusted for demographics), and reports results for other dimensions of the income distribution (that is, aggregate welfare, poverty, and polarization). Section 2.3 is devoted to identifying problems generated by the measurement errors typically encountered in household surveys and to assessing the impact of such errors on the ability to measure, and hence understand, inequality.

Section 2.4 places the results of section 2.2 in an international perspective by comparing inequality in Latin America to other regions in the world. This analysis draws on recent studies that have pulled together large data sets with inequality information from many countries.

Household per capita income is derived from three main components: remuneration of assets (including labor and human capital), financial transfers, and household demographics. Section 2.5 considers inequality statistics on these variables that have been computed from the sample of household surveys and drawn from recent studies by other authors.

Section 2.6 goes beyond the distribution of income to present information on the distribution of some goods and services with which people are especially concerned. Most of the section focuses on evidence of inequality in school attendance and educational mobility, although statistics on inequality in health, political representation, crime victimization, and some basic social services (for example the provision of clean water) are also presented and discussed. Finally, section 2.7 provides concluding remarks.

2.1. Some conceptual issues

As discussed in chapter 1, it is safe to state that most people have preferences for social fairness and associate the concept of unfairness to some sort of inequality. Differences arise at the stage of defining the variable(s) considered most important to equalize among individuals in order to attain a fairer society. A first choice to be made is between outcomes and opportunities. Should we try to reduce disparities in outcomes (for example, income or consumption levels), or instead guarantee equality of opportunities to achieve those outcomes? Many authors have argued in favor of the second alternative.[1] According to this view, inequality should not be a societal concern if it arises between people subject to the same constraints; is the consequence of individual choices regarding the effort invested in improving outcomes; or is related to other variables for which people should be accountable. Unfortunately, the concept of opportunity is difficult to define and measure, and hence in practice it is usually abandoned in favor of the analysis of inequality in outcome variables (see box 1.1 in chapter 1 for an example of an attempt to measure it.)

Probably the most relevant outcome variable to compare among individuals is the intertemporal living standard, that is, the "average" well-being of people over their entire lifetimes. However, conceptual and, in particular, data-related limitations restrict the comparison of living standards to time periods much shorter than a lifetime. As a result, surveys usually capture dimensions of well-being for periods no longer than one year.

Within the group of variables usually measured in a household survey, consumption is generally considered to be the preferred overall measure with which to approximate living standards.[2] It has three main advantages over its main competitor, household income. First, if people can borrow and lend (as can most people at least in small amounts, for short periods of time, and in informal markets), consumption is more closely associated with individual well-being than is income.[3] Second, underreporting is usually a less severe problem in relation to consumption than income. Third, most surveys report gross income rather than after-tax income, even though the latter is a more relevant indicator of welfare and usually more reflective of consumption levels.

Consumption can be estimated from household surveys conducted in many countries. In particular, the Living Standards Measurement Surveys (LSMS) project of the World Bank makes use of questionnaires designed to measure consumption, or at least expenditures. Unfortunately, consumption surveys are not common in Latin America. The great majority of countries in the region conduct surveys without questions related to consumption or expenditure. In our sample of 20 countries, in only five were a minimum of two expenditure surveys conducted in the last decade.

For this reason, the measurement of social unfairness in Latin America has been mainly associated with the measurement of inequality in the distribution of household income. Although the current study includes information on other variables, it largely follows that tradition. The implicit assumption is that current household income, as measured in household surveys, is highly correlated to individual opportunities and intertemporal living standards. Although these correlations are surely positive and probably high, it is difficult to know how distorted the picture drawn from household survey income data is in comparison to reality.

It is important to be aware that, in focusing on household income inequality, it is possible to implicitly consider as unfair situations that are not (for example, two people may have different incomes due only to the different levels of individual effort or because they have different income profiles associated with the same mean income in intertemporal terms). It is also possible to assess as fair situations that are not (for example, an unskilled prime-age worker who will remain relatively poor the rest of her life and a college student who will be rich in the future may currently have the same income).

In addition to the analysis of household income or consumption inequality, the literature on measuring inequality increasingly reflects concern over other variables (for example, schooling, health status and services, and political representation). Two arguments are behind this concern. The first states that individual well-being depends on factors beyond consumption of goods and services, including health status, security from crime and violence, degree of freedom, and respect for human rights. One possible analytical strategy is to try to value such factors in monetary terms, add them to income or consumption, and measure inequality only in the aggregate. A less ambitious approach is to measure inequality in different variables without any attempt to aggregate the results.

A second argument states that societies have a particular concern with the distribution of certain variables, such as consumption of basic education and health services. Even if these aspects were included in the computation of total consumption, there would be normative arguments for assessing inequality separately for each variable. To inform consideration of these arguments, section 2.6 presents statistics on the distribution of school enrollment, health status and services, political representation, safety, and coverage of some basic social services.

There is great interest in measuring inequality among individuals. However, individuals usually live in households and share a common budget. This fact implies that an individual's well-being depends on the resources available in, the size and structure of, and norms of sharing within the household. The most commonly used indicator of individual well-being is household per capita income, that is, total household income divided by the number of persons in the household. Although widely used, this variable ignores three relevant factors: (1) consumption-related economies of scale within the household, which might, for example, allow a couple to live with less than double the budget of a person living alone; (2) differences in needs among individuals that are a function of age and gender (such differences are behind the adjustments often made for adult equivalents); and (3) unequal allocation of resources within the household.[4]

Following the tradition in Latin America, this chapter considers inequality measures for the distribution of household per capita income among individuals, although statistics that take points (1) and (2) above into consideration are also computed. There is also considerable interest in inequalities between groups or categories of individuals, for example, inequalities drawn along ethnic, racial, and gender lines. This subject is presented briefly in the following pages, but is treated in more depth in chapter 3.

Summing up, the ideal objective would be to measure the degree of social unfairness in Latin American countries. Due to conceptual and data-related limitations, we have measured inequality in the distribution of household income, adjusted for demographics, and complemented these statistics with indicators of inequality in the distribution of other dimensions of well-being. Although the limitations of this approach are evident, the authors believe that the statistics provided in this chapter are useful to help characterize and understand social unfairness in the region.

2.2. Income inequality and beyond

Despite the many caveats associated with household surveys, they remain the most reliable and appropriate source for distributional analysis. A data set of household surveys for most Latin American countries since 1989 was prepared for this report. The sample is introduced first, followed by some basic inequality statistics and discussion of the limitations of the data. A set of tables provided in the statistical appendix from the household surveys and other sources forms the basis for the following discussion.

The data

The authors were able to assemble a data set containing 52 household surveys covering the period 1989–2001. The sample comprises approximately 3.6 million individuals surveyed in 20 countries: Argentina, Bolivia, Brazil, Chile, Colombia, Costa Rica, the Dominican Republic, Ecuador, El Salvador, Guatemala, Honduras, Jamaica, Mexico, Nicaragua, Panama, Paraguay, Peru, Trinidad and Tobago, Uruguay, and República Bolivariana de Venezuela. The sample is fully representative of most of Latin America but only partially of the Caribbean countries, which do not regularly conduct or publish household surveys.[5]

For most countries, the sample contains three observations corresponding to the early 1990s, mid-1990s, and the late 1990s, 2000, or 2001. In each period, the sample represents more than 92 percent of the region's total population. All household surveys included in the sample are nationally representative. The exceptions are Argentina and Uruguay, where surveys cover only urban residents but nonetheless represent more than 85 percent of the total population in both countries.[6] All surveys record a basic set of demographic, education, labor, and income variables at the household and individual levels. Although differences exist among countries, the surveys are roughly comparable in terms of the type of questionnaire and sampling techniques used.

Table A.1 presents the main characteristics of each household survey. The table shows the names of the surveys, their coverage (urban or national), and the sample size (in number of individuals). For reference, the population estimates of each country are presented in column (v). Household income is reported in all surveys. Those surveys that also cover expenditures are indicated in column (vi). All surveys have specific questions related to labor income and nearly all also cover nonlabor income (that is, capital income, property income, profits, and transfers), although they differ in terms of the detail of the questions and the possibility of separating out different sources of nonlabor income. Surveys that include questions related to nonmonetary income and the implicit rent of own housing are also marked in the table.

Most surveys were obtained through the Program for the Improvement of Surveys and the Measurement of Living Conditions in Latin America and the Caribbean (MECOVI), a joint effort of the Inter-American Development Bank (IDB), the World Bank, and the United Nations Economic Commission for Latin America and the Caribbean (ECLAC). This program promotes improvements in the collection, organization, and analysis of household surveys in the region. Other surveys used in this chapter are part of the LSMS program; these usually yield richer data because they include questions on social services and expenditures.

This study is not the first one to analyze inequality in Latin America based on a set of household surveys. Altimir (1994) and Morley (2001) at ECLAC, Wodon and others (2000) at the World Bank, and, in particular, Székely and his co-authors (2000 and 2001) at the IDB, have gathered information from household surveys to analyze income distribution in the region.[7] Compared to these studies, the current sample covers more countries, provides more information on some countries (mainly Argentina), and includes surveys for 2000 and 2001. This study also presents a larger set of statistics across countries and over time that are related to several dimensions of inequality (that is, in addition to household income) and to inequality in the distribution of relevant demographic and socioeconomic variables.

The authors made all possible efforts to make statistics comparable across countries and over time by using similar definitions of variables for each country and year and by applying consistent methods of processing data. However, perfect comparability is not assured, since the coverage of and questionnaires used in household surveys differ among countries and frequently also within countries over time.[8] Three ways of alleviating comparability problems are adhered to throughout the chapter. First, when major changes in methodology or coverage occur, ways of assessing the impact on inequality statistics are provided. For instance, in Bolivia the household survey was urban in 1992 and nationally representative in 1996. Two sets of statistics are therefore presented for Bolivia in 1996: one for the whole sample and one for those urban areas also surveyed in 1992.

Second, in addition to presenting statistics for more general variables (for example, household income from all sources), more specific variables with fewer problems of comparability (for example, wages from primary jobs for male prime-age workers) are also considered. Third, the tables document the particularities of each survey that may blur comparisons with other countries and years. (Most of this information is available on the Web site of this study. Readers interested in technical details are advised to visit the site.) Although every effort has been made to clean the data and present consistent statistics, the reader interested in a specific country is advised to consult country-specific literature.

Income inequality in the 1990s

This section uses the data set to study income inequality across countries and over time. It first takes a look at the most analyzed distribution in Latin America: distribution of household per capita disposable income among all individuals in the population. Population weights are used in the calculations and missing and zero-income observations are discarded. Following the practice of national statistical offices, the authors use a broad definition of the household but exclude servants and renters and their families. Both monetary and nonmonetary incomes are considered when that information is available. Although most income sources are included (that is, labor, capital, profits, property rents, and transfers), some potentially relevant items are ignored (for example, the implicit rent from own-housing, in-kind gifts, and government in-kind transfers). Estimates of some of these variables are available in only a few surveys and are of dubious quality.

The relevant concept for welfare analysis is net income rather than gross income. In household surveys in the region, some income sources are generally reported after labor and income taxes (for example, earnings of salaried workers), while some others are typically not (for example, earnings of non-salaried professionals or capital income). In addition, cash transfers are reported in surveys but the value of government in-kind transfers (such as the provision of education and health services) is ignored. This differential treatment calls for a detailed analysis of the distributional incidence of taxes and public spending. Unfortunately, this analysis is rarely done on a regular basis since it poses numerous theoretical challenges and demands information not typically included in household surveys. This chapter follows the usual practice of computing statistics over the distribution of income reported in the surveys. (See chapter 9 for a survey of studies of the incidence of taxes and government spending.)

Table A.2 shows one of the most tangible measures of inequality: the income shares of different income strata.[9] People are sorted according to their household per capita income and divided into ten groups of equal size (called deciles). In all the Latin American countries, the share of total income held by the poorest 10 percent of the population has been always less than 2 percent, while the share of the richest 10 percent has been always higher than 30 percent. The first panel in figure 2.1 shows the income shares by decile in the three largest economies of the region: Argentina, Brazil, and Mexico. In these three countries, income shares slowly increase at a rate of less than two percentage points between consecutive deciles along most of the distribution. Differences between deciles are greater in the upper quarter of the distribution, especially between deciles 9 and 10. This

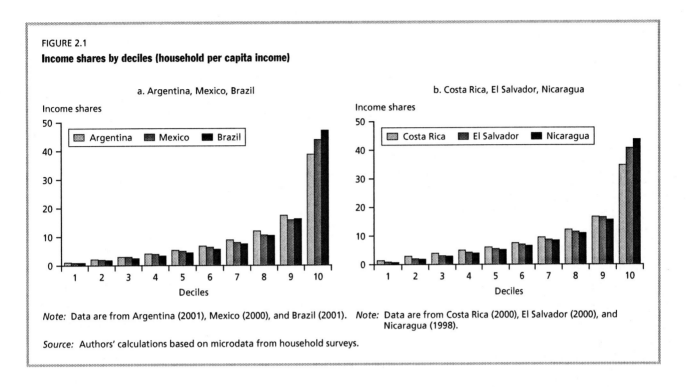

FIGURE 2.1

Income shares by deciles (household per capita income)

a. Argentina, Mexico, Brazil

b. Costa Rica, El Salvador, Nicaragua

Note: Data are from Argentina (2001), Mexico (2000), and Brazil (2001).

Note: Data are from Costa Rica (2000), El Salvador (2000), and Nicaragua (1998).

Source: Authors' calculations based on microdata from household surveys.

income gap is more than 20 percentage points in Argentina and more than 30 in Brazil.

Inequality is lower in Argentina, since the income share for each of deciles 1–9 is greater than in the other two economies and, consequently, the top decile share is smaller. The comparison between Brazil and Mexico is also clear: the income share of each of the eight poorest deciles is higher in Mexico, implying lower inequality. The second panel of figure 2.1 replicates the analysis for three Central American countries. Nicaragua is the most unequal economy of the three, while Costa Rica appears to be substantially more equal than the rest.[10]

Column (xi) in table A.2 reports the income ratio between the average individual in the top decile and a typical person in the bottom decile. This ratio ranges from 16 in Uruguay (in 1989) to values above 60 in several countries. In column (xii), individuals at the outer limits of these deciles are compared, that is, the poorest in the top decile are compared with the richest in the bottom decile. The income ratios are much smaller than in the previous column, a fact driven by the presence of a few individuals with extremely large household incomes compared to even the incomes of most people in the top decile.[11] It has been argued that Latin American distributions are characterized by large differences between the rich and the middle class. To show these differences more closely, column (xiii) in table A.2 provides the income ratio

between a person located at the 95th percentile and one located at the 80th percentile.

To illustrate the long "upper tail" of the distributions, figure 2.2 shows a histogram of the household per capita income distribution in Mexico for 2000, ignoring the richest 1 percent of the population. Most people are concentrated in the first quarter of the income line. Including the richest 1 percent would make the graph illegible, as most of the population would be concentrated in a small segment very close to the origin.

In the academic literature, more sophisticated measures of inequality are preferred to simple statistics on income shares and ratios. Table A.3 presents a set of commonly used indices: the Gini coefficient, the Theil index, the coefficient of variation, the Atkinson index, and the generalized entropy index with different parameters.[12] All indices are designed to increase as the distribution becomes more unequal. By far, the most used one is the Gini coefficient, which in the sample ranges from 42.2 in Uruguay for 1989 to 61.2 in Brazil for 1990.[13]

Although widely used, household per capita income is probably not the best available measure of individual well-being based on household income, as it ignores household economies of scale and differential needs by age. An individual's *equivalized* household income is defined as total household income divided by $(A + \alpha_1 \cdot K + \alpha_2 \cdot K_2)^\theta$ where A

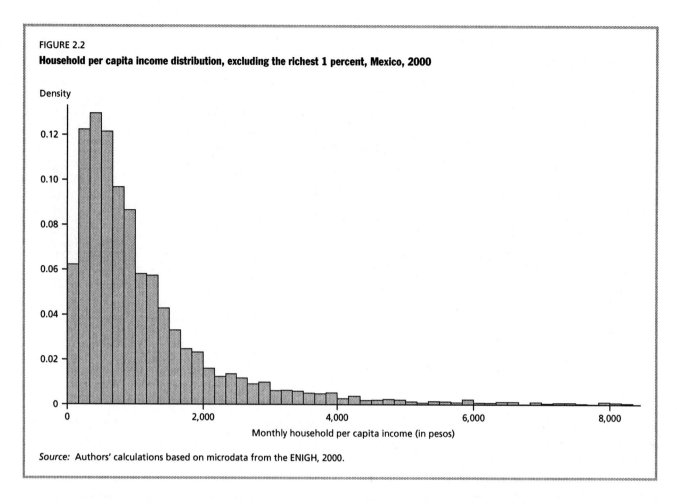

FIGURE 2.2

Household per capita income distribution, excluding the richest 1 percent, Mexico, 2000

Source: Authors' calculations based on microdata from the ENIGH, 2000.

is the number of adults, K_1 the number of children under 5 years old, and K_2 the number of children between 6 and 14. Parameters α allow for different weights for adults and children, while θ regulates the degree of household economies of scale. Following Deaton and Zaidi (2002), intermediate values of the αs ($\alpha_1 = 0.5$ and $\alpha_2 = 0.75$) and a rather high value of θ (0.9) as the benchmark case are applied.[14] Statistics for the distribution of equivalized household income constructed in this way are presented in tables A.4 and A.5. Table A.6, which reproduces the Gini coefficient of that distribution for all the countries in the sample, is the basic input for figures A.2, A.3, and A.4.

Inequality has risen in most South American economies during the last decade (see first panel of figure A.1). Argentina experienced by far the biggest jump (7.7 Gini points between 1992 and 2001).[15] Venezuela follows with an increase of nearly 4 Gini points.[16] The income distribution has also become more unequal in Bolivia, Chile, Ecuador, Peru, Uruguay, and possibly Paraguay (see below for a discussion of the Paraguay). Colombia has not

experienced significant changes in inequality. Brazil is the only South American economy where there has been a clear reduction in inequality in the 1990s, although this change was small enough to not change Brazil's position as the most unequal country in the region relative to all other countries for which information from the 1990s is available. (Guatemala was more unequal by some measures than Brazil at the end of the decade, but there is no information for earlier periods.) Most of these results are in accordance with those found in other studies for the period 1990–1999 (Morley 2001, Székely 2001, and Wodon and others 2000). These studies, however, overlooked the two most relevant distributional changes in the region: the large increase in inequality in Argentina and the distributional improvement in Brazil.

In Central America and the Caribbean, changes have been milder (see second panel of figure A.1). The income distribution has remained remarkably stable in Jamaica, Nicaragua, and Panama and has become more equal in Honduras and somewhat more unequal in Costa Rica and

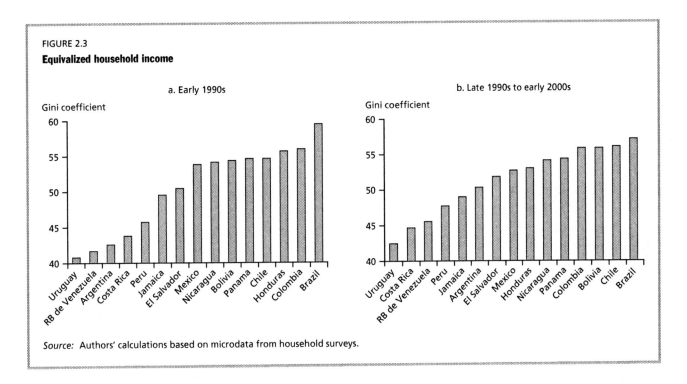

FIGURE 2.3

Equivalized household income

a. Early 1990s

Gini coefficient

b. Late 1990s to early 2000s

Gini coefficient

Source: Authors' calculations based on microdata from household surveys.

El Salvador.[17] Inequality indices went down in Mexico by 2000, although not enough to confirm that the fall is really significant in statistical terms (see below for a discussion on this point). Initial analysis by the Government of Mexico of the 2002 survey finds a larger further decline in inequality, but this was not available in time to include in the analysis for this report.

The assessment of inequality patterns is quite robust with regard to the choice of inequality measures. It is interesting to note, however, that the share of the poorest deciles has increased significantly only in Brazil and Panama, while it has shrunk in most of the region's economies. Consequently, for instance, the Atkinson index with inequality-aversion parameter 2 (see column (vi) in tables A.3 and A.5), which gives more weight to changes affecting the poorest individuals than the Gini coefficient, generates a somewhat more pessimistic picture of distributional changes in the region.

It should be noted that less unequal countries have performed worse on average than more unequal countries. While the distribution has become more unequal in Argentina, Uruguay, and República Bolivariana de Venezuela (three low-inequality economies), it either has not changed or has become more equal in Brazil, Colombia, Mexico, and Panama (four mid- to high-inequality economies). The standard deviation for the distribution of Gini coefficients in the region fell substantially in the last decade, from 6.1 to 4.6.

Although Latin America has traditionally been very homogeneous compared to other regions of the world, it has become even more so in distributional terms in the last ten years.

Figure 2.3 illustrates this fact. In the early 1990s, countries fell into three groups: (1) those with low inequality (relative to regional standards), comprising Argentina, Costa Rica, possibly Peru, Uruguay, and República Bolivariana de Venezuela; (2) those with high inequality; and (3) Brazil, which stood out as significantly more unequal than the rest. Ten years later, the differences among groups are not so clear. A sort of convergence of inequality levels seems to have taken place. Figure A.3 shows this distributional convergence for the three largest economies of the region. Although still significantly different, the income distributions of Argentina, Mexico, and Brazil have rapidly become more alike during the last decade.

A decade of differential changes has had some impact on the inequality ranking of countries in the region. Argentina moved up the inequality ladder, closer to the mid- and high-inequality group; Bolivia and Chile also rose in the rankings; and Colombia, Costa Rica, and Honduras all moved down. In spite of having the largest reduction in inequality in the last decade, Brazil remains at the top of the list of these countries.

As a result of the reported changes, the average Gini coefficient across countries increased almost 1 point in the period (from 50.5 to 51.4). The population-weighted average, however, shows a small decrease (from 51.9 to 51.5) because of the positive performance of Brazil and Mexico and the stability of Colombia, the three most populated countries in the region.

Table A.7 reports the Gini coefficient for the distribution of household income divided by alternative equivalent scales. In columns (vii) and (viii), distributions in urban and rural populations are separated wherever possible. In some countries inequality is higher in cities, while in others it is higher in rural areas. However, in most countries inequality differences between urban and rural areas appear to be minor. Household surveys do not usually properly capture nonlabor and nonmonetary income. Columns (ix) to (xii) report the Gini coefficient for the distribution of household per capita income, including as income sources only labor income, monetary income, labor monetary income, and labor monetary income in urban regions. These are the most homogeneous household income variables to compare across countries.

According to some, inequality only has normative significance for the distribution of variables that are beyond the control of individuals. This idea may indicate, for instance, concern about the distribution of total household income and not household income adjusted for demographics, since fertility decisions are (mostly) under the control of individuals. Without judging the validity of this argument, column (xiii) shows the Gini coefficient for the distribution of total household income. Finally, table A.7 reports the Gini coefficient for the distribution of equivalized household income for people in certain age ranges in order to control for factors related to the lifecycle.

Most of the qualitative results related to inequality trends and cross-country comparisons do not significantly vary when any of the distributions in table A.7 are considered instead of the household per capita or equivalized income distributions given in tables A.3 and A.5. There are a few ranking reversals and changes in trends as different income variables are considered, but the main results remain quite robust despite these methodological changes.

A brief history of income inequality in Latin America since the 1950s

This section combines information from the data set prepared for this report with evidence from other sources for previous decades to draw a general picture of trends in income inequality in the region. Unfortunately, the view of this issue becomes increasingly blurred as one goes back in time. As recently as the 1970s, many countries did not conduct national surveys or even any household surveys. In fact, it was only after World War II that countries around the world started to conduct household surveys and to compute inequality statistics in a systematic way. Mexico and some Caribbean countries (including Barbados, Guyana, Jamaica, and Trinidad and Tobago) were the first in the region to participate in that trend in the 1950s.

Only Mexico has continued with a systematic program of surveying household incomes and expenditures. The available statistics for that country show a mild increase in income inequality in the 1950s and the first half of the 1960s (Felix 1982, Fields 1989, and Altimir 1996b). There is some evidence that inequality also increased in some of the countries in the region where distributional statistics became available in the 1960s (such as Brazil, Costa Rica, Chile, and Uruguay).[18]

Most countries either consolidated or introduced household surveys in the 1970s. The picture of income inequality from that decade on is therefore clearer. Some international organizations (including ECLAC, IDB, and the World Bank) shed additional light on the issue by generating periodic reports depicting the level, structure, and trends of income inequality in the region. Table A.8 indicates signs of changes in inequality trends in most Latin American countries in the last three decades. During the 1970s, inequality increased significantly only in the Southern Cone countries (that is, Argentina, Chile, and Uruguay).

In contrast, several countries in Latin America (the Bahamas, Colombia, Mexico, Panama, Peru, and República Bolivariana de Venezuela) experienced equalizing changes, while others showed stable distributions. The 1980s was a "lost decade" in distributional terms, as well as in terms of growth. Most countries suffered a significant increase in the level of income inequality. In about half, inequality continued to increase in the 1990s, although in most cases at a slower pace. As a result of the patterns described above, most countries in the region now have more unequal income distributions than they did around 1970, and very likely than they did at the end of World War II. There are some exceptions, but for the majority of Latin American countries the economic changes of the last half-century have been mainly disequalizing.

The previous evidence refers to countries in the region considered separately. Londoño and Székely (2000) compute inequality indicators for the region as a whole by calculating a Lorenz curve using the percentiles of each country. They conclude that inequality fell in the 1970s, increased in the 1980s, and increased a bit more in the first half of the 1990s. The average income ratio of top to bottom quintiles went from 22.9 in 1970 to 18.0 in 1982, back to 22.9 in 1991, and then to 24.4 in 1995. Londoño and Székely (2000) also conclude that both the level and the change of overall inequality are mainly due to differences within rather than across countries. In fact, in the last 20 years a slow convergence in per capita income has occurred among countries in the region. Consequently, the increase in regional inequality is due exclusively to disequalizing changes in the income distributions within countries.

Having described the main changes in the region as a whole, the rest of this section is devoted to presenting a broad picture of income inequality patterns by country.

Inequality has dramatically increased in *Argentina* during the last three decades.[19] The Gini coefficient for the household per capita income distribution in the Greater Buenos Aires area increased from 34.5 in 1974 to 53.8 in 2002 (CEDLAS 2003). Even if observations for the recent years of economic crisis are ignored, the trend toward an increase is noticeable. None of the other Latin American countries has experienced such deep distributional changes as Argentina.[20]

Inequality also increased in neighboring *Uruguay* during the 1990s, although the increase was smaller. Moreover, there were no significant distributional changes in Uruguay in the 1970s and 1980s. As a consequence of these divergent patterns, the distributions of Argentina and Uruguay, once almost identical, now are significantly different. The third country in the Southern Cone, *Chile,* has always had higher inequality indicators, but that country's income distribution became more unequal during the 1970s and 1980s. Although this "storm" seemed to end in the 1990s (Ferreira and Litchfield 1999), there are no signs of distributional recovery; in fact, inequality measures increased slightly during the last decade (see Contreras and others 2001).

Brazil has traditionally been the most unequal economy in the region. The Brazilian economy experienced a significant increase in income inequality during the 1980s (Ferreira and Litchfield 1996), but since then inequality has stabilized and even started to decline (Neri and Camargo 1999). As mentioned above, a drop in income inequality in Brazil during the last decade has been identified.

Due to the limited number and changing nature of household surveys, distributional information for *Bolivia* and *Paraguay* before the mid-1990s is scarce. Inequality appeared to increase slightly in Bolivia during the 1990s, a result that is confirmed by other studies (Morley 2001, Székely 2001). Paraguay did not have reliable national household surveys until the mid-1990s. In order to gain some insight on the evolution of inequality, the authors of the current study computed the Gini coefficient for two years, 1990 and 1995, using only data from the metropolitan area of Asunción; the finding was a sizable increase in inequality.[21] Inequality seems to have decreased during the second half of the 1990s in Paraguay, although possibly not enough to compensate for the increase that occurred during the first half.[22]

Income distribution in *Colombia* and *República Bolivariana de Venezuela* became more equal in the 1970s and more unequal in the 1980s. In the 1990s, there was no recovery from the distributional losses of the 1980s; inequality continued to increase in República Bolivariana de Venezuela and the pattern for Colombia was stable (see also Ocampo and others 1998, Székely 2001). In Peru, although there is no clear evidence that income distribution became more unequal in the 1970s and 1980s, data for the 1990s suggests a significant movement toward a greater concentration of income. Studies that use expenditure data have had similar results. The distribution seems to have also become somewhat more unequal in neighboring *Ecuador,* at least in the second half of the 1990s.

The income distribution in *Mexico* has changed in different directions in the last three decades. After improving in the 1970s, the distribution became substantially more unequal in the 1980s. In the 1990s, despite important economic changes and shocks, income distribution has remained remarkably stable (however, as noted above, preliminary results for 2002 indicate a reduction in inequality). The tables in this section illustrate this fact, which has also been highlighted by other authors (Morley 2001, Székely 2001).[23]

The inequality pattern for *Panama* is similar. In *Costa Rica,* the distribution remained stable for decades at low levels of inequality (Londoño and Székely 2000). Despite a small increase in inequality during the 1990s, *Costa Rica* remains one of the most equal countries in the region (see also Trejos 1999). Inequality is much higher in the other Central American countries. The evidence suggests no significant inequality changes in *Nicaragua,* a drop in *Honduras,* and a small increase in *El Salvador* during the

1990s. Only one household survey is available for *Guatemala*, on the basis of which the country emerges as one of the most unequal countries of the region.

Once more widespread among Caribbean countries, household surveys are now scarce in the region. This makes monitoring the social situation and designing poverty reduction policies in the subregion much harder. For the handful of countries where data is available, however, some trends can be discerned. During the 1970s and 1980s, inequality increased in the *Bahamas* and decreased in *Trinidad and Tobago*, according to Fields (1989) and the World Institute for Development Economics Research (WIDER) (2000). Some studies report mild inequality increases in the *Dominican Republic* (Hausman and Rigobón 1993). Income distribution has remained quite stable in *Jamaica* in the last decade, as shown in this and other studies (Chen, Datt, and Ravallion 1995, World Bank 1999). Inequality in the Caribbean seems to have always been significantly lower than in the rest of Latin America.

It is always tempting to account for inequality patterns with a simple explanation, for instance by referring to a few macro variables. Inequality decreased in the 1970s during times of relative economic prosperity and increased during the "lost decade" of the 1980s. According to this simple view, the recovery of the 1990s should have brought significant distributional improvements. However, there is no evidence that this happened. Of course, many changes that occurred in the 1990s can be blamed for the lack of distributional improvement, but their consideration would result in more complex explanations. A sign of this complexity is the multiplicity of distributional patterns across relatively homogeneous countries that result from the evidence provided in this chapter. (Discussion of the inequality determinants in the region is deferred to part II of this report.)

Are the levels of inequality in the region's income distributions high? The answer seems to be "yes" without the need for much qualification of the question. That current inequality levels in the region are high is illustrated in three ways: (1) compared to previous decades, (2) compared to countries in other regions of the world, and (3) according to the perceptions of people throughout Latin America. This section has shown evidence for point (1), while the next section is devoted to consideration of point (2).

Regarding point (3), evidence is of course more elusive. According to a recent survey in various Latin American countries on perceptions about various economic and social issues by Latinobarómetro,[24] nearly 90 percent of the population considers the current income distribution in their countries to be "unfair" or "very unfair" (see figure 1.3 and table A.9). The correlation between the level of income inequality as measured by the Gini coefficient for the equivalized household income distribution and the proportion of "very unfair" answers (or the sum of "unfair" plus "very unfair") is positive but only marginally significant. The unconditional relationship between the change in the Gini coefficient during the 1990s and the perception of justice in the income distribution seems to be nonsignificant.

Consumption inequality

As discussed in section 2.1, household consumption is a better measure of well-being than income. Unfortunately, only a few countries in the region conduct expenditure surveys on a regular basis, with most of them participants in the World Bank's Living Standards Measurement Study project. Only Ecuador, Jamaica, Nicaragua, Mexico, and Peru have conducted more than one expenditure survey in the last decade.[25] The inequality patterns that can be traced with that information do not differ significantly from the one depicted in this paper using income data (WIDER 2000). As expected, inequality levels are much lower when computed over the distribution of expenditures, as people tend to smooth their consumption from more volatile income profiles. However, the changes over time are similar: inequality increased in Peru, probably also in Ecuador, and stayed roughly unchanged in Jamaica, Mexico, and Nicaragua.[26]

Other dimensions of the distribution

Inequality is just one dimension of income distribution. This section briefly considers three other relevant dimensions: polarization, aggregate welfare, and poverty.

Polarization

The notion of polarization refers to relatively homogeneous clusters of households or individuals that identify with each other and are antagonistic toward or alienated from other clusters. A case of maximum polarization in terms of income would be one in which half the population is penniless and the other half shares total income equally among its members. A central conjecture that motivates research on polarization is that differences between homogeneous groups can cause social tension. Some indices have recently been developed to measure income polarization.[27] These measures depend on three factors: (1) the number of groups and their relative sizes, (2) the degree of equality within each group ("identification"), and (3) the degree of income differences among groups ("alienation"). Intuitively, higher levels of identification and alienation would increase polarization. It is worth noting that polarization can increase when inequality decreases (and vice versa). For instance, some transfers from the middle class to the poor and the rich can lead to both lower inequality and higher polarization (see Esteban and Ray 1994). Thus, the analysis of income polarization is complementary to that of income inequality.

From the sample of household surveys, the authors computed two bipolarization indices for each country and year: the Wolfson Index, which divides the distribution at the median income, and the Esteban, Gradín, and Ray 1999 (EGR) Index, which finds the optimal income cut-off point. Table A.10 shows the results for these bipolarization measures, along with the Gini coefficient, for both the distribution of household per capita income and the distribution of equivalized household income.

As with inequality measures, polarization increased in several South American countries and remained stable in Central America, the Dominican Republic, and Jamaica. Argentina, Bolivia, Uruguay, and Venezuela experienced the largest increases in polarization. Among the economies with falling bipolarization measures, there are cases in which inequality increased, for example Chile. (Note that in tables A.2 and A.4, the share of the top decile increased significantly in Chile in the last decade, driving inequality measures up.)

Among the main losers of the distributional changes of the 1990s were people in deciles 7 to 9, that is, people who are considered according to bipolarization measures as belonging to the same "class" as the winners in the top decile. This fact weakens measured "identification" within the high-income group, and in turn drives bipolarization measures down. Between 1995 and 1999, Paraguay exhibited an opposite pattern: the share of the top decile went down, while the share of deciles 7–9 increased significantly, implying a decline in inequality but an increase in bipolarization that was driven by a tighter identification within the high-income group.[28]

Theories of polarization in economics emphasize the importance of group-based differences. There is, of course, a much stronger tradition of analysis of groups in other social science disciplines. Issues of social class are discussed in box 2.1, while differences among ethnic, racial, and gender groups are the subject of chapter 3.

Aggregate welfare

To assess the aggregate welfare of an economy, both the mean and the inequality level of the income distribution should be taken into account. It could be the case that inequality increases but everybody's incomes go up. In that case, most people would agree that aggregate welfare in an economy has increased despite the growth in inequality. Since the performance of an economy should not be assessed only by considering inequality statistics, the opposite mistake of just looking at average statistics—which is very common in the economics field—should be avoided as well. Average income may rise but inequality may also increase in such a way that some people suffer reductions in their real incomes, which may then translate into a negative assessment of the overall performance of the economy, according to some value judgments.

Table A.14 presents welfare measures for all the countries in the sample that have more than one observation. Each column shows the value of a given aggregate welfare function for a given country and year. Values are rescaled so as to make the first observation for each country equal to 100. Four social welfare functions are considered. The first uses the average income of the population; according to this value judgment, inequality is irrelevant. In columns (ii) to (iv) and (vi) to (viii), three widely used functions that take inequality into account are considered.[29] In the first panel, real per capita gross domestic product (GDP) from national accounts is taken as the average income measure and combined with the inequality indices shown in table A.3, in order to obtain rough estimates of the value of aggregate welfare according to different value judgments.[30] For various reasons, per capita income from household surveys differs from estimates in the national accounts, so in the second panel of table A.14, the exercise is repeated using information only from household surveys.[31]

Most Latin American economies managed to grow during the 1990s, but in many the income distribution became more unequal. This combination led to ambiguous results for aggregate welfare in some cases. In all ten economies portrayed in figure A.3, real per capita GDP increased during the 1990s. However, in Peru and Venezuela, according to value judgments that attach more weight to the poorest individuals (Atk(2) in figure 2.4), welfare declined, while in others, such as El Salvador and Uruguay, the welfare increase

BOX 2.1
Social class

The concept of *social class* is an analytical tool widely used in sociology and other social sciences, but mostly ignored in modern economics. The term refers to "discrete and durable categories of the population characterized by differential access to power-conferring resources and related life chances" (Portes and Hoffman 2003). In practice, social classes are usually defined in terms of income sources. Portes and Hoffman (2003) recently presented evidence on class structure and trends in Latin America, based on information from household surveys gathered by ECLAC (2000).

In that study, five groups are considered: capitalists, professionals and executives, petty entrepreneurs (or the petty bourgeoisie), formal workers, and informal workers. The first two groups comprise the "dominant" class. Empirical estimates are rough. Capitalists are operationally defined as owners of firms with more than five workers, while professionals and executives work in the public sector and in firms employing five or more workers. The petty bourgeoisie includes owners of small firms, own account professionals, and technicians. Formal workers are defined as those in the public sector or in firms with five or more workers.

Based on information from ECLAC (2000), the first panel of table A.11 shows the relative occupational income of each social class for each country and year. Except for a few countries, there are no clear signs that the "dominant" class, defined in this very narrow way, has become richer in relative terms during the 1990s. In addition, in most countries the share of low-paid informal workers in the population has not increased significantly since the 1990s, according to the second panel of table A.11.

Using the definitions in Portes and Hoffman (2003), the authors of the current study have applied the data set to compute the class structure in Argentina and Brazil, the two paradigmatic cases of distributional changes in Latin America used in this analysis. The main results are shown in table A.12. Compared to Argentina, Brazil has a significantly higher share of informal workers and a lower share of petty entrepreneurs and formal workers. The second panel of table A.12 shows average individual income for each class relative to that of petty entrepreneurs. In Argentina, capitalists, professionals, and executives gained significantly in relative terms compared to petty entrepreneurs and, in particular, to informal workers. In addition, the income gap between formal and informal workers widened during the 1990s in Argentina.

In contrast, relative incomes across classes were pretty stable in Brazil. The same conclusion applies when considering equivalized household income instead of individual income (as indicated in the third panel). The fourth panel of table A.12 shows that the "dominant" classes receive around 20 percent of total income. These estimates, however, are very likely affected by the difficulties in including capitalists and landlords in household surveys and by the problem of underreporting of income. Finally, the fifth panel of the Table shows Gini coefficients within classes. Inequalities within groups are lower in Argentina than in Brazil, although the gaps are narrowing.

There is a sizable degree of income overlap among social classes. Figure A.5 shows the relative income of each percentile of the within-class distributions in Argentina and Brazil. Both graphs show substantial income overlapping across classes, especially among capitalists, professionals, and petty entrepreneurs on the one hand, and between formal and informal workers on the other. Table A.13 shows cross-tabulations of the deciles, based on the distribution of individual income and the class structure. Around 75 percent of capitalists declare incomes that place them in the top two deciles of the individual income distribution. However, it should be noted that those deciles also include around 80 percent of all professionals and executives, more than 60 percent of petty entrepreneurs, more than 15 percent of formal workers, and around 10 percent of informal workers. Of course, informal workers are more concentrated in the bottom deciles of the income distribution. It is interesting to note that informal workers are increasingly moving toward the bottom deciles in Argentina, in contrast to a more stable situation in Brazil.

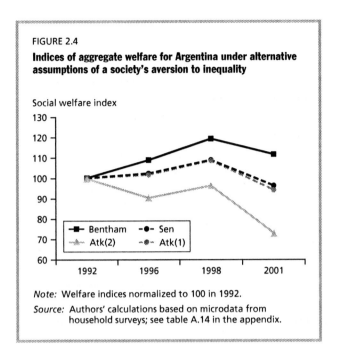

FIGURE 2.4

Indices of aggregate welfare for Argentina under alternative assumptions of a society's aversion to inequality

Social welfare index

Note: Welfare indices normalized to 100 in 1992.

Source: Authors' calculations based on microdata from household surveys; see table A.14 in the appendix.

was significantly smaller than growth in GDP. In Argentina, the contrast is more dramatic: despite an 11 percent increase in per capita GDP measured by national accounts between 1992 and 2001, aggregate welfare decreased according to all the value judgments implicit in the calculations that do not neglect distributional issues. The increase in inequality was large enough to offset the growth in mean income. In contrast, aggregate welfare unambiguously increased in Costa Rica and Chile despite disequalizing distributional changes. In Brazil and Panama, growth in aggregate welfare was fueled by both a growing per capita income and a more equal income distribution.[32]

The scope of these exercises is limited, as it is assumed that aggregate welfare is a function only of household income. Other factors—including freedom, security, political power, access to basic services, and health status—should also be considered as arguments for individual well-being. A comprehensive welfare study including these aspects is beyond the scope of this chapter. However, section 2.5 below provides statistics on the distribution of some of the variables that, arguably, influence individual utility.

Poverty

Although inequality and poverty are different concepts, they are closely related. Changes in income-related poverty can be thought of as the result of changes in average income and inequality. For instance, a growing economy with stable levels

of inequality would end up reducing the number of people whose incomes fall below an absolute poverty line. In fact, the significant fall in poverty in Latin America during the 1970s was fed by growing economies with either stable or more equal distributions. The story in the 1980s was exactly the opposite: falling incomes and more unequal distributions combined to generate a tangible increase in poverty statistics. The 1990s again showed a different combination: despite some disequalizing changes in income distribution, the strong recovery of several Latin American economies generated a reduction in the poverty indicators both for the region as a whole and in most countries (see Wodon and others 2000 and 2001, Székely 2001, and Sala-i-Martin 2002). Overall, in the last three decades the region has experienced a substantial decline in the incidence of poverty.[33]

Table A.15 summarizes part of the large body of literature on poverty indicators in the region.[34] It should be emphasized that poverty measures are very sensitive to the explicit and implicit assumptions made by researchers (Székely and others 2000). Thus, caution is required when comparing results obtained by different methodologies. The general trend during the 1990s was toward a reduction in income poverty. In the mid-1990s, various authors found that there were 1.5–2 percent fewer poor people in the region than at the beginning of the decade (Wodon and others 2001, Londoño and Székely 2000). This reduction is mainly explained by the performance of Brazil, where the headcount ratio fell around 7 percentage points.

Chile was the other country that had an extraordinary performance in terms of poverty reduction (around 16 percentage points). Colombia (until the late 1990s), Costa Rica, and Panama also managed to reduce poverty thanks to stable income distributions and growth. On the other hand, in Mexico the percentage of poor people increased about 5 percentage points during the first half of the 1990s. Much of the literature fails to report the increase in poverty in Argentina, even though the official headcount ratio in Greater Buenos Aires went from 17.8 in 1992 to 25.9 in 1998 and to 35.4 in 2001. That poverty increase, also noticeable in the rest of the country, took place during a period of growing per capita income. Venezuela is the other case where, despite a growing economy, the increase in inequality pulled poverty rates up significantly.

Figure A.4, based on data from Székely (2001), shows the poverty headcount ratio of most countries in the region on the basis of a poverty line of US$2 a day (adjusted for differences in purchasing power across countries) in the late 1990s. High-income countries with relatively low inequality, such as Uruguay, República Bolivariana de Venezuela, and Argentina, have relatively low poverty levels. Chile has recently joined this group due to its growth performance, despite being a high inequality country. On the other hand, low-income countries with high inequality, such as Bolivia, El Salvador, Guatemala, Honduras, Nicaragua, and Paraguay, have very high poverty levels.

2.3. Measurement-related issues and data limitations

Although household surveys are the most appropriate source of information for distributional analysis, they have many limitations. It is important to make these limitations explicit in order to ensure that statistics are interpreted with caution and to identify areas for future improvements. While most limitations are present everywhere, some are particularly important in Latin America.[35] Probably the main difference between household surveys in the region and in other less developed parts of the world is the lack of expenditure-based questionnaires in most Latin American countries. As noted in section 2.1, expenditures are a better measure of living standards than income, especially in less developed areas. The extension of consumption-based questionnaires in the region is certainly one of the main areas in need of attention by national and international agencies.

Does use of income rather than expenditures overstate Latin America's inequality relative to other regions?

It may be that Latin America appears to be more unequal than other regions that only report information on expenditures because of systematic differences between income and expenditure inequality. There are two reasons why, in any given country, incomes are generally more unequally distributed than consumption expenditures financed by those same incomes:

- Households dislike sudden variation in their consumption patterns, and thus tend to smooth consumption patterns over time. For a given individual, consumption flows therefore behave almost like the averages of income streams over time (see Friedman 1956). The law of large numbers implies that the cross-sectional dispersion of the distribution of

consumption will thus be smaller than that of the distribution of income at any point in time.

- It is generally argued that income is recalled and measured with a greater level of error than is consumption (see Deaton 1997), adding to variance (and therefore inequality) in the distribution of current incomes. In particular, underreporting can be the result of several factors. These include a deliberate decision by the respondent to misreport; the absence of questions that could capture some income sources (for example, the implicit rent from housing for homeowners); or the difficulty of recalling or estimating income from certain sources (for example, earnings from informal activities, in-kind payments, home production, and capital income). This problem probably implies a downward bias on the measured living standards of both poor people, who rely on a combination of informal activities or production for their own consumption, and of rich people, who derive a larger proportion of income from nonlabor sources and are probably more prone to underreport.

Whatever the sources of difference between income- and expenditure-based information, what can be said about how Latin America would compare with regions in which inequality is only measured in terms of consumption?

A new study by Elbers and others (2003) sheds some initial light on this question. The study takes advantage of a 1996 pilot household survey conducted in Brazil's northeastern and southeastern regions. Known as the *Pesquisa sobre Padrões de Vida* (PPV), that survey is modeled on the World Bank's LSMS. The PPV is a multimodule integrated survey that collects data on both household consumption and income. Fairly detailed information on consumption expenditures is also collected, making it possible to impute values of consumption streams from items such as housing and food products made at home. While generally viewed as a high-quality survey, the PPV has a small sample size and limited geographic coverage, and is therefore not widely used to study inequality at the national level.

Elbers and others (2003) employ a recently developed methodology to impute consumption from the PPV survey into Brazil's traditional (income-based) PNAD survey.[36] This approach allows the authors to estimate consumption-rather than income-related inequality in Brazil, based on the same underlying data from the PNAD household survey.

FIGURE 2.5

Brazil's consumption inequality in international perspective

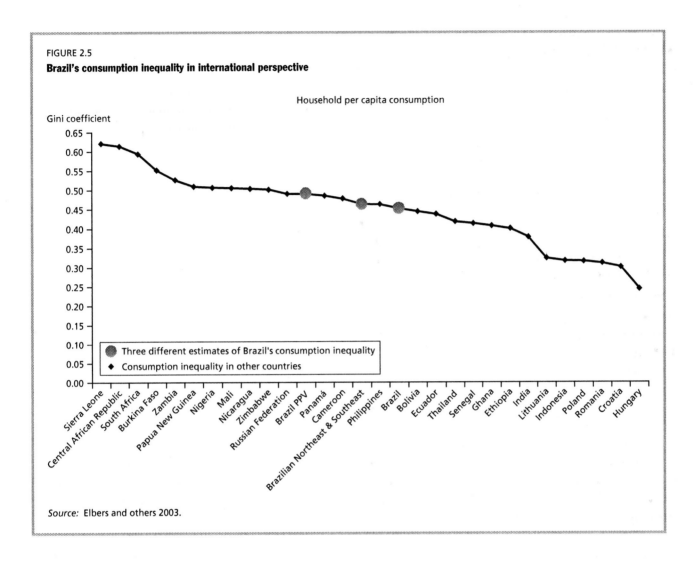

Source: Elbers and others 2003.

Figure 2.5 indicates that when inequality is measured in the PNAD on the basis of the Gini coefficient of imputed consumption, Brazil's inequality is less extreme. This new Gini coefficient in Brazil as a whole is measured at around 0.45, compared with around 0.6 for household per capita income. If attention is given only to the northeastern and southeastern regions, inequality is a bit higher, at 0.46. Inequality in these two areas, measured directly with the PPV household survey data, is a bit higher still, at 0.49.

All three of these measures are, however, significantly below those observed in a number of other countries. It is interesting to note that, with the exception of Russia and Nicaragua, most of the countries with high levels of consumption inequality are in Africa, which is also a high-inequality region (and possibly also one with weaker statistical traditions and so less accurately measured consumption). While still unequal by international standards,

Brazil is less obviously an outlier. To the extent that similar concerns can be raised about the quality of income data in other Latin American countries, inequality in the whole region, relative to that in other regions, may be lower than has traditionally been assumed.

Income volatility and mobility

A related concern arises from the fact that there is considerable income volatility within Latin America. When incomes are volatile from month to month, measured inequality tends to reflect an overestimation of underlying inequality. De Ferranti and others (2000) showed that aggregate volatility of real private consumption in Latin America was almost three times as high as in the developed economies between 1960 and 1999. During the same period, it was slightly higher than in most countries in Asia, but lower than in Sub-Saharan Africa. This aggregate volatility translates into high levels of risk and uncertainty at a more disaggregated level. In Brazil, for instance, the mean income of the poorest fifth of the population fell by more than 30 percent during the 1982–1983 recession, rose by more than 30 percent during the 1984–86 boom, fell by some 12 percent in 1990–1991, and then rose again by 15 percent in 1994–1995. Volatility in both gross national disposable income and real private consumption is also very high—indeed higher than in the rest of Latin America and in the Caribbean countries (World Bank, 2003e). Under the standard assumption that consumers are averse to intertemporal volatility in their consumption path (or averse to risk), this sort of roller coaster clearly reduces social welfare.

Income variations over time are caused by a number of factors. As discussed above, a large self-employed sector is usually characterized by more volatility than is the formal sector, since profits adjust to changes in demand and cost conditions directly but wages are usually more protected. The rate at which firms close tends to be much higher among small firms in the informal sector than among large firms in the formal sector (see Levenson and Maloney 1998). However, in Latin America real wages have often oscillated quite dramatically as a result of high and often unstable inflation rates combined with imperfect indexation mechanisms. In addition to wages, income may also be affected by changes in employment status. Unemployment risk is of increasing concern in Latin America, particularly for young people and women, as reviewed in de Ferranti and others (2000).

In rural areas, climatic events represent an additional source of risk, beyond those which arise from terms-of-trade and other macroeconomic shocks. A study of household strategies for coping with the downturn in agricultural production in El Salvador in 1997 (Conning, Olinto, and Trigueros 2000) found that landless workers, who tended to rely on agricultural employment prior to the crisis, were hit the hardest.

What does the evidence of large income volatility in Latin America (reviewed in more detail in de Ferranti and others 2000) imply in the context of a study of inequality? There are three basic implications:

- As the volatility of current income increases, so does the gap between inequality in current income and inequality in permanent income. This is one factor behind the large difference between income inequality and consumption inequality measures in Brazil discussed above. Consumption is a better indicator of permanent income.

- To the extent that people are risk-averse, volatility is costly in terms of social welfare. On the one hand, long-run interpersonal inequalities may be overestimated by focusing on current incomes. On the other hand, some of this measurement reflects inequality in the incomes of the same people over time, which is detrimental to individual (and thus social) welfare for reasons having to do with preferences for lower risk. Although this is less of a problem to the extent that people can smooth out patterns of consumptions, it is only cost-free if capital markets (including, importantly, insurance markets) are perfect.

- Some of what appears to be intragenerational short-term mobility is simply volatility by a nicer name. Some of the evidence on mobility in Latin America is discussed in box 2.2, but the point here is that evidence of large, short-term disruptions in wage or income distributions is likely to reflect high risk and volatility.

The absence of multiyear panel data in the region means that very little is actually known about intragenerational mobility in Latin America (however, see Graham and Pettinato 2002 for a discussion of results of a study in Peru). If and when more becomes known, it is likely that analysts will face trade-offs between welfare gains (arising from lower inequality during multiple periods when later incomes are less predictable on the basis of earlier incomes) and welfare losses (arising from aversion to income fluctuation over time). These trade-offs will be the same as those that result from mobility and volatility trends observed in more developed countries. Gottschalk and Spolaore (2002, p. 193), for instance, find that "When aversion to income fluctuations and (beyond-the-veil) risk are introduced, those larger costs offset the benefits stemming from reduced multi-period inequality. Consequently, Germans and Americans end up obtaining similar net benefits from mobility, although for very different reasons." Recently, this sort of careful thinking about mobility has challenged earlier facile assertions that higher inequality in the United States than in Europe was not problematic, since mobility was also higher there.

BOX 2.2
Mobility in Latin America: What little is known?

Since the idea of intragenerational short-term mobility is strongly related to volatility—or at least the two concepts are not easily separable—the literature usually focuses more on intergenerational long-term mobility. The main variables used in this kind of analysis are generally assets or choices related to education and occupation, which can be good proxies for permanent income. With these two variables, Valéria Pero (2003) studied the Brazilian case and showed that the country does not have significant educational or occupational intergenerational mobility.

In fact, Brazil has one of the lowest levels of intergenerational educational mobility in the world. According to Behrman, Gaviria, and Székely (2001), Latin American countries have lower intergenerational educational mobility than developed ones. Furthermore, comparing Brazil and the other Latin American countries, there is evidence that Brazil has an even lower level of mobility (Menezes-Filho 2001). The main reason for this phenomenon is the fact that educational performance in Brazil is associated more with family background—in particular the schooling of parents—than it is in other countries.[a]

The educational levels of individuals and their parents are highly correlated, in the sense that sons of parents with little education also have little education. According to Paes de Barros and others (2001), the schooling of parents appears to be the most important variable in explaining educational performance in Brazil. Moreover, the schooling of mothers seems to have a stronger effect than that of fathers on educational performance. Based on the literature, Pero (2003) goes further, concluding that "The influence of parents' schooling on educational performance is stronger for men than women, for black than nonblack, and for residents in the Northeast than in the Southeast."

Nevertheless, Bourguignon, Ferreira, and Menéndez (2003), as well as others, point to an increase in educational mobility over time. According to this conclusion, an additional year of schooling for parents means a larger increase in schooling for older cohorts than for younger ones. A complementary analysis (Pero 2003) indicates that it is possible to find evidence that educational mobility is more noticeable among less educated individuals. Thus, indications that educational mobility is rising for young cohorts could be related to the fact that educational policy is closing the gaps related to family background in Brazil.

In keeping with points presented above, members of the younger generation should be able to achieve better positions in the labor market in comparison to their parents. In other words, an increase in occupational mobility could be expected as each generation becomes more educated. Although the data suggest this pattern—since more than half the sons in Brazil are in different occupational classes from those of their fathers—the occupational mobility rate in that country seems to be very low compared with other countries, most of which are developed (Scalon and Ribeiro 2001).

In some sense, the occupational mobility rate can be considered a good indicator of development. According to Pero (2003), mobility can result from "economic growth and its impacts on job creation and on sectoral and occupational composition and demographic aspects" and may be a consequence of "distribution of opportunities, upon which the society builds mobility channels to match people efficiently in the social structure in a fair system."

This perspective is corroborated by analyses of different Brazilian states, since there is greater mobility in more developed areas. The literature concerned with educational and occupational mobility in Brazil indicates that during the 1970s, mobility was the result of industrialization and urbanization processes. On the other hand, this does not appear to be true with regard to the distribution of opportunities. Silva and Roditi (1988)—using a log-linear model to test the hypothesis of constant circular or relative mobility patterns over time—argue that the distribution of opportunities have not changed significantly. However, Scalon and Ribeiro (2001) assert that there is a trend toward a more even distribution of the achievement of social positions, even though Brazilian society is rigid in comparison to other countries.

In conclusion, Pero (2003) finds that occupational mobility increased in Brazil between 1973 and 1996. Pero also suggests that other channels of mobility were more important in determining position in the social structure than occupation or class inheritance. The Brazilian data also indicates that mobility currently tends to be more related to positional changes than to the creation of new positions.

a. Contrary to common sense, variables such as the training of teachers and infrastructure (for example, books, computers, and night courses) are not that important in explaining educational performance. The key point is that although these variables have a positive effect, they account for just a small part of the level of education as a whole.

Issues of coverage and measurement of incomes

A further issue concerns how comprehensive and accurate are questions related to income. All household surveys in Latin America include questions on monetary income from salaried work, but some use very simple (and therefore less reliable) questions and many do not include estimates of nonsalary and nonmonetary payments. Among those countries that focus on this issue, efforts to obtain correct estimates vary significantly. All countries make some effort to capture income from self-employment and capital income. However, the intensity of these efforts varies among countries and sometimes also within countries over time. Differential misreporting behavior among respondents and varying efforts in the survey design can distort inequality comparisons among countries. If these behaviors and efforts change over time, they can also distort the view of inequality trends.

Researchers apply three kinds of strategies to alleviate these problems. The first is to restrict the analysis to more homogeneous variables that are subject to fewer problems of misreporting. Typically, people look at the distribution of labor income or, in an even more restricted approach, at the distribution of monetary wages from salaried work in urban areas (see section 2.4). Of course, the cost of doing this is ignoring a sometimes sizable part of the overall income distribution. The second strategy is to apply some grossing-up procedures. Income from a given source in the household survey is adjusted to match the corresponding value in national accounts. This adjustment usually leads to inflating capital income relatively more than the other income sources, and hence generates higher inequality estimates.

Finally, a third strategy is to estimate some incomes based on other pieces of information in a survey. For instance, the implicit rent from own-housing can be estimated using hedonic price regressions if a survey records some housing characteristics and the amount paid by renters in the rental sector (see Fay and others 2002). In addition, multivariate regressions can be run to estimate wages for workers who do not report or clearly misreport wages, but do report individual characteristics (for example, education and age).

Since surveys differ with regard to the severity of these problems, adjustments should be made on a case-by-case basis. This is a task that goes beyond the scope of this chapter. Researchers who have made different types of adjustments have generally found that most results for inequality trends within countries are robust.[37] Results across countries are somewhat less robust in the face of methodological changes. Székely and Hilgert (1999) find that some inequality rankings among Latin American countries vary as a wide range of adjustments are performed to deal with the informational issues sketched here. However, even when there might be some changes, the general picture remains robust: low-inequality and high-inequality countries remain in their groups regardless of the methodology used for the analysis.

A common observation among users of household surveys is that they do not typically include "very rich" individuals; millionaires, wealthy landlords, powerful entrepreneurs, and capitalists do not usually show up in the surveys. The highest individual incomes in surveys conducted in Latin America correspond primarily to urban professionals. This fact may be the natural consequence of random sampling (that is, there are so few millionaires that it is unlikely that they would be chosen by a random sample-selection procedure to answer the survey), nonresponse, or extensive underreporting. The fact is that rich people in the surveys are "highly educated professionals obtaining labor incomes, rather than capitalist owners living on profits" (Székely and Hilgert 1999). The omission of this group surely implies underestimation of inequality of a size that is difficult to predict.

Real rather than nominal incomes should be used in any distributional analysis. If prices faced by all households were the same, the distinction would be irrelevant. However, prices usually differ by location. If two households located in different regions have the same nominal income but face different prices, they will have different living standards. Despite the fact that many authors have highlighted the importance of considering spatial variations of prices in a distributional study (for example, Deaton 1997, Ravallion and Chen 1997), price adjustments are rarely performed in countries that do not routinely collect information on local prices as part of household surveys.

Unfortunately, most Latin American countries fall into this category. Some countries have regional price information, which is useful but does not solve the problem since price dispersion may be high within a single region (especially between urban and rural areas). However, the inequality results in this study appear to be quite robust when adjustments for regional prices are made. For instance, in Argentina the Gini coefficient for the distribution of household per capita income for 2001 slightly decreases from 52.2 to 51.9 as regional prices are taken into consideration. For

Chile in 2000, the Gini coefficient increases from 57.1 to 57.3 when this is done.

Is measured inequality over- or understated?

Is "real" inequality lower or higher than the estimates derived here from household surveys? Unfortunately, the answer is not clear. Some factors lead to an underestimation of inequality (for example, misreporting of capital incomes or the absence of very rich people in the surveys), while others result in an overestimation (for example, using monthly income instead of permanent income or consumption). More work is definitely needed in this area. However, it should be noted that the key concern here is not to know the exact level of inequality of a country in a given year, but instead to make time and cross-country comparisons. The authors implicitly assume in this analysis that factors that bias the measurement of inequality remain stable among countries and over time.

It is necessary to avoid either of the two extreme positions taken toward household surveys, that is, either to discard them or to use them without qualifications. Even with all their limitations in mind, household surveys provide valuable information for a distributional analysis and are the best available source of data with which to generate representative distributional statistics of the population. However, it is important to be aware of their drawbacks. Despite important steps taken by Latin American governments and international organizations in the last decade (for example, the MECOVI program), there is still a long way to go before a more reliable, richer, and more homogeneous set of national household surveys is available. In this regard, Latin America lags behind some other less developed regions.

Sample variability and confidence intervals

Measures of the different dimensions of a distribution are subject to sample variability problems because they are derived from surveys, not census data. If a sample consisted of only two individuals, indicators would surely vary widely over time even when the population remains completely unchanged, since two different individuals would be randomly selected each year. This problem can be alleviated but not completely eliminated through the use of larger samples. This point is illustrated here by assessing the robustness of some inequality comparisons with the help of confidence intervals estimated using bootstrapping techniques. This method provides interval estimations and

dispersion measures for inequality indices in a simple and efficient way.[38]

Table A.16 shows the estimated Gini coefficient for the distribution of household per capita income for each country and year, its bootstrapped standard error, the coefficient of variation, and the corresponding confidence interval for a 95 percent level of significance.[39] Given the large size of samples in most household surveys, the Gini coefficients are estimated with high precision. This is reflected in the low values of the standard errors. Column (iii) shows that the standard error is almost always smaller than 1 percent of the estimated coefficient. However, in many cases this is enough to cast doubt over the statistical significance of the inequality changes. For instance, although the recorded Gini increased in Mexico between 1996 and 2000, the two confidence intervals overlap and make the change in the Gini coefficient insignificant, that is, consistent with when different samples are taken from a population with a stable income distribution.

2.4. Inequality in Latin America in perspective

This brief section is devoted to placing the evidence from the previous section in geographical perspective. How unequal are Latin American economies compared to the rest of the world?

In the last 10 years, several studies have surveyed and computed inequality measures across countries and over time. Deininger and Squire (1996) put together a large data set of quintile shares and Gini coefficients for most countries since World War II. This panel data set—which greatly stimulated the empirical study of the links between inequality and other economic and political variables—was updated and extended in the World Income Inequality Database, a joint project of the United Nations University, WIDER, and the United Nations Development Programme (WIDER 2000).[40] Using these and other secondary sources, Milanovic (2002), Bourguignon and Morrison (2002), and Sala-i-Martin (2002) recently computed income distributions for the world and its regions.[41] Other authors have used microdata to compare distributions from different regions of the world. Bourguignon, Ferreira, and Leite (2003) and Székely and Hilgert (2001) have compared Latin American countries with some developed countries at the microdata level.

This empirical literature unambiguously suggests that Latin America is the region with the highest levels of inequality in the world, and that this has been true for as long as statistics have been kept.[42] Each bar in figure 2.6 indicates the value of the Gini coefficient for the distribution of household per capita income in countries located in four "regions" of the world.[43] Inequality in Latin America is higher than in Asia, Eastern Europe, and the developed countries.[44] Income inequality in the least unequal Latin American country (Uruguay) is higher than in the most unequal country in Eastern Europe and the industrialized countries, and not too much different from that in the most unequal country in Asia. The nine most unequal countries in the sample are in Latin America. In addition, the 14 economies included in the graph are all among the 20 most unequal countries in the sample.

Figure 2.6 refers to income inequality. When inequality is measured with regard to the distribution of household expenditures, the conclusions are similar. Using information from the same source (WIDER 2000), the average Gini coefficient in the seven Latin American countries for which expenditure data from the 1990s are available (44.0) is far above the average Gini coefficient in Asia (36.6) and Eastern Europe (30.4) and slightly higher than in Africa (43.3).[45]

Has Latin America always been more unequal than the rest of the world? The most widely cited source to answer this question has been table 5 of Deininger and Squire (1996), which is reproduced here in table A.17. The table, which shows nonweighted averages of Gini coefficients by region, indicates that at least since the 1960s, inequality in Latin American countries has been higher than in any other region of the world. With the exception of countries in Sub-Saharan Africa, the differences in Gini points between Latin America and other regions are large. This gap narrowed in the 1970s and became wider again in the 1980s. There was no clear pattern in the 1990s, when Latin America performed better than some regions in distributional terms (for example, Eastern Europe) and worse than others (for example, South Asia).

It is sometimes argued that inequality is related to the state of development in a country and comparisons should therefore be made that control for this factor. Londoño and Székely (2000) use regression analysis to compute the difference between actual inequality and expected inequality given the level of development of many countries in the world. The difference for Latin American countries is positive; that is, the region suffers from "excess inequality," which Londoño and Székely (2000) find has fluctuated around 13 Gini points over time.

Although widely cited, Deininger and Squire's table should be interpreted very cautiously. Among its problems

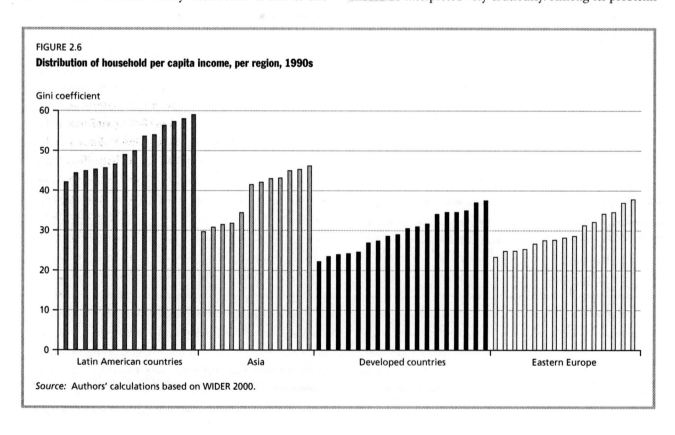

FIGURE 2.6
Distribution of household per capita income, per region, 1990s

Gini coefficient

Source: Authors' calculations based on WIDER 2000.

TABLE 2.1

Gini coefficients of the distribution of household per capita income: Common sample countries, decadal averages by region

Region	1970s	1980s	1990s	Overall average
Levels				
Latin America and the Caribbean	**48.4**	**50.8**	**52.2**	**50.5**
Asia	40.2	40.4	41.2	40.6
OECD	32.3	32.5	34.2	33.0
Eastern Europe	28.3	29.3	32.8	30.1
Changes		*70s–80s*	*80s–90s*	*70s–90s*
Latin America and the Caribbean		2.4	1.3	3.7
Asia		0.2	0.8	1.1
OECD		0.2	1.7	1.9
Eastern Europe		1.0	3.5	4.5
Difference in Gini points: LAC vs.				
Asia	8.3	10.4	10.9	9.9
OECD	16.1	18.3	18.0	17.5
Eastern Europe	20.2	21.6	19.4	20.4

Source: Authors' calculations based on WIDER 2000, Smeeding and Grodner 2000, Székely 2001, and estimates for Latin America.

are four issues: (1) the sample of countries used to compute the regional statistics is unbalanced, (2) income inequality statistics are mixed with expenditure inequality measures, (3) some of the figures that are averaged come from studies that use different methodologies, and (4) data from the 1990s are very scarce.[46] Some of these problems are corrected in table 2.1, in which Gini coefficients are computed from a common sample of countries, come from a small set of studies and hence are methodologically more consistent, and use income as the living standard variable. The general picture is not very different from table A.17. Inequality in Latin America has been significantly higher than in Asia, OECD countries, and Eastern Europe in the last three decades. There are no signs that this gap is narrowing.[47]

In a recent study, Bourguignon and Morrison (2002) computed world income inequality statistics since 1820, including information at the regional level. Table A.18 shows three inequality measures computed for five regions since 1950. The figures reflect nonweighted and population-weighted averages across countries or groups of countries.[48] Although for some regions the statistics go back to 1820, inequality measures for Latin America start in 1950.[49] Once again, the region emerges as very unequal compared to the rest of the world. The last panel of the table shows the difference in inequality between Latin America and the rest of the regions in terms of Gini points. There is no evidence that the gap between Latin America and the rest of the regions has narrowed in

the last 50 years. The story at the level of individual countries is similar: the five Latin American countries/subregions considered in the study have been among the eight most unequal countries/subregions in the world since 1950.

As mentioned before, there are no consistent statistics for inequality before the 1950s. To calculate world distribution between 1820 and 1950, Bourguignon and Morrison (2002) assume no changes in distribution in Latin America, arguing that "the absence of strong evidence suggesting the distribution was much less unequal during the 19th century." They also refer to Malthus's suggestion that in 1820 inequality was much larger in Mexico than in England. In chapter 4 of this report, it is argued that extreme inequality emerged soon after the Europeans began to colonize the Americas.

In another recent study, Milanovic (2002) computes regional distributions in which all individuals are treated equally as inhabitants of a given region (see table A.19).[50] Latin America again appears as a region of high inequality. However, Asia is currently the region with the highest Gini coefficient. This is mainly due to the great disparities in national incomes across countries in that region (for example, Japan, Hong Kong (China), and the Republic of Korea in comparison with India or Bangladesh). In the decompositions performed by Milanovic and Yitzhaki (2002) with the same data set, only 7 percent of overall inequality in Latin America is due to between-country group inequality.

By contrast, the contribution of the between-country Gini coefficient is 39 percent in Africa, 72 percent in Asia, 39 percent in Eastern Europe and the former Soviet Union, and 18 percent in Western Europe, North America, and Oceania. Compared to the rest of the world, Latin America is a region comprising relatively similar countries, within which high inequality prevails.

Summing up, although there are many methodological drawbacks related to the available evidence, differences in magnitude are sufficiently large to indicate that inequality in Latin America has been greater than in the rest of the world since at least World War II, with the possible exception of Sub-Saharan Africa. Moreover, there are no signs that this gap has narrowed over time. Changes in inequality have been more or less similar on average to those found in the rest of the world in the last half century. The widespread drop in inequality in the 1970s was probably more pronounced in Latin America, but this relative gain was lost in the 1980s when inequality in the region increased more rapidly than in the rest of the world. During the 1990s, inequality increased in Latin America at about the global average rate.

It is interesting to note that the position of most Latin American countries in the ranking of global inequality has been nearly the same during the last several decades, despite changes in the economic, social, and political environment.

The last five decades have witnessed economic booms and crude recessions, inward growth models and export-led growth strategies, widespread public sector interventions and extensive promarket reforms, dictatorships and democracies, yet in none of the region's countries did any of these scenarios change the income distribution to make it significantly more similar to distributions in other parts of the world.

This observation suggests an important point: Latin America seems to be more unequal than the rest of the world for reasons beyond the economic cycle or particular economic policies. These factors have undoubtedly played an important role in shaping income distribution, a role that should be studied and better understood. However, there seem to be underlying factors that are stronger determinants of inequality levels in the region. Several chapters in this report elaborate this point (see part II).

Which parts of the Latin American income distributions differ most from the rest of the world? Inequality, for instance, may be higher in Latin America because of greater income concentration in the middle class and lower concentration in the bottom strata, compared to other regions. Tables 2.2 and 2.3 suggest that this is not the case. Latin American distributions are mainly characterized by a higher income share among the rich relative to countries in

TABLE 2.2

Distribution of household per capita income, 1992 (income shares by deciles and vintiles)

Regions	Latin America (i)	Africa (ii)	Asia (iii)	Eastern Europe (iv)	Developed countries (v)	World without LA (vi)	Difference (i)–(vi) (vii)
Deciles							
1	1.6	2.1	2.6	2.2	2.5	2.4	−0.8
2	2.4	3.0	3.5	3.8	3.4	3.4	−1.0
3	3.0	3.7	4.8	5.1	5.3	4.8	−1.8
4	3.4	4.6	5.8	5.7	6.3	5.7	−2.2
5	5.0	5.5	6.5	7.5	7.3	6.7	−1.8
6	6.0	6.5	7.5	8.2	8.6	7.8	−1.7
7	7.6	8.6	9.0	9.4	10.5	9.5	−1.9
8	9.0	10.5	10.5	10.8	12.2	11.1	−2.2
9	14.0	13.3	12.4	12.8	14.8	13.5	0.5
10	48.0	42.2	37.4	34.7	29.1	35.1	12.9
Total	100.0	100.0	100.0	100.0	100.0	100.0	
Vintiles							
19	10.8	11.3	9.7	8.9	10.7	10.3	0.5
20	37.2	30.8	27.7	25.8	18.5	24.8	12.4

Source: Authors' estimates based on Bourguignon and Morrison 2002.

TABLE 2.3

Distribution of household per capita income, 1990s (quintiles)

	LAC (i)	Sub-Saharan Africa (ii)	East Asia & Pacific (iii)	South Asia (iv)	Eastern Europe (v)	Middle East & North Africa (vi)	Developed countries (vii)
1 and 2	13.2	14.1	18.1	21.7	22.2	17.8	18.4
3 and 4	33.8	33.5	37.5	38.4	40.0	36.8	41.8
5	52.9	52.4	44.3	39.9	37.8	45.4	39.8
Total	100.0	100.0	100.0	100.0	100.0	100.0	100.0

Source: Authors' estimates based on Deininger and Squire 1996.

other regions.[51] Who are the losers from this "excess share?" The tables suggest that the eight bottom deciles in Latin America have lower income shares than they do in the rest of the world. If anything, the "losses" seem to be larger for middle-income groups. If a typical Latin American distribution had to mimic a typical income distribution in the rest of the world, the income share of the top vintile (the richest 5 percent of the population) would have to be reduced and the proceeds distributed more or less evenly across the poorest 80 percent of the population.

Despite its high inequality, Latin America performs better in terms of poverty levels (when measured by standardized international poverty lines) than do some other less developed regions of the world, primarily because of the region's higher per capita income. Poverty is lower in the region than in Africa and Asia (see table A.20). World poverty has been significantly reduced in the last decade. The Latin American record is better than that of Africa, Eastern Europe, and South Asia, but not nearly as good as East Asia's.

2.5. Looking inside household income

Section 2.2 considered the distribution of household equivalized real income among individuals. This variable can be written as, $(Y^L + Y^{NL})/(AE^\theta.P)$, where Y^L stands for household total labor income, Y^{NL} represents household total nonlabor income, AE are the number of equivalent adults in the household, θ is a parameter for consumption economies of scale, and P is the price index for the bundle consumed by the household. Differences in well-being among individuals, which are approximated by differences in equivalized household income, depend on differences in each of the factors in this equation. Since differential prices are not studied in this paper due to a lack of information and θ is

assumed to be fixed, this leaves three sources of differences: labor income, nonlabor income, and family size and structure. These three components are discussed below.

Labor income

Labor is the main income source for most individuals. This role is magnified in household surveys, since most nonlabor sources are usually not well represented. Column (i) in table A.21 shows that the share of labor sources in total reported income is more than 80 percent in most Latin American countries—substantially greater than what is recorded in national accounts. The table also shows the Gini coefficient for the distribution of individual labor income in columns (vii) to (ix). Most of the conclusions in section 2.2 on inequality rankings and trends remain valid when the analysis is restricted to individual labor income.[52] Wodon and others (2001) perform source decompositions of the Gini coefficient, and conclude that about three-quarters of the Gini coefficient for the distribution of per capita income can be attributed to the contribution of inequality in the labor income distribution, since that source represents a very large share of total income in household surveys.

Education

Individuals earn labor income from the use of their endowment of productive "labor assets," such as physical capability, human capital, and connections. This section deals mostly with one of these assets, formal education. Although education is certainly very important as a determinant of income, its central position in the literature is also based on its observability in surveys and censuses. This contrasts with the difficulty of obtaining statistics for other relevant income determinants, such as natural ability, labor market connections, on-the-job training, and work ethics.

Table A.22 shows the average number of years of formal education for adults aged 25–65 by income quintile and by age and gender group for each country and year.[53] There are significant differences across countries in the average years of education. Although in Argentina, Chile, and Panama that average is around ten years, in Guatemala, Honduras, and Nicaragua the corresponding figure is less than six years. These differences hold for all income quintiles, although the gap between the Southern Cone and the rest of Latin America is wider for the poorest quintile.

One remarkable phenomenon in table A.22 is the substantial increase in the average years of education in all Latin American countries during the 1990s, which continued a process initiated decades ago. In most countries, education increased in all income groups, except in Argentina and Peru, where years of education among adults from the poorest households decreased. Figure 2.7 shows that the gap in years of education between the bottom quintile and the top quintile increased not only in these two countries, but also in more than half of the countries in the sample.[54] The education gap has widened in Brazil and Mexico from already large values by Latin American standards, despite a sizable increase in years of education in the bottom quintile of the income distribution.

Another remarkable fact evident in table A.22 is the reversal of the gap in years of education between men and women. In all Latin American countries, men older than 50 have more years of education than women of the same age, but the difference is in favor of women in the 10–30 year age bracket.[55] For the working age population (aged 25–65), years of education are slightly greater for women in some countries (including Argentina, Brazil, Jamaica, Panama, Trinidad and Tobago, Uruguay, and República Bolivariana de Venezuela) and somewhat higher for men in the rest of the region's countries.

In table A.23, people are divided according to age and household income quintile. For most countries, the gap in years of education between the top and bottom quintiles is wider for young adults than for older people, which suggests increasing educational inequality in the last few decades. For instance, in Bolivia in 1999 the gap was 7.8 years for people aged 51–60, 8.5 years for people aged 41–50, and 9.1 for individuals in their 30s. This trend is a sign of an unbalanced increase in education in Bolivia that is also present in most

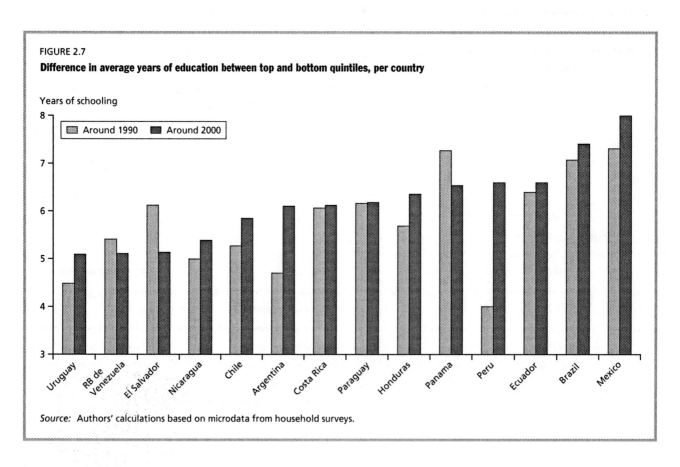

FIGURE 2.7

Difference in average years of education between top and bottom quintiles, per country

Years of schooling

Legend: Around 1990, Around 2000

Countries (left to right): Uruguay, RB de Venezuela, El Salvador, Nicaragua, Chile, Argentina, Costa Rica, Paraguay, Honduras, Panama, Peru, Ecuador, Brazil, Mexico

Source: Authors' calculations based on microdata from household surveys.

Latin American countries in the sample. Figure 2.7 shows that only in Chile and Mexico is the educational gap between the poor and the rich substantially lower in the cohort aged 31–40 than in the cohort aged 51–60. Table A.23 also shows that during the last decade, the gap in years of education between top and bottom quintiles for youth aged 21–30 has not shrunk in almost all of the Latin American countries. This is also the case for children aged 10–20 in most countries, with the exception of Brazil, Chile, Ecuador, Mexico, and Panama.

Recently, effort has been made to gather educational information from most countries in the world. Table A.24 summarizes data from an updated version of Barro and Lee (2000). All figures in the table correspond to adults over 25. Results for the 1990s are in general consistent with our estimates. The Latin American average for years of schooling is almost at the level of the world mean and has also increased in the last four decades at rates similar to the world mean.

Thomas, Wang, and Fan (2002) calculated Gini coefficients over the distribution of years of education for 140 countries for the period 1960–2000. Data for Latin American countries and regional averages are reproduced in table A.25. Educational Gini coefficients for the region are close to the world mean, higher than in the developed countries and Eastern Europe, slightly lower than in Asia, and significantly lower than in Africa. This ranking has not substantially varied in the last four decades. Table A.28 shows the results of computing educational Gini coefficients from the current sample of household surveys. The Southern Cone countries (that is, Argentina, Chile, and Uruguay), Jamaica, Panama, and Trinidad and Tobago have the lowest inequality levels.

Educational Gini coefficients fell for most of the Latin American countries during the 1990s. This result is not inconsistent with the widening gaps illustrated in figure 2.6. In the case of Brazil, as indicated in table A.22, between 1990 and 2001 years of education increased from 1.9 to 3.0 in the bottom quintile and from 8.9 to 10.4 in the top quintile. The absolute difference in years of education between the rich and the poor has increased (as is shown in figure 2.4), but the ratio has decreased. This latter effect is captured by the Gini coefficient, a measure of relative rather than absolute differences among individuals.[56]

Table A.27 shows an alternative rough measure of education: the self-reported literacy rate by income quintile. Most countries have made substantial progress and some have achieved nearly 100 percent literacy. However, the percentage of illiterate people is still very significant among the poor, reaching more than 30 percent in several countries.

In the analysis of the labor market that follows, the adult population is classified into three educational groups according to years of education: low (less than 8 years of schooling), medium (9–13 years of schooling), and high (more than 14 years of schooling). This roughly corresponds to unskilled, semiskilled, and skilled workers.[57] Table A.28 shows the shares of each educational group in the adult population. The share of adults with high levels of education has significantly increased in all the Latin American countries in the sample, especially among women.

Hourly wages: Returns to labor assets

Investing in education usually pays in the labor market, especially in terms of higher hourly wages. Looking at the distribution of hourly wages is important for two reasons. On the one hand, most of the differences in average earnings among educational groups are due to differences in hourly wages and much less to differences in hours of work or unemployment rates. The second reason the distribution of hourly wages is relevant is because of normative issues. If people were completely free to choose hours of work and family size, the distribution of hourly wages (and some inherited assets) would become the primary concern in an equality-of-opportunity scenario of social fairness.

Table A.29 shows the Gini coefficients for the distribution of hourly wages for different groups of workers. Most of the conclusions drawn from previous tables hold here. The distribution of hourly wages has become more unequal in Argentina, Peru, Uruguay, and República Bolivariana de Venezuela, but also in countries like Colombia and Nicaragua where household income inequality did not significantly change. In contrast, hourly earnings inequality decreased in Brazil. For the rest of the countries, changes have been small and the levels usually depend on the group for which inequality is computed.

The literature has stressed the relevance of studying wage gaps among educational groups as main determinants of inequality in hourly earnings. The "wage premium" earned by skilled workers has always been a major topic of interest for labor economists and other social scientists. Table A.30 shows wage gaps among three educational groups. For instance, in Brazil in 2001, the hourly wage in the primary job of a skilled worker was on average 6.5 times more than that of an unskilled worker. All numbers in the table are higher than 1, meaning that more educated workers on average have higher hourly earnings. The wage premium for skilled workers increased in most countries during the 1990s, even in economies in which household income inequality did not significantly change or even decreased, such as Brazil (see also figure 2.8). In contrast, the wage gap between semi-skilled and unskilled workers (column (iii) in table A.30) did not significantly increase in most countries and decreased in some (see figure 2.9).

The figures in table A.30 are unconditional means. In order to investigate further the relationship between education and hourly wages, the authors ran regressions of the logarithm of hourly wage in the primary job on educational dummies and other control variables (that is, age, age squared, regional dummies, and an urban/rural dummy) for men and for women.[58] Table A.31 shows the results of these Mincer equations. For instance, in Argentina in 2001, a male worker between 25 and 55 years old with a primary education degree earned on average nearly 22 percent more than a similar worker without that degree. Completion of

secondary school implied a wage increase of 40 percent over the earnings of a worker with only a primary school education; in other words, the *marginal* return of completing secondary school versus only primary school is 40 percent.

The wage premium for a college education is an additional 76 percent. In Argentina, returns on primary and secondary school education have not significantly changed in the last decade. In contrast, there was a large jump in returns on college education (from 54 to 76 percent). That jump was also noticeable for working women and for both male and female urban salaried workers. Although not of the magnitude of the changes seen in Argentina, the marginal returns to college education increased in several other Latin American countries during the 1990s, particularly for urban salaried workers, confirming the results from the unconditional means (see figure 2.10).[59]

Mincer equations are also informative with regard to two interesting factors: the role of unobservable variables and the gender wage gap. The error term in the Mincer regression is usually interpreted as capturing the effect on hourly wages of factors that aren't considered in household surveys, such as natural ability, connections, and work ethics. An increase

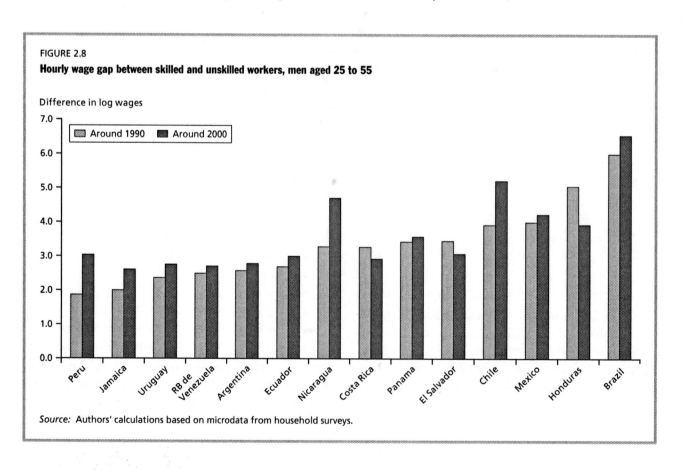

FIGURE 2.8

Hourly wage gap between skilled and unskilled workers, men aged 25 to 55

Difference in log wages

Source: Authors' calculations based on microdata from household surveys.

FIGURE 2.9

Hourly wage gap between semi-skilled and unskilled workers, men aged 25 to 55

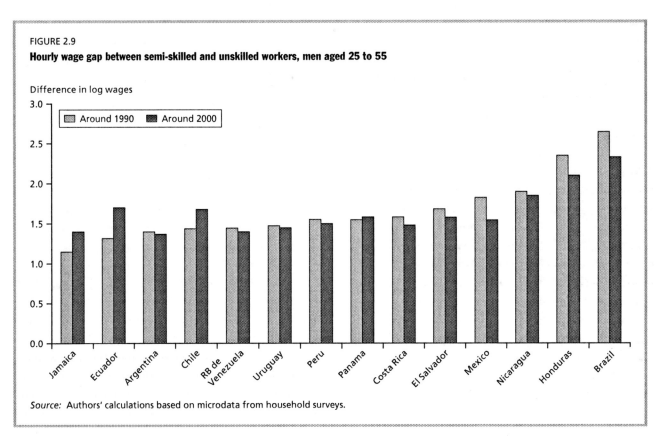

Source: Authors' calculations based on microdata from household surveys.

FIGURE 2.10

Increase in hourly wages for college-educated workers, men aged 25 to 55

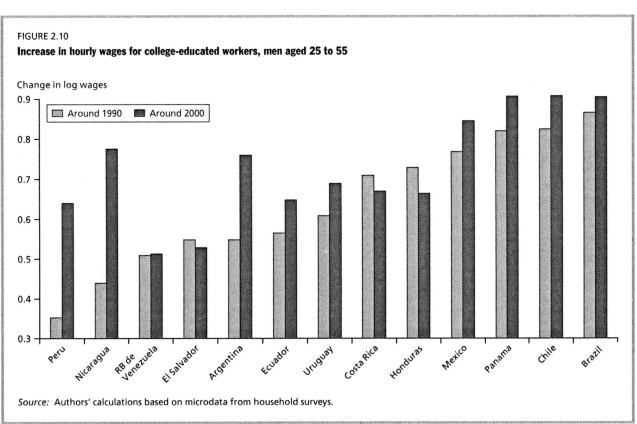

Source: Authors' calculations based on microdata from household surveys.

61

in the dispersion of this error term may reflect an increase in the returns on such unobservable factors in terms of hourly wages (Juhn, Murphy, and Pierce 1993). Table A.30 shows the standard deviation of the error term of each Mincer equation. The returns on unobservable factors have clearly increased in Argentina and República Bolivariana de Venezuela, while there were either no clear changes or reductions in the rest of the Latin American countries.

Another way of investigating the influence of factors other than education on inequality is to compute the distribution of hourly wages *within* each educational group. Table A.33 does this for prime-age males. Again, Argentina and República Bolivariana de Venezuela stand out from the rest of the countries due to significant increases in inequality within all educational groups. In most countries, inequality increased among skilled workers and did not increase (or even decreased) for others. Chile provides one of the clearest examples of this trend, since the distribution of hourly wages has become significantly more equal for workers with low and medium levels of education and more unequal within the skilled group.

The coefficients in the Mincer regressions are different for men and women, indicating that they are paid differently even when they have the same observable characteristics (that is, education, age, and location). To further investigate this point, the authors simulated the counterfactual wage that men would earn if they were paid like women. The last column in table A.32 reports the ratio between the average of this simulated wage and the actual average wage for men. In all cases this ratio is less than one, reflecting the fact that women earn less than men even when controlling for observable characteristics.[60] This result has two possible interpretations: it is either the consequence of discrimination against women or the result of men having more valuable unobservable factors than do women (for example, that they are more attached to their work). It seems that the gender wage gap has shrunk in all countries during the last decade (see also figure 2.11). Brazil has the widest gap between men and women, while in Argentina, Colombia, Mexico, and Peru the gap is narrower than in the rest of the region. Chapter 3 in this report focuses more on this aspect.

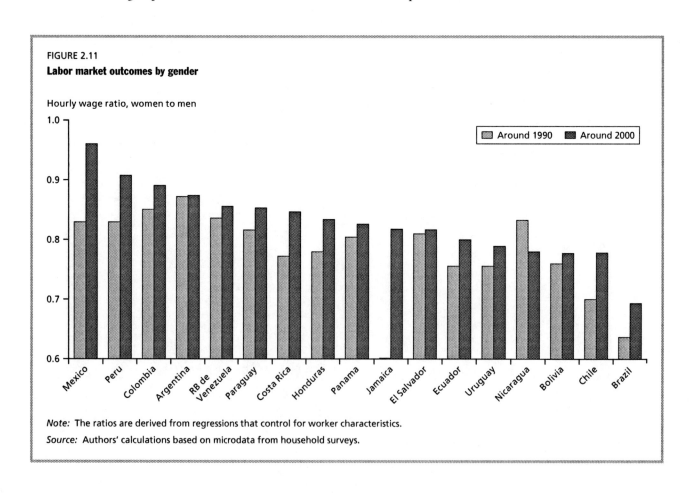

FIGURE 2.11
Labor market outcomes by gender

Hourly wage ratio, women to men

Around 1990   Around 2000

Note: The ratios are derived from regressions that control for worker characteristics.
Source: Authors' calculations based on microdata from household surveys.

The use of labor assets: Hours worked, participation, and unemployment

Are the differences in hourly wages reinforced by differences in hours worked? Table A.34 suggests that the opposite is true. Correlations between hours worked and hourly wages are negative and significant in all countries. Also, the second panel shows that in most countries, workers with low levels of education tend to work longer hours than workers with more years of formal education. However, this gap is narrowing in most Latin American countries, with hours worked decreasing for the unskilled and increasing for the skilled during the last decade (see figure A.6). See box 2.3 for the description of a set of decompositions that sheds additional light on the structure of inequality in hourly earnings.

So far, this discussion has focused on the group of workers in the labor market. However, some able-bodied people may decide not to work or may not find a job even after actively looking for one. Table A.36 contains basic statistics on employment, unemployment, and duration of unemployment by education and gender. People with a college education participate in the labor market more than other groups. In addition, the employment rate for men is much greater than for women. There does not seem to be a clear pattern of changes in the employment gap between skilled and unskilled workers. Differences in employment rates among educational groups have increased in some countries and decreased in others.

The unemployment rate for the unskilled is higher than for the skilled in more than half of the countries in the sample. Also, in most countries the difference between the unskilled and the skilled with regard to unemployment has become larger over the last decade (see figure A.7), implying a disequalizing effect on the income distribution. Labor patterns differ among countries. While unemployment increased in South America, it either decreased or remained low in the rest of Latin America. Finally, the last panel of table A.36 reports shorter but increasing spells of unemployment for the unskilled.

Nonlabor income

Income from nonlabor sources, once a primary object of interest for economists, is not at the center of inequality studies today. This is due in part to the increasing relevance of labor as a main income source, and in part because of the difficulties of getting reliable information on nonlabor income sources.

Column (ii) in table A.21 shows the share of nonlabor income in Latin American household surveys, while column (x) presents the Gini coefficient for the distribution of that variable. Nonlabor income comprises capital income, profits, rents, and various types of transfers (that is, both private and public, including pensions). The coverage of nonlabor income sources varies greatly among surveys. While, for instance, some countries include detailed questions on income from capital and rents, some include only a general, vague question and others don't broach the subject at all.

Capital income, land rents, and profits are highly concentrated in the richest stratum of the income distribution

---

BOX 2.3
Some simple decompositions

A rough but illustrative way of investigating what is behind a distribution is to perform simple decompositions. A population is divided into groups according to a given variable, and total inequality is expressed as a combination of inequality between and within groups. Table A.35 shows the results of performing decompositions of the Theil inequality index computed over the distribution of wages for working adults aged 25–55. The table suggests that even though formal education is an important factor in accounting for differences in wages in all Latin American countries, the roles of gender and age are small. This does not imply that, for instance, differences in wages between men and women are negligible, but instead that these differences are very small compared to differences in wages within each of the two gender groups.

The role of location (urban or rural) varies across countries. For instance, the wage gap between urban and rural areas accounts for 11 percent of overall wage inequality in Bolivia and just 2 percent in República Bolivariana de Venezuela. In many Latin American countries, the relevance of urban-rural differences has decreased during the last decade.

See also Wodon and others 2000 for similar decompositions with a smaller sample.

(see table A.37). An increase in the share of these income sources (for example, an increase in the rate of return on capital) may imply a disequalizing change in the income distribution. Inequality trends and differences across countries can then be accounted for by differences in the share of these nonlabor sources. Unfortunately, capital income and land rents and profits are seriously underestimated in household surveys. In nearly all countries, the share of all of these income sources is 2–4 percent (see column (iii) in table A.21).[61] Given this minor role, neither the reported level nor the changes in household income inequality discussed in this chapter are driven by capital income. As mentioned in section 2.2, the inequality that can be measured on the basis of household surveys essentially stems from differences in labor income and demographic factors.

The previous discussion suggests that if good estimates of individual capital income and profits were available, the measured level of inequality would be a good deal higher. What about trends in inequality? According to the United Nations National Account Statistics, the Latin American countries' average share of nonlabor sources in the GDP did not significantly change during the 1990s. Harrison (2002) shows that during the period of 1960–1997, the average labor share in Latin American countries was almost constant (or slightly decreasing in some cases).

In a recent paper, Gollin (2002) finds that the labor share, when appropriately measured to include those workers who are self-employed or employed outside the corporate sector, does not vary much across countries or time periods.[62] On the other hand, there does seem to be some short-run volatility in shares that are possibly associated with crises (see chapter 8). The evidence of no significant changes in the share of labor and nonlabor sources increases confidence in the reported inequality changes obtained from household surveys that mostly ignore capital income. However, it is clear that more effort and resources should be devoted to improve the measurement of capital income, rents, and profits in Latin American household surveys.[63]

Transfers are an important component of nonlabor income. People receive private and public transfers, the latter in the form of cash subsidies and in-kind programs such as free education and health. The third panel of table A.37 shows the distribution of cash transfers, excluding pensions. Perhaps surprisingly, the distribution is pro-rich, meaning that higher shares of total transfers go to high-income strata, probably as a consequence of the greater relevance of private

transfers relative to public income support programs.[64] This pattern, however, seems to be changing, since the share of the bottom quintiles in total cash transfers has been increasing during the last decade.

In some countries, the main item in nonlabor income is pensions. In Argentina, Brazil, Panama, and Uruguay, pensions account for more than half the value of nonlabor income (see column (v) in table A.21). Pensions are also concentrated in the upper-income strata, although to a smaller degree than is capital income (see table A.37).

Land is one of the most important assets in agrarian economies such as those in Latin America. Table A.38 reproduces data on the distribution of operational holdings of agricultural land assembled by the United Nations Development Programme (UNDP) (1993) and Deininger and Olinto (2000) (who in turn mainly used the decennial United Nations Food and Agriculture Organization World Census of Agriculture). The data do not include adjustments for soil quality, land improvements, or communal tenure arrangements and refer to operational rather than ownership distribution. Deininger and Olinto (2000) highlight the fact that the distribution of land is more concentrated than the distribution of income, and also that the variation across countries is higher than that of income. Again, Latin America emerges as a very unequal region compared to other regions in the world.[65] Table A.39 reproduces the Gini coefficients for operational holdings of agricultural land in Latin American countries.

Housing is probably the main asset that most people own. Several household surveys in Latin America report whether a house is owned by the family who lives in it, although very few report the property or rental value of the dwelling. Table A.40, derived from the sample of household surveys used in this report, presents for each income quintile the share of families owning a house (that is, both the building and the lot). Housing ownership is widespread along the income distribution. In fact, in several countries the share of poor people who own a dwelling is higher than the corresponding share for the rich. However, figure A.8 shows that in most countries in the last decade, housing ownership among the rich has grown relative to the poor. Poor families live in houses that are smaller (in terms of number of rooms) than do rich families. Since poor families also tend to be larger in size, the number of persons per room is significantly greater. Differences across income quintiles have not significantly varied over time in most Latin American countries.

Fay, Yepes, and Foster (2002) find that the distribution of housing values is more unequally distributed than income in Chile and Peru. They find that in the last decade, housing markets have increasingly excluded the poor, a conclusion that with different intensities is also evident in Argentina, Bolivia, Brazil, Colombia, Honduras, Jamaica, Mexico, and Uruguay.

Family size and structure

The resources available to each person depends on the number of people with whom an individual has to share total household resources. Size and composition of the household are therefore key determinants of an individual's economic well-being. Table A.41 shows the number of children under 12 years of age by parental income quintiles and by education of the household head. The table reveals significant differences in means, with the Southern Cone nations, Jamaica, and Panama being the areas where families are of smaller size. All nations have experienced substantial reductions in the number of children per household during the last decade. In most, reductions have been generalized

across the income strata. The exception is Argentina, where the number of children under 12 in the bottom quintile increased between 1992 and 2001. In most Latin American countries, the ratio of the number of children in the bottom and the top quintiles has increased in the last decade, thereby contributing to higher income inequality (see figure 2.12).[66]

Table A.42 shows household size by equivalized income quintiles and by education of the household head. The results are similar to those in the previous table. Countries differ with regard to average family size and the gap between poor and rich families. Most show a similar pattern of falling number of persons per household in each part of the income distribution, with the exception of Argentina and Uruguay, where poorer families have become larger.

Inequality is reinforced if marriages take place between persons with similar income potential. Table A.43 presents some simple linear correlations that suggest the existence of assortative mating in all Latin American countries (see also chapter 6 and Fernández, Gunerm, and Knowles 2001). Men with more years of formal education tend to marry women with a similar educational background, as shown in column (i).

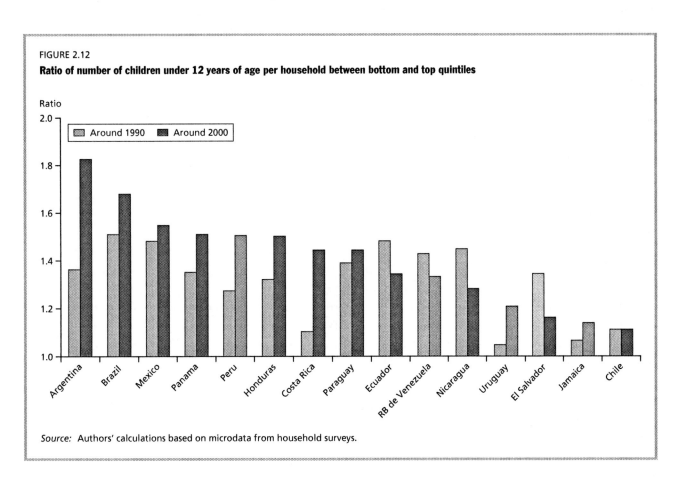

FIGURE 2.12

Ratio of number of children under 12 years of age per household between bottom and top quintiles

Source: Authors' calculations based on microdata from household surveys.

BOX 2.4

Social capital and trust

Social capital has been broadly defined as the set of informal rules embedded in social relations and society's institutional arrangements that enable members to achieve their individual and community objectives (Coleman 1990). Social interactions, in particular repeated interactions, produce obligations and expectations among individuals that generate trust among people, in turn easing and promoting cooperation and participation. This idea has spurred a growing body of research that tries to assess the influence of social capital on a wide range of economic and political outcomes.[a]

Measuring social capital is not an easy task. Most of the literature at the country level has relied on the World Values Surveys, which include microdata for 30 mostly developed countries in response to questions about interpersonal trust and civic engagement. Using Latinobarómetro surveys, the authors of this report constructed two measures of social capital: a measure of *interpersonal trust* and a measure of *institutional trust*.[b] Averaging out

results for the period 1996–2001, they found that interpersonal and institutional trust increase with age and subjective income and decrease with education and perception of income inequality (see table A.46).[c]

This box was primarily written by Matías Busso.

a. The literature has found that higher levels of social capital are associated with higher economic growth (Knack and Keefer 1997), increased judicial efficiency, lower government corruption (La Porta and others 1997), and improved local government efficiency (Putman 1993).

b. The question used to construct the measure of *interpersonal trust* is: "Can you trust most people?" If the person answers affirmatively, then trust is given a value of 1; otherwise it is given a value of zero. The variable *institutional trust* was constructed as a simple average of eight questions. Latinobarómetro asks "How much can you trust the following organizations? Government, congress, the judiciary, the church, the military, police, political parties, and TV." To construct the index of institutional trust, the authors arbitrarily assign a value of 1 if respondents say "a lot," 0.66 if they say "something," 0.33 if the answer is "a little," and 0 if it is "not at all."

c. The results of multivariate regression analysis, controlling for country-fixed effects, confirm the unconditional results shown in table A.46.

This is one of the factors that contribute to a positive correlation of hourly wages within couples, as shown in column (ii). There is no evidence of changes in the degree of assortative mating in the last decade, according to these simple statistics. Finally, columns (iii) and (iv) show positive, though small, correlations in hours of work, both when considering and excluding people who do not work.

Concern over child labor has increased recently. Table A.44 shows the proportion of working children between 10 and 14 years of age. Unfortunately, many surveys do not report labor statistics for younger children. While child labor is negligible in some countries, it is a strong phenomenon in others. There are significant differences in child labor across income strata.

In some countries, household surveys report the race or ethnicity of individuals. Based on that information, table A.45 presents the ratio between nonwhites and whites with regard to wages and household per capita income. In all countries for which information is available, nonwhites earn less and are poorer than whites. This is discussed in more detail in chapter 3.

Finally, some rough estimates of the distribution of social capital—and of the related concepts of interpersonal and institutional trust—are reported in table A.46 and discussed in box 2.4.

2.6. Inequality beyond income

Most of the empirical studies that aim to measure the fairness of social arrangements focus on the distribution of individual welfare. However, in the real world people seem to care also—and probably especially—about the distribution of particular goods and services. It is likely that more people would support programs that seek to guarantee equality in basic education and health care than programs aimed at reducing income or total consumption inequality. This specific egalitarianism is further supported by normative arguments based on the idea of equality of opportunity (see Tobin 1970 and Roemer 1996, among others). This section provides statistics on inequality distribution for some of the variables for which people show particular concern: school enrollment, basic health status and services, political representation, safety from crime, and some basic social services (for example, the provision of clean water). Having a basic level of these variables is often seen as a right, and hence inequality is viewed as particularly disturbing to the extent that it impinges on the realization of this right.

School enrollment

Guaranteeing equality of access to formal education is one of the goals of most societies. The authors have used the sample of household surveys to calculate school enrollment statistics by income strata in order to compute inequality measures of school attendance and to investigate the issue of educational mobility that links the education of children and youth to that of their parents.

Table A.47 shows school enrollment rates by equivalized income quintiles. The table indicates, for example, that among Brazilian children aged 6–12 in the bottom quintile, 70 percent attended school in 1990 and 93 percent in 2001. For the top quintile, 96 and 99 percent attended school in 1990 and 2001, respectively. These numbers reflect three important phenomena: (1) attendance rates increase along with household income, (2) enrollment rates have increased over time for all quintiles, and (3) the gap in attendance rates between poor and rich children has significantly narrowed during the last decade.

Are these results applicable to other age brackets and countries? The first result is quite general: in all countries, schooling rates increase along with income. The differences between poor and rich are smaller for children of primary school age and larger for youth of college age. Differences are also very large for children under five years of age.[67] The second result is also quite general: enrollment rates have increased over time among all income distribution points in nearly all countries. On average, increases have been greater in pre-primary school, followed by high school, college, and finally primary school, where several countries are close to achieving nearly universal schooling.

The third result—the shrinking gap in enrollment rates between the poor and the rich—is quite general for children under 12 (see figure 2.13).[68] However, the gap has widened in some countries for youth aged 13–17 and has become larger in most countries for youth aged 18–23. Differences in college attendance between the poor and the rich have increased throughout the region over the last decade.

The level of inequality in the distribution of conditional probabilities of attending school can be viewed as a measure of inequities in access to education. The authors estimated these conditional probabilities from logit models of the attendance decision, using parental equivalized income, age, gender, location, and parental education as independent variables.[69] The Gini coefficients for the distribution of these conditional probabilities for different age groups are reported in table A.48 for each country and year. The higher the Gini coefficient, the higher the differences in the probability of attending school among children of the same age, after controlling for the independent variables. These differences can be due to parental income, but also to parental education, location, and gender, all of which are implicitly considered here to be unacceptable sources of differences in access to education.

Inequality in the probability of being enrolled in school is low for kids aged 9–12 (see column (i) of table A.48). Countries that have nearly achieved full enrollment naturally have a Gini coefficient close to 0. Chile, and especially Brazil, have experienced large decreases in this measure. Column (ii) shows the Gini coefficient for the distribution of conditional probabilities of attending secondary school for youth aged 15–17 who finished primary school. Gini coefficients have been falling over the last decade in many countries. One notable exception is Brazil, where good results in primary school are not replicated at the high school level. Table A.48 also shows substantial differences in the Gini coefficients across countries, from a negligible 4.5 in Argentina to 26.2 in Brazil. Column (iii) shows similar statistics for high school graduates aged 19–21.

Inequities are in general higher in college than in high school, even when the analysis is restricted to those youth who completed the previous educational level. In two-thirds of the countries, dispersion in the distribution of probabilities of attending college for those who finished high school increased during the period considered. The last column in table A.48 (also shown in figure A.9) summarizes inequalities for all educational levels. The Gini coefficient for the distribution of conditional probabilities of attending college for all youth aged 19–21 significantly fell in half of the Latin American countries in the survey, and increased or did not significantly change in the rest.

Educational mobility

The analysis of schooling decisions is closely related to the topic of educational mobility. The concept is simple: if family

FIGURE 2.13

School enrollment rates by age and country

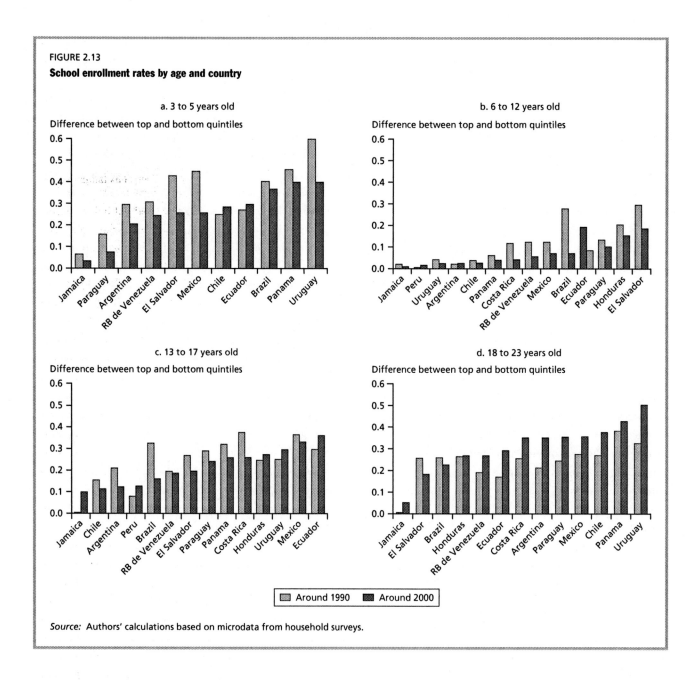

Source: Authors' calculations based on microdata from household surveys.

background explains a child's opportunities, then social mobility is low. As we have seen in previous sections, during the 1990s many Latin American countries experienced an increase in income inequality. High inequality is often seen as less worrisome when it is combined with high social mobility than when it occurs in a context of low social mobility.

Ideally, mobility for opportunities or for living standards would be computed. However, surveys in Latin American countries do not have long panels to allow this step. This section therefore follows the methodology developed in Andersen (2001) to provide estimates of *educational* mobility,

that is, the degree to which parental education and income determine a child's education. The dependent variable is the schooling gap, defined as the difference between (1) years of education that children would have completed had they entered school at a normal age and advanced one grade each year, and (2) actual years of education. In other words, the schooling gap measures years of missing education. The Educational Mobility Index (EMI) is defined as 1 minus the proportion of the variance of the school gap that is explained by family background. In an economy with low mobility, family background would be important and thus the index would be small (for technical details see Andersen 2001).

Table A.49 shows the EMI for teenagers (aged 13–19) and young adults (aged 20–25) in all Latin American countries in the sample. Educational mobility is relatively high in the Southern Cone and the Caribbean. There have not been substantial improvements in mobility in the region as a whole (see figure A.10). In many countries, the EMI has not significantly changed over the last decade, while in others it has decreased for both age groups. Only in Brazil and Panama are there unambiguous signs of higher mobility.

Health

Inequality in health is causing growing concern in both the public policy arena and the academic literature. This concern has translated into a better understanding and measurement of disparities in health status and services indicators. The Demographic and Health Surveys (DHS) program is the main initiative in gathering information on a large number of health variables, as well as data on respondents' demographic, social, and economic characteristics (see <www.worldbank.org\poverty\health\data>. Table A.50, developed with information from that program, presents statistics for different health status measures and health service indicators for each Latin American country in the sample and for the average of other regions in the developing world. These are presented by quintile of socioeconomic status, defined in terms of the ownership of assets in the household rather than as income or consumption.

Along with the statistics for each quintile, each panel of the table shows the concentration index (CI), a measure of the extent to which a particular variable is distributed unequally across the income strata (see Lambert 1993). "Bads," like child mortality, are usually more common among poor households. In this case, the CI is negative. The higher the CI in absolute value, the more concentrated the "bads" are in the poor households. In contrast, "goods," such as immunization, are more frequent in the richer percentiles. In this case, the CI is positive. The higher the CI, the more concentrated the "goods" are in the most affluent households. In sum, if a region has values of CI close to zero, health inequalities are assessed to be relatively low.

Panel A of table A.50 provides statistics on two measures of health status: under-five mortality and underweight

children. As expected, inequalities in health exist to the disadvantage of the poor. Latin America stands out as a region of relatively good average health status measures, but also as a region of high inequality (see also Wagstaff 2001). The concentration index for the region is, in absolute terms, larger than the world mean for both under-five mortality and underweight children. Some countries, such as Bolivia, Brazil, the Dominican Republic, and Peru have very high levels of inequality.

Under-five mortality among Peruvians in the top quintile is lower than in the countries in East Asia included in the DHS program (that is, Indonesia, the Philippines, and Vietnam). In contrast, under-five mortality in the bottom quintile is higher in Peru. Health inequality measures for prevalence of diarrhea (see panel B) are also relatively high in Latin America, with Peru and Brazil again standing out as particularly unequal countries. In contrast to the inequality statistics on health status, inequality in services such as immunization, basic antenatal care, and attended delivery in Latin America do not seem higher than in other developing regions of the world. At any rate, the disparities are worrisome. In Peru, while a medically trained person attends nearly all deliveries of babies in the top quintile, that proportion is only 14 percent for babies in the bottom quintile.

Wagstaff and Watanabe (2000) computed measures of inequality for stunting, underweight, and wasting, working with a sample of 20 countries and ranking individuals by equivalized consumption.[70] Latin American countries in the sample systematically appeared at the top of the inequality rankings. The most negative concentration index for stunting and underweight was in Peru and for wasting in Nicaragua. Using consumption as a welfare indicator, Wagstaff (2000) reports that inequality in under-five mortality is particularly high in Brazil compared to other countries in the world.

A related topic that is also attracting increased attention in public debate and from policymakers across Latin America is the extent and distribution of physical and mental disabilities. Because of conceptual issues, sampling frames, and reporting difficulties, the true extent of disability is seldom easy to infer from standard household surveys. Nonetheless, progress has recently been made with regard to both the measurement and understanding of disabilities in Latin America—and of the relationship of these aspects with distribution and poverty (see box 2.5).

BOX 2.5
Disability and distribution

The linkage between poverty and disability is strong, with evidence suggesting that causality goes in both directions. Poverty can cause disability through malnutrition, poor health care, and dangerous living conditions. Disability can cause poverty by preventing the full participation of disabled people in the economic and social activities in their communities, especially if the proper support systems and accommodations are not available. As many as 15–20 percent of the poor in developing countries have disabilities.

One problem in studying the link between income, poverty, and disability is the difficulty in obtaining high quality data, especially data that can be used to make comparisons across countries. The rate of disability found in household surveys and censuses varies dramatically. This variation results from differing measures of disability, different data collection techniques, and different reactions to survey questions by respondents. For example, the rate of disability in Paraguay was measured as 1 percent, but in Uruguay and Brazil it was measured as 16 percent (see table A.51). It is unlikely that a common definition and comparable quality data would have yielded such disparate rates of disability across reasonably similar, neighboring countries. In fact, a 1991 census in Brazil measured the rate of disability at 0.9 percent. The higher rate measured in 2001 was not the result of an explosion of disability in Brazil, but of the use of better measurement techniques.

What is disability? Disability refers to a long or short-term reduction in a person's activity resulting from an acute or chronic condition. Table A.52 shows the breakdown of the disabled population by type of disability, in countries with available data. But disability goes beyond the description of a particular medical condition.

Disability is multi-faceted, complex, and difficult to define. In fact, it is best understood as the interaction between a condition and a host of personal, social, and environmental factors. The International Classification of Functioning, Disability, and Health (ICF) developed by the World Health Organization (WHO) explicitly recognizes that any evaluation of a person's functioning and

disability must incorporate the physical and cultural context in which they live, and so also includes a list of environmental factors.

In 2001, following the ICF methodology, the Brazilian census broadened the scope of questioning, including questions on degrees of impairment (including mental, physical or motor, sight, and hearing aspects). Some preliminary findings include:

- More women than men are disabled, mainly because women live longer and disability is more common among the elderly. Fifty-four percent of disabled people in Brazil are women.
- Disability rates vary across racial groups. More than 17.5 percent of blacks have a disability, compared to 13.8 percent of whites.
- Disability is linked to poverty. The poorest areas in Brazil present higher shares of disabled people: in the ten states with the highest rates of disability, eight are located in the Northeast, one in the Center-West and one in the North. Moreover, 40.1 percent of disabled people earn less than minimum wage, compared to 29.6 percent of nondisabled people.
- Disability is negatively correlated with education, and thus with permanent incomes. The incidence of disability falls from 22 percent among those with no formal education, to 20 percent among those with 1–3 years of schooling, to 16 percent among those with 4–10 years of schooling, and to 15 percent among those with more than 10 years of schooling.

A deeper analysis of data and broader data collection methods across the region are necessary in order to explore further the relationship between disability and the distributions of education and income. Greater understanding should pave the way to better policies that can help break the links between poverty and disability.

Political representation

Disparities in income and wealth interact with disparities in representation and political influence. More influential groups tend to have higher economic rents, while wealthier individuals tend to have more political influence. Statistics on inequality in political influence are naturally very hard to obtain. In recent papers, Samuels and Snyder emphasize legislative malapportionment as a measure of inequality in representation (see for instance Samuels and Snyder 2001). Malapportionment is a discrepancy between the share of legislative seats and the share of population within electoral districts, and implies a failure to uphold the "one person, one vote" rule.

Table A.53 shows measures of malapportionment in both chambers of congress or parliament in several Latin American countries. A score of x percent means that x percent of seats are allocated to districts that would not receive those seats in cases of perfect apportionment. The table suggests that malapportionment is significantly higher in Latin America than in the rest of the world.[71] Note, however, that although malapportionment is linked to inequality in political representation, it does not necessarily imply a bias against the poor. There is clearly a need for more empirical work in this field. Issues of power and political representation are discussed in more depth in chapters 4 and 5.

Safety from crime

Safety from crime is one of the top concerns of the Latin American population. The available evidence suggests that the region has the highest rates of homicide and crime victimization in the world (see for instance Shrader 2001). The probabilities of being victim of a crime are not uniform along the income distribution. Although rich people are a more valuable target to criminals, they also have better means with which to protect themselves against crime.

Recent studies have tried to assess whether crime has a higher impact on poor people than on rich people. Since national victimization surveys are rarely available, researchers use a variety of other sources. Gaviria and Pagés (1999) use Latinobarómetro surveys from 1996 to 1998 to compute crime victimization across quintiles of a socioeconomic index based on the ownership of durable goods and household characteristics. Table A.54 reproduces these results, generally indicating that victimization moderately increases with wealth in all countries.[72]

Di Tella, Galiani, and Schargrodsky (2002) use a survey specially designed for victimization analysis and conclude that in Buenos Aires, "although high-income households used to suffer a significantly higher home victimization rate than low-income households, the difference has now turned nonsignificant. For street robberies, both groups show similar augments in victimization." Fiszbein, Giovagnoli, and Adúriz (2002) use a national household survey in Argentina and find that the rate of households that reported being a victim of crime or violence in the previous six months is not significantly different along the income distribution. Crime is also a large problem in some countries in the Caribbean, such as Haiti and Jamaica (see, for instance, World Bank, 2003f).

Basic services

Tables A.46 and A.48 report statistics by income strata on access to some basic services, including water, hygienic restrooms, and electricity.[73] The size of the gaps between the poor and the rich in terms of these services varies widely across Latin America. Figure 2.14 is informative with regard to these gaps, which tend to be larger for hygienic restrooms than for electricity and water, where coverage is more widespread. At any rate, in several countries the difference in the fraction of households with direct access to water or with electricity in the house is more than 30 percentage points between the top and bottom quintiles. Figure 2.14 shows that the gaps in the access to water, hygienic restrooms, and especially electricity have significantly narrowed in most countries in the last decade. Information on access to a telephone is also included, although arguably it is not a basic social service.[74] Access to a telephone has dramatically increased in the region, especially for the wealthiest households.

2.7. Conclusions

This chapter has presented and analyzed statistics on different dimensions of inequality in Latin America, setting the stage for the following chapters of this report. As discussed above, a data set of household surveys from 20 Latin American countries was assembled and used to compute statistics on the distribution of a wide set of variables. Results drawn from various authors complete the picture of inequality presented in the preceding pages.

The authors emphasize the need for improvements in data collection. The measurement of living standards in the

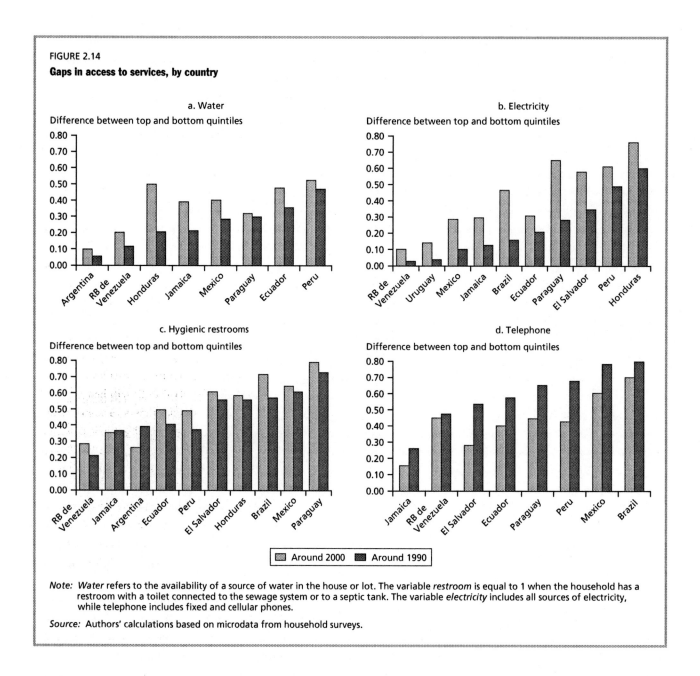

FIGURE 2.14

Gaps in access to services, by country

a. Water
Difference between top and bottom quintiles

b. Electricity
Difference between top and bottom quintiles

c. Hygienic restrooms
Difference between top and bottom quintiles

d. Telephone
Difference between top and bottom quintiles

Around 2000   Around 1990

Note: Water refers to the availability of a source of water in the house or lot. The variable *restroom* is equal to 1 when the household has a restroom with a toilet connected to the sewage system or to a septic tank. The variable *electricity* includes all sources of electricity, while telephone includes fixed and cellular phones.

Source: Authors' calculations based on microdata from household surveys.

region has some shortcomings that blur the picture of inequality and hamper the possibilities of conducting comparative analysis. Governments and international organizations should move toward standardization of questionnaires across countries (without losing valuable idiosyncratic components), improvement in capturing nonlabor and nonmonetary income, generalization of consumption surveys, and introduction of long panel surveys. Data availability is currently particularly poor in the Caribbean, where recent household surveys were completed in only 3 out of 15 countries.

The existing data, however, are useful to provide at least preliminary answers to relevant questions on inequality levels, trends, and structure. The tables provided in the statistical appendix provide useful information on the distribution of household income, as well as on labor, educational, and demographic variables by country and year.

Income inequality has increased in Latin America since World War II. During the 1990s, the trends were not uniform across countries. On average, inequality has increased in South America and remained stable in Central America, the Dominican Republic, and Jamaica. Two paradigmatic cases of changes in inequality are the neighbors Argentina and Brazil. Argentina, once a very low-inequality country by Latin American standards, has experienced dramatic disequalizing changes in recent decades. In contrast, inequality has fallen significantly in Brazil, the most unequal country in the region. The evidence presented in this chapter suggests a movement toward convergence in the country-by-country inequality levels for the whole region. Latin American economies, already quite homogeneous in terms of inequality, are becoming even more uniform.

The available evidence suggests that Latin America is and has been the most unequal region in the world. Differences in inequality with respect to the rest of the world have not significantly changed in the last 50 years. The assessment of Latin America as a high-inequality region is not restricted to income. The same conclusion arises when considering the distribution of consumption, land holdings, health status, and some measures of political representation.

This chapter has also analyzed other dimensions of distribution beyond inequality. Fueled by growth in GDP, poverty measures fell and aggregate welfare increased in most Latin American countries during the 1990s. However, increases in inequality have reduced the positive effects of growth: in several Latin American countries, the assessment of the performance of the economy is less optimistic when distributional issues are considered.

Although there are many contributing factors, household income inequality computed from household surveys is in particular the result of an unequal distribution of education, combined with high wage premiums for skilled workers and decreasing fertility rates due to improvements in income and education. The intensity of these three factors seems to have increased in most Latin American countries during the 1990s.

Finally, this chapter examined the information on non-income measures of inequality, including health status, crime victimization, political influence, and access to basic services. In some cases, notably in health status, the region is highly unequal by international standards. This may also be true of political influence, but cross-country information is weaker in this area. Basic services are typically unequally distributed, but less so than with regard to income, while the weak information on crime victimization that exists suggests that this aspect may be at least relatively equally distributed.

Notes

1. See Le Grand 1991 and Roemer 1996 and 1998 for overviews of this debate.

2. See Deaton 1997 and Deaton and Zaidi 2002 for arguments supporting the use of consumption as the best welfare indicator.

3. In fact, according to the life-cycle theory, with full access to capital markets current consumption should be closely associated to intertemporal living standards.

4. See Buhmann, Rainwater, Schmaus, and Smeeding 1988 and Deaton 1997 for discussions on these points.

5. Only the Dominican Republic, Jamaica, and Trinidad and Tobago are included in the sample. The quality and frequency of household surveys in the Caribbean are significantly lower than in the mainland Latin American countries. For instance, although household surveys in Guyana and St. Lucia are available, the authors were not able to compute consistent household income statistics for these countries.

6. For reference purposes, the authors have worked with some surveys that cover only urban areas in Bolivia, Colombia, and Paraguay in the early 1990s.

7. See IDB 1998, Londoño and Székely 2000, Székely and Hilgert 1999 and 2001, and Székely 2001.

8. Whenever a trade-off arises, the author has generally decided to preserve comparability within a country over time rather than across countries.

9. For some countries, income definitions have varied over time. Although statistics for alternative definitions have not been computed for the sake of brevity, and in most cases the tables provide a single line for each country and year. For instance, although the survey in El Salvador for 2000 includes nonmonetary income, in the tables statistics are given without those incomes in order to preserve comparability with previous surveys in that country. Alternative results for El Salvador, as well as for the Dominican Republic, Honduras, Paraguay, Peru, Uruguay, and República Bolivariana de Venezuela are available upon request. The main results reported in the paper do not vary in any of these cases because alternative income definitions are considered. During 2001, Argentina was in a deep recession. For reference, tables A.2 and A.3 also include statistics for 1998, when the economy was still growing. The surveys excluded some areas of Bolivia in 1992, Colombia in 1992, and Peru in 1991. For reference, all the statistics for Bolivia in 1996, Colombia in 1996, and Peru in 1994 were computed using, alternatively, the whole national survey or only the observations from the areas covered in the early 1990s. The label *regional* in Peru refers to all regions covered in the 1991 survey (which excluded Costa Rural, Selva Urbana, and Selva Rural).

10. Data for Nicaragua include nonmonetary income, while data for Costa Rica and El Salvador do not. However, ignoring nonmonetary payments from the Nicaraguan survey does not significantly alter the

results of the inequality comparison among these three countries (see also table A.7).

11. The richest individual in the household survey of Mexico in 2000 has an income 18 times greater than the median individual in the top decile. That gap (18 times) separates the median individual in the top decile from a person in the poorest second decile of the overall income distribution. This is an example of the long "upper tail" of the distributions.

12. See Lambert 1993 and Cowell 1995 and 2000 for details on these inequality indices.

13. The Gini coefficient ranges from 0 (complete equality) to 100 (all national income concentrated in the hands of one individual). It is also common to present that coefficient in terms of the [0,1] interval, instead of the [0,100] interval.

14. There is room for debate as to the appropriate value of these measures. For a case for a lower value of θ, see Lanjouw and Ravallion (1995). The best practice is to test the robustness of any conclusions against different assumptions, but space did not allow presentation of the results.

15. Even ignoring the most recent economic crisis, the inequality increase is very large (around 5 Gini points between 1992 and 1998).

16. The survey in Venezuela for 1989 is not strictly comparable with 1995 and 1998, since it does not include nonlabor income and nonmonetary payments. However, ignoring these incomes in 1995 and 1998 does not significantly modify the results. For instance, the Gini coefficient for the distribution of household per capita income in 1995 goes from 46.9 with all income sources to 46.7 with only labor monetary income.

17. The survey frame changed significantly in the Dominican Republic between 1995 and 1997, making the results of the comparisons difficult to interpret.

18. See Fields 1989 for Brazil, Gonzales-Vega and Cespedes 1993 for Costa Rica, and Altimir 1994 and 1996a for the remaining countries.

19. See Altimir 1986 and Gasparini, Marchionni, and Sosa Escudero 2001, among others, for documentation of similar inequality trends in Argentina.

20. This pattern is hardly attributable to informational problems, such as the urban coverage of the household survey. More than 85 percent of Argentineans live in cities and significant migratory movements have not occurred in the last three decades.

21. This result is in line with those reported by ECLAC 1996a, Morley and Vos 1997, and Robles 1999.

22. A decrease of nearly 3 points in the Gini coefficient between 1995 and 1999 was identified, even after eliminating an extreme outlier in the 1995 survey. Székely and Hilgert (1999) do not find

significant changes between 1995 and 1998 and report an increase between 1998 and 1999. On the other hand, Gonzalez (2001) finds a drop of 1 point in the Gini coefficient between 1998 and 1999.

23. The Gini coefficient actually fell around 1 point, which is just within the limit to be considered a nonsignificant change from a statistical point of view (at a 95 percent confidence level).

24. Latinobarómetro is an annual survey of public opinion that started in 1995. Data is gathered in 17 Latin American countries.

25. One LSMS survey is available for parts of Brazil for 1996–1997, Guatemala for 2000, Guyana 1992–1993, and Panama for 1997.

26. See Chen and others 1995, World Bank Development Indicators Database (1998–2000), and various World Bank Poverty Reports on these countries.

27. Readers interested in technical details can consult Esteban and Ray 1994, Wolfson 1994, Esteban, Gradín, and Ray 1999, and a note by Matías Busso on the Web site of this study.

28. The next step in the research agenda would be to consider measures of polarization with more than two groups.

29. These include one proposed by Sen (equal to the mean times 1 minus the Gini coefficient) and two proposed by Atkinson (CES functions with two alternative parameters of inequality aversion). See Lambert (1993) for technical details.

30. The sources for GDP figures are World Bank 2000b and World Development Indicators Database.

31. See Gasparini and Sosa Escudero 2001 for a more complete justification of this kind of study.

32. Note that in Panama the share of the bottom deciles increased, leading to a fall in inequality indices with greater weights in that part of the distribution (for example, the Atkinson Index with a parameter equal to 2).

33. The estimates range from 37 percent (Londoño and Székely 2000) to 53 percent (Sala-i-Martin 2002).

34. This study does not attempt to compute poverty statistics with our sample of household surveys because the World Bank has recently issued a report on poverty in Latin America and the Caribbean (Wodon and others 2001) and frequently produces Poverty Reports in several countries in the region.

35. For reviews on the usual limitations of household surveys for distributional analysis, see Deaton 1997, Gottschalk and Smeeding 2000, and Atkinson, Brandolini, and Smeeding 2002.

36. See chapter 2 and table A.1 in the statistical appendix for more details on the PNAD survey.

37. For example, Gasparini and Sosa Escudero (2001) found that the measured increasing trend in income inequality in Argentina is robust when the three types of adjustments mentioned above are made.

38. The implementation of the bootstrap method here follows Sosa Escudero and Gasparini 2000. For more theoretical references on the subject, see Biewen 2002, Davidson and Duclos 2000, and Mills and Zandvakili 1997.

39. Results for other variables and indices are available from the author upon request.

40. Tabatabai (1996) at the International Labor Organization also made an independent effort to put together distributional statistics for many countries in the world.

41. Secondary data sets have some problems that were recently reviewed by Atkinson and Brandolini (2001) and Atkinson, Brandolini, and Smeeding (2002).

42. Deininger and Squire (1996), for instance, highlight the "familiar fact that inequality in Latin America is considerably higher than in the rest of the world."

43. The Gini coefficients are taken from the UNU/WIDER-UNDP World Income Inequality Database. All countries with at least one observation in the period 1991–1999 with the quality rating "reliable data" are included. When several observations are available for a given country, the most recent data point has been used.

44. Africa is not included in this graph, since there are not enough observations on income inequality in that region.

45. The data set includes observations for Bolivia, Ecuador, Guyana, Jamaica, Mexico, Nicaragua, and Peru. This set of countries does not have an average Gini coefficient for the household per capita income distribution that is significantly different from the overall mean for Latin America (that is, it is just 0.4 Gini points higher).

46. For instance, in the sample Brazil has 15 observations from 1960 but observations end in 1989. Being a country with very high inequality, omitting Brazil in the 1990s reduces the regional value for that decade and biases the results for the decadal changes.

47. The exception is the gap with Eastern Europe, a region that suffered strong distributional transformations in the 1990s.

48. For instance, for the case of Latin America, Bourguignon and Morrison (2002) consider five "countries" (Brazil, Mexico, Argentina/Chile, Colombia/República Bolivariana de Venezuela/Peru, and a group of 37 smaller countries).

49. Most statistics are obtained from Maddison 1992, Deininger and Squire 1996, and Altimir 1996b.

50. Notice that this is not international inequality within a region obtained by averaging (with or without weights) national levels of inequality.

51. This fact is also highlighted in IDB 1998.

52. Two exceptions are Colombia and Nicaragua, where the Gini coefficient for the distribution of individual labor income significantly increased in the 1990s, while the Gini coefficient for household income remained unchanged.

53. Educational systems differ across countries and sometimes also over time within countries. See the Web site of this study for details on the construction of educational variables. The variable years of education are recorded in most surveys. For those in which it is not, we have estimated it from the maximum educational degree attained by people and their age. Years of education are truncated at a maximum of 17.

54. This fact would have been even more noticeable if years of education had not been truncated at 17.

55. Bolivia and Guatemala are the two clearest exceptions to this pattern.

56. The Gini coefficient as most of the inequality indices, is scale-invariant (see Lambert 1993).

57. In addition, this roughly corresponds to (1) completion of primary education or less, (2) completion or noncompletion of secondary education, and (3) at least some higher education.

58. See Wodon and others 2000 and Duryea and Pagés 2002 for estimates of returns on years of education in several Latin American countries.

59. Nicaragua and Peru experienced changes in the returns on skilled labor similar to those in Argentina.

60. The only exception is Mexico in 1996; nonetheless, the coefficient is not significantly different from 1.

61. Only Chile has a share higher than 10 percent, which may be the consequence of a better survey design. This higher share does not seem to account for the high inequality level in Chile, which is still one of the highest in Latin America when the analysis is restricted to the distribution of labor income (see table A.7).

62. Bernanke and Gurkaynak (2002) replicate and update Gollin's (2002) calculations for a larger sample of countries. They find that labor shares in Latin America are higher than those computed directly in the UN National Account Statistics. Moreover, the heterogeneity among Latin American countries seems to be lower.

63. The need for more reliable information on capital income has been emphasized again as recent studies have cited the distribution of nonlabor assets as a key determinant in income distribution, income mobility, and growth. See Birdsall and Londoño 1997, Deininger and Squire 1998, and Deininger and Olinto 2002.

64. The only exception to this pattern is Chile.

65. Cardoso and Helwege (1992) report that the largest 7 percent of land holdings in Latin America account for 77 percent of the land. See also Thiesenhusen 1995 for more evidence.

66. The absolute difference in the number of children has also increased in many countries (see Table 5.20).

67. In some countries, statistics refer to schooling only for children 5 years of age or older, since no information is recorded for younger children. See the Web site of this study for details.

68. Of course, it could be the case that the gap in attendance rates narrows down, but the gap in the quality of education becomes larger.

69. This analysis follows Gasparini 2002.

70. "Stunting" is used to describe a condition in which children fail to gain sufficient height given their age. The term "wasting" refers to a situation in which children have failed to achieve sufficient weight given their height.

71. Samuels and Snyder 2001 show that this result holds when controlling for institutional variables.

72. The question in Latinobarómetro used for the study is: "Have you or any member of your family been assaulted, robbed, or victimized in any way during the past 12 months?"

73. Water refers to the availability of a source of water in the house or on the building lot. The variable restroom is equal to 1 when the household has a restroom with a toilet connected to a sewage system or septic tank. The variable electricity includes all sources of electricity. Some definitions and classifications differ among surveys, so comparisons should be made carefully. See the Web site of this study for more details on the definitions for specific countries.

74. The variable *telephone* includes fixed and cellular phones.

CHAPTER 3

Group-Based Inequalities: The Roles of Race, Ethnicity, and Gender

L ATIN AMERICA IS A RACIALLY AND ETHNICALLY DIVERSE REGION, WITH MEN AND WOMEN, AFRO- AND Euro-descendents, and indigenous and nonindigenous people actively pursuing higher living standards for themselves and their families. However, levels of well-being are not equal across races or ethnic and gender groups.

The extent of inequality in well-being and the reasons for such differences have been the focus of various regional and country studies. The most notable study on indigenous groups, by Psacharopoulos and Patrinos (1994), concludes that indigenous people are systematically poorer than nonindigenous people and that this pattern can be largely traced to fewer "endowments"—education, job experience, family structure, and occupation—as well as to other causes, such as differential preferences, institutions, social relations, cultural norms, and discrimination. In terms of gender analysis in the Latin American region, Psacharopoulos and Tzannatos (1992), find that across the region, women's earnings and labor force participation are consistently lower than men's and can also be traced to "endowment" and other effects. Regional studies on race are scarce, with country-level studies of Brazil making up the bulk of the research.

This chapter investigates the extent to which inequality within and between racial, ethnic, and gender groups contributes to national inequality. Standard measures of inequality are applied to racial, ethnic, and gender subgroups and these results are aggregated up to the national level. This chapter will focus primarily on wage inequalities and inequality in endowments that impact wages. It draws on sociological and anthropological work, but the bulk of the information is based on economics and derived using economic tools. Although race, ethnicity, and gender are all examined in this chapter, this approach does not suggest that the underlying factors that lead to group-based inequalities in any one of these dimensions necessarily are responsible for the observed group-based inequality with regard to the other dimensions. Instead, the patterns and underlying factors that lead to differences according to race, ethnicity, and gender need to be considered and understood separately for each category.

The following chapter has four sections in addition to the current introduction. Section 3.1 describes circumstances related to gender, race, and ethnicity in Latin America and considers some conceptual issues encountered in analyzing these demographic groups. Section 3.2 uses descriptive statistics to outline the extent of inequality within and between the different demographic groups (defined as white and Afro-descendents, Indo- and Afro-Guyanese, and indigenous and nonindigenous depending on the country), within which the gender variable cuts across racial and ethnic group lines. Inequality throughout the lifecycle is examined in terms of education, sector of employment and occupation, household formation, wealth and access to services, and labor income. Section 3.3 uses econometric tools to clarify how differential returns on characteristics and differential levels of education, fertility, and sector of work contribute to the observed inequality between individuals' labor incomes and to the contribution of race, ethnicity, and gender to national inequality. Finally, section 3.4 provides concluding remarks.

3.1. Who are the people of Latin America?

Table 3.1 shows that an estimated 17–30 percent of the Latin American population identify themselves as Afro-descendents, with Brazil having the largest concentration of such citizens. Some 44.7 percent of Brazilians identify themselves as being black or of mixed race (*preto* or *pardo*), which is the equivalent of nearly 80 million people. The next largest Afro-descendent populations in Latin America are in Colombia (25 percent), Nicaragua (13 percent), and República Bolivariana de Venezuela (10 percent), while the majority of the populations of most Caribbean countries identify themselves as Afro-Creole. More than 80 percent of the citizens of Haiti, Barbados, Grenada, *Guadeloupe,* Jamaica, St. Vincent and the Grenadines, and St. Lucia claim African descent.

Although indigeneity rates have been historically much higher, only 10 percent of the population of Latin America identify themselves as indigenous today (see box 3.1 and table 3.1). These rates vary strongly across countries: the majority of Bolivians and Guatemalans are identified as indigenous, comprising 71 and 66 percent of the national populations, respectively. Peru (47 percent) and Ecuador (38 percent) also have sizable indigenous populations. Indigenous populations in the Caribbean countries are rarely quantified, but when they are they appear as a small proportion of the population (table 3.1).

With the exception of Belize, Costa Rica, French Guiana, and the Dominican Republic, one half or more of the population of Latin America is female (table 3.1), with women making up the majority in nearly one-half of the countries. It is not unusual for women to make up a higher proportion of a population than men, since women tend to have higher longevity and are less prone to die prematurely from violence (Jacobsen 2002).

The evolution of race, ethnicity, and gender as concepts

Ethnicity and race

The unique colonial history of Latin America forms the basis for the conceptualization of race and ethnicity and related policies today (see also chapter 4). Sociologists argue that in Latin America, the population of European

TABLE 3.1

Distribution of Afro-descended, indigenous, and female populations in the Americas and the Caribbean, various years (percent)

Country	Afro-descendents[a]	Indigenous	Female[b]
Latin America			
Argentina	—	1.0[c]	51
Bolivia	2.0	71.0[c]	50
Brazil	44.7[c]	0.4[e]	51
Chile	—	8.0[c]	50
Colombia	25.0[g]	1.8[f]	51
Costa Rica	2.0	0.8[a]	49
Ecuador	10.0	38.0[c]	50
El Salvador	—	7.0[c]	51
Guatemala	—	66.0[c]	50
Honduras	5.0	15.0[c]	50
Mexico	0.5	14.0[e]	51
Nicaragua	13.0	5.0[c]	50
Panama	73.5	10.0[e]	50
Paraguay	3.5	1.5[e]	50
Peru	9.7	47.0[c]	50
Uruguay	5.9	0.4[e]	51
RB de Venezuela	10.0	0.9[c]	50
Caribbean			
Antigua and Barbuda	97.9	—	52
Bahamas	85.0	—	51
Barbados	95.8	—	51
Belize	57.0	19.0[d]	49
Bermuda	61.3	—	52
Cuba	62.0	—	50
Dominican Republic	84.0	—	49
French Guiana	42.6	4.0[d]	49
Grenada	84.0	—	50
Guadeloupe	87.0	—	51
Guyana	42.6	6.0[d]	52
Haiti	100.0	—	51
Jamaica	91.4	2.0[d]	51
St. Lucia	90.3	—	51
St. Vincent and Grenadines	95.0	—	50
Suriname	41.0	6.0[d]	50
Trinidad and Tobago	43.0	—	50
Other			
Canada	2.2[f]	1.0[d]	50
United States	12.3	0.9[e]	51

— not reported.
Note: Table includes data from 2000 for Latin America and the United States, except: Afro-descendents from 1992 for Bolivia, Guatemala, Paraguay, Peru, and Venezuela; 1990 for Ecuador and Panama; 1995 for Nicaragua; and 2001 for Canada. Indigenous from 1999 for Canada. Data are for 2001 for Colombia, 1999 for Honduras, and 1997 for Uruguay. For the Caribbean, all Afro-descendent data are for 1999 and all indigenous data are for 1999. The gender data are for 2000.
Sources: [a]Florez, Medina, and Urrea 2001 for all figures except: [b]UNDP 2000, [c]Mahoney and Vom Hau 2002, [d]Deruyttere 2001, [e]National census data, [f]World Bank 2003a, [g]Vice-presidencia de la República de Colombia 2002.

BOX 3.1

Distribution of the population of the Americas: An historical evolution

The racial and ethnic composition of the Americas changed substantially following the arrival of the Europeans. The graph below shows that in 1570, nearly 100 percent of the Americas was populated by people identified as "indigenous," but by 1825, nearly 40 percent of Spanish America, 80 percent of Brazil, and 98 percent of the United States and Canada were considered nonindigenous. The share of African and indigenous descendents dropped by 1935 as Euro-descendent populations in the Americas continued to grow rapidly and the assimilation of indigenous people into European-style institutions continued.

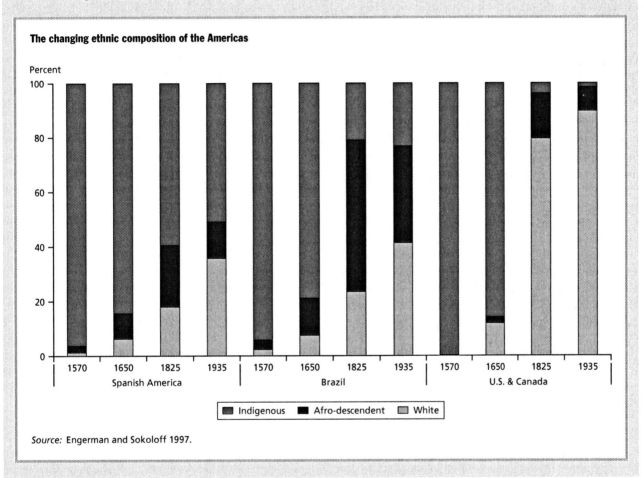

The changing ethnic composition of the Americas

Source: Engerman and Sokoloff 1997.

descendents strove for ethnic unity in order to build national unity that could counter the newly arriving colonists and help to control the nonwhite population through assimilation with the primarily indigenous (rather than Afro-descendent) populations (Agier 1995). Privately, however, individuality has been emphasized and mobility has been seen as a result of "self-whitening" and wealth rather than movement of a group as a whole; race and class status were thus linked.

Given the history of the development of racial and ethnic identity in Latin America, racial and ethnic differences have often been denied in favor of the claim that countries in the region are "post-racial," that is, a single mixed community (Graham 1990). Racial inequality that is recognized has been treated either as the result of an incomplete process of national integration or as an expression of class-based inequality. With this mindset, differences between racial or ethnic groups have been attributed to socioeconomic influences that happened to be correlated with, but are not caused by, power structures (Torres-Saillant 1998). Discussions on race and ethnicity have been combined with those on poverty and class, thereby ignoring many specific aspects that contribute to intergroup differentials. It has also been claimed that Latin America was more racially tolerant than the United States, for example, with its history of legalized segregation, suppressed ethnic and racial identity, and rights movements. This claim has formed the basis for an ideology of racially and ethnically blind national policies focused on poverty reduction.

This conceptualization is, however, changing as racial and ethnic disparities in well-being are increasingly acknowledged in academic and policy circles and reflected in social movements. In the mid-1970s, scholars began to argue that, despite ideologies of integration, differences in well-being between demographic groups are partly based on racial and ethnic discrimination. More recently, sociologists have theorized that racial or ethnic inequalities are a result of a history of power relations that create an uneven playing field by setting up a situation in which endowments, opportunities, and expectations differ by demographic group (Baiocchi 2001). These theories are becoming salient as ethnic and racial groups increasingly reshape their cultures and raise their voices for equal rights and a greater share of opportunities in their countries (Arocha 1998). This shift has also led to increased demands and efforts to include ethnic and racial groups in national statistical exercises (see box 3.2), and to address the difficult identification and measurement issues that arise in those contexts (see box 3.3).

Due to the nature of colonization in the Caribbean, racial identity evolved differently than the way it did in the rest of Latin America. Racial lines were more starkly drawn under colonial rule, a factor that—partly due to the absence of plantation owners—facilitated the maintenance of the white population largely separate from the ethnic and Afro populations. This physical distance in turn fostered a social distance between whites and blacks. Planters identified with

---

BOX 3.2

Todos Contamos: National census and social inclusion

"I have a problem with this census questionnaire, I am not included", said José Chalá after listening to a presentation on Ecuador's 2000 census. Mr. Chalá was referring to absence of data on Ecuadorans of African descent. His status in this census is hardly unique. Not all countries in Latin America and the Caribbean include a category to account for those of African descent, which limits a government's ability to address inequality and to inform policies and programs oriented toward poverty reduction and social inclusion.

The World Bank and other multilateral organizations have been working with governments in Latin America to rectify this shortcoming. In November 2000, the government of Colombia, with the sponsorship of international organizations, held the first *Todos Contamos* ("Everyone Counts") conference to raise awareness among demographers, government census personnel, and indigenous and Afro-descended individuals and organizations in Latin America, about the need to include questions on race and ethnicity in national censuses. By 2002, 10 countries in the region included a racial or ethnic self-identification question in their censuses.

A follow-up workshop, *Todos Contamos II: National Census and Social Inclusion,* was held in Lima, Peru in October 2002. It brought together more than 100 representatives from 18 countries throughout Latin America to take stock of progress made, discuss lessons, explore methodologies, and share examples of how census questions can be further improved. At the end of the conference, each participating country revealed a plan of action that included six key aspects: (1) incorporating racial and ethnic questions into national censuses and refining existing questions; (2) integrating in a systematic manner the question of race and ethnic self-identification in national household surveys and poverty analyses; (3) fostering greater participation by ethnic groups in data collection; (4) disseminating information that is already available; (5) implementing capacity-building programs to help translate data into social inclusion-oriented policies; and (6) promoting national *Todos Contamos* conferences and supporting country-to-country learning exchanges. Progress has been made as Latin America slowly moves toward a better understanding of who really makes up the region's population.

England much more than *haciendaros* (large estate owners) did with Spain, with the result that planters in the Caribbean did not develop a sense of national identity. Instead, a stronger sense of subordinate racial identities developed over time. Once the fight for independence did ensue, the black political elite became stronger and continued to reinforce black racial identity in many Caribbean countries (Safa 1998, Torres-Saillant 1998).

As the racial composition of Latin America continues to change, another racial and ethnic group has recently established a presence in Caribbean countries. Migrants from India have formed sizable Indo-Guyanese and Indo-Trinidadian populations. These groups continue to grow, integrate into society, and increasingly compete with the Afro-Guyanese and Afro-Trinidadians for economic, social, and political positions in their adopted countries (Safa 1998).

Gender

While racial and ethnic variables are newly recognized as important factors in explaining differences in well-being among demographic groups, gender has a longer history of acceptance as a salient variable that affects the likelihood of poverty and inequality. Many Latin American countries have had strong women's movements that began in the 1970s and 1980s, resulting in an ever-increasing presence of women in the economy, political arena, and society as a whole. All governments in the region now have Women's Offices or Women's Ministries.

Over time, women's well-being has improved relative to men's, whether because of better opportunities for women, changing needs of society that have altered gender roles, or the worsening of men's situations. Maternal mortality has decreased, women's educational attainment is approaching or surpassing that of men (particularly in the English-speaking Caribbean countries), women's labor force participation continues to increase, and the wage gap is decreasing over time. In addition, women's involvement in political, cultural, and intellectual realms continues to grow, with participation rates in senior government in many countries exceeding those in the United States and some other Organisation for Economic Cooperation and Development (OECD) countries. These successes are not equally experienced by all women, however, as those living in urban areas who are not indigenous or of African descent are making gains at a much faster rate than are women in rural areas or those of indigenous or African descent (World Bank 2000f, 2002c).

Despite these gains, gender disparities in various measures of well-being still exist and new challenges continually face societies. Women still lag behind men in most indicators of well-being—including wage gaps, control over resources, political voice, and health care—but meanwhile there are increasingly notable trends of disadvantage among men, including shorter longevity, greater alcoholism, and higher suicide rates than women (Jacobsen 2002). In Brazil and the Caribbean countries, male educational attainment rates are lagging and difficulty in obtaining and maintaining employment is increasing, in turn placing male-oriented gender issues firmly on the agenda.

The Roots of Difference

Observed differences between subordinate and dominant groups are commonly attributed to discrimination (broadly construed), but the process of creating these differences involves a complex interaction between individual choice, opportunities, and the institutions with which individuals interact throughout their lifetimes. Two insights come from sociological perspectives on the formation and persistence of group-based differences. (See Heller and Mahoney 2003 for a discussion of concepts and processes related to such differences.) First, they are fundamentally *relational,* that is, interactions that occur between groups shape the behaviors, dispositions and attitudes of both subordinate and dominant groups. In the language of economists, such interactions determine "preferences," which should be seen as products of social relations. Second, an important reason for the persistence of what Tilly (1999) refers to as *durable* inequalities, is that they serve organizational purposes, allowing people in workplaces, schools, and other areas of activity to use group-based differences to influence how they interact with others. As Tilly (1999, p.7) states:

> Durable inequality among categories arises because people who control access to value-producing resources solve pressing organizational problems by means of categorical distinctions. Inadvertently or otherwise, those people set up systems of social closure, exclusion, and control.

Generally, the outcomes that can be observed today—such as wages, labor supply, housework time, and access to services—are the result of a lifelong process of accumulation of experiences, human capital, preferences, and constraints. At each stage of life, decisions are made and events occur that

BOX 3.3

The challenge of racial, ethnic, and gender identification and measurement

Race, ethnicity, and gender are difficult concepts to measure due to the social underpinnings of these demographic groupings. Individuals are commonly classified into race based on phenotype; into ethnicity by language, customs, and dress; and into gender by biology. However, inherent in these definitions are power relationships, behaviors, and expectations that are not easily observed or classified (Baiocchi 2001). Despite the difficulty in defining race, ethnicity, and gender, many countries in Latin America have made great strides in identifying the demographic composition of their populations. All census data now identify the sex of respondents, although the identification of race or ethnicity is less common.[a]

Assignment of a person to a *racial category* is difficult. Although "race" is based on observable physical characteristics that do not change over a lifetime (for example, skin color, hair type, and facial features), racial mixing over the years has led to a continuum of physical characteristics in all Latin American countries. For example, table 3.2 illustrates the high degree of disagreement on racial classification among Brazilian individuals and census interviewers. The racial category self-reported by individuals tends to be "whiter" than that identified by the interviewer. Among those individuals identified as "black" by the interviewer, only 57.9 percent also identified themselves as black, whereas 39.8 percent replied that they were of mixed race and the remaining 2.2 percent identified themselves as white. In addition, race seems to be strongly tied to economic status, suggesting that the meaning of "race" is in part socially, rather than completely biologically, constructed; wealthier classes tend to be "whiter." This is supported by classifications of race based on both self-reporting and interviewer perceptions, where the discrepancy between white and nonwhite increases with economic status (Florez, Medina, and Urrea 2001).

The difficulty of identification is exacerbated in the case of *ethnicity*, because linguistic or cultural practices, which may change over a lifetime, are used for classification, as opposed to the relatively fixed biological features used for racial identification. Even if a person is identified as indigenous, this is a crude measurement since many distinct indigenous groups are present in Latin American countries. The Guatemalan National Living Standards survey (ENCOVI),

for example, counts 23 ethnolinguistic indigenous groups; poverty, inequality, access to services, education, demographic, and labor force statistics differ greatly amongst these groups, even though all are classified as "indigenous" (World Bank 2002b, Edwards and Winkler 2002).

The absence of a precise method for ethnic identification is highlighted in the contrast between individual and interviewer perceptions of ethnicity. This contrast differed more in the classification of indigenous groups than in the identification of racial groups. Individuals in a Peruvian survey tend to *mestizar-se* (racially mix themselves), rather than "whiten" themselves. One-half of those who were identified by the interviewer as "white" self-identified as *mestizo* (mixed race), while two-thirds of those identified by the interviewer as "indigenous" declared themselves as *mestizo* (see table 3.3).

The identification of a person's *gender* is less controversial since gender and sex are highly correlated variables. However, they are different concepts. While "sex" is identified by those basic biological attributes that differentiate males and the females, "gender" is taken to refer to the full ensemble of norms, values, customs and practices that are correlated with a particular sex but contribute to much wider social differences between women and men (Kabeer 1994 and Kabeer and Subrahmaniam 2000). When women take on traditional "male" roles—such as unmarried women who are the sole breadwinners and have no childcare responsibilities—they behave more similarly to unmarried men than to women with more traditional female roles (Cunningham 2000, Bosch and Maloney 2003). The social connotation of "gender" is therefore difficult to capture through a single variable, although the high correlation among sex and gender roles allows for the sex variable to serve as a proxy.

These measures of racial, ethnic, and gender classification by statisticians are clearly far from perfect. Thus, any analysis using these measures (including the statistical analysis in this chapter) must take into account measurement errors when using the variables of "race," "language spoken," and "sex" to capture the complex biological-social concepts of race, ethnicity, and gender.

a. Censuses in 14 of the 35 Latin American countries do not ask about racial or ethnic origin and even fewer labor force or household surveys ask related questions (Florez, Medina, and Urrea 2001).

TABLE 3.2

Interviewer perception versus self-perception of race—Brazil, 1997 (percent)

		White	Mulatto	Black	All
		Interviewer classification for all			
	All	56.9	31.7	13.4	
		Interviewer versus self-classification			
	White	88.6	20.2	2.2	56
Self-classification	Mulatto	11.0	71.0	39.8	33
	Black	0.4	8.8	57.9	11
	Total	100.0	100.0	100.0	100

Source: Telles and Lim 1999.

create opportunities for or constraints on the next stage of life. Thus, the reason for observed outcomes today can be partly attributed to past events, sometimes all the way back to childhood, and can in turn be formed by historical processes of group formation and intergroup interactions. These experiences and decisions are affected by how individuals and groups view themselves and how dominant groups behave toward them. Such processes occur within the context of the formal and, especially, informal institutions that present opportunities or barriers at each stage of formation.

From birth, individuals are socialized to conform to their biological, demographic, and social group. Males and females, indigenous and nonindigenous, rich and poor, develop collective expectations and acquire preferences that comply with the rules of behavior, emotions, and expectations that are assigned to individuals based on the group to which they belong. Collective identities are constructed as products of social histories. There is, of course, individual variation within groups, but that is formed in relation to group-based characteristics.

Although some roles are based on biology (such as childbirth for women), many are based on assumptions of differences between groups (for example, an assertion that white men are more capable than women or nonwhite individuals), obsolete societal arrangements (women care for the household, indigenous people work in the fields), or an assignment of roles used to create or sustain a social hierarchy. This process of molding individual motivations, preferences, and behaviors is driven by cultural and social contexts (Baron and Hannan 1994), thus potentially translating biological differences into social differences.

Social differences influence individual choices throughout the lifecycle. In response to unequal social histories and life changes, subordinate groups often develop patterns of behavior, practices, and dispositions that influence lower aspirations, or acquire "constraining preferences." For example, the behavior of children as a "girl" or "boy" may be partly biological, but it is also largely based on the preferences that a parent or society teaches children based on their (biological) sex. This behavior in turn shapes choices of how to behave in school, both of which influence the selection of career, and all three of which affect the choice of family formation and employment. These patterns subsequently lead to the contemporaneous differences in such aspects as wages, labor force participation, assets, and family roles. A similar argument can be made for children of different ethnic or racial groups.

Discrimination: The costs of engaging with different groups

Discrimination is a key factor that influences the accumulation of skills and experiences of individuals and groups during their lifetimes. It is also part of the relational, historically formed interactions between groups. In the economic approach, discrimination is defined as a process of

TABLE 3.3

Interviewer versus self-perception of ethnicity—Peru, 2000 (percent)

		Interviewer classification				
		White	Mestizo	Indigenous	Other	Total
	White	55	10	8	3	13
	Mestizo	45	87	74	55	79
Self-classification	Indigenous	0	2	18	1	6
	Other	0	1	1	41	2
	Total	100	100	100	100	100

Source: GRADE 2001, as cited in Gacītúa-Marió and Wodon (forthcoming).

83

unequal treatment of individuals due to characteristics that are unrelated to the decision at hand and which lead to differentially observed outcomes. Discrimination is classified into two broad categories.

- *Pure discrimination* is a differential treatment of individuals because they possess characteristics that are "distasteful" to the discriminator. For example, if an employer is not comfortable working with Afro-descendents, the employer will compensate for this discomfort by penalizing Afro-descendents at a rate that is equal to the value of the cost of the unhappiness that the employer feels. This is realized through not hiring Afro-descendents, hiring them at lower wages, or giving them fewer opportunities than those given to otherwise observationally equivalent white counterparts (Becker 1971).

- *Statistical discrimination* is differential treatment of individuals based on observable characteristics that are correlated with certain undesired behaviors, but which may or may not accrue to the person in question. For example, women are more likely than men to leave the labor market due to childbearing, so employers may offer less training to female than to male employees since there is a higher probability that they will not be with the firm for as long as otherwise equivalent men. All women in the firm would then receive less training, even though the original motivation for lower pay may not apply to certain individual women.

It is often difficult to disentangle which observed differences are due to the behavior of the group adversely affected and which are due directly to discrimination. Of course, no one would choose lower wages over higher wages, all else being equal, but choices may have been made earlier in life that are unobservable to the researcher—such as the choice to select a lower-paying career that is more compatible with family responsibilities rather than choosing a higher-paying career that allows little personal time—but that affect observed wages. Thus, it is not possible to measure the degree to which discrimination is responsible for differential outcomes (Becker 1971, Altonji and Blank 1999). However, as noted above, such "choices" by subordinate groups, can themselves be products of histories of exploitation and unequal conditions.

A key conclusion of this line of thinking is that it is impossible to precisely identify the degree to which employer and worker preferences, employer and worker constraints, and institutions lead to observed differential outcomes among individuals from various demographic groups. However, it is possible to analyze how the outcomes would differ if some of these cross-group differences were controlled for (see box 3.4 for an example). Although gender, race, and ethnic differences are explained through the same model, they should be understood differently due to the relative importance of different factors for each group.

This chapter primarily focuses on income and educational inequality and the processes that take place earlier in life that may be responsible for the observed income differences among groups. Thus, the chapter uses data to measure the differences between men and women, indigenous and non-indigenous people, Indo- and Afro-descendents, and white and Afro-descended residents in Latin America at each stage of the lifecycle with regard to educational attainment (childhood), occupational and sector of employment, family formation (youth/early adulthood), and observed contemporary wages (adulthood).

Although the empirical work presented in this chapter is representative of the type of approach generally taken to analyze inequality, the approach does not definitively solve the puzzle of how to attribute the observed differentials to the different potential causes. Nevertheless, it does delineate the extent of differences between groups and provides some clues about how institutions, choice, and discrimination may be the source of the observed differences.

3.2. Inequality among individuals during the lifecycle

This section presents differences in levels of education, participation in occupation and employment sectors, family structure, wealth, access to services, and income among different racial, ethnic, and gender groups. Where possible, gender is considered jointly with race or ethnicity. The objective of this section is not to compare the distribution of these variables along ethnic or racial lines across countries, as underlying histories and resulting institutions make such cross-country comparisons meaningless. Instead, the following discussion presents various examples of inequality related to race and ethnicity across Latin America, thus revealing the great range of differences that exist throughout the region.

BOX 3.4

What if we do hold "all else constant?"

Men and women make different choices throughout their lifetimes that lead to different labor market outcomes. Thus, comparisons by sex are simplistic since they assume that men and women respond identically to incentives and are treated the same in the labor market. The table below shows that by successively holding factors constant between men and women, the gap between men's and women's labor force participation and wages decreases.

Women in Argentina, Brazil, and Costa Rica are 30–40 percentage points less likely to work than are men and they earn lower wages. However, when the sample tested is limited to young individuals—whose human and social capital have not diverged as much by gender as that of older individuals—with the same level of education, the labor force participation gap falls to 10 percent, while the wage gap does not show a clear trend. When the sample is further limited to only those individuals who are not married and do not have children (two key variables that particularly affect women's labor force participation and performance), the labor force participation gap disappears and the wage gap shrinks. In other words, some of the difference in labor market outcomes are due to personal choices made throughout life that are not directly related to the labor market.

Labor market outcomes for different groups

	Argentina	Brazil	Costa Rica
Difference in labor force participation rates			
All men and women	31.5	30.4	39.6
Age 25–35, university education	9.8	8.27	7.9
Age 25–35, university education, no spouse or children	–2.34	0	0
Ratio of female to male wages			
All wage earners	0.98	0.65	0.9
Wage earners, age 25–35, university education	0.88	0.68	0.9
Wage earners, age 25–35, university education, no spouse or children	0.98	0.75	0.94

Source: Authors' calculations.

Educational attainment is unequal by race and ethnicity, but not by gender

Men and women have increasingly similar levels of education in Latin America. This is particularly true in urban areas (see table 3.4), where women's educational attainment exceeds men's accumulated education in several countries, especially among younger age groups. While more women than men are illiterate in the age group 55–70 in all countries, this same pattern holds true only for youth in the Dominican Republic, El Salvador, and Peru.[1]

However, when examining the sample according to racial and ethnic characteristics, gender equality is not universal. The education level of indigenous women in Bolivia and Guatemala lags behind that of men from the same ethnic group. This difference may reflect the education gap in rural areas, or it may demonstrate that gender—and the preferences and discrimination associated with it—has a greater effect on parents' decisions to send their sons or daughters to school in indigenous households (figure 3.1). By contrast, women of Afro descent in Brazil and Guyana have a small advantage compared with men in the same group.

Within each country, the white/nonindigenous/Indo populations have higher levels of education than the indigenous/Afro-descended groups, but no single education level is strictly segregated by race or ethnicity. Indigenous and Afro-descended people are clearly over-represented among the least educated (figure 3.1) and under-represented among the most educated. For example, 63 percent of indigenous Bolivian women have primary school education or less, compared to 38 percent of nonindigenous Bolivian women.

TABLE 3.4

Ratio of female to male educational attainment and literacy

	Year	Female/male education	Female/male illiteracy, by age	
			20–24	55–70
Argentina	1997	—	0.33	2.80
Bolivia	1999	—	0.99	4.09
Brazil	1999	1.03	0.55	1.24
Chile	1998	1.00	0.87	1.22
Colombia	1998	0.97	0.96	1.62
Costa Rica	1998	0.97	—	—
Dominican Republic	1996	0.88	1.42	1.45
El Salvador	1997	0.92	1.22	1.75
Honduras	1998	1.00	0.71	1.42
Mexico	1999	0.96	—	—
Nicaragua	1998	0.99	0.63	1.70
Paraguay	1999	0.95	0.64	3.00
Peru	1997	0.96	1.13	5.09
RB de Venezuela	1996	1.04	0.45	2.02

— data not available.
Source: Author's calculations based on microdata from household surveys.

This illustrates both the education gap by ethnicity and that a large proportion of nonindigenous Bolivian women also have this low level of education. Thus, even though the education system does not strictly leave behind men and women of only one ethnic or racial group, certain groups are more left behind than others. The single group that is left behind the most is indigenous women, who lag behind white/nonindigenous/Indo-Guyanese women due to racial and ethnic gaps and behind indigenous men due to a gender factor that does not appear to be as strong among white/nonindigenous groups or Afro-descended groups.

The explanation for higher educational attainment among white, nonindigenous men and women has been attributed by various researchers to the following factors:

The rural-urban divide A collection of studies for Latin America finds that any difference in school attendance and performance between rural and urban schools nearly disappears in Ecuador, Peru, and Bolivia when controlling for the location of the school (García Aracil and Winkler 2002 for Ecuador,

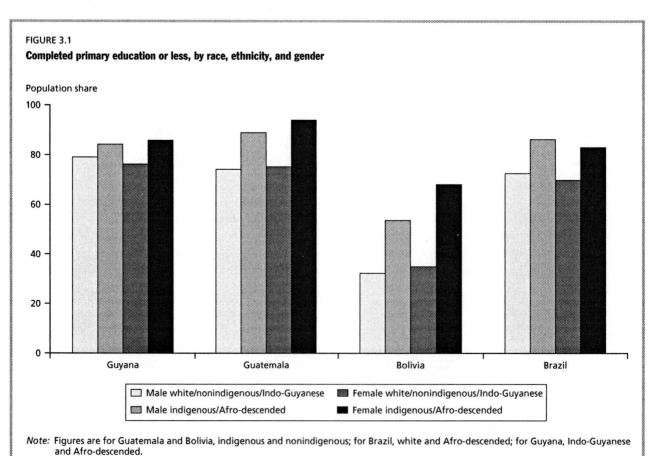

FIGURE 3.1

Completed primary education or less, by race, ethnicity, and gender

Note: Figures are for Guatemala and Bolivia, indigenous and nonindigenous; for Brazil, white and Afro-descended; for Guyana, Indo-Guyanese and Afro-descended.

Source: Authors' calculations based on microdata from household surveys.

Saavedra and Cardenas 2002 for Peru, and McEwan and Jimenez 2002 for Bolivia). However, Saavedra and Cardenas (2002) caution that there is a great deal of heterogeneity among schools within rural or urban areas as well.

Discrimination in schools   Is racial discrimination a factor in schooling? Oliveira Barbosa (2002) suggest that in Brazil, racial discrimination is not a factor in teacher evaluations of students, but that social position of the student is. Since Afro-Brazilian students are over-represented among the poor (Henriques 2001), this suggests that racial discrimination is conflated with socioeconomic discrimination. Conversely, girls (not controlling for race) experience positive discrimination in teacher evaluations. On the other hand, Albernaz, Ferreira, and Franco (2002) find evidence of Afro-Brazilian children doing less well after controlling for social status and school quality.

Intergenerational transfer of low levels of education   Many studies have found that parents (especially fathers) pass on their low levels of education to their children (Arias, Yamada, and Tejerina 2002 for Brazil, Sosa and Marchionni 1999 for Argentina, García Aracil and Winkler 2002 for Ecuador, and McEwan and Jimenez 2002 for Bolivia). The causes of the strong intergenerational transfer of low levels of education are unknown, but it may be due to the underestimation by parents of the value of education, the lower ability of racial (and ethnic) minorities to convert education into earnings (Valle Silva 2001), or a lack of funding for low-educated parents to send children to school.

Poverty and child labor   Poverty is cited as a reason behind school dropouts (Gacitua and Wodon, forthcoming, World Bank 2001a), whether due to the direct cost of attending school (that is, for uniforms, books, transportation, and supplies) or to the opportunity cost of school attendance (that is, forgone labor market earnings). Since the poor are over-represented among indigenous and Afro-Latino groups, they are more likely to be in this situation. Furthermore, these children are more likely to hold jobs (Psacharopoulos and Patrinos 1994).

Quality of education and available markets   Education—particularly beyond secondary school—is pursued largely in preparation for the job market. Girls, however, have another market that they may enter: the marriage market. Preparation for the marriage market does not occur in schools, but in the home (Knaul 2001). Thus, girls who live in remote areas where job opportunities are limited, such as rural indigenous communities, may find that dropping out of school and learning skills in the home will return a higher investment than education.

Employment sectors and occupations are highly segregated

Another factor that affects individual welfare is occupational and sectoral choice. Observed variations by race, ethnicity, and gender in occupations and sectors of work are correlated with differences in earning potential and well-being.

Sectoral allocation is noticeably gender-specific across countries. In all three countries considered in table 3.5, a

TABLE 3.5

Difference in the probability of being in each sector, by race and by gender (percent)

	Difference by race/ethnicity for men			Difference in probabilities, by gender, for white/nonindigenous		
	Bolivia	Guatemala	Brazil	Bolivia	Guatemala	Brazil
Formal sector employee	−3.4	−8.2	−4.5	−3.3	−9.9	−7.5
Informal sector employee	−8.1	4.1	5.1	−16.7	−16.0	−1.9
Public sector employee	−1.3	2.6	−0.6	−1.3	−2.0	0.6
Self-employed	23.9	7.7	−2.4	−4.7	−9.2	−11.3
Nonincome earner	−11.2	−1.0	3.5	26.0	37.1	20.2

Note: A negative value indicates that the probability is greater that a white/nonindigenous male is in that sector relative to an Afro-indigenous male (left columns) or relative to a female of the same race/ethnicity (right columns). Formal sector employee is defined as an individual whose employer pays social security benefits for the worker (Bolivia and Guatemala) or a Brazilian worker with a *carteira assinada* (signed work contract).
Source: Author's calculations based on microdata from household surveys.

TABLE 3.6

Share of sector that is female (percent)

	Labor force	Formal wage	Self-employed	Informal wage
Argentina[a]	39	36	36	47
Brazil[a]	43	38	38	56
Chile	33	28	40	—
Costa Rica[a]	40	38	35	50
El Salvador	40	32	54	—
Nicaragua	34	32	29	—
Paraguay	38	37	38	—

— not reported.
a. Cunningham (2001), data from 1995 for Costa Rica and Brazil, 1997 for Argentina. Formal wage employee is identified for Argentina and Costa Rica as an individual whose employer pays social security benefits and in Brazil as a person with a *carteira assinada* (signed work contract).
Source: Authors' calculations, 1998, for all except as indicated in note a.

TABLE 3.7

Occupational distribution, by gender

	Year	Duncan index[b]	Domestic worker (percent) Female	Male
Argentina[a]	1999	29	15	1.0
Brazil	1999	41	22	1.0
Chile	1998	31	15	0.2
Colombia	1998	31	8	0.2
Costa Rica	1998	41	17	0.2
El Salvador	1997	—	9	0.3
Honduras	1998	36	10	0.6
Mexico		31	—	—
Nicaragua	1993	—	14	0.3
Paraguay	1999	—	21	0.8
Peru		36	—	—

— not reported.
a. World Bank 2001b.
b. Percentage of the men and women who would have to trade occupations to create gender equality in all occupations.
Source: Authors' calculations based on microdata from household surveys.

much higher proportion of white and nonindigenous women than white or nonindigenous men are nonincome earners, meaning that they are not in the labor force or are unpaid workers.[2] Compared to the subset of women who do work, men comprise a disproportionate share of the urban formal sector, while the other sectors are more mixed.

Table 3.6 shows women's share of the labor force and of the formal, self-employed, and informal wage sectors; only in Paraguay does women's participation in the sectors reflect their participation in the labor force as a whole. Conversely, in El Salvador, 40 percent of workers are women but only 32 percent of the workers in the formal sector are women. Even in the modern economies of Chile and Argentina, women are underrepresented in the formal sector by 5 and 3 percentage points, respectively. On the other hand, women are overrepresented in the lower paying informal wage sector, comprising more than half of the informal wage workers but less than half of the labor force (Cunningham 2001).

Occupation

Men and women are not equally represented across occupations. Men are particularly overrepresented in the manufacturing sector—in which more than 80 percent of jobs are held by men in most countries—while women hold approximately 60 percent of service sector jobs even though they comprise only 40 percent of the labor force in most countries. Other sectors are more mixed and more closely represent women's share of the labor force. For women and men to be equally represented in the labor force, approximately 29–41 percent of men and women would have to exchange occupations (table 3.7).[3]

A higher proportion of women than men are in low-paying service occupations regardless of racial or ethnic background. Women also dominate the high-paying managerial field, but here there is more segregation along racial and ethnic lines. Figure 3.2 shows that white and nonindigenous (Indo-Guyanese) women are particularly engaged in service sector work, and nonwhite women are not far behind. In Bolivia, for example, 28 percent of nonindigenous women and 15 percent of indigenous women with jobs are employed in the service sector. This compares to less than 10 percent of men of either ethnic category.

One explanation for women's high participation in the service sector is their overrepresentation as domestic servants. In Argentina, for example, domestic service is the occupational category with the largest proportion of the female labor force, at 15 percent (World Bank 2001b). More than 20 percent of the female labor force is employed in domestic service in Brazil and Paraguay, while fewer than 1 percent of men are employed as domestic workers (table 3.7).

Domestic work is often pointed to as the most vulnerable of jobs due to its isolated nature, the full dependence of

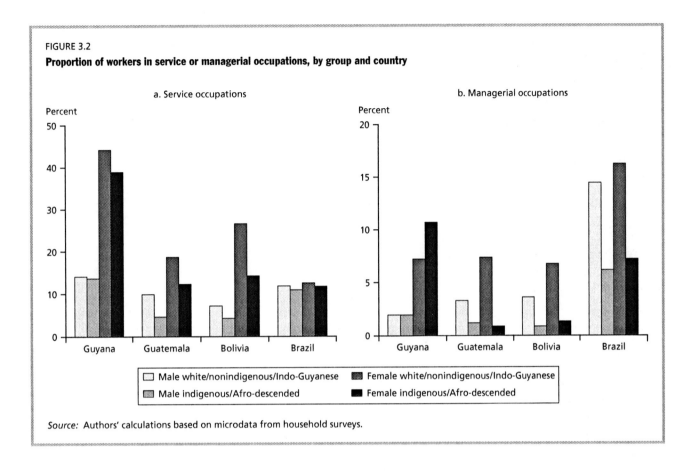

FIGURE 3.2

Proportion of workers in service or managerial occupations, by group and country

a. Service occupations

b. Managerial occupations

Legend:
- ☐ Male white/nonindigenous/Indo-Guyanese
- ▨ Male indigenous/Afro-descended
- ▦ Female white/nonindigenous/Indo-Guyanese
- ■ Female indigenous/Afro-descended

Source: Authors' calculations based on microdata from household surveys.

the worker on the employer, limits on career advancement, and the excessive work hours for domestic workers who live with their employers and thus are essentially at their workplace 24 hours a day, 6 days a week. However, interviews with domestic workers reveal that there are positive factors associated with this type of work. A sample of Argentine domestic workers, for example, report leaving low-paying formal sector jobs to return to the domestic service sector, in which employers are more flexible in terms of work hours, salary payments, and bonuses than are formal sector employers (World Bank 2001b).

A different pattern emerges in the high-paying managerial sector, in which differences in participation are based more on race or ethnicity than on gender. In Guatemala, Bolivia, and Brazil, nonindigenous or white women are most represented in the sector, followed by nonindigenous or white men. The trend deviates in Guyana, where women are more in the managerial sector than men; this is due to men's high participation in agricultural and manufacturing occupations.

Family formation

The choice of family formation, in terms of spouse, children, and extended family, is an important factor that determines future access to earning opportunities. Perhaps more important, however, is the fact that the gender roles associated with being a wife or a husband, or being a parent or not, influence one's work and nonwork life (see box 3.5).

Most individuals in Latin America are married with children. More than 50 percent of households are headed by a couple that is married or in a consensual union with children present in the household, while another 20 percent are headed by a couple without any children. Single mothers are household heads in 5–14 percent of Latin American households, while less than 1 percent of households are headed by single fathers. Unmarried heads of households account for the remaining 15 percent of the sample.

Women are twice as likely as men to be unmarried without children, partly due to their longevity when husbands have died and children have moved out of the house, a factor that in turn results in a large proportion of elderly women

Women's other job: housework

Married women's contribution to caring for their own homes and families is equivalent to a full-time job. Mexican women who do not hold jobs in the labor market spend an average of 49 hours each week taking care of their homes and families, while those in the labor market still spend a substantial amount of time engaged in home care—33 hours weekly. This compares to the 5.5 hours contributed by husbands each week, with an extra 30 minutes of housework added to this figure if wives are employed. Thus, women's work in the home is not simply a "specialization of labor," since even when women work in the labor market they still undertake the majority of housework.

Even before arriving in the labor market, housework is assigned according to gender. Daughters contribute 14 hours weekly helping their mothers, while sons spend the same time as their fathers (that is, 5–6 hours weekly).

Average weekly hours spent on housework, by household member*

	If wife employed	If wife not employed
Wife	32.8	48.9
Husband	6.1	5.5
Teenage daughter	14.3	14.0
Teenage son	6.2	5.5

*Only households with a married or consensual union household head, spouse present.
Source: Encuesta Nacional de Empleo Urbano, Mexico, 1999.

who care for themselves. A broad breakdown of this structure shows that household structures generally do not differ across racial and ethnic group lines. Differences are greater according to the gender of the head of household: male-headed households are approximately one person larger than female-headed households. It turns out that this is not due to differences in the numbers of children, but rather reflects the missing male partner in female-headed households.

Across the four-country sample, no single race or ethnicity has larger families. Afro-Brazilian and indigenous Guatemalan men have households that are a half-person larger, on average, than those of white and nonindigenous

men, but Guatemalan households headed by men have roughly 4.5 people, regardless of the ethnicity of the household head.

Extended families are more prevalent in households headed by women, but this household arrangement is not particular to specific ethnic or racial groups. More than two-thirds of male-headed households do not include family members beyond a spouse and children, a proportion that is similar among households headed by indigenous men. In contrast, approximately half of households headed by women include family members besides a spouse and children. This is particularly true of indigenous female-headed households in Bolivia and Guatemala and in Afro-Guyanese female-headed households. However, female-headed households make up fewer than 30 percent of households in Guyana and 20 percent of households in Bolivia and Guatemala, making nuclear households the dominant model in society.

Households headed by indigenous and Afro-descended people have less wealth

Assets and access to services are proxies for wealth and well-being. Assets are an intertemporal measure of wealth since they are accumulated over time and may be converted into income at any point. Public services also add value to a household by improving quality of life and decreasing demands on household time.

Households headed by white and nonindigenous people generally own more assets than those headed by Afro- or indigenous people. Table 3.8 shows the average dwelling size per capita (measured by number of rooms) and rates of ownership of an automobile, refrigerator, and home. Dwelling area per capita is larger in female-headed households, which partly reflects the smaller average number of people living in such households. In addition, houses inhabited by white or nonindigenous families are larger than those inhabited by Afro or indigenous families. However, Afro-Brazilians are marginally more likely to own their homes than are white Brazilians. In terms of ownership of durable goods, households headed by nonindigenous men and women are more likely to own both automobiles and refrigerators, and male-headed households are more likely to own automobiles.

Inequality by race rather than gender is most notable in terms of access to services. In the three countries considered in table 3.9, households headed by white or nonindigenous people have greater access to water, sewage systems, electricity,

TABLE 3.8

Asset ownership, by race, ethnicity, and gender (percent)

	Rooms per capita	Own home	Auto	Refrigerator
Guatemala				
Nonindigenous male	0.58	—	20.4	38.5
Indigenous male	0.37	—	5.7	9.8
Nonindigenous female	0.82	—	10.6	46.7
Indigenous female	0.56	—	2.9	9.7
Brazil				
White male	2.0	73.1	—	84.2
Afro-male	1.8	74.7	—	70.4
White female	2.9	72.8	—	85.2
Afro-female	2.4	74.8	—	73.6

— missing data.
Source: Author's calculations based on microdata from household surveys.

TABLE 3.9

Access to services by race, ethnicity, and gender (percent)

	Water	Sewage systems	Electricity	Garbage collection
Guatemala				
Nonindigenous male	75.0	44.1	78.3	30.7
Indigenous male	64.6	23.0	59.0	8.7
Nonindigenous female	81.6	58.2	85.6	37.4
Indigenous female	71.5	31.2	67.2	12.9
Bolivia				
Nonindigenous male	41.5	52.2	81.2	—
Indigenous male	16.2	29.7	55.8	—
Nonindigenous female	38.3	59.1	84.3	—
Indigenous female	18.2	36.9	64.3	—
Brazil				
White male	99.9	47.4	95.4	78.8
Nonwhite male	99.8	40.7	89.0	65.4
White female	99.9	50.0	96.4	81.7
Nonwhite female	99.8	43.1	90.7	69.5

Source: Authors' calculations based on microdata from household surveys.

and garbage collection than do Afro- or indigenous-headed households. For example, in Bolivia more than 50 percent of households headed by nonindigenous men or women have access to sewage systems compared to 30 percent and 37 percent of households headed by indigenous men and women, respectively. Within ethnic or racial groups, households headed by women seem to have particularly high levels of access to public services.

Access to services is greater for all urban dwellers compared to any group of rural dwellers. For example, in Guatemala, although 56 percent of households headed by rural white men and 56 percent of households headed by rural indigenous men have access to water, 85 percent of households headed by urban indigenous men have access to that service. Similarly, 68 percent of households headed by nonindigenous rural women and 55 percent of households headed by indigenous rural women have access to electricity, while 83 percent of households headed by indigenous urban women have electricity. These differences highlight the general pattern of urban-rural differentials being much greater than ethnic differentials with regard to access to services. However, since indigenous people are disproportionately represented in rural and marginal urban areas, they experience more of the burden of limited access in such areas.

FIGURE 3.3

Wage gaps by race/ethnicity and gender

Ratio of group mean wage to white male wages

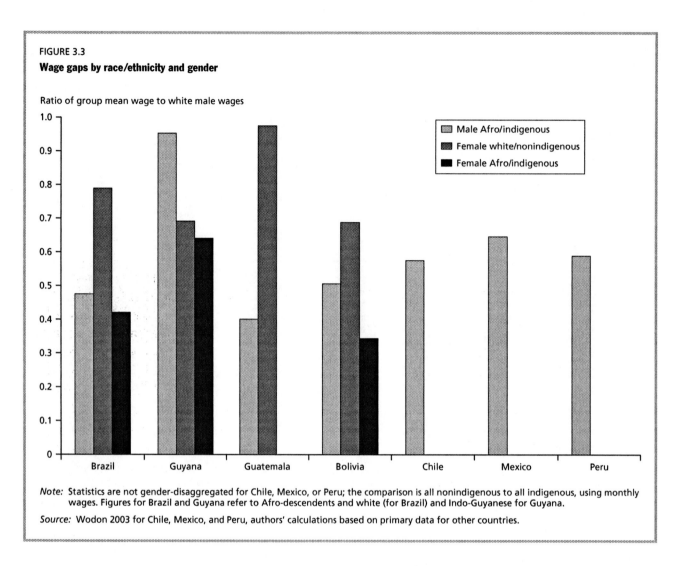

Note: Statistics are not gender-disaggregated for Chile, Mexico, or Peru; the comparison is all nonindigenous to all indigenous, using monthly wages. Figures for Brazil and Guyana refer to Afro-descendents and white (for Brazil) and Indo-Guyanese for Guyana.

Source: Wodon 2003 for Chile, Mexico, and Peru, authors' calculations based on primary data for other countries.

White/nonindigenous men have the highest average income, but all groups have high within-group inequality in wages

Within racial and ethnic groups, women have lower earnings than men, although the gap narrows in urban areas. National figures show that women earn 60–80 percent as much as do men of the same race and ethnic group (figure 3.3). This compares to a national gender wage ratio of 0.78 in the United States in 2002.[4] In urban labor markets—disregarding racial and ethnic variables—the gender wage gap is not very large. Figure 3.4 shows that women in urban areas earn lower wages than do men, but that the wage gap hovers around a ratio of 0.85; the average hourly earnings for women in Argentina and Costa Rica actually exceed the hourly average wages of men.[5]

White and nonindigenous people earn the highest wages in Latin America. Data from across the region show that white/nonindigenous men and women have higher average earnings than do Afro- or indigenous men or women.[6] Among the countries in figure 3.3, indigenous men earn 40–65 percent less than nonindigenous men. A similar pattern exists between white Brazilian and Afro-Brazilian men, with the latter group earning 48 percent of the wages earned by the former. In addition, a similar gap exists between the wages of women of different races. This pattern differs in Guyana, however, where Afro- and Indo-Guyanese men (and women) earn very similar average wages (Indo-Guyanese have a slight edge).

When putting together race, ethnicity, and gender, two lessons emerge. First, indigenous/Afro-descended women earn the lowest wages among the four groups while white/nonindigenous/Indo men earn the highest. Among the countries in figure 3.3 that allow disaggregation of statistics according to race, ethnicity, and gender, nonwhite

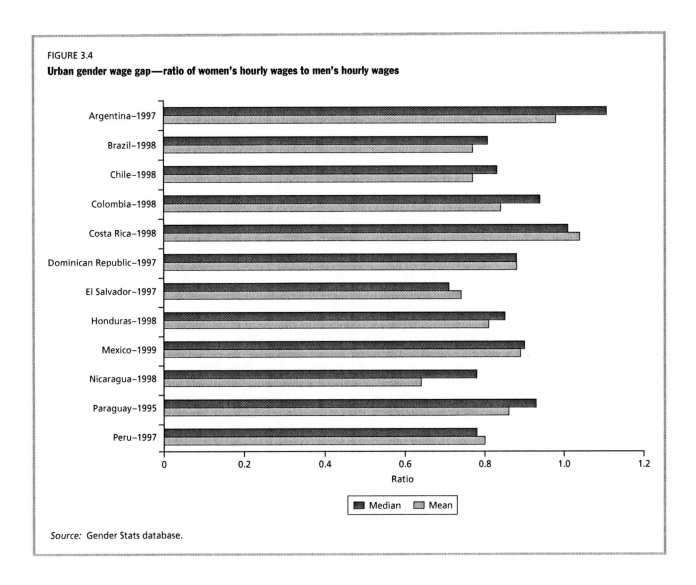

FIGURE 3.4

Urban gender wage gap—ratio of women's hourly wages to men's hourly wages

Source: Gender Stats database.

women earn 35 percent (Bolivia), 42 percent (Brazil), and 64 percent (Guyana) of white men's wages. Second, race and ethnicity play a greater role in wage gaps than does gender. In three of the four countries in figure 3.3, white/non-indigenous women have higher earnings than indigenous/Afro-Brazilian men. Only in Guyana do Afro-descended men have wages that exceed those of the Indo-Guyanese women.

Sources of wage inequality

A standard Oaxaca-Blinder decomposition (table 3.10) shows that wage differentials between racial and ethnic groups are driven more by differences in productivity-related characteristics than by differences in the returns to those characteristics.[7] Guyana is the exception (for a discussion of the methodology used, see box 3.6).[8] Two characteristics are most responsible for the wage gap—inequality in the education

level and racial-ethnic disparities in urban-rural residence—and reflect the heterogeneity in characteristics described earlier in this chapter. In terms of the contribution of the return on various characteristics that drive the observed wage gap, the high wage premium placed on education enjoyed by white/nonindigenous workers is not experienced by the Afro/indigenous workers. In the case of Guyana, neither differences in characteristics nor returns on characteristics explain the wage gap between racial groups; however, there is little difference in the observed wages that can be explained.

For all four countries, differences in returns on productivity-related characteristics (coefficients) are the driving force behind the gender-based wage differentials group. Indeed, the similarity in women's and men's characteristics serves to mitigate rather than increase the

TABLE 3.10

Decompositions of group mean log wage differentials

	Differential	Attributed to differences in characteristics	Attributed to differences in coefficients
Decompositions of white/nonwhite men wage differentials			
Bolivia	0.94	0.57 (61%)	0.37 (39%)
Brazil	0.62	0.47 (76%)	0.15 (24%)
Guatemala	0.72	0.44 (61%)	0.28 (39%)
Guyana	0.01	−0.04 (−400%)	0.05 (500%)
Decompositions of white men and women wage differentials			
Bolivia	0.29	−0.07 (−24%)	0.36 (124%)
Brazil	0.41	−0.12 (−29%)	0.53 (129%)
Guatemala	0.92	0.14 (15%)	0.78 (85%)
Guyana	0.56	0.01 (2%)	0.55 (98%)

Source: Authors' calculations based on microdata from household surveys.

BOX 3.6

Oaxaca-Blinder decomposition methodology

The standard methodology for identifying the factors behind the difference in wages between two groups is the Oaxaca-Blinder methodology. The method quantifies the portion of the wage differential that can be attributed to a difference in characteristics between two groups and the proportion that is due to the difference in payoffs from those characteristics (that is, the differences in coefficients associated with those characteristics in a regression framework). To generate the estimate, each member of the sample (i) is assigned to one of two groups, defined as m and f. The first step is to estimate the wages for each group separately, using a standard Mincerian wage equation:

$$(1) \quad Ln(Y_{i,m}) = \alpha_m + \beta_m X_{i,m} + \varepsilon_{i,m}$$

$$(2) \quad Ln(Y_{i,f}) = \alpha_f + \beta_f X_{i,f} + \varepsilon_{i,f}$$

Where $Y_{i,m}$ is earnings of individual i in group m, $X_{i,m}$ is a vector of productivity-related characteristics of individual i, $\varepsilon_{i,m}$, is the error term, and α_m and β_m are the coefficient estimates for group m; the same pattern is followed for group f. Subtracting equation (2) from equation (1) and

rearranging the equation gives equation (3).

$$(3) \quad Ln(Y_m) - Ln(Y_f) = (\overline{X}_m - \overline{X}_f)\hat{\beta}_m + (\hat{\beta}m - \hat{\beta}_f)X_f$$

Estimated $(\hat{\beta})$ and observed mean values $(\overline{X})$ are plugged into equation (3) to give the difference in the wages for each group. The first term on the right-hand side of the equation quantifies the amount of the wage differential that can be attributed to the difference in observed productivity characteristics and the second term on the right-hand side gives the amount that can be attributed to the difference in returns to productivity characteristics. X-bars are vectors, where each component is the average level of that productivity characteristic in group m or f. The β_m and β_f are taken from equations (1) and (2). Commonly, the contribution of each term to the overall distribution is stated as a proportion. The contribution of each productivity characteristic in X can also be calculated using equation (3).

Source: Oaxaca 1973.

gender-based wage differential in Bolivia and Brazil. While the difference in returns (coefficients) is largely driven by returns on education, returns related to all characteristics prove important. Although the gap in returns is commonly interpreted as "discrimination," this is only part of the story.

The male-female difference in returns on characteristics also captures the effects of those variables that were not controlled for in the vector of endowments, including actual job experience, preferences, pre-market effects, and mismeasured variables.[9]

TABLE 3.11

Within-group inequality share (for distributions of labor income)

	All	White/Indo-Guyanese nonindigenous men	Afro-descended indigenous men	White/Indo-Guyanese nonindigenous women	Afro-descended indigenous women
Theil (1)					
Bolivia	0.60	0.47	0.53	0.56	0.69
Brazil	0.65	0.60	0.51	0.59	0.50
Guatemala	0.78	0.73	0.55	0.67	0.69
Guyana	0.32	0.32	0.29	0.41	0.26
Theil (0)					
Bolivia	0.73	0.52	0.69	0.61	0.82
Brazil	0.58	0.56	0.45	0.53	0.44
Guatemala	0.86	0.72	0.65	0.85	0.85
Guyana	0.29	0.27	0.27	0.34	0.26
Gini					
Bolivia	0.56	0.51	0.53	0.54	0.60
Brazil	0.57	0.56	0.51	0.54	0.49
Guatemala	0.61	0.59	0.54	0.58	0.61
Guyana	0.39	0.37	0.39	0.43	0.37
90th percentile wages/ 10th percentile wages					
Bolivia	35.4	14.5	32.6	20.4	39.0
Brazil	10.4	13.7	8.8	10.0	9.0
Guatemala	36.8	23.2	26.2	43.2	42.8
Guyana	5.5	4.3	5.0	4.9	5.2
50th percentile wages/ 10th percentile wages					
Bolivia	9.8	4.2	10.7	5.9	9.6
Brazil	2.6	3.4	2.5	2.5	2.8
Guatemala	10.3	6.3	7.5	12.8	8.0
Guyana	2.6	2.3	2.0	2.4	2.6

Source: Authors' calculations based on microdata from household surveys.

In addition to inequality between groups, there is great inequality *within* gender, racial, and ethnic groups, especially among women (table 3.11). Using the Theil coefficient as a measure of income inequality, white and nonindigenous men appear to have the most unequal wages in Brazil and Guatemala. However, indigenous women's incomes in Bolivia are the most unequal and Indo-Guyanese women have the highest Theil coefficient among the Guyanese groups.[10] Considering the ratio of the 90th and the 50th percentile wages to the 10th percentile wages suggests that wage inequality is greater among women than men, since the women's ratios tend to exceed those of men in Guatemala and Guyana and somewhat in Bolivia. This high variance may reflect the greater heterogeneity among the female than the male labor force in terms of actual experience, training, and work choice.[11]

The factors behind national inequality: Within-group inequality

In statistical terms, national wage inequality is mostly explained by within-group, rather than between-group, differences.[12] Table 3.12 shows the contribution to national inequality of the within- and between-group inequalities for the two Theil indices of the four countries in the study, as well as for all persons, among men by race and ethnicity and among white/nonindigenous/Indo persons by gender.

In each case, within-group inequality accounts for the greatest proportion of overall inequality. In no case does between-group inequality account for more than 14 percent of overall inequality. Similarly, inequality between women and men accounts for less than 3 percent of national inequality. Thus, measures of national inequality between individuals is largely due to heterogeneity within racial, ethnic, and

TABLE 3.12

Theil index decompositions (for hourly wages)

	Theil (1)	Theil (0)	Within-group inequality	Between-group inequality
Four-way partition				
Bolivia	0.60		0.53 (88%)	0.07 (12%)
		0.73	0.66 (90%)	0.07 (10%)
Brazil	0.65		0.57 (88%)	0.08 (12%)
		0.58	0.50 (86%)	0.08 (14%)
Guatemala	0.78		0.69 (88%)	0.09 (12%)
		0.86	0.75 (87%)	0.11 (13%)
Guyana	0.33		0.31 (94%)	0.02 (6%)
		0.29	0.28 (97%)	0.01 (3%)
Inequality among men by race/ethnicity				
Bolivia	0.55		0.50 (91%)	0.05 (9%)
		0.67	0.62 (93%)	0.05 (7%)
Brazil	0.63		0.57 (90%)	0.06 (10%)
		0.57	0.51 (89%)	0.06 (11%)
Guatemala	0.76		0.69 (91%)	0.07 (9%)
		0.77	0.69 (90%)	0.08 (10%)
Guyana	0.31		0.31 (100%)	0.00 (0%)
		0.27	0.27 (100%)	0.00 (0%)
Inequality among whites/nonindigenous/Indo by gender				
Bolivia	0.51		0.50 (98%)	0.01 (2%)
		0.57	0.55 (96%)	0.02 (4%)
Brazil	0.62		0.60 (97%)	0.02 (3%)
		0.57	0.55 (96%)	0.02 (4%)
Guatemala	0.74		0.72 (97%)	0.02 (3%)
		0.79	0.77 (97%)	0.02 (3%)
Guyana	0.35		0.34 (97%)	0.01 (3%)
		0.30	0.28 (93%)	0.01 (7%)

Source: Authors' calculations based on microdata from household surveys.

gender groups, and not to the differences between demographic groups. This is not to say that between-group differences are not important. As shown earlier in this chapter, they are in fact substantial and facilitate understanding of poverty. Moreover, group-based differences may be of particular societal concern (Kanbur 2000), or may be particularly durable because of the role they play in maintaining overall differences (Tilly 1999 and chapter 4).

3.3. Would income inequality decline if returns to human capital were more equal?

The discussion in the preceding pages shows that, starting in childhood, people from different racial, ethnic, and gender groups face different circumstances and accumulate different levels of human capital characteristics. This partly explains the varying wage distributions between groups, but the question emerges as to whether differences in treatment according to race, ethnicity, and gender have measurable effects on overall inequality. In other words, if all persons

were treated alike, would overall measures of income inequality go down? Or is inequality so high—both overall and within gender, racial, and ethnic groups, including the advantaged groups in society—that such changes would have little effect on the overall level of inequality?

This question is examined here in two steps. First, the returns on characteristics of the white/nonindigenous/Indo and/or male group are applied to the Afro/indigenous and/or female group in order to simulate wages, which are then used to generate inequality measures. This allows us to understand how national inequality would change if everyone were rewarded the same as the relative "wage-dominant" group.[13] Second, both the returns on characteristics and the conditional distributions of some of the personal characteristics that affect wages—education level, sector of employment, and children (that is, fertility)—of the white/nonindigenous/Indo and/or male group are applied to the Afro/indigenous and/or female group in order to simulate wages, which are then used to generate national inequality measures. This step facilitates understanding of how equalizing the playing field in terms of both returns on characteristics and wage-related characteristics would affect national inequality.

The simulations are based on data from four recent household surveys from four countries: Brazil (1996), Bolivia (1999), Guatemala (2000), and Guyana (1999). These countries were chosen because their surveys asked questions regarding racial and ethnic status as well as a number of other variables of interest, including occupational sector, educational attainment, household composition, and earnings. Together, these surveys provide a range of information, including cases in which the wage-disadvantaged group is in the majority (Bolivia), the wage-disadvantaged group is in the minority (Guatemala), and the wage-disadvantaged and wage-advantaged groups are of relatively similar size (Brazil

and Guyana). Hence, minority versus majority status and its relation to wage-disadvantage can be considered separately. In addition, the definition of wage-disadvantaged group in some cases follows racial lines (Brazil and Guyana) and in other cases is more obviously drawn along ethnic lines (Bolivia and Guatemala). Also evident are different levels of female participation in the paid labor force and different educational distributions.[14]

Equalizing returns on endowments

The inequality measures from observed and simulated wages are shown in table 3.13. Wage inequality that is calculated from observed wages is shown in column (a) and inequality measures from simulated wages is shown in columns (b)–(d), where the simulated wages are generated by equalizing the

TABLE 3.13

Individual earnings and inequality measures, based on actual and simulated earnings within racial and gender groups

		Equalize returns only			Equalize returns and the distribution of some characteristics		
	Observed (a)	Equal treatment by race/ethnicity within gender (b)	Equal treatment by gender within race/ethnicity (c)	All segments treated as white/nonindigenous/Indo men (d)	Equal treatment by race/ethnicity within gender (e)	Equal treatment by gender within race/ethnicity (f)	All segments treated as white/nonindigenous/Indo men (g)
Theil(1)							
Bolivia	0.60	0.53	0.56	0.51	0.57	0.58	0.55
Brazil	0.65	0.61	0.64	0.63	0.64	0.66	0.65
Guatemala	0.78	0.75	0.79	0.76	0.75	0.76	0.79
Guyana	0.32	0.35	0.32	0.34	0.36	0.31	0.33
Theil(0)							
Bolivia	0.73	0.63	0.68	0.59	0.66	0.72	0.65
Brazil	0.58	0.57	0.58	0.57	0.58	0.59	0.59
Guatemala	0.86	0.85	0.89	0.84	0.81	0.77	0.86
Guyana	0.29	0.31	0.27	0.29	0.31	0.28	0.30
Gini							
Bolivia	0.56	0.54	0.55	0.53	0.55	0.56	0.55
Brazil	0.57	0.56	0.57	0.56	0.56	0.59	0.57
Guatemala	0.61	0.61	0.62	0.61	0.59	0.60	0.63
Guyana	0.39	0.41	0.38	0.40	0.40	0.39	0.40
90th percentile wages /10th percentile wages							
Bolivia	35.4	24.3	31.3	22.2	26.9	34.0	26.6
Brazil	10.4	11.8	12.2	12.1	14.2	15.5	16.7
Guatemala	36.8	32.5	27.2	23.9	30.3	28.3	21.4
Guyana	5.5	5.4	4.7	4.9	5.3	4.7	4.7
50th percentile wages /10th percentile wages							
Bolivia	9.8	7.5	9.7	7.1	7.6	9.9	7.7
Brazil	2.6	2.9	2.9	2.9	3.5	3.3	4.2
Guatemala	10.3	9.3	7.9	7.2	8.7	7.5	5.8
Guyana	2.6	2.4	2.2	2.3	2.5	2.2	2.3

Source: Authors' calculations based on microdata from household surveys.

returns on characteristics across groups. Within the "equal-ize returns only" section, three columns are presented. The first simulation (column (b)) considers what would happen to the overall earnings distribution if white/nonindige-nous/Indo and Afro/indigenous receive the same returns on characteristics within gender groups, while the second sim-ulation considers what would happen if women were treated like men within each racial and ethnic group (column (c)). The third simulation considers what would happen if both women and Afro/indigenous people received the same return on characteristics as did white/nonindigenous/Indo men (column (d)). Columns (e)–(g) are considered in the discus-sion in the next section.

If everyone were rewarded the same for their character-istics as are white/nonindigenous/Indo- men (that is, com-paring columns (a) and (d)), inequality would not uniformly increase or decrease across the sample. It would stay the same or decrease in Bolivia and Guatemala (depending on the inequality measure used) and increase in Guyana. A decrease in inequality in Bolivia is expected, since non-indigenous men there have the lowest within-group inequal-ity of the four groups.

Equalized returns among racial or ethnic groups (column (b)) explain the great proportion of the observed changes in the overall Theil index (column (d)). In Bolivia, Guatemala, and Guyana, changes in the simulated Theil indices by race

(that is, by holding gender constant) are greater than those in the simulated Theils by gender (that is, by holding race constant). The increased inequality in Guyana is due to the greater wage inequality among Indo-Guyanese, compared to Afro-Guyanese of both genders. The equalization of returns by gender has more to do with the decrease in the differ-ences between certain parts of the whole distribution, but is not strong enough to drive the overall inequality in the distribution.

Equalization of returns on the distribution of characteristics

As argued earlier in this chapter, characteristics accumulated throughout the lifecycle that affect current wages vary greatly by gender, race, and ethnicity. In addition, returns on these characteristics (in other words, endowments) leads to dif-ferent observed wages. To consider what would happen if dif-ferent groups *both* had similar characteristics *and* received the same compensation for various factors affecting their earn-ings, simulations were run of earnings distributions for wage-disadvantaged groups in those cases in which they would accumulate endowments (including education, sector of employment, and, for women, number of children) and be compensated by the same earnings mechanism as the advan-taged groups (box 3.7).

BOX 3.7
Econometric methodology

In order to perform a multistage simulation—in which human capital-related characteristics as well as returns on human capital can be considered—the authors uti-lized the microeconometric simulation method devel-oped in recent work by Bourguignon, Ferreira, and Leite (2002). The method expands the standard earnings decomposition method (the Oaxaca-Blinder method, described in box 3.6) by allowing some of the variables in the earnings equation to be determined by earlier processes that are also estimated separately by group. Thus, a distribution of characteristics is simulated and substituted rather than using the mean values of char-acteristics, as is done in the standard Oaxaca-Blinder method. While Bourguignon, Ferreira, and Leite (2002) apply their method to considering differences in

household income distribution across countries, this approach is readily modifiable to considering the same factor—this time in the form of individual income and earnings distributions—across demographic groups within a country.

In order to walk through this process, imagine two groups, X and Y. Here earnings for group X are simulated under the assumption that they are treated like group Y.

The first step in this process is to estimate education level for members of group Y as a function of age, mother's level of schooling (when available), and region. Then education is simulated for members of group X by using their values for age and mother's level of schooling and the estimated coefficients from the education equation for group Y. A ran-domly generated error term for each X-person is then drawn from a normal distribution that is standardized to reflect the X-group's error term variance. (See Bourguignon, Ferreira, and Lustig 1998 for details on how this methodology works.)

The second step, for women in group X only, is to estimate the number of children for group Y as a function of age, mother's level of schooling, region, and education. The number of children is simulated for members of group X by substituting their values for age, mother's level of schooling, and (simulated) education in the fertility equation for group Y. A randomly generated error term for each X-person is then drawn from a normal distribution standardized to reflect the X-group's error term variance.

The third step is to estimate the sector of employment for group Y as a function of age, mother's level of schooling, education, household composition, and (for women only) number of children in the household. The sector is simulated for members of group X by using their values for age, mother's level of schooling, household composition, (simulated) education, and (for women only) the simulated number of children in the sectoral choice equation for group Y. A randomly generated error term for each X-person is then drawn from a normal distribution standardized to reflect the X-group's error term variance.

The fourth step is to estimate monthly earnings for group Y as a function of age, mother's level of schooling, education, occupational sector, and region. Then earnings are simulated for members of group X by using their values for age, mother's level of schooling, (simulated) education, and (simulated) sector. A randomly generated error term for each X-person is then drawn from a normal distribution standardized to reflect the Y-group's error term variance.

Steps 1–3 utilize multinomial logit as the estimation technique, since people fall into distinct groups, while step 4 utilizes Ordinary Least Squares (OLS) as the estimation technique to deal with the continuous earnings distribution with a build up at the zero earnings point.

The figures below show graphically the type of output that is generated from these successive levels of simulation, so that it is possible to see how each additional underlying stage brings the simulated earnings distribution for the wage-disadvantaged group closer to that of the wage-advantaged group. In this case, actual and simulated earnings are presented for white and indigenous men in Guatemala. The largest effect comes from simulating the earnings distribution for indigenous men, using the coefficient estimates from their Mincer wage equation:

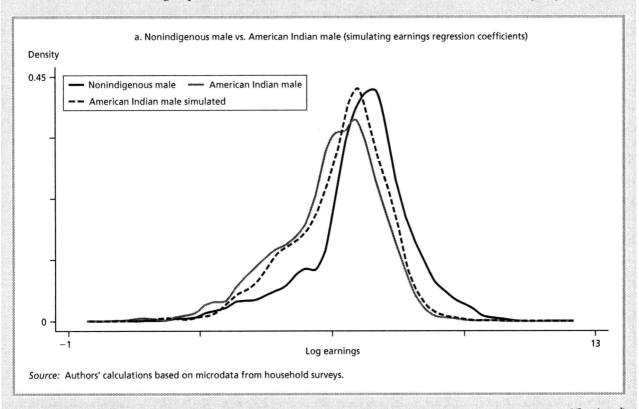

a. Nonindigenous male vs. American Indian male (simulating earnings regression coefficients)

Source: Authors' calculations based on microdata from household surveys.

(Continued)

BOX 3.7 **(continued)**

There is little difference between the simulated densities on the above graph and the following one, which presents the distribution while simulating education:

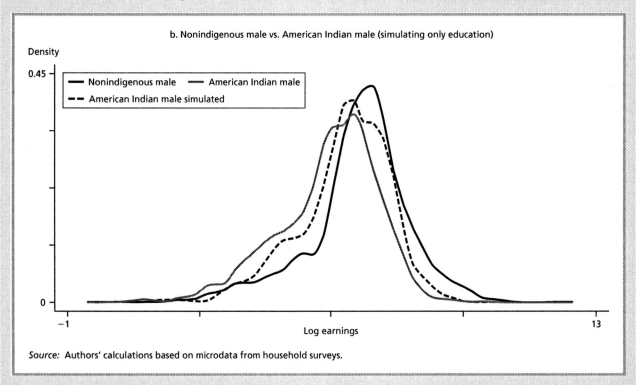

b. Nonindigenous male vs. American Indian male (simulating only education)

Density

0.45

— Nonindigenous male   ···· American Indian male

‑‑ American Indian male simulated

−1

Log earnings

13

0

Source: Authors' calculations based on microdata from household surveys.

Finally, the last graph shows that simulated occupational sector and education are not major factors in causing the distributions to move closer together:

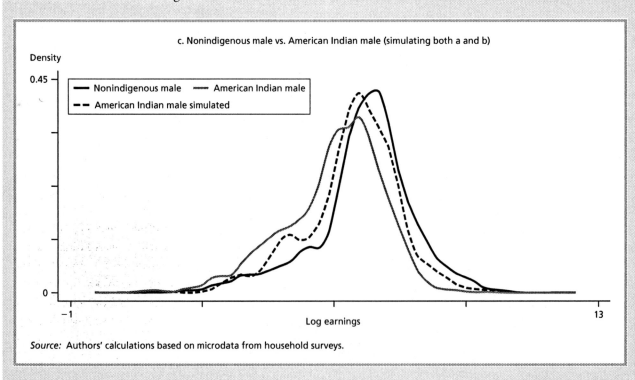

c. Nonindigenous male vs. American Indian male (simulating both a and b)

Density

0.45

— Nonindigenous male   ···· American Indian male

‑‑ American Indian male simulated

−1

Log earnings

13

0

Source: Authors' calculations based on microdata from household surveys.

The multistage procedure simulates endowments according to the same process through which the male and/or white/nonindigenous/Indo group accumulated these characteristics. The simulation procedure also allows for the effects of possible discrimination in access to or variation in the choice of educational attainment and employment sector (as well as the feed-through to fertility outcomes in the case of women) to be considered directly. In addition, it then becomes possible to consider the effects of potential discrimination in terms of earnings, once an individual has a particular educational level, employment sector, and family structure.

Equal treatment by race, gender, and ethnicity explains some, but not most, of the differences in wage distributions

The result of these simulations for each country can be visualized in figures 3.5 and 3.6. Figure 3.5 shows a simulation for men in Bolivia, in which indigenous men are given the earnings specification of nonindigenous men.[15] Note that the spread of both actual earnings distributions is significant (as shown earlier in table 3.4 regarding the various inequality measures). The simulated distribution for indigenous men shifts somewhat closer to the distribution for nonindigenous men, but continues to display a significant spread, as was observed for Guatemala in box 3.7. This remaining gap is due, at least in part, to the difference in parental education levels across the two ethnic groups, which reflects a historical heritage of ethnic differences across generations.

Figure 3.6 performs a similar exercise as that in figure 3.5, this time for Guyana by comparing Indo-Guyanese men to Indo-Guyanese women, in which the latter group is given the earnings specification of the former. Note again the continued spread in the simulated distribution for white women, even as the distribution conforms more closely to the distribution for white men.

These results, which are consistent with results for the other two comparisons (indigenous men to indigenous women and nonindigenous women to indigenous women) for Bolivia and Guatemala, and also with similar graphs generated for Brazil and Guyana, point to results from a formal calculation of inequality measures (presented in tables 3.13 and discussed below). Racial and gender differences in inequality contribute little to national inequality, compared to the large wage inequality observed within any single demographic group and the contribution of this spread to national inequality.

Inequality increases when endowments are equalized

Equalizing both returns and the distribution of some endowments—so that education, occupation, and fertility levels of the nondominant group are modified to be close to that of the dominant group—has the effect of returning the inequality measures back to their original levels. Returning to table 3.13, the set of columns entitled "equalize returns and the distribution of some characteristics" replicate the set entitled "equalize returns only," but also allow for certain characteristics of the simulated group to be distributed in the same way as those from the white/nonindigenous/Indo or male group. Thus, columns (e)–(g) show the level of inequality if the effect of those earlier events and decisions (that is, education, occupation choice, and fertility) were determined in the same way in each group.

While inequality decreased overall (but increased for Guyana) when only the returns on characteristics were equalized, it increased again when some of those characteristics were also equalized. A comparison of observed (column (a)) and completely simulated (column (g)) overall inequality shows almost identical Gini inequality measures. The Gini coefficient remains unchanged in Bolivia and actually increases in Brazil under the simulations that address gender differences (apparently because treating women like men in the Brazilian system increases the overall spread of earnings).

In the case of the Theil indices, there is also little noticeable change and little similarity in the direction of change across countries, particularly for the Theil (1) measures. There are more noticeable changes in the 90/10 and 50/10 ratios, with general reductions in these ratios relative to the base case in Bolivia, Guatemala, and Guyana and increases in the case of Brazil. However, significant spread remains in all four countries' earnings distributions under any of these scenarios, particularly in Bolivia and Guatemala.

The last result suggests that the way in which endowments are generated for white/nonindigenous/Indo or male individuals creates greater within-group inequality than do returns on these endowments. This can be rigorously tested by decomposing the Theil indices generated by the full simulation into within- and between-group inequalities and comparing this result to the within- and between-group

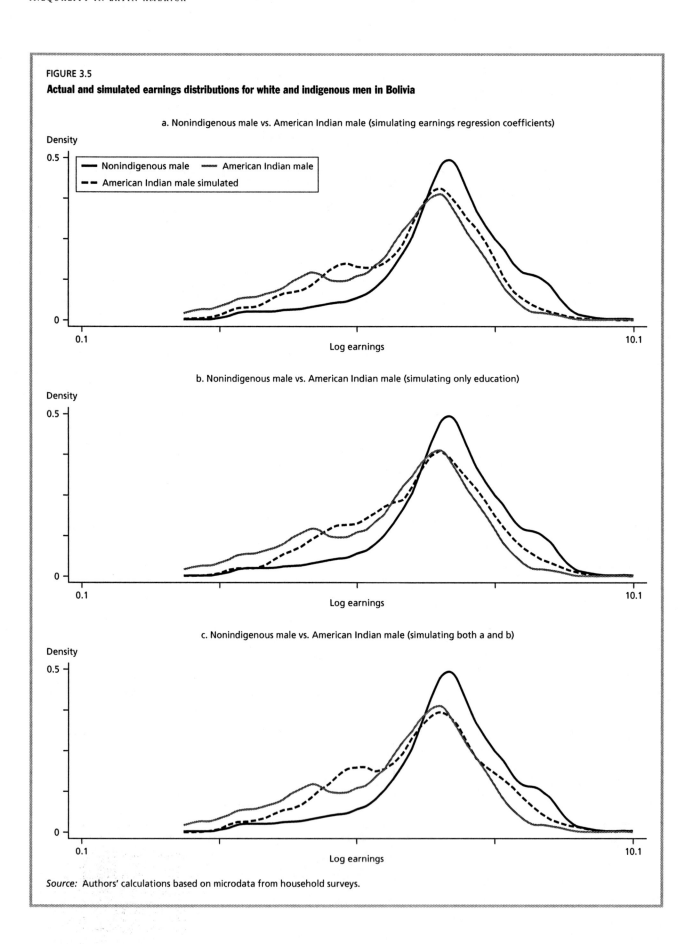

FIGURE 3.5

Actual and simulated earnings distributions for white and indigenous men in Bolivia

a. Nonindigenous male vs. American Indian male (simulating earnings regression coefficients)

Density

— Nonindigenous male ···· American Indian male
- - American Indian male simulated

Log earnings

b. Nonindigenous male vs. American Indian male (simulating only education)

Density

Log earnings

c. Nonindigenous male vs. American Indian male (simulating both a and b)

Density

Log earnings

Source: Authors' calculations based on microdata from household surveys.

102

FIGURE 3.6

Actual and simulated earnings distributions for Indo-Guyanese men and women

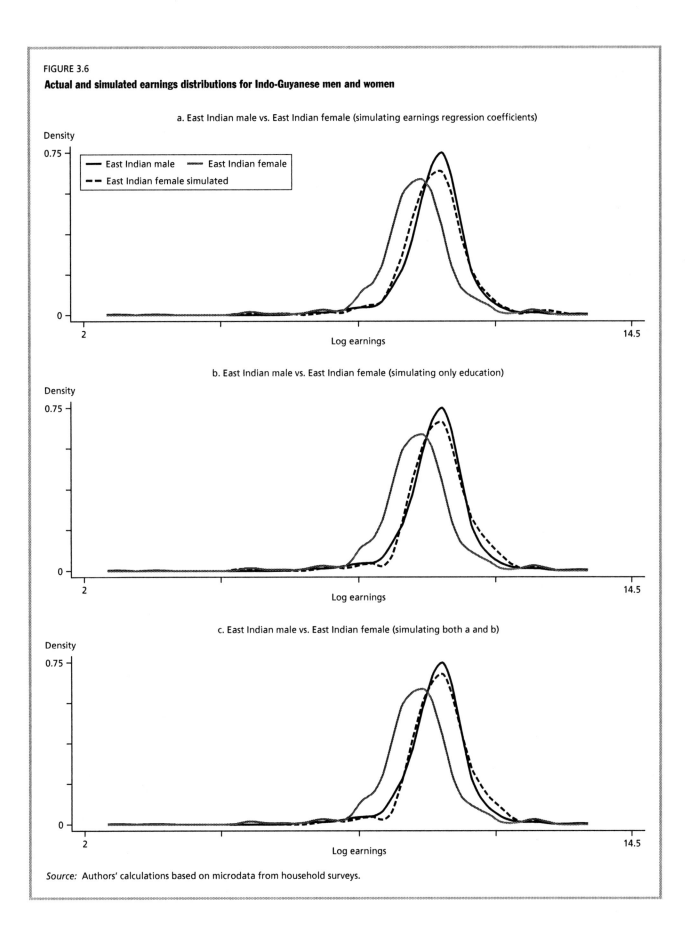

a. East Indian male vs. East Indian female (simulating earnings regression coefficients)

b. East Indian male vs. East Indian female (simulating only education)

c. East Indian male vs. East Indian female (simulating both a and b)

Source: Authors' calculations based on microdata from household surveys.

measures for both the observed wages and partly simulated (that is, with returns on endowments) wages. Although inequality did not change when using simulated wages from the wage-dominant group's return on characteristics and their distribution, the nature of the inequality did change. In other words, nearly all inequality can be attributed to within-group inequality.

National inequality does not uniformly decrease when leveling the playing field

Section 3.2 described a range of notable differences between racial and ethnic groups and between men and women, many of which appear to be of a type that would affect the ability of members of these groups to earn a reasonable income and achieve a reasonable standard of living within their societies. Such differences are related to educational attainment, employment sector participation and occupation, household structure, and dependency ratios.

Given the differences in the way race, ethnicity, and gender apparently interact with advantage and majority status across the four countries studied, it is striking to notice the relatively similar levels of inequality and results from the simulations reported above. Indeed, it appears that these differences, while creating different average levels of income, actually contribute little to the spread of earnings, that is, to earnings inequality.

These results may run counter to what might have been expected given the widespread nature of beliefs among both social scientists focusing on Latin America and the broader public concerned with the effect of demographic factors on income distribution. The difference in results may be partly due to limited comprehension that within-group variation is so much larger than between-group differences, when measured in terms of inequality indices that are based on differences between all individuals or households.

At the same time, there are a number of other reasons that the results presented here might differ from those generated from other sources. These require further exploration before the current results can be asserted as the standard against which others should be measured. First, some of the social science evidence relates to differences in dimensions other than income, and thus is not necessarily relevant to understanding income differences. For instance—to the degree that much of the sociological literature is concentrated on describing and understanding power relationships within societies and households—it is not possible to characterize dimen-

sions related to power other than relative earnings contributions (or potential for earnings).

Second, there may be some important determinants of income missing that are correlated with race, ethnicity, and gender. The estimated equations presented here do not explain fully variations in education, employment sector, fertility, or earnings.[16]

Third, the regional controls used in the current study may capture racial and ethnic (and, though less likely, gender) differences to some degree. To the extent that there are differential distributions of racial and ethnic groups between rural and urban areas and between regions of a country, the controls used here may downplay the linkage between location and difference.

Fourth, other important dimensions of income inequality may not have been captured due to the focus on labor income. An additional step, that of considering what would happen if unearned income (for example, pensions, interest, rent, and returns on equity) were distributed equally, would provide an important addition to the research reported herein. It is more difficult to obtain this type of information, although other studies (notably Bourguignon, Ferreira, and Leite 2002) have also considered unearned income distribution before calculating household income distributions.

Finally, these results do not relate inequality measures to the relative normative importance of between- and within-group differences. As already noted, there are many reasons why societies may be particularly concerned with within-group differences on grounds of social justice and because of the particular historical and organizational role such differences can play.

3.4. Conclusions

The evidence presented in this chapter confirms that racial, ethnic, and gender inequalities exist across Latin America, along a number of dimensions and for a variety of different measures. White/nonindigenous men and their households have more—in terms of labor income, formal sector jobs, assets, and education—than does any other ethnic or racial group, including in comparison to women. However, not all white/nonindigenous men are wealthy; instead men and women, whites and Afro and Indo groups, and indigenous and nonindigenous people are represented in all advantaged and disadvantaged sectors of society.

On average, women earn less than men, and nonwhite workers have much lower earnings than white workers. A closer look at the wage distribution shows that these average tendencies do not persist across the distribution. Instead, while the poorest part of the population is relatively evenly divided among white/nonindigenous women and Afro or indigenous men and women, white/nonindigenous women have a larger presence than Afro or indigenous individuals higher up the distribution. The exception is Guyana, where gender is the more important variable.

Guyana is an important special case, since its inclusion in the sample shows that being of Afro descent does not necessarily allocate a person to a position of inferiority. Although Afro-Brazilians have situations similar to those patterns observed for the indigenous in countries with high indigenous populations, Afro-Guyanese fare nearly as well as Indo-Guyanese. Instead, the gender divides are much greater in the Guyanese economy. This suggests that the power structure along racial lines is a greater determinant than simply phenotypical characteristics. In Guyana, this is a rapidly evolving structure.

Finally, the mix of being female with being indigenous or of Afro descent is highly disadvantageous—indigenous and Afro-descended women are at the bottom of any distribution, even in Guyana. Thus, the "double strike" concept seems to apply in that inequalities arising from being female and from the nondominant racial or ethnic group combine into a particularly difficult position.

The within-group inequality measures and graphs presented in this chapter showed a high degree of inequality within demographic groups and much overlap between groups. When distributions were plotted separately for different groups, the mode of the Afro/indigenous distribution fell to the left of that of the white/nonindigenous/Indo group (both for men and women). However, examination of the wage distributions for each group showed a high degree of overlap among them, suggesting that within-group variations are larger than between-group differences. Comparisons of inequality measures across countries also showed that no one ethnic, racial, or gender group consistently experiences greater inequality.

The simulations presented in this chapter showed that even when the playing field is leveled, within-group inequalities persist. Equalizing those factors that determine employment and wages—education, sector of employment, and fertility—decreases the spread in the wage distribution in some countries but increases it in others. Hence, measured overall income inequality (in terms of the amount of the spread in incomes, not the difference in mean incomes by group) cannot be assumed to be greatly affected or even decreased by a leveling of the playing field along racial, ethnic, and gender lines.

Using various measures of inequality and simulated wages from four countries, national wage inequality may increase or decrease if the processes that determine wages for white/nonindigenous men also determine the wages of women and Afro/indigenous men. Naturally, however, a decrease in wage and income inequality that is based on racial, ethnic, and gender factors is of great value in itself, since it would reduce one of the major horizontal inequities in the region—one that has deep historical roots and great durability.

Notes

1. Throughout the rest of this chapter, unless otherwise noted, the statistics for Bolivia, Brazil, Guatemala, and Guyana are generated by the authors using: *Encuesta Continua de Hogares,* 1999 for Bolivia; *Pesquisa Nacional por Amostra de Domicilio,* 1996 for Brazil; *Encuesta Nacional sobre Condiciones de Vida,* 2000 for Guatemala; and *Survey of Living Conditions,* 1999 for Guyana.

2. Cunningham (2001) shows that nearly all unpaid Mexican workers are married women, with 10 percent of married working women citing unpaid work as their sector of employment. The majority of these women are married to men who declare themselves "self-employed." Thus, these appear to be family businesses to which women contribute and from which they are likely to share in the fruits of their labor to a limited degree.

3. One-digit occupational categories give crude estimates of the Duncan Index, due to the heterogeneity of jobs within occupations. For example, in Peru, both physicians (0.21 percent of men and 0.08 percent of women) and midwives (0.01 percent of women and 0 percent of men) are classified as "professional occupations." The gender segregation within these occupations is lost using the one-digit occupational categories, while it clearly emerges when physician and midwife are treated as distinct occupations. The interpretations of the labor market greatly change when more disaggregated occupational codes are used. The Brazilian data show that the Duncan Index is 0.41 when using one-digit occupational codes for 7 occupations but is 0.62 when using 35 occupations, indicating that another 20 percent of men and women would have to switch occupations for the distribution of occupations to be equal by gender.

4. This figure refers to median weekly earnings for year-round, full-time workers; see ftp://ftp.bls.gov/pub/news.release/History/wkyeng.01172003.news.

5. The statistics presented in Figure 3.4 are based on hourly wages. Since women tend to work fewer average hours per month, as compared to men, the use of hourly wages to construct the gender wage gap is more accurate than the use of monthly wages, which are commonly reported by statistical agencies.

6. Monthly wages are used for Chile, Mexico, and Peru. Hourly wages are a more appropriate comparison variable than monthly wages since the number of hours worked by each group differs.

7. This has been found for other studies using Latin American data. These studies include MacIsaac and Patrinos (1995), which uses Peruvian data and finds that 50–70 percent of the log earnings gap between indigenous and nonindigenous men is due to differences in characteristics. Patrinos, Velez, and Psacharopoulos (1994) find that 78 percent of the difference between the Spanish and Guarani speakers is due to differences in characteristics. In addition, Patrinos (1997) points out variation in the proportion attributable to characteristics among the various ethnic groups within Guatemala.

8. Using a standard set of characteristics, including age, educational attainment, occupational sector, and rural-urban location for a four-country sample, the decomposition for two of the possible group comparisons—white/nonindigenous versus Afro/indigenous men and white/nonindigenous men versus women—are calculated. (Details of the estimation are in the companion working paper Cunningham and Jacobsen 2003.)

9. For example, age is a proxy for labor force experience and is a good measure for both men and women if they have similar levels of education (which they do) and they both work full-time after completing school. However, a smaller proportion of women than men are in the labor force and women enter and exit the labor force with greater frequency than men. As a result, "actual experience" is impossible to measure for women, leading to a poor estimate of the returns due to age for women and greater deviation from men's better measured returns. The claim that the "other" is an upper bound for discrimination is also not entirely correct, since discrimination may even be greater than the value of the "other" proportion; however, some of the omitted effects decrease the observed discriminatory effects.

10. For the formal definitions of the Gini, Theil (1), and Theil (0) index, as well as a discussion of index decomposition, see Litchfield (1999).

11. Hourly wage is used to calculate the statistics for Bolivia, Brazil, and Guatemala in tables 3.4 and 3.5. This controls for the higher variation in women's monthly work hours. The Guyana data does not permit using a similar control, since a variable for the number of hours worked monthly is not reported.

12. The relative contribution of inequality within and between demographic groups to national inequality can be estimated by decomposing the inequality measure into these two components. While it is not possible to do this with the Gini index or with the wage ratios, the Theil index is decomposable in this fashion.

13. This is necessarily a partial equilibrium analysis, since the assumption is made that increasing everyone's rewards to match those of the wage-dominant group will not result in an overall downward pressure on returns, as may occur in a general equilibrium model.

14. The authors attempted to estimate a relatively similar specification for each of the four countries. While this did not affect the ability to create counterfactuals (since they are all within-country), it does make the results more comparable across countries in terms of understanding that the results capture the same effects in each country. Hence, although the particular levels of education vary for each country, for instance, the educational variable enters in a similar way into each country's specification. Full numerical results from these simulations are reported in the companion working paper for this chapter, Cunningham and Jacobsen (2003).

15. Note that other counterfactual states could have been used in the simulation process, for instance by attributing to white men the earnings specification of nonwhite men or utilizing weighted intermediate values of the white and nonwhite male coefficients for the simulation coefficients. However, this particular version of the counterfactual has interpretive appeal as it addresses directly the "what if" scenario of members of the disadvantaged group being treated as if they were members of the advantaged group, under current labor market conditions.

16. Omitted variables would have to be correlated with these demographic factors in order to be important explanatory variables for demographic differences in earnings. Another aspect of "goodness of fit" is that nonsystematic factors perhaps matter more in the societies studied here than in other societies; that is, these earnings functions are potentially inherently more stochastic. However, this stochastic factor would still have to differ systematically by demographic group, in that certain groups are more likely to have a higher variance in earnings due to stochastic factors.

PART II

The Determinants of Inequality in Latin America

CHAPTER 4

Historical Roots of Inequality in Latin America

IT IS WELL KNOWN THAT NO OTHER REGION HAS AS EXTREME INEQUALITY IN WEALTH OR INCOME AS Latin America. This chapter addresses some basic questions about the roots of this inequality. Has Latin America always been more unequal than other regions? What does the historical record reveal about comparative inequality?

Following Engerman and Sokoloff (1997, 2000, 2002) and Acemoglu, Johnson, and Robinson (2001, 2002), the authors of this chapter argue that the contemporary situation cannot be understood without recognizing that extreme inequality emerged soon after the Europeans began to colonize the Americas half a millennium ago, and has been reflected in the institutions they put in place. Both this initial inequality and institutions were shaped largely by the factor endowments that the Europeans found in Central and South America, rather than the nature of the colonial powers themselves. Although these colonies ultimately gained independence and the development of technology and the world economy brought about important changes, extreme inequality persisted into the 19th and 20th centuries because the evolution of political and economic institutions tended to reproduce and reinforce highly unequal distributions of wealth, human capital, and political influence.

The difficulties of overcoming gross disparities in circumstances became all the more formidable during the late 19th century, when major increases occurred in the relative returns on land—an asset with extraordinarily concentrated ownership—and on education, in which Latin American societies were slow to invest. A legacy of political institutions bordering on authoritarianism also spurred inequality by discouraging the evolution of truly consolidated democracies. Finally, the "burden of history" must be considered. If the currently very high levels of inequality in Latin America are the result of long historical processes, does this mean that they are immutable? What can be done to turn this pattern around?

4.1. Factor endowments, inequality, and institutions

Although factor endowments, technology, and relative scarcity have important implications for inequality, their effects are filtered through economic, social, and political institutions. Economic and political institutions define and enforce property rights and provide the legal framework within which markets and other voluntary agreements between private agents are organized. Thus, they have a fundamental impact upon the distributions of income, capital, and political standing. There is no doubt that the colonies established by the Europeans in South and Central America were characterized by extreme inequality from the beginning, but institutions ultimately account for its persistence. The basis for the initial inequality is in some ways easy to understand. There were very few Europeans among much larger populations of indigenous peoples and slaves, but they were greatly advantaged by their higher levels of human capital (that is, knowledge of technology and the sorts of legal and economic institutions established in the colonies), wealth, and legal standing. However, it is institutions that must be considered to gain understanding of why this inequality persisted for nearly 500 years and generated patterns that can still be seen today.

Brazil, like many other European colonies with soils and climates suitable for cultivating sugar—the most valuable commodity in world trade from the late 16th through the 18th centuries—rather quickly developed a vibrant agricultural sector oriented toward exploiting the country's comparative advantage. With the "technology" of gang labor, sugar could be produced at a very low cost on large slave plantations. Brazilian planters tapped the readily available supply made possible by a world market in slaves. In the country's first 250 years, roughly 70 percent of the immigrants to this Portuguese colony arrived in chains. Europeans could do very well in Brazil's booming economy, which attracted more than 25 percent of those people who chose to come to the Americas through 1760. Although the fraction of the population that was white and privileged rose over time (from 7.4 percent in 1650 to 23.4 percent in 1825), the structure of Brazilian society did not change, and remained dominated by a small but entrenched elite.

Spanish America also came to be characterized by extreme inequality early in its history. The most powerful country in Europe during the 16th century, Spain was the leader in colonizing the New World. It chose to focus its efforts on areas such as Mexico and Peru, establishing colonies that were characterized by both a substantial native population surviving contact with the European colonizers and by distribution among a privileged few of claims to enormous blocs of land, mineral resources, and native labor. Among the many examples of institutions that aided members of the elite and offered little to the bulk of the population were the *encomienda* (which gave Spanish conquistadors the right to Amerindian labor), the *mita* (a system of forced labor used in the mines), and the *repartimiento* (the forced sale of goods to Indians, typically at highly inflated prices).

The resulting large-scale estates and mines, established early in the histories of these colonies, were to some degree based on pre-conquest social organizations in which Native American elites extracted tribute from the general population. These arrangements endured even when principal production activities were lacking in economies of scale. Although small-scale production was typical of the grain agriculture sector during this era, the essentially nontradable property rights to tribute (in the form of labor and other resources) from rather sedentary groups of natives gave

landholders the means and the motive to operate on a large scale.

The small group of elites that enjoyed large rents had the political power to protect their interests, and protect them they did. Severe restrictions on trade routes and on further immigration from Europe bolstered their position and hindered the ability of regions of New Spain without substantial native populations (such as Argentina and Uruguay) to attract resources or otherwise compete with colonial centers in Bolivia, Mexico, and Peru until late in the 18th century. Despite their small share of the population—less than 20 percent as late as 1825—people of European descent living in Spanish American benefited from greater wealth, human capital, and political influence than did the rest of the population, and were therefore able to shape policies and institutions to their advantage. These circumstances in turn perpetuated extreme inequality, and conditions changed little after the colonies gained independence. The elites maintained effective control in the new republics and the fundamental basis for economic inequality remained the same.

It is illustrative to consider what happened to the European colonies in the northern part of North America, where initial conditions were quite different and a much greater degree of equality prevailed. This relative equality, however, was not due to the original intentions of the colonial powers or of the early colonizers. When the English set up their colony at Jamestown, Virginia, in 1607, for example, the original plan was inspired by the experience of the Spaniards in Latin America. The English looked for gold and tried to capture the local Algonquian chief Powhatan, in the hope that this would empower them in the same way that the capture of Atahulapa had for Pizarro in Peru in 1532. This strategy proved to be an utter failure, however, and a new strategy had to be developed when the colonists starved and the Virginia Company went bankrupt (see Morgan 1975).

In addition, the English, French, and Dutch learned that there was no gold and few indigenous people to exploit, and that the soils and climates of North America would not support the production of highly profitable crops such as sugarcane (and thus large slave plantations). The reality was that land was cheap and labor was costly. Such circumstances were radically different from those found elsewhere in the hemisphere, and fostered a remarkable degree of equality. Virginia and other colonies had to compete with each other to attract migrants by providing favorable working conditions to even unskilled laborers coming to North America as indentured servants. Attempts to establish tenant agriculture and the hierarchical social structures of England—such as in Maryland under Lord Baltimore and in Pennsylvania under William Penn—were repeatedly frustrated by the reality of factor endowments and initial circumstances. Labor scarcity made for high wages, but also low returns on land, and thus limited prospects for attaining gentlemanly status. In the words of David Galenson, the noted economic historian of colonial America (Galenson 1996, p. 144):

> Although the establishment of large estates to be worked by tenants and landless laborers was the initial model on which these proprietary colonies were usually based, the greater economic power conferred on settlers by the New World's labor scarcity prevented these English tenures and practices from effectively taking hold, and proprietors were often forced to adapt by simply selling their land outright to settlers.

Relatively few Europeans chose to migrate to New England and Canada (net migration to these areas was actually negative during the early period), but those who did came to enjoy greater equality, protection of the law, and institutions that were in the long run more conducive to widespread participation in the commercial economy, investment, and

economic growth. The populations of these colonies grew primarily due to a healthy excess of births over deaths until early industrialization got under way, and consequently European perceptions of the opportunities available in the region changed. From these conditions emerged a society in which the population was relatively homogeneous and there was relative (compared to most of the hemisphere) equality in wealth, human capital, and ultimately political influence.

Of course, Native Americans and African Americans did not enjoy the same conditions as did whites. However, these groups accounted for a much smaller proportion of the population than in colonies established elsewhere, and the pattern of institutions in the United States was established before the arrival of large numbers of slaves (see table 4.1).

What was key to the formation of colonial institutions was not the identity of the colonizing power, but rather the initial conditions in the colonies (see Engerman and Sokoloff 1997 and Acemoglu, Johnson, and Robinson 2001). Thus, British colonies such as Guyana, British Honduras, and Jamaica developed degrees of inequality, economic structures, and institutions that looked very much like those in neighboring colonies established by other European powers. Similarly, Spanish colonies that had small populations of Native Americans, such as Argentina, Costa Rica, and Uruguay, seemed to follow significantly different paths of

TABLE 4.1

The distribution and composition of the population in New World economies (percent)

Colonial region and year	Composition of population			Share in New World population
	White	Black	Native American	
Spanish America				
1570	1.3	2.5	96.3	83.5
1650	6.3	9.3	84.4	84.3
1825	18.0	22.5	59.5	55.2
1935	35.5	13.3	50.4	30.3
Brazil				
1570	2.4	3.5	94.1	7.6
1650	7.4	13.7	78.9	7.7
1825	23.4	55.6	21.0	11.6
1935	41.0	35.5	23.0	17.1
United States and Canada				
1570	0.2	0.2	99.6	8.9
1650	12.0	2.2	85.8	8.1
1825	79.6	16.7	3.7	33.2
1935	89.4	8.9	1.4	52.6

Source: Engerman and Sokoloff 1997.

institutional development than did those with factor endowments that disposed them toward extreme inequality. The sharp contrasts in many institutional dimensions between Costa Rica—which had relatively few Native Americans—and Guatemala is well-known.

Another example, however, concerns a broader pattern influencing the capabilities of local governments. The lowest level of Spanish administration was the *cabildo,* a council that at least nominally had the power to levy taxes and held responsibility for administering municipal services such as schools. The *cabildo* was generally appointed by higher officials, who were themselves appointed by the Spanish Crown. Yet there was the possibility for a *cabildo abierto,* or open council, where all the *vecinos,* or citizens, could meet to express their opinions and attempt to influence policy. This institution was the closest thing to a truly democratic entity in Spanish Latin America. Noting that these meetings were seldom (if ever) held in many areas, such as colonial Peru, Lang (1975, p. 28) has suggested that:

> Relative insignificance was often the best guarantee that a town would retain all of its privileges unrestricted by subsequent clashes between the *cabildo* and various bureaucratic bodies. Santiago and Buenos Aires . . . considered to be marginal and undesirable places, convened the *cabildo abierto* numerous times during the Hapsburg era.

Thus, the political variation within the Spanish colonies strongly supports the notion that it was initial conditions that mattered most for the development of institutions.

4.2. The persistence of inequality: The colonial period

Patterns of inequality persisted once they were established during the early colonial period. This occurred because the initial nexus of institutions survived, as did the rationale for these institutions. Even though the century after the conquest of the continent saw a huge collapse of the indigenous population of Latin America (the conventional estimate being that the 1492 population declined by about 90 percent during the following century), exploiting Indian labor and resources remained the most attractive strategy whenever it was feasible. Colonial institutions often responded to the population collapse simply by allowing for more efficient exploitation of the remaining indigenous peoples. In Peru, the reforms of Viceroy Toledo in the 1570s concentrated the

indigenous into urban centers in order to be better able to mobilize them to work in the silver mines of Potosi. Even the Bourbon reforms in the second half of the 18th century were meant only to rationalize and increase the efficiency of the system (from the point of view of the Spanish state), not to fundamentally alter it.

The situation was similar in the United States, despite the fact that very different sorts of institutions persisted there. For example, even though the British Crown was at times able to effectively intervene and restrain or overrule colonial legislatures (such as when Charles II abolished the practice of universal male suffrage in Virginia), they remained a vital force.

4.3. The persistence of inequality: Post-independence

Like the United States, most of Latin America had fought for, and won, independence from their colonial masters by the early 19th century. Despite the rhetoric of the revolutionary movement—and the fact that nearly all of the new countries were nominal democracies—the political break from Spain appears to have yielded little or no reduction in the extent of inequality throughout the continent as a whole. Indeed, in most Latin American societies, inequality probably increased during the following decades.

On the face of it, this appears to be much harder to account for than persistence of inequality during the colonial period. The fundamental reason for the persistence of extreme inequality appears to have been the continued pattern of institutional change that favored the interests of the elite and provided the bulk of the population with only limited access to economic opportunities. Given the disparities in resources that were a legacy of the colonial period, it should be no surprise that the Creole elite were quickly able to regain effective control of the independent countries and determine the general structure of institutions.

Indeed, in several cases, most notably Mexico, independence was favored precisely because it enabled domestic elites to avoid liberalizing currents that were emerging from Spain. This was particularly true after the writing of the Cadiz Constitution in 1812. Peter Bakewell (Bakewell 1997, p. 377) sums up the consensus on this issue when he notes that "Mexican independence in 1821 has long been viewed as a reaction to the liberalism of the revived Spanish Cortes, a rejection by influential conservative Creoles." Thus, independence did not fundamentally alter the structures of political power in Latin America.

An important study of institutional persistence in 19th century Latin America is that by Woodward (1966) on Guatemala. He shows that the economic life of Guatemala during the colonial period was controlled by a merchant guild called the Consulado de Comercio, the members of which continued to control the economy after independence. As Woodward (1966, p. 34) notes, "The merchants continued to hold their exclusive court privilege until 1871. Little or no change was made in the basic concept of justice before that year. As in the 1790s, in the 1860s the wealthy, aristocratic merchants continued to rely on their own court to interpret justice in the best interests of their own class, and in maintaining their leadership over the commerce of the land." Woodward also points out (1966, p. xiv) that "This seemingly paradoxical existence of a royal institution under a republican government is explained by the nature of the government which ruled Guatemala from 1839 to 1871. Republican in form . . . the monopolistic position of the Consulado was consistent with the policies and objectives of the regime."

As noted above, truly representative institutions never really developed during the colonial period in Spanish America, while the relatively representative legislative assemblies were established quite early in most of the British colonies in North America. This contrast in political inequality, along with corresponding variation in economic inequality, endured into the 19th century and beyond. The persistence of these radical disparities in the distribution of political power can be seen by examining both the laws governing who was entitled to vote, as well as the fraction of the population that actually participated in elections.

Since most of the societies in the Americas were nominally republican democracies by the mid-19th century, this sort of information had a direct bearing on (although it likely understates) the extent to which elites—whose position was based largely on wealth, human capital, race, and gender—were able to wield disproportionate influence in the formation and implementation of government policies. The understatement arises not only from the advantages elites had in making effective use of informal channels of political influence (including an approach based on the force of arms), but also from the fact that many elections were accompanied by fraud and, in the absence of an effective secret ballot, explicit or implicit coercion (see Graham 1990 on the case of Brazil).

Table 4.2 summarizes information about how the right to vote was restricted across New World societies in the late 19th and early 20th centuries. The estimates reveal that although it was common in all countries to give the right to vote only to adult males until the 20th century, the United States and Canada were the clear leaders in doing away with restrictions based on wealth and literacy, and a much higher proportion of the population voted in these countries than anywhere else in the Americas. Not only did the United States and Canada adopt the secret ballot and extend the franchise to even the poor and illiterate much earlier—although restrictions were reintroduced in the United States in the 1890s at the expense of African Americans—but the proportion of the population that voted was at least a half-century ahead of even the most progressive and most equal countries in South America (namely, Argentina, Costa Rica, and Uruguay).

It is a remarkable testament to the extent of political inequality in Latin America and the Caribbean that as late as 1900 none of the countries in the region had a secret ballot system or more than a minuscule fraction of the population casting votes. The Australian ballot (a system of state-provided ballots with provisions to ensure secrecy) was not introduced until 1958 in Chile and 1988 in Colombia. Before this time, political parties directly issued their own ballot papers. Baland and Robinson (2003) show that these circumstances had dramatic effects on voting patterns in Chile, effectively allowing conservative parties to control elections in rural areas since landowners could use the threat of job dismissal to regulate the voting behavior of workers.

The great majority of European nations, as well as the United States and Canada, achieved secrecy in balloting and universal adult male suffrage long before other countries in the western hemisphere, and the proportion of the populations that voted was always higher (often by as much as 4–5 times). Although many factors may have contributed to the low levels of participation in Latin America, wealth and literacy requirements—in addition to the absence of secrecy—were serious binding constraints. Some countries, such as Barbados, maintained wealth-based suffrage restrictions until the mid-20th century, but most European societies joined the United States and Canada in moving away from economic requirements over the course of the 19th century. However, whereas the states in the United States frequently adopted explicit racial limitations on voting, when they abandoned economic requirements (that is, when the constitutional amendments following the Civil War ended the practice), Latin American countries typically chose to screen according to literacy.

TABLE 4.2

Laws governing the franchise and the extent of voting in selected countries, 1840–1940

Period and country	Year	Lack of secrecy in balloting	Wealth requirement	Literacy requirement	Percent of the population voting
1840–80					—
Chile	1869	No	Yes	Yes	1.6
	1878	No	No	No[a]	—
Costa Rica	1890	Yes	Yes	Yes	—
Ecuador	1848	Yes	Yes	Yes	0.0
	1856	Yes	Yes	Yes	0.1
Mexico	1840	Yes	Yes	Yes	—
Peru	1875	Yes	Yes	Yes	—
Uruguay	1840	Yes	Yes	Yes	—
	1880	Yes	Yes	Yes	—
Venezuela	1840	Yes	Yes	Yes	—
	1880	Yes	Yes	Yes	—
Canada	1867	Yes	Yes	No	7.7
	1878	No	Yes	No	12.9
United States	1850	No	No	No	12.9
	1880	No	No	No	18.3
1881–1920					
Argentina	1896	Yes	Yes	Yes	1.8[b]
	1916	No	No	No	9.0
Brazil	1894	Yes	Yes	Yes	2.2
	1914	Yes	Yes	Yes	2.4
Chile	1881	No	No	No	3.1
	1920	No	No	Yes	4.4
Colombia	1918[c]	No	No	No	6.9
Costa Rica	1912	Yes	Yes	Yes	—
	1919	Yes	No	No	10.6
Ecuador	1888	No	Yes	Yes	2.8
	1894	No	No	Yes	3.3
Mexico	1920	No	No	No	8.6
Peru	1920	Yes	Yes	Yes	—
Uruguay	1900	Yes	Yes	Yes	—
	1920	No	No	No	13.8
RB de Venezuela	1920	Yes	Yes	Yes	—
Canada	1911	No	No	No	18.1
	1917	No	No	No	20.5
United States	1900	No	No	Yes[d]	18.4
	1920	No	No	Yes	25.1
1921–40					
Argentina	1928	No	No	No	12.8
	1937	No	No	No	15.0
Bolivia	1951	—	Yes	Yes	4.1
Brazil	1930	Yes	Yes	Yes	5.7
Colombia	1930	No	No	No	11.1
	1936	No	No	No	5.9
Chile	1920	No	No	Yes	4.4
	1931	No	No	Yes	6.5
	1938	No	No	Yes	9.4

(continued)

TABLE 4.2

(continued)

Period and country	Year	Lack of secrecy in balloting	Wealth requirement	Literacy requirement	Percent of the population voting
Costa Rica	1940	No	No	No	17.6
Ecuador	1940	No	No	Yes	3.3
Mexico	1940	No	No	No	11.8
Peru	1940	No	No	Yes	—
Uruguay	1940	No	No	No	19.7
RB de Venezuela	1940	No	Yes	Yes	—
Canada	1940	No	No	No	41.1
United States	1940	No	No	Yes	37.8

a. After having eliminated wealth and education requirements in 1878, Chile instituted a literacy requirement in 1885 that seems to have contributed to a sharp decline in the proportion of the population that was registered to vote.
b. This figure is for the city of Buenos Aires, and likely overstates the proportion that voted at the national level.
c. The information on restrictions refers to national laws. The 1863 Constitution empowered provincial state governments to regulate electoral affairs. Afterward, elections became restricted (in terms of the franchise for adult males) and indirect in some states. It was not until 1948 that a national law established universal adult male suffrage throughout the country. This pattern was followed in other Latin American countries, as it was in the United States and Canada to a lesser extent.
d. There were 18 states—7 in the South and 11 elsewhere—that introduced literacy requirements between 1890 and 1926.
Source: Engerman, Haber, and Sokoloff 2000.

The contrast between the United States and Canada, on the one hand, and the Latin American countries, on the other, was not so evident at the outset. Despite the sentiments popularly attributed to the Founding Fathers, voting in the United States was until early in the 19th century largely a privilege reserved for white men with significant property holdings. By 1815, only four states had adopted universal white male suffrage, but as the movement to do away with political inequality gained strength, the rest of the country followed suit. Virtually all new entrants to the Union extended voting rights to white men (with explicit racial restrictions generally introduced in the same state constitutions that did away with economic requirements), and older states revised their laws in the wake of protracted political debates.

The politically and economically key states of New York and Massachusetts made the break with wealth-based restrictions in the 1820s and the shift to full white adult male suffrage was largely complete by the late 1850s (with North Carolina, Rhode Island, and Virginia being the laggards). The relatively more egalitarian populations of the western states were the clear leaders in the movement. The rapid extension of access to the franchise in these areas not coincidentally paralleled liberal policies toward public schools, taxes, and access to land, as well as other policies that were expected to be attractive to potential migrants.

Labor scarcity was a crucial element in determining the initial level of inequality across New World colonies, and continued to have an important effect on the level of political inequality even within the United States. It is striking that the pioneers in extending suffrage (such as new states being formed in Argentina, Uruguay, and the United States) did so during periods in which they were striving to attract migrants. The right to suffrage was often one of a set of policy measures that were thought to be attractive to those contemplating relocation. When elites—such as holders of land or other assets—want common men to locate in the polity, they may choose to extend access to privileges and opportunities even in the absence of the threat of civil disorder. In fact, a polity (or one set of elites) may find itself competing with another to attract labor or whatever else is needed. (See Acemoglu and Robinson 2000 for cases in which the franchise was extended under threat of civic disorder.) Alternative explanations, such as the importance of national heritage, are not very useful in identifying why Argentina, Costa Rica, and Uruguay pulled so far ahead of their Latin American neighbors, or why other British colonies in the New World lagged behind Canada with regard to the pace at which access to suffrage was extended.

Differences in the distribution of political power had a feedback effect on both access to economic opportunities and investment in public goods in such a way as to in turn influence the long-term direction of institutional development and inequality. Educational institutions provide a highly relevant example because increases in a society's levels of schooling and literacy have been related to many socioeconomic changes conducive to growth, including higher labor productivity, more rapid technological change, and higher rates of commercial and political participation. Moreover, in addition to promoting growth, public investment in education also has a major influence on the distribution of the benefits of growth.

Although most New World societies were so prosperous by the early 19th century that they had the material resources needed to support the establishment of a widespread network of primary schools, before the 20th century only a few made such investments on a scale sufficient to serve the general population. The United States and Canada were exceptions in terms of leadership in investing in institutions of primary education. Virtually from the time of early settlement, the North Americans seemed to have generally been convinced of the value of providing children with a basic education, including the ability to read and write. It was common for schools to be organized and funded at the village or town level, especially in New England.

The United States probably had the most literate population in the world by the beginning of the 19th century, but the common school movement—which got under way in the 1820s following the movement to extend the franchise—put the country on an accelerated path of investment in educational institutions. Between 1825 and 1850, nearly every northern state that had not already done so enacted a law strongly encouraging or requiring localities to establish free schools that were open to all children and supported by general taxes (Cubberley 1920). Although the education movement made slower progress in the South, schooling had spread sufficiently by the mid-19th century that more than 40 percent of the school-age population was enrolled and nearly 90 percent of white adults were literate (see table 4.3). Schools were also widespread in early 19th century Canada. However, the northernmost English colony lagged behind the United States by several decades with regard to establishing tax-supported schools with universal access, even though its literacy rates were nearly as high.

The rest of the hemisphere trailed far behind the United States and Canada in primary schooling and the attainment

TABLE 4.3

Literacy rates in the Americas, 1850–1950

Country	Year	Age group	Rate[a] (percent)
Argentina	1869	6 and above	23.8
	1895	6 and above	45.6
	1900	10 and above	52.0
	1925	10 and above	73.0
Barbados	1946	10 and above	92.7
Bolivia	1900	10 and above	17.0
Brazil	1872	7 and above	15.8
	1890	7 and above	14.8
	1900	7 and above	25.6
	1920	10 and above	30.0
	1939	10 and above	57.0
British Honduras	1911	10 and above	59.6
(Belize)	1931	10 and above	71.8
Chile	1865	7 and above	18.0
	1875	7 and above	25.7
	1885	7 and above	30.3
	1900	10 and above	43.0
	1925	10 and above	66.0
	1945	10 and above	76.0

(continued)

TABLE 4.3

(continued)

Country	Year	Age group	Rate[a] (percent)
Colombia	1918	15 and above	32.0
	1938	15 and above	56.0
	1951	15 and above	62.0
Costa Rica	1892	7 and above	23.6
	1900	10 and above	33.0
	1925	10 and above	64.0
Cuba	1861	7 and above	23.8
			(38.5, 5.3)
	1899	10 and above	40.5
	1925	10 and above	67.0
	1946	10 and above	77.9
Guatemala	1893	7 and above	11.3
	1925	10 and above	15.0
	1945	10 and above	20.0
Honduras	1887	7 and above	15.2
	1925	10 and above	29.0
Jamaica	1871	5 and above	16.3
	1891	5 and above	32.0
	1911	5 and above	47.2
	1943	5 and above	67.9
	1943	10 and above	76.1
Mexico	1900	10 and above	22.2
	1925	10 and above	36.0
	1946	10 and above	48.4
Paraguay	1886	7 and above	19.3
	1900	10 and above	30.0
Peru	1925	10 and above	38.0
Puerto Rico	1860	7 and above	11.8
			(19.8, 3.1)
Uruguay	1900	10 and above	54.0
	1925	10 and above	70.0
RB de Venezuela	1925	10 and above	34.0
Canada	1861	All	82.5
English-majority counties	1861	All	93.0
French-majority counties	1861	All	81.2
United States			
North whites	1860	10 and above	96.9
South whites	1860	10 and above	91.5
Total population	1870	10 and above	80.0
			(88.5, 21.1)
	1890	10 and above	86.7
			(92.3, 43.2)
	1910	10 and above	92.3
			(95.0, 69.5)

a. In some cases, the figures for whites and nonwhites, respectively, are reported in parentheses.
Source: Engerman, Haber, and Sokoloff 2000.

of literacy. Even the most progressive Latin American countries, such as Argentina and Uruguay, were more than 75 years behind the United States and Canada. These societies began to boost their investments in public schooling at roughly the same time that they were experiencing an economic boom and intensifying their efforts to attract migrants from Europe, which was well before they implemented a general liberalization of the franchise.

While this association might be interpreted as providing for the socialization of foreign immigrants, it also suggests that elites may have been inclined to extend access to opportunities as part of an effort to attract the scarce labor for which they were directly or indirectly competing. The latter perspective is supported by the observation that major investments in primary schooling did not generally occur in any Latin American country until the national governments provided the funds; in contrast to the pattern in North America, local and state governments in Latin America were not willing or able to take on this responsibility on their own. Most of these societies therefore did not achieve high levels of literacy until well into the 20th century. Fairly generous support was made available, however, for universities and other institutions of higher learning that were more geared toward the children of the elite.

Two mechanisms help explain why extreme levels of inequality depressed investments in schooling. First, in settings where private schooling predominated or parents paid user fees for their children, greater wealth or income inequality generally reduced the proportion of the school-age population enrolled, which in turn held per capita income constant. Second, greater inequality likely exacerbated the collective-action problems associated with the establishment and funding of universal public schools, either because the distribution of benefits across the population was quite different from the incidence of taxes and other costs or simply because the heterogeneity of the population made it more difficult for communities to reach consensus on such public projects. Where the wealthy enjoyed disproportionate political power, they were able to procure schooling services for their own children and to resist being taxed to underwrite or subsidize services for others. Although the children of the elite may have been well educated, not everyone was so fortunate. Furthermore, it is a fact that no society has ever realized high levels of literacy without public schools.

Another example of how the evolution of institutions in Latin America contributed to the persistence of extreme

inequality is land policy. Virtually all the economies in the Americas had ample supplies of public land well into the 19th century and beyond. Since the respective governments of each colony, province, or nation were regarded as owners of this resource, they were able to influence the distribution of wealth—as well as the pace of settlement for effective production—by implementing policies to control the availability of land, set prices, establish minimum or maximum acreages, provide credit for such purposes, and design tax systems. Because agriculture was the dominant sector everywhere, questions of how best to employ this public resource for the national interest and how to make the land available for private use were the subject of policy debates, if not political struggles, in many countries. Land policy also became an instrument with which to shape the labor force, because it either encouraged immigration by making land readily available or influenced the regional distribution of labor (or supply of wage labor) by limiting access to and raising the price of land.

There were never major obstacles to acquiring land in the United States, the terms of which became easier over the course of the 19th century (Gates 1968). The well-known Homestead Act of 1862—which essentially made land free in plots suitable for family farms to all those who settled and worked the land for a specified period—was perhaps the culmination of a policy of promoting widespread access to land. Canada pursued similar policies: the Dominion Lands Act of 1872 closely resembled the Homestead Act in both spirit and substance. Argentina and Brazil instituted similar changes in the second half of the 19th century as a way to encourage immigration, but these efforts were much less directed toward providing land to smallholders, and were thus less successful, than the programs in the United States and Canada.

In Argentina, for example, a number of factors explain the contrast in outcomes. First, the elites of Buenos Aires—whose interests favored keeping scarce labor in the province rather than in the capital city—were much more effective at weakening or blocking programs than were their urban counterparts in North America. Second, even those policies nominally intended to broaden access to land tended to involve large grants to land developers (with the logic that allocative efficiency could best be achieved through exchanges among private agents) or transfers to occupants who were already using the land (including those who were grazing livestock). Policies in Argentina thus generally conveyed public lands to private owners in much larger and concentrated holdings than did policies in the United States and Canada. Third, the processes by which large landholdings might have broken up in the absence of economies of scale may have operated very slowly in Argentina. Once land was in private hands, its potential value for grazing may have set a floor on land prices that was too high for immigrants and other ordinary would-be farmers to manage, especially given the general underdevelopment of mortgage and financial institutions.

Argentina, Canada, and the United States all had an extraordinary abundance of virtually uninhabited land to transfer to private hands in order to bring this public resource into production and serve other general interests. In societies such as Mexico, however, the issues at stake with regard to land policy were very different. Good land was relatively scarce and labor was relatively abundant. Here the lands in question had long been controlled by indigenous peoples, but without the existence of individual private property rights.

Mexico was not unique in pursuing policies, especially in the final decades of the 19th and the first decade of the 20th century, that had the effect of conferring ownership of much of this land to large nonindigenous landholders. The 1856 Ley Lerdo and the 1857 Constitution had established methods of privatizing public lands in a manner that could originally have been intended to help indigenous farmers enter a national land market and commercial economy. Under the regime of Porfirio Díaz, however, these laws became the basis for a series of new statutes and policies. Between 1878 and 1908, regulations resulted in a massive transfer of public lands (more than 10.7 percent of the national territory) to large holders, such as survey and land development companies, either in the form of outright grants for services rendered by the companies or for prices set by decree.

Table 4.4 presents estimates of the fractions of household heads (or a near equivalent) that owned land in agricultural areas in the late 19th and early 20th centuries in Argentina, Canada, Mexico, and the United States. The figures indicate enormous differences across the four countries regarding the prevalence of land ownership among the adult male population in rural areas. On the eve of the Mexican Revolution, the figures from the 1910 census suggest that only 2.4 percent of household heads in rural Mexico owned land. This figure is astoundingly low. The dramatic land policy

TABLE 4.4

Land ownership rates in rural regions of Mexico, the United States, Canada, and Argentina in the early 1900s (percent)

Country, year, and region	Proportion of household heads who own land[a]
Mexico, 1910	
North Pacific	5.6
North	3.4
Central	2.0
Gulf	2.1
South Pacific	1.5
Total rural Mexico	2.4
United States, 1900	
North Atlantic	79.2
South Atlantic	55.8
North Central	72.1
South Central	51.4
West	83.4
Alaska/Hawaii	42.1
Total United States	74.5
Canada, 1901	
British Columbia	87.1
Alberta	95.8
Saskatchewan	96.2
Manitoba	88.9
Ontario	80.2
Quebec	90.1
Maritime[b]	95.0
Total Canada	87.1
Argentina, 1895	
Chaco	27.8
Formosa	18.5
Misiones	26.7
La Pampa	9.7
Neuquén	12.3
Río Negro	15.4
Chubut	35.2
Santa Cruz	20.2
Tierra del Fuego	6.6

a. Land ownership is defined as follows: In Mexico, household heads who own land; in the United States, farms that are owner-operated; in Canada, occupiers of farmland who own that land; and in Argentina, the ratio of landowners to the number of males between the ages of 18 and 50.
b. The Maritime region includes Nova Scotia, New Brunswick, and Prince Edward Island.
Source: Engerman and Sokoloff 2002.

measures taken in Mexico at the end of the 19th century may have succeeded in privatizing most of the public lands, but they left the vast majority of the rural population without any land at all. The evidence obviously conforms well with the idea that in societies that began with extreme inequality (such as Mexico), institutions evolved in such a way as to greatly advantage the elite in terms of access to economic opportunities, and thus contributed to the persistence of extreme inequality over time.

In contrast, the proportion of adult males who owned land in rural areas was quite high in the United States, at just below 75 percent in 1900. Although the prevalence of land ownership was markedly lower in the South, where African Americans were disproportionately concentrated, the overall picture is one of land policies (such as the Homestead Act) that provided broad access to this fundamental type of economic opportunity. Canada had an even better record, with nearly 90 percent of household heads owning the agricultural lands they occupied in 1901. The estimates of landholding in these two countries support the notion that land policies made a difference, especially when compared to Argentina. The rural regions of Argentina constitute a set of frontier provinces, where one would expect higher rates of ownership than in Buenos Aires. The numbers, however, suggest a much lower prevalence of land ownership than in the two North American economies.

Nevertheless, all of these countries were far more effective than was Mexico in making land ownership available to the general population. The contrast between the United States and Canada, with their practices of offering easy access to small units of land, and the rest of the Americas (as well as the contrast between Argentina and Mexico) is consistent with the argument that the initial extent of inequality influenced the way in which institutions evolved, and in turn fostered persistence in the degree of inequality over time.

Land policies in Mexico and Argentina reflect another general pattern in the way that institutions evolved. As technology and market conditions changed, institutions adjusted because societies—as well as the segments of the populations that had real influence—sought to take advantage of the new circumstances. The late 19th century was a period of falling transportation costs and extraordinary growth in world trade. Among the greatest beneficiaries of this development were relatively land-abundant countries in the Americas, such as Argentina and Uruguay, which were now in a better position to exploit their strong comparative advantage in agriculture. Increased access to vast international markets in chilled beef, grains, and other agricultural products dampened ratios of wage rates to land rents (see the estimates of Williamson 1999, O'Rourke and Williamson 2002, and Bértola and Porcile 2002). Given the already high concentration of land ownership, the effect of this improved integration of world

markets was likely another factor that reinforced inequality. In his assessment of the case of Argentina, Scobie (1964, p 5.) certainly thought this to be the case:

> Those whose forebears had been able to acquire and keep enormous land grants or who now secured estates enjoyed a gilded existence. Lands whose only worth had been in their herds of wild cattle, land which could be reached by horseback or oxcart, land occupied largely by hostile Indians underwent a total transformation. British capital had built railroads. Pastoral techniques had been improved and the resources of the pampas were being used more thoroughly. Immigrants, newly arrived from European poverty, were available . . . as sharecroppers, tenant farmers, or peons to raise corn, wheat, or alfalfa. Under such conditions, land provided an annual return of from 12 to 15 percent to the owner and land values often rose 1000 percent in a decade. Those who already had land, power, or money monopolized the newly developed wealth of the pampas.

By creating new market opportunities in Latin America and increasing the value of land, the integration of world markets may have stimulated efforts by elites to influence the sorts of land policies discussed above, with the aim of capturing a greater share of potential gains for themselves. This flexibility in altering institutions to serve the purposes of the politically and economically powerful in response to changing circumstances is also evident in many other areas of economic policy, such as the regulation of financial institutions and foreign trade. What was good for the elites was likely not good for reducing inequality or spurring economic growth. In terms of these aspects, the Latin American economies fell far behind their neighbors to the north over the course of the 19th century.

4.4. The 20th century

This chapter has suggested that Latin America entered the 20th century with very high levels of inequality, which virtually all of the evidence discussed elsewhere in this volume indicates persisted during the rest of the century. For example, the estimates of Calvo, Torre, and Szwarcberg (2002) for Argentina suggest that the extent of inequality changed little during the 20th century. This is consistent with the evidence in Diaz-Alejandro (1970) and Randall (1978). A study of inequality in Colombia since the 1930s by Londoño (1995) likewise argues that inequality in the 1990s was at about the same level as it was in 1938. Similarly, a study of income distribution in Mexico by Reynolds (1970) found that little change occurred between the 1940s and the late 1960s.

Explaining the persistence of inequality is again problematic. During the course of the 20th century, Latin American societies underwent significant social, economic, and political changes. Urbanization increased considerably and the role of agriculture declined. Thus, the highly inegalitarian pattern of landownership that characterized Latin America ought to have become less and less significant as a determinant of income inequality. In contrast, educational attainment still lagged behind that of North America, and there was a large amount of catching up to do, as the numbers in table 4.3 indicate.

In addition, modernization moved nearly all countries in the direction of more open and democratic politics. Even if democracy was perhaps relatively shallow and unconsolidated, it seems to have undergone a significant change compared to the 19th century. Moreover, several countries, including Bolivia, Mexico, and Nicaragua (and possibly Colombia, depending on the interpretation of *La Violencia,* the period of violence in the 1950s) underwent dramatic social revolutions, while others, such as Peru after 1968, implemented radical redistributive policies.

This pattern in Latin America also contrasts with what we know about Europe, where economic inequality appears to have fallen dramatically during most of the 20th century (Morrison 2000). It is also different from the pattern seen in the United States, where measures of inequality indicate a marked decline from the 1930s through the 1960s, before a recent upturn began (see, for example, Goldin and Katz 1999).

What accounts for the radically different courses of countries throughout the Americas? Why did inequality apparently remain unchanged in the face of the types of social and economic transformations that led to falling inequality elsewhere? Unfortunately, there is little research on this topic, and given the severe limitations of the evidence it is possible only to offer some intelligent, but nevertheless speculative, conjectures. (These are explored in somewhat more depth in the next two chapters of this report.)

First, it is surely the case that mass education has been of low quality in Latin America, especially when compared to North America. Pritchett (2001) has pointed out that mass expansions of educational enrollment in the last 40 years appear to be uncorrelated with economic growth, which is consistent with the idea that educational expansion can take place without radically transforming inequality. The most plausible explanations for Pritchett's findings are either that educational quality is often so low that there is no impact on development, or that the social payoff from education depends on other institutions in society. This latter idea may also be important for explaining the disappointing impact of educational expansion on inequality in Latin America. Despite the increase in education, there are still deeply ingrained patterns of social exclusion and discrimination in Latin America that are hard to break down and which prevent poor people from becoming upwardly mobile. This may be why even apparently radical changes, such as the Bolivian revolution, end up having little effect on inequality (see Kelley and Klein 1981).

Another possible explanation for the failure of educational reform to reduce inequality is the type of development strategy that evolved in Latin America starting in the 1930s. This approach, which was based on looking inward, import substitution, and isolation from world markets, may have reduced incentives for investments in education and skill building. It is significant that countries that adopted export-oriented development strategies in the 20th centuries (for example, Mauritius and Singapore) often also experienced declining inequality.

These effects may have been reinforced by the factor endowments of Latin America. Even in the 20th century, many economies were dominated by the export of primary commodities, such as oil in Venezuela; coffee in Brazil, Colombia, and Central America; bananas in Central America; sugar and bananas in the Caribbean; and copper and nitrates in Chile. It has been argued (for example, by Leamer and others 1999) that commodity-intensive development reduces the returns on education, which may have been another factor in reducing the impact of educational expansion on inequality.

Finally, it is also possible that in the presence of imperfect financial markets, changes in the structure of the economy from agriculture to industry have little effect on inequality. Although there are no comparative data on this connection, it seems likely that the ownership of industry in Latin America is much more concentrated, and financial markets much less developed, than in North America. Haber (2002a) has shown how banking was very tightly controlled in Mexico compared to the United States. For example, in

1910 the United States had roughly 25,000 banks and a highly competitive market structure. In contrast, Mexico had 42 banks, 2 of which controlled 60 percent of total banking assets and virtually none of which actually competed with another bank. This example, and others like it, suggest that financial markets in Latin America were also very thin and monopolized (see the essays in Haggard, Lee, and Maxfield 1993). Without access to financial markets, poor people stayed poor.

Although the focus of this chapter is economic inequality, it is hard to separate this issue from political inequality. Political inequality both causes and is caused by economic inequality. Just as in the 19th century, one of the central reasons for the persistence of inequality in the 20th century may be the prevalence of authoritarianism in Latin America. Although democratization has taken place throughout the region, this process has usually been unconsolidated and limited in what it can achieve.

Moreover, those popular democratic parties that have been able to obtain power have also often been driven by narrow political considerations and opted for policies that were dramatic in the short run but conveyed little in the way of lasting benefit. For example, in Argentina, despite the fact that policy under the first administration of Perón in the late 1940s and early 1950s significantly reduced inequality, these effects quickly unraveled when the military took over in 1955 and did not lead to lasting improvements in terms of inequality. Chapter 5 discusses these issues further.

4.5. The 21st century and beyond

If the roots of Latin American inequality lie deep in history, is there anything that can be done about it today? What do historical processes tell us about the future evolution of inequality in Latin America? Certainly the recognition of the powerful factors that shaped and allowed extreme inequality to persist for centuries in Latin America does not inspire optimism, but a historical perspective reminds us that changes that take a generation or two to be realized should perhaps not be considered to be so slow. Although it is impossible to conceive of a quick-fix solution, there is abundant and impressive historical and cross-country evidence that democracy (or political equality), equality in the distribution of human capital, and economic equality tend to develop together.

It is generally difficult to attack economic inequality directly (for example through redistribution measures) without harming some of the incentive structures thought critical to ensure processes of economic growth. For that and other reasons, more indirect policies that would broaden effective access to economic opportunities—not just for the current population, but, more importantly, for future generations—would be preferable. Such policies would include not only major investments in extending access to high-quality education, but also efforts to provide more equal access to political influence and to the protection of laws more generally. The historical experiences of Europe and the United States suggest that the most reliable ways to induce falling inequality are to promote sustained educational investment and asset accumulation by the poor and to ensure avenues for social and economic mobility. In general, this may entail solving market and other institutional failures that discourage the poor and their children from making the sorts of investments that would help them succeed in an increasingly global economy.

CHAPTER 5

State-Society Interactions as Sources of Persistence and Change in Inequality

THE PREVIOUS CHAPTER EXAMINED HOW INITIAL FACTOR ENDOWMENTS AND EARLY INSTITUTIONAL development played a central role in the generation of egregious levels of inequality in Latin America. The next two chapters consider the nature of the political and economic processes that continue to shape inequality in the region today.

This chapter discusses both political and social factors and seeks to fill in the interactions between social and political institutions, power, and governance that were summarized in two sides of the triangle used to portray the conceptual framework presented in chapter 1 (figure 1.1). In assessing both current problems and possibilities for change, the current chapter's primary focus is on the performance of the state, which is viewed as a product of historically-formed state-society relations. The state is examined in terms of a syndrome, or malaise, that is characterized by unequal social relations and "weak" governing capacities. "Weak" has a specific meaning: doing a poor job of providing public goods such as macroeconomic stability, property rights and citizenship, and basic services such as education, health, water, sanitation, roads, electricity, and social protection.

In all of these areas, failures in state action are typically regressive, hurting the poor and weak disproportionately. They are also, in most areas, bad for overall development. Where states fail in providing *public goods,* wealthy members of society typically can either exert private influence over the state for selective delivery, or can opt out of the system. For example, elites can shift savings abroad and develop private means of protecting property rights and their personal security. Poor and middle groups live with the consequences.

With respect to *services,* some Latin American states historically did a reasonable job of providing services for elites (for example through the early formation of universities in many countries). However, most did a poor job of broad-based provisioning; by 1925, only Argentina and Uruguay had achieved literacy rates of 70 percent or higher (see table 4.3). In 2000, literacy was still only 65 percent in Guatemala, 77 percent in Nicaragua, and 87 percent in Brazil (and considerably lower for poorer groups in all

countries, as indicated in table A.27). At the same time, while most countries in the region have made substantial progress in expanding basic education coverage, a major challenge related to school quality remains unsolved for most of the public school systems in the region (de Ferranti and others 2003). Wealthy groups again have greater options for either exerting influence on public service provisioning for themselves or opting out for private provision.

Similar patterns can be identified with regard to other services. Although most Latin American states have developed social welfare systems since the early 20th century, these are often best characterized as "truncated" systems that only reach formal sector workers, leaving out the neediest segments of the populations (see chapter 9). These issues are tightly linked to the *tax effort,* which reflects the underlying implicit social contract that conditions the willingness of all groups—but especially elites and middle groups—to pay taxes in return for effective state action.

Why has this pattern of weak and truncated state actions persisted? Addressing this question involves taking some tentative steps into a complex terrain. There is considerable heterogeneity in conditions across the region, and it would be impossible to do justice to the issues in a short chapter. Yet, as seen in chapter 4 on the historical formation of high inequality in Latin America, the links among economic, political, and social conditions are fundamental. Attempting to understand these links is central to any enterprise that seeks to draw conclusions on policy options. There is an immense literature on

the issues of state-society relations in Latin America, especially in the fields of political science and sociology. This chapter does not seek to present new theories, but rather has the more modest objective of drawing on major strands in the existing literature—on both Latin America and elsewhere—to help inform understanding of the ways in which state-society relations can be a force for both the persistence and transformation of economic, social, and political inequality.

To motivate the discussion, figure 5.1 shows bivariate correlations between selected indicators of social difference, state

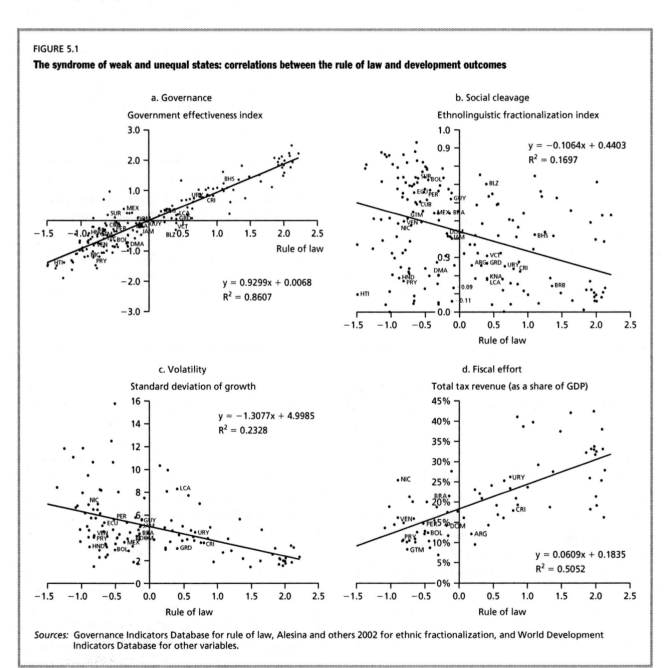

FIGURE 5.1

The syndrome of weak and unequal states: correlations between the rule of law and development outcomes

Sources: Governance Indicators Database for rule of law, Alesina and others 2002 for ethnic fractionalization, and World Development Indicators Database for other variables.

capacity, and economic performance, with the "rule of law" used as an anchor for the graphs. An ethnic fractionalization index is used as a (highly imperfect) measure of unequal social relations, though similar results are obtained with a Gini coefficient of income inequality. The rule of law can be thought of as a rough proxy for a state's performance in providing the public goods of protection of property and citizenship rights, government effectiveness is a proxy for bureaucratic capacity to provide broad-based public services, and macroeconomic instability and tax effort are two of the outcome measures. These are only correlations, but they may capture the two-way patterns of causality between inequality and state performance.

The remainder of this chapter is divided into two main sections. The first discusses the origins of weak and unequal state performance in state-society interactions, including a discussion of why the process of democratization has been halting and lengthy, as well as insufficient to effect a transformation in political and social inequalities. The second section turns to the question of how to effect change in order to achieve more effective and equal states, a condition that is characterized here as the move toward a new "political equilibrium."

5.1. Political and social structures as forces for the reproduction of inequality

Chapter 4 on the historical roots of inequality in Latin America posed a puzzling question: why has inequality persisted in the region, in spite of significant social, economic, and political changes? This section addresses this question and discusses how enduring features of political institutions and social structures have limited the scope for equalizing public actions, and thus contributed to reproduction of inequality in the region long after its colonial origins faded. Has inequality in the region persisted simply because of the lateness of changes (especially the arrival of universal suffrage), or are there other forces that are preventing democracies in the region from becoming more potent drivers of equalizing changes? It is argued that while the late arrival of competitive democracy is a relevant fact, the evolution of the institutional structure in the region in response to, and in defense of, the predominant elite interests has been a fundamental cause of the persistent inequality, rather than the type of regime in place.

Institutional evolution has taken a variety of forms within the region. However, the underlying characteristics of state relationships have been strikingly similar across different patterns of political and social development in the region. The main commonality is the theme of a two-way causal relation

between historically-formed, unequal social and political structures and relatively weak and regressive states (as evidenced in the areas of the provision of public goods and basic services, noted in the introduction to this chapter). In some cases—for example the Dominican Republic, El Salvador, Guatemala, Honduras, Nicaragua, or Paraguay for much of the past century—this has typically taken the form of traditional authoritarian or oligarchic regimes characterized by profound exclusion of the bulk of the population, as well as high levels of state capture by small groups of elites.[1]

In Argentina, Brazil, and Mexico, where industrialization advanced to a relatively greater extent, significant processes of incorporation of the working classes into the political structure occurred. However, this trend was both partial (that is, primarily of only the formal working class) and effected in a way that tended to perpetuate relations based on patronage, which typically created vested interests among middle-class groups as well as elites (Cohen 1989, Middlebrook 1995, O'Donnell 1973). In countries such as Bolivia, Ecuador, or Peru, where deep and complex social and ethnic divisions have existed, the processes of incorporation have tended to be even less complete, even for the formal working class, and to be marked with conflict. Traditional oligarchic politics was often replaced with "populist" outsider movements (for example, Bolivia's 1952 revolution, Ecuador's *Velasquismo*, and Peru's *Aprismo*), which raised hopes among the underprivileged without building an effective state to cater to their general demands.[2]

While formally operating in electoral democracies, elite-dominated political parties in Colombia and Venezuela in the second half of the 20th century grew increasingly disconnected from their popular support bases and pursued patronage-driven policies.[3] The challenge of political incorporation was exacerbated by weak democratic consolidation, as well as periodic unconstitutional transitions, especially during the Cold War period. Chile, Costa Rica, and Uruguay to varying degrees developed states that were, when under democratic auspices, more effective in providing public goods and redistributive services, although both Chile and Uruguay suffered periods of repressive authoritarian rule.[4]

Unequal social relations and weak states: twin facets of negative institutional legacies

Unequal relations and clientelism
The persistence of unequal social relations between elites and poorer groups is classically manifested in the form of

clientelist relations, which are characterized by the unequal, although reciprocal, exchange of favors, benefits, or rents for support or acquiescence.[5] In a clientelist system, citizens do not base their support for candidates and parties according to their political preferences in particular issue areas; instead, their support is contingent upon particularistic material incentives. Rather than pursuing public policies that address the shared needs of a broad segment of society (as might a disciplined programmatic party with broad geographic coverage), clientelist politicians generally draw support from relatively narrow, geographically-defined constituencies and concentrate on providing tangible material goods (that is, support for patronage) that is narrowly targeted to a specific group of supporters in exchange for their support.[6] Clientelist practices enable the poor to make isolated efforts to attain local goods, but these rarely form the basis of broad-based policy initiatives that address the underlying causes of poverty and inequality.

The other side of clientelistic, or patronage-based, systems is the absence of broad, organized alliances of social groups pressing for sustained improvements in their collective welfare and public services (for example, general improvements in mass education). This condition has reduced incentives for political elites to strengthen the capacities of the state to provide such services. Strengthening the state in this sense would have required considerable investment to improve its capacities to raise revenues through taxation and to organize its administrative apparatus. Given that the elites already had selective access to public goods, such as security of property, and to basic services (that is, either through the market itself or through appropriation of the limited state functions), it was often not rational to make these investments in state building. In cases of the partial incorporation of poorer groups into national systems of service provision, especially in the middle-income countries, new vested interests were created, for example to sustain the "truncated" welfare state.

The importance of clientelism in both rural and urban settings has been documented throughout the region, for example in Brazil (Leal 1948, Carvalho 1997), Mexico (Cornelius 1977, Grindle 1977), Colombia (Schmidt 1977, Archer 1990), Peru (Stokes 1995), and Venezuela (Powell 1977). More traditional forms of clientelism, often linked to powerful local personalities, are probably of greater importance in the relatively less developed parts of the region, that is, in less developed countries (see box 5.2 on the Dominican

Republic) and in poorer sub-regions such as northeastern Brazil or the southern states of Mexico. However, clientelism is not by any means peculiar to Latin America or developing countries. It has been an important aspect of the political history of many (perhaps most) Organisation for Economic Cooperation and Development (OECD) countries, for example in the political machines of U.S. cities and at both a local and national level under Christian Democrats in Italy (Shefter 1994). Where Latin America is distinctive is in the depth and resilience of clientelist structures.

An additional, particular feature of the relationship between states and subordinate groups in many Latin American countries in the mid 20th century was a more formal "corporate" form of inclusion, in which governments brought working class or peasant movements into national, institutionalized, patronage-based systems. These processes were typically marked by co-option. Such conditions were exemplified by the highly "successful" incorporation of labor, peasants, and other functional groups in society in Mexico, which was fully institutionalized by Lázaro Cárdenas into a remarkably stable form of state-party organization under the *Partido Revolucionario Institucional* (PRI). In Argentina, Juan Perón successfully co-opted a previously independent union movement into the corporate wing of Peronism. Co-option of groups was also reflected in the less successful attempts by the Bolivian *Movimiento Nacional Revolucionario* to emulate the PRI-style form of governance and state formation after the 1952 revolution, which succeeded in first bringing the peasant movement under the patronage of the national movement, but failed to provide the economic and services support that might have made land reform a success (see chapter 7 on land reform).

In most cases, however, these incorporation processes simply transferred unequal social structures to the formal political arena by reproducing unequal vertical relations at the national political level. Although corporatism is increasingly a phenomenon of the past, its heritage persists in many areas that are relevant to current policy, including widespread vested interests that have accrued to the formal working classes and public sector servants. This phenomenon is evidenced in dualistic labor structures (see chapter 8) and the truncated welfare state (see chapter 9).

Clientelism and corporatism—and more generally the vertical forms of inclusion of subordinate groups—have also left a damaging legacy in terms of political organization. It worked against the development of programmatic parties (either those that represented working classes or more conservative forces), which was an important part of the political evolution of most European countries and the United States (Shefter 1994). Chile is one of the exceptions to this pattern in Latin America, in the sense of having a long history of genuine programmatic parties, especially those that represent both the middle- and working class. As discussed below, political scientists attribute Chile's relative success in developing an effective and redistributive state after its transition to democracy in part to the continuity of party performance originating in the country's earlier history (Valenzuela 1977).

In some cases, corporatism allowed for more blatant forms of political subordination, as well as state capture by some of the more privileged interest groups. Political scientist James Malloy (1979) describes how the corporatist arrangements in Brazil's social security systems—initially developed by the authoritarian government of Getúlio Vargas as a way to preempt radicalization of the working class—were eventually captured by the organized labor in the formal sector as the movement gained a series of policy concessions from the state, as well as privileged access to state rents at the cost of workers outside formal organizations.[7]

Although unequal, vertical social relations have been a general phenomenon in Latin America, in many countries they have been overlaid and reinforced by ethnic and racial divisions. This is most apparent in Brazil, much of the Caribbean, the Central Andes, parts of Central America, Colombia, and Mexico. As discussed in chapter 4, these divisions reach back to profoundly unequal conditions that emerged in the colonial period. Such relational inequalities have had major effects on processes of socialization, collective expectations, and daily interactions, in turn affecting behaviors and conditions related to school, work, and social interactions.

For example, in an ethnographic study of poor black women in a sugarcane-producing area of northeastern Brazil, Scheper-Hughes (1992) documents the harsh dilemmas faced by the poor in seeking to manage their daily lives, with many hoping to find the "good patron" who will solve their problems. Such stories are repeated in sociological and ethnographic studies in the region (see Calderón and Szmukler 2004). Such group-based differences continue to affect both the design and implementation of policy and, as in other parts of the world, magnify the challenges of forming the social and political base through which public goods and services are provided by the government. (See box 5.1 for evidence from the United States and Europe.)

Weak state capacity

The implementation of political actions to reduce inequality, either through the overt redistribution of assets or the efficient production of public goods, requires adequate institutional capacities of the state apparatus. Most Latin American countries have relatively "weak" states relative to OECD comparators and other developing countries of similar income levels, and therefore typically score low on a range of governance indices, for example the rule of law, government effectiveness, and corruption (Kaufmann, Kraay, and Mastruzzi 2003). As noted above, this means, in particular, relative weaknesses in providing the public with goods such as the rule of law, citizenship, and protection of property rights, and with basic services such as quality primary and secondary education.[8] Such weaknesses are reflected in the difficulties a number of the states in the region face with regard to raising revenues.

The potential for the state to enact pro-equity changes is also constrained by informal political realities, whereby the excessive influence of elites and some well-organized middle-class groups (such as unions) on public decisions often results in the effective "capture" of the state. For public actions to be effective against entrenched interests, the state itself needs to be more or less autonomous from such influence. Many Latin American states have historically faced difficulties with state capture in its most blatant form, as in the oligarchic domination by the so-called 14 families in El Salvador, the dynastic rule of the Somozas in Nicaragua, the long personalist rule of Stroessner in Paraguay, the "partidocracia" in Venezuela, and the recent case of Vladimiro Montesinos in Peru during the 1990s. In addition, more subtle, everyday manifestations of the uneven application of the rule of law, which discriminates against the poor, also occur.

International evidence of the salience of state capture comes from international surveys of executives by the World Economic Forum. Representatives of firms were asked questions on the extent in their countries of excessive or illegal influence of powerful conglomerates, firms, or individuals on state policymaking (figure 5.2). Such unequal influence (or "crony bias") is correlated with a more negative assessment of the fairness and impartiality of courts and the enforceability of court decisions, less secure

BOX 5.1

Racial inequality and social spending: evidence from the United States and Europe

The impact of group-based differences is not limited to Latin America and the Caribbean; it has had a profound effect on social policy in the United States as well. Although the United States and Europe enjoy comparable levels of economic prosperity, the United States invests considerably less of its resources into social programs and public goods. The United States spends approximately 16 percent of its gross domestic product (GDP) on social programs, in contrast to the European average of 25 percent. Not surprisingly, the United States also registers levels of income inequality that are substantially higher than its European counterparts. A quantitative comparison of the United States and Europe reveals the influence of a history of racial inequality on these phenomena (see Alesina, Glaeser, and Sacerdote 2001).

Since African Americans are overrepresented in the lowest income brackets, the white majority tends to view social spending and redistributive policies as disproportionately benefiting minorities, effectively undercutting support for policies that would reduce levels of inequality.[9] Loury (2002) has explored the often subtle ways in

which a history of racial stigma can continue to have salience in contemporary behavior and policy-making. Alesina, Baqir, and Easterly (1999) find lower spending on publicly provided services in less racially homogeneous areas. Since universal programs would benefit the population as a whole, including the "undeserving" poor, average Americans tend to vote for more limited government expenditures on transfers or services targeted to the poor.

In contrast, racial differences were historically much less important to overall social interactions and policy formulation in European nations during the 20th century. Europeans were more likely to view the poor as unfortunate and did not stigmatize them as members of a socially undesirable group. This historical absence of racial inequality helps explain the differing levels of social spending in the United States and Europe. More recent racial and ethnic tensions in Europe and, in some countries, the related rise of far-right, anti-immigrant parties, further illustrates the point that the central issue of concern is the interactions between group-based differences and policy choice, and not an intrinsically "European" preference for redistributive policies.

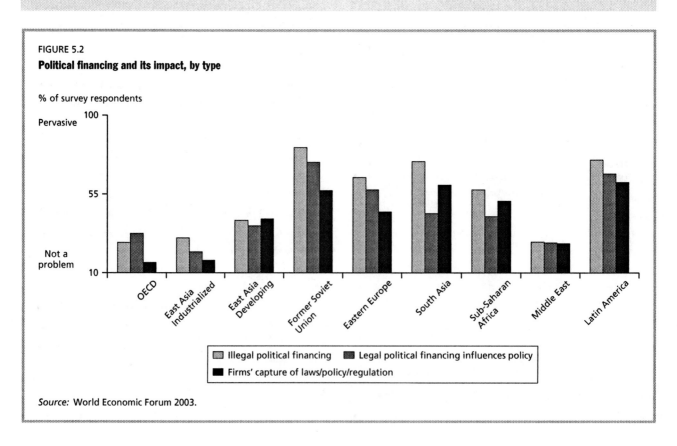

FIGURE 5.2

Political financing and its impact, by type

% of survey respondents

Legend:
- Illegal political financing
- Legal political financing influences policy
- Firms' capture of laws/policy/regulation

Source: World Economic Forum 2003.

property rights, lower levels of tax compliance, and higher levels of bribery.

Views of firms on unequal influence over policies, in international perspective

The importance of state capture in the region is supported by careful documentation of key episodes in the history of lawmaking in Mexico by Haber (2002a) and by country-specific surveys. For example, in surveys of firms and public officials in Peru in 2001, some 80 percent of respondents judged that there was a "high impact" of bribes given to parliamentarians to shape laws, the judiciary to influence decisions, and public officials to shape ministerial decrees. A slightly lower proportion of respondents reported significant levels of "state capture" of affected regulatory agencies, and much less with regard to the Central Bank (see figure 5.3). A similar pattern was found in a survey of firms in Colombia, but with "only" about 60 percent reporting influence on the judiciary.

The weakness of the rule of law and property rights has in turn led to the partial "privatization" of these public spheres by the rich and the powerful, including in some cases by organized segments of the middle classes. This trend has occurred at the cost of poorer and subordinate groups, who have lacked the power or wealth to exert such influence. Property rights are of particular interest in light of their potent influence on investment and growth. In some countries where general protection of property rights has been absent, alternative means of protecting the elites' rights emerged.

In a major study of Mexico, Haber, Maurer, and Razo (2003) use historical, political, and economic analysis to show how property rights were selectively enforced, especially in the turbulent period of 1910–1929. Governments made selective, credible commitments to subsets of asset holders, guaranteed by third-party actors who shared in the rents. The third-party actors varied with the asset and period, including local military factions (for example, agricultural products during the revolution), the United States (for example, for oil), and the union movement (in the industrial sector). These arrangements were institutionalized in the corporate state created under the PRI and supported investment

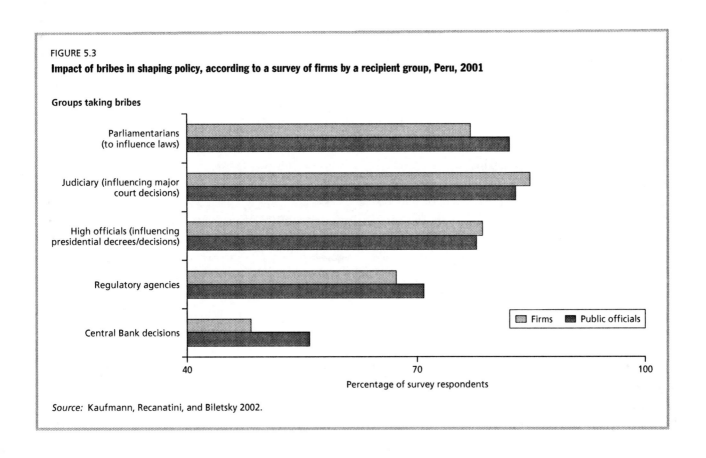

FIGURE 5.3

Impact of bribes in shaping policy, according to a survey of firms by a recipient group, Peru, 2001

Groups taking bribes

Source: Kaufmann, Recanatini, and Biletsky 2002.

and rapid growth that lasted till the 1980s debt crisis. However, this economic improvement came at the cost of a pattern of development that was both inefficient and inequitable, since selective protection of rents and rent-sharing were central to the institutional basis for growth.[10]

A more extreme case of elite influence and state capture is Guatemala. Starting in the late 1800s, landed elites and the military have exercised strong influence over the Guatemalan state (Heller and Mahoney 2003). The 1870s were marked by the rise of export agriculture, controlled primarily by landed plantation coffee elites. The state encouraged the growth of the coffee industry by catering to the needs of coffee elites, providing infrastructure to service export agriculture and implementing coercive labor policies over the indigenous population to secure plantation labor. The economic base of the elites has evolved, but high levels of state capture and exclusion have persisted to the present day. In the second half of the 20th century, the exclusionary politics unfolded in violent conflict and extreme repression by the state, especially of indigenous groups. These events finally culminated in the 1996 Peace Accords, but even today the Guatemalan state's capacity for public goods provision is quite limited. Guatemala collects only 8 percent of gross domestic product (GDP) in taxes and spends 6 percent of GDP on social sectors.

Costa Rica provides a contrasting example: since the 1870s, the state has maintained substantial autonomy from dominant class actors, including the coffee elite. (See Paige 1997 and Mahoney 2001 for comparative discussions.) This pattern was coupled with increasing political openness, the mobilization of class interests through political parties, and the channeling of demands through democratic institutions. In turn, the societal demand for services rose, to which the state responded with programs of broad-based provisioning, notably in basic education. Costa Rica raises 18 percent of GDP and spends 17 percent of GDP from taxes and other sources on social sectors (see table 9.2 and figure 9.3).

The case of the Dominican Republic further illustrates how an extreme form of clientelism can combine with other institutional characteristics to crystallize in a political equilibrium of a small state with limited service provision (see box 5.2). In sum, clientelism induces politicians to provide targeted goods (such as small-scale public works) in highly visible ways to specific constituencies (such as local communities). In the absence of a programmatic political party

with a national reach, individual politicians, including the president, cannot credibly offer a major public policy initiative (for example, educational reform) and expect to receive electoral support. Cognizant of the governing elites' inability to commit to a major policy reform, the electorate would prefer to vote for locally prominent candidates who promise to deliver tangible public works or public employment programs.

Institutional legacies of inequality and the limits of democratization

This section focuses on the process of democratization in Latin America. On the one hand, an authoritarian legacy (see chapter 4) and the dynamics induced by fragmented social structures and weak states led to the delayed and halting consolidation of democracy, with periodic bouts of unconstitutional threats and authoritarianism (especially during the Cold War period). On the other, when democracy did return to the region in the 1980s, it proved insufficient to transform the region to one with genuinely equal citizenship and effective, inclusive states (O'Donnell 1998b).

These processes can be understood in terms of the broader question of how poorer and subordinate groups are incorporated into the polity. The ineffectiveness of politically legitimate representation mechanisms, especially broad-based programmatic political parties, in including the poor has often created tensions and dynamics that were inimical to sustained redistributive change (Collier and Collier 1991, Rueschmeyer, Stephens, and Stephens 1992). These same dynamics have had significant impacts not only on frequent regime changes in the mid-20th century throughout Latin America, but also the prospects for democratic consolidation in more recent years (Collier and Collier 1991).

When social and economic modernization began to put strains on the traditional exclusionary politics in the early 20th century, political elites and society responded in a variety of ways to this new dynamic. As discussed above, in more economically advanced countries (including Argentina, Brazil, and Mexico), elites attempted to incorporate "popular" sectors (primarily organized urban labor) through state-dominated corporatist arrangements. In some cases (notably Argentina and Brazil, but also Chile and Uruguay), these incorporation processes led to the radicalization of segments of the popular sector, which in turn triggered authoritarian reactions from the military, backed by the countries' economic elites.

BOX 5.2

Clientelism and the underprovision of public services in the Dominican Republic

Politics in the Dominican Republic has been characterized by a strong clientelist tradition, whereby parties rarely compete for votes on the basis of national policy issues, and by strong presidentialism, whereby presidents dominate the national political scene but rely on the support of local political bosses to obtain votes. A combined effect of these institutional characteristics is significant emphasis on government provision of targeted goods (in other words, public works), low spending on public goods (for example, education), and low overall spending.

The clientelist tradition in the Dominican Republic is the legacy of 30 years of the repressive, personalist dictatorship of Trujillo from 1930 to 1961, which stifled the development of credible political parties with clear and credible stances on public policy issues. Absent disciplined parties with clear policy reputations, presidents face greater challenges from political rivals even within their own party and cabinet. These rivals are always interested in laying their hands on portions of public expenditures in order to provide patronage goods to their own personalized constituencies. Responding to this, presidents have under-

taken relatively little public spending and concentrated it in the presidency. For example, in the Dominican Republic, almost 30 percent of total public investments in 2000 were executed by the Ministry of the Presidency.

Presidents could push for improved public sector financial management to better monitor spending by line ministries, in principle increasing presidential willingness to allow more delegated spending and greater accountability. However, they are reluctant to do this since (unlike Alberto Fujimori in Peru) they have only a limited ability to counter efforts by rivals to use resources as they see fit, even if a sophisticated system of public sector financial management makes those uses completely transparent. The inability to tightly control expenditure execution, however, gives the president a strong incentive to keep overall expenditure levels low. In the end, the government provides highly targeted patronage goods and under-provides public goods such as high-quality public primary education that could have made a dent in inequality in the country.

Source: Keefer 2002.

In countries where initial incorporation was more limited (such as Ecuador and Peru), political exclusion offered a fertile ground for populism, as exemplified by the leftist military regime of Velasco and the *Aprista* administration of García in Peru or by new parties and "outsider" movements. In earlier periods, this trend was evidenced by periodic indigenous insurrections (for example, in the Yucatan, Mexico) or in millenarian movements of withdrawal, such as the Canudos movement in northeastern Brazil. In the 20th century, political exclusion and populism were manifested in violent civil conflict, notably in parts of Central America, Bolivia, and Peru. Especially in the Cold War, post-Cuban Revolution atmosphere, social tensions tended to spur repressive, authoritarian reactions, as in Guatemala (1956), Chile (1973), and El Salvador (1980s), to name a few of the more violent examples.

Populism did have redistributive aims—or at least rhetoric—manifested in both authoritarian and democratic regimes, but the movement was also a symptom of unequal, vertical institutions through which charismatic leaders

periodically emerged with promises to the masses that were not mediated by institutional structures. However, populist leaders were in most cases ineffective precisely because of their charismatic, personalist status, and were incapable of effecting change in overall patterns of privilege and institutional processes. In the case of Velasco in Ecuador, Conaghan (1995, p. 446) comments: "Velasco's early success was the product of his close ties to traditional elites. Unlike classic populism in Latin America (for example, Peronism), Velasco never produced real material and political advances for lower-class supporters . . . He did, however, school an entire generation of politicians in how to win political power without building organizations or refining party platforms. His career seemed to underscore the unimportance of party and the dominance of personality . . ." In other countries, reforms (such as the Peruvian land reform) were implemented incompletely, failed to resolve distributional struggles, and spilled over into macroeconomic instability (notably in Argentina, Bolivia, and Peru). The result was that previous "gains" in redistribution were reversed.

The contemporary history of Argentina vividly illustrates how a nation's inability to successfully deal with the question of political inclusion has stymied the development of an effective state, with periodic unresolved distributional struggles and a steady worsening of inequality (see chapter 2). In Argentina, the incorporation of the poorer groups (especially urban workers) started in the 1940s under the populist regime of Juan Perón, who mobilized industrial workers into state-sanctioned (and controlled) labor unions and introduced a series of policy measures aimed at addressing their needs (including large increases in worker wages and benefits and the creation of a social security system). There was a large increase in labor share under Perón that was then sharply reversed when he was out of power (see figure 5.4, which illustrates a long time series of labor shares in Argentina).

The government's relationships with organized labor was highly dependent on Perón's personal relations and charismatic appeal rather than institutionalized mechanisms of representation. In the words of Snow and Wynia (1990, p. 138), "The material benefits obtained by the workers during the Perón administration were essentially gifts from above rather than the result of working-class demands." Following the ouster of Perón in a coup, democratic and military regimes alternated until a more extensive period of democracy set in during the 1980s. The second period of rising labor share, 1967–1974, was one of relatively good economic performance and strong labor union pressure, both under dictatorship and the elected Peronist government. However, this culminated in economic crisis and the 1976 coup, with a sharp reduction in labor share. This pattern exemplifies a broader international pattern of crises often "resolving" underlying distributional struggles, with losses being borne by formal labor (see chapter 8 and Diwan 2001).

If Argentina represents a case of extreme regime instability masking the underlying persistence of unequal social relations and a weak state, Venezuela is a case in which formal democracy has failed to resolve distributive conflicts throughout the 20th century. Venezuela has therefore not been evolved into a redistributive state capable of fostering inclusive development. Although the country maintained a healthy economic performance and democratic stability during the 1960s and 1970s, once its oil-dependent

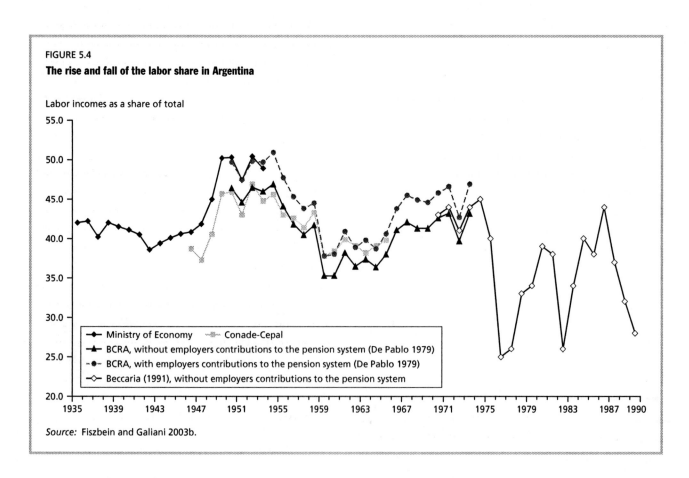

FIGURE 5.4

The rise and fall of the labor share in Argentina

Labor incomes as a share of total

Legend:
- Ministry of Economy
- Conade-Cepal
- BCRA, without employers contributions to the pension system (De Pablo 1979)
- BCRA, with employers contributions to the pension system (De Pablo 1979)
- Beccaria (1991), without employers contributions to the pension system

Source: Fiszbein and Galiani 2003b.

economy ran into trouble in the 1980s, successive governments failed to adjust economic policy and, in turn, faced an escalating crisis in governance.

For a long time, oil revenues have provided Venezuela with a relatively easy source of fiscal revenues with which to finance the expansion of public services, but have also sharply limited the incentive of political elites to invest in strengthening the state's tax capacity. When the role of oil revenues role as a social lubricant weakened in the 1980s and 1990s, the original elite group that established 20th century democracy increasingly came to serve to protect the privileges of new elites—those associated with established parties—and to ossify the country's democratic institutions.

As in the case of Argentina, the country's inability to resolve distributive conflict in a peaceful and sustainable manner is vividly illustrated by the current stand-off between a populist president and ardent opponents.

Democratization constituted an important shift in the political opportunity structure, but it was not a sufficient condition for change. This was precisely because the process of democratization interacted with the institutional structures of unequal social relations and weak states and, in particular, the weak agency of subordinate and middle-class groups relative to the influence of elites. The result was weak effective demand for change on the part of states. In addition, unequal structures tended to persist under democratic auspices.

BOX 5.3

Are there political and social reasons for the contrast between Latin America and East Asia?

East Asia is often characterized as a region of growth with equity *par excellence*. Reality is more complex, and some East Asian countries have experienced significant increases in inequality in the past two decades (Ahuja and others 1997). However, it is clear that a number of countries in the region—from Japan to (most recently) Vietnam—have experienced long phases of high growth with moderate levels of inequality. Moreover, this pattern has occurred in many countries when they had authoritarian governments.

Based on an extensive literature on the underpinnings of East Asian success, two strands are of particular relevance to the current discussion. First, successes almost always involve broad alliances between elites and subordinate groups, especially peasants during the early phases of transition. This pattern reflects many factors, including long traditions of smallholder agriculture; land reforms during periods of major political transition (that is, in China, Republic of Korea, and Taiwan, China); the need to deliver incomes and services to peasants in the face of external threats to national security (Korea and Taiwan, China); and threats of peasant-based revolutionary movements (Indonesia).

These alliances did not necessarily involve grassroots mobilization, but it was in the interests of elites to economically include poorer groups. In Malaysia, this action took the particular form of improving the position of the historically poorer ethnic group of *bumiputeras* (Malays), but was effected by a government that both directly depended on that group for its primary social and political base (under the rule of Mahathir) and also recognized the need to protect the property rights of other domestic and foreign investors. Unequal social relations therefore had less salience in East Asia.

Second, successful cases of simultaneous growth and equality evolved a form of economic management that combined a degree of bureaucratic autonomy with close linkages to major interest groups. Such "embedded autonomy" (Evans 1995) was a central element of the successful development of states that emerged in the region. This was by no means a clean affair, and often coexisted with cronyism and corruption. However, for major development choices—from export drives in Korea to dealing with macroeconomic crises in Indonesia prior to the deep economic and political crisis of 1998—embedded autonomy facilitated the pursuit of pro-development paths rather than protection of vested interests. States were effective in key areas of providing public goods and services.

The key contrast with Latin America should not be seen in terms of a spectrum of authoritarian and democratic systems, but in terms of how East Asia's political and social histories—which evolved under different external environments—underpinned more inclusive and effective institutional structures.

Sources: World Bank 1993, Teranishi 1997, Evans 1995, Heller 2001.

Clientelism can function under democracy, as well as under authoritarianism (see Shefter 1994 and Chubb 1983 for OECD countries and Hagopian 1996 for the persistence of clientelist politics in Brazil). Group-based social inequalities also show great persistence across formal regime changes. A comparison between Latin America and East Asia is useful. Although there has been plenty of cronyism and corruption in East Asia, other factors in the social and political structures of most countries in that region have led to the construction of states that have been both more effective and redistributive during both authoritarian and democratic periods.

5.2. The potential for equalizing political and social change

The first section of this chapter sought to explain how institutional forces cause inequalities to persist. With this in mind, how can societies break with the history of unequal social relations and weak states? Success will depend upon developing institutions that are resilient to the predations of the rich and powerful and can tackle vested interests. For most countries in the region, success also involves strengthening the implicit social contract that underpins an adequate tax effort with which to finance government spending.

The authors argue here that there is potential for change. Some features of the regional context are favorable. Although democratization alone has not so far led to a swift transformation of social relations and political structures, it remains an important *potential* catalyst for change in the opportunity structure. While the authors do not seek to address international influences in this chapter, it is worth noting that with the passing of the Cold War and the globalization of information flows, awareness of human rights, and connectivity of social movements, the pressure and potential for inclusive political and social change may be higher than it was in the past. (See Castells 1997 for a discussion of the relationships between identity formation, globalization, and information.)

In addressing these issues, the authors take the view that political agency matters. History and institutions are also important, but are not determinist sources of action. This is based on a reading of country and local experiences in Latin America that are discussed in the following sections. This position echoes debates on whether governments in OECD countries can affect conditions of inequality. Drawing on an analysis of experiences across the OECD and a structured comparison between Spain and the United Kingdom in the 1980s, recent work (Boix 1998) shows that the different preferences of political parties with respect to inequality were acted upon when governments were elected, especially in the domain of structural policies (see box 5.4).

Programmatic parties, conceived of as "organized coalitions of interests around ideas" (Boix 1998, p. 14) are less well-developed in Latin America, but the principle that coalitions of interests and ideas can lead to different policy choices that influence distribution is directly relevant. Under what conditions are there effective coalitions for change? How do these coalitions interact with the different initial institutional conditions that prevail across Latin America? Even though the region (with the exception of Cuba) has not seen major change in its distributional patterns based on fundamental political and social transformations, some experiences are already promising. The section below focuses on change both at the level of countries and at the sub-national level.

The potential for more effective and redistributive states at the national level

Patronage vs. programmatic parties in a democratizing context

Despite being an insufficient force to foster a more effective and redistributive state, democratization did help bring into the political arena generalized demands for state action in the social sphere throughout Latin America in the 1990s. These demands were undoubtedly heightened in the wake of the period of economic crisis and worsening income inequality during the 1980s. Most governments did respond to these problems in one way or another. Social spending grew significantly in most countries, with part of the growth (except for large increases in pension outlays) being progressive in impact because of the expansion of basic services such as education, health, water, and sanitation to parts of the population that had previously not been served (see chapter 9). However, there were large variations in the effectiveness of such actions in terms of outcomes, and an expansion in public spending as such did not reflect any change in the underlying political equilibria.

Both in Latin America and throughout the history of Europe and the United States, changes to political equilibria that underpin more effective and redistributive states have occurred both from within and outside of existing state

BOX 5.4

Political agency and the potential for redistributive strategy in rich countries: lessons from the OECD

A comparison of the different paths taken by governments in the OECD finds that institutional determinism does *not* hold true, at least in certain domains of public policy. Although both social democratic and conservative parties support growth, very different strategies have been pursued to this end. This is particularly the case with regard to distributional choices related to the trade-off between employment and equality on the one hand and efficiency on the other. During the 1970s and 1980s, social democratic governments chose strategies based on significantly higher public capital formation, human investment, and tax efforts, and maintained a larger public business role in the economy. In contrast, conservative governments chose lower investment in physical and human capital, lower taxes, and privatization.

The contrast in policies among types of governments can be clearly seen in a comparison between two programmatic parties in the 1980s: the British Conservatives under Margaret Thatcher and the Spanish Socialists under Felipe González. These parties were based initially on very different electoral coalitions. The British Conservatives appealed to the middle and upper classes and sought to expand their base in the former, for example through

housing policy and encouragement of broad-share ownership through privatization. That party successfully reduced the power of vested interests, notably in the union movement. In contrast, the base of the Spanish Socialists was initially among the working and lower-middle classes. Although there was some erosion of support from the former group due to its need to pursue a tight macroeconomic policy, this was compensated by a significant expansion of support due to policies that expanded social benefits.

The point of the comparison here is not to evaluate the impact of policy choices; this would require both a careful assessment of instrumental effects of policies and normative views on inequality and unemployment. It is, however, noteworthy that Britain experienced a very large increase in inequality in the 1980s, by the standards of rich countries. Spain experienced a small decline in its (already lower) level of inequality. Moreover, some observers argue that the substantial expansion in social welfare was a key complement to the extensive industrial restructuring associated with Spain's opening up and integration into Europe.

Source: Boix 1998.

structures. The key question is whether new or reformed parties or groups, when they attain power, adopt the potent tools of patronage in order to shore up support or pursue collective goals.[11] In the following discussion, different cases of transition within Latin America are considered, with boxes used to illustrate areas of policy action.

Chile is a good example of how the pre-existence of programmatic parties combined with relative bureaucratic autonomy to facilitate a transition toward political equilibrium with a more effective and redistributive state. Where these pre-conditions are weak, change has occurred either because of the internal mobilization of new parties or "outsider" movements. Brazil illustrates both in the form of the Cardoso and Lula administrations. Latin America also has a variant of the outsider movement, that is, of a populist leader who appeals strongly and directly to a (disaffected) populace, but is weakly embedded in organizational structures or local mobilization. This is itself a product of the weakness of party

traditions and fragmented societies, and is a case illustrated by Peru. The general weakness of programmatic parties in the region—a product of historical patterns of political evolution—makes the challenge of improving the state harder, and in turn makes the role of other actors in society (including business associations, unions, grassroots movements, and nongovernmental organizations) even more important.

Chile has been relatively successful in consolidating an effective and redistributive state, including a significant degree of redistribution of services; however, the country has not been able to reduce its high level of income inequality. Unusually for Latin America, Chile benefited from a long history of party formation along class-based rather than vertical corporatist lines, as well as a tradition of a relatively autonomous and competent public administration. The first democratic administration pursued a policy of "growth with equity."[12] This approach was implemented by balancing the fruits of market-oriented economic policies (introduced by

BOX 5.5
Increased equity through taxation and social spending in a democratic Chile

The Aylwin administration's (1990–1994) equity-enhancing policies included an increase in taxes to finance expanded social spending. The tax reform was moderately progressive (at least in intention), raising the share of government revenues generated through direct taxes from 18 percent to 24 percent and increasing the share of corporate and upper-income personal taxes within the direct tax category. Tax reform was accompanied by an arrangement to earmark a specific share of revenues for social spending.

Between 1990 and 1994, social spending increased by almost 50 percent. This had little impact on the high level of measured income inequality during the same period, which was largely driven by the effect of market forces on labor incomes. However, there were significant reductions in other dimensions of inequality, reflecting the redistributive character of social spending: if the imputed value of social benefits is included, the distribution of "income" improved significantly in the 1990s (see chapter 9 and Bravo,

Contreras, and Millan 2002). Many vulnerable segments of society, such as the elderly and the poorly educated, experienced large gains in well-being, and the benefits of economic growth were distributed more or less equally across regions.

The reform package, which was the first piece of major legislation by the *Concertación* coalition, was politically negotiated in order to assuage the conservative economic elites of the government commitment to fiscal responsibility and moderate economic policies without radical redistributive efforts. This negotiated settlement reflected not only the relative political strengths of the conservative elites and the Aylwin government (which lacked a majority in Congress), but also what the parties comprising *Concertación* had learned from experiences in the 1970s, when radicalism eventually culminated in a brutal coup and nearly two decades of authoritarianism under Pinochet.

Sources: Boyland 1996, Weyland 1997.

the former military government) with the objective of achieving social equity and justice by systematically strengthening social policies (see box 5.5).

As a result, key public goods were delivered, inflation was brought under control, and fiscal prudence was maintained. There were no major challenges to property rights, and a significant expansion of citizenship rights (relative to the authoritarian era) was complemented by a strong increase in broad-based, targeted services. With macroeconomic and social stability apparently assured, an investment boom occurred that in turn sustained rapid growth and poverty reduction. Democratic administrations also invested in modernizing the public administration, building on already solid (by regional standards) administrative capacities. Today, Chile is known for its effectiveness and the probity of its public administration, as well as for its achievements in the realm of economic and social policies.[13]

The Chilean mix of prudent macroeconomic policies with gradual social sector reform might appear to be a sensible yet predictable outcome of a good government. However, in so many other countries (including several in Latin America), similarly strong social desires for redistribution

have resulted in unsustainable economic populism. Why was Chile in the 1990s able to avoid a similar fate, and instead succeed in introducing a progressive policy reform agenda without jeopardizing business confidence and macroeconomic stability?

One plausible explanation is found in the encompassing nature of key political institutional actors and the relations among them. The institutional backbone of Chile's "growth with equity" approach was the broad center-left alliance of the *Concertación,* which comprised 17 political parties around the core of the Socialists and the Christian Democrats. Deprived of access to state patronage during the struggle against the military dictatorship in the 1980s, these parties evolved throughout the decade into moderate, pragmatic political entities with strong ties to social organizations (particularly labor unions) and a solid commitment to pluralist, representative social democracy.

As the negotiated democratic transition allowed conservative forces to retain significant institutional advantages, the *Concertación* deliberately chose a consultative form of governance—a so-called "politics of agreements"—whereby the government discussed every important piece of legislation not only with coalition partners, but also with opposition parties and social organizations.[14] Such negotiated settlements were possible because both the political parties and key societal organizations involved (in particular labor and business confederations) had broad, encompassing bases of representation and support.[15] In the face of strong demand for social equity and expectations for prudent economic management, actors managed to achieve sensible compromises on a broad national agenda instead of pursuing parochial, sectoral interests.[16]

If Chile has, by Latin American standards, formed a relatively effective (and redistributive) state, why does it remain one of the most unequal societies in the region in terms of income? (See chapter 2.) Three factors are relevant. First, Chile's historical formation (especially during the 19th and first half of the 20th century) has always involved a mixture of relatively high degrees of constitutional rule and of concentration of wealth, which is in part associated with the importance of mining in the economy. Second, most observers agree that there were significant increases in inequality in the 1970s (with the transition to the Pinochet regime) and the 1980s, which is evident both in the income data (see chapter 2 for a brief discussion and references) and also in the consolidation of the position of major conglomerates (Schamis 2002). Third, shifting income distributions is always a slower process than, for example, increasing access to services, due to the centrality of market forces in determining wage distributions.

As discussed in a recent World Bank report (de Ferranti and others 2003), international integration was a catalyst for skill-biased technical change in countries such as Chile, initially leading to a sharp increase in skill premiums and wage inequality. However, the large expansion in schooling (especially at the tertiary level) appeared by the end of the 1990s to be offsetting such powerful demand-side forces.

Like Chile, Brazil went through a negotiated transition from an authoritarian military government. Throughout the dictatorship and even during the democratic transition, the continued importance of unequal social relations, the lack of programmatic parties, and the strength of special interest groups characterized Brazil's political economy. Although Brazil did inherit a relatively effective state in terms of bureaucratic capacities in certain state functions, such as industrial promotion (Evans 1979, Schneider 1991), the effective provision of key public goods—notably macro stability, property rights, and citizenship—was not part of the legacy of the country's military rulers.

Brazil's political institutions have traditionally fostered political deadlock.[17] The institutional fragmentation of the Brazilian political system—in which a large number of interest groups and individual politicians, unconstrained by cohesive party discipline, engage in the exchange of short-term political favors—is not conducive to redistributive change. Instead, powerful and well-organized groups successfully lobby to press for or protect their own interests and privileges, which in turn largely reflect the underlying inequality of political power in Brazilian society. Such weak governance is clearly illustrated by the dynamics of the process of forming a constitution in the late 1980s, as well as by difficulties that the country has since faced in reforming its regressive social security system (see box 5.6).

Since the mid-1990s, the Cardoso and the Lula administrations have consistently pursued a policy mix of a strong commitment to macroeconomic stability, social development, and building state capacities for revenue collection and service delivery.[18] Actions by both governments have no doubt been constrained by the institutional fragmentation of the Brazilian political system.[19] Nonetheless, the achievements made and the consistency with which these governments have pursued more equitable policies are notable.[20]

Pro-equity policies have been pursued by these two reformist governments, each of which has different partisan origins. Cardoso's party, the PSDB, was created as an internally mobilized group by defectors of the PMDB—which was itself the outgrowth of the "opposition" party created by the military and traditional politicians during the authoritarian period—as an attempt to overcome the PMDB's clientelist orientation. Lula's PT, on the other hand, was an outsider movement during the authoritarian period (and thus lacked access to state patronage for mobilization) and developed as a genuine horizontal alliance between unions and other mainly lower-class groups, including poorer households dependent on the informal sector.[21]

Despite these differences, both parties found opportunities to govern the country in a gradually maturing democratic environment. These developments suggest that multiple possibilities for positive political agency exist even in a difficult governance environment, which may also indicate that Brazil is in a time of transition to a political equilibrium that is more favorable for the reduction of inequality.

Peru under Fujimori illustrates how an outsider leader can be effective in breaking through established institutional

BOX 5.6

Failed redistributive efforts in a fragmented democracy: social security reforms in Brazil

Following a democratic transition in 1985, Brazil spent nearly two years debating and drafting a new constitution. The National Constitutional Assembly (ANC) operated within a highly fragmented political system, in which loose coalitions of weakly organized parties and numerous special interest groups engaged in targeted political bargaining.[a] As a result, the 1988 Brazilian Constitution is an incoherent and complex document that simply pulls together a very broad range of special interests expressed through the ANC.[b] Although the Constitution includes a strong social component—including the universal nature of basic services such as education and health—it also cements a number of special privileges of powerful interest groups, such as granting public servants excessively generous and fiscally unsustainable pension benefits.[c]

The incoherence of the Brazilian Constitution has necessitated endless attempts by subsequent governments to amend the document in order to introduce major reforms, most notably (but not exclusively) reforms of the social security system. Already in the constitutional debate, proposals by technocrats in the Ministry of Social Security aimed at making the social security system distributionally fairer—for example calling for universal social security coverage, improvements in the pension benefits of poor rural workers, the diversification of social security taxes, and an age-based threshold for receipt of the time-of-service pension—were defeated by various interest groups. Business interests opposed the diversification of social security taxes, while urban unions and pensioners challenged the proposed restrictions on time-of-service benefits. Public sector unions achieved a major concession when

virtually all government employees—regardless of whether or not they had been recruited through a competitive qualification process or had ever made contributions to the pension system—would be "reclassified" as tenured civil servants eligible for generous pension benefits.

In the mid-1990s, the Cardoso administration attempted a major overhaul of the social security system. Although progress was made, some of the most far-reaching reform proposals, especially those affecting the entrenched interests of public sector unions, were defeated.[d] The recently elected Lula administration is now embarking on another major reform attempt to gradually bring the very generous public sector pension regime more in line with the private sector regime. Although the reform has not gained final approval, the government has already had to make several important concessions vis-à-vis its original proposal, again reflecting the power of corporate interests in the areas of public service, the military, and the judiciary.

a. The National Constitutional Assembly (ANC) was the same national congress that had been elected in 1985, and thus tended to reflect the parochial and short-term political interests of legislators, as well as their vulnerability to special interest group pressure.
b. By one count, at least 383 separate groups representing diverse occupational and functional interests pressed for inclusion of their agendas in the Constitution—vividly illustrating the collective action problem caused by the fragmented, vertical, corporatist structure of state-society relations in Brazil (Vianna 1998).
c. See Reich 1998 for an analysis of the constitution-making process.
d. This case is analyzed in detail in Melo 1998.
Sources: Weyland 1996b, Vianna 1998, Melo 1998.

structures in a time of crisis. A decade after the democratic transition occurred, Fujimori inherited almost the exact opposite attributes of an effective and redistributive state: hyperinflation; a violent conflict with the *Sendero Luminoso* (Shining Path) guerrilla movement; uncertain property rights; weakened citizenship rights; and a collapse of the state's capacity to raise revenues and deliver services, especially in poorer areas. In the early 1990s, Fujimori substantially improved the provision of public goods—especially with regard to macroeconomic and social stability—by

ending the conflict with *Sendero* and supporting a major expansion in basic services, in particular to poor, rural populations.

How was this done? Instead of reforming the state to upgrade its overall capacity (as both Chile and Brazil have attempted to do), "islands" of effective state action were created, notably in customs and taxes (in order to provide revenues to support spending), in macro-management, and in the concentration of a set of service delivery programs in the presidential administration. These actions involved

BOX 5.7
Neopopulism and policies on social funds in Peru

The case of Peru highlights both the possibility (at least in the short run) and the difficulty of sustaining equality-enhancing policies through outsider, "neopopulist" leaders.[a] Under President Fujimori, traditional sources of authority and intermediation between citizens and the state were weakened because he relied upon direct, personal appeals to poorer citizens. Traditional political parties all but disappeared, and government became much more centralized.

An important example is the centralization of FONCODES and other social programs under immediate control of the Presidency. This shift both enhanced service delivery and helped Fujimori garner electoral support outside party structures. One study finds that FONCODES expenditures increased significantly in the three months prior to national elections, and that projects were directed to provinces in which their political effect was likely to be largest. Between 1991 and 1993, FONCODES expenditures favored core supporters and marginal voters. After a disappointing result in a national referendum held in 1993, the Fujimori administration redirected resources in an attempt to buy back the vote in turncoat provinces. Since Fujimori targeted poorer constituents, FONCODES projects tended to favor the poorest provinces, with the result that the program had a redistributive function.

Although evaluations of the pro-poor impact of FONCODES on poverty have been positive, the program has often been criticized for its politicization and for a design that bypassed local governments. Consistent with Fujimori's other policy and political actions, FONCODES did little to contribute to the institutional development and empowerment of local governments.

a. See Roberts 1995 on the concept of neopopulism and its application to the Fujimori regime.
Sources: Schady 2000, World Bank 2001c.

breaking through existing clientelist institutional structures (for example, through closing parliament) or circumventing them (for example, by avoiding traditional bureaucratic channels). Political support was sustained by initially widespread approval for the improvements relative to the preceding crisis; the delivery of services to the poor, albeit in a form of a national clientelist project (see box 5.7); and, increasingly, connections with the rich. However, this situation had high costs in terms of undermining democratic institutions, including the capture of the judiciary and parts of the media.

In terms of political structure, the Fujimori experience has parallels with the model of the populist leader who reaches across institutional structures and promises redistribution, but who has the resolve and capacity to challenge vested interests and maintain macro-level stability, and uses authoritarian methods when needed. At the beginning of Fujimori's rule, the depth of the economic crisis and a discredited political elite facilitated change.

However, the charismatic outsider leader model is inherently risky, and ultimately unsustainable because of the lack of an institutional base of representation to link the governing elites to the poor. In the case of Peru, costs were massively higher than could have been imagined. The lack of institutional constraints on the authoritarian and personalized presidential behavior—exacerbated by the well-documented abuse of power by Montesinos, Fujimori's close associate—led to a steady and systematic undermining of the rule of law with respect to property rights and citizenship, and the eventual loss of legitimacy and collapse of the regime.[22] There have been important gains in the subsequent transition to democracy, but the road from unequal social relations and a weak state is long, and one that is made more difficult with a socially fractured population, high expectations, and the absence of programmatic parties.

Other problematic or incomplete transitions
Other countries in Latin America have had failed or problematic transitions to democracy (albeit with less dramatic forward and backward shifts than in Peru). Guatemala, a classic case of unequal social relations and a weak state, signed Peace Accords in 1996 and achieved some gains in taxes and

service provision from a very low base level, including some symbolic provisioning of bilingual education. However, at the national level there were few signs of major transition from a polity captured by old elites and new drug- and crime-related interests. Also symbolic was the proposal for a multicultural constitution (now increasingly common in the region), which was rejected in a referendum. As discussed in box 5.2, the Dominican Republic, despite a relatively good growth performance, also remains mired in a low-level equilibrium with high levels of patronage and a weak tax effort.

Bolivia is a more complex case. Starting from a situation of deeply clientelist structures and a weak state, the country pursued a number of measures to strengthen governance and accountability. It restored macroeconomic stability in the mid 1980s, and sought wide-ranging reforms in public administration, but it is not clear if these significantly transformed clientelist relations. Finally, Bolivia took innovative measures to support democratic decentralization (see below), which were intended to increase the influence of poorer, including indigenous, groups.

At the same time, Bolivia has been swept by waves of anger that coalesced in the formation of groups in a largely indigenous-based protest movement, which forced the resignation of President Sánchez de Lozada in late 2003, reminiscent of the earlier ouster of President Mauhad in Ecuador. (However, Ecuador had registered a less clear commitment to policy and structural reforms than had Bolivia.) In both cases, the protest movement fits the mold of a classic outsider movement of poor, indigenous groups allied with vested interests, such as teachers unions. The movement's strength flowed from a combination of severe adverse shocks to the economy (including the emblematic destruction of coca production in Bolivia) and a long history of social and political exclusion and disillusionment with the political class and capacity of government.

Transition at the sectoral level

Even when the realm of national-level politics remains inhospitable to equity-enhancing change, transition away from clientelistic modes of governance has been possible at the sectoral level in a number of countries. Well-known examples in the region include EDUCO, an effective community-based school program in El Salvador, and the Family Health Program in the State of Ceará, Brazil (for details, see Tendler 1997). Political dynamics of transition at the sectoral level is well illustrated by the case of Mexico's targeted anti-

poverty programs *Programa Nacional de Solidaridad* (National Solidarity Program, or PRONASOL), a strongly clientelistic policy instrument,[23] and its successor PROGRESA (currently called *Oportunidades,* or "Opportunities"), better conceived technically as a policy lever for long-term poverty reduction (see box 5.8 and chapter 9).

The role of democratic decentralization

Can political and administrative decentralization lead to local political and social transformations? (See de Ferranti and others 2000 for a general discussion.) The process of decentralization has in its very nature bred a large variety of experiences, since new opportunities for greater political autonomy have interacted in diverse local political, social, and economic contexts. Absent proactive national compensatory policies, decentralization would generally increase inter-jurisdictional inequalities, for example through the greater capacity of richer jurisdictions to raise taxes that could then be applied to the provision of better economic and social services.

In some cases, local democratization, symbolized by the election of mayors, has actually changed the opportunity structure for local action for aspiring leaders and local movements. This has been referred to as a "silent revolution" (Campbell 2003). Yet outcomes are contingent upon precisely the types of issues raised in the preceding discussion of national conditions and transitions. How embedded are unequal social relations and how strong or weak is the local state, in the sense of its capacity to provide (local) public goods and services? Decentralization will be disequalizing if it strengthens the hands of local elites, but equalizing if it is associated with local democratic processes that favor poorer groups and lead to more effective state action.[24]

That good local governance can make a positive difference to state performance is illustrated by the cases of Porto Alegre (Brazil) and Bogotá (Colombia), where major changes in patterns of action on the part of governments and citizen groups have fostered cultures of citizenship, which have in turn led to a successful break with the social and cultural bases of inequality that have defied national-level public intervention. Clearly, local contexts matter with regard to the distributive outcomes of decentralization, as illustrated by the Bolivian experience with decentralization, in which outcomes of the explicitly pro-community decentralization process have depended on the political and social contours of newly created municipalities.

A job wel

BOX 5.8

Transition at the sectoral level? Mexico's targeted antipoverty programs

Although much of the funding for *Programa Nacional de Solidaridad* (National Solidarity Program, or PRONASOL) was apparently directed toward the poor,[a] several studies have found that political variables heavily influenced the allocation of the program's resources.[b] Aside from its politicized management, PRONASOL's programmatic focus on infrastructure investments—the largest area of funding was basic services, such as water, sewage treatment, and electricity—was visible and effective for the purpose of generating electoral support. PRONASOL was effectively replaced by PROGRESA (currently called *Oportunidades,* or "Opportunities"), which focused primarily on investment in human development within more technocratic decision-making processes.[c] Impact evaluations of PROGRESA have been more favorable than evaluations of PRONASOL.[d] An analysis of the political determinants of PROGRESA allocations found that although electoral considerations appear to be somewhat related to funding patterns, poverty level has by far been the best predictor of PROGRESA expenditures (Menocal 2001).

What accounts for this episode of depoliticization of antipoverty programs in Mexico? The shift coincided with the democratization, or at least pluralization, of Mexican politics. The change in this program can be seen in the context of President Zedillo's response to the economic crisis of the period and general dissatisfaction with the politics surrounding spending by PRONASOL, which was a flagship program under his predecessor President Salinas. With each report of corruption of social funds under Salinas, pressure on Zedillo to act in an "above-board" manner increased.[e] His response took various forms, including a politically driven process of decentralization. The case of PROGRESA is one of a redesigned *centrally* managed program, shaped to both have a tighter link to the extreme

poor and to be less vulnerable to use as an instrument of patronage. PROGRESA illustrates that even in a clientelist political environment, technical design of a policy can make a difference in terms of both development impacts and the scope for political manipulation.

a. With regard to health care, government programs benefited more than 4 million people in 1985. An additional 3.4 million people were aided by PRONASOL's hospitals in areas with large indigenous populations, and 1.6 million families benefited from new clinics. With regard to education, PRONASOL's *Escuela Digna* program benefited 4 million students. In 1989–1990, 5 million people benefited from a drinkable water and sewage program, and another five million benefited from rural electrification projects. By 1992, PRONASOL spending as a share of overall public spending on social sectors had reached 12.34 percent (Lustig 1994).

b. One study (Molinar Horcasitas and Weldon 1994) found that the federal government spent more in areas where concurrent local and federal elections were scheduled and that PRONASOL funds were targeted not to states in which the PRI traditionally dominated, but to marginal states that were not necessarily the poorest in Mexico but where the opposition party *Partido Revolucionario Democrática* (the Democratic Revolutionary Party, or PRD) was strong. Another study (Diaz-Cayeros, Magaloni, and Weingast 2002) found that the PRI targeted electorally marginal municipalities and withheld funds from PRD-dominated municipalities, but spent little on municipalities where it had a big margin of victory. Where the PRI won by a small margin, it spent the most.

c. At the end of 1999, PROGRESA covered approximately 2.6 million families, or about 40 percent of all rural families and one-ninth of all families in Mexico. At that time, the program operated in almost 50,000 localities in more than 2,000 municipalities and 31 states.

d. The International Food Policy Research Institute (IFPRI) concluded that PROGRESA had significantly increased enrollment of boys and girls in secondary school, reduced illness among beneficiaries by 12 percent for children and 19 percent (in terms of job-related sick days) for adults, reduced stunting caused by nutritional deficiencies, and increased calorie consumption and dietary diversity. For a summary of IFPRI results, see http://poverty.worldbank.org/library/view/5561.

e. By decentralizing expenditures, primarily to PRI governors, and then letting those politicians decide who got what, Zedillo may in effect have been allowing for the political use of these funds but at the same time keeping himself at arms length from criticism.

Two cases of a shift to more effective and redistributive local states

Deep democratic decentralization One of the best-documented cases of local-level transition from clientelism is that of Porto Alegre. This process was facilitated by the introduction of local elections and then by the election of the *Partido dos Trabalhadores* (Workers Party, or the PT). Subsequent

dynamic interactions between local groups, party, and government—through which the PT has repeatedly been reelected—have allowed the government to learn from its experience and democratization to take root (see box 5.9).

When opportunity was created by national political and governmental decentralization, local capacities were propitious because of the presence of an externally mobilized party and

BOX 5.9

Popular budgeting in Porto Alegre: explaining a transition to a new political equilibrium

Municipal budgets have long been the domain of rent-seeking elites in Brazil. Politicians, bureaucrats, business interests, and local powerbrokers have typically colluded in controlling the allocation of city resources. The participatory budgeting (PB) system represents an important change in the traditional configuration of power interests, since as a bottom-up process it has significantly shifted decision-making powers from traditional elites to ordinary citizens. The role of the PT—an ideologically cohesive and programmatically left-of-center party—as the catalyst of change has been critical, since it created the "opening from above" and provided the ongoing support that has made PB possible.

In contrast to the more hierarchical, rigid, and organizationally insulated character of most Latin American socialist parties, the PT is deeply embedded both organizationally and ideologically in civil society. From the time of its establishment in 1980, the PT has been a social movement party, having been formed as an alliance of progressive elements within the church, unions, peasant associations, human rights groups and an array of revolutionary organizations. Created as an instrument of struggle against an authoritarian regime and associated corporatist structures, during its first decade of existence the PT, in the words of Rebecca Abers, "constantly sought to maintain ties to a multitude of grassroots social movements and developed highly decentralized internal structures."[a]

The close and dynamic relationship between the PT as a formal organization and its social movement partners has created a number of synergies. Most obviously, the PT has provided a critical brokerage function by creating the formal spaces and political opportunities in which a range of social movements and civic organizations have been able to articulate their demands, exchange ideas, and propose reforms. However, if the political opening and the opportunity structure for PB was created from above, it is civil society that provided the critical informational resources for the PB and fostered its mobilization. In opting for the introduction of PB, the PT piggybacked on demands first presented to an earlier administration by the Union of Neighborhood Associations of Porto Alegre (UAMPA), which had called for popular, community-based "control of the definition of the city budget." A wide range of civic organizations (including neighborhood and church-based groups, women's organizations, nongovernmental organizations, and unions) then provided the mobilizing networks, innovative ideas, and participatory practices that came to define the PB. With every year, neighborhood delegates to the budget council became increasingly better at linking local demands to city-wide needs and objectives (Abers 1996, 2000b, Biaocchi, 2001).

a. Abers 1996, p.37.

the local traditions of associational activity. It was, however, the development of the institution of participatory budgeting (PB) that facilitated the split from clientelist structures. The design of the PB process—by which delegates are allocated to the budget council in proportion to the level of participation by associations in open forums—has stimulated associational activity. PB has also had the effect of promoting horizontal coalition building; this contrasts with the past when neighborhoods processed demands vertically through political patrons, with the effect of severely compromising their associational autonomy and weakening civil society.

State action in Porto Alegre has been successful in key public arenas, especially in service provision, a trend that has both improved conditions across the city and had a strong

redistributive element. A rising tax effort is evidence of a broader willingness to support the project, as has been the reelection of the PT. Although Porto Alegre is a good illustration of a shift to a new political equilibrium, caution should be exercised in drawing specific institutional lessons, especially on the process of PB. By Brazilian and regional standards, the city enjoys a high degree of social inclusion. PB has been exercised in a little more than 100 municipalities in Brazil (out of a total of more than 5,500). Assessing the actual determinants and impact of PB will require examining some of the 100 or so other cases of the process in Brazil.

Entry of outsider political entrepreneurs and mobilization of middle-income group support Bogotá provides a second case of a dramatic shift in the performance of local government in a large city. Bogotá's political transformation has unfolded against the backdrop of a national political scene characterized by power-alternating and power-sharing agreements between the two established political parties, based on the post-*violencia* accord among the elites. This context helped embed, at both the national and local levels, a particularly well-entrenched form of clientelism, through which the tradition of exchanging favors for political support persisted in a wide range of areas (for example, jobs and local public works). This pattern has often been stronger in poor areas in both urban and rural settings.

As in Brazil, opportunity has been created in Bogotá by the advent of mayoral elections and electoral competition. However, in this case the transforming event appears to have been electoral victories by outsider political entrepreneurs who were not part of the patronage-based party systems, rather than (as in Porto Alegre) a programmatic political party with a strong grassroots base. These entrepreneurs have chosen to pursue changes in governmental practice and state-society interactions that shifted the domain of political competition from the capacity to deliver patronage to the capacity to deliver public goods (that is, a cleaner city, reduced violence) and broad-based services, notably in education and transport. Such competition was reflected in the alternation between two mayors, Mockus and Peñalosa. Mockus, in particular, placed great emphasis on building new coalitions with a range of social groups and on changes in the culture of citizenship.

The effects of these institutional changes are evident in large improvements in city performance, both in terms of the level of provisioning of services and (although more anecdotally) in the quality of service delivery. The modernization of Bogotá's public transport system resulted in a dramatic decrease in accident deaths from around 1,300 per year in the early 1990s to less than 800 by 2001. Government efforts to improve public safety resulted in the reduction of homicides per 1,000 inhabitants from 80 in 1993 to 31 in 2001. Net enrollment in primary and the secondary schools improved from 85 percent in 1993 to 91 percent in 2001, with the secondary level showing the most dramatic increase.

Similarly positive tendencies were registered with regard to other indicators of social service delivery, such as public health, water, and sanitation provision. Trends are also, again emblematically, reflected in a rise in tax effort—tax burden per resident increased from 39,000 pesos in 1988 to 86,000 pesos in 1999—while at the same time the city government implemented a series of administrative modernization measures and kept its operational expenses (such as personnel costs) more or less constant, thus allowing increased revenues to finance the expansion of public services (Maldonado 2003).

The experience of Bogotá shows how change is possible when electoral competition attracts talented outsiders to the political arena, who can then use their position to effect changes in political cultures and state effectiveness. Why did this occur in Bogotá and not in some other cities? The authors do not have a complete answer to this question, but suggest that it is driven by an interaction between the degree to which clientelist structures are entrenched with the capacity of individuals and groups to make use of new alliances to effect change. Both international and Latin American experience suggests that institutionalizing such changes will be of great importance, in terms of both building constituencies for autonomous bureaucracies and societal demands for performance in the provision of collective goods.[25]

How local institutional context affects the potential for shifts

Throughout this chapter, the authors have emphasized the importance of the institutional context within which a particular political equilibrium of unequal social relations and effective state may evolve into different patterns of governance. The critical role of local context is visible in quasi-experimental settings of nationwide decentralization processes, whereby political opportunity structures open up more or less equally across a given country, and yet each local jurisdiction develops its own path of institutional evolution. A crucial question is how local political agency can capitalize on the new opening in the local political arena. As the cases of Porto Alegre and Bogotá demonstrate, the strength of local associational activities and the quality of competitive elections are important elements of these local contexts.[26] When these factors interact positively with each other, political incentives and capacities for building an effective, redistributive local government are enhanced. When one or both of these factors is missing, the potential of democratic decentralization is likely to be underexploited.

One of the most radical cases of decentralization in the 1990s is Bolivia's *Participación Popular* (popular participation), which aimed to strengthen citizens' ability to oversee the actions of municipal governments and hold them accountable. This process introduced institutional mechanisms of social control, including vigilance committees and territorial base organizations (known as OTBs) that were charged with overseeing municipal government performance and the "constructive vote of censure," a formal procedure to remove mayors on account of poor performance. Decentralization in Bolivia brought about significant shifts in the allocations of public investments from a range of sectors—including transport, hydrocarbons, energy, education, urban development, and water and sanitation—and the apparent equalization of their geographic distribution. (For a more detailed analysis see Faguet 2000.) This evidence indicates that decentralization in the aggregate has brought about positive distributive consequences by allowing local demands to drive public resource allocations.

However, a closer look at Bolivia's experience, at least in the initial phase of popular participation, shows varying experiences across municipalities in terms of improvements in local governance. Oversight and participatory instruments—in the form of vigilance committees, the OTBs, and the constructive vote of censure—sometimes became attractive targets for political parties and interest groups, thereby weakening accountability and transparency. In those localities where traditional parties remained strong (and civic associational activities weak), vigilance committees tended to function less

effectively. This may be because the committees were co-opted by the traditional elites or because both municipal governments and the committees became arenas for open conflict. Instead of being used as an ultimate means of holding mayors electorally accountable for their performance, the constructive vote of censure was often abused as a tool of partisan conflict. In a sample of 38 of the 311 municipalities surveyed in a recent World Bank study (World Bank 2000c), 92 mayors came and went between 1996 and 2000, or 2.4 mayors per municipality in less than four years. It is hard to imagine that effective governance could emerge in such a context.

The influence of varying local institutional context in the same country is also illustrated by a comparison of medium-size cities in Colombia that underwent the same nationwide process of political decentralization (see box 5.10).

These city-by-city cases illustrate the potential for beneficial cycles of change that bring about complementary or joint shifts in different areas of local governance, citizenship, and public services. Pro-poor, participatory development patterns have in some cases gone hand-in-hand with pro-business and local economic development initiatives, better local education services, reduced corruption, resource mobilization, and changes in the work culture of public sector labor. Dynamic mayors have also been important in creating positive change, but they work within a system and the incentive to be a mayor depends on the context. Holding

---

BOX 5.10

Local contexts and the transition from clientelism: Ibagué versus Pasto

Colombia went through a major political and functional decentralization, but effects varied across municipalities depending on initial conditions. A clientelist political culture developed into an institutionalized art form in Ibagué, which was essentially run as a well-controlled political machine. In Pasto, one study on the 1970s asserts that "the totality of the municipal budget is devoured by the parasitic bureaucracy created by the clientelist machinery."[a]

The key facilitating changes in the political environment at the city level, which altered the opportunity structure, included the introduction of democratic mayoral elections in 1988 and the subsequent radical decentralization of responsibilities and resources in 1991. However, the results of these events varied sharply, with the biggest difference seen between Ibagué and Pasto. Ibagué remained politically

mired in old structures—at least until the election of a businesswoman in the late 1990s—and appears to have made limited progress in tackling corruption and improving services. In Pasto, in contrast, an apparently transformative change took place under the mayoral leadership of Antonio Navarro (one of the ex-leaders of the recently legalized M-19 movement), who brought about radical changes in city governance, promoted openness and transparency, and reduced corruption. This shift also led to new alliances, especially with local business associations and citizen groups.

a. Velásquez, 1982, as quoted in Angell, Lowden and Thorp (2001) p. 51.
Source: Angell, Lowden, and Thorp 2001.

that office is more attractive for talented and ambitious individuals in Colombia than, for example, in Chile, where political decentralization has advanced much more slowly. However, when basic political and social institutional structures are achieved in the "right" way or radically improved, there is potential for shifting to better and more equal institutions, with subsequent gains in multiple areas.

5.3. Conclusions

History has bequeathed Latin America with unequal social relations and weak states, in degrees that vary across the region. Clientelist and patronage-driven relationships, backed by varied political and social cultures across groups, tend to perpetuate inequalities. Weak states—in the sense of low capacities to deliver the public goods of macroeconomic stability, ensure property and citizenship rights, and deliver basic services—are pernicious contexts for inequality, as they are particularly vulnerable to the predations of the rich and organized middle-income groups (such as public sector unions).

Nonetheless, both international and Latin American experiences illustrate the potential for change. This is most likely to occur when there are shifts in the opportunity structure (including via electoral competition) and strengthening of the capacities of poorer groups to articulate their interests and organize, often in alliance with middle-income groups and progressive elites. These processes may take various forms. In the long run, the (much maligned) political parties have a crucial role to play, provided they are formed along programmatic or policy lines, rather than the more common tradition of vertical, patronage-oriented parties.

Where programmatic parties are absent, change is often effected by political outsiders in the form of political entrepreneurs or movements. This can be an important catalyst for breaks with history. However, such outsider-driven changes are only likely to be sustainable if they become embedded in formal institutions, especially those that create the capacity of lower and middle groups to articulate their goals and interests and organize for an effective and redistributive state. There have been cases of significant shifts in government action within a few years, primarily at the local level (as noted in the cases of Bogotá and Porto Alegre). However, more often a shift to a new political equilibrium involves a series of advances and difficulties, as appears to have occurred in Bolivia, or a series of steps that come to be seen as a strategic transition, as may be occurring in Brazil.

Important complements, but not substitutes, for changes from within or outside the system include measures to increase transparency and public debate, to strengthen public administrative capacities, to sustain societal pressure, and to increase the capacity for effective government. These measures could take the form of a variety of transparency initiatives that are already underway in various parts of the world, such as citizens' scorecards to independently assess the performance of government agencies in serving citizens (for example, in Bangalore, India, and the Philippines); efforts, promoted by both governments themselves and some nongovernmental organizations, to improve transparency in public budgets (such as Argentina's "*Lupa Fiscal*"); and the careful use of information technology to modernize information management systems (for example, Brazil's SIAFI, which the media uses to report on the federal government's budget management).

Various countries in the region, such as Bolivia, Brazil, and Peru, have begun to institutionalize various forms of public consultations and participatory governance for government planning purposes. Although not all of these initiatives may be resounding successes, since their impact inevitably depends on local conditions, they represent a promising approach to enhancing citizen voice and accountability. Traditional measures to strengthen state bureaucracies, such as modernization of administrative procedures, training of personnel, and organizational restructuring, will continue to be necessary. However, the implementation record in this area is mixed at best, and supply-side interventions to strengthen administrative capacities are unlikely to be effective unless they are appropriately tailored to local conditions and backed by clear political demands emerging from a well-functioning political accountability arrangement (Burki and Perry 1998, World Bank 2000e, World Bank 2003a).

In closing, the question of whether history is fate can be revisited. This report places considerable emphasis on the centrality of history in explaining current conditions. Institutions—in the sense of the formal and informal "rules of the game" of social interaction—can be seen as the crystallization of historically-formed interactions between power and wealth. However, as the case discussions above show, the interpretation of how change takes place is *not* institutionally deterministic. Rather, the authors see institutional change as occurring in response to the political and social agency of different groups, as well as to external forces that include economic factors.

How this change takes place will be a function of the dynamic evolution of the capacities of different groups to make effective demands on the state, and of the pattern of political opportunities, of which the capacity of the state to respond is a key element. The bottom line is: change is possible, even though it does not come about easily or frequently. Under certain conditions under which opportunities arise, it is the voluntary actions of political and social actors operating within specific institutional constraints that determine the courses of change.

Notes

1. See Paige (1997) and Mahoney (2001) on the Central American countries, Hartlyn (1998) on the Dominican Republic, and Abente (1995) on Paraguay.

2. For analyses of these dynamics, see Malloy and Gamarra (1988) on Bolivia, Cotler (1978) on Peru, and Martz (1983) and Quintero (1980) on Ecuador.

3. See Archer (1990) on Colombia and Levine (1973), Coppedge (1994), Karl (1995), and Rey (1990) on República Bolivariana de Venezuela.

4. See Valenzuela (1977) and Garretón (1989) on Chile and González (1991) on Uruguay.

5. Originally understood as relationships between "patrons" (for example, landlords and local strongmen) and their "clients" (for example, peasants) in traditional agrarian societies, clientelism has shown remarkable resilience and "survived" industrialization and urbanization (see Powell 1970).

6. Recent empirical work that tries to model the effects of clientelism on policy outcomes under different assumptions all point to the same conclusion: clientelism results in less than optimal levels of public goods production. Although not all public goods would directly impact inequality reduction positively, it is safe to assume that inequality is unlikely to decline in the *absence* of more public goods production. Representative work includes Keefer (2002) and Robinson and Verdier (2002), as summarized by Ames 2003.

7. By contrast, *societal* corporatist arrangements that emerged in several West European countries in the post World War II period served as mechanisms for building national-level class compromises. For representative work in this area, see Schmitter and Streeck (1985) and Katzenstein (1984) and (1985).

8. This does not mean Latin American states were weak in all dimensions. Indeed, there were many instances of strong and effective action harnessed by elites to perpetuate their positions, at times through the use of violence.

9. While racial attitudes are the most powerful predictors of social spending, other categorical inequalities play a role as well. Historically, ethnicity has divided the U.S. working class and hampered class-based demand formation, as immigration introduced ethnic divides in the working class. Workers in the United States have not developed class solidarity to the degree that they have in Europe, U.S. workers have frequently identified according to ethnicity rather than class. In the early part of the 20th century, for example, newer immigrant groups (mainly of Catholic background) were not viewed as potential class partners by the "older" Protestant working class. Indeed, many of these newer Italian and Irish immigrants pressed their demands through clientelistic ties to local level political machines in many urban centers. These clientelistic networks impeded broader class ties and the subsequent articulation of class-based demands.

10. See Fernando Henrique Cardoso's classic study on "associated-dependent development" (Cardoso 1973) for an argument linking the specific industrialization strategy pursued by Brazil in the mid 20th century, the country's political development, and inequality.

11. Externally mobilized parties, typified by European labor or socialist parties, characteristically sustained the strong programmatic traditions that evolved in their formation once they were in office, whether at local or national levels. For internally mobilized parties or political groupings, behavior depended on history and context and, in particular, on whether a tradition of bureaucratic autonomy and independence had *already* been established prior to the process of party formation. If such a tradition existed, the ruling party's capacity to deploy the tools of patronage were sharply diminished and the incentive to sustain support through a programmatic orientation grew correspondingly stronger. Where bureaucratic autonomy was weak, patronage tended to persist, if with new masters (Shefter 1994).

12. This policy was based on three pillars: (1) change in governance style to ensure inclusive, participatory processes appropriate to a renewed democracy; (2) maintenance of economic stability and growth; and (3) commitment to social justice.

13. Chile constantly ranks high among developing countries in various indicators of good governance and state capacity, such as Transparency International's corruption index. See Marcel (1999) for a detailed account of Chile's public sector modernization efforts during the 1990s.

14. For example, the 1990 labor reform was based on a "national agreement" between the government, the *Central Unitaria de Trabajadores* (Central Workers Union), and the *Confederación de la Producción y el Comercio* (Confederation of Production and Trade) and

resulted in a 22 percent increase in the real minimum wage between 1990 and 1992. See Foxley and Sapelli (1999).

15. The adoption of negotiated approaches was also facilitated by the fact that the conservative elites had to some extent been discredited by their association with the Pinochet regime.

16. Equally important was the improved quality of the state in terms of both policymaking and administration. A series of policy and institutional changes implemented during and since the dictatorship had reduced or even eliminated the scope for patronage politics (for example, the uniform tariff that limits the scope of private sector lobbying; privatization of the social security system that limits politicians' incentives to increase pension benefits by increasing public spending; the independence of the central bank that prohibits it from financing fiscal deficits; and the strict, executive-centered budget process that limits the scope of congressional logrolling and financing of pork barrel projects by inflating the budget). For more details, see Foxley and Sapelli (1999).

17. There is a growing literature on the institutional roots of Brazil's governability problems. Some representative work is found in Ames (2001), Mainwaring (2000), and Stepan (2000).

18. The Cardoso administration launched deep reforms of the public administration that involved constitutional changes (Bresser Pereira 1998). Although some achievements were registered, the outcomes fell short of the fundamental objectives of the reform due to resistance from the public sector unions, sometimes supported by the Judiciary (Rinne 1999 and Melo 1998). During the two Cardoso administrations, the federal government's capacity for revenue collection was enhanced significantly. The Lula administration is now trying to bring to the national level the principles of transparency and participation that served PT administrations well in various municipalities. In the social arena, the Cardoso administration introduced several policy innovations. These include FUNDEF, a formula-based distribution of a portion of the education budget to either states or municipalities based on the number of primary-level students enrolled in schools in their jurisdiction that has had a positive incentive effect on coverage expansion, and *Bolsa Escola* and other conditional cash transfer programs that have recently been combined into the larger *Bolsa Família* program, the Family Health program pioneered in the State of Ceará that uses family health agents to promote preventive health at the community level. The Lula administration has placed a new focus on social efforts, such as the flagship Zero Hunger and Youth Employment programs, and is also attempting to scale up some successful innovations like conditional cash transfer programs.

19. For example, both the Cardoso and Lula administrations have had to share cabinet posts with coalition partners that are neither programmatic nor grassroots based, and to negotiate with governors. This ensures engagement in the traditional forms of political exchanges of votes in congress, with the subsequent release of public expenditures and other aspects.

20. The Cardoso administration was more successful in these areas of positive action that did not threaten the deep vested interests in Brazilian society, compared to major structural reforms that implied some kind of redistribution. While it is too early to assess the Lula administration's performance, that government has shown willingness not only to build on the successful achievements of the previous government, but also to tackle some of the entrenched privileges through structural reforms, most notably the reform of the public sector pension regime.

21. For the PT, the union movement was central, but it was not structurally incorporated into the state in the way the main Mexican union confederation was (see Heller and Mahoney 2003).

22. Property rights were threatened, for example through targeted tax raids on political opponents, while citizenship rights were undermined through excess military and police actions in the name of counter terrorism. This latter factor resulted in many accusations of human rights abuses as well as the manipulation and extortion of the regime's opponents by Montesinos.

23. PRONASOL was inspired and created directly by President Carlos Salinas de Gortari (1988–94), who concluded in his own doctoral thesis that federal spending in rural communities did not produce sufficient popular support for the regime and that the poor relationships between government agencies and beneficiaries were to blame (Salinas 1978).

24. Between and within jurisdictional effects can interact in a way that adversely affects inequality, particularly if poorer jurisdictions are systematically more unequal and weak in institutional terms.

25. In this context, it is too soon to interpret the implications of the recent election of a left-leaning candidate in Bogotá. It is hopefully a sign not of a rejection of the institutional shifts facilitated by previous mayors, but rather of a shift toward a more mature pattern of electoral competition across programmatic lines that is sustained by both social demands and new bureaucratic traditions.

26. Even in a nondecentralizing, patronage-laden context, such as Mexico under Salinas, electoral competitiveness at the local level appears to have significant impact on government performance. Thus, there is evidence that even PRONASOL, the centrally controlled antipoverty program with a well-documented politicized management, produced better outcomes in those municipalities characterized by a competitive electoral environment (Hiskey 1999).

CHAPTER 6

Economic Mechanisms for the Persistence of High Inequality in Latin America

THIS CHAPTER TURNS TO ECONOMIC MECHANISMS AND THE DISTRIBUTION OF HOUSEHOLD PER capita income. This focus complements the discussion of political and social mechanisms that were reviewed in chapter 5; in a sense, the current chapter constitutes a different prism through which the same, interrelated, set of phenomena can be viewed. Despite the various conceptual and data quality caveats highlighted in chapters 1 and 2, it remains the case that household per capita income is probably the variable most commonly used to construct a distribution, against which inequality is then measured. In addition, as indicated in chapter 1, income helps shape personal freedoms and affects political power and patterns of participation, thus feeding back into the broader set of attributes with which this book is concerned.

Household income distributions are not simple constructs, however. They are the result of a complex process, in which initial opportunities available to individuals interact with their educational, professional, and personal choices. Both opportunities and choices are in turn shaped by the institutional environment in which people live, including such aspects as family values; the quality of schools; labor market institutions (for example, hiring and firing rules, the size of the informal sector, the size and role of unions, and the prevalence of minimum wages); and the nature of state taxes and transfers. For given individual trajectories, the household income distribution also depends on the pattern of household formation, from the choice of partner to reproductive decisions.

Even though it is essential to acknowledge the complexity of the processes that lie behind an income distribution, progress in understanding these processes can only be made by tackling such complexity analytically. This chapter takes the view that income distributions are determined by the following logical sequence. The first aspect considered is patterns of individual asset accumulation, which determine the distributions of the assets that people later use to generate income. The second concern is how, given these assets, people choose where to work, that is, which sectors of employment, jobs, and types of contracts are chosen. Third, the chapter looks at how remuneration rates in these jobs are determined. Fourth, how individual earnings combine into household incomes is examined from the perspective of household formation. The fifth issue considered is nonlabor income, with particular emphasis on the state taxes and transfers that lead from the primary to the secondary income distribution. Box 6.1 lays out this logical sequence schematically. It can be seen as a slightly more detailed version of the link between the "assets and opportunities" and "outcomes and incomes" presented in figure 1.1 in chapter 1.

This representation can be thought of as a sequence of functionals of distributions, as follows. Think of I (Z, w) as the joint distribution, over the population, of all relevant innate characteristics (Z) and inherited family wealth (w). Then let X denote the set of acquired human capital characteristics, such as health status and educational attainment. P (X, Z, w) may then represent the joint distribution of family wealth and both innate and acquired human capital characteristics throughout the population. The process

---

BOX 6.1

Schematic representation of household income determination

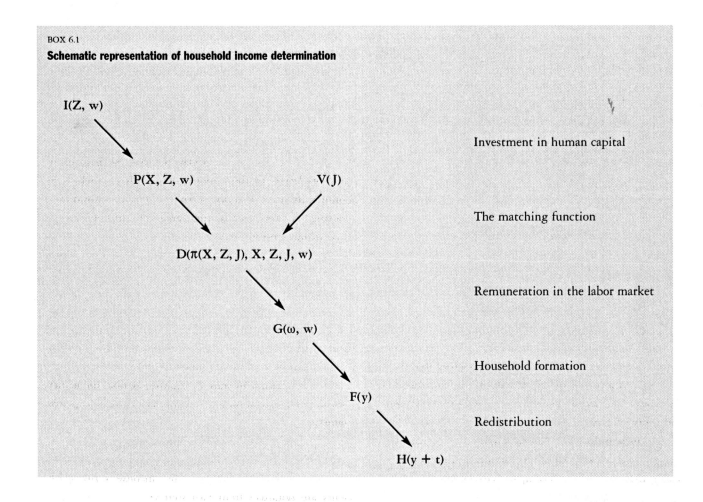

I(Z, w)

Investment in human capital

P(X, Z, w)   V(J)

The matching function

D(π(X, Z, J), X, Z, J, w)

Remuneration in the labor market

G(ω, w)

Household formation

F(y)

Redistribution

H(y + t)

---

through which P is generated from I is enormously complex in practice, but can be thought of as a human capital formation functional. In reasonably abstract terms, this depends on Z and w and is mediated by a number of family and educational institutions.

Once we have a distribution P of the relevant characteristics of potential workers and a distribution V of job attributes (J) across all potential vacancies, then the process by which labor market institutions allocate workers to vacancies (or to unemployment) is often called a "matching function" (see, among others, Pissarides 1990). These matches are characterized by sets of attributes of workers and jobs, as well as by the productivity of the match π (X, Z, J).

The labor market does not only match workers and vacancies—important though that task is. It also generates wage rates. These rates determine how firms remunerate workers, which is generally a function of the productivity of the match. However, if the labor market is segmented, remuneration may also be a function of elements of J. In addition, if signaling is at play or discrimination of some sort exists, elements of X and Z may affect the wage rate ω through channels other than productivity. In the simplified scheme presented here, all of these processes are subsumed under the remuneration functional, which leads from the distribution of match attributes among matches (D) to an individual earnings distribution G, which is here written jointly with wealth.

Once a joint distribution of individual wage rates and wealth (G) has been determined, the distribution of household incomes is obtained through two processes: (1) the combination of individuals into households, including the outcome of their reproductive decisions, and (2) the return on nonhuman wealth, designated as nonlabor income. These processes are subsumed here under the household formation functional. Finally, this primary income distribution is converted into the secondary income distribution after allowing for the state's redistribution through taxes and transfers. When pension incomes are mediated through the state (except when they are kept in individual accounts), this sort of income will also be included, given the extent of interpersonal redistribution that generally exists.

This scheme is perforce synthetic. It does not pretend to do justice to the full complexity of the processes represented. Having focused on labor incomes, this framework was particularly reduced-form with regard to portfolio decisions for physical and financial wealth and the remuneration functions for those assets in capital markets. However, as with more developed models, the essential purpose of analytical tools is often to abstract from details on some fronts in order to shed light on other aspects of reality. This framework is used to facilitate the investigation of some of the mechanisms through which income distributions in Latin America are currently reproduced.

A comparative approach is taken throughout the chapter, drawing both on cross-country correlations and on detailed microeconometric pair-wise comparisons, in order to shed light on the following question: What factors account for Latin America's excess income inequality vis-à-vis the rest of the world? For each step in the above conceptual framework for income determination (that is, asset accumulation, labor market matching and remuneration, household formation, and government redistribution), the authors investigate how Latin American countries compare with other countries.

There are two reasons why cross-country regressions were not run in order to explain inequality levels. First, the model used here to determine income inequality (which was discussed in chapter 1) emphasizes circular causality flows between incomes, political power, the distribution of assets, and the nature of institutions. These variables are jointly determined and it would be incorrect to specify a single-equation model. Second, cross-country data scarcity would not allow for a meaningful estimation of a single-equation model even if it were appropriate (which it is not).[1] Instead, the authors present bivariate scatter plots and report the associated correlation coefficients. These diagrams offer insight into the position of Latin American nations within the set of observations. They are *not* to be interpreted as being suggestive of causality. This information is complemented by the results of two pair-wise comparisons of income distributions: Brazil and the United States and Chile and Italy. Naturally, given the enormous diversity within Latin America, and the even greater variations outside the region, these comparisons are meant to be illustrative rather than comprehensive.

6.1. Asset distributions: Education and land

It is possible that one reason why income inequality remains so high in Latin America is that the ownership of assets—which generates incomes—is itself fairly concentrated in the first place. As was shown in chapter 4, concentration in the ownership of land and other natural resources played a central role in the birth of inequality in colonial Latin America. Today, for the vast majority of the population in the region, total wealth is held predominantly in the form of two assets: education and housing. For residents in rural areas, the distribution of agricultural land is also critical. Housing values are difficult to measure and information about their distribution is very hard to obtain. (What little is known about the distribution of housing assets in Latin America is summarized in chapter 7.) Most of the following section focuses on the relationship between the distributions of education and (rural) land on the one hand, and that of income on the other.

It seems natural to start by looking at how inequality measures for education and income are correlated across countries. This can be done using the international set of Gini coefficients for years of schooling compiled by Thomas, Wang, and Fan (2002), based on the Barro and Lee (2000) data on educational indicators. The "income" Gini coefficients are obtained from two sources: table A.3 in the statistical appendix of this report for the Latin American countries and the *World Development Report* 2003 database for all other countries.[2] Figure 6.1 plots the sample of 68 countries for which information on both dimensions is available. Latin American countries are indicated by their country acronyms.

One problem with scatter plots such as figure 6.1 is that, whereas all Gini coefficients in the Latin American database are based on income distributions, those in the *World Development Report* database are based on both income distributions and distributions of consumption expenditure, depending on the country. Since these are obviously not strictly comparable, the indicator on which a country's Gini coefficient is based is indicated by denoting income Gini countries with full circles and expenditure Gini countries with empty circles. Correlation coefficients are also reported for the sample that includes all countries (ρ_{ic}) and for the sample that includes only countries with Gini coefficients that refer to income distribution (ρ_i). This latter group is more comparable to the Latin American countries included

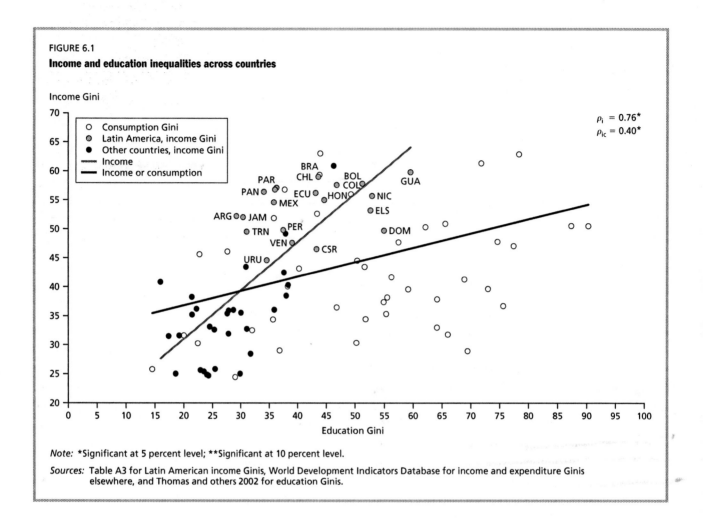

FIGURE 6.1

Income and education inequalities across countries

Income Gini

$\rho_i = 0.76^*$
$\rho_{ic} = 0.40^*$

Legend:
- ○ Consumption Gini
- ◉ Latin America, income Gini
- ● Other countries, income Gini
- ⋯⋯ Income
- — Income or consumption

Education Gini

Note: *Significant at 5 percent level; **Significant at 10 percent level.

Sources: Table A3 for Latin American income Ginis, World Development Indicators Database for income and expenditure Ginis elsewhere, and Thomas and others 2002 for education Ginis.

in the analysis.[3] This convention is followed in a number of figures throughout this chapter.

Another problem with scatter plots is that of interpretation. Figure 6.1, like all other cross-country scatter plots presented in this chapter, shows *covariance patterns* between income inequality (on the vertical axis) and some other variable (on the horizontal axis). As indicated above, the authors believe that most of these variables are jointly determined. These diagrams should therefore *not* be interpreted as suggesting a direction of causation. Simple regression lines (of the income-related Gini coefficient on the x-variable) are drawn exclusively for purposes of illustration.

The correlation across countries between educational and income inequality is clearly positive and significant. The Pearson correlation coefficient between the Gini indices is 0.76 for the income-only sample and 0.40 for the joint income and education sample. These numbers are significant at the 1 percent level in both cases. They are also somewhat

higher than both the figure of 0.27 found by Castelló and Doménech (2002), who used their own education-related Gini coefficients, and the income-related coefficients from Deininger and Squire (1996), although this latter figure was also significantly positive.

Figure 6.1 also shows that Latin American countries do not have particularly high levels of educational inequality by world standards. Instead, they are concentrated toward the middle range of the horizontal axis, with educational Gini coefficients ranging between 0.29 (Argentina) and 0.60 (Guatemala). According to Castelló and Doménech (2002), the average Latin American Gini coefficient for education is lower than that of every other developing region, except for the transitional economies. Figure 6.2 further illustrates this by plotting the Lorenz curves of years of schooling for two Latin American countries (Chile and Nicaragua) that are close to opposite ends of the regional spectrum of educational inequality and alongside the curve

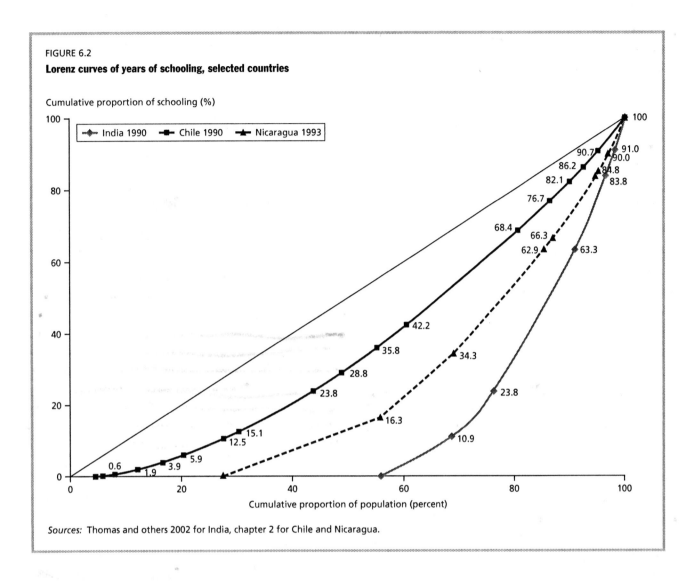

FIGURE 6.2

Lorenz curves of years of schooling, selected countries

Cumulative proportion of schooling (%)

Legend: India 1990 — Chile 1990 — Nicaragua 1993

Cumulative proportion of population (percent)

Sources: Thomas and others 2002 for India, chapter 2 for Chile and Nicaragua.

for India. Although income inequality in both Chile and Nicaragua is higher than India's expenditure inequality, inequality in years of schooling is unambiguously higher in India.

Since they do have high income inequality levels, Latin American countries tend to also have some of the highest levels of income inequality *conditional on* educational dispersion in the world. All Latin American countries plotted in figure 6.1 lie above the regression line of the joint sample, and most also lie above the regression line of the income-related sample. In other words, in light of the average cross-country relationship, Latin American countries appear to have "too much" income inequality, given their levels of inequality in years of schooling.

This finding suggests that other factors may play a greater role in accounting for the region's egregious inequality levels,

as discussed further below. However, before jumping to the conclusion that educational disparities are definitely not the reason for high income inequality in Latin America, it should be noted that years of schooling is a very imperfect measure of the value of the human capital stock embodied in a person. In particular, this indicator does not convey the quality of the education achieved during a given period. It is therefore possible that the ratio of income to education inequality in Latin America simply reflects the fact that disparities in human capital accumulation in this region occur to a greater extent (that is, compared to other parts of the world) because of differences in the quality of education among various schools, rather than because of differences in the number of years of schooling among individuals.

It is difficult to test this hypothesis, however, because the quality of education is very hard to measure in a comparable manner. It is put forth simply as a caveat against concluding that education differentials are unimportant in explaining Latin America's high income inequality, since true human capital inequality may be understated as a result of inadequately capturing quality differentials. Two pieces of evidence suggest that this possibility is worth exploring.

The first comes from the most recent attempt to compare student achievements internationally through the Organisation for Economic Co-operation and Development (OECD) Program for International Student Assessment (PISA) (2000). This exercise was undertaken for 31 countries, only 4 of which do not belong to the OECD. One of these was Brazil. Since Mexico belongs to the OECD, there are two Latin American countries in this sample, which otherwise includes rich countries, some transition economies, and the Republic of Korea. Table 6.1 reports the means, the coefficients of variation, and the 90th to 10th percentile ratios for test scores with regard to the three dimensions for which they are reported in OECD 2001: literacy/reading, mathematics, and sciences.

The results are striking. In terms of absolute levels, Mexico and Brazil rank at the bottom of the table on every scale, with the lowest mean scores of all 31 countries. Even the internal ranking is consistent, with Mexico always scoring above Brazil. In terms of the two measures of dispersion in test scores (or "quality inequality") used here, results are more mixed for Mexico, where the 90th to 10th percentile ratios are the 13th, 6th, and 21st highest in the literacy, mathematics, and scientific scales, respectively. However, dispersion results are still rather stark for Brazil, for which the 90th to 10th percentile ratios rank 5th highest in literacy but 1st highest in both mathematics and science. The coefficients of variation present a similar picture, as can be easily seen in table 6.1.

These findings imply, first and foremost, that any comparison of educational distributions across countries that relies on years of schooling as a measure should be treated with considerable circumspection. If test scores are any indication, what students learn in any given year varies considerably across countries. At the same time, looking beyond country means, this finding also suggests that variations in the quality of education *within* countries, while present everywhere, appear to be more pronounced in some Latin American countries than in the OECD.

It would be tempting to read into the latter finding that the educational inequality of Latin American countries, measured along the horizontal axis of figure 6.1, was systemati-

cally understated. On the basis of a comparison between a single Latin American country (Brazil) and the OECD sample, however, it is possible that similar (or even worse) quality differentials exist in other developing countries.[4] In particular, there are no data on quality dispersion for countries in Africa and South Asia, which tend to lie to the right of those in Latin America in figure 6.1.

The second piece of evidence on the importance of differences in educational quality comes from a study of "educational production functions" in Brazil, which uses test score data from the 1999 wave of the national primary education examinations known as the Sistema de Acompanhamento do Ensino Básico (SAEB). Using hierarchical linear models (which permit an identification of the sources of inter- and intra-school variation in achievement scores), the study found that 28 percent of the total variation in the sample occurred across schools. Most of this variation was accounted for by differences in the mean socioeconomic levels of students in these schools, indicating that sorting plays a large role in the determination of educational outcomes. However, variables related to the quality of school infrastructure (such as whether classrooms are systematically stuffy or noisy) and to the educational attainment of teachers were also significant. This finding indicates that disparities in the quality of educational services being provided throughout Brazil contributed to disparities in the ultimate value of those services to students.[5]

This brief foray into issues pertaining to the measurement of the *quality* of education serves mainly as a caveat to the apparent simplicity of the visual message conveyed in figure 6.1. The issue of quality is a reminder of how imperfectly information on years of schooling captures human capital accumulation for the purposes of making comparisons or aggregation within countries; this is even more evident with regard to international comparisons. Analyzing quality also raises the possibility that educational inequality in Latin America might be understated with respect to countries in other regions. If that is the case, income inequality conditional on educational inequality might not be so high for this region. However, this possibility is by no means established, given the severity of the data limitations. The balance of the analysis so far must still be that—since Latin America has very large income-related differentials but not very high education-related ones— educational inequality cannot be the sole source of very high income inequality in the region.

TABLE 6.1.

Variation in student performance in PISA 2000 examinations

Country	Reading/literacy scale			Mathematical scale			Scientific scale		
	Mean score	Coeff. of var.	90th/10th percentile	Mean score	Coeff. of var.	90th/10th percentile	Mean score	Coeff. of var.	90th/10th percentile
Australia	528	0.19	1.66	533	0.17	1.55	528	0.18	1.61
Austria	507	0.18	1.62	515	0.18	1.61	519	0.18	1.59
Belgium	507	0.21	1.79	520	0.20	1.76	496	0.22	1.82
Canada	534	0.18	1.59	533	0.16	1.51	529	0.17	1.56
Czech Republic	492	0.20	1.66	498	0.19	1.67	511	0.18	1.62
Denmark	497	0.20	1.68	514	0.17	1.55	481	0.21	1.77
Finland	546	0.16	1.52	536	0.15	1.47	538	0.16	1.52
France	505	0.18	1.62	517	0.17	1.58	500	0.20	1.74
Germany	484	0.23	1.85	490	0.21	1.77	487	0.21	1.77
Greece	474	0.20	1.74	447	0.24	1.93	461	0.21	1.75
Hungary	480	0.20	1.69	488	0.20	1.71	496	0.21	1.74
Iceland	507	0.18	1.62	514	0.17	1.53	496	0.18	1.59
Ireland	527	0.18	1.60	503	0.17	1.54	513	0.18	1.60
Italy	487	0.19	1.63	457	0.20	1.69	478	0.21	1.72
Japan	522	0.16	1.54	557	0.16	1.50	550	0.16	1.53
Korea	525	0.13	1.40	547	0.15	1.48	552	0.15	1.48
Luxembourg	441	0.23	1.81	446	0.21	1.70	443	0.22	1.76
Mexico	422	0.20	1.72	387	0.21	1.77	422	0.18	1.62
New Zealand	529	0.20	1.73	537	0.18	1.63	528	0.19	1.67
Norway	505	0.21	1.73	499	0.18	1.62	500	0.19	1.64
Poland	479	0.21	1.76	470	0.22	1.79	483	0.20	1.70
Portugal	470	0.21	1.76	454	0.20	1.72	459	0.19	1.68
Spain	493	0.17	1.58	476	0.19	1.65	491	0.19	1.67
Sweden	516	0.18	1.61	510	0.18	1.62	512	0.18	1.62
Switzerland	494	0.21	1.75	529	0.19	1.64	496	0.20	1.71
United Kingdom	523	0.19	1.66	529	0.17	1.57	532	0.18	1.64
United States	504	0.21	1.75	493	0.20	1.72	499	0.20	1.71
OECD Total	499	0.20	1.71	498	0.21	1.75	502	0.20	1.71
OECD Average	500	0.20	1.70	500	0.20	1.70	500	0.20	1.70
Brazil	396	0.22	1.76	334	0.29	2.19	375	0.24	1.88
Latvia	458	0.22	1.82	463	0.22	1.81	460	0.21	1.75
Liechetenstein	483	0.20	1.72	514	0.19	1.67	476	0.20	1.67
Russian Federation	462	0.20	1.70	478	0.22	1.79	460	0.22	1.77
Mean	493.82	0.19	1.68	493.52	0.19	1.67	493.12	0.19	1.68

Source: OECD 2001.

A similar message arises from a rather different type of analysis that compares the microdata on the income distributions of two countries in much greater detail. One recent study (Bourguignon, Ferreira, and Leite 2002) compared the household income distributions for Brazil and the United States by simulating what the Brazilian distribution might look like if certain aspects of U.S. economic behavior were "imported" into Brazil. It found that replacing the Brazilian conditional distribution of education with that of the United States—but changing nothing else—would reduce the Brazilian Gini coefficient by 6.4 points (from 0.569 to 0.505), which corresponds to just over half of the total Gini gap between the two countries.

Other inequality measures had even more impressive declines in this analysis. For example, the Theil index fell from 0.644 to 0.460, or more than 60 percent of the Brazil-United States Theil gap. Figure 6.3 illustrates this exercise in a more disaggregated manner through plots of the differences in logarithms between the mean incomes of each 100th of the Brazilian and U.S. distributions (normalized to have the same mean) in the solid line, as well as the difference between the counterfactual "Brazil with the U.S.

FIGURE 6.3

Difference in mean incomes per hundredth of the mean-normalized distribution: U.S.–Brazil and U.S.–Brazil (with U.S. conditional distribution of education)

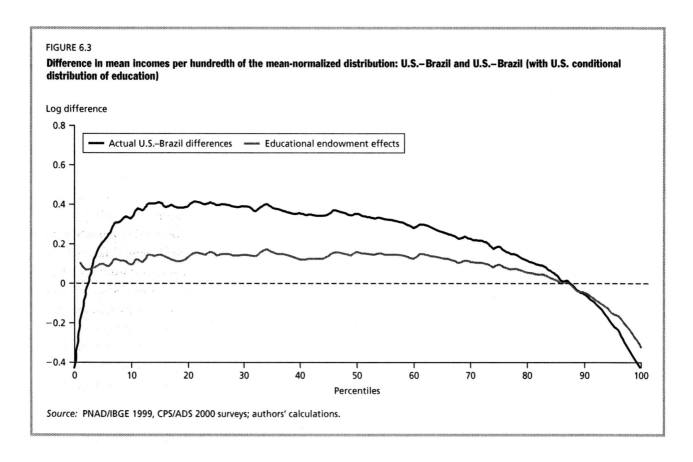

Source: PNAD/IBGE 1999, CPS/ADS 2000 surveys; authors' calculations.

conditional distribution of years of schooling" and the U.S. distribution. Like the comparisons across countries, this more disaggregated exercise suggests that educational disparities account for an important share of Latin America's high income-related inequality, but are not the only explanatory factor.

A contrasting message comes from countries in Latin America with greater average educational attainment (and less educational inequality). A similar microeconometric comparison between Chile and Italy found that "importing" the parameters of the Italian conditional distribution of education into Chile accounted for only 2 of the 20 Gini point difference between the two countries. Chile's Gini stood at 0.557, Italy's at 0.357, and Chile with an Italian distribution of education moved to 0.537. Factors other than the structure of education lie behind the sources of differences in income inequality between these two countries.

The search for other possible sources for Latin America's "excess inequality" therefore continues, in part by considering another asset of great importance for poor people. In chapter 4, the historical process that led to high inequality in Latin America was based on the fact that some of the

products in which the region developed an early comparative advantage (such as sugar and cocoa) were most efficiently produced on large slave plantations. This fact, along with large power differences between groups, led to the development of societies that were polarized between slaves and slave owners, or between large landowners and indigenous workers or small landholders. Is inequality in land ownership still abnormally high in Latin America? Could this factor still be driving income inequality even in today's mostly urban societies?

To investigate this possibility, figure 6.4 plots the income and expenditure Gini coefficients used in figure 6.1 against land-related Gini coefficients from the Deininger and Olinto (2000) data set. Data are available for both Gini coefficients for 75 countries, all of which are plotted below. (Those in Latin America are once again denoted by their country abbreviations.)

Evidence of correlation across countries is a little more mixed with regard to the association between land and income inequality. The simple correlation coefficient for the joint sample is 0.22 and is only significantly different from zero at the 10 percent level. However, for the income-only

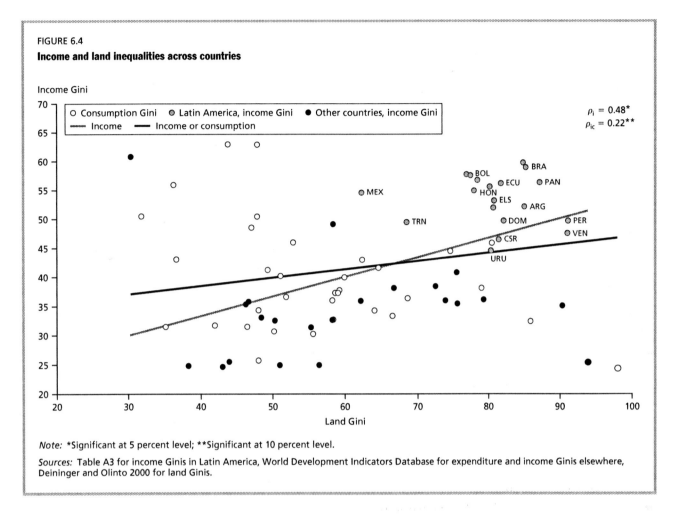

FIGURE 6.4

Income and land inequalities across countries

Income Gini

Legend:
○ Consumption Gini   ◉ Latin America, income Gini   ● Other countries, income Gini
‑‑‑‑‑ Income   ▬▬ Income or consumption

$\rho_i = 0.48^*$
$\rho_{ic} = 0.22^{**}$

(Plotted country labels: BOL, BRA, ECU, PAN, MEX, HON, ELS, ARG, TRN, DOM, PER, CSR, VEN, URU)

Land Gini

Note: *Significant at 5 percent level; **Significant at 10 percent level.

Sources: Table A3 for income Ginis in Latin America, World Development Indicators Database for expenditure and income Ginis elsewhere, Deininger and Olinto 2000 for land Ginis.

sample, it is 0.48 and significant at the 1 percent level. All in all, there does appear to be a positive association between land and income inequalities across countries, although it is weaker than the one that exists between education and income inequalities.

In regional terms, however, Latin America's inequality ranks seem to be closer for land and income. The cluster of the region's countries has moved from the upper-middle of figure 6.1 to the upper-right quadrant in figure 6.4. Latin America is overrepresented among the highest Gini coefficients in the world, with regard to both income and land. It is still the case, however, that Latin American income inequality conditional on land inequality is higher than the world average, suggesting that—as is the case for educational disparities—considering land dispersion on its own can result in an underestimation of income inequality in Latin America. The search for the culprits of inequality must continue beyond the realm of asset accumulation and into the functioning of the labor market.

6.2. Job match quality

According to the schematic representation of household income determination presented in box 6.1, once individuals are endowed with a basic allotment of human and other assets, they decide whether or not to participate in the labor market and are matched up with a job vacancy. Their earnings will depend to a large extent on the characteristics of this match. It follows that the distribution of earnings across the population might well depend on the nature of labor force participation, unemployment, and the formal or informal nature of the labor market.

It turns out that total labor force participation, as reported by the International Labour Organization (ILO) for 116 countries, is essentially uncorrelated with inequality in the joint sample. (The correlation coefficient is –0.04, with a p-value of 0.66). In the income sample only, however, the correlation is negative (–0.42) and significant. It is also the case that this latter result is driven to a rather large extent by relatively low rates of female labor force participation in

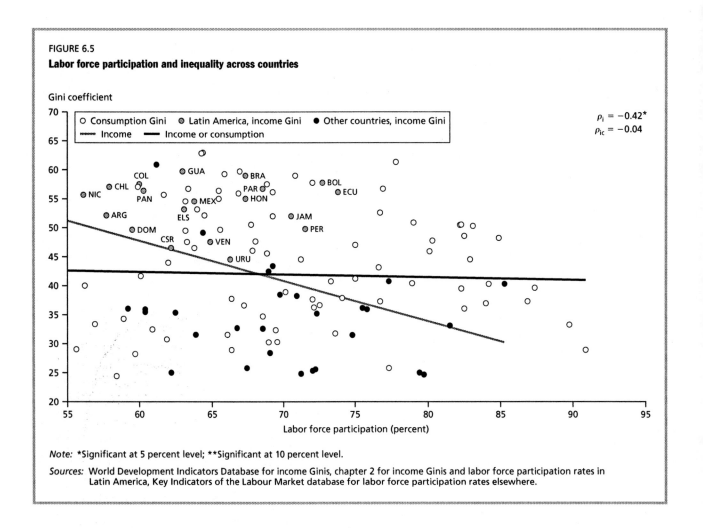

FIGURE 6.5

Labor force participation and inequality across countries

Gini coefficient

$\rho_i = -0.42*$
$\rho_{ic} = -0.04$

Note: *Significant at 5 percent level; **Significant at 10 percent level.

Sources: World Development Indicators Database for income Ginis, chapter 2 for income Ginis and labor force participation rates in Latin America, Key Indicators of the Labour Market database for labor force participation rates elsewhere.

Latin America compared to more developed regions, which report low income Gini coefficients and have higher overall labor market participation rates. The scatter plot illustrating these patterns is presented in figure 6.5.

Overall, there does not seem to be evidence of a significant covariance pattern between labor force participation and inequality across countries. An exception to this occurs when only income-reporting countries are considered, which excludes much of Africa and Asia. Nevertheless, what does remain true is that Latin American countries lie overwhelmingly above both regression lines. In this data set, the coefficient of a Latin American dummy included in a cross-country regression of income inequality on total labor force participation would be significantly positive, as it would have been in similar regressions using education and land Gini coefficients.

Similarly, no clear pattern of correlation emerges from the joint cross-country distribution of inequality and unemployment rates. Figure 6.6 presents the plot for total

unemployment rates, once again drawn from the ILO database. The correlation coefficient is insignificant in the pooled sample and –0.34 and significant at the 5 percent level in the income-only sample. The latter result is likely to be spuriously driven by a positive correlation between unemployment and gross domestic product (GDP) per capita, as well as by the negative correlation between inequality and GDP per capita in the sample. Once again, all Latin American countries lie above both regression lines. This time, however, they are more spread out along the horizontal axis—along which, in this case, the unemployment rate is measured—than was the case in previous graphs, suggesting that Latin American countries have less in common in terms of their unemployment rates than they did, for instance, with respect to patterns of land or education distributions.[6]

The situation is somewhat different when we consider the extent of duality in the labor market, as measured by the share of informal sector employment in total employment.

FIGURE 6.6

Unemployment and inequality across countries

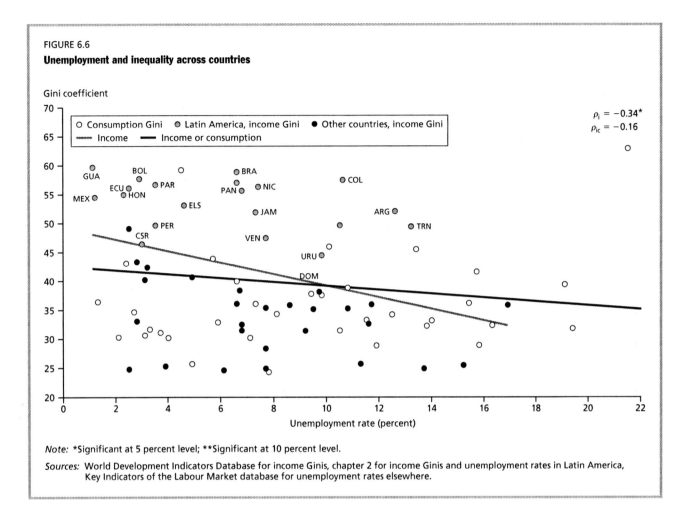

Note: *Significant at 5 percent level; **Significant at 10 percent level.

Sources: World Development Indicators Database for income Ginis, chapter 2 for income Ginis and unemployment rates in Latin America, Key Indicators of the Labour Market database for unemployment rates elsewhere.

The scatter plot of this share and the income Gini coefficients is shown in figure 6.7. The correlation coefficient between the two is 0.35 and significant at the 2 percent level in the pooled sample.[7] Latin American countries lie along the middle ranges of informality, between African countries to the right and more developed countries to the left, and remain above the regression line.

The positive association between a large informal sector and income inequality across countries may reflect the fact that the informal sector is quite heterogeneous. It includes, among others, unpaid family workers, voluntary owners of small family businesses, street vendors who cannot find work elsewhere, employees in small firms who receive training in their first jobs, young mothers earning pocket money, and well-educated owners of small firms that are just being established. The heterogeneity of the informal sector contributes to the difficulty in understanding its nature and may explain why it tends to be more unequal than the formal sector.

A comparison of mean earnings across sectors reinforces the claim of heterogeneity (Cunningham and Maloney 2003). Clearly, unpaid workers are at the bottom of the earnings distribution.[8] Employees in small firms tend also to earn lower average wages than do formal sector employees. However, average earnings for self-employed workers are very similar to the wages of formal sector employees, although the variance of wages is higher for the former group.[9]

Many factors help explain the higher inequality among the self-employed. First, self-employment is a risky venture, so the self-employed may require higher wages to compensate for the extra insecurity that they absorb by owning their own businesses. Second, the selection process for survival in the self-employment sector typically leads to a broader distribution of earnings for any given level of human capital, compared to what would be obtained if workers were all salaried with nonstochastic, smoothly increasing wages relative to human capital. Since the self-employed have full

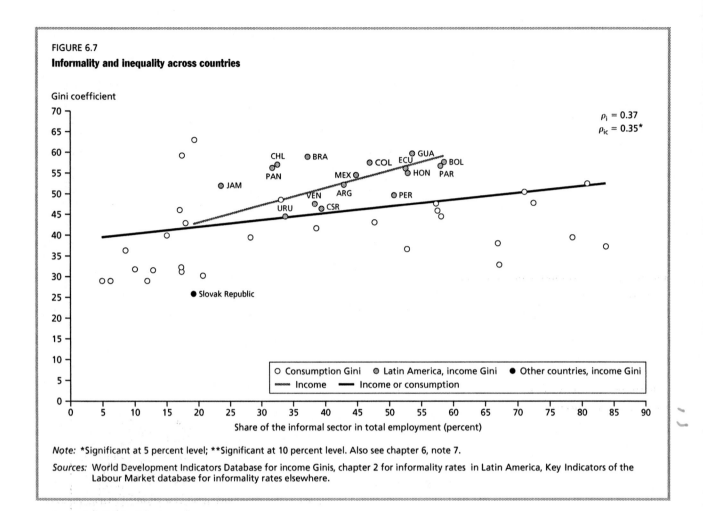

FIGURE 6.7

Informality and inequality across countries

Gini coefficient

$\rho_i = 0.37$
$\rho_{ic} = 0.35^*$

Share of the informal sector in total employment (percent)

○ Consumption Gini   ◎ Latin America, income Gini   ● Other countries, income Gini
····· Income   — Income or consumption

Note: *Significant at 5 percent level; **Significant at 10 percent level. Also see chapter 6, note 7.

Sources: World Development Indicators Database for income Ginis, chapter 2 for informality rates in Latin America, Key Indicators of the Labour Market database for informality rates elsewhere.

information about their abilities and do not pay efficiency wages, their returns best approximate marginal productivity, unlike employees who are hired based on the few characteristics that employers can observe.[10]

Third, inequality among the self-employed may simply capture measurement error, since regular employees report wages but the self-employed may not accurately report profits. Due to the abstract and difficult task of estimating forgone earnings from capital investments, the self-employed are likely to overestimate their earnings, thus leading to unequal earnings between two particular observations within a sample that actually have the same net earnings.

In Latin America, inequality is greater among the self-employed than among salaried workers. The informal sector comprises 30–70 percent of the labor force and is made up mostly of self-employed individuals. As shown in table 6.2, evidence from six Latin American countries indicates that earnings inequality in the self-employment sector is double the degree of inequality that exists in the wage sector. Most

of this inequality is within groups, while that between groups is very small in all countries except Chile.[11]

These findings suggest that a greater level of labor market informality contributes to higher inequality through a composition effect—that is, greater weight in a sector with higher within-group inequality—rather than through large differences in means between the formal and the informal sector, as a more traditional approach might have predicted. It may also be the case that increases in the share of the informal sector during the 1990s might have exerted some upward pressure on overall inequality in countries such as Colombia, Costa Rica, and Mexico (see Cunningham and Santamaría 2003).

Overall, the picture that arises from this analysis of the quality of job matches and income inequality is murkier than the picture from asset distributions. The correlation coefficients between education and land inequalities on the one hand and income inequality on the other are convincingly positive. However complex the process of joint determination might be, the

TABLE 6.2

Wage work and self-employment in selected countries, 1995

	Argentina	Bolivia	Chile	Colombia	Uruguay	RB de Venezuela
Share of the self-employed in the labor force	26%	56%	29%	33%	26%	37%
Theil index, all workers	0.362	0.642	0.735	0.667	0.398	0.340
Theil index, self-employed	0.484	0.819	0.867	0.972	0.499	0.470
Theil index, wage workers	0.295	0.430	0.411	0.433	0.350	0.264
Inequality decomposition						
Within-group	0.355	0.642	0.639	0.653	0.395	0.340
Between-group	0.007	0.001	0.096	0.013	0.004	0.000

Source: Wodon and Maloney 2000.

covariance between asset inequality and income inequality does seem to be borne out, both by the cross-country data and by the microeconometric comparisons between Brazil and the United States. In contrast, the microeconometric comparison between Chile and Italy found only small effects of educational assets on the distribution of income.

On the other hand, no association was identified between income inequality and either labor force participation or unemployment. Once again, this is consistent with findings from a microeconometric comparison of Brazil and the United States by Bourguignon, Ferreira, and Leite (2002). Importing the occupational structure from the United States onto Brazil (which is conditional on observed worker characteristics) had very little effect on inequality. A similar result is found when Italy's occupational structure is imported onto Chile.

The microeconometric studies confirm the view that occupational structure variables play a smaller role in accounting for Latin America's excess inequality than do either educational or land endowments. The one exception might be the extent of labor market informality due to the prevalence of greater income disparities within the informal sector, as discussed above. This tentative conclusion suggests that rigid labor market institutions, such as high hiring and firing costs, may contribute to more rather than less inequality (see Heckman and Pagés-Serra 2000). Other labor market institutions also play a role in the context of the determination of labor market remuneration or wage formation, as discussed below.

6.3. Remuneration in the labor markets

In addition to its allocative role, through which workers and vacancies are matched, the labor market affects income distribution directly through the determination of wage rates paid to different workers holding different jobs. One stan-

dard way in which economists view the determination of earnings is through the human capital model, originally developed by Gary Becker and Jacob Mincer. If education and experience increase a worker's productivity, then earnings ought to vary positively with each of these factors, even when controlling for the other. A standard Mincer equation is therefore as follows:[12]

$$(1) \quad \log(e_i) = b_0 + b_1 s_i + b_2(age - s_i - 6) + b_3(age - s_i - 6)^2 + \varepsilon_i$$

Where s_i captures the years of schooling of individual i, and e_i measures that person's earnings or wage rate. It follows that, for a given distribution of education (the dispersion of which may be measured by the Gini coefficient, as shown in figure 6.1), earnings inequality should rise with the coefficient b_1 in equation (1) above. In figure 6.8, the familiar income Gini coefficients are plotted against the Mincer coefficients (b_1) for the 33 Latin American and OECD countries, on which Fernández, Gunerm, and Knowles (2001) estimated equation (1) above on household survey microdata. The result is the highest correlation coefficients reported in this chapter: 0.70 in the pooled sample and 0.81 in the income-only sample, with *p*-values of 0.000 in both cases. In this (unfortunately small) sample of countries, it seems that returns on education in the labor market are closely associated with income inequality. Latin American countries lie in the upper quadrant of the diagram, with high estimated Mincer coefficients and high income inequality.

The microeconometric comparison of Brazil and the United States provides further support for the conclusion that higher returns to education in Latin America are an important factor in accounting for the region's high levels of inequality. Replacing Brazil's structure of returns with that of the United States

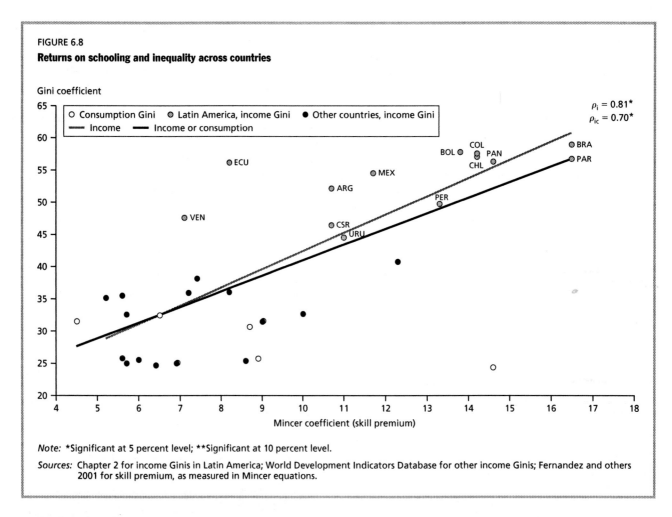

FIGURE 6.8

Returns on schooling and inequality across countries

Note: *Significant at 5 percent level; **Significant at 10 percent level.

Sources: Chapter 2 for income Ginis in Latin America; World Development Indicators Database for other income Ginis; Fernandez and others 2001 for skill premium, as measured in Mincer equations.

led to a reduction of 4 points in the Gini coefficient, or about one-third of the total gap. Even more revealing is the fact that jointly replacing Brazil's conditional distribution of years of schooling and returns structure with those of the United States led to a reduction of 7.5 Gini points, from 0.569 to 0.494. This change represents a full 60 percent of the difference in Gini coefficients between the two countries.

The disaggregated impact of the simulation on the entire distribution can be gauged from the information provided in figure 6.9(a), in which the thick, solid line shows the actual differences between incomes per percentile in the United States and Brazil. The dotted line represents the differences between the Brazilian distribution and the simulated distribution for Brazil with the U.S. returns and occupational structures, while the thin solid line in between those two lines represents the differences between the Brazilian distribution and the simulated distribution for Brazil with U.S. returns and occupational and educational structures. It is clear that the combination of returns on

education and its actual distribution in the population accounts for an important part of the difference between the income distributions of Brazil and the United States.

An analogous picture for the Chile-Italy comparison is shown in figure 6.9(b). Here the actual differences between the mean-normalized incomes per percentile between Italy and Chile are represented by the thick, uppermost line. The dotted line represents price effects, that is, the difference between Chile "as is" and Chile with the Italian structure of labor market returns. Just above the dotted line, the thin solid line depicts the differences between Chile with the Italian returns structure and conditional educational distribution. There is very little difference between these lines, indicating that almost all the difference related to education flows from differences in returns on education. A substantial share of the distributional difference between the two countries is accounted for. In fact, the Gini coefficient for that counterfactual distribution (0.445) lies approximately midway between the coefficients for Chile (0.557) and Italy (0.357).[13]

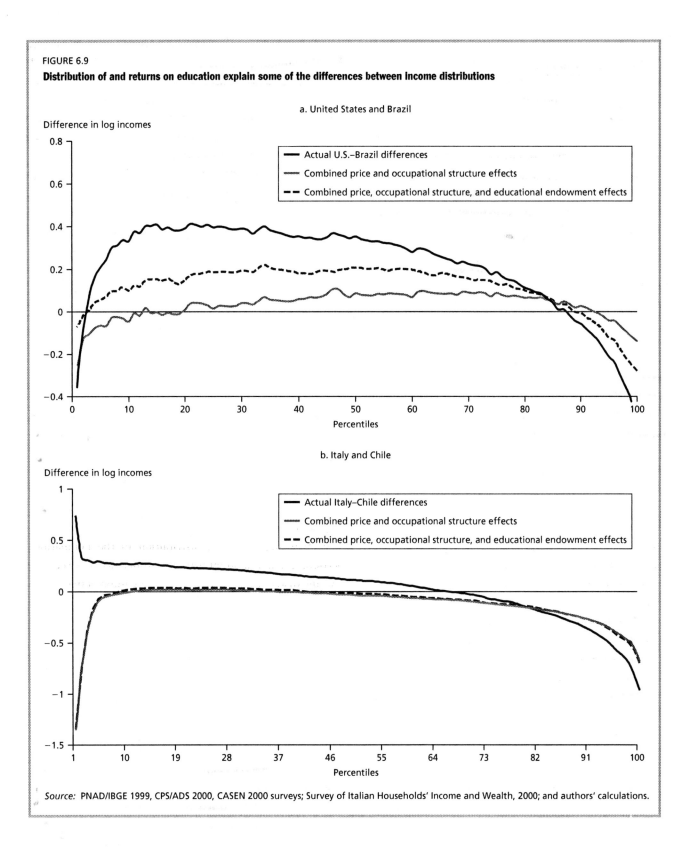

FIGURE 6.9

Distribution of and returns on education explain some of the differences between income distributions

a. United States and Brazil

Source: PNAD/IBGE 1999, CPS/ADS 2000, CASEN 2000 surveys; Survey of Italian Households' Income and Wealth, 2000; and authors' calculations.

The evidence does provide support for two conjectures: (1) Latin America is characterized by higher than average returns to human capital, particularly education, and (2) this is an important part of the reason for the region's "excess inequality." Why returns to education are so high in Latin America remains something of an open question. To some extent, the obvious but not terribly helpful answer is that the ratio of demand for highly skilled workers to their supply is too high, while the ratio of demand for low-skilled workers and their supply is too low. This conclusion in turn begs the question of why this is the case.

It seems inevitable that part of the reason lies in the changing pattern of comparative advantage for middle-income countries. As Wood (1997, p. 49) puts it: "The economic world of the 1960s and 1970s consisted effectively only of developed and middle-income countries, and thus the middle-income countries had a comparative advantage in goods of low skill intensity. In the 1980s, when low-income Asia started to realize its own comparative advantage in goods of low skill intensity, the comparative advantage of middle-income countries shifted to goods of intermediate skill intensity." The popular analogy is that the wages of poor Latin Americans are set in Beijing, but those of highly educated Latin Americans are set in New York.

It is logical to recognize that this intermediate position between countries with an abundance of skilled labor and those with an abundance of unskilled labor must have some bearing on return structures in Latin America. However, such understanding should not rule out consideration of the following views:

- The political economy of high agency inequality throughout the history of Latin America has had an impact by limiting the supply of schooling, which has in turn resulted in a lower ratio of skilled to unskilled labor supply than would otherwise have been the case.[14]
- Most of the recent increases in wage differentials by skill in Latin America (as elsewhere) appear to be driven by skill-biased technical change, rather than by static trade effects of the type usually associated with the Stolper-Samuelson theorem in Hecksher-Ohlin trade theory. The authors' views on that debate do in fact generally favor this interpretation, as comprehensively set out in de Ferranti and others 2003.[15]

In fact, the authors agree with both of these views. The higher than usual rates of return on human capital in Latin America

seem to arise from an historical pattern of underinvestment in education combined with an intermediate position in the world trading system, which implies that most sectors in the region involving low-skilled, intensive labor are "price-takers." The way in which these differentials between wages and skill levels have evolved recently appears to be driven predominantly by process-related, managerial, and technical innovations, which in many cases have been mediated through international trade and foreign direct investment.

Before concluding this section, it is important to say a word about labor market institutions in Latin America. Even though wage rates, like all prices, ultimately depend on demand and supply conditions, these interact through institutions. In addition, since labor markets are—due to heterogeneity and information asymmetries—particularly complex, related institutions are particularly important.[16] This chapter has already argued that hiring and firing costs, as well as other regulatory features, may affect workers' decisions about whether to enter the formal or informal sectors, which in turn has implications for the overall distribution of incomes.

Wage-setting is also affected by other institutions, such as labor unions or the prevalence of minimum wages. Whereas in most OECD countries, unions succeed in compressing wage scales and reducing overall wage inequality in covered sectors (and often throughout the economy, through collective bargaining spillovers), this effect is not robust in Latin America. In some countries, such as Brazil, unions actually appear to have the opposite effect: unionized workers appear to have greater wage disparities than nonunionized workers, and unionization appears to contribute to greater wage dispersion in the economy as a whole. (See Cunningham and Santamaría 2003 for a brief survey of the evidence.)

Arbache (2002) argues that this trend is largely due to the fact that Brazilian unions, unlike those in most other countries, are organized according to professional categories. Employers thus bargain separately with various unions that represent different grades of employees and are concerned only with their own salaries. In contrast to more integrated labor movements, there is little pressure to have compressed wage scales. More generally across Latin America, the limited impact of unions appears to largely be a result of both low levels of union participation and the fact that the spillover effects from unionized to nonunionized workers (the so-called bargaining coverage rates) are small (see Cunningham and Santamaría 2003).

Minimum wages, on the other hand, do appear to have the potential to generate equalizing effects on wage distributions in Latin America. In Colombia and Brazil, for example, a 1 percent increase in the minimum wage results in increases along the formal sector wage distribution, with effects greatest below the minimum wage and diminishing across the wage distribution (Maloney and Núñez 2000, Neri, Gonzaga, and Camargo 2001). Although the spillover (or "lighthouse") effects of minimum wage rises can be felt quite far up the wage distribution in these two countries, they are much larger among low-wage workers. The overall effect of this pattern is clearly to reduce inequality.

It should be noted that the scope for the minimum wage to be used as a policy variable that can reduce inequality is obviously limited by the fact that at some point employment effects may become too great (see Angel-Urdinola 2003). In addition, if the minimum wage is used to index public sector liabilities (such as pension outlays, in the case of Brazil), the opportunity costs of public funds in terms of other forgone equitable expenditures may outweigh any equity gains in the wage distribution.

6.4. Household formation

Latin America's position in the world has now been considered in terms of a number of covariates of income inequality levels: dispersion in asset distributions (education and land); indicators of labor market matching (participation, unemployment, and informality rates); and a key indicator of returns to human capital (estimated Mincer coefficients). Moving further along the schematic determination of household incomes depicted in box 6.1, the authors suggest that the process of household formation affects how earnings distributions are transformed into household income distributions.

In particular, how men and women sort themselves into couples matters a great deal. Consider two societies with identical earnings distributions. Household income inequalities would clearly be different if in one of them the highest-earning woman married the lowest-earning man (and so on), while in the other the highest-earning woman married the highest-earning man (and so on). Income inequality would be much higher in the latter society than in the former. More generally, this example simply suggests that when shifting from earnings distributions to distributions of household income per capita, marital sorting may be an important factor.

Figure 6.10 plots Gini coefficients related to both income and marital sorting for all 33 countries (once again only in Latin America and the OECD), which were computed by Fernández, Gunerm, and Knowles (2001). The marital

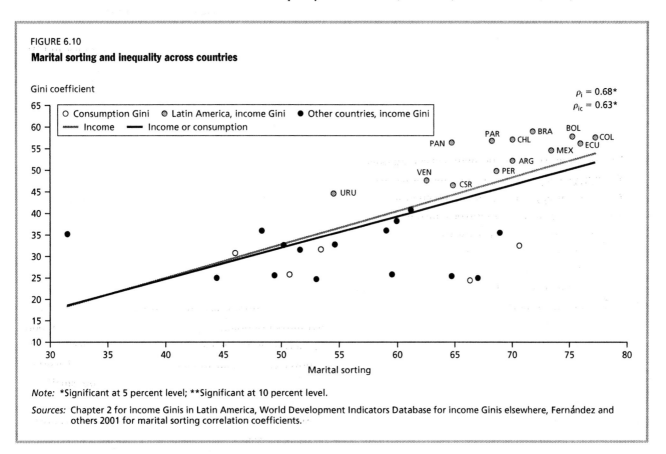

FIGURE 6.10

Marital sorting and inequality across countries

Note: *Significant at 5 percent level; **Significant at 10 percent level.

Sources: Chapter 2 for income Ginis in Latin America, World Development Indicators Database for income Ginis elsewhere, Fernández and others 2001 for marital sorting correlation coefficients.

sorting coefficients are defined as Pearson correlation coefficients for years of schooling between husbands and wives among couples within a country. The correlation coefficients between marital sorting and income inequality in this sample are high: 0.63 in the pooled sample and 0.68 in the income-only sample (with *p*-values of 0.000 in both cases). As before, most plausible models of household formation and income determination would suggest the existence of considerable simultaneity in this relationship: in more unequal societies, men may be likelier to marry women from the same social stratum and with similar education levels. At the same time, if education increases labor market participation and earnings, this will likely contribute to the persistence of income inequality in the future.

Although whom a person lives with is important, it does not fully determine household composition. Income per capita will also depend on how many children a person has and on the age structure in the household. Figures 6.11 and 6.12 capture these two dimensions, albeit imperfectly, through two commonly used demographic variables: the youth dependency ratio (defined as the ratio of the number of persons

ages 0–15 to the number of persons ages 16–64) and the old-age dependency ratio (defined as the ratio of persons ages 65 or over to the number of persons ages 16–64).

These ratios are very imperfect measures, since they represent simple population shares that do not take into account the correlation between total household size and total household income. The latter factor clearly matters for how dependency ratios affect the distribution of household per capita income. Be that as it may, the correlation coefficients considered here are still significant in both cases: 0.50 in the pooled sample and 0.84 in the income-only sample for youth dependency, and −0.56 in the pooled sample and −0.83 in the income-only sample for old-age dependency.[17] In this sample of 121 countries, a larger share of youth in a population is associated with higher inequality—primarily because of a negative correlation between the number of children in the household and household per capita income—while a larger share of the elderly in a population is associated with lower inequality.

The detailed Brazil–United States comparison by Bourguignon, Ferreira, and Leite (2002) also found that

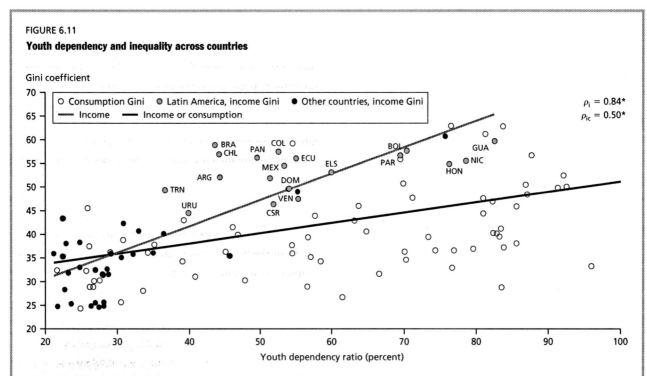

FIGURE 6.11

Youth dependency and inequality across countries

Gini coefficient

Note: *Significant at 5 percent level; **Significant at 10 percent level.

Sources: Chapter 2 for income Ginis in Latin America, World Development Indicators Database for income Ginis elsewhere and dependency ratios. Dependency ratios of youth are defined as 0- to 15-year-old population as a proportion of total workforce, that is, total population = 16- to 64-year-olds.

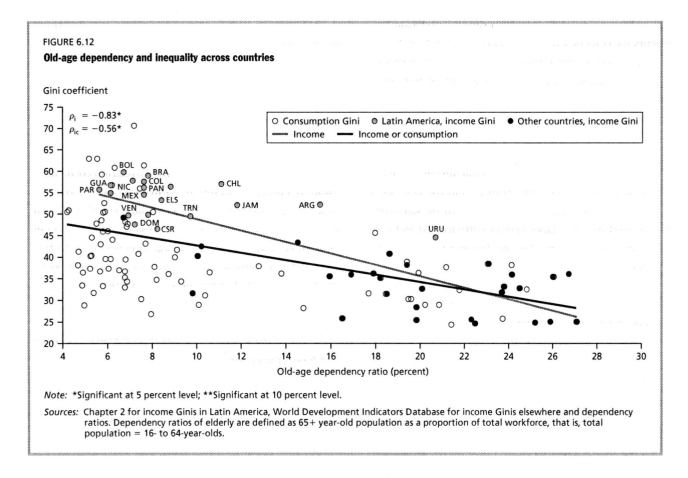

FIGURE 6.12

Old-age dependency and inequality across countries

Note: *Significant at 5 percent level; **Significant at 10 percent level.

Sources: Chapter 2 for income Ginis in Latin America, World Development Indicators Database for income Ginis elsewhere and dependency ratios. Dependency ratios of elderly are defined as 65+ year-old population as a proportion of total workforce, that is, total population = 16- to 64-year-olds.

replacing Brazil's larger family sizes with those prevalent in the United States helped reduce inequality, although not by very much. When combined with the changes reported in figure 6.9, importing the parameters from a multinomial logit model for the number of children in U.S. households into the Brazilian model led to a further decline of 1 point in the Gini coefficient. Figure 6.13 once again plots the differences between incomes in Brazilian and U.S. households, with the thick solid line referring to actual mean-normalized differences. The dotted line refers to the counterfactual distribution for Brazil with U.S. educational, occupational, and returns structures. The solid line between these two lines corresponds to the simulation that incorporates demographic effects. It can be seen that the effect is to further reduce Brazil's inequality and to bring the simulated distribution closer to that of the United States. In this specific case, it is also apparent that the effect of demographic behavior is not as quantitatively important as are the effects related to both the distribution of and returns to education.

Because the incidence of this aggregate spending is likely to matter a great deal for the relationship between public intervention and inequality, it would be ideal to examine more disaggregated categories of spending. Since internationally comparable data on the incidence of public programs are scarce, however, it is difficult to disaggregate much. Here only one category of public spending is considered, which due to its commonly universal coverage is not usually regressive: public expenditure on primary education. Figure 6.15 plots the income-based Gini coefficients against the ratio of this expenditure per student to per capita GDP. As one would expect, the correlation coefficients are even lower (–0.51 in the pooled sample and –0.67 in the income-only sample) and remain significant. A similar result is obtained if, instead of considering public expenditure on primary education, the ratio between government transfers to nonprofit institutions and households and GDP is used (International Monetary Fund Government Finance Statistics database). This correlation is shown in figure 6.16.

Figures 6.14–6.16 suggest that states do in fact play an active role in affecting the distribution of disposable household income through their basic taxation and public expenditure choices (see chapter 9). This is not to suggest that the

FIGURE 6.13

The role of reproductive behavior in accounting for differences in income distribution between Brazil and the United States

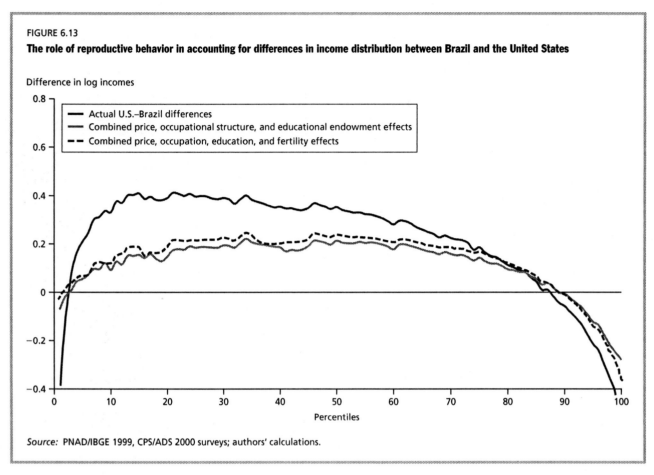

Source: PNAD/IBGE 1999, CPS/ADS 2000 surveys; authors' calculations.

FIGURE 6.14

Total public spending and income inequality

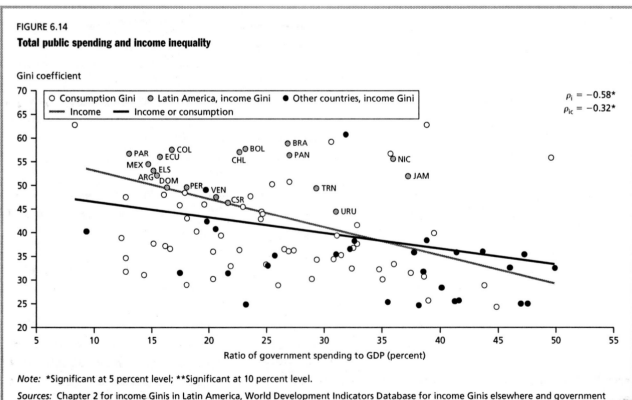

Note: *Significant at 5 percent level; **Significant at 10 percent level.

Sources: Chapter 2 for income Ginis in Latin America, World Development Indicators Database for income Ginis elsewhere and government spending-to-GDP ratios.

FIGURE 6.15

Public expenditure on primary education and income inequality

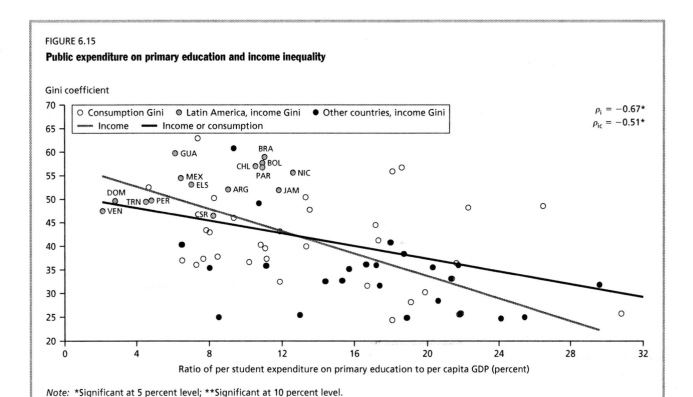

Gini coefficient

$\rho_i = -0.67*$
$\rho_{ic} = -0.51*$

Ratio of per student expenditure on primary education to per capita GDP (percent)

Note: *Significant at 5 percent level; **Significant at 10 percent level.

Sources: Chapter 2 for income Ginis in Latin America, World Development Indicators Database for income Ginis elsewhere and per student expenditure on primary education-to-per capita GDP ratios.

FIGURE 6.16

Public income transfers to households and income inequality

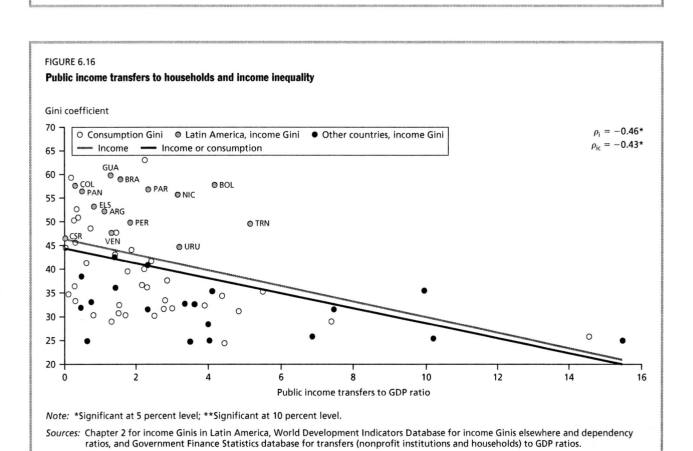

Gini coefficient

$\rho_i = -0.46*$
$\rho_{ic} = -0.43*$

Public income transfers to GDP ratio

Note: *Significant at 5 percent level; **Significant at 10 percent level.

Sources: Chapter 2 for income Ginis in Latin America, World Development Indicators Database for income Ginis elsewhere and dependency ratios, and Government Finance Statistics database for transfers (nonprofit institutions and households) to GDP ratios.

influence of the state on distributional outcomes is limited to taxation and spending levels. There clearly are a number of other important channels through which state institutions affect the distribution of power and income (such as the degree to which decisionmaking processes are democratic and participatory). Nevertheless, the primary impact of the state as an economic actor is indeed felt through the raising and spending of revenue. In addition, although the direction of causation is once again impossible to ascertain from the figures provided here, it is clear that at least some categories of public expenditure (such as on primary education and transfers) are negatively correlated with income inequality.

Interestingly, whereas Latin American countries are reasonably spread out along the horizontal axis in figure 6.14—indicating a large variation across the region in ratios of total public expenditure to GDP—they are rather concentrated toward the left in figures 6.15 and 6.16. This suggests that the region tends to lie toward the low end of the international range of public spending per student in primary education and transfers, relative to GDP.

The cross-country nature of these comparisons means that they are limited to aggregate indicators of public spending. The incidence patterns of the aggregate amounts spent are not taken into account, even though the impact of the state on distribution can clearly vary enormously among countries with the same expenditure-to-GDP ratio. Distributional impacts depend on who receives the benefits of such spending. Latin America has often been singled out as a region where the richer and more powerful segments of society appropriate large shares of the benefits of public programs for themselves (see, for example, International Development Bank 1998, United Nations Economic Commission for Latin America and the Caribbean 2001, and chapter 9 of this report). This pattern would tend to increase the importance of the public expenditure component in accounting for the region's high levels of inequality beyond what is suggested by figures 6.14–6.16.

This conclusion is confirmed by what Bourguignon, Ferreira, and Leite (2002) found in terms of the comparison between Brazil and the United States discussed above. In that

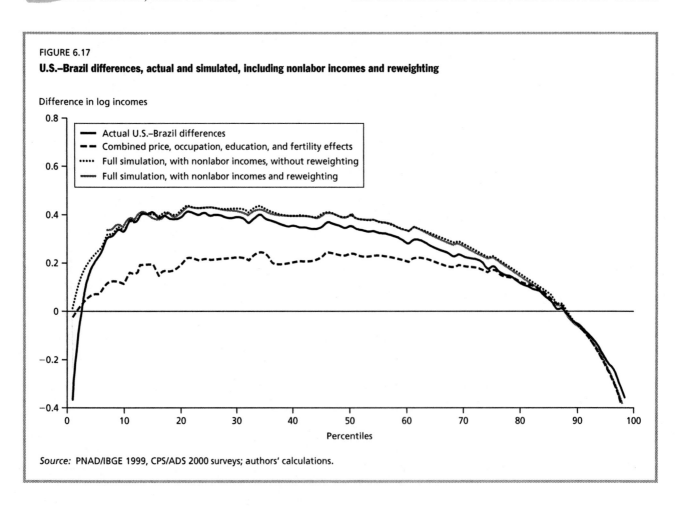

FIGURE 6.17

U.S.–Brazil differences, actual and simulated, including nonlabor incomes and reweighting

Difference in log incomes

Legend:
— Actual U.S.–Brazil differences
– – Combined price, occupation, education, and fertility effects
····· Full simulation, with nonlabor incomes, without reweighting
⋯⋯ Full simulation, with nonlabor incomes and reweighting

Percentiles

Source: PNAD/IBGE 1999, CPS/ADS 2000 surveys; authors' calculations.

study, when the impact of importing the parameters of the U.S. conditional distribution of nonlabor incomes to Brazil is simulated, the Gini coefficient is reduced by more than 3.5 points. When combined with the other effects previously discussed (that is, the distribution of education, the structure of returns, and occupational and demographic structures), the distribution of nonlabor incomes practically closes the inequality gap: the simulated Brazilian Gini coefficient (incorporating all the changes) now comes within 1.7 points of the United States. Other measures of inequality are also comparably near their U.S. "target levels."

The interesting thing with this result is that the bulk of the change is due to pensions, which account for 83 percent of total reported nonlabor income in Brazil. Figure 6.17 reproduces the main curves shown in figure 6.13, that is, the actual Brazil-United States differentials and the intermediate simulated distribution corresponding to Brazil with imported U.S. parameters for educational endowments and returns and occupational and demographic structures. Figure 6.17 adds the curve that combines all of the imported

U.S. parameters with those for nonlabor incomes. This curve comes quite close to the actual differences between mean-normalized Brazil and the United States. Most of this effect is due to replacing the conditional distribution of retirement pensions in Brazil (which are primarily publicly funded, at least in part) with that of the United States.

Whereas retirement pensions as a share of total income decline with household income per capita in most countries (including the United States), they make up a rising share of the total in Brazil, as indicated in figure 6.18.

A similar (although somewhat weaker) equalizing effect of nonlabor incomes is observed in the comparison between Chile and Italy. As counterfactual income distributions for Chile are simulated by importing various elements of the Italian distribution, the inequality gap between the two countries progressively narrows. Importing just the conditional distribution of nonlabor income (which includes all public transfers) contributes two Gini points, or one-tenth of the gap between the two countries. When this simulation is combined with all other simulated parameters (that

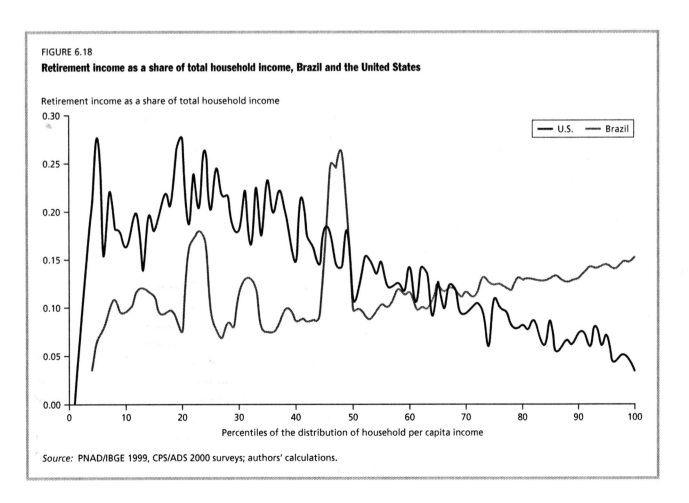

FIGURE 6.18

Retirement income as a share of total household income, Brazil and the United States

Retirement income as a share of total household income

Source: PNAD/IBGE 1999, CPS/ADS 2000 surveys; authors' calculations.

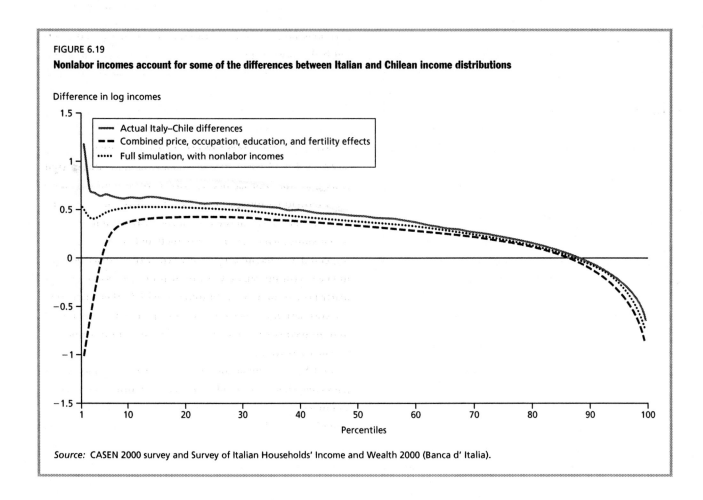

FIGURE 6.19

Nonlabor incomes account for some of the differences between Italian and Chilean income distributions

Difference in log incomes

Source: CASEN 2000 survey and Survey of Italian Households' Income and Wealth 2000 (Banca d' Italia).

is, for the structure of returns, the distribution of education, occupational behavior, and reproductive choices), it adds almost three Gini points. This complete simulation changes the Chilean Gini coefficient from 0.557 to 0.391, which is not too far from the Italian "target" of 0.357.

Figure 6.19, which is analogous to figure 6.18, expands the Chile-Italy comparison represented in figure 6.9(b). The thick solid line at the top represents, once again, differences in the logarithm of incomes accruing to corresponding percentiles of the Italian and Chilean distributions after means were equalized. The dashed line at the bottom represents the same differences between Italy and a counterfactual distribution for Chile after the Italian returns and occupational, educational, and reproductive structures were imported. Finally, the dotted line between these two lines represents the same differences when the conditional Italian distribution of nonlabor incomes (including public transfers) is also incorporated into the simulated Chilean distribution.

It is interesting to note that although the impact of the Italian conditional distribution of nonlabor incomes on the

Gini for Chile was not large, it had a significant effect on the lowest relative incomes in that country. Whereas the previous stages of the simulation succeeded in making the top 80 percent of the Chilean income distribution look more similar to that of Italy, they failed to raise the incomes of people at the bottom of the distribution. At this stage, the Italian structure of nonlabor incomes had a substantial positive impact on the bottom 20 percent of the Chilean distribution.

Since most income from self-employment among the poor is usually reported as labor income, this is unlikely to represent the effect of capital incomes. It is more likely to represent the effect of larger and better targeted public transfers and benefits. As in the case of the Brazil-United States comparison, this microeconometric evidence supports the view—suggested by the pattern of correlations across countries—that Latin American states are relatively unsuccessful at transferring resources to their poorest citizens, and that this is one factor behind the region's excessive inequality.

6.5. Conclusions

Drawing on a schematic representation of the determinants of household incomes, this chapter considered Latin America's position in the world in terms of six broad groups of factors: (1) the distribution of the assets that underlie income generation; (2) the structure of occupation and employment across the labor force and the labor market institutions that influence them; (3) the structure of remuneration in the labor market and, in particular, returns to education; (4) patterns of household formation and composition; and (5) the level and incidence of taxes and public spending.

The preceding discussion was framed in terms of the correlation between indicators pertaining to each of the first five areas and income-based Gini coefficients, and complemented by two specific country comparisons of disaggregated income distributions: Brazil and the United States and Chile and Italy. These two comparisons are clearly not representative of Latin America as a whole, but interestingly the information that they provide resonated well with the patterns emerging from correlations across countries.

Cross-country diagrams provided illustrations of joint distributions, or patterns of correlation. These cannot be interpreted in causal terms, since in general both variables are determined jointly through economic and political processes. An additional caveat is that the correlations presented were all pair-wise, and hence did not control for other attributes. Multivariate regressions on the cross-section were run, but—in addition to the usual problems of data comparability and interpretation often ascribed to them—this analysis suffered from the fact that two of the variables that were most closely correlated with income inequality (namely the Mincer and the marital sorting coefficients) were only available for a nonrandom sample of 33 countries. The results of the regressions were therefore so problematic that they were left unreported.

The balance of the evidence presented—whether from the international correlations or from the more detailed comparison between Brazil and the United States—suggests that four factors are jointly responsible for Latin America's high income inequality. These are: (1) a moderately unequal distribution of educational endowments; (2) the prevalence of high rates of return on education in the labor market, which may operate through specific institutions; (3) household formation patterns with high levels of marital sorting and a large, negative correlation between the number of children

and household income per capita; and (4) the role of high but badly targeted public spending. In addition to these four key factors, it should also be noted that some of Latin America's excess inequality may be illusionary and due to the predominance of income rather than expenditure surveys (see chapter 2.)

Strikingly, there is apparently no single culprit that can be blamed for Latin America's inequality. The interaction among all the four factors described above reinforces each one's individual role and generates the final outcome. This is particularly clear in the case of the distributions of years of schooling, which are not extremely unequal by developing country standards. It is only when these distributions interact with unusually high returns on education (particularly post-secondary education) and with higher than average correlation coefficients between spouses that they lead to high inequalities in earnings, and therefore in income.

Finally, both the cross-country correlations and the Brazil-United States comparison also pointed to the role of the regressive incidence of public finance in failing to reduce—and indeed in some cases in exacerbating—inequality in the secondary distribution of income. (The magnitude of this phenomenon and the areas in which it is most pronounced are discussed in chapter 9.) The general picture that arises is therefore consistent with a view of the world in which wealth and educational inequalities are self-perpetuating, often through decisions taken within political systems. The pattern of taxation and public expenditure is not exogenously determined in a social and political vacuum. It is also likely to be influenced by the distributions of education, income, and political power, as discussed in other parts of this report.

Notes

1. Since data for Mincer coefficients and marital sorting coefficients are only available in comparable form for 33 countries, and some of these have no reliable Gini coefficients, the best cross-country regression model would have 19 degrees of freedom. The authors did run such regressions, and found almost no significant partial correlations. Given the variety of omitted variable, simultaneity, and attenuation biases from which the specification might have suffered, the authors were unable to conclude much from those results, and therefore present the bivariate correlations merely as a descriptive tool.

2. In all cases, the Gini coefficient used was for the latest available year in the respective database.

3. This is clearly a relative statement. Income variables collected from different survey instruments across countries are not strictly

comparable. However, they are generally held to be more closely comparable among themselves than in relation to consumption expenditure variables, given that sources of measurement errors are quite different across the two concepts and agents tend to choose consumption streams that are inter-temporally smoother than income streams.

4. This is the case particularly because quality dispersion in Mexico (the other Latin American country in the sample) was rather average in relation to the OECD sample.

5. The study also found that, even when controlling for socioeconomic status, black students performed worse than did nonblack students (see chapter 3). In addition, even after controlling for a number of attributes related to family and education, students in private schools significantly outperformed those in the public school system. See Albernaz, Ferreira, and Franco (2002).

6. It should be noted, however, that both this greater dispersion in Latin American countries and the low correlation coefficients might be the consequence of a large measurement error in the unemployment variable, which in turn could result from the fact that statistical agencies and labor ministries in different countries define and collect data on unemployment rates in widely disparate ways.

7. The pooled sample is the only relevant one in figure 6.7, since there is only one country in the income-only sample that is not in Latin America: the Slovak Republic.

8. The category of "unpaid" workers may simply reflect a misreporting of income, particularly if the worker is a relative of the "employer." Most unpaid workers are the spouses of a firm owner. In Mexico, for example, 10 percent of married women are unpaid workers, compared to the members of almost no other family group (Cunningham 2001). With this in mind, unpaid workers may actually receive their income "in-kind" if the firm owner shares the income throughout a household.

9. The comparison of these two groups is difficult since it is nearly impossible to quantify the value of the social security benefits that formal sector workers will receive, the value of "being one's own boss," or the value of low job security.

10. This difference also implies that standard wage regressions will have less explanatory power in the self-employment sector, as found by Rees and Shah (1986) and Borjas and Bronars (1989). In fact, Rees and Shah found that in the United Kingdom there is no significant relationship between self-employed earnings and human capital variables.

11. If the level of self-employment in Latin American countries was similar to that encountered in most OECD countries (that is, about 10 percent versus an average of more than 30 percent in the countries included in table 6.2), the within-group component of the inequality indices would be much lower because within-group inequality is lower among salaried workers. As a result, the inequality indices for Latin America would also be lower.

12. This equation can, of course, be augmented to allow for other determinants of earnings in segmented markets (such as sector or region of activity) or in cases where there is discrimination (such as that related to race and gender).

13. Note that the impact of adding the educational effects to the price effects is much larger in the Brazil-United States case than in the Chile-Italy case. This arises from the fact that the Chilean distribution of years of schooling is much closer to that of Italy than the Brazilian distribution is to that of the United States.

14. See Bourguignon and Verdier (2000) for a model in which high inequality slows down educational expansion through a political channel.

15. As one would expect, this is not clear for every country. The pattern of wage differentials in Brazil during 1988–1995, for instance, is quite consistent with a standard Stolper-Samuelson interpretation. See Gonzaga and others (2002).

16. See Blau and Kahn (1999) and DiNardo, Fortin, and Lemieux (1996) for discussions on labor market institutions in developed countries.

17. The p-values were 0.000 in all four cases.

PART III
Policies for Lower Inequality

CHAPTER 7

Policies on Assets and Services

T HE THIRD PART OF THIS REPORT TURNS TO THE QUESTION OF WHAT CAN BE DONE IN SPECIFIC policy-related arenas to reduce inequality in Latin America. How can public action lead to greater equity with a minimal cost in terms of efficiency and, in turn, result in faster and more effective poverty reduction? In the next three chapters, the authors combine a discussion of practical choices for public action with recognition of the centrality of the broader social and political processes that were discussed in chapter 5.

There are multiple, complex areas for action, since inequalities are linked to almost all aspects of economic and social policy. There is no way that a report of this length can do justice to the full spectrum of issues. The authors therefore seek to cover a broad range of concerns, in the spirit of providing an overview of some of the major policy questions. Although this pursuit is not comprehensive—and it certainly cannot go into the depth that any particular area warrants—the aim here is to draw out key themes and contribute both to debate and more in-depth analysis.

Possible areas for public action are organized into three categories. This chapter focuses on influences on the distribution of assets (an issue closely linked to service provision), with emphasis on education; property rights, land, and housing; and the provision of infrastructure.

Chapter 8 considers policies that affect how economic institutions function, moving from the micro to the macro level. Evidence on the overall effect of market-oriented policies and on the particular role of labor markets is considered, followed by macro-level policies and shocks. Chapter 9 then looks at factors that influence the secondary distribution of income (that is, taxes and transfers), with a particular focus on measures that can help manage risk and, specifically, conditional cash transfer instruments. An important consideration when examining policy options is the assessment of tradeoffs, particularly between distributional and efficiency goals. Whenever feasible, this question is discussed in general terms, although country-specific analysis would be required to develop a more definitive assessment.

In part II of this report, it was argued that the interaction between the distribution of assets and institutions makes the most fundamental difference with regard to both the distribution of well-being in a society and the dynamics of change. Unequal assets and unequal institutions lower the well-being of poorer groups and are associated with political structures and sociocultural processes that lead to the perpetuation of inequality. This chapter focuses on how a more equal distribution of assets can be achieved in Latin America in three areas: education; property rights, land, and housing; and infrastructure. Although by no means exhaustive, this chapter provides enough material to highlight some of the major themes and potential areas for public action.

7.1. Education

Education lies at the center of the perpetuation of inequality, both reflecting and influencing unequal economic conditions, power, and social status. Education also has the potential to reduce inequalities. This perspective is central to thinking in many disciplines, from economists who view more equal education as a means of achieving more equal labor income to social scientists who see new forms of education as essential to changing the aspirations, outlook, and behaviors of subordinate groups.[1]

The interactions between education and the various dimensions of inequality are complex. The discussion in chapter 6 indicated that a relatively equal distribution of education across the population is no guarantee of equal income. By international standards, Latin America has on average middling levels of education inequality but high levels of income inequality. Some societies, such as Chile, have relatively extensive and equal education by Latin American standards (that is, an average of ten years of education and a Gini coefficient of 24 for 25- to 65-year-olds in 2000), but also high income inequality. Even broad-based and high quality education systems, such as those in France, can deeply reflect and perpetuate patterns of social difference, as documented in the classic work of French sociologist Pierre Bourdieu (1984).

The embedded and complex relationship between education and society should inspire caution when confronted with the simple view that more education can solve high levels of inequality with regard to income, power, and social status. However, this is not to say that education does not matter. It most certainly does; education has been central to every case of a successful and equal development process, in both economic and political terms. This fact applies to the U.S. experience in the 19th and 20th centuries, the European experience (most notably during Scandinavian transitions), the Japanese process of development after the Meiji restoration, and in almost all the East Asian success stories, from the Republic of Korea to Vietnam.

Moreover, the importance of education appears to be increasing as global integration intensifies and the transition to urban, industrial, and service-based societies takes hold. Education is quickly becoming the most important economic asset for the majority of the population, a factor that only reinforces the need to expand access to quality education. Most countries have made significant progress on basic education, placing priority on expanding secondary schooling, democratizing college education, and strengthening quality throughout the system (de Ferranti and others 2003). As noted in chapter 2, many countries have experienced increases in the premium placed on a college education. Yet most of Latin America's college systems are still primarily the domain of the children of elites, who often

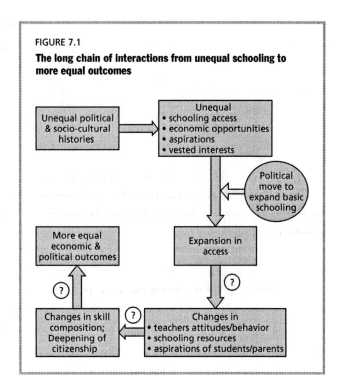

FIGURE 7.1

The long chain of interactions from unequal schooling to more equal outcomes

benefit from sizeable subsidies. Democratizing tertiary education, and increasing access to bright but poorer kids, is important for reasons related to both efficiency and equity.

The following pages examine the potential for public action to effect a large and equalizing expansion of education that can also support greater equality in other dimensions. Most notable among such aspects is income, for which there is much more information on quantitative relationships.

Figure 7.1 represents some of the complexities of these processes. It is useful to draw a distinction between first-stage reforms that are primarily about expanding access to basic education via increased schools and teachers, and second-stage reforms that focus on both equitable access throughout the system and the achievement of high levels of quality. The latter are typically more complex politically and institutionally, thus raising questions about uncertainties in the chain of changes. Most Latin American countries have made the push toward universal basic education, although some have not completed that process. All are engaged to varying degrees in second-stage reforms.

The primary focus here is on service delivery and use as the major levers that states and social groups have to effect change in educational attainment. The first issue considered is the recent dynamics of educational expansion. Then the potential impact of a future large-scale expansion on income inequality is examined through structured comparisons between Latin America and more developed regions. With this foundation in mind, the central challenge of what can be done to improve educational equality is discussed.

Recent dynamics of educational expansion

How fast have societies in Latin America pursued an educational transition? Education dynamics of the recent past suggest that Latin American countries show some signs of breaking with a political and social history of education-based mechanisms for exclusion. There is a great variety of experiences, and all countries in Latin America have launched significant educational expansions in the past decades. However, last year's World Bank report on educa-

tion in the region (de Ferranti and others 2003) emphasized that on average education expanded more slowly in the region than in other regions of the world, especially East Asia and the European periphery.

A picture of past expansions can be obtained by using the data assembled for this report to look at how educational attainment varies across cohorts.[2] The current education of the 51- to 60-year-old cohort reflects educational efforts launched 40–50 years ago. Low levels of average education in a country, or within a cohort, are typically associated with high inequality of education. (Actual types of inequalities are discussed below).

The patterns in Latin America can be roughly classified into four typical past processes, as illustrated for four selected countries in figure 7.2. In the first group are countries with

FIGURE 7.2

Education dynamics in selected countries; years of schooling of men and women by age group

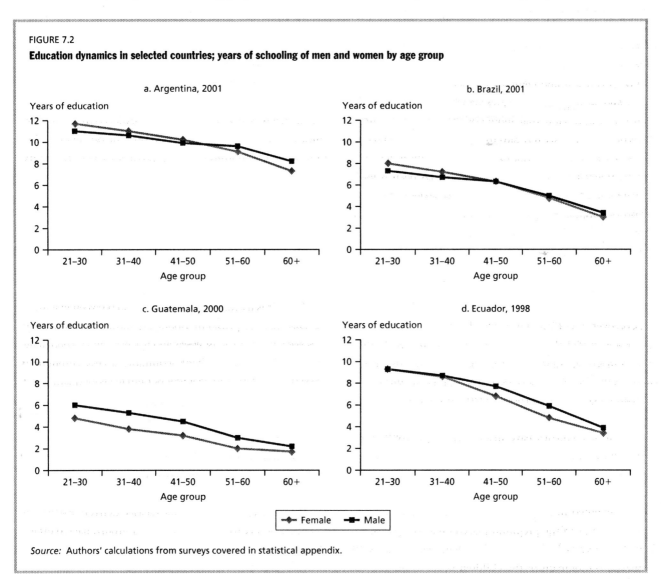

Source: Authors' calculations from surveys covered in statistical appendix.

relatively high levels of educational provisioning in the middle of the 20th century, followed by subsequent expansion, especially the Southern Cone countries. This group ended up with average years of schooling comparable to Spain and Malaysia in 2000.[3] Second, there is a group that started with a lower level of education, but had a major expansion in recent decades. This includes some countries with a high concentration of indigenous people, including Mexico, Peru, Ecuador, and Bolivia. It is noteworthy that at least in Bolivia, Mexico, and Peru, the 20th century was in part characterized by episodes of major social mobilization or revolution with socially inclusive aims, such as strong societal pressures to expand education. Third, Brazil stands out as a country with a dismal historical legacy but a much more recent acceleration in provisioning. Fourth, there is a set of countries in which educational provisioning has continued to be very low despite recent progress; this is especially the case in the poor Central American societies of Guatemala, Honduras, and Nicaragua (as well as, undoubtedly, Haiti).

The evolution of educational inequality can be illustrated by comparing educational attainment for different categories of the same cohort (see table A.23). Doing so confirms continued large inequalities, especially in those countries where overall progress has been relatively weak or late. Table 7.1 compares Brazil and Jamaica. There has been important progress in Brazil in the recent past, but the differences between the bottom and top income quintiles remain very large: 7.1 years in 1990 and 6.9 years in 2000 for 21- to 30-year-olds. Of equal concern is the fact that there is also a large gap in the years of education

TABLE 7.1

Years of education by income quintile for Brazil and Jamaica, men and women aged 21–30

Quintiles	First	Second	Third	Fourth	Fifth	Average
Brazil						
1990	3.0	4.4	5.7	7.3	10.1	6.6
2000	4.3	5.7	7.2	8.8	11.2	7.6
Jamaica						
1990	9.7	9.0	10.0	9.7	10.8	10.0
1999	9.3	9.5	10.0	10.2	10.5	10.0

Source: Calculations from microdata; see table A. 23 in statistical appendix.

attained by 10- to 20-year-olds (many of whom are still in school), which barely changed (from 3.7 to 3.6 years) between 1990 and 2000.

In contrast, Jamaica has continued to have a remarkably equal educational profile: 21- to 30-year-olds in all income quintiles had more than nine years of education in both 1990 and 2000, with a top-to-bottom quintile difference of only one year. (This is partly because of unusually low tertiary education enrollments in Jamaica at all income levels.) In terms of incomes, Jamaica is more equal than Brazil but is still unequal by international standards, with a Gini coefficient of 49 in 2000. The patterns and sources of income difference must therefore work in domains other than acquisition of years of education.

Group-based differences are still large among racial but not between gender groups

In terms of categorical, or group-based, variations, chapter 3 showed that there continue to be large differences in educational attainment between ethnic and racial categories. In Brazil, Bolivia, Guatemala, and Peru, the wages of prime-age, nonwhite men are on average half those of whites, and the difference in mean per capita incomes is even lower. (See table A.45 in the statistical appendix). Differences in education always account for the larger share of the differences that are revealed in the labor market. As figure 7.3 shows, progress in reducing black-white differentials in schooling has been much slower in Brazil than in South Africa. Years of schooling for South African blacks are lower than for Brazilian whites among older age cohorts, but higher among younger ones.

In contrast, with respect to gender women have made significant advances relative to men. Among younger cohorts in most countries, women are at an educational advantage, at least with respect to years of education attained. This also applies to gender differences among blacks in Brazil, but does not apply to indigenous groups in Bolivia and Guatemala, where girls continue to have lower attainment and enrollment.

Spatial differences have remained large during educational expansions, at least in some countries. This is markedly so in the case of northeastern Brazil and the southern states of Mexico. In the latter case, which includes Chiapas, Guerrero, and Oaxaca, there is also a strong overlap with differences associated with indigeneity.

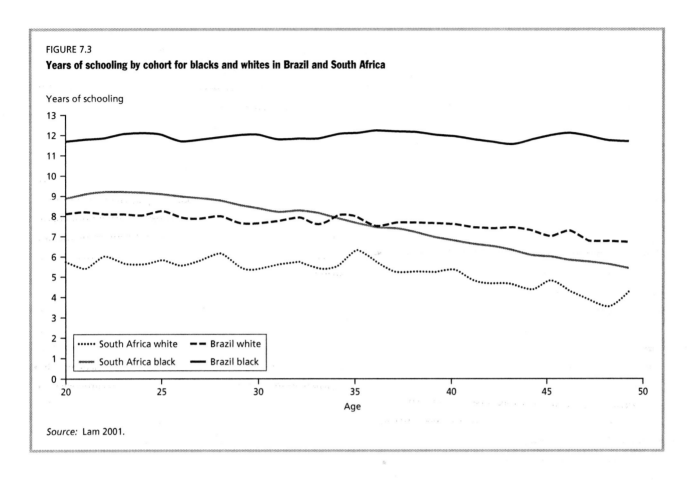

FIGURE 7.3

Years of schooling by cohort for blacks and whites in Brazil and South Africa

Years of schooling

Legend: ······ South Africa white   – – Brazil white   ~~~~ South Africa black   — Brazil black

Age

Source: Lam 2001.

Tertiary education is increasingly the most salient divide

One of the key correlates of advantage in the past 10–15 years has been achievement of tertiary education. In 19 out of the 20 countries for which data exist for the end of the 1980s and 1990s (Guatemala is the exception), marginal returns to tertiary education are substantially above the returns to secondary education (see table A.31).[4] Furthermore, for 11 of the 17 countries for which time series have been produced, marginal returns to tertiary education rose during the 1990s.

These differences in tertiary education make some of the trends in expansion of enrollment particularly worrisome from the perspective of future inequality dynamics. As noted in chapter 2, a compression of differences in enrollment at the primary school level has occurred between income categories, in turn a consequence of the crowding-in of excluded groups. Experiences have been varied at the secondary level, with neither clearly equalizing nor unequalizing patterns seen across countries.

However, in the 1990s differences between the top and bottom quintiles in the enrollment of 18- to 23-year-olds widened substantially in all countries except Brazil, El Salvador, and Honduras, all three of which had the highest levels of inequality in tertiary enrollments in the region (see figure 2.13 in chapter 2). There are high and often rising inequalities related to tertiary education, which gives the greatest gains and (as discussed below) receives the highest subsidies. Moreover, the privileged access to tertiary education is in many countries associated with either private secondary schooling—which is affordable only to the better-off—or with passage through higher-quality public schools.

The importance of educational quality

Educational levels are only part of the story. Of at least equal importance is the quality of education. As discussed in last year's World Bank report (de Ferranti and others 2003) and in chapter 6, issues of low quality appear to be pervasive throughout Latin America. Those countries that have participated in international tests have scored substantially below the Organisation for Economic Cooperation and Development (OECD) average or scores for high performers elsewhere (especially some East Asian and Eastern European countries). This is shown in the results for Chilean and Colombian students in the Third International Mathematics and Science Study (TIMSS), test and for Brazil and Mexico in a standardized test undertaken by the OECD. These results reflect not only a lower average but a wide dispersion in Latin America. Only 4.4 percent of Brazilian students and 8.6 percent of Mexicans scored above the OECD average.

Differences in educational quality are strongly associated with other dimensions of inequality, especially the socioeconomic status of households. As one illustration of this link, table 7.2 shows the differences in test results among Brazilian students by self-identified racial category. This information shows large deficits for nonwhites, which are higher for blacks than for people with mixed blood. Between one-third and one-half of the deficit is associated with differences in the socioeconomic status of individuals or with the condition of schools. A slightly higher proportion of the deficit is attributable to both socioeconomics and school conditions taken together. Thus, poorer, nonwhite students get both worse results and worse schools, and there remains an additional effect associated with race. This problem is typically interpreted as the product of some combination of race-based differences in family or social experiences and expectations or factors in the schooling experience that are not captured in data on schooling conditions (for example, the social distance between teachers and students, poorer teaching skills, and cultural aspects of the curricula).

The importance of socioeconomic status in determining test results is a common finding. An analysis of Brazilian and Mexican schools by the OECD (2001) found that only 20 percent of differences in test results can be explained by differences in school quality and that overall, about half of the variation in student test scores occurs within schools, with the other half explained by differences between schools (see table 7.3). However, with regard to differences between schools, more than half of the difference is due to measured gaps in the socioeconomic status of students.

The possible transformation of education in the future

What would Latin American countries look like with more equal educational conditions? The answer depends on three factors: the distribution of both the quantity and quality of education; the pattern of remuneration in the labor market; and the mechanisms that translate such remuneration into household income distributions. Indirect effects of expanded education on fertility and labor force participation would also play a role. The relative increase in the supply of more educated workers would tend to reduce the wage premia paid to these workers, but what actually happens is a product of both interactions with demand-related side effects and the influence of formal and informal institutions.

In light of the incomplete understanding of the determinants of wage structures, this report does not seek to model or predict changes. However, as reported in chapter 6, two paired comparisons were undertaken, between Brazil and the United States and Chile and Italy. Brazil and Chile are both unequal societies even by Latin American standards, yet have very different educational structures; Chileans have higher and more equally distributed education levels. The United States is a rich country with high levels of education, and has relatively flexible labor markets by OECD standards. Italy also has a highly educated workforce, but is relatively equal and has more policy and institutional interventions in place in the labor market.

TABLE 7.2

Mathematics test results for Brazilian students who identify themselves as black or of mixed blood, compared with white

	Observed difference	Difference adjusted for SES	Difference adjusted for schooling conditions	Difference adjusted for both SES and school
Mixed blood (pardo)	−16	−9	−8	−7
Black (preto)	−24	−18	−14	−13

Source: SAEB 1999 INEP, 8ª série Matemática.
Note: The standard deviation of math tests is 50; all differences shown are statistically significant. SES = socioeconomic status.

TABLE 7.3

Schools account for only a small part of variance in student learning outcomes

	Share of total variance in test results for all students (percent)			
	1. Due to differences in student performance within schools	2. Due to differences across schools	3. Fraction of total variation attributable to school student background and differences across schools	4. Share of total variation in student test performance that is school-specific and not attributable to student background differences across schools (column 2 minus 3)
Brazil	55	45	25	20
Russian Federation	63	37	17	20
Czech Republic	48	52	4	18
Korea, Republic of	62	38	14	24
Mexico	46	54	32	22
Developed country average	66	34	20	14

Source: OECD 2001, Annex B1, table 2.4.

The two paired comparisons led to the contrasting results that were presented in chapter 6.[5] In the case of the Brazil-United States comparison, differences in the distribution of educational endowments and returns to education explained about two-thirds of the difference in overall income inequality. This suggests that benefits of an equalizing education expansion exist for Brazil, which could in turn induce movements toward the more equal returns observed in the United States. However, for the Chile-Italy comparison, the difference in inequality in educational endowments hardly explained any of the difference in income inequality. Much more was due to the pattern of returns to education and the greater equality associated with unobserved factors in Italy. This would suggest that the sources of the differences in income inequality between the two countries stem from factors other than the structure of education.

A related exercise for the poor Brazilian northeastern state of Ceará yielded results that were also consistent with a cautious assessment (Ferreira and Leite 2004 and World Bank, 2003d). That study simulated a large educational expansion and, instead of making a comparison with another country, explored the implications of a plausible range of changes in the pattern of returns on skills. Even with a strong equalizing shift in the pattern of returns, the overall influence on income inequality was small, in part because expanded basic education induced entry of relatively low-skilled women into the labor market. In contrast, the effect on poverty was substantial.

In addition to these comparisons across countries and possible long-run changes, an educational expansion has potentially significant transitional effects. When there are high returns to tertiary education (and convex returns overall), as well as relatively small groups of tertiary graduates, there can be a temporary rise in overall inequalities. This is because initial expansion of tertiary enrollments will tend to increase the share of the highly paid. Only when this group becomes sufficiently large will overall inequality decline.

These simulations should be considered as accounting exercises that provide some quantitative information on what might occur if the educational (and other) characteristics of Latin American countries were to shift substantially. Simulations are certainly not predictions. However, they suggest that although equalizing education expansion is undoubtedly of fundamental importance, it would be unwise to assume that education alone would lead to a transformation of income inequality.

Policy choices for educational transformation

What are the political, policy-related, and institutional conditions that would lead to an equalizing expansion of education, in terms of both quantity and quality? Both policy formulation and implementation matter. Experiences in Latin America and elsewhere suggest that there is no magic bullet for attaining higher quality and more equitable education systems. There are many promising experiments in decentralization, demand-side measures, transparency, and testing, but none alone is a panacea. The way in which systems operate depends on the context, that is, on the patterns of interactions emphasized in this report, in which economic factors are intertwined with political, social, and cultural influences. General work on service provision (World Bank 2003a) has emphasized the varieties of influence and accountability that determine the design and execution of policy. These relationships occur both via indirect paths of influence on governmental decisionmaking and the direct interactions between communities and households on the one hand and service delivery organizations and frontline workers on the other.

The shape of an expanding education system

As emphasized by de Ferranti and others (2003), the overall way in which an education system expands makes a significant difference with regard to its equity properties. A major theme developed in that report was the need for extensive expansion from the bottom up, in keeping with the path of East Asian and Scandinavian countries. For most countries in Latin America, this approach would imply a particular focus on a large expansion of secondary education. However, this type of expansion alone is not enough.

First, of equal importance is the need to address the potentially adverse effects of the "massification" of education, especially through measures that both ensure high quality and prevent the large-scale opting-out of education by members of the middle class, whose political support for quality education is crucial. This makes the issues around accountability and teacher performance fundamental. Second, there is a strong need to improve access to tertiary education—which is primarily the domain of elites—both to ensure that societies make effective use of the pool of potential talent in the population and to create incentives and opportunities for all groups taking part in secondary-level schooling.

Societal commitment and resources

Discourse in Latin America is strongly proeducation, typically emphasizing the right of everyone to at least a basic education. This trend is often linked to the rising demands for higher skills as a result of globalization. However, actual behavior and conditions result in a more mixed picture.

Resource allocations are indicative of the level of commitment of national or local governments. However, differences in total resource allocations explain only part of the differences in educational outcomes. According to international standards, most Latin American countries have already allocated significant resources to education. The share of gross domestic product (GDP) spent on education at all levels in the region fell from 3.7 percent to 2.9 percent between 1980 and 1990, but then rose to 4.8 percent by 1995. This trend compares with 2.6 percent on average for East Asian developing economies (de Ferranti and others 2003).

The real issue at hand is the allocation and effective use of resources. In this regard, there are large differences among countries. Figure 7.4 illustrates three very different patterns of spending across primary, secondary, and tertiary levels. Chile has seen a large, equalizing convergence across these levels; Mexico has experienced steady growth at all levels, thereby maintaining unequal patterns; and Brazil has a large bias toward tertiary education, which receives seven times more funding than does secondary education.

Issues also exist that are related to the distribution of resources across inputs. Especially in the wake of macroeconomic crises, there has been a tendency in Latin America to cut nonpersonnel-related expenses disproportionately, resulting in a situation in which a high proportion of spending is on teachers. In contrast, all "production function" analyses find that the marginal effect of nonsalary spending is many times higher than spending on teachers. This reflects the priority that both governments and teachers' unions place on the relative protection of personnel.

Finally, there are questions to be asked about the depth of support for education spending. Are citizens, businesses, and policymakers eager to improve education and enthusiastic about tax-based support, especially in an increasingly globalized world? This is not always clearly the case. At least for some poorer regions, there appears to be some resistance to educational expansion on the part of modernizing business elites, who often prefer lower-cost labor and training, subsidies, and tax advantages from governments rather than concerted efforts to expand secondary education (see box 7.1). It is particularly interesting that this echoes the 20th century experience of the southern states in the United States, which also pursued a relatively low-tax, low-education, cheap-labor course as part of efforts to attract private investment.

This pattern underscores a more general message: the need for civic efforts to facilitate high-quality, broad-based education, including access to tertiary education. Economic incentives do matter, but are insufficient, and may not always

FIGURE 7.4

Spending by education level in Chile, Mexico, and Brazil

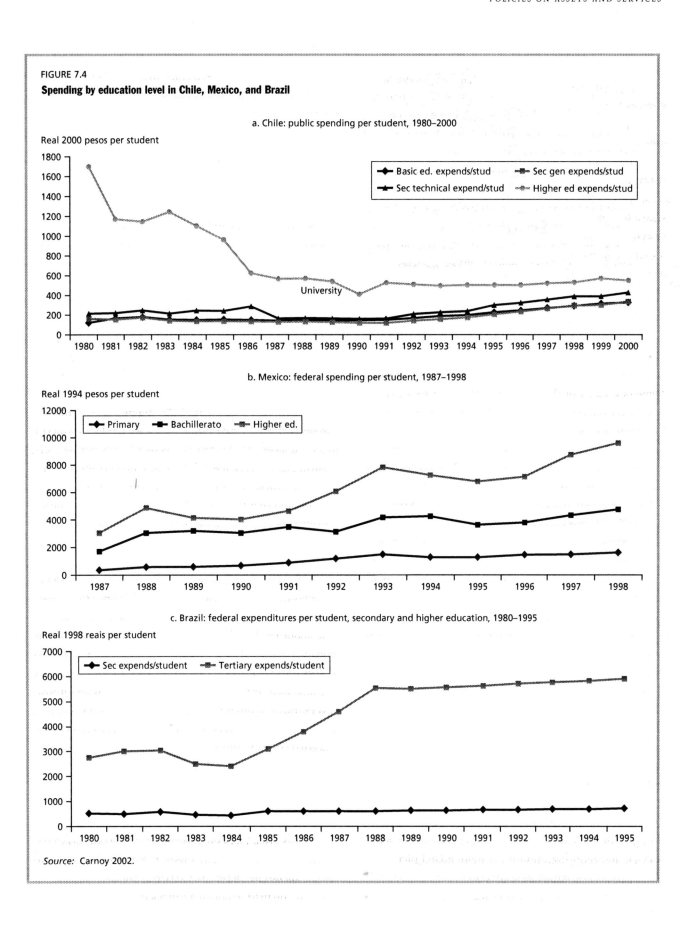

a. Chile: public spending per student, 1980–2000

Real 2000 pesos per student

Legend: Basic ed. expends/stud | Sec gen expends/stud | Sec technical expend/stud | Higher ed expends/stud

b. Mexico: federal spending per student, 1987–1998

Real 1994 pesos per student

Legend: Primary | Bachillerato | Higher ed.

c. Brazil: federal expenditures per student, secondary and higher education, 1980–1995

Real 1998 reais per student

Legend: Sec expends/student | Tertiary expends/student

Source: Carnoy 2002.

BOX 7.1

Business elites and the fear of education: Is there a low-road trap? Evidence from northeastern Brazil and the southern United States

In light of the current combination of democratization and allegedly surging demands for developing skills in a world of economic reform and globalization, it would seem that fear of, or resistance to, education would be a part of past history. In conducting background work for this report, Judith Tendler (2003) explored a specific, surprising dimension of this issue in the context of attitudes among business elites, who constitute an important, somewhat neglected source of demand for education.

Drawing on fieldwork in northeastern Brazil, other surveys of the business world's attitudes in Brazil, and the historical experience of the southern United States, Tendler found that "modernizing" business elites (including those who have relocated from southeastern Brazil) prefer workers with only basic education. This is generally considered sufficient for workers to rapidly catch up to productivity levels that prevail in higher-wage areas, especially when combined with on-the-job training. (Comparable results were found in surveys referred to in Tendler 2003 in other parts of Brazil). Minimum education levels are also seen as key to maintaining a more docile and less mobile workforce with weak aspirations to advance to less grueling service sector jobs. This preference is in contrast to the typical public discourse of the business sector on the value of education. However, it is consistent with a survey of Brazilian elites by Elisa Reis (1999), who found that business elites were unwilling to support increased spending or taxes on education, despite the fact that they often named education as an important factor in poverty reduction.

The low-education preferences of business elites are in practice supported by specific policies of northeastern Brazilian state governments. In particular, as in other poor regions (notably the southern United States), state governments have emphasized low wages and tax breaks as sources of competitive advantage. This tendency has been complemented by an array of specific training and infrastructure subsidies that help firms upgrade their own labor forces but take away resources from the greater collective need of generalized educational upgrading, especially at secondary levels. These patterns seem to make up a "low road" to globalization that keeps northeastern Brazil (and similar poor areas and poor countries) in a low education/high inequality equilibrium relative to the alternative of broad-based, tax-financed educational upgrading.

Source: Tendler 2003.

---

be supportive of educational upgrades (as described in box 7.1 with regard to the business world's preference for only basic education). This is consistent with historical experiences of education expansion. As noted in de Ferranti and others 2003, the "Great Transformation" of education in the United States during 1910–40 was due to a range of economic and societal factors, including high rates of return on secondary education, campaigns by school administrators, and egalitarian features of the schooling system. Societal pressures that served to change the collective expectations of all participants mattered, as they did during earlier periods of education expansion in the United States (Goldin 1999 and 2001).

Decentralization, accountability, and teacher performance

The skills and performance of teachers, as well as their interactions with pupils, are key to the quality of schooling, and thus also to the distribution of schooling quality. In many countries, the teaching profession has been greatly affected by the patterns of political and institutional development discussed in chapter 5. Teaching appointments are often part of clientelistic forms of patronage (see Angell and others 2001 on the case of Colombia). Teachers' unions are usually important forces, whether as elements of historical corporatist structures (in Mexico, for example) or as sites for political mobilization (as in Bolivia). This fact provides a context for reform efforts.

Considerable experimentation with education reforms has taken place in Latin America, including decentralization both at the school and local government level (see Di Gropello 2003 for a review). However, there has been little rigorous evaluation of the impact of decentralization on the quality of service delivery and educational outcomes, and even less on distributional effects.[6] With respect to increased school autonomy, EDUCO in El Salvador has been frequently cited as a major experiment in greater school autonomy that allowed educational expansion for poorer groups without a loss in quality. Most studies of this and similar reforms find a significant impact either on educational achievement or on intermediate variables, such as teacher management and learning, with a positive but weaker link occurring between autonomous decisionmaking in pedagogical processes and learning. Schools that are more active in tracking and monitoring teacher activity are likely to be more successful in increasing student achievement.

By contrast, little evidence exists on the impact of decentralization of local or intermediate governments on educational achievement. Actual performance is likely to be context-specific. For example, Angell and others (2001) document significant differences in the extent to which local education reform was effectively pursued across municipalities in Colombia. Pasto stood out for the vigor of its local reform efforts, which were part of an overall shift to more effective local governance and facilitated in part by the election of a dynamic outsider mayor (see chapter 5). This is an area in which further experimentation would be highly useful, along with ongoing monitoring and evaluation.

A more contentious issue is that of vouchers. Advocates see vouchers as having the potential to increase school quality by allowing households to exercise choice among different schools, which would in effect apply competitive pressures on educational systems to improve performance. It is also argued that vouchers can benefit the underprivileged by allowing poor kids to choose better schools. On the other hand, critics fear that vouchers will heighten the polarization among schools and between students that do well and those who don't, and undercut the morale of teachers more than they spur better teaching. International evidence on these points is ambiguous (Gauri and Vawda 2003).

The effects of vouchers are not clearcut, judging from the results of the two main experiments with the system in Latin America: a large-scale expansion in Chile and a five-year experiment in Colombia that was targeted toward low-income neighborhoods. Some studies of the Chile case find modestly higher test scores, but this is not a robust result; others argue that neither overall quality nor the achievement gap between subsidized and nonsubsidized elite schools has changed (see, for example, Hsieh and Urquiola 2003). In Colombia, vouchers were allocated through a lottery, which allowed for a quasi-experimental evaluation that found that winners scored 0.2–0.3 standard deviations higher on standardized tests, after controlling for other characteristics of students and their families (see Angrist and others 2002. Note that the program was discontinued in 1997.) A tentative conclusion is that vouchers targeted toward poor children in urban areas—where there is significant school choice—may play a useful role. However, vouchers do not appear to be as important an instrument as the conditional cash transfers referred to below, which also involve transfers for education but with different design characteristics.

Proactive support for excluded groups

Although broad-based expansion of education systems helps to expand coverage to poorer groups, there is also a strong case to be made for special action to include those students that have historically suffered educational deficits due to location, socioeconomic class, or culturally based inequalities. Ongoing experiments therefore suggest the need to work on both the demand and supply sides of the education issue.

With respect to the demand side, there is evidence that scholarships conditional on school attendance have positive effects on deprived groups. These include *Oportunidades* (previously known as PROGRESA) in Mexico and *Bolsa Família* (previously *Bolsa Escola*) in Brazil, among others. (These are discussed in more detail in chapter 9, since an important element of the design is redistributive transfers targeted toward poor families.) In the case of *Oportunidades*, geographic targeting has led to the relatively high participation of indigenous people (although those in the most remote areas without schools are not reached) and specific grants for girls, who in this group suffer higher dropout rates than boys. Such programs have become one of the core instruments for providing incentives for excluded groups to enter school.

On the supply side, bilingual education is of particular relevance to indigenous people. Indigeneity is not coterminous with speaking indigenous languages, especially in the context of the major migrations of indigenous or mixed blood groups to urban areas. However, for many of the more rural and poorer indigenous groups, language is an important aspect of both their learning experience and cultural identity. Ethnographic and other case study evidence documents the role of social distance in schooling, which can be amplified by language factors. This is not solely an issue for traditional indigenous groups; work by Portes and

BOX 7.2

Bilingual education: Preserving cultural heritage without being left behind

Research shows that for students whose "home" language is not the dominant language in a society, those in bilingual education schools have higher reading comprehension levels than those who learn in only the dominant language. Bilingual education schools typically teach skills in the child's native language and then transfer these skills to the use of the nationally dominant language.

Those in favor of this educational model argue that simultaneously immersing a student in a new language and a new skill does not allow the student to learn either very well, thus accounting for low performance on reading tests. Conversely, those who are against this model claim that by teaching a child in his or her native language first immediately puts them at a linguistic disadvantage that cannot be overcome later in the education process. This debate is partly settled by empirical evidence, which shows that the bilingual education approach provides equal or higher reading competencies to children across the world, in such diverse countries as Canada, Guatemala, Haiti, Nigeria, the Philippines, and the United States. Preliminary work in Guatemala further suggests that bilingual education is cost-effective in terms of learning outcomes.

Source: Patrinos and Vélez (1996); additional information provided by Harry Patrinos.

Rumbaut (2001a) on migrants (especially Latino and Asian) to the United States finds analogous problems, which can become more acute in the case of the children of migrants who are torn between two cultures. Bilingual education can play a role both in terms of enhancing education, since initial learning in a mother tongue seems to help students, and managing cultural transitions by reducing social distance and making learning more relevant to children (see box 7.2). One issue in this context that has not been addressed in core educational work is the position of Afro-descended children. In this case, the issue is not so much language as more subtle cultural aspects of social difference that an education system can accentuate or active design can help combat. This is an area for further research and efforts.

Toward more democratic tertiary systems

Tertiary education systems are predominantly the domain of elites, and are typically highly subsidized (though much more so in Brazil than in, for example, Chile). This trend is both inefficient and inequitable. The talent pool is reduced and the intergenerational transmission of wealth and elite status is facilitated. Reforming tertiary education is often contentious, with (understandable) resistance to subsidies for less advantaged groups. There are, however, experiments underway that seek to make attending a university more affordable to the poor and to make the quality of different universities more transparent. As discussed by de Ferranti

and others (2003) a number of measures will need to be taken, including overcoming credit and information constraints for potential applicants, increasing cost recovery for public universities (in light of high private returns), and linking public resources to performance. A particular issue is whether to introduce affirmative action programs based on race, ethnicity, or class. This is currently a controversial issue in Brazil with respect to Afro-descended groups. The evidence is clear that such groups are both greatly underrepresented in tertiary education and suffer a series of disadvantages in schooling and socialization processes. Achieving a more equal society in Brazil would require greater representation. The goal of affirmative action programs in that country would be to build an education system that allows talented Afro-Brazilians (as well as the indigenous and poor) to advance through the educational system.

The experience with affirmative action in the United States provides some lessons, including with regard to the complexity of the issue. In July 2003, the U.S. Supreme Court ruled on a case that supported the goal of including racial diversity in the objectives of recruitment policies, but ruled that mechanistic means of doing so (as in across-the-board adjustment in test scores) are not constitutional. Although the authors of this report do not have a clear basis for being for or against affirmative action in college recruitment in the Brazilian case, there is no question that action of some kind is needed to increase the chances that poor and talented Afro-Brazilians will gain access to tertiary education.

Educational reform "against the odds?"

First-phase reforms involving access to and expansion of basic education often command broad support from various stakeholders, including politicians, teachers' unions, and parents. However, second-phase reforms that are needed to deal with problems of quality—including for poorer groups—typically involve measures that affect the conditions of work for teachers and increase the power of parents and communities. At the tertiary level, reform can involve dealing with the vested interests of universities and students who are part of richer groups in society. Is making education more equal therefore a classic political economy case of reform "against the odds," in which benefits are diffuse but costs are associated with concentrated and organized groups?

Actual experiences show that reforms do occur, with the role of different groups varying across cases. This is seen in a five-country study of Bolivia, Brazil (in the state of Minas Gerais), Ecuador, Mexico, and Nicaragua by Grindle (2002; see also discussion in Ames 2003). Efforts in all five countries involved decentralization to the state, municipality, or school, and to differing degrees involved providing training and career advancement opportunities to teachers and promoting student testing, parental involvement, and curricula reform. Teachers' unions were often found to be sources of resistance. However, in every case except Ecuador, significant reforms were undertaken that involved leadership from the executive branch (that is, by presidents or ministers of education) and persistent action by reform teams.

Do unions have to be the villains in reform processes? Maceira and Murillo (2001) argue that it is necessary to take into account the market position, beliefs, and alliances of teachers unions, but that engagement and negotiation with worker representatives can be a source of both sensible design and, importantly, greater buy-in by stakeholders. Indeed, in at least one of Grindle's (forthcoming) cases (the Brazilian state of Minas Gerais), unions appear to have been advocates for reform and to have long called for greater democracy in education. Similarly, the Colombia teachers' union has significant progressive elements, especially in the pedagogic movement, that favor decentralization, greater school autonomy, and teacher appointments by open competition rather than clientelism (Angell, Lowden, and Thorp 2001).

7.2. Property rights, land, and housing

Property rights matter for both growth and inequality. Security of property rights is essential to investment, and property rights were featured in the original "Washington Consensus" as one of the ingredients for growth.[7] Links between property rights and inequality may also be a factor in the bivariate association between measures of polarization and of the credibility and predictability of property and contractual rights (figure 7.5). On the one hand, greater polarization may be a source of challenges to property rights, if manifested in distributive struggles (as argued by Keefer and Knack 2000). Such challenges can be in the form of outright expropriation or the more subtle form of changes in policies, such as taxes, that affect returns to property.

On the other hand, unequal political structures can cause inequalities in both the ownership and security of property rights. Unequal land ownership has been a central feature of Latin American history (see chapter 4) and remains prevalent in many parts of the region today. However, inequalities in security are also prevalent, as made clear by typically weaker land rights in poorer urban areas (de Soto 1989 and 2000). Furthermore, in politically unstable societies, one solution has been to generate institutional mechanisms for *selective* commitments on property rights that typically involve tight alliances between political and economic elites, as discussed in chapter 5 (see Haber, Maurer, and Razo 2003 for a detailed discussion on the case of Mexico).

More secure property rights for all will thus generally be good for equity, especially if they influence patterns of investment by households and property owners across the income distribution. However, there are potential tradeoffs. Where property ownership (as opposed to the security of property rights) is very unequally distributed, a case can be made for redistribution. Nonetheless, threats of expropriation for redistributive purposes will lower the investments of property owners, in turn reducing growth (and possibly employment). These issues are discussed below, first in the context of rural land and then with regard to urban areas, which also includes the consideration of housing.

Rural land reform

Inequalities in land ownership have been at the center of the historical formation of social, income, and political inequalities in Latin America (see chapter 4). The typical pattern in the region has been the creation and maintenance of large landholdings for groups of colonial origin, followed in most countries by the extensive appropriation of land by elites after independence in both the 19th century, and, in some countries in the 20th century. A wide range of mechanisms were

FIGURE 7.5

Polarization and property rights across countries

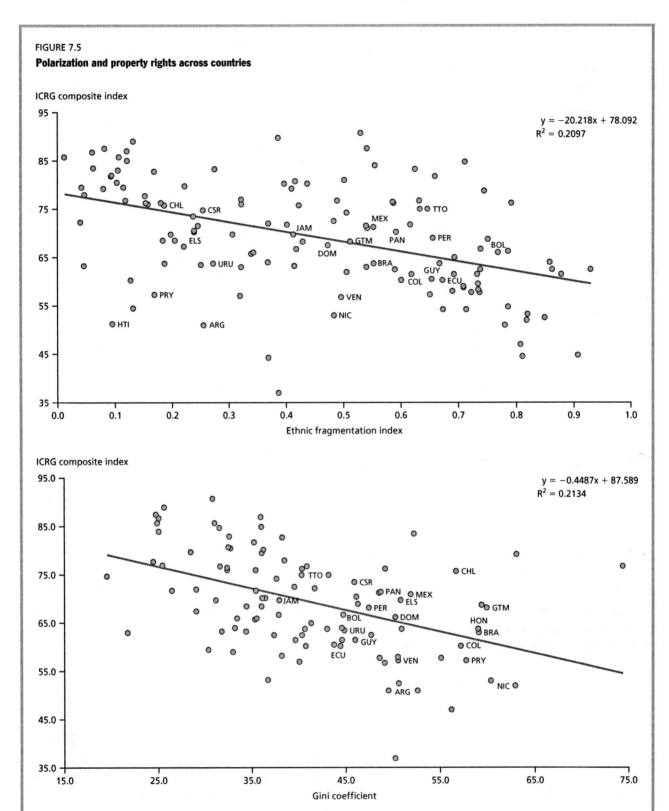

Source: Authors' calculations, based on the ethnic fragmentation index in Alesina and others 2002, income Gini coefficients calculated for this report, and the composite index from the *International Country Risk Guide* (ICRG) that is a proxy of credibility and predictability of property and contractual rights. (See Knack and Keefer 1997 for a discussion.)

TABLE 7.4

Gini coefficients for the distribution of operational holdings of agricultural land across regions

Region	Deininger and Olinto (i)	UNDP (ii)
Latin America	0.81	0.74
Middle East and North Africa	0.67	0.56
North America	0.64	
Sub-Saharan Africa	0.61	0.51
Western Europe	0.57	
East and South Asia	0.56	0.52

Note: Column (i) shows averages for the 1950–1994 period. Column (ii) shows values around 1981.
Source: Deininger and Olinto 2000 and UNDP 1993.

used to effect this process, including expropriation of indigenous lands during both the colonial period and the 19th century (for example in El Salvador, Guatemala, and Mexico), control of labor through slavery to make land productive (notably in sugar production in Brazil), forced labor requirements, debt peonage, imported indentured labor, and vagrancy laws. These mechanisms were complemented by interventions related to taxes, inputs, and other market-related aspects.

Comparative information on the inequality of land ownership is unreliable, since standard measures don't adjust for land quality and use. With this word of caution in mind, tables 7.4 and 7.5 show the commonly quoted land-related Gini coefficients. For Latin America as a whole, the Gini coefficient was 0.81 in the second half of the 20th century, compared with 0.56 in Asia.[8] As discussed in chapter 4, the prevailing pattern of landholding and production became intimately linked with forms of political domination and the weak influence of subordinate groups, trends that were supported by the neglect of education and other social services.

Although the frontier settler countries of Argentina, Chile, and Uruguay had small indigenous or Afro-descended populations, they also developed highly unequal patterns of land ownership. Argentina and Uruguay had, if anything, slightly higher than average levels of inequality, in large part because of the extensive pattern of livestock production. Chile's relatively modest land inequality, represented by a Gini coefficient of 0.64 around 1981, was influenced by land reforms of the 1960s and early 1970s. (Under the Pinochet

TABLE 7.5.

Gini coefficients for the distribution of operational holdings of agricultural land in Latin American countries

	Deininger and Olinto		UNDP
	1950–1979 (i)	1980–1994 (ii)	1981 (iii)
Antigua	0.74		
Argentina	0.86	0.85	
Bahamas	0.90	0.87	
Barbados	0.90	0.93	
Belize	0.72	0.71	
Bolivia		0.77	
Brazil	0.83	0.85	0.86
Colombia	0.85	0.77	0.70
Costa Rica	0.81		
Chile			0.64
Dominican Rep.	0.80		0.70
Ecuador	0.86		0.69
El Salvador	0.83		
Grenada	0.78	0.74	0.69
Guatemala	0.86		
Guyana		0.68	
Honduras	0.75		0.64
Jamaica	0.81	0.81	
Mexico	0.59		
Nicaragua	0.80		
Panama	0.71	0.87	0.84
Paraguay	0.86	0.78	0.94
Peru	0.94		0.61
Puerto Rico	0.73	0.77	
Suriname	0.73		
Trinidad	0.68		
Uruguay	0.82	0.80	0.84
RB de Venezuela	0.92		

Note: The values for each country correspond in column (i) to the first value in the 1950–1979 period and in column (ii) to the most recent observation during the 1980–1994 period.
Source: Authors' calculations based on Deininger and Olinto 2000 and UNDP 1993.

government, these reforms were only partly reversed, with a significant component of distribution to small and medium farmers.) Costa Rica—for reasons related to socio-economic structure and political transition in the late 19th century—developed a system of political influence that gave substantial influence to small and medium farmers over the shaping of policy, along with an associated early broadening of suffrage and the provision of basic education. This process was associated with relatively equal land distribution in the Valle Central, the most populated and important area of the country. Outside this area, land was unequally distributed, which explains the high overall Gini coefficient.

Redistributive land reform has long been advocated both as a source of greater short-run equity and efficiency and as a measure to support the transition to a more rapid and equal development path.[9] However, it is important to recognize the complexity of the relationship between land size and productivity. Current thinking on the land size-efficiency relationship in Latin America recognizes this complexity.[10]

For most crops and under normal conditions of availability of mechanical services, production is neutral with regard to scale for a wide range of farm sizes, starting with fairly small areas of one or two hectares. For grains and other field crops that require a small labor input and little management, the relevant area can be large (that is, up to several hundred hectares). For farms growing labor-intensive crops (mostly fruit and horticulture) or when management requirements are substantial (because of such factors as varying soil conditions, erratic weather conditions, frequent pest incidence, and mixed farming), returns on production begin to decline rather quickly. This is because under similar technology and market conditions, family farms are generally more efficient than wage-labor farms with regard to managing labor and ensuring quality management practices.

For crops that require immediate processing (like coffee, sugar, or African palm), small farm size is not a problem at the farm level (that is, in terms of production), but can be a disadvantage at the industry level if coordination between farmers and mills is inadequate. For coffee, farm size is not a significant problem because processing—in which timeliness is essential—is carried out on the farm with simple means. However, processing can make a difference for sugar, palm oil, and banana production; for these crops, both wage-labor plantation systems and family farm systems have proved to be competitive. Industrial crops that do not require immediate processing (such as cotton, a variety of oil seeds, and to some extent cocoa) tend to be grown competitively on small and medium family farms.

Large farms often have advantages in terms of access to input and output markets, financing, and contracting of technical assistance. This can sometimes offset diseconomies of scale associated with management and labor supervision. The advantages of large farms could potentially be replicated by small and medium farms if they coordinated input and output needs through cooperatives or similar associations, as is done in many parts of Europe. However, in situations of marked agricultural dualism—which are typical in Latin American countries—the small farm sector usually remains disadvantaged with respect to access to financial and technical services.

In addition, small, poor farms are generally located on marginal land, often in mountainous areas, that offer poor conditions for commercial farming. The advantage of large farms has frequently resulted from an array of distortions in policy induced by the political influence of landed elites. Such distortions range from output, input, and credit subsidies to the public provisioning of infrastructure to meet the needs of large farmers (see Binswanger, Deininger, and Feder 1995).

This situation suggests that small farms can be efficient alternatives for production, but that this depends on conditions specific to particular crops and associated factors such as marketing and credit. The importance of context in turn implies that attention should be given to the likely heterogeneity of conditions. In one review of empirical work in six countries, López and Valdés (2000a, 2000b) found that the contribution of land to per capita income is low (even though returns on production are typically either constant or decreasing), especially when compared with other factors of production such as human capital.

However, recent work on Mexico by Finan, Sadoulet, and de Janvry (2002) (summarized in box 7.3) finds a more complex relationship between land size and welfare, with the potential for making large, poverty-reducing gains from levels of land ownership as low as one or two hectares. These authors also emphasize the powerful influence of other household characteristics, including education and indigeneity, and of the economic context, with roads having a strong influence on productivity and household welfare.

There is also some evidence of the dynamic advantages of lower land inequality. The negative influence of land inequality on subsequent growth has been documented in econometric work, as illustrated by the bivariate relationship shown in figure 7.6. Such cross-country results are only suggestive, as has been emphasized throughout this report. Earlier chapters have discussed a range of potential mechanisms through which land inequalities may be associated with lower growth. These include the impact on policy distortions and, perhaps more profoundly, links with the creation of weak and unequal institutions that dampen growth prospects. In contrast, work that interprets the sources of rapid East Asian growth has often emphasized

BOX 7.3

The poverty reduction potential of land in rural Mexico

A major question that arises when developing land policy is the effect of increased land on the welfare of the poor. Although almost all studies find a positive impact both on production and income, empirical work on several Latin American countries by López and Valdés (2000a and 2000b) concludes that the effect of land on the size of income is low for small farmers. This implies that only large increases in land would lift poor rural farmers out of poverty. Work on rural households in Mexico by Finan, Sadoulet, and de Janvry (2002), based on a 1997 survey, casts important light on this issue. These authors use a methodological approach (specifically, semiparametric regression techniques) that allows for highly nonlinear relationships with land size. They also explore the impact of complementary factors and use a broad welfare measure that captures the multiple dimensions of well-being, as well as income alone.

There are two main results of this approach. First, access to even a small plot of land can raise household welfare significantly: for small landholders with at most one hectare of land (which means 30 percent of farmers in the survey), an additional hectare increases welfare by an average of 1.3 times the earnings of an agricultural worker. (This is illustrated in the figure below, which shows the peso value of marginal increases in land.) This pattern is partly due to the fact that land can facilitate the more effective deployment of a household's labor resources in the context of imperfect labor markets and local unemployment. As the size of land increases, its marginal value falls to a much lower level.

Second, there are important complementarities between land and other influences. Finan, Sadoulet, and de Janvry (2002) explore this by comparing farming households with different characteristics and decomposing the differences in asset holdings and differences in these assets across households. This is shown in the figures (a–c) below. The first figure (a) explores the impact of nonland assets for households with low levels of education (group A) and high education (group B). The bottom line (W_A) shows the estimated relationship between welfare and land size for households with low education. The second line (W_{A1}) estimates the relationship for group A, assuming that its

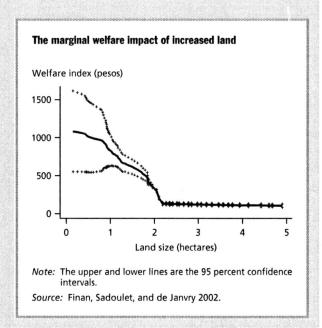

The marginal welfare impact of increased land

Welfare index (pesos)

Note: The upper and lower lines are the 95 percent confidence intervals.

Source: Finan, Sadoulet, and de Janvry 2002.

members had the nonland assets and the same returns as the members of group B. The third line (W_{A2}) adds in the higher returns received by group B. Finally the top line shows the relationship between land size and nonland assets, returns on education, and returns to land for group B. The combination of differences in nonland assets and differences in returns on these assets explains a high proportion of the gap.

The second figure (b) undertakes a similar exercise between indigenous and nonindigenous households. Results show that nonindigenous households not only possess higher nonland assets, but also get higher returns on these assets; there is an unexplained premium of 55 percent of the welfare differential. If indigenous households had the same return on their assets as do nonindigenous households, they would only require access to less than 3 hectares to reach the poverty line, compared with the 15 hectares needed given the returns they actually receive. Finally, the third figure (c) shows the impact of road access; the infrastructure context has a powerful impact on returns and on the efficacy of increased land in improving welfare. These results underscore the importance of developing an integrated strategy for rural development, including the need to understand the special conditions faced by indigenous groups.

BOX 7.3   **(Continued)**

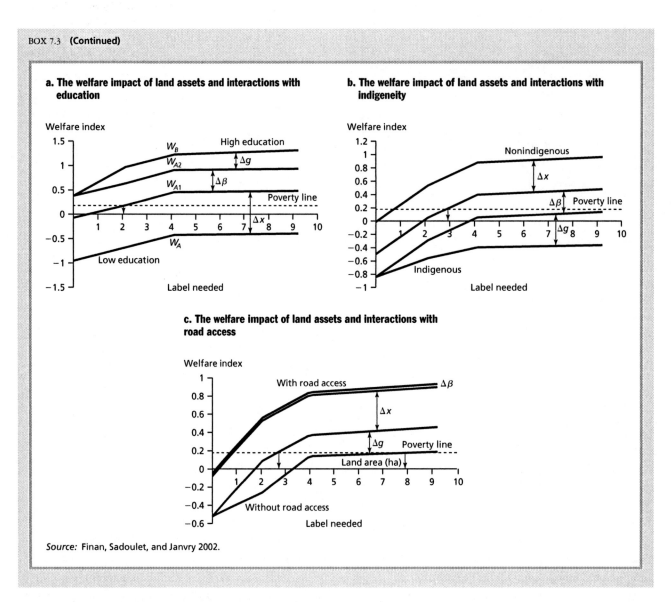

a. The welfare impact of land assets and interactions with education

b. The welfare impact of land assets and interactions with indigeneity

c. The welfare impact of land assets and interactions with road access

Source: Finan, Sadoulet, and Janvry 2002.

how relatively equal land distributions, combined with the political imperative to provide benefits to peasants, have resulted in policy choices that favor the broad-based provisioning of economic and social services.[11] This pattern has fostered a relatively dynamic rural base and the upgrading of the labor force that contributed to the industrial takeoff.

The history of "incomplete" land reforms in Latin America

Despite the resistance and influence of landed elites, it is notable how much redistributive land reform actually occurred in Latin America during the 20th century. The Mexican revolution led the way, and was followed over the decades by large-scale reforms in Bolivia, Chile, Cuba,

El Salvador, Nicaragua, and Peru (see table 7.6). These were sometimes motivated by peasant mobilizations, but also— especially during the Cold War era and in the wake of the Cuban revolution—by pressure from above and outside, including from the United States under the Alliance for Progress. These forms of pressure had the joint objectives of increasing the well-being of peasants and reducing the probability of a rural communist insurgency.

Throughout the 20th century, the possibility of redistributive land reform was also politically facilitated by rising urbanization and the growing importance of urban relative to rural elites. In some cases (Chile for example), alliances between the peasantry and urban-based, social democratic movements formed the political foundation for land reform. Yet the results were largely disappointing. By the late 1980s,

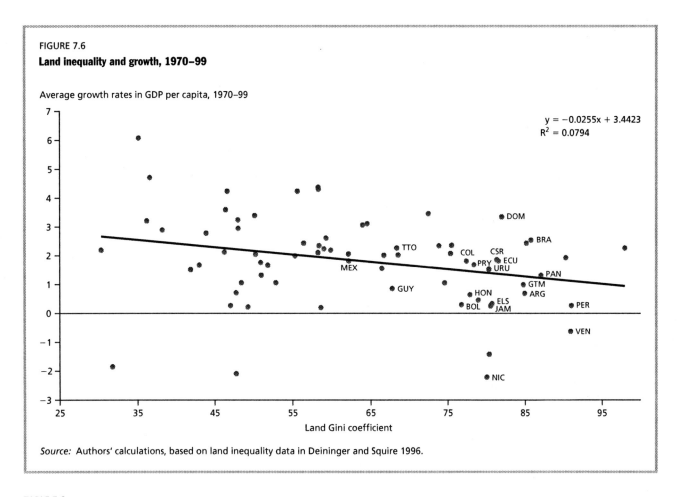

FIGURE 7.6

Land inequality and growth, 1970–99

Average growth rates in GDP per capita, 1970–99

$$y = -0.0255x + 3.4423$$
$$R^2 = 0.0794$$

Source: Authors' calculations, based on land inequality data in Deininger and Squire 1996.

TABLE 7.6

Selected land reforms in Latin America in the 20th century

		Area		Beneficiary households	
	Period	Total (thousand hectares)	Share of arable land (%)	Number (thousands)	Share of rural households (%)
Mexico	1915–76	13,375	13.5	3,044	67.5
Bolivia	1953–70	9,792	32.3	237	47.5
Peru	1969–79	8,599	28.1	375	30.8
El Salvador	1932–89	401	27.9	95	16.8
Nicaragua	1978–87	3,186	47.1	172	56.7
Chile[a]	1973	9,517	60.1	58	12.7

a. The numbers for Chile refer to the partial reversal of the redistributive land reforms of the previous decade, for which data are not available.
Source: World Bank 2003b, p. 182.

de Janvry and Sadoulet (1989) were lamenting the "lost game of Latin American land reform" because of the lack of significant redistribution and the growing influence of medium and large farmers on the state as Cuban-style threats diminished. The predominance of first authoritarian and then economically liberalizing democratic regimes further contributed to the lack of interest in radical land reform in the 1980s and 1990s. As a measure of international opinion, the World Bank's 1990 *World Development Report* (World Bank 1990) judged land reform to be good for poverty reduction in principle, but to rarely be feasible except under the unusual circumstances of colonial action or revolution.

What happened with the major land reforms of the 20th century? They clearly did not usher in the hoped-for transformation of social and economic inequalities in Latin America. Nor, for the most part, did they generate the kind of vibrant smallholder sectors that were so important in furthering East Asia's dynamic development path. However, the reason was not because land reform was in principle ill-conceived. Rather, major land reform efforts were often poorly designed—notably where ill-fated production cooperatives were emphasized—and, more fundamentally, were "incomplete" (de Janvry and Sadoulet 2002b).

This incompleteness existed both with respect to the generation of competitiveness in the post-reform sector and to giving power to peasants, whether in terms of direct or implicit influence over decisionmaking (the latter being a feature of East Asian successes even under authoritarianism). Although the communist transition (particularly in China and Vietnam) and communist threat (in much of the rest of East Asia) made governments respond to the interests of the peasantry, the threat of Cuban-style revolutions in Latin America spawned halfhearted land reforms and heightened repression, at least until the democratization movements of the 1980s ensued.

The political agency of landed elites was one of the factors behind the weaknesses in reforms. A specific element was the economic response to the threat of land redistribution, or the heightened insecurity of property rights. This in particular induced both low levels of tenancy and the eviction of tenants, followed by shifts into more capital- or land-intensive forms of production, such as livestock production (Binswanger, Deininger, and Feder 1995, de Janvry and Sadoulet 1989). In some cases, resistance took the form of the suppression of rural movements, tenant evictions, or large-scale violence between peasants and governments or other forces associated with landed elites. This occurred, for example, in Colombia, El Salvador, and Guatemala during the 20th century. Even in countries where major violence did not occur, the effect on the whole society of such "premature ejection" of labor from productive land was strong, and increased inequalities by placing greater pressure on marginal lands, rural, nonfarm production, and urban unskilled labor markets (see Binswanger, Deininger, and Feder 1995, Conning and Robinson 2002).

The "incompleteness" of land reform processes also played out in a variety of settings. In both Mexico and Bolivia, a genuine large-scale transfer of land from haciendas to peasants occurred in the wake of revolutions. However, in both cases long-term productivity has been low and stagnant and rural poverty has been deep and persistent. In Mexico, there was initially strong state support for the newly created *ejido* sector—a system of communal lands based on expropriated private landholdings—with regard to efforts related to irrigation, credit, and technical assistance. The poor performance of the sector may in fact partly reflect weaknesses in longer-term support, but an important element was an underlying problem in the design of land management.

Restrictions on tenancy and the subdivision and sale of land undermined incentives for production and structural change (World Bank 2001c). The 1992 reforms were a response to these problems (as discussed below). The *ejido* sector was also incorporated into vertical, clientelistic patterns of political relationships, backed by food-related programs and the provisioning of local works that helped sustain rural support, in particular for the *Partido Revolucionario Institucional* (Institutional Revolutionary Party, or PRI) (Fox 1993). There is evidence of the evolution of unequal power within *ejidos* that provided local counterparts of statewide and national forms of clientelism (World Bank 2001c).

In Bolivia, the failure to generate a competitive and influential peasant sector was much starker. The land reform occurred mainly in the *Altiplano* and valleys, with little action taking place in the then sparsely populated *Oriente*. Relatively egalitarian land structures were formed in the former areas, but there was again a failure to support peasant-based production. This failure had political roots. The horizontal alliances that were a force behind the 1953 revolution were quickly reoriented toward vertical incorporation of these groups into the new national structures, notably within the leading political agent of the revolution, the *Movimiento Nacional Revolucionario* (National Revolutionary Movement, or MNR).

With this change, the peasantry entered a new phase and took on a new form of neglect (albeit without haciendas, or estates, controlling them), except for their continuing important role in providing votes when elections were held. The restructuring of unequal vertical relationships overlapped with the continuation of identity-based differences despite, or perhaps because of, the much greater predominance of indigenous groups in Bolivia than in Mexico.[12] Meanwhile, in the Bolivian *Oriente*, where soils and agroecological conditions were better, a concentration of land occurred behind the backs of the legislature, often in a corrupt fashion. Only during the 1990s did elements of a more broadly inclusive national project reemerge under a "pluricultural" constitution. This effort did build on some of the social changes of the 1950s, notably the granting of legal status to and the potential influence of "base groups" that were typically a syncretic mix of indigenous structures and rural unions. However, progress in land reform remained slow, and reemerged as a central issues in new waves of protest in 2001–2003.

Both Peru and Chile introduced collective land reforms. Peru's case is both instructive and tragic, especially with respect to the dynamics of change in the poorer Sierra (the strongly indigenous Andean region). The reforms were part of an ideology of giving power to the peasants. As President General Velasco Alvarado said in 1969 after seizing power, "Peasants, the landlords will no longer eat your poverty!" (Seligmann 1995, p. 1). However, during the course of implementation, the Peruvian land reforms had features of "high modernist" projects (Scott 1998) that favored the larger-scale cooperative production of expropriated haciendas over support to smallholder agriculture.

The reforms also failed to provide complementary services and favored an integrationist cultural agenda rather than the empowerment of indigenous aspirations. Despite (or partly because of) attempts to shift the highly unequal balance of power in land-related court cases to peasants, land disputes and local conflict were rife. With worsening aggregate economic conditions in the 1970s and 1980s, service provision to poor rural areas remained dismal and poverty worsened, even as deep, old resentments were stirred and new aspects of expectation, mobilization, and conflict emerged. The dismantling of agrarian reform cooperatives took place in the early 1980s, with the parceling of land occurring as an implosive phenomenon rather than as a counter reform. Credit and extension services were cut back and the new *parceleros* (parcel owners)—many of whom were agricultural workers with little entrepreneurial experience—were left on their own, with disastrous results.

Even important educational advances had mixed effects. The first major cohorts of indigenous groups with an education emerged with hopes of attaining modern jobs, but in reality faced miserable economic opportunities. Local teaching was one outlet, but low-paid school teachers became a source of radical resentment. This in turn provided fertile ground for the emergence of the violent and millenarian *Sendero Luminoso* (Shining Path) movement, which is much closer in approach to the Khmer Rouge in Cambodia than to traditional guerrilla movements in Latin America. The main victims of both *Sendero* and the military effort to respond to the movement were poor rural peasants.[13] Political and economic order was finally restored under the semi-authoritarian regime of Alberto Fujimori (1990–2000), who reversed some of the earlier land reforms (especially those affecting the more fertile coastal areas) and undertook substantial expansion of social and infrastructural services to peasants through a kind of national-level clientelistic project.[14] However, little was done to strengthen the competitiveness of peasant-based agricultural production.

Other land reform efforts also remained largely mired in problems related to failure to achieve competitiveness, notably under cooperative structures (Cuba and Nicaragua under the Sandinistas) or in sites of conflict (El Salvador). With the shift to a heightened emphasis on markets starting in the mid-1980s, issues of redistributive land reform took a much lower place on the agenda. (On the Washington Consensus list, the important issue of property rights was typically interpreted as a message of increasing those of existing incumbents, thus implying that the redistribution of property rights was to be avoided.)

Major 20th century efforts for direct land reform were disappointing. Did the past 15–20 years of market liberalization yield better results by providing an incentive regime for labor-intensive agricultural development? There were positive developments in terms of the reduction of inefficient distortions in product, input, and credit markets that had been created under the influence of landed elites. In some cases, this helped bring down land prices (World Bank 2003b). The reduced protection of import-substituting industries (through tariffs or the overvaluation of real exchange rates) shifted incentives to tradable production and helped some parts of the agricultural sector—though not producers of subsistence or other nontraded products, which are often important among the rural poor (see Schiff and Valdés 1992 for a review).

The last few decades also sparked high hopes that labor-intensive, export-oriented agriculture would help solve the employment and rural poverty problem and, at least implicitly, render the politically difficult challenge of land reform unnecessary. Chile appeared to be a model for this process. Under the rule of Augusto Pinochet (1973–1990), about one-third of expropriated lands were restituted to their large-scale owners and most of the remainder was allocated as private parcels averaging around 20 hectares. When growth took off (following the economic crisis of the early 1980s), export-oriented agricultural expansion was a central component. During the 1980s, there was an enormous expansion in nontraditional agro-exports.

Chile was not alone. Other cases—involving in large part the successful association of small farmers and processing and exporting companies—include the development of nontraditional exports, for example, decorative plants, palm kernels, and tropical fruits, on the Atlantic coast of Costa Rica; vegetable production in Guatemala; successful exports to the United States of fruits and vegetables by irrigation farmers in northern Mexico; production of tropical fruits and vegetables for international markets in northeastern Brazil; soya and wheat production in Paraguay; and the recent expansion of palm oil exports from Colombia. Yet while advocates saw such developments as a source of growth and jobs, critics emphasized the adverse effect that they had on the rural poor, primarily in the form of reduced access to land, uncertain work, and rising food prices.

A comparison between export-oriented agriculture in Chile, Guatemala, and Paraguay by Carter, Barham, and Mesbah (1996) provides insight into the question of who benefited from such agro-export booms. The study found that outcomes were contingent on initial conditions, types of crops, patterns of support, and the induced processes of structural change. In Chile, for example, the agro-export boom was dominated by medium to large farmers, in part due to the information, packaging, and marketing requirements of fruit production.[15] With new pressure on the traditional crops grown in the smallholder sector, there was a substantial amount of selling out to large farmers, with almost 60 percent of the *parceleros* who had received land under the Pinochet land reform selling their land by the late 1980s. This exclusionary pattern (in terms of landownership) was partly offset by the rapid growth in employment on the large farms, but the new jobs were mostly seasonal and paid stagnant or declining wages.

In contrast, in the Guatemalan highlands smallholders have been the main actors in the boom in winter vegetable crops. These crops are 50–300 percent more labor-intensive than traditional crops. In this case, changes in land owner-

ship involve transfers from medium to small producers. This pattern is attributable to four factors: the high levels of labor interactivity required in the production process (where smallholders have an advantage); an initially highly fragmented land ownership structure in this part of Guatemala; contractual linkages with processors that also facilitated working capital; and the ability of farmers to pursue self-insurance strategies by mixing exports with food crops.

In Paraguay, both the pattern of initially adopting soya and wheat and the induced structural changes were exclusionary. This was because of a prevailing mixture of technical factors (some crops required less labor interactivity), economic institutions (smallholders lacked the means to access working capital), and initial land allocation processes (the frontier region had relatively large land allocations and a land market that facilitated unequal agrarian change).

There is no guarantee that small farmers or rural workers will be major beneficiaries of agro-export booms. Agro-exports can favor poor farmers or workers, but the degree to which this actually happens depends on both technical factors and the institutional context. Although smallholders have often been favored by labor interactivity in some of the agro-export crops and initially fragmented land holdings, most competitive biases work against them. This trend is due to the labor- and skill-intensive character of most production processes, price-quality measurement issues, the perishability of many crops, the extended gestation periods of some investments, and the lack of complementary insurance markets. Similarly, as the case of Petrolina-Juazeiro in northeastern Brazil illustrates (see chapter 8), export production on large farms can be consistent with decent work for agricultural laborers, but this again depends on the institutional context. In this case, the critical issue was the nature of interactions between the union movement and modern farms.

New opportunities and options

Land reform had moved to the bottom of the policy agenda by the end of the 20th century, reflecting shifts in the tides of opinion and disappointments over earlier efforts. Yet the issues that spurred reform have not gone away. Rural poverty remains pervasive and is almost always deeper than urban poverty. Agro-exports can help alleviate the situation, but will not be an automatic solution. The context of the early 21st century provides potential opportunities for intensified action. There is heightened concern today over poverty and social exclusion and continued demands from established movements (such as the *Movimento Sem Terra* in Brazil and indigenous groups in many countries). Perhaps most important, more recent experience suggests that land reforms can be designed to be effective and to reflect lessons learned from the mistakes of the past.

An approach involving multiple paths and activities is outlined below. There is no single "high modernist" or other route to rural development and agrarian change. It is increasingly understood that there are multiple exit paths out of rural poverty, including migration, intensified smallholder production, and unskilled and (increasingly) semiskilled work on farms and in rural nonfarm activities and small towns. Transfers for redistribution and risk management can also play a complementary and transitional role (see chapter 9).

This complexity implies the need to avoid standardized solutions. One example involves plot size. "Unviable" plots for agricultural production can in fact play an important role in income generation and diversification, even when the bottom 20 percent of rural households typically gets only 30–50 percent of its income from agriculture.[16] As discussed in box 7.3, increasing land to the 1–2 hectare range in Mexico can have a significant impact on poverty. More broadly, achieving competitiveness is a factor of overall spatial strategies, local participation, and linkages between agricultural and nonagricultural sectors, as emphasized in "*la nueva ruralidad.*" (Food and Agriculture Organization and the World Bank 2003). In addition, as noted above, support for smallholder production also involves tackling remaining distortions that favor large-scale production and developing infrastructural and institutional services to support smallholder production. Finally, agrarian change is often intimately connected with the identity-based inequalities and subsequent needs for and policies on social incorporation that were major themes in chapters 3 and 7.

Both farmers and countries across Latin America—as well as the extent to which land reform is on the political and economic agenda throughout the region—vary greatly. It is important to distinguish between countries (and among areas within countries) with regard to where existing land rights are and are not contested. The former applies to parts of Bolivia, Brazil, and Colombia (for example in parts of the Bolivian *Oriente*). In these cases, agrarian reforms with some expropriatory elements may have a role to play, with their design depending on both political and technical

considerations. In Colombia, recent legislation allows for the confiscation of the lands of druglords. The situation is different in countries where the land rights system has legitimacy, such as in the Southern Cone countries or where there are no lands to redistribute (for example, in the Bolivian highlands, Mexico, and Peru).

Five approaches to land reform are outlined below. It should be noted that in all of these examples, infrastructural, technical, and institutional support tailored to local conditions is essential to ensure competitiveness.

Strengthening tenancy markets   As already noted, the tenancy market in Latin America is severely underdeveloped relative to other parts of the world, especially when compared with developed countries. The primary reasons for this are weak property rights and a lack of conflict resolution mechanisms, sometimes combined with prohibitions on renting (for example, pre-1992 in the Mexican *ejido* sector). Yet rentals can be a major mechanism for the redistribution of land access, with significant efficiency gains. Renting is also often part of the land acquisition "ladder" for small producers. There is a strong case to be made for tackling existing disincentives to rent (see below for an example from Mexico post-1992). There are also a variety of experiments that seek to support tenancy and deserve careful tracking and evaluation; examples include the Landless Workers' Consortium and Sharecropper and Rural Leasing Exchange in Brazil and group rentals in Honduras.

Land titling   Insecure property rights can reduce production growth because of reduced incentives to make investments and the limited ability to use land as collateral for credit. According to surveys conducted in the early- to mid-1990s, about 63 percent of farmers in Chile, Colombia, Honduras, and Paraguay lacked legal title to their land (López and Valdés 2000a). Empirical work on Honduras and Paraguay has identified significant impacts of this trend, for example an increase in per capita income by 5 percent in Honduras. However, most benefits were captured by medium and large farms. Work on Asia suggests that land titling alone is insufficient. To reap significant benefits, titling should be complemented by a fair and effective legal system, cadastral surveys, and implementation of enforcement mechanisms, in addition to actions that enhance competitiveness in terms of infrastructure and other economic services.

Community- and market-based land reform   In the early 1990s, the World Bank and other agencies became associated with a new approach to land reform. This involved decentralized and voluntary land sales backed by both credit and grants for land purchase (in addition to complementary actions to enhance competitiveness). Such assistance is needed because land prices typically exceed in-use values due to other sources of land value (for example, as an investment and source of security and status), and even after distortionary policies are removed. There are some interesting experiments under way, notably in the *Cédula da Terra* project in Brazil, but rigorous evaluations on them are not yet available. There are also disadvantages to this approach, especially those associated with fiscal cost. In addition to upfront fiscal subsidies, a contingent fiscal liability applies if farmers default on loans used for land purchase. These fiscal costs may limit the potential for scaling up community- or market-based land reform. Nevertheless, this approach may be a valuable instrument for some groups of farmers, especially under conditions in which there is mutual acceptance of the legitimacy of land ownership by both the seller and the purchaser.

Negotiated recuperation of lands   There are substantial but underutilized opportunities for recuperation of lands for use by poor people at a relatively low cost. This includes the potential distribution of public lands. In Bolivia, the government has identified 900,000 hectares of land suitable for settlement; in the Dominican Republic there is a backlog of already expropriated land. This approach may also involve recuperation of illegal settlements, given the potential welfare dimensions of this process. There are also opportunities for negotiated deals in areas where land title is ambiguous, that is, where partial release of land with uncertain title is conducted in return for titling of the smaller part. The mayor of Brasilia has an ongoing scheme of this kind, and a comparable scheme is under way in the Dominican Republic. Many Latin American land reforms have incomplete titling and present new opportunities. Releasing land in return for greater security of the remaining plot can be an attractive deal for landowners.

Land reform and indigenous, communal processes   One aspect of land reform that is of particular relevance to indigenous groups involves collective rights to land. Indigenous cultures often have effective ways of managing property that balance the need to provide security and incentives for investment with mechanisms for regulating the overuse of common resources. (See chapter 1 in World Bank 2003b for a review of such methods.) Indigenous groups in Ecuador and Bolivia have succeeded in obtaining collective rights that involve restitution of ancient claims. When traditional mechanisms work well, such approaches can be both equitable and efficient solutions, but there is also a risk of maladaptation to dynamic processes of social and economic change. With rapid change, problems of insecurity, conflict, and overuse of common property become more important. In addition, indigenous sociocultural systems can perpetuate traditional patterns of inequality. Institutional design needs to be shaped in a way that simultaneously allows for change and integrates transparent, local democratic processes so that decisions can be made as local land policy evolves.

An example of the transition from collective toward more individual landholdings is the *ejido* (communal land) sector in Mexico. The 1992 land reforms, which involved changes to the 1917 constitution, were the product of a political compromise between those resistant to change in the *ejido* sector and advocates for a full-blown shift to property rights. The resulting hybrid reform may have been a judicious choice. The self-governance of *ejidos* was strengthened through the effective recognition of their legal standing and autonomous decisionmaking power over internal matters, and in particular by allowing members to decide on the form of land ownership within their entity (including full individual property titles). Land rental was fully supported and sales were legalized but restricted to others within the *ejido*, except when a community decision was made to shift to *dominio pleno*, or fully individualized titles. In addition, an independent system of agrarian justice was set up to administer a wide range of land disputes.

Some 50 million hectares and 3 million households have had land regularized under the *ejido* reform, including 1 million households that previously had no land rights at all.[17] No major sell-off or concentration of landholdings has occurred, as feared by some. Panel data for 1994–1997 show that those who participated in *ejidos* also experienced rising incomes, primarily because of an expansion in off-farm work. An extensive program of resolution of conflicts over land was also established and there is some evidence of greater transparency and deepening in governance within *ejidos*, which have been subject to both external party influence and substantial internal inequalities in power. The agenda remains unfinished, however, especially in areas where land disputes and other conflicts are severe; this is particularly the case in the southern states, which are poorer and have a higher concentration of indigenous people than other areas. Nonetheless, the *ejido* process still represents a complex reform that may facilitate a process of modernization without the sudden removal of existing mechanisms that provide security (World Bank 2001c).

Urban land and housing

With regard to urban areas, the focus is placed here on the housing issue, which has important links with issues of land tenure.[18] For most people in urban areas, housing is the single most valuable item they will ever own. For the poor and much of the middle class, home ownership and the accumulation of consumer durables are typical asset-building strategies. Expenditures on housing account for an average of 25 percent of household consumption. What happens to the distribution of housing is likely to have a strong impact on asset inequality in any given country.

Homeownership itself is not highly correlated with income (see table A.8). Homeownership often, but not always, increases along with an individual's income. In Argentina and Ecuador, for example, it is higher in the poorest quintile than in the second and third quintiles. In addition, homeownership even among the very poor is quite high (above 60 percent for most countries), with the exception of Ecuador and Colombia. A large proportion of poor homeowners have informal tenure; in Mexico, for example, a survey of the country's poor urban neighborhoods shows that only about half the homeowners had a formal title to their land. Even in Argentina, where the housing market is quite mature, a full 18 percent of all homeowners lack a full set of titles.

Despite relatively equal access to homeownership, in the countries for which data are available the overall distribution of housing wealth is extremely unequal, even more so than inequality in incomes (see table 7.7). Chile in 2000 is a partial exception, with housing wealth inequality similar to income inequality. This may be the result of a widely praised homeownership program. The distribution of housing wealth appears to be less stable than income distribution, but it is unclear whether this is due to greater measurement errors or real trends (Fay, Yepes, and Foster 2002).

Is housing a good asset to hold? Being a homeowner brings advantages of a constant flow of services and frees liquidity-constrained households from having to generate a

TABLE 7.7
Distribution of housing wealth in Brazil, Chile, and Peru

	Peru		Chile		Brazil	
	1991	1999	1992	2000	1992	1999
Housing wealth Gini	0.66	0.72	0.69	0.59	0.73	0.66
Income Gini	0.45	0.44	0.56	0.57	0.56	0.57
Share of housing value held (percent):						
Income quintile 1	14	4	17	11	7	8
Income quintile 2	17	6	11	13	9	9
Income quintile 3	18	9	13	17	13	13
Income quintile 4	25	18	17	22	20	20
Income quintile 5	25	62	42	38	52	50

Note: The housing wealth Gini coefficient shows that the "poor" are nonowners with zero housing wealth. This measurement is therefore not strictly comparable with the share of housing value that is held by the various *income* quintiles. The Brazil data are from Reis and others (2000) and the other data are from Fay and others (2002).

fixed sum for rent every month. This can be important in times of crisis. For example, in Uruguay 10 percent of people who did not own the house in which they live had to move following the economic crisis in order to cut down on housing costs. Housing services can also be monetized quite easily by taking in renters or additional household members.[19] However, being a homeowner may also have some downsides, for example by tying the poor to locations that are disadvantageous for work or unsafe due to crime or natural disasters. It is unclear how liquid housing markets are in poor neighborhoods.

Most governments in the world have pursued active homeownership policies. Throughout Latin America, these have typically taken two forms: mortgage subsidies that benefit the middle and upper classes and the provision of "low-income" housing of a size and value that is typically beyond the means of the low-income population. In Mexico, about one percent of GDP is spent on housing subsidies that largely benefit the middle and upper classes, substantially more than is spent on *Oportunidades,* the country's largest targeted social program.[20] Developed countries, on the other hand, have been more successful with their homeownership policies. Two good examples are the United States and the United Kingdom, where a secular trend of decreasing wealth inequality has been associated with the spread of popular assets such as housing and consumer durables (Davies and Shorrocks 2000).

Most low-income families in Latin America acquire housing through informal markets, the main characteristic of which is the gradual acquisition and upgrading of housing. It is estimated that informal housing accounts for about one-quarter of all urban homes in Latin America (Angel 2000), varying from a low of 10 percent in Buenos Aires to a high of 59 percent in Bogota (ECLAC 2000). Low-income families are concentrated in informal housing for several reasons. The avoidance of cumbersome regulation and excessive standards can lead to substantially cheaper houses. (In Buenos Aires, for example, the cheapest formal sector house or apartment costs 2.7 times the median income; similar housing in an informal settlement costs 0.8 times the median income.) The informal sector also offers the opportunity to live in houses that are built gradually as financing resources become available. In the informal sector, the gradually built house consists completely of equity, and can be lived in, sold, rented, or passed on as family patrimony, however modest and incomplete.

While informal housing is the most common choice for low-income families, it has disadvantages from a public policy point of view. The informal sector is poor at performing the collective action role of ensuring that settlements have adequately defined rights of way, properly titled properties, and access to urban services such as water and sanitation. Failure to plan properly for these aspects means greater capital outlays in the future, for example to resettle families away from high-risk areas (such as floodplains), replot rights of way so that emergency vehicles and collective transport can access communities, and untangle legal claims on property that can take years or decades to resolve.

An effective and equitable public policy should be based on a good understanding of the informal sector, and seek to work on both the demand and supply sides of the housing and land markets. To a large extent, policies have evolved. In the 1960s and 1970s, the public sector sought to directly provide low-income housing, typically linking it to clearing out slums and relocating populations in new settlements, which were often in more distant, cheaper locations that made transportation and other aspects of daily life costly and inconvenient. As a result, the poor would often sell their new houses and move into informal settlements closer to town. Gradually, projects began to focus more on upgrading slums, but high costs and the absence of cost-recovery policies resulted in government agencies running out of resources. The 1980s saw a greater emphasis on reforming housing financing and the financial performance of related govern-

ment agencies. Today, public policies aim for a more integrated approach and are adopted to support demand through property rights, mortgage financing, and the rationalization of demand subsidies. This approach in turn helps to promote institutional development and to organize supply by providing infrastructure for residential land development, regulating land and housing development, and coordinating the building industry.

High supply costs are often due, at least in part, to regulatory or market failures. Many national or local governments impose minimum land use and housing standards that place housing out of reach for large segments of the population. Moreover, cities in many countries suffer from a scarcity of serviced land, usually because of the cumbersome process required to develop land. In Ecuador, the laws governing residential development have created a cumbersome approval process for residential subdivisions that averages 16 months and imposes costs estimated at 30 percent of the value of new homes.

Public policies to ease supply-side constraints focus on lowering costs, increasing the supply of serviced land, and engaging residents in the provision of housing. This requires administrative reforms to:

- Make land tenure regularization and land transactions easier. Peru offers an excellent example of successful reforms of this type. In just over five years, the COFO-PRI project regularized 1.6 million lots and registered more than 1.2 million titles by streamlining administrative and legal processes and adopting a large-scale approach to regularizing vast tracks of illegal housing.
- Make buildings and land subdivision regulations more flexible and allow for reduced norms and standards. Experience in Brazil and elsewhere has shown that with flexible standards, a house can be built at about half the price of a formal housing unit.
- Allow for and encourage progressive provision of infrastructure, whereby public investment focuses on major trunk infrastructure and leaves to the residents (in partnership with developers) the process of installing connections to their plots.
- Develop innovations in materials and reduce system installation and material costs.

On the demand side, the main objective is to ease the financial constraints of the poor. This can be done through small savings schemes; by pooling group savings into community trusts and linking the trusts to national housing finance programs; by providing access to staged and progressive loans and technical assistance; by encouraging community-based production and employment; and through small targeted subsidies in the form of up-front capital grants for people who cannot afford a down payment. Developing financing strategies to meet the demand for low-income housing also helps stimulate the interest of private sector entrepreneurs in development and construction. A number of countries have successfully experienced such demand-side interventions. Perhaps the most successful example of a direct subsidy is Chile's Unified Subsidy and Basic Housing Program, which enrolls the lowest income groups in a savings program that eventually allows them to acquire a house through a combination of savings, a direct subsidy (which varies according to income but cannot exceed about US$4,000), and an optional mortgage credit. Again, these programs are flexible in that they allow participants to purchase an old or a new housing unit or to build a house for those that already own a plot.

In recent years, these principles—along with a greater emphasis on community participation and cost recovery—have been applied to a new generation of very successful

programs to upgrade slums. One of the better known is the case of El Mezquital, a low-income informal settlement with a population of close to 40,000 people on the outskirts of Guatemala City. In this community, an average public investment of US$1,200 per household has stimulated substantial increases in private investment and has resulted in significant improvements in the quality of life (for example, infant mortality rates fell from 80 to 20 per 1,000 live births in four years) and an increase in land values by a factor of 11. In El Mezquital, community participation extends beyond the simple contribution of labor to involvement in planning, implementation, and evaluation of all activities. Management capacity is promoted by working through the community. Both project funding and contracting are carried out directly by a community association. Community-based organizations ensure that the costs of investments are recovered and that families pay for the consumption of urban services.

Land and property taxation

The issues discussed in this section are linked with the tax issues discussed in chapter 9. Land and property taxes are substantially underdeveloped in Latin America relative to OECD comparators (as shown in figure 7.7). Even though

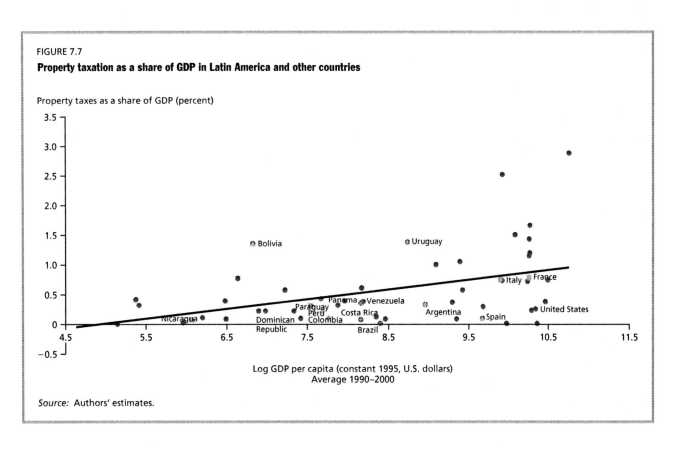

FIGURE 7.7

Property taxation as a share of GDP in Latin America and other countries

Property taxes as a share of GDP (percent)

Log GDP per capita (constant 1995, U.S. dollars)
Average 1990–2000

Source: Authors' estimates.

these are not elastic taxes, they could play a much larger role and yield benefits in terms of efficiency, equity, and local government functioning. Technical issues related to this shift exist, but are not insuperable. In the context of rising decentralization, the current emphasis on social inclusion, and the need for more accountable local government, the time has come to have a major push for a substantially greater use of these instruments in both rural and urban areas. A new tax-related strategy could be politically linked to local reform and development, whether through agrarian change or urban land development.

7.3. Infrastructure services and the distributional impact of privatization

This section turns to the relationship between infrastructure provision and inequalities. Infrastructure services can have large effects on the level and distribution of well-being. Yet infrastructure provision is also embedded in the political economy of Latin American societies. The amount, efficiency, and equity of infrastructure provision has been compromised in particular by clientelistic structures and the persistently low tax effort typical in much of the region. Since the 1980s, there have been major attempts to reform infrastructure provision, both through privatization and reforms within the public sector. Some of these have brought substantial benefits for both efficiency and equity. However, these changes are incomplete, with problems remaining in regard to the process and regulation of privatization (which partly explains its extreme unpopularity) and, in most countries, a strong need for both more spending and deepening of reforms within the public sector.

Why infrastructure matters

Infrastructure can have both direct and indirect effects on well-being. Access to and use of electricity, roads, telephony, clean water, and improved sanitation has intrinsic value: in many societies, access to at least some of these categories of basic infrastructure is considered a right that should be extended to all citizens. There are also important indirect effects on incomes, via the influence of roads on access to markets and jobs, and of electricity and telephony on the productivity of small and large enterprises. Finally, there are indirect influences on health, education, and security, for example through access to schools and clinics. As discussed in chapter 2 and illustrated in table 7.8, access to infrastructure remains unequal, especially in poorer countries such as Bolivia and Honduras. In addition, even where access is reasonably equal there are large differences in consumption that are correlated with income. Often differences in access are magnified by differences in quality, with lower quality in peri-urban and rural areas. Infrastructure expansion has the potential to equalize income and other dimensions of well-being if it increasingly integrates poorer groups into regional and national systems of production, commerce, and service provision.

Evidence of the influence of infrastructure on incomes is provided in recent country level analyses (Calderón and Chong 2004, Calderón and Servén 2003). This work explores the cross-country relationship between infrastructure, growth, and inequality by using an international data set of both developing and developed countries. It is not surprising that infrastructure is correlated with growth: higher-income countries can afford the investment in infrastructure. What is of particular interest in these analyses is

TABLE 7.8

Access to selected services for top and bottom quintiles, selected countries (percent)

Country (ranked by income)	Water		Sewerage		Electricity		Telephones	
	Top quintile	Bottom quintile	Top quintile	Bottom quintile	Top quintile	Bottom quintile	Top quintile	Bottom quintile
Uruguay (1989)	98	80	82	28	100	89	n/a	n/a
Brazil (1992)	n/a	n/a	87	17	99	60	61[a]	2[a]
Mexico (1992)	96	63	91	28	99	75	54	3
Colombia (1996)	96	60	92	35	98	81	71	12
Bolivia (1996)	86	26	49	4	93	21	59[b]	1[b]
Honduras (1990)	89	49	55	4	80	15	n/a	n/a

Notes: a: 1995, b: 1999.
Source: National household surveys analyzed for this report.

their attempt to disentangle the influence of infrastructure on both growth and inequality. The analyses use data on the stock of telecommunications, electricity, and land transportation (roads and railways) and examine the relationship between expansions in indices of infrastructure stocks and subsequent changes in growth and inequality. (Technically, this is done by using panel data methods such as the Generalized Method of Moments to minimize endogeneity problems, as well as to control for various other influences.)

These studies find that more and better quality infrastructure both enhances growth and reduces income inequality. With respect to growth effects, it is quantity, not quality, that is significant in the econometric analysis. After controlling for a range of other influences on growth, Calderón and Servén (2003) find that about a quarter of the variation in Latin American growth in 1996–2000 relative to 1981–85 can be explained by differences in infrastructure stocks. With respect to income inequality, both the quantity and quality of infrastructure has a significant negative influence: more and higher quality infrastructure is associated with lower inequality, after controlling for other influences (such as initial income, education, financial assets, and health). Calderón and Chong (2004) estimate that an increase in infrastructure equivalent to moving up one quartile of the global distribution of infrastructure stocks is linked with a reduction in the Gini coefficient of 2.2 points in a five-year period and 12 points in the subsequent 35 years. Such a long-run effect is equivalent to a shift from the level of inequality prevailing in Brazil to that in Costa Rica.

Even the most careful cross-country analysis has to be treated with some caution given the multiple, interacting influences at play. It is therefore important to complement this type of evidence with micro analyses. When this is done, there is evidence of the positive influence of infrastructure. For example, in Guatemala (which has low levels of infrastructure provision), infrastructure is strongly correlated with the profitability of microenterprises (table 7.9). Econometric analysis that controls for other influences on profitability and seeks to deal with the endogeneity of infrastructure[21] further supports the view that access to electricity, water, and telephony have large, significant influences on incomes: expansion of these services to poor, underserved populations can lead to equalizing income increases. Similarly, in El Salvador, panel data on incomes in rural areas finds an association between expanded infrastructure and proximate influences on incomes (such as time to market),

TABLE 7.9

Enterprise profitability and access to infrastructure in Guatemala (net income of owner in quetzales per worker hour)

Coverage	Basic service	
	Yes	No
Electricity	8.0	3.4
Piped water	7.9	4.7
Fixed phone	15.9	4.6
Cellular phone	20.2	5.2

Notes: Refers only to enterprises that operate in dwelling. The null hypothesis of equality of profits between enterprises covered and not covered is rejected in all cases at either 99 or 95 percent levels of significance.

Source: World Bank calculations using the ENCOVI 2000 survey (Instituto Nacional de Estadística, Guatemala), World Bank 2002b.

with disproportionate gains accruing to poorer groups (World Bank, forthcoming). In an analysis of the effect of rural road rehabilitation in Peru, Escobal and Ponce (2002) find a significant impact of road quality on income, especially in terms of wage employment. (This study seeks to control for reverse causation, that is from incomes to rural roads, by matching households in areas close to rehabilitated roads with those in other areas that did not benefit from the intervention.)

This selective review of macroeconomic and microeconomic evidence supports the premise that infrastructure matters with regard to both the level and distribution of well-being. Other work, provides evidence on additional dimensions, notably education and health (see Fay and others 2003). This finding complements the role of other assets (such as education and land), as illustrated, for example, by the discussion of farming in Mexico in box 7.3. The rest of this section turns to issues in the provision of infrastructure.

Latin American problems in infrastructure delivery: Finance and institutions

The 1980s debt crisis resulted in the culmination of long-standing problems in infrastructure provision in Latin America. Although conditions varied across the region, the primary symptoms of insufficient infrastructure were low levels and unequal provision of infrastructure services, dismal quality, and lack of financing. This malaise can be seen as a product of deeper institutional conditions, as discussed in chapter 5. Throughout the region, infrastructure was traditionally provided by public utilities or government departments. It is therefore useful to place infrastructure concerns in the context of differing intellectual perspectives on the role of public or private enterprise, and to distinguish three views (La Porta and López-de-Silanes 1999):

- The "social welfare" view, in which public enterprises can pursue goals set by governments that reflect society's broader interests (including those related to equity), as opposed to the "narrower" profit motive of private firms.
- The "agency" view, in which economic incentives are crucial to behavior (especially that of managers) and public provisioning raises special challenges in providing sufficiently "high-powered" incentives.
- The "political economy" view, in which the owners and managers of both public and private enterprises are embedded in political structures and reflect the groups and distributional alliances that they are a part of.

The first perspective, on social welfare, formed the overt ideological basis for the nationalization of public utilities and, in many countries, large parts of the tradable industrial sector. Sometimes this process has been more closely linked to nationalist ideologies (as in Mexico) or "populist" projects with vaguely socialist or national socialist leanings (as in the case of Peronism in Argentina). However, the principle in all its various forms is essentially that public ownership could better protect the national patrimony, support the expansion of employment, and provide goods and services for all.

By the 1970s and early 1980s, public enterprise sectors throughout Latin America were increasingly tattered, characterized by low productivity, bloated payrolls, and the rising drain on government budgets. There were also high levels of inequality in supply in the utility sector (which still holds to some degree, as discussed in chapter 2), with significant segments of the population at the bottom of the income distribution rationed out of the public provision of electricity, water, sanitation, and telephony. The middle and upper classes benefited from low prices but suffered from low service quality, especially with respect to obtaining new connections. These conditions best fit a combination of the agency and political economy views.

The public provision of infrastructure was typically embedded within the broader clientelistic patterns of relationships that long defined state-society interactions. In most

of the region in the middle of the 20th century, nationalization formed part of the broader process of incorporation of various domestic groups into the state (see chapter 5). Nationalization generally involved the expropriation of foreign actors, while beneficiaries included domestic businesses (as both suppliers and consumers of goods and services at low prices), formal workers, and urban consumers (Murillo 2002). This resulted in specific dynamics of behavior on the part of these enterprises for clientelistic purposes (Foster 2002, World Bank 2003a).

Politicians maintained control over the public sector by appointing and dismissing managers and providing subsidies to support unsustainable enterprises. In return for this patronage, utilities were obliged to do political favors in the form of providing jobs, keeping tariffs down, and allocating new investment and public works contracts on the basis of political criteria. This pattern undermined incentives for efficient performance and, in turn, resulted in high costs, excess employment, and a lack of internally generated resources to finance badly needed expansions in service coverage. With the fiscal crises of the 1980s, money from the national budget also dried up. Customers had little if any power to hold providers directly accountable for services and national elections were much too broad a mechanism through which to express discontent with specific utilities.

Most countries responded to this crisis in service provision with significant institutional reforms. Privatization dominated the discourse of the late 1980s and 1990s, even though it formed only one element of the reforms pursued. These also included decentralization of water provision (mainly to municipal levels) and attempts to corporatize national utilities that remained in the public sector. However, privatization is of particular interest in light of its centrality in debates over the relationship between reforms and inequality. For advocates, privatization seemed to offer a straightforward solution to the twin problems of a lack of finance for infrastructure expansion and severe inefficiencies: using the institutional transition to facilitate a genuine break with the past. Fiscal proceeds from sell-offs only added to the attraction. Although distribution was emphasized less, there were hopes that solving the financing problem would both allow expansion to underserved populations who had been rationed out under old models, and yield benefits by releasing resources for social spending.

Privatization was pursued across the region under diverse political regimes. These included, in the words of Murillo

(2002, p. 462), "not only right-wing regimes such as Pinochet's in Chile, Chamorro's in Nicaragua, and Calderón Sol's in El Salvador, but also . . . old populist parties like the MNR in Bolivia, the Peronists in Argentina, and the PRI in Mexico [which] led the push to privatize . . . even though they had previously been the champions of nationalization." Executive power and technocratic designs undoubtedly played important roles in reform efforts. However, a richer account of policy design reveals preferences for change as products both of political constituencies and of the updating of beliefs in light of new information (Murillo 2002). Moreover, it is a mistake to see the post-reform world as one of diffuse benefits, free of the rent-seeking and unequal influence that were features of the pre-reform, clientelist, protectionist model.

Under privatization, new rents and gains were afforded to particular groups—notably domestic conglomerates and wealthy individuals—that politicians could make use of to support old or create new constituencies. Beliefs, fiscal crises, external pressures, and a common culture among decision-making elites in the region facilitated convergence. However, the way in which beliefs were updated was influenced by the views and socialization experiences of political elites, leading to varying political biases in the design of privatization. Chile under Pinochet pursued an approach that was friendly to foreign capital, distrustful of state control, and had no overarching regulatory agency. Mexico, which was more nationalist and statist in tradition, placed more restrictions on foreign participation (93 percent of privatizations went to domestic businesses, according to Schamis 2002) and had more regulatory structures. Argentina, which was less nationalist and had a populist-statist tradition, was open to foreign capital but sought strong, independent regulation (with mixed effects across agencies). These institutional choices have affected the subsequent evolution of privatization.

What were the overall patterns of change? First, there was a substantial expansion of private investment, especially in telecoms and electricity and to a lesser extent in water, roads, and railways. As a result, the private sector in the region now serves some 85 percent of domestic telephone consumers, 50 percent of domestic electricity consumers, and 15 percent of domestic water consumers (Foster 2003). However, with the exception of telecoms, the growth of private investment was insufficient to offset a drastic decline in public investment (figure 7.8), such that overall investment declined sharply from 3.5 percent of GDP in the first half of the 1980s to 2 percent in the second half of the 1990s. This shift helped release resources for the expansion in social spending (see chapter 9), but at the cost of a further reduction in infrastructure provision relative to comparators. In relation to the East Asian "tigers,"[22] the infrastructure gap rose substantially. For example, with regard to electric power generating capacity, the median infrastructure stock in East Asia grew from 90 percent of Latin America's in 1980 to 230 percent in 2000; with regard to paved roads, the ratio rose from 780 percent to 1560 percent (Calderón and Servén 2003).

Second, expansions in service access did occur due to private and public investment (figure 7.9). Impacts of this investment on inequalities in access varied depending on initial conditions. Where the middle class and elites were already covered, the expansion that did occur typically went to the poor, as exemplified by water and electricity service in Argentina. However, where access was initially low, the beneficiaries of expansion were typically the nonpoor, especially those in the middle of the distribution. This pattern is consistent with the general dynamics of service expansion, which typically function along the income distribution (see chapters 2 and 9 with regard to social service provision).

Third, privatization became highly unpopular. This became evident in the streets of Arequipa, Peru, in June 2002, when days of rioting against the planned privatization of water and electricity services occurred. The privatization plan was viewed as a betrayal, a selling off of national assets that would only benefit the rich and, most likely, new foreign owners. Such sentiments have echoed across the region, from the dominantly negative view on electricity privatization expressed in the Mexican Congress to the intense feelings and violent action against the botched water privatization process in Cochabamba, Bolivia. A negative view of privatization is also reflected in the sharp fall in assessments of privatization in public opinion surveys conducted by the organization Latinobarómetro (see figure 7.10). Across the countries surveyed, on average only 22 percent of people thought that privatization had benefited their country, which marked a sharp decline since 1998. Firms surveyed held a similarly negative (and declining) view of privatization.

The remainder of this section first looks at the distributional effects of privatization and then at the policy issues related to equitable expansion of infrastructure in both the public and private sector.

FIGURE 7.8

Public and private investment in selected infrastructure sectors in Latin America, 1980–98

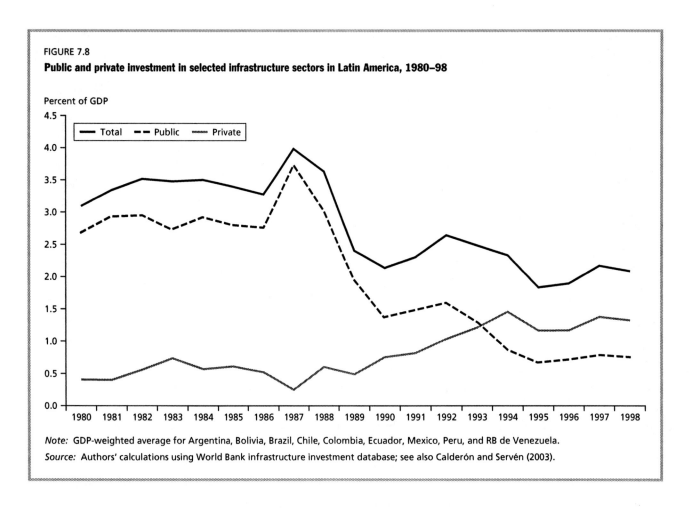

Percent of GDP

Note: GDP-weighted average for Argentina, Bolivia, Brazil, Chile, Colombia, Ecuador, Mexico, Peru, and RB de Venezuela.

Source: Authors' calculations using World Bank infrastructure investment database; see also Calderón and Servén (2003).

The effects of infrastructure privatization

A range of work has examined the impact of the privatization of utilities and other companies on profitability, efficiency, a variety of distributional effects, and financing.

Most analyses find significant gains in profitability and efficiency following privatization. This can be illustrated with partial measures of productivity; for example, sales per worker in Chile, Mexico, and Peru, rose by 88, 92, and 112 percent, respectively. In Argentina, output per worker rose by 46 percent, while in Brazil the ratio of costs to sales implied a 45 percent increase in efficiency.[23] More comprehensive estimates of efficiency changes in Argentina—which account for joint effects on improvements across inputs and outputs—also indicate annual efficiency gains ranging from 1 percent for electricity distribution to 6 percent for water (Estache 2002). How were these gains distributed among consumers, workers, firms, and the government?

With respect to economic analyses of privatization and inequality, there have been three recent research projects with a Latin American orientation.[24] The qualitative results are

similar and are illustrated here by a cross-country study of Argentina, Bolivia, Mexico, and Nicaragua that applied common techniques to assessing the impacts of privatization on inequality in the electricity, telecommunications, and water sectors (McKenzie and Mookherjee 2003). All analyses come with an empirical warning: it is difficult to undertake a clean comparison of the experience of privatization with that of continued public ownership under changed economic or managerial conditions, since there are never precisely similar companies or conditions to facilitate such an evaluation. Thus, most analyses are of a before-and-after character with attempts to obtain approximate comparisons when feasible.

Consumers

Impacts of privatization on consumers are due to effects in three areas: increased access, prices, and quality. Such effects tend to reach consumers who are on average poorer than those who already have access; as noted above, the extent of poverty orientation depends on the initial distribution.

FIGURE 7.9

Increases in access to infrastructure, by income decile in Argentina and Nicaragua

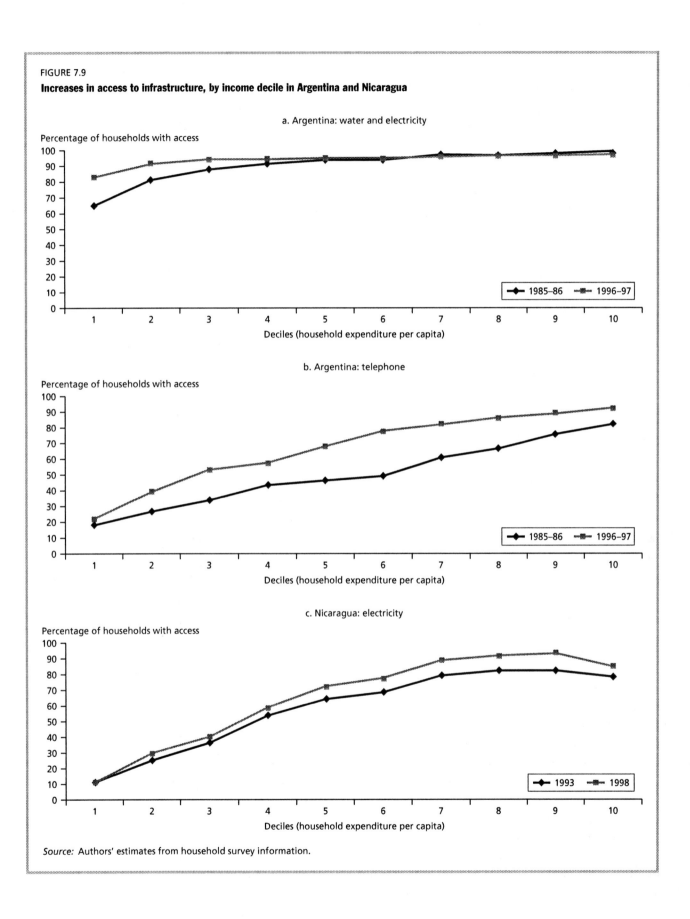

a. Argentina: water and electricity

Source: Authors' estimates from household survey information.

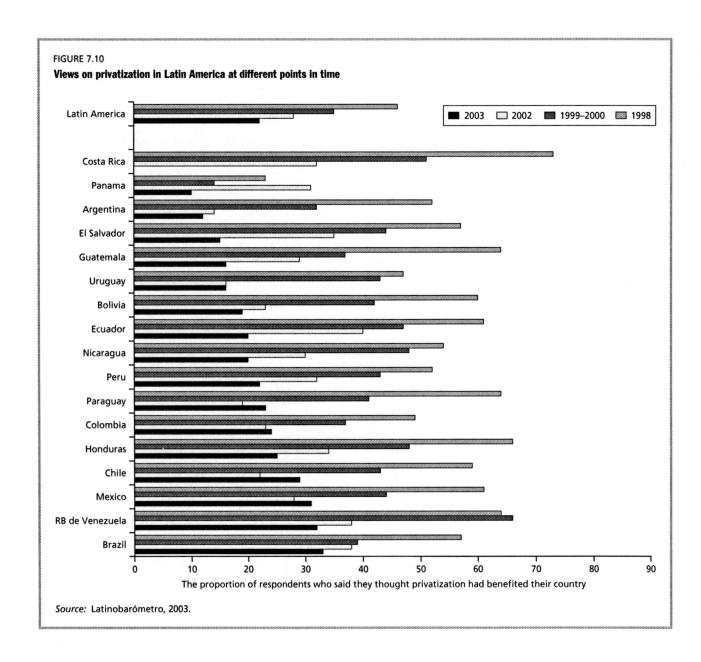

FIGURE 7.10

Views on privatization in Latin America at different points in time

The proportion of respondents who said they thought privatization had benefited their country

Legend: ■ 2003 □ 2002 ■ 1999–2000 ▥ 1998

Source: Latinobarómetro, 2003.

Critics often argue that privatization leads to higher prices, which in turn finance higher profits. In fact, price changes vary greatly depending on initial conditions and patterns of change, especially with regard to the balance between gains in efficiency, the need to compensate for historically subsidized prices, and the regulatory and institutional framework that determines profits. A case can also typically be made for tariff rebalancing so that tariffs reflect costs (for example, between local and long distance charges for telephony, across sectors for water and electricity, and between connection and consumption charges in all cases). In the four-country study (McKenzie and Mookherjee 2003), a wide variety of effects were noted, with prices falling in five out of the ten cases studied and rising in the other five (table 7.10). Even within Bolivia, there were sharp contrasts between real price declines in water in the La Paz/El Alto region and large increases related to the infamous Cochabamba water privatization project. Also noteworthy is the large increase in prices for telephony in Mexico, which may have been associated with the granting of a monopoly for several years to the group that won the privatization contract. Finally, with respect to quality, the available evidence is of significant improvements following privatization, in terms of indicators such as reliability and waiting times for

TABLE 7.10

Price changes after privatization

	Argentina		Bolivia		Mexico		Nicaragua	
	Before	After	Before	After	Before	After	Before	After
Telephones	100	84	100	92	100	148		
Electricity	100	67	100	126			100	124
Water	100	84			100	109		
La Paz/El Alto			100	90				
Cochabamba			100	143				

Note: Table shows real price indices, relative to the Consumer Price Index, with preprivatization prices set at 100.
Source: McKenzie and Mookherjee 2003.

connection. (Again, privatization may not have been necessary to secure such improvements, as the experience of the Peruvian public water company in Lima illustrates.)

An analysis of the overall impact of consumer effects on poverty and inequality suggests generally small changes, largely because households devote only small shares of their budget to infrastructure services.[25] In all cases, the effects on inequality were minor. In all but one, effects on poverty were positive but not large. For example, in Argentina access and the price effects of electricity and telephony were associated with minor effects on income inequality and a 1–1.5 percent reduction in poverty. In Bolivia, privatization and water in the La Paz/El Alto region was also associated with little change in inequality and a 1–1.5 percent reduction in poverty. In contrast, the large price increases following the Cochabamba water privatization project did increase poverty by some 2 percent. In Nicaragua, large increases in the welfare of those who gained access to electricity (in the order of 12–16 percent in the bottom three deciles of income distribution) were roughly offset by welfare declines, which were in turn due to price increases for those who already had access.

A significant study by Galiani, Gertler, and Schargrodsky (2002) on Argentina estimates the impact of water privatization on child mortality, a key nonmonetary measure of welfare, by exploiting the variation over time and space between municipalities with and without privatized water. Child mortality fell an additional 5–7 percent in areas with privatized water services and an estimated 24 percent in the poorest municipalities, with the decline in mortality associated with reductions in deaths from water-borne infectious and parasitic diseases.

Workers

Extensive job layoffs in privatized enterprises are probably the most publicized and politicized aspect of apparent cost, a pattern that follows naturally from the analysis of the public company as a clientelist provider of jobs. Large layoffs of regular workers have indeed occurred in Latin America. A cross-country study by the International Development Bank (Chong and López-de-Silanes 2003) estimates total losses in employment in privatized companies from about 23–25 percent in Argentina, Chile, and Peru to around 40 percent in Colombia and more than 50 percent in Mexico. Firm-specific effects can be larger. Ennis and Pinto (forthcoming) estimate losses of 75 percent in privatized utilities in Argentina (that is, electricity, natural gas, water, telecommunications, airlines, and railways), and indicate that if those workers who were laid off had received zero income, poverty would have risen from 29.5 to 32.0 percent.

However, the net effects or layoffs depend on the labor market and macroeconomic situation. All studies find that *net* employment effects are less adverse than gross losses, and are sometimes positive. In the case of Mexico, López-Calva and Rosellón (2002) used panel surveys to follow the experiences of individual workers. They found that 45–50 percent of laid-off workers found jobs in the same sector within a year, without any loss of social security or health benefits. Only 0.5 percent of workers were unemployed for a full year. This pattern of generally positive gains is common for the medium term. In the Peruvian telecommunications sector, employment rose from 13,000 to 34,000 jobs between 1993 and 1998. About 145,000 new jobs were created in the same sector in Brazil during that period. Even in Argentina, which had large losses due to a slack labor market, the share of employment in privatized utilities had recovered to almost its pre-privatization levels (around 7 percent) by 1996, suggesting that the long-term trajectory of employment was similar to that for overall employment.

Effects on wages have been varied. In Argentina, economy-wide wages rose following privatization, although the impact of privatization itself may have been mildly depressing because public sector workers commanded a 10 percent premium. However, the impact is unlikely to have been significant, and would have been offset by the increased hours of the workers who shifted to the private sector (Ennis and Pinto forthcoming). In Mexico, La Porta and López-de-Silanes (1999) found that wages increased in the privatized sectors; the pace of the increase was fastest for blue-collar workers, implying that part of the large efficiency increases were passed on to workers. One of the countries in which wage effects may have been significant and negative is Nicaragua, where reallocation involved some 5–7 percent of the workforce and the public sector wage premium was significant (20 percent in urban and 29 percent in rural areas in 1993).

Fiscal effects

Fiscal gains were one of the drivers of privatization. There were often large fiscal gains from sales, followed by increased tax receipts from profitable private companies. Capital receipts ran as high as US$25 billion in Argentina and US$33 billion in Mexico. The distributional effects of these receipts depend on how they were applied by governments, most of which used part of the gains to retire debt. In addition to positive stabilization effects, doing so allowed for reductions in debt service and created fiscal room for the expansion in social spending that characterized most economies in the 1990s. As discussed in chapter 9, this expansion was generally mildly or significantly equalizing. However, it is noteworthy that some governments ended the decade with higher indebtedness despite gaining large capital receipts from privatization, as was markedly the case in Argentina and Brazil. This pattern is consistent with the use of fiscal expansions by governments to postpone distributional struggles to the future (see chapter 8), which makes the challenge of achieving growth with greater equity all the more difficult in the present.

Finally, privatizations have often been undertaken with less than full transparency, which was dramatically the case in Nicaragua. During the period of active privatization in the 1990s, receipts were running at 2.5 percent of GDP every year, yet this had no fiscal implications for or effects on social spending. Given the poor standing of Nicaragua in terms of corruption, it is highly likely that the money that disappeared went to a few rich individuals or groups. The more recent privatization of electricity raised 5 percent of GDP, 80 percent of which actually accrued to government reserves and supported future, if not present, public spending (Freije and Rivas 2002).

Domestic business sector effects

Did privatization lead to excess profits for domestic and foreign capitalists? In most cases profits did go up, but often from a starting point of unsustainable, loss-making positions. In addition, a proximate source of these gains was the large layoff of surplus workers. However, as just discussed, layoffs were typically associated with net expansions in employment at the sectoral level. Reasonable profits are a necessary part of private production, and the search for profits is key to the realization of productivity gains under the "agency" interpretation of enterprise performance.

The more relevant question is whether profits were excessive. A study of all privatizations in Mexico found that profits in the noncompetitive sector were not, on average, significantly above the competitive sector (La Porta and López-de-Silanes 1999). A more recent study focusing on utilities finds suggestive evidence of higher profits in noncompetitive than competitive sectors following privatization in Chile, Mexico, and Peru, but not in Colombia (Chong and López-de-Silanes 2003). However, the increase in profits following privatization was not larger in noncompetitive than in competitive sectors. To the extent excess profits existed, they likely reflected regulatory failures, preferences of governments for higher profits to support their tax base, or specific features of the design of privatization. In some cases, explicit or implicit profit guarantees were made that were put in place to attract investors or to maximize fiscal benefits from higher sales prices. Typical cases involved the Mexican and Peruvian telecommunications sectors, where a specified period of monopoly was guaranteed. As noted earlier, prices increased in the former case. In 2002, the charge structure pursued by Peruvian telecoms became a source of public controversy since it was higher than Latin American standards, even though this had been legally agreed to as part of the original sale. Finally, much less is known about illegal gains, although accusations are common (as previously noted with regard to the missing millions of dollars in Nicaragua).

Who gained control of the privatized assets? There is some evidence of the consolidation of gains by domestic conglomerates, along with a relatively small number of international companies. Schamis (2002) has documented how domestic conglomerates and large-firm business elites in Argentina, Chile, and Mexico were major protagonists and beneficiaries of the privatization process. In the case of Chile under Pinochet, this situation was associated with a revolving door of individuals moving among major conglomerates, the state, and newly privatized companies. In Mexico, such conditions were part of a long tradition of close forward and backward linkages between business and the state (see Haber 2002b), but also marked a change in the patterns of alliance. While the historical influence of business associations representing medium-sized firms (which were judged to be backward and protectionist) was reduced, connections with large-scale conglomerates increased (Schamis 2002). These processes involved new forms of distributional alliances in pursuit of rents.

An overall assessment

The preceding analysis of experiences in various countries suggests that utility privatization brought substantial benefits, but that room for criticism remains. There is widespread evidence that greater efficiency has resulted, although higher profits and productivity were often achieved in part by laying off excess workers. There is also evidence that many privatizations led to increased access by poorer groups, that price increases declined as often as they rose, and that net employment effects were often positive within a sector. Moreover, severance pay at least partly shielded the blow of worker layoffs, with aggregate effects on income inequality typically being very small.

Poverty impacts are almost always beneficial and can be significant when large increases in access occur, with apparently few exceptions (Cochabamba in Bolivia being one). On the other hand, there is also evidence that privatization has been associated with increased power on the part of conglomerates and their foreign partners, as well as with relatively high profits in noncompetitive sectors. Finally, accusations of favors being given or corruption taking place during the privatization process have often been made. Such concentrated gains by a few actors, whether made legally or illegally, combined with losses by workers, help to explain the apparent paradox that privatization is deeply unpopular even though it has often yielded significant benefits.

Consumers also now expect decent service from their utilities, and no longer use the dismal service levels of the 1980s as a benchmark (Estache 2003).

Policies for equitable infrastructure expansion

Privatization alone did not solve the financing and institutional malaise that afflicted the infrastructure sector in the 1980s. In light of the importance of infrastructure to both growth and equity, there is a need for both policies to restore public sector provisioning and a strengthened policy and regulatory framework for private provisioning. A case can also be made for specific subsidy policies on distributional grounds, for both the public and private sectors.

Restoring public spending and extending public sector reforms

The case for restoring public spending on public infrastructure is vividly illustrated by figure 7.8, as well as the previous analysis of Latin America's widening infrastructure deficit with respect to other regions. Measures to close the gap are good for both growth and inequality. Some sectors—sanitation and rural water and roads, for example—are likely to remain in the public sector in the long run. Moreover, the private sector may also need a stronger public presence if demand is insufficient. However, achieving this will require both facing issues of finance and tackling persistent institutional challenges in public provisioning.

The financing issue is intimately connected to Latin America's relatively low tax effort and relatively high debt burden. As discussed in chapter 9, raising taxes in ways that minimize both efficiency costs and regressive effects is central to a more equitable development path, provided that resources are used effectively. User charges that reflect costs can make an essential contribution, although this has to be balanced with distributional objectives (see below).

Effective use of resources in the infrastructure sector depends equally on institutional problems. Resolving agency-related hurdles and avoiding the clientelistic use of utilities—two factors that were important motivations for privatization—remain major challenges for the public sector. *Obras* (public works) are still a classic tool of patronage. Institutional reforms can bring gains in terms of efficiency and equity under public auspices, especially if actions are taken to separate policymaker from provider under a strong agreement, increase transparency, and strengthen the direct voice of all consumers, especially those who have previously been excluded.

Indirect evidence for this process is provided again by the Bolivian case, in which the privatized La Paz/El Alto water utility was compared with the cooperative water utility in Santa Cruz. It performed better, but the gains were significantly smaller than those seen in a before-and-after comparison. Another example from the same sector is the Lima water company known as SEDAPAL. Even though the company has so far remained under public ownership, it has undertaken a series of reforms (including with regard to corporatization and outreach) and has achieved substantial improvements in both efficiency and access. On the other hand, a recent review of experience in the regulation of municipalized water companies concluded that many adhere to a clientelistic model, although at local levels (Foster 2003). That review also argues for the need to improve and expand civil society, strengthen regulation (as well as civil society's knowledge of regulatory decisions and processes), and align central finance with the realization of regulatory goals.

Strengthening privatization processes and regulating private production

While assessment of the effects of privatization on efficiency and equity provided here is substantially more positive than that provided by opinion surveys in Latin America, there are nonetheless key areas where improvements can be made. Privatization in principle facilitates the separation between policymaker and provider, but remains susceptible to informal and "revolving door" ties and to excess power on the part of the provider. Independent regulators have to be part of the solution, at least in noncompetitive sectors, but they largely do not yet perform the central role of protecting the public interest, especially when governments and operators have a common interest in high profits and associated high taxes (Estache 2003). However, classic problems of regulatory capture or relative weakness remain, especially in the context of large private firms with highly qualified, well-paid staff. Ensuring the legal, budgetary, and staffing independence of regulators can help. In Argentina, for example, a stronger legal framework for electricity and gas regulators was associated with better regulatory performance than that seen in other sectors (Estache 2002, Foster 2003).

Also important is the process of privatization itself. The post-privatization market structure is influenced by the extent to which an activity has natural monopoly charac-

teristics, but can also be affected by design. It is now recognized that the process of electricity privatization in Chile (as was the case in Great Britain) created firms with substantial monopoly power, and thereby missed an opportunity to create a more competitive market. It is a fact that once a system is privatized, it can be harder to change the structure. This not only increases economic (and perhaps political) influence, but can make the task of any regulator more difficult.

Complementary to design specifics are questions of transparency and participation, in both the privatization process (in order to support measures to minimize corruption) and in production. Such questions can involve participatory engagement by groups with weak influence. For example, the case of water privatization through *Aguas Argentinas* involved a redesign of the approach to access after complaints were heard on the local level (Estache, Foster, and Wodon 2002). Factors such as openness, the presence of watchdogs, and independent analysis as a means of increasing public information and debate are also important. Participation can reduce incentives for collusion between providers and policymakers (potentially in both public and private models). In France, the indirect expression of voice—via the potential to vote out mayors who fail to design effective agreements with local water companies—provides an example. Publishing and explaining regulatory decisions, establishing appeals processes, and involving consumers can help increase the independence of regulators, despite the fact that consumer involvement has generally been low in Latin America (World Bank 2003a).

User charges and subsidies

User charges that cover costs are essential to the financial viability of utilities in both the public and private sectors. However, the extent to which specific charges reflect costs needs to be balanced against the distributional objectives of assuring basic levels of supply to all groups. Should such distributional goals be handled by the general tax and benefit system? There are in fact good arguments for explicitly including equity considerations within the pricing policies of utilities: most societies view at least some infrastructure services as basic needs, and so are concerned with actual consumption of utility services; general welfare systems are far from perfect; and paying attention to social concerns may be essential to the social acceptance of private production (Gómez-Lobo and Contreras 2000).

As noted above, during the 1980s, many utilities had pricing policies that were bad on both efficiency and equity grounds. Prices did not cover costs, but subsidies rarely reached the poor, who typically did not have access to services. Regressive subsidy policies have persisted in some cases, especially in some public utilities. In Mexico, electricity subsidies are large (substantially greater than the flagship poverty-focused *Oportunidades* program) and regressive, if somewhat less so than in the past.

Subsidies to ensure access to and basic consumption levels by the poor are desirable, but pose challenges with regard to targeting that are common to the social sectors (see chapter 9). Although discussion of design details is beyond the scope of this chapter, some general points can be made here.

It is generally desirable to have low connection fees in order to encourage uptake, as well as subsidies to encourage basic levels of consumption. If the fiscal position of a country allows, it is also desirable to include subsidies in the public budget, so that utilities don't have to cross-subsidize by "taxing" other consumers (as is the case in Chile, for example). However, doing so will not always be feasible, especially in cases in which the fiscal position is tight. In assessing the pre-crisis performance of privatized utilities in Argentina, Estache (2002) argues that efficiency gains were insufficiently passed on to consumers, and that cross-subsidies for poorer groups are likely to be necessary in any practical solution. The Colombian water utilities finance subsidies through higher tariffs for richer consumers, for example.

It is therefore clear that choices exist between subsidizing categories of consumption (as in the case of lifeline tariffs, that is, basic tariffs at low rates) or categories of consumers, which would include an assessment of the capacity of different consumers to pay for services. For example, Chile makes use of a national proxy-means test (known as the *ficha* CAS) to determine water subsidies, reaping substantial savings from spreading the administrative burden of means assessment across many programs. Colombia has a geographic targeting system, based on the classification of a geographic area within a municipality into one of several socioeconomic strata. Despite this apparently less precise method, the Chilean and Colombian schemes have similar targeting properties: both are progressive, but both make significant errors of exclusion and inclusion (Gómez-Lobo and Contreras 2000). Subsidy design should therefore be shaped around the characteristics of a country and a particular service, and be subject to regular monitoring and evaluation.

7.4. Conclusions

This chapter has focused on assets in three major areas: education; property rights, land, and housing; and infrastructure. Discussions on each area have emphasized the intimate links with institutions (in the broad sense in which the word is used in this report). These three areas are undoubtedly significant in any quest for greater equity, and there are strong complementarities between them. However, this is not a comprehensive list of aspects that should be explored; other areas related to asset formation are also important, and health is one important omission here. Although this chapter could only sketch issues and options in these three central areas, it has nonetheless supported the view that a major, serious, redistributive effort to promote asset distribution is indeed feasible, and substantial scope exists for asset creation strategies that are good for both growth and equity. Making sure this happens will both require and support critical, complementary changes related to equalizing political action and social agency, and potentially help shift the cycles of inequality from vicious to virtuous.

Notes

1. Paulo Freire (1970) is a classic example.

2. Some biases are inherent in these patterns, since poorer, less educated people on average lead shorter lives.

3. See table 4.2 in de Ferranti and others (2003). These interregional comparisons are made on the basis of the Barro and Lee (2001) data set. All numbers presented for intraregional comparisons are taken from the microdata analyzed for this report; note that there are discrepancies between these sources.

4. These are the marginal returns on finishing an educational level obtained from Mincer equations, as indicated in table A.31 in the statistical appendix.

5. For a brief discussion of the methodology used, see chapter 6; for details, see Bourguignon, Ferreira, and Leite (2002).

6. Recent studies on Latin American schooling include Glewwe and others (1995), King and Ozler (1998), Paes de Barros and Mendonca (1998), Jimenez and Sawada (1998), and Eskeland and Filmer (2002). See also Wossmann (2000) for a cross-country study.

7. The "Washington Consensus" refers to the set of market-oriented policies that were commonly adopted in Latin America in the late 1980s and 1990s. See chapter 8 for a discussion.

8. A recent analysis of Colombia makes an adjustment for land characteristics (see World Bank 2003b). However, this leads to only a modest reduction in the Gini coefficient for land distribution from 0.93 to 0.85.

9. There is a large body of literature on this point; (see chapter 1 of World Bank 2003a) for a review.

10. This synthesis is based on comments from José María Caballero. For a review, see Chavas (2001).

11. For one of many overall syntheses, (see World Bank 1993). For an approach that emphasizes the centrality of political support of the peasantry, see Teranishi (1997).

12. See Klein (1992) for a general history and Gray-Molina (2002) on children of the 1953 revolution.

13. See Seligmann (1995) for an ethnographic account of agrarian reform and its aftermath in a poor area of Cusco province in the Andes. McClintock (1998) discusses *Sendero Luminoso* in a comparative analysis with El Salvador.

14. Just as PRONASOL was in part an instrument for gathering rural votes for President Salinas in Mexico in the 1990s, so at times was the social fund FONCODES in Peru. As with many social funds, FONCODES combined genuine success in service provision and a strong propoor orientation with the goal of maintaining political support. See Schady (2000) and Paxton and Schady (2002) for more on this and related points.

15. It is also important to note that the foundation of major successes was partly established through government projects that were launched during the Frei and Allende administrations. This was relevant in the cases of temperate fruits, relocation of dairy from the Central Valley to the south, and the development of timber for cellulose production.

16. See World Bank (2001a) for an example of multiple paths toward rural development in Brazil; figure 4 in de Janvry and Sadoulet (2002b) on shares of off-farm incomes in six Latin American countries; and Lanjouw and Ravallion (1999).

17. These *avecindados* and *posesionarios* occupied land within *ejidos,* but were not formally members and therefore lacked traditional rights of land use.

18. This subsection is based on inputs from Marianne Fay and Anna Wellenstein.

19. In Uruguay, for example, 6.8 percent of the households in the bottom quintile of the population merged with other households in order to reduce housing expenses.

20. This includes spending by the federal government and implicit finance subsidies provided by the quasi-public pension fund and housing lenders INFONAVIT and FOVISSSTE, which are funded through loan repayments and compulsory savings (5 percent of payrolls) from private and public sector employees, respectively.

21. Endogeneity can arise since causation may also flow from greater profitability to the use of modern utilities. The analysis used community-level access as an instrument to deal with this issue, at least partially.

22. Hong Kong (China), Indonesia, Republic of Korea, Malaysia, Singapore, Taiwan (China) and Thailand.

23. Estimates from a synthesis by the IDB (2002). See also the extensive analysis of the privatization process for Mexico in La Porta and López-de-Silanes (1999), which identifies large efficiency gains in both competitive and noncompetitive sectors.

24. These were conducted under the auspices of the World Institute for Development Economics Research (WIDER), the IDB (2002), Chong and López-de-Silanes (2003), and the Latin American and Caribbean Economic Association (LACEA)/World Bank/IDB Network on Inequality and Poverty (summarized in McKenzie and Mookherjee 2003). For earlier work on this subject, see Galal and Shirley (1994) and Estache, Foster, and Wodon (2002).

25. To quantify access effects, this study estimated the "virtual" prices associated with rationing of access, by estimating the price level that would cause zero consumption.

CHAPTER 8

Policies on Markets and Institutions

THIS CHAPTER DISCUSSES THE RELATIONSHIP BETWEEN MARKETS AND INEQUALITY. IN TERMS OF the conceptual framework presented in chapters 1 and 6 (see figure 1.1), such an exploration involves moving from policies that affect asset distributions (the subject of chapter 7) to policies that influence market returns to these assets. In turn, the role of one set of institutions, those that are directly linked to market outcomes, must be considered. The subject of this chapter is only part of the broader question of how and to what extent institutions influence inequality (the central role of political and social institutions was discussed in chapter 5). Links among all factors will be considered and referred to at various points throughout this chapter.

The question of the impact of market-oriented reforms on inequality is one of the more controversial areas of debate in Latin America. The issue is often framed in black and white terms: have market-oriented (and macroeconomic) policy reforms been a curse or a cure for Latin America's ills of slow growth and high inequality? This report takes a more nuanced view. As the structure of the third, current part of the report indicates, institutions affecting markets are only one domain of economic policy that is relevant to distribution (and growth, of course.) It is also important to look separately at different market-related institutions, and to recognize that the consequences of markets will depend on the structure of asset ownership and social and political structures.

This chapter first looks at overall evidence on the relationship between structural market-based reforms and inequality. It then briefly surveys issues in the labor market, recognizing that this area in particular warrants a much fuller treatment than there is room for here. Particular focus is placed on the relationship among macroeconomic crises, policy responses, and inequality, which is a major concern in Latin America. Both the review of evidence and new work undertaken for this report support the view that financial crises will typically be regressive, a fact that underscores the importance of strengthening policies to avert crises and developing both policies and institutions that ensure more equitable resolutions to crises when they do occur.

8.1. Markets and inequality

Over the past two decades or so, most countries in Latin America have undertaken major policy reforms that have opened their economies to greater market influence. Structural changes have included the substantial liberalization of trade and domestic financial policy, opening up of capital accounts, privatization of state-owned companies, and tax reforms that entail more uniform tax treatments and greater reliance on value added taxes. The following section reviews these overall issues (see chapter 7 for a more detailed treatment of the privatization of infrastructure).

The initial driver for policy reforms in Latin America was economic crisis and the imperative to restore growth. There are numerous accounts of both the reform process and its effects on growth. (For a recent example, see Loayza, Fajnzylber, and Calderón 2002 and Burki and Perry 1998.) Two important conclusions can be drawn from these analyses. First, there is consensus that many reforms were indeed undertaken. To illustrate, figure 8.1 presents reform indices constructed by Sam Morley, then of the Economic Commission for Latin America

FIGURE 8.1

The extent of policy reforms in Latin America, with country and policy variations

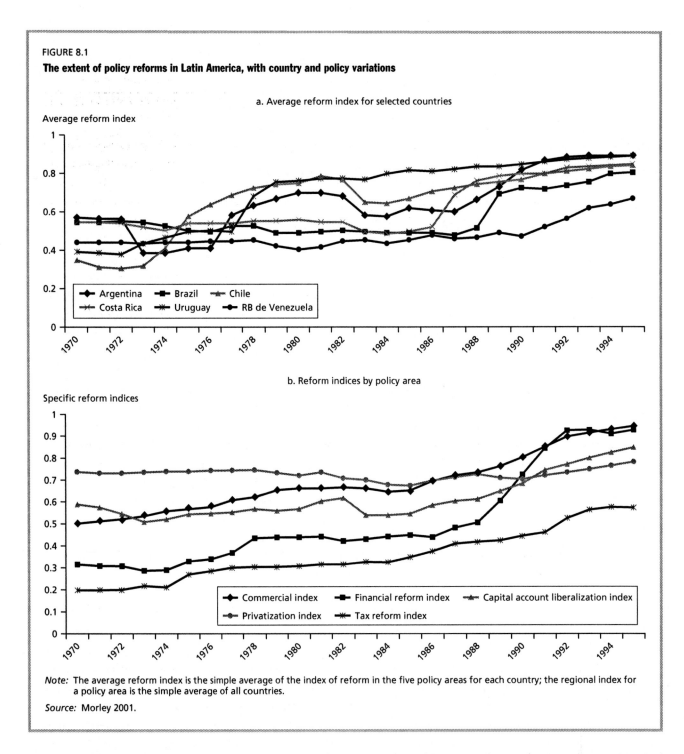

a. Average reform index for selected countries

Average reform index

Note: The average reform index is the simple average of the index of reform in the five policy areas for each country; the regional index for a policy area is the simple average of all countries.

Source: Morley 2001.

and the Caribbean (ECLAC), that are based on earlier work by Eduardo Lora of the Inter-American Development Bank (IDB). Although such indices pose difficulties,[1] they nonetheless provide support for the view that there has been a significant move in the direction of more liberal, market-oriented policies throughout the region.

Significant variation has occurred both across countries and reform categories. Among a few countries selected as illustrations, Chile and Uruguay were early and strong reform-ers on many dimensions, but Argentina and Costa Rica had caught up with them by the mid-1990s. Brazil has undertaken fewer reforms on average, while the República Bolivariana de Venezuela has been a laggard. In terms of the type of reform that has taken place, a steady and large wave of reform in trade liberalization has occurred since 1987, followed by a burst of reform in the financial sector around 1990, and significant capital account opening in the 1990s. Tax reform has been slower. Privatization started at a relatively high level—since many countries did not have large public sectors—and then underwent less change, although important and high profile privatization processes did take place in some countries.

Second, there is a somewhat weaker consensus that reforms had a positive impact on growth, but that this effect was more muted than originally hoped for. Reforms helped, but didn't lift Latin America up onto East Asian-style growth paths. A recent analysis that includes reform indices as well as other structural factors such as education and governance (2003) finds that the reform response of countries in Latin America has been in line with results based on global experience. However, achieving rapid growth requires far more than a specific set of market-oriented reforms. As Rodrik (2003, p. 2) has argued in a review of growth strategies, "First-order economic principles—protection of property rights, market-based competition, appropriate incentives, sound money and so on—do not map into unique policy packages. Reformers have substantial room for creatively packaging these principles into institutional designs that are sensitive to local opportunities and constraints." (For a general discussion on this topic, see Lindauer and Pritchett 2002.)

The achievement of growth has complex institutional underpinnings. There is aggregate evidence that the quality of institutions is a powerful determinant of sustained long-term growth, although debates continue over the relative importance and independence of "institutions" and market-oriented policies that foster greater economic integration. Some authors argue at one extreme that "institutions rule over policies," while others believe that the role of institutions is overstated in some of the recent literature on economic growth.[2] A fair statement might be that both perspectives matter and that there are causal interrelations in both directions.

The issue of concern here is the potential impact of market-oriented reforms on inequality, a subject about which there are diverse views. Box 8.1 outlines two opposing views, each of which is intellectually coherent. Those reform advocates who have focused on questions of inequality anticipated strong, positive effects. Others predicted disequalizing consequences. The approach of this report—which has emphasized the strong interactions between markets, institutions, and sociopolitical factors—would suggest that theory is ambiguous, and will often be context-specific. What does empirical work suggest?

BOX 8.1

Alternative views on the potential impact of market-oriented reforms and inequality

Theoretical expectations of the relationship between reform and inequality are diverse. At the risk of putting forth a slightly caricatured perspective, two of the currents of thought prevalent in debates in Latin America (as well as elsewhere) are outlined here.

In the blue corner. Market-liberalizing reforms are equalizing for three central reasons:

(1) Rent reduction. A panoply of state controls has only served to create "rents," that is, opportunities for gains based on protected privileges that were systematically appropriated by the rich and powerful. These rents also entailed efficiency costs. Market liberalization reduces rents and opportunities for corruption, allowing people to receive income that is in line with their economic worth, not their influence.

(2) Reduction of distortions. Trade protection, domestic regulation, and financial repression maintain a systematic bias against labor, including unskilled labor, which encourages industry over agriculture, import

substitutes, and capital-intensive production choices rather than labor-intensive exports.

(3) Access to markets. Deepening markets would have significant equalizing effects, since most often the poor are precisely the ones with the weakest market access.

In the red corner. Neoliberal policies are disequalizing because they dismantle systems of support and protection that nurture employment growth, provide institutional support for agriculture, and facilitate widespread social provisioning. The chill winds of international competition hurt the weak and benefit the strong. This is especially true for those companies and individuals with an initial basis for economic strength in terms of economic capital, skills, access to financial systems, and international and domestic connections, and which are therefore best positioned to benefit from market opportunities. Liberalization also reduces the power of labor, both by making capital more accessible and by withdrawing state-mandated protections for workers.

The big picture suggests that there is no simple story

Chapter 2 presented patterns of change in income inequality over the past decade and reviewed the literature on evidence from previous decades. Some patterns emerged from that analysis, with a number of countries showing mild distributional improvements in the 1970s, many experiencing a worsening in the 1980s, and a subset of South American countries showing slight worsening in the past decade. However, the dominant pattern is of resilient high inequality under a wide array of policy regimes.

Moreover, every pattern has its exception. In the past decade, Brazil and Mexico both implemented major reforms and have, respectively, experienced a small reduction in inequality and no clear trend. In the 1970s and 1980s, Chile experienced growing income inequality. Eagerness for an overarching explanation might attribute this trend to the vigorous shift toward market-oriented policies under the Pinochet regime, starting in the 1970s. However, there was a lot more going on in Chile than market liberalization. The military junta explicitly sought to reverse the redistributive measures of the previous government and destroy the power of organized labor. The variety of country experiences suggests a multiplicity of distributional stories across relatively homogenous countries.

The lack of any dramatic or obvious pattern is further illustrated by looking at the simple bivariate relationships between reform effort and changes in income inequality. In figure 8.2, the change in the average reform index between 1980 and 1995 is compared by country, with the change in income inequality measured by the Gini coefficient at the beginning and end of the 1990s. (This is a rough form of calculation that allows for possible lags between reforms and effects. A similar lack of a bivariate relationship was found between the *level* of reform and the *change* in inequality.) As indicated, no clear pattern emerges.

Attempts to disentangle effects suggest modest and mixed effects

With the words of caution given above, attempts to disentangle the effects of market-oriented policy reforms on the income dimension of inequality can be examined. The lack of an obvious bivariate pattern, as illustrated in figure 8.2, may hide more complex causal effects. (As frequently emphasized, this is only one dimension of inequality that is of interest. Chapters 2, 7, and 9 discuss some important gains in the distribution of spending and access to associated services, which in many

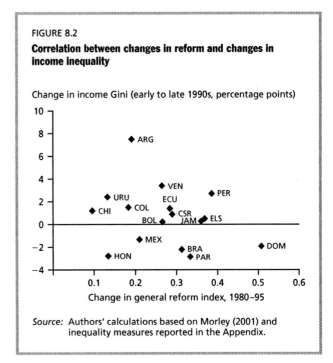

FIGURE 8.2

Correlation between changes in reform and changes in income inequality

Change in income Gini (early to late 1990s, percentage points)

Source: Authors' calculations based on Morley (2001) and inequality measures reported in the Appendix.

cases have helped reduce inequalities in well-being and opportunities.) Several studies on market-oriented policy reforms have been conducted, especially those associated with ECLAC (see in particular Morley 2001). Also notable are a cross-country review in Berry (1998) and a cross-country analysis of effects on wage inequality by Behrman, Gaviria, and Székely (2001). An additional important study is by Ganuza, Taylor, and Morley (1998), although it focused on the effects of reforms on poverty rather than on inequality.

These studies generally compare changes in measures of income inequality in relation to changes in policy, using reform indices such as those put forth by Lora (2001) (as illustrated in figure 8.1) or other similar work. Cross-country analysis in particular exploits variations in the timing of different reforms to look for statistical associations with changes in inequality. Table 8.1 summarizes results from this approach, along with recent work undertaken at the World Bank (as background for this report) on a global database (see López 2003). The latter was conducted within the same overall framework as the growth study referred to above (Loayza and others 2002).

Most studies find modest negative effects on household or individual income inequality in at least some areas of policy change. However, the effects are not always statistically robust and different studies find different effects for different categories of policy reform. For example, Morley (2001) finds slightly negative effects of trade liberalization

TABLE 8.1

Effects of policy reforms on inequality: Estimates from three studies

Study	Morley/ECLAC	Behrman, Birdsall, and Székely	López
Variable	Gini index	Wage differentials	Gini index
Trade liberalization	+	0	+
Financial liberalization	0	+	+
Capital account liberalization	–	+	
Tax reform	+	+	
Privatization	0	–	
All	0	+	

Note: + means inequality increasing; – indicates inequality reducing, 0 means no robust effect.
Source: Morley (2001) and Behrman and others (2001) address Latin America; López (2003) uses a global database.

on income distribution, while Behrman, Birdsall, and Székely (2001) find positive influences of trade liberalization but negative effects of financial liberalization on wage inequality.

It appears that market-based policy reforms have been neither a curse nor a cure for income inequality, as the opposing views presented in box 8.1 would have suggested. On balance, the evidence suggests mild disequalizing effects. Modest and complex effects could well have been lost in a sea of other variables that bring about changes in inequality, both in terms of economic assets and the broader set of sociocultural and political variables that can be forces for sustaining or changing income differences.

Although general cross-country studies do not lead to firm conclusions, one category of work is more persuasive. There is an emerging consensus that economic integration is a force behind the transmission of skill-biased technical change in the labor markets of many countries. This is based on a careful analysis of labor market trends conducted through a prism of interactions between the relative supply and relative demand of different skill categories. A number of country studies and the new work conducted for last year's World Bank report (de Ferranti and others 2003) have applied such a supply-and-demand framework.[3] Since this approach was detailed in that report, only a brief summary of the results is provided here.

It is unambiguous that many countries have experienced rising demands for workers who are educated through the

tertiary level that typically outweighs increases in the relative supply of these workers. The extent of increase in this premium varies across countries, but has been particularly strong during various periods in Argentina, Chile, Colombia, and Mexico, and present but weaker in Brazil. By contrast, there has not been a significant rise in the premium placed on workers with a secondary education (primarily because the substantial expansion in the relative supply of workers with secondary schooling largely offset increases in demand).

There has been debate in the economic literature as to whether these observed changes are due to the classical effects of increased trade, in which those countries with relatively abundant unskilled labor would (in simple models) have experienced rising demand for such labor and subsequent increases in the wages of the unskilled.[4] According to this account, the fall in relative demand for unskilled labor in Latin America would have been caused by the entry into world markets of such labor-intensive giants as Bangladesh, China, India, and Indonesia.

In fact, economic analysis identifies a different pattern of generalized biases against the unskilled and in favor of the skilled across both more and less labor-intensive industries. This provides support for the view that the dominant source of the observed changes is what economists refer to as skill-biased technical change (SBTC). It should be noted that such skill-biased changes can come from many sources, including technological advances in the layman's sense (for example, owing to information technology), as well as changes in the occupational and sectoral composition of work organization that favor tertiary or secondary school graduates.

Although significant changes in labor market policies have not occurred, there is some evidence that some shifts have sharpened trends toward rising wage differentials, owing in particular to declines in unionization and a more binding minimum wage (particularly in the case of Colombia). More generally, it is possible that the combination of easier access to capital and periodic crises have weakened the bargaining power of labor (see section 8.3 for more on this point).

Finally, although the classical effects of trade on wage inequality have not occurred, economic integration and liberalization—including the expansion of trade, financial liberalization, and Foreign Direct Investment (FDI) inflows—appear to have a mediating influence that has spurred technological, sectoral, and work organization changes, which have in turn led to rapid growth in the relative demand for skills.

This is probably the strongest evidence to support the view that polices that spur economic integration often lead to increases in wage inequality. This process reflects a tradeoff between growth and distribution, at least during economic transition. A growing demand for skills has been associated with processes of innovation and economic change that are central to Latin America getting on a faster growth path. Moreover, there is some evidence that such change is once-off. For example, both Chile and Mexico—the two countries that have gone furthest in terms of international economic integration—appear to have experienced a leveling off in the past few years (see discussion in de Ferranti and others 2002 and 2003). It should also be noted that increases in wage inequality have not been systematically associated with rising income inequality in terms of household-level per capita incomes, as discussed in chapters 2 and 6.

What can be done so that market-based reforms have more equalizing effects?

The effects of both opening up markets and economic integration are complex, and some of them may be once-off or temporary. However, the existence of likely disequalizing economic pressures in already highly unequal societies is an important issue. What can be done to offset such disequalizing effects? Potential policies can be organized into four categories, as follows.

(1) *Complementary measures to provide more equal assets across households and groups.* The assets that individuals, households, and groups possess have a powerful influence over their capacity to respond to new market opportunities. This is illustrated by differing returns on educational levels, but also applies to other economic assets such as land and infrastructure. Policies should facilitate a rapid expansion of educational attainment in response to increased demand for and premiums placed on skills, and support broader access to land and infrastructure (as discussed in chapter 7).

(2) *Sequencing of policy changes.* Economic development involves a process of creating and destroying jobs, firms, and economic activities. Part of the dynamic that empirical trends indicate is a more rapid destruction than creation of activities for the unskilled. Some countries have managed to create new productive activities while simultaneously shielding old, less productive ones. This is perhaps most dramatically

illustrated in the case of China, where dynamic non-state activities (for example, town and village enterprises) and private firms expanded significantly in the 1980s and 1990s, whilst large numbers of unproductive jobs in state firms were preserved.

This was also the case in Japan during its high-growth era. Internationally competitive export industries grew while inefficient domestic sectors (for example, agriculture and construction) were preserved through explicit public policies (which were in turn facilitated by political pressures and underpinned by substantial electoral malapportionment). However, the Japan example also illustrates the risk of such an approach: it is difficult to stop protecting inefficient sectors. In the 1980s, when the Japanese economy looked strong, observers declared victory for the Japanese model of capitalism (that is, a system with strong state intervention via industrial policy with strategic foresight). However, once the Japanese economy began to perform poorly in the 1990s, the weight of opinion shifted to favor the U.S. model, in which the market presumably operates to clear inefficiency out of the system in at least some areas. The U.S. agricultural sector is an important counterexample that again illustrates the political difficulties of ending protection of a politically influential sector.

Policy change is an important area that is influenced by both economic design and political economy. However, this report has neither conducted original work on this issue, nor found a clear synthesis from existing work. Nonetheless, it can be suggested that these factors may be quite significant in some cases. For example, opening up an economy at a high and fixed exchange rate (with significant declines in the price of capital in Argentina being one result) may have contributed to large job losses among relatively unskilled workers. Sorting out these issues will clearly require much more careful work in the future.

(3) *Measures to provide safety nets or "ropes."* The process of job destruction can lead to temporary or permanent income losses, with adverse effects on various aspects of both social and psychological well-being. A central part of a well-functioning market economy is the provision of safety nets to catch those who are hurt, or of safety "ropes" to help limit their fall. To the extent that these exist in Latin America, they have

tended to be unequal in scope; options for reform are discussed in chapter 9.

(4) *Deeper markets and a more equal investment environment.* Markets are by no means uniform with regard to both their reach and effects. An important part of the objective of achieving more equal effects through market-oriented policy reform involves the deepening of markets to provide more equal opportunities for all potential market participants. Doing so will require increased attention to the economic, political, and sociocultural factors that contribute to the unequal effects of markets.

It should be remembered that the investment environment is central to the dynamics of economic change and job growth (Stern, forthcoming). The determinants of an investment environment are complex, including market opportunities, access to inputs, infrastructural quality, the extent to which transactions are associated with corruption, and the role of government agents in facilitating or obstructing the wide variety of measures needed for investment and production by firms.

Important for the present focus is the fact that, although the investment "environment" connotes a public good, in most cases conditions stray significantly from that quality. A public good implies that its benefits would be the same for everyone and the actions of some agents would not affect the position of others. In most Latin America societies, it is more realistic to talk of a series of investment environments for different groups of firms, which are influenced by market structure, property rights, a firm's characteristics, political influence, and social connectivity (as discussed in chapter 5). In other words, investment environments are embedded in unequal sociocultural and political structures.[5]

It will be necessary to pay more attention to factors that influence both inequalities in the investment environment and market access and inequalities among individuals and households. Doing so will require careful empirical analysis that combines economic and social science approaches. A recent analysis by Hellman and Kaufmann (2003) on the relationship between "inequalities of influence" in the business sector and the quality of the institutional environment is suggestive of the importance of these issues. This issue is also closely related to one of the general themes of this report: that there is a circular relationship between weak institutions and inequalities of power, wealth, and position.

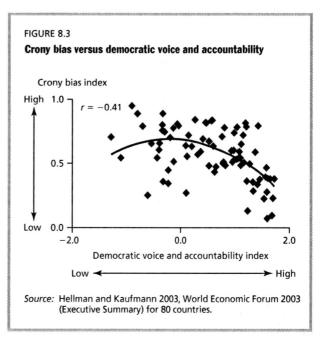

FIGURE 8.3

Crony bias versus democratic voice and accountability

Crony bias index

Source: Hellman and Kaufmann 2003, World Economic Forum 2003 (Executive Summary) for 80 countries.

Hellman and Kaufmann (2003) construct an index of "crony bias," which is "perceived by the firm as the difference between the firm's characterization of the influence of individuals or firms with close, personal ties to political leaders and the influence of its own business or trade association on recently enacted laws, rules, and regulations affecting their business" (Hellman and Kaufmann 2003, p. 9). In extreme cases, state capture, or the use of illegal means by private groups to obtain favorable government policies, result. This phenomenon has been well documented in the case of Russia and other successor states of the former Soviet Union, but there is also evidence from global analyses and recent business surveys that attests to at least the perception of its importance in many other places. (See Kaufmann, Kraay, and Mastruzzi 2003 for a summary of the results of surveys.)

A global survey finds an inverted U-shaped relationship between the crony bias index and an index of voice and democratic accountability, as indicated in figure 8.3 and using data from the World Bank governance database. The highest level of crony bias occurs in societies with intermediate levels of democratization, which is typical of most of Latin America. Apart from providing advantageous influence to the large and powerful, crony bias is also associated with weakness in public institutions, as discussed in chapter 5. In societies with high levels of crony bias, firms trust and use the courts less, pay fewer taxes, and have less secure property rights; bribery is also more prevalent. Figure 8.4

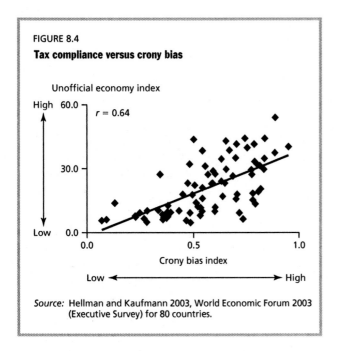

FIGURE 8.4

Tax compliance versus crony bias

Unofficial economy index

Source: Hellman and Kaufmann 2003, World Economic Forum 2003 (Executive Survey) for 80 countries.

illustrates this problem in relation to the extent of unofficial business activities. Hellman and Kaufmann (2003) suggest that these patterns can lead to a self-reinforcing dynamic, with lower support for public institutions perpetuating the weakness of institutions and, in turn, a greater likelihood of capture by more influential groups.

As always, one should be cautious about overinterpreting cross-country results, and new in-depth work will be needed to explore these mechanisms further. However, it is worth noting that the themes considered here are consistent with a current focus in the political economy literature: the new distributional coalitions that emerged post-liberalization and could take advantage of new means of securing better deals. (See Schamis 2002 for a discussion on this point in the context of privatization.)

A complementary issue concerns the role of business associations, especially those that represent small and medium firms. As noted above, the crony bias index is itself largely a product of the perceptions of these groups. Related cross-country work finds a positive relationship between the importance and activity of such associations and measures of institutional performance. This is consistent with case study evidence of the potential role of such associations in transitions away from clientelist and patronage-based relationships between government and business. There is literature on this issue from developed countries, and Angell, Lowden, and Thorp (2001) document related patterns in

their comparative analysis of experiences in different medium-sized Colombian cities.

The policy agenda related to crony bias involves building the institutional basis for increased transparency, less corruption, better corporate governance, and more effective regulation. This is likely to involve alliances between new forms of governance (as discussed in chapter 5) and business associations, especially those that represent small and medium firms.

Although reducing unequal influence at the "top" and strengthening the effectiveness of institutions will provide general support for more equal treatment across firms, there are also special issues related to the informal sector to consider. Participants are highly heterogeneous, including the self-employed, micro and small firms, and medium and large firms with informal practices (especially with regard to employment). Extensive literature on conditions and policy exists, and two key points can be made in this context. First, there is an agenda of proactive measures to improve the business and investment environment for small and medium firms that is rooted in some of the fundamental questions of market failure and weak influence that were discussed in chapter 1. This agenda is likely to involve a range of areas of action, including reducing excess regulation, strengthening property rights, providing infrastructure, streamlining bureaucracy, and deepening financial markets (see de Soto 1989 and 2000 and Tendler 2002, among others). Second, this agenda is not institution-free, but is very much about the forms of political and social interaction that exist in the broader societal context. As one example, the spectacular success of the "Third Italy" small-scale sector was not a product of government favors, but of vibrant associational activity that provided specific services to firms in order to facilitate the processes of formalization and recognition of workers rights (see box 8.2).

8.2. Labor market policies and inequality[6]

Can well-designed labor policy and institutions lead to greater equality without the occurrence of major losses in efficiency? As with overall structural policies, there are sharply divided opinions on this question. One school of thought argues that inflexibilities in the labor market and high levels of protection and privilege for formal workers are sources of higher inequality between "insiders" and "outsiders" with respect to formal labor policies and institutions, as well as sources of lower growth in "good" jobs. Another

BOX 8.2

The evolution of small-scale firms in the "Third Italy"

The expansion of the small firm sector in central and north-eastern Italy is one of the great economic successes in the second half of the 20th century. This change contributed to the absolute and relative economic and social transformation of the region. Modena, for example, went from being a high unemployment region in the early 1950s, ranking 40th amongst Italy's 95 provinces in terms of per capita income, to the top of the list in 1980 and one of the wealthiest areas in Europe.

Part of this story provides lessons on the dynamics of small firms in developing countries today. As Criscuolo (2002) discusses in a case study of firms in Bologna and Modena, dynamic growth emerged neither in the form of special government favors nor generalized burden-relieving or deregulation. In the developing country context, Tendler (2002) has argued that such approaches risk confining the small firm sector to social policy, and rendering it vulnerable to the exchange of favors or relief for political support.

Two elements of Criscuolo's (2002) diagnosis are worth highlighting here. First, central to the dynamics of the sector and its interactions with the state was vigorous associational activity. The *Confederazione Nazionale dell'Artigianato* (National Confederation of Artisans, or CNA) emerged from anti-fascist resistance in the 1930s and 1940s, and had close connections with the communist movement. It became the key actor for the small scale sector in terms of interactions with governments on policy and supporting small firms in effecting change in organization and practices.

Second, the type of policies and practices adopted strongly favored what would now be termed formalization. Ideologically committed to worker rights, and pragmatically committed to productivity growth, the CNA was an important advocate for good working conditions and efficient organization. The major type of instrument it used was what Criscuolo terms "development burden-relieving," or the provision of a range of both administrative services (around accounting, payroll management, and fiscal counseling) and production-targeted support (around producers' consortia, industrial sites, and innovation centers). These activities helped small firms both comply with the formal regulations that the CNA advocated and sustain high levels of productivity growth.

A remarkably dynamic small-scale sector emerged as a product of mobilization and the central role of deliberate, proactive, and persistent support of association. This helped artisan firms pursue the "high road" to small business development. While institutional context is intrinsically specific to geography and history, there are potentially valuable lessons to be learned for deepening markets in Latin America.

Source: Criscuolo 2002.

---

school of thought argues that state policies on labor are essential to ensure decent working conditions, reduce the risk of exploitation of the vulnerable, and provide reasonable levels of income security against job loss, sickness, and old age. Sorting through these issues is a major (and important) undertaking (see World Bank 1995 for an overall discussion). The design of labor policy is complex, and the literature on the issue is expansive. Specifics need to be carefully worked out in particular contexts. As with many issues covered in this report, the current discussion is restricted to a few general policy themes.

Current labor policy and institutions are an unholy compromise in much of Latin America. To the extent that they make a difference to labor market outcomes, this assessment holds true in the context of partial coverage. In some cases, such coverage is associated with differential privileges, which impose implicit costs on outsiders; social security provisions in many countries are an important example. There are also areas in which labor institutions lead to inflexible and inequitable outcomes.

Teachers unions are an example of a labor institution that has often (though not, of course, always) been an impediment to reforms that would lead to higher quality and more equitable schooling, which is an area of fundamental importance to the expansion of more equal capabilities. (Such cases reflect "opportunity hoarding," in the language of sociologists.) More generally, while unions often have helped improve the working conditions of their members, this rarely leads to greater equality. Estimated effects are usually negligible. In the case of Brazil, unions seem to lead to greater inequality of wages. This is because, in contrast to Organisation of Economic Co-operation and Development (OECD) countries, unionized workers tend to be in the more skilled and better-paid part of the overall wage distribution.

The other side of this situation is that large segments of the workforce are not covered by union action, protected in terms of health standards, discrimination, or abuse, or provided with even basic forms of income security. Many Latin American countries are reasonably flexible in overall labor market adjustments (though there are important differences between, for example, relatively flexible Mexico and Argentina), but flexibility is the flip side of having large informal sectors that are weakly covered by formal working conditions. Minimum wages generally have modest and mildly equalizing effect on the structure of wages, but this is offset by reductions in employment, especially for young, low-skilled, and female workers (World Bank 2004). Where significantly binding, as in Colombia, minimum wages probably contribute to lower levels of formal employment.

Large informal sectors are symptomatic of both weak formal employment growth and a high ratio of the costs to the benefits of formalization, whether for employers or workers. However, this does not imply that workers in the informal sector are necessarily worse off, or that they are queuing up for better work in the formal sector. The key word is heterogeneity. Many informal sector participants are self-employed entrepreneurs who are in that sector out of choice because of higher returns or preferred working conditions. (See Maloney 2003 for a survey of issues related to informal sector employment.) In some cases, households may adopt diversified employment strategies, with one worker maintaining a formal job in order to secure social security and health benefits and others pursuing informal activities.

However, informal work can also be more susceptible to socially based inequalities. As Heller and Mahoney (2003) argue, because the informal sector is largely outside the reach of the state and transactions within it are largely extra-legal, success is often dependent on networks and on noninstitutionalized mechanisms of reducing transaction costs. In other words, "Access to capital, control of space and markets, enforcement of transactions, and maintaining buyer and seller networks thus all involve controlling access to a resource or a network by erecting strong boundaries of ethnicity, gender, community, and race. Criminal networks,

with their deeply reified blood ties, rituals of membership, and high existence costs are only the extreme case" (Heller and Mahoney 2003, p. 41).

A number of directions that could be taken to achieve a more equitable labor policy are put forth here, in the spirit of seeking to both extend worker rights to all and increase the flexibility in those sectors of the labor market that are relatively protected. These policies can generally be framed in terms of increasing incentives for formalization by both reducing costs and increasing benefits.

First, policies that support the informal sector are needed (as noted in the preceding section). In particular, Latin American countries should seek innovative ways to increase the productivity of firms in this sector and facilitate their participation in formal institutions. The informal sector should not be viewed exclusively as a pool of workers left out of formal employment due to excessive regulations, but rather as a group of entrepreneurs, and their employees, that need support and amenable policies in order to grow and succeed. Such policies include the reduction of transaction costs, the availability of credit and formal mechanisms through which to operate, and, most importantly, labor laws that permit firms to adapt to changing economic conditions.

Second, labor market laws and minimum wage-setting procedures should be assessed carefully in each country. Dual objectives should be to remove excessive rigidity and to reduce the impact of minimum wages on unemployment. More specifically, removing excessive rigidity means giving employers and employees alike efficient mechanisms with which to adapt to the business cycle, which would then be reflected in higher formal employment rates in the long run. Regarding minimum wages, it is important to ensure that the mechanism used to set them be based not only on purchasing power, but also on considerations related to productivity and employment.

If managed effectively, these policies can be consistent with greater support for workers. This can be done through both reduced informality and the spinoff effects of a generally more supportive approach to labor in terms of institutional functioning. Figure 8.5 illustrates the tradeoff between more rigid protection and informality. However, note that Costa Rica has both more rigidity (as proxied by an index of the costs of firing workers) and lower levels of informality than does the Dominican Republic. In an in-depth comparison of the labor markets in these two countries, Itzigsohn (2000)

FIGURE 8.5
Labor market rigidity and informality

Informal sector share of total employment

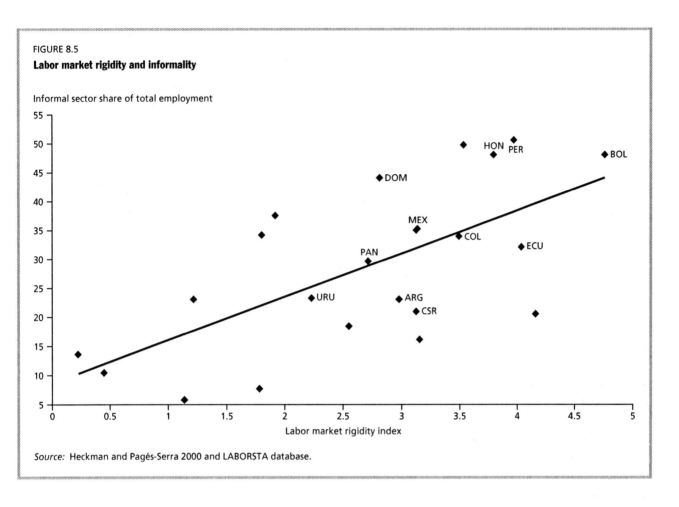

Source: Heckman and Pagés-Serra 2000 and LABORSTA database.

argues that this pattern is the product of an overall strategy in Costa Rica that was more supportive of worker rights and working conditions than efforts in the Dominican Republic. The effects of this approach were therefore as much a result of the impact on the functioning of institutions as of the details of policies.

Third, reforms in the area of social security should continue to be made with the intention of achieving a more equitable form of risk management for all workers and households (see chapter 9).

Fourth, unions have a central role to play in both the workplace and society, but the context in which they function influences the distributional effects of their activities. Where unions have become means for protecting privileges that impose costs on others—especially those who are less fortunate—then more flexibility will be of greater value. There is a contrast between those union movements that were effectively incorporated into vertical state structures (Mexico, for example) and those with stronger horizontal affiliations (as in Brazil). The latter will be more likely to act in the

interests of broader groups of poor workers and households. (This is not, however, to say that they will not still seek to vigorously defend the interests of their members.)

Finally, there is no inherent inconsistency between unions, state regulation, and integration into the global economy via a high productivity route. This is illustrated by a case study of union involvement in export-oriented, high-value crops in northeastern Brazil (box 8.3). Unions have been an important element of a shift toward a path to integration that has benefited both workers and firms, primarily at a local level in a specific industry. Cases in which productivity has increased cooperation at a national level are probably harder to find in Latin America, in contrast, for example, to the role of the Swedish union movement in that country's development (de Ferranti and others 2002).

8.3. Inequality and macroeconomic crises

Macroeconomic instability has been the bane of long-term economic performance in Latin America. Periodic crises have been sources of pervasive and deep social scars. In recent decades,

BOX 8.3

Unions, firms, and the expansion of high-value export crops in Petrolina-Juazeiro in northeastern Brazil

A study on the evolution of worker-firm relationships in the high-value export crop sector in Petrolina-Juazeiro underscores the potential positive role of unions in increasing both productivity and the well-being of workers. In a seemingly unpromising environment of landless agricultural laborers, union activity was an important ingredient in the shift to work practices that both offer better working conditions and achieve high productivity— as well as, importantly, high quality—in a successful area of export agriculture. This outcome was facilitated by a combination of market conditions and the strategy and history of institutional actors. The critical importance of timing for quality in the agricultural process (for example in harvesting grapes) gave the workers potential leverage. The rural union had to significantly change its strategy from focusing on its traditional base among small farmers in order to represent the interest of landless workers. In addition, the farm owners were primarily large-scale firms from southeastern Brazil with experience in collective bargaining, in contrast to the more traditional large-scale sugar farmers of the northeast who were accustomed to more repressive and conflictive labor relations.

Source: Damiani 2003.

the 1980s debt crisis brought to a halt an extended period of growth in much of the region, albeit growth that occurred on highly unequal terms. By the beginning of the 1990s, most countries appeared to have gained a sounder macroeconomic policy footing, and market-based debt reductions had helped reduce the debt overhang. Yet crises continued to hit the region in the subsequent decade. The 1994–1995 Mexican and the 2001–2003 Argentine crises will be remembered as much as the steady gains in health and education that occurred throughout the region during this time.

The causes of crises—as well as of optimal macroeconomic, financial, and debt management policies to prevent and manage crises—is an immense area of study. The literature and debates are not summarized here, but instead crises are examined through the prism of the concerns and approaches contained in this report. Are there any causal links between weak and unequal institutions and crises? What are the distributional consequences of crises? Does the perspective of this report cast light on feasible policy options that are better for reducing inequality and managing crises? Each of these questions is considered in turn.

What causes macroeconomic crises? Proximate and deep factors

Earlier parts of this report explored how weak and unequal institutions can be self-sustaining with regard to long-term development processes and underlying policy choices. Some institutional weaknesses may actually be functional for the powerful. Can weak and unequal institutions also be a source of macroeconomic instability and the unequal resolution of crises?

The usual suspects for crisis causation have traditionally been faulty macro-level policies, especially those associated with excessive public spending, overvalued exchange rates, and loose monetary management. There are well-documented links between such factors and volatility, high inflation, and currency and banking crises. These have correctly received significant attention—not least of all by international financial institutions—with the objective of achieving better macroeconomic policies to prevent crises. In the wake of the 1980s debt crisis, realistic exchange rates and prudent fiscal and sound monetary policies were central to the policy platforms being advocated for, and eventually adopted by, countries in Latin America. There were important gains that have, in particular, been associated with large reductions in inflation. Most studies find that lower inflation tends to have positive effects on income distribution.

Substantial gains in these policy areas seem to have ushered in a period of stability. However, this changed with the 1994–1995 Mexican crisis, the ripple effects of the East Asian and Russian crises in 1997 and 1998, and macroeconomic difficulties in countries such as Argentina, Bolivia, and Venezuela starting in 2000. All problems had clearly not been solved. In the economics field, these and other crises (including those that occurred in Europe during the 1990s) helped spawn a range of new thinking. Recent perspectives have emphasized asymmetric information problems in financial markets, the possibility of multiple equilibria with high and

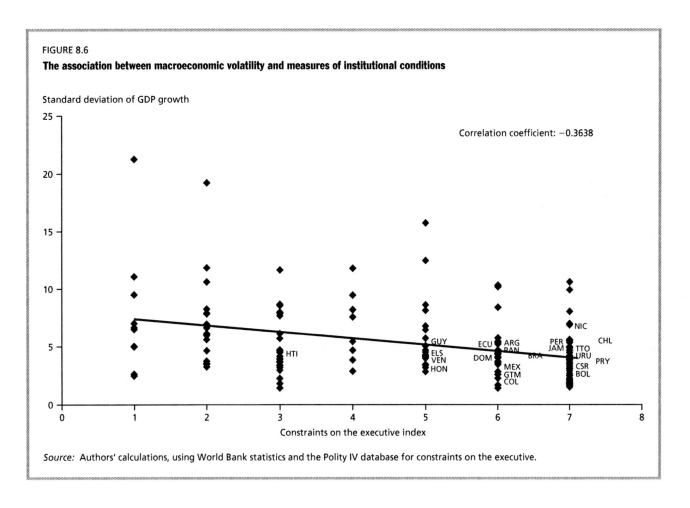

FIGURE 8.6

The association between macroeconomic volatility and measures of institutional conditions

Standard deviation of GDP growth

Correlation coefficient: −0.3638

Constraints on the executive index

Source: Authors' calculations, using World Bank statistics and the Polity IV database for constraints on the executive.

low external capital flows, currency balance sheet mismatches in government and the corporate and financial sectors, and weak financial sector regulation and performance.[7]

Even when fiscal and monetary policies are reasonably sound (as they were in much of East Asia before crisis ensued), surges in capital inflows reinforced by premature or poorly designed capital account liberalization, as well as weak prudential regulation and supervision, have led to the excessive accumulation of short-term external debt and credit booms. This pattern rapidly reversed when the booms ended, and led to sharp domestic asset price declines and large currency devaluations. These problems in turn resulted in widespread corporate bankruptcy and deep recessions.

One theme of relevance to this report can be emphasized here. As in many areas discussed in other chapters, economic processes interact with institutional conditions. Weak institutions (which are related to inequality in ways discussed in chapters 4 and 5) may have a causal influence on the occurrence of crises. There is a suggestive association between weak institutions and macroeconomic volatility, as illustrated

by the bivariate relationship between a measure of the extent to which the executive is constrained by national institutions and the standard deviation of growth in gross domestic product (GDP) (figure 8.6). This association says nothing about causation, but some studies do provide an empirical basis for the inference of some causal processes on the relationship.

An example of empirical work on crises is a recent study by Acemoglu and others (2002) that explores the relationships among macroeconomic policies, institutions, and macroeconomic volatility. It argues that the strength of institutions is a principal long-term causal force behind volatility, which can be manifested through macroeconomic policies or other factors (box 8.4).

This analysis is useful, but does not explore the specific mechanisms of crises. Two are likely to be of importance and to lie at the intersection of concerns over inequality: management of distributional conflict and the relationship between unequal influence and the functioning of the financial system.

BOX 8.4
Institutions, macroeconomic policy, and volatility

Recent work by Acemoglu and others (2002) explores the relationships among institutions, macroeconomic policy choices, and economic volatility. Countries that have had faulty macroeconomic policies (such as excessively expansionary fiscal policy, loose monetary policy, and overvalued exchange rates) have also experienced higher macroeconomic volatility, as well as lower growth, in the past few decades. The question is whether the end of the story is that governments make the "mistake" of choosing bad policies that then cause volatility.

An alternative view is that both the choice of policy and economic volatility reflect underlying institutional weaknesses. By institutions, the authors are concerned with a *"cluster of social arrangements* that include constitutional and social limits on politicians' and elites' power, the rule of law, provisions for mediating social cleavages, strong property rights enforcement, a minimum of equal opportunity, and broad-based access to education, etc."[a] (Also see the discussion in chapter 5.) The key argument in this regard is that institutional weaknesses will tend to lower investment and increase volatility and policies, for example through the inability to manage distributional struggles.

Cross-country evidence in support of this argument is provided by exploring the empirical relationship between macroeconomic policies—an indicator of institutional strength using an index of constraints on the executive from the Polity IV database—and measures of economic volatility, including the standard deviation of growth and largest declines in output. The empirical challenge is that both macroeconomic policies and institutions are likely to be endogenous, or to reflect the influence of omitted variables. To deal with this, the authors use an identification strategy based on the substantive view that extractive institutions formed in colonial periods can have a persistent negative influence on contemporary institutional conditions (see chapter 4.) Such extractive institutions are more likely to evolve in situations where there is relatively modest settlement, which allows for the use of an index of settler mortality during the colonial period. This measure of the hospitality of the environment is correlated with recent institutional measures, but there is no reason why it should have any direct influence on current macroeconomic policies.

When the analysis of influences on volatility is undertaken using settler mortality as an instrument to identify the exogenous, historically determined component of recent institutional conditions, the relationship between macroeconomic policies and volatility largely disappears, while measures of institutional strength remain robustly significant. This trend applies both when macroeconomic policies are treated as exogenous (which would generally bias the results to favor the influence of such policies, if these variables are actually endogenous), or if lagged values of macroeconomic policies are used as instruments. There is weak support for the role of exchange rate overvaluation, but not for the role of inflation or measures of public spending and deficits. The authors suggest that where underlying institutional weaknesses exist, they can spill over into crises in various ways, sometimes through macroeconomic policy mechanisms and sometimes via microeconomic routes. This is further illustrated by case study analyses of Argentina and Ghana.

Source: Acemoglu and others 2002.
a. Acemoglu and others 2002, p. 4.

With respect to the management of distributional conflict, there is a tradition of work that focuses on how fights between groups can have potent influences on the conduct of macroeconomic policy. (See Bates 1981 for a seminal piece on this subject.) The interaction between distributional struggle and institutional weakness is illustrated in cross-country work by Rodrik (1999). That analysis seeks to explain the varying impacts of the shocks of the 1970s on growth in terms of the interaction between latent social conflict or distributional struggles on the one hand, and institutions for conflict management on the other. The study looks in particular at differences in growth during 1960–1975 and 1975–1989, periods when most of Latin America suffered a significant decline in economic growth while East Asia actually experienced accelerated growth; this difference occurred despite the fact that both regions experienced shocks.

Countries that experienced the largest declines in growth were not necessarily those that suffered the greatest shocks, but rather those with a combination of more divided societies (as measured by indices of inequality or social difference between groups) and weak institutions for conflict management (as proxied by indicators of the quality of governmental institutions, the rule of law, democratic rights, and social safety nets). In Rodrik's (1999) analysis, more conventional influences on economic vulnerability—including economic openness, the share of government consumption, and levels of indebtedness—become insignificant predictors of growth collapse once the measures of latent conflict and institutions for conflict management are introduced. The discussions in this report (especially in chapters 4 and 5) support the view that Latin America is generally a region of high social cleavage and weak institutions, including weak constraints on the power of elites, when compared with East Asian and OECD countries.[8]

Completing this type of story would require careful case study research. A vivid contemporary example is Venezuela, where social-political conflict and the associated stoppage by the oil industry directly led to approximately a 26 percent drop in GDP from March 2002 to March 2003. Less dramatic episodes also occurred earlier, with the government's ability to engineer "social pacts" increasingly exhausted from the mid-1980s on, a trend that in turn limited society's ability to resolve distributional conflict through semicorporatist settlements. This is an interesting example precisely because Venezuelan democracy was founded on the basis of an explicit pact between the government and the elites, as well as on the deliberate use of distributional—but not redistributional—public policies stemming from the abundant public resources generated by oil revenues. This scheme worked for a while: Venezuela succeeded in maintaining remarkable macroeconomic stability and quite respectable levels of growth during the 1960s and 1970s.

The second area in which institutional weaknesses may be associated with crises is the links between unequal influence of the corporate sector and the functioning of the financial system. As noted in section 8.1, "crony bias" is associated with a range of weaknesses in institutions. To the extent that this phenomenon weakens the lending practices and prudential behavior of the financial sector, it can have a pernicious influence both on crisis causation (via excessive credit expansion) and crisis dynamics (through poor portfolios). This is of particular importance to interpretations of some of the more recent crises that were not based on fiscal laxity.

The studies referred to here are by no means the last word in empirical investigation of interactions among macro-level policies, institutions, and volatility with regard to both cross-country analysis and, perhaps more importantly, in-depth case studies. As noted earlier, an extensive economics literature on the sources of crisis already exists. Questions related to institutional weakness and links to inequality intersect with only some of the mechanisms discussed in that literature. Macro-level policy choices of course have an effect at least in the short- to medium-term, and the functioning of the financial system will be central to whether crises occur and how severe they are. The mechanisms whereby institutional weaknesses interact with distributional struggles to form a source of volatility require considerably more exploration. Nonetheless, there is a need to bring these issues back to the center of an analysis of crises.

The distributional consequences of macroeconomic crises

Macroeconomic crises affect society in multiple ways. Four economic channels of influence are emphasized in most research: the impact of reduced demand on jobs, wages, and enterprise income; changes in prices; public spending cutbacks; and changes in the value of assets.[9] As households and communities respond to these effects, secondary effects can be felt in terms of household decisions on schooling or health, the increased work of women and other secondary workers, depletion of financial assets, and reliance on social networks for support.

Many observers also emphasize the costs of macroeconomic crises to the social fabric, as individuals are forced into illegal activities or as young men and women adapt to adverse opportunities by shifting into cultures of drugs, violence, or prostitution rather than skills acquisition and productive work. Adverse effects can be persistent (a phenomenon known as "hysteresis" in the jargon of economists), for example through losses in organizational, human, or social capital that can take considerable time to rebuild. As one example, it is striking that personal violence in Latin America increased in the 1980s and then did not go down even when economies recovered in the 1990s. (For more on this subject, see Fajnzylber, Lederman, and Loayza 2000.)

This section looks at three categories of evidence related to the effects of macroeconomic crises. First, the results of studies on income distribution, as measured by household surveys and via spending, are summarized. Second, information on the distribution between labor and capital is discussed. Third, distributional aspects of the resolution of crises through financial sector channels are considered. While these two latter sources are relatively new and represent early research efforts, they have a particular bearing on the issues discussed throughout this report.

Effects on income distribution

Are the costs of crises unequally distributed? It is often asserted that the poor suffer most when a crisis hits. Past work actually reveals a mixed picture in this regard. With respect to influences on incomes, evidence from household surveys typically finds losses across all strata that are partially disequalizing in some cases but not in others. For example, Lustig (2000), in reviewing 20 Latin American crises, found small increases in the Gini coefficient in 15 cases that compared post- with pre-crisis periods, but small declines in others. De Janvry and Sadoulet (2000) reviewed 48 instances in 12 countries in Latin America between 1970 and 1994 and found asymmetric effects between recessions that tended to increase income inequality and periods of positive growth, which in effect led to a ratcheting up of inequality over this period.

Morley (2001) found that during the 1980s, recessions typically led to increases in inequality, while recoveries were associated with lower inequality. However, Morley also found no clear pattern of response to macroeconomic crises during the 1990s. On the basis of worldwide evidence, Ravallion and Chen (1997) found no overall pattern of change in the income distribution during episodes of macroeconomic decline in most regions, with increases and declines occurring in roughly equal proportion. The major exception in the 1990s was the successor states of the former Soviet Union, which experienced significant increases in inequality during episodes of large-scale income decline. (These were clearly associated with the large-scale institutional changes taking place during the transition from socialism (World Bank 2000d).

Although there is some evidence that recession increases inequality, some of the time, most of these results suggest that there is no general pattern of the influence of adverse shocks on income distribution (or at least not on that part of the distribution captured by surveys; see below). This is further borne out by case study evidence, for example with regard to the contrast between Mexico and Argentina in recent years. With respect to the Mexican Tequila crisis,

TABLE 8.2

Changes in real per capita income across the income distribution in Mexico, 1992–2000

	Increase in real per capita income (in percent)			
Deciles	1992–94	1994–96	1996–98	1998–2000
1	21.3	−23.4	0.1	21.9
2	10.0	−19.9	4.9	14.1
3	11.9	−21.6	4.6	21.7
4	7.5	−22.1	9.6	17.3
5	6.1	−22.4	14.2	13.7
6	7.6	−20.0	9.0	11.3
7	6.0	−20.9	13.9	19.6
8	8.6	−22.6	11.9	16.4
9	8.7	−21.5	11.5	12.5
10	14.5	−24.1	20.4	5.6
Top 5%	17.5	−24.7	22.2	4.7
Top 1%	18.4	−23.9	37.0	−3.5

Source: Authors' calculations from Mexican household income and expenditure surveys.

López-Acevedo and Salinas (2000) found relatively high losses in the top decile of the income distribution, for which the share of total income declined from 42.3 percent in 1994 to 40.7 percent in 1996. This was the main force behind the fall in the Gini coefficient from 0.534 to 0.519 during this period. Table 8.2 shows the pattern of income decline that occurred between 1994 and 1996.

Why did richer groups in Mexico lose out in the crisis? It might have been expected that the rich would be particularly hard hit by losses in financial income in the wake of the asset price declines associated with the currency and financial crisis. In fact, the opposite appears to have occurred, at least on average. The decline in the share of the rich was instead driven by sharp declines in labor earnings in the financial and other high-paying service sectors. By contrast, the contribution of financial income to total income increased (table 8.3), with growth in real financial income per capita at the top of the distribution rising from 6 percent for the top decile to 14 percent for the top 1 percent of the income distribution.

Evidence on financial income from household surveys is generally weak, covering only a fraction of total financial trends in a country. Although these results should be treated with caution given the usually weak coverage of capital income, the apparent capacity of the rich to increase their financial income during the crisis is striking.[10] It is possible that this occurred because of earnings on money that was successfully shifted out of the country just before the crisis,

TABLE 8.3

Financial income during the 1994–96 crisis in Mexico

Deciles	Mean financial income per capita (in 2000 pesos)		Share of financial income in total income (percent)		Real increase in financial income per capita (percent)
	1994	1996	1994	1996	1994–1996
1	20.5	16.9	1.8	2.0	−17.5
2	26.3	26.1	1.6	2.0	−0.8
3	56.8	33.5	2.7	2.0	−41.0
4	47.1	38.8	1.9	2.0	−17.5
5	65.3	67.5	2.1	2.8	3.3
6	107.4	90.4	2.9	3.0	−15.8
7	141.0	134.9	3.2	3.8	−4.3
8	161.8	147.2	2.8	3.3	−9.0
9	257.3	264.7	3.2	4.2	2.9
10	1,444.1	1,535.0	7.1	10.0	6.3
Top 5%	2,524.1	2,833.4	8.8	13.1	12.2
Top 1%	7,416.5	8,448.1	13.1	19.4	13.9

Source: Authors' calculations from Mexican household income and expenditure surveys.

and that consequently experienced capital gains when the exchange rate collapsed. This is only a partial picture, and large asset price movements occurred that imposed capital losses on those holding Mexican assets, especially assets that were denominated in pesos. (The role of the financial sector in redistribution is discussed further below.)

The finding that labor earnings became slightly more equal during Mexico's crisis is consistent with findings by Sánchez-Páramo and Schady (2002) in a study of six major Latin American countries, which indicated that the premium placed on tertiary education tends to fall during crises. This premise is also consistent with an international analysis of influences on income distribution by López (2003) that finds banking crises to have equalizing effects on measured income after controlling for a range of other factors. Again, for most countries, measured household income is dominated by labor income, and capital income is severely underreported.

In Argentina, the recent crisis has so far led to a substantial worsening in inequality, with an increase in the Gini coefficient from 0.49 in 1999 to 0.55 in 2002. (In contrast to Mexico, reported financial income in Argentina is so small as to be implausible and is therefore not analyzed.[11]) As a result, the ratio of income between the top and bottom deciles rose from 15 times in 1999 to 28 times in 2002 (compared to 11 times in 1990). The differences between the two cases are undoubtedly complex, but one of the more striking contrasts lies in labor market adjustment.

Mexico has long had a pattern of adjustment at the bottom of the labor market in which firms and workers adjust through lower real wages—whether based on shifts into lower-paying work (for example, in the informal sector) or declines in real wages that are facilitated by inflation. During the Tequila crisis, unemployment spiked, but then declined rapidly to the 3 percent range a couple of years later. At the top of the labor earnings distribution, by contrast, the pre-crisis period had seen large increases. This was especially true in leading sectors such as high-paying services and finance, which were hit hard by crisis.

In contrast, Argentina shifted to a high unemployment labor market even during the relatively good times of the 1990s. This change was influenced by high layoffs due to restructuring, the relatively low relative price flexibility associated with a fixed exchange rate and low inflation, and, possibly, the influence of labor market policies.[12] The Argentine crisis further increased unemployment, which rose to 21.5 percent in May 2002 before declining to 17.8 percent in October of that year. The spike in inflation after the exchange rate devaluation was a source of large real wage declines and a sharp rise in poverty.

A comparison of Argentina and Mexico suggests a general lesson: the way in which crises affect household distribution is conditional on the structure of the labor market, the sectoral incidence of adverse shocks, and the way that the labor market adjusts.

The above discussion refers to the evolution of income differences as measured in household surveys, which capture three channels of influence: labor market changes, relative prices, and returns to nonhuman capital assets. Although no overall pattern of distribution effects is evident, it is important to emphasize that impacts on poverty are unambiguously adverse, since declines in income push some nonpoor people into poverty and deepen the poverty of those who are already poor before a crisis. Even an equiproportionate decline in incomes across the income distribution is likely to hurt those at the bottom most; a 10 percent decline in income for those in poverty is more costly in terms of well-being than it is for those in the middle or upper parts of the distribution.

This result applies with even greater force to households living in extreme poverty, which generally have insufficient resources with which to purchase adequate food or pay for medical expenses, especially during deep or protracted recessions. (See de Ferranti and others, 2000.) In addition, particular individuals and households can experience much larger drops in income, a phenomenon that is hidden in data based on averages. Large income declines for individuals and households are concerns that are distinct from chronic poverty on both welfare and political grounds. (See Pritchett 2001 for an analysis of Indonesia.) This fact has implications for the design of safety net instruments, as discussed in chapter 9.

The other main channel that has been studied in past research concerns the distribution of public spending and the consequential distribution of services and transfers. Two general processes are important in this regard. First, in the aggregate, public spending in most Latin American countries tends to be procyclical, expanding in good times and contracting in bad (see chapter 9). This trend is driven by political pressures to increase spending when the going is good, the strongly procyclical nature of private market sentiments, and the proclivity for "sudden stops" in market flows when the going is bad (see de Ferranti and others 2000 and Calvo and Reinhart 2000 for more on this point). Sharp reversals in capital flows are also associated with the lack of credibility given to countercyclical fiscal policies because of asymmetric information problems: it is difficult for markets to distinguish between a prudent countercyclical fiscal policy and fiscal laxity, especially when governments have not proven able to produce surpluses in good times.

This trend in turn affects the capacity to finance deficits and increases the burden of debt service because of exchange rate depreciations for foreign and domestic dollar-denominated

debt and rising risk premiums. During the economic slowdown of the late 1990s, two exceptions to this rule were Chile, which had developed both the credibility and the budgetary processes to run a countercyclical policy, and Bolivia, a country dependent on concessional finance and therefore spared the vicissitudes of private market sentiments. In the case of Bolivia, the deficit rose from 3.5–3.7 percent of GDP in 1999 and 2000 to 7 percent in 2001 under International Monetary Fund (IMF) programs.

Second, when crises induce spending declines, there is a tendency to protect those categories of spending that are practically, legally, or politically more difficult to adjust. This includes debt service (except when crises are very deep and countries stop paying), permanent public employment, and social security entitlements (notably pensions for retired public sector workers). Maintaining teachers and nurses on the public payroll can help keep basic social services going, although there can be discontinuities when crises are deep and workers don't get paid, or when declines in real wages become very costly in terms of morale and complementary inputs.

Moreover, there is evidence that cuts disproportionately hurt programs (especially discretionary ones) that are relatively progressive. Just as many programs tend to function along the income distribution as they expand, thereby crowding in poorer groups (see chapter 9), spending cuts work in the opposite fashion (see Ravallion 2000 and 2002). Of particular concern are cutbacks in targeted transfer programs, the resources of which decline or fail to expand as needs rise alongside an increase in poverty.

The distribution between capital and labor

Household surveys are relatively good at capturing labor income and some transfers, but are particularly weak at capturing capital income. Yet the distribution between labor and capital income is an important part of the story. This issue can be examined using information from national accounts. Doing so involves considering the functional distribution of income between workers and owners of capital rather than the personal distribution across households. There is evidence that the share of income going to labor decreases during crises and that there is some persistence in this redistribution.[13]

The underlying sources of information for labor and capital shares in national accounts are different from those contained in household surveys. While household surveys ask household members where they work, how much they earn, and what they spend money on, national accounts are based primarily on information from production sources (that is, surveys of firms, estimates of agricultural production, and sales statistics). Detailed information on the composition of value added is typically only available periodically—for example from agricultural and industrial censuses and special surveys of service sectors—so that estimates of the functional distribution of income are likely to contain substantial inaccuracies. This is especially the case when the informal sector is significant.

The data on labor shares provided here cover primarily formal work. Because of all the limitations discussed in chapter 2, household surveys are the preferred instrument for obtaining direct measures of the well-being of households and of changes over time. However, national account sources may be superior in capturing what is happening to all sources of income, including capital income. The fact that capital income and the incomes of the rich appear to be relatively poorly captured by the surveys adds another dimension to

the interpretation of what happens during crisis episodes. In order for patterns of change in the distribution of income in the national accounts to reflect real changes, any biases or inaccuracies have to be the same during the entire cycle. This may not be the case during economic downturns, for example if informal labor incomes are underestimated and the relative share of this source of income rises.

With these now familiar caveats on the quality of the data in mind, the resulting patterns can be examined. Using a global database, Diwan (2001 and 2002) examines the relationship between crises (in currency, banking, or both) and labor shares. These studies find that labor shares systematically fall during crises and don't fully recover afterward, a cross-country result that is illustrated for four countries in Latin America in figure 8.7. The cross-country pattern is highlighted by the case of Mexico, where the labor share fell sharply in 1982, steadily recovered during the following decade, weathered the more moderate macroeconomic setback of 1989, and then fell significantly following the

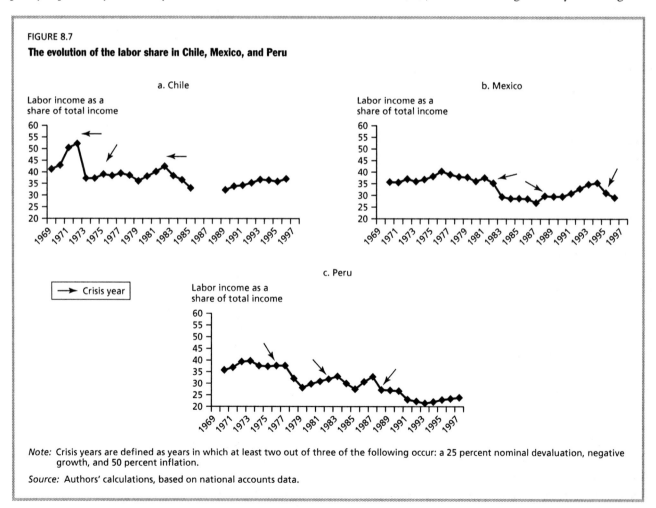

FIGURE 8.7

The evolution of the labor share in Chile, Mexico, and Peru

a. Chile

Labor income as a share of total income

b. Mexico

Labor income as a share of total income

→ Crisis year

c. Peru

Labor income as a share of total income

Note: Crisis years are defined as years in which at least two out of three of the following occur: a 25 percent nominal devaluation, negative growth, and 50 percent inflation.

Source: Authors' calculations, based on national accounts data.

1994–1995 crisis. The flip side of this pattern, of course, is that the shares of corporate and financial sector capital income rise relative to wages. There are also significant interactions with structural variables. In particular, closed trade, capital controls, and fiscal deficits are associated with higher labor shares in normal times, but also with large falls in labor shares when crises occur.

What are the mechanisms behind these trends? There are both proximate and deep explanations. In terms of proximate factors, labor market and prices channels tend during crises to lead to a disproportionate drop in the portion of value added that workers obtain through a diverse combination of wage and employment declines. Worker and household adjustments—whether occurring through shifts into lower-paying informal work or the increased labor force participation of secondary workers—do not compensate for the relatively adverse effects on initial employment conditions. (If they do, it is not captured in the data.) With regard to capital, most Latin American countries have relied significantly on external savings to finance investment (leaving them with high debt burdens and vulnerable to capital outflows) and on large movements of asset prices when confidence falls. Interest rates are typically increased to reduce capital flight, thereby also protecting domestic financial income.

At a deeper level, the interpretation of causes depends on the underlying view of how labor market outcomes are determined. In a world in which wages are determined by marginal productivity—and are therefore subject to the multiple influences of institutional or policy-related effects on wages, from minimum levels to severance pay—the explanation should be sought in the disproportionately high decline in labor productivity, relative to returns on capital, that occurs during crises. It is not clear why this pattern ensues.

Alternatively, if bargaining or, more broadly, power relationships are an important influence on private and public wages, the explanation lies in a decline in the relative power of workers during a crisis. Under this premise, crises can be seen as mechanisms for the resolution of distributional conflicts that are not tackled during good economic times. The latter is the preferred interpretation of Diwan (2001 and 2002), who sees crises as mechanisms that societies use to "digest" social losses across groups. Labor is relatively immobile and so typically bears a higher proportion of the cost.[14] Further exploration of this issue will require in-depth research on case studies. Fizsbein and Galiani (2003), in initial work on the Argentine case, find large changes in the labor share around the time of crises, which at least in some cases appear to be associated with the resolution of political fights between formal labor and other interests at the expense of labor. This is perhaps most clearly the case in the episode of high inflation and stabilization under the Argentine military government in the 1970s.

The impact of financial sector "adjustments" on income distribution

While the evidence surveyed here provides an important part of the picture, it still leaves out some of the larger issues at play. In particular, currency and financial crises are both driven by, and cause, large movements within the financial system, which in turn have significant fiscal consequences for the future. According to a survey of 40 banking crises, the average fiscal costs were 14.7 percent of GDP. These costs were incurred because of a variety of resolution tools, including guarantees for depositors and creditors, liquidity support, repeated capitalizations, and public debt relief. While the costs are distributed over many years, these are clearly nontrivial amounts. In addition, they have often been larger, as table 8.4 illustrates, for Latin America and countries hit by the East Asian crisis. Mexico's Tequila crisis cost 19.3 percent and Chile's 1981–83 crisis cost 41 percent of GDP. The bailout of Banco Intercontinental in the Dominican Republic in 2003 (which is still too recent to be included in table 8.4) is estimated to have cost between 14 and 17 percent of GDP (see World Bank 2003g). The bill for the current Argentina crisis is not yet in. By contrast, the Savings and Loans crisis in the United States during the 1980s cost just 3.2 percent of GDP.

TABLE 8.4

Total fiscal costs of selected banking crises

Country and episode	Fiscal cost (in percent of GDP)
Argentina, 1980–82	55.1
Brazil, 1994–96	13.2
Chile, 1981–83	41.2
Ecuador, 1996–	13.0
México, 1994–	19.3
Venezuela, RB de, 1994–97	22.0
Indonesia, 1997–	50.0
Korea, 1997–	26.5
United States, 1981–91	3.2

Source: Honohan and Klingebiel 2000.
Note: Costs refer to both fiscal and quasi-fiscal outlays and are the accumulated total.

What are the distributional dimensions of financial crises? Are richer financial sector participants bailed out at the expense of poorer groups outside the financial system? Do richer participants within the financial system gain (relatively speaking), or receive higher levels of protection for their losses, when crises occur? In background work for this report, Halac and Schmuckler (2003) found evidence of adverse distributional effects of crises through both effects. Large, foreign depositors enjoyed the greatest level of compensation, and sometimes capital gains, in crises in Argentina, Ecuador, and Uruguay, while small depositors suffered capital losses. In addition, there is evidence that large borrowers with close connections with banks particularly benefited from crises in Chile, Ecuador, and Mexico. This is illustrated here with case study evidence from Mexico and Argentina.

There is no direct, survey-based evidence of the household impacts of financial sector changes. An assessment therefore has to be formed on the basis of indirect evidence. The total size of the Mexican bailout is estimated at $112 billion (Honohan and Klingebiel 2000), with a large additional amount spent trying to prevent crises from occurring with regard to liquidity support, sovereign bond swaps, and the financing of large investors who withdraw money from projects. Halac and Schmuckler (2003) use the $23 billion decline in the Central Bank's reserves between February and December 1994 as a proxy, thereby calculating a total fiscal and quasi-fiscal cost of the crisis of $135 billion. This amount represents about one-quarter of Mexico's GDP in 2000 and some four times the $33 billion received in capital receipts from privatization during the 1990s.

Winners and losers in the large financial transfers in Mexico can be roughly assessed by examining the characteristics of different social groups. Those whose losses were partially or wholly compensated by the workouts were shareholders, depositors, and borrowers. Shareholders in Mexico are primarily wealthy individuals and families. With respect to depositors, evidence of the distribution of deposits for Mexico City in 2000 found that only 14 percent of the population has a savings/debit account and a much smaller proportion a checking account or time deposit. Among those who have any type of account, 84 percent of deposits are held by individuals in the top half of the distribution, with 36 percent of individuals from the top 10 percent of the distribution.

Deposit holdings are clearly highly skewed even within Mexico City, which is a relatively well-off part of the country.

The bulk of borrowers were from the formal and, in particular, the large-scale corporate sector. Owners of this sector are typically wealthy and workers come from the middle of the income distribution. Most of the beneficiaries of the financial transfers were therefore well-off by Mexican standards. It is possible that there were secondary benefits in employment stemming from financial support measures, but international evidence on bailouts does not find any association between the size of a resolution and output.

Transfers that took place were financed by higher budgetary surpluses than would have otherwise been needed in the absence of financial crisis. The distribution between higher taxes and lower spending is hard to judge in terms of its relation to the counterfactual without a financial transfer. However, the main tax instrument, the value added tax (VAT), is essentially a flat tax in terms of income distribution; in other words, the poor and the rich pay in equal proportion. As discussed in chapter 9 and noted above, spending expansions typically crowd in poorer groups. Assuming that this would have occurred in Mexico in the late 1990s, poorer groups disproportionately lost out from the lower spending than would otherwise be the case. This indirect evidence suggests that the winners were predominantly in the top part of the distribution (including some of the very wealthy), while the losers were spread throughout the distribution, with a probable bias toward poorer groups.

The ongoing Argentine crisis provides a second case. The effects of the crisis are still being worked through, and the design and final fiscal costs of any bailout are still unknown. Nonetheless, it is possible to look at changes within the financial sector that occurred in the context of the very large reductions in well-being (and increases in inequality) associated with rising unemployment, falling wages, and spending cuts. A central element of financial management was the asymmetric "pesification" of loans and deposits. Debtors enjoyed a conversion of their pre-crisis debts at a rate of one peso to the dollar, while deposits were converted at 1.4 pesos to the dollar; the market price of the dollar at this time was 1.7 pesos.

Depositors also faced restrictions on cash withdrawals on bank accounts and experienced forced reprogramming of pesified time deposits. Since the peso depreciated to almost 4 per dollar in 2002 (before stabilizing at closer to 3 in the first quarter of 2003), depositors suffered further capital losses compared to the counterfactual of an earlier conversion to dollars. In addition, banks suffered a large capital loss

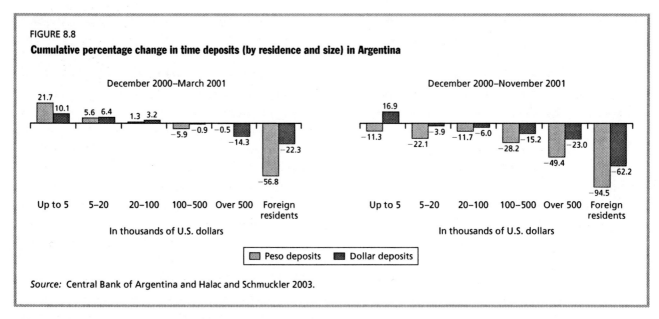

FIGURE 8.8

Cumulative percentage change in time deposits (by residence and size) in Argentina

December 2000–March 2001 · December 2000–November 2001

In thousands of U.S. dollars

Up to 5   5–20   20–100   100–500   Over 500   Foreign residents

☐ Peso deposits   ■ Dollar deposits

Source: Central Bank of Argentina and Halac and Schmuckler 2003.

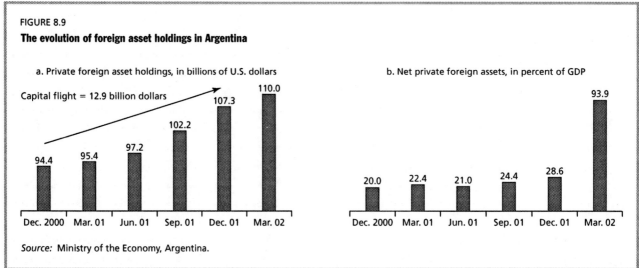

FIGURE 8.9

The evolution of foreign asset holdings in Argentina

a. Private foreign asset holdings, in billions of U.S. dollars

Capital flight = 12.9 billion dollars

b. Net private foreign assets, in percent of GDP

Source: Ministry of the Economy, Argentina.

from the asymmetric pesification, but the government has sought to finance this with a "compensation bond" that is currently estimated at 14.6 billion pesos (roughly 12 percent of Argentina's current GDP). The story is far from over, however, and other mechanisms are likely to emerge, the cost of which will once again be paid for in the form of either higher taxes or lower spending.

Depositors experienced large losses in Argentina; of particular interest is the question of which ones were most affected. There is striking evidence of the pattern and timing of changes in both peso and dollar deposits (figure 8.8). Large deposit holders were moving money out of both peso and dollar deposits between December 2000 and March 2001, well before the final unraveling of the economy in December 2001

(and before the currency crash and financial sector adjustments that caused the capital losses occurred). Although withdrawals became more widespread during 2001, small depositors continued to keep money in the country in dollar deposits.

The scale of capital flight amounted to about US$12.9 billion in the year ending in December 2001 (figure 8.9). Those who got their money out experienced large capital gains in terms of purchasing power in Argentina, a consequence of the steep real exchange rate depreciation. Private net foreign assets in the first quarter of 2002 were equivalent to 94 percent of GDP, up from between 20–30 percent in preceding years. As was speculated above, it is possible that a similar phenomenon may have been behind increases in the financial income of the top decile during Mexico's

Tequila crisis, as reflected in the (undoubtedly incomplete) data provided in household surveys.[15]

An assessment of distributional dimensions of the financial effects of crises has to rely on indirect evidence of the type illustrated by these cases. A tentative conclusion is that financial sector crises can lead to large, disequalizing redistributions. Some large financial sector participants were able to avoid losses—or even to achieve gains—by anticipating the crisis, while crisis resolution mechanisms largely protected richer groups.

What can be done?

Countries in Latin America have relatively high levels of macroeconomic volatility and crisis-related risk, and there is evidence to support the view that fundamental reasons for this stem from weak and unequal institutions. Many countries are on a path of lower growth and higher inequality, with a greater proclivity for disruptive attempts at redistribution. Others, notably Chile, have developed strong mechanisms for economic management and encompassing coalitions that effectively manage potential distributional conflicts (see chapter 5) and allow for relatively rapid and steady growth with continued high inequality.

What does this pattern imply for policy choice? Macroeconomic management clearly is not a policy with which to facilitate the exercise of immediate "client power" over service delivery. However, there should be a role for public debate that indirectly influences both policymakers and the relationship between policymaking and actors or organizations that manage policy directly (such as ministries of finance, central banks, and financial regulators). The discussion below organizes policy implications into four areas, with emphasis first placed on the role of fundamental social and political aspects, and suggestions then given for three areas that may help bridge the apparent gulf between proximate and deep solutions.

Social and political fundamentals

The diagnosis that institutions matter with regard to crises might naturally lead to fixing institutions, in keeping with the view that the world is easily amenable to such solutions. Some of the measures of the past 15 years have been taken in this vein. Examples are the granting of autonomy to central banks, policies on fiscal rules at national or local levels, greater transparency in fiscal and financial accounts, and strengthening of the institutional basis of financial systems. While these

steps have often had positive effects, the analysis here suggests that such measures will not be panaceas in situations that involve complex underlying problems and weak institutions.

A striking example of such situations is Argentina, which was a poster child for the international financial community during the 1990s. This role had a strong foundation, since Argentina seemed to have broken out of its chronic instability and poor performance through a series of measures that moved the country along a more prudent path. However, problems spilled over into other directions in an example of the "seesaw" effect. In other words, when underlying conflicts and institutional weaknesses are not resolved, the domains of action are pushed into new areas (Acemoglu, Johnson, and Robinson 2002).

Manifestations of this trend in Argentina were weak fiscal control over the provinces, continued debilitating corruption, and strained relations between the executive and the judiciary. These problems interacted with policy mistakes—including pegging to the wrong currency and applying expansionary fiscal policies during the economic boom, deep structural problems (such as a de facto "dollarized" financial system), and a weaker international environment—to produce the deep economic and social crisis of the recent past. (See Perry and Serven 2002 for a review of the economic causes of the crisis.)

Where crises are products of underlying social and political structures, the long-run solution must involve changes in these domains or, as Robinson (2002) has termed it, the move toward a new "political equilibrium." Doing so would involve effective, inclusive, and accountable political and other types of institutions, a goal that is closely linked with tackling issues related to inequality in influence, recognition, and wealth, constraining clientelistic practices, and abuses of power (as discussed in chapter 5).

In a good political equilibrium, everything tends to go right. Choices of policies and specific institutional arrangements are of great importance, but as instruments of the polity rather than as a means of protecting society from the vagaries of politicians, or "politician-proofing" (as phrased in Robinson 2002). This is completely consistent with recent work on economic performance that emphasizes the absence of specific, generalized policy and institutional solutions to economic challenges; instead, successes occur when societies shape solutions to fit specific contexts. (See Rodrik 2003 for a discussion on this segue.) Such solutions are, of course, constrained by the rules of arithmetic and fundamental economic conditions; for example, budgets have to be financed and prices do make a difference to behavior.

Chile provides an illustration of this perspective. As discussed in chapter 5, following its transition to democracy, the country has been characterized by a relatively encompassing coalition of political and social actors and extensive consensus on the strategic directions of social and economic policy. These circumstances have entailed maintaining sound macroeconomic policy and supporting property rights and open trade in the context of inclusive and equitable policies, especially in the area of public spending. Chile has been one of the few countries in Latin America that has managed to pursue countercyclical policies during good times, and recently adopted a fiscal rule that institutionalizes this approach. These processes are products of a reasonably effective political equilibrium.

Distributionally inclusive risk-management institutions

The importance of safety nets in mitigating the costs of crises is a longstanding focus for policy advisors, especially in the wake of the 1980s debt crisis (see World Bank 1990) and the East Asian crisis. Support for safety nets has become standard in programs supported by the World Bank and the IMF. Since creating new institutions and programs during a crisis is a bad idea, it has been argued that such safety nets should be developed independently of a crisis, and designed to kick in automatically when crises hit. (For more on this, see de Ferranti and others 2000, Ferreira, Prennushi, and Ravallion 1999, and World Bank 2000b.)

The problem is that this rarely occurs and safety nets are usually fiscally constrained (especially during crises) and inadequate relative to the problem. There are also risks that such targeted programs are captured and exploited politically. The Trabajar (work) program, established under the Menem administration in Argentina, was correctly renowned for its highly effective targeting of the poor (see Jalan and Ravallion 1999 and 2003). However, the program also became known for local political capture, and lost political support with the change in government in 1999. This led to significant delays in building a more modified and extensive program, known as Jefas y Jefes de Hogares (head of household) some time after the new crisis occurred.

Safety nets for the poor are often treated as policy add-ons. In this regard, the issue can be seen as part of the incompleteness of inclusion of subordinate groups in overall social and political arrangements in a society. As O'Donnell (1999a) has argued, while broad provisioning for risk was central to the process of inclusion of the working classes in Europe, this same process generally didn't occur in Latin America. Germany's Bismarckian welfare state was a response to the distributional threat from the Marxist Social Democrats. The Beveridge welfare state in the United Kingdom was a response to a history of mobilization by lower class groups, the unifying experience of the Second World War, and the shadow of the depression in the 1930s. By contrast, the weak and vertical forms of incorporation of subordinate groups in Latin America (as discussed in chapter 5) led to truncated forms of social risk management that divided the formal working class from outsider groups.

Such political economy considerations imply the need for more comprehensive risk management institutions that appeal to middle class groups as well as to the poor and that provide "safety ropes" for a broad segment of the population, not just a highly targeted net for the very poor. (Gelbach and Pritchett 1997, Sumarto, Suryahadi, and Pritchett 2003). The mix of programs will depend on conditions in specific countries, but will also typically involve politically acceptable, comprehensive transfers for the extreme poor (notably those linked to human capital formation), various forms of labor-based measures (from public works to unemployment insurance), and measures for the young and old that can be expanded during times of recession. (These aspects are discussed further in chapter 9.)

Putting broad-based risk management at the center of policymaking has an important corollary in macroeconomic policy. The design and performance of safety nets has a powerful influence on macroeconomic policy options (Bourguignon 2000). Designing broad-based risk management institutions to manage distributional losses and conflicts will effectively free up macroeconomic policy to more efficiently respond to shocks.[16]

Policymaking when not in crisis: Exercising "superprudence" in fiscal, financial, and debt policies

The material surveyed here suggests a pessimistic conclusion on the capacity of societies in Latin America to effectively manage crises in an equalizing fashion. When shocks occur, the cards are stacked against discretionary choices and behaviors that favor poorer groups. Rich, powerful groups have both more information and more influence; when all groups strive to protect their wealth and incomes, this influence is likely to be exercised. This problem is seen in the initial results of patterns of adjustment and distribution of workouts within the financial sector; in the relatively limited coverage of safety nets; in poor track records related to the distributional dimensions of spending cuts; and in cross-country evidence of mechanisms to resolve distributional struggles. Although it is important to keep seeking mechanisms through which to make distributional resolutions more equitable, doing so underscores the importance of developing institutions during noncrisis periods that can automatically foster better responses during crises.

This statement has a possibly surprising implication. In public debates, adopting a less stringent macroeconomic stance is often portrayed as a distributionally progressive approach, whether in good times or bad. While there will always be specific judgments made about the distributional impacts of a range of fiscal and monetary policy options, the analysis here suggests that taking a "superprudent" position over the course of the cycle provides greater hope of supporting a more equal development pattern. On one level, this sharply reinforces the common prescription to break pro-cyclical policy positions. Macroeconomic restraint in good times will facilitate automatic stabilizers and a sensible easing of policies to be applied in a disciplined fashion when adverse shocks occur. Building fiscal rules and institutions that help overcome both the political economy-related pressure to deplete potential surpluses in good times and informational asymmetry problems—and hence improve credibility in countercyclical fiscal policies during downturns—therefore become a major priority (Perry 2003). This strategy would in particular provide the macroeconomic foundation for broad-based, self-expanding safety nets.

Countercyclical fiscal policy, while eminently desirable, has been elusive in Latin America, domestically for political economy reasons and externally because of the herd-like swings of private sector sentiment (de Ferranti and others 2000). In 2002 and early 2003, the region was in the down-swing of a private lending cycle. This sharpened macro-level pressures, forced defensive monetary strategies, and increased domestic costs. Yet the retreat of private loan resources from Latin America has had the positive side effect of leaving the region's external nontrade inflows dominated by foreign direct investment and remittances, both of which are much less volatile sources of financing (with remittances often displaying a countercyclical pattern) that form a healthy base for long-term development.

However, history suggests that when the next upswing occurs, private lenders will be back and borrowers (especially in the private corporate sector) will be happy to receive their loans. There is some evidence that a structural break occurred after the Russian crisis, and that flows are unlikely to return to the levels that prevailed in 1996–1997 for some time; in the long run, this is likely to be a good thing. The interactions among external debt, crisis, and distribution suggest that most countries in Latin America should be more debt-averse than in the past.

Indeed, Latin American economies have remained excessively vulnerable to the reversal of capital flows due to a combination of moderate to high public debt levels, excessive reliance on foreign and dollar-linked domestic debt, low export and tax ratios, weak prudential regulation and supervision, and procyclical fiscal policies. The implication is that the best course for macroeconomic policy in the region to take, from the point of view of reducing poverty and inequality, would be twofold: increasing public sector savings and adopting superprudent regulatory and supervisory practices in the financial system during good economic times, while at the same time increasing the level of openness of economies, developing long-term domestic capital markets, improving debt management, and increasing tax ratios. Since it will take time to achieve the latter objectives, the authors recommend the generation of cyclically-adjusted public sector surpluses for a period of time for countries with high debt burdens, in order to reduce vulnerability to shocks and the likelihood of crisis.

This recommendation implies the importance of paying attention to private sector indebtedness, balance sheet currency mismatches, and patterns of capital inflows. There is also a prima facie case to be made for managing short-term capital inflows, although the verdict is out on whether policies such as Chile's to tax such inflows have had significant, lasting effects. Technical issues on the feasibility and design of measures to manage capital flows are left for another report. Developing long-term capital markets in domestic currency is also critical, not just for governments but for the corporate sector as well, in order to overcome the dilemma between undertaking major currency or rollover liquidity risks.

A superprudent stance implies confronting distributional conflicts in the tax and spending decisions that are made during good times. The buildup of debt in the 1970s and 1990s in many Latin American countries—despite the substantial privatization receipts of the latter period—helped avoid distributional struggles, as the cases of both Brazil and Argentina illustrate. Debt also allowed for expansions in social spending without confronting unaffordable entitlements to the nonpoor (such as public sector social security commitments in Brazil), and actually facilitated new expansions in spending (especially at the provincial and state levels in both countries). However, this trend only shifted the distributional conflicts to the future.

In cases in which fiscal policy is limited, at least in the short run, the financial sector policy becomes all the more important. This is especially true because the evidence presented above suggests that a lot of distributional action takes place between the financial sector and the rest of the economy, as well as within the financial sector itself. Taking action in good times will generally be more efficient and less costly than any rescue package offered in the aftermath of a crisis, and may be more politically feasible than restrictive fiscal policy when the going is good.

Governments can encourage market discipline and improve regulation and supervision to strengthen the financial system. This includes, among other things, a sound contractual and regulatory environment, rigorous monitoring that fosters risk awareness, risk-based capital requirements (including risks arising from currency mismatches), and countercyclical provisioning requirements. Banks on average create too few provisions in good times and are then forced to increase them during cyclical downturns, thus magnifying losses (Laeven and Majnoni 2002).

A good example of countercyclical provisioning requirements is the system established in late 1999 by the Bank of Spain (Banco de España 1999). The Spanish regulation seeks to deal with the movement of solvency risks throughout the economic cycle by requiring "statistical loan loss provisions," in addition to both general and specific provisions for loans classified as doubtful. In other words, provisions must be set aside in order to cover transactions that have not yet been specifically identified as doubtful assets, but for which experience shows that a risk may exist. These provisions are built up in good times and then shifted into specific areas of provision in bad times (without passing through the income statement) as the loan portfolio decays. Also important is the design of deposit insurance and the desirability of having explicit, limited, and funded deposit insurance systems rather than blanket protection, whether or not the latter is explicit or implicit.

Distributional resolutions within crisis

It is now standard advice to protect propoor spending and increase safety net spending when crises hit. While the past record is not good (chapter 9), moving in the direction of broad-based risk management institutions and superprudence during good times will increase the probability that it will occur. On the fiscal front, more attention could be given to increased, temporary taxation on luxuries, such as cars and other consumer durables. Even if the quantitative impact is not large, this action would serve as a political signal of a government's efforts to share the burden of crises more equitably, and may also facilitate negotiations in other spheres. The risk is that these measures will not be removed after the crisis passes. It would therefore be wise to focus on a very few, high profile items for a limited time, for example by adopting "sunset" clauses that require formal legislative renewal after a certain period.

The analysis of the financial sector workouts in Mexico and Argentina underscores the importance of policies that limit adverse redistributions through pro-rich resolution processes. This approach can be considered in terms of distributions both between the financial sector and the rest of the economy and within the financial system. With regard to the former, the major question to be considered is the costs of *not* bailing out. Cross-country evidence indicates that resolution policies increase fiscal costs without reducing output declines (Honohan and Klingebiel 2000). This implies financial redistributions in favor of the relatively rich, without the often-asserted gains in protecting employment.

However, discontinuity is likely to arise if a financial system were to collapse, with major consequences in terms of economic conditions. Assuming that some action is necessary to avoid financial collapse, what designs make sense? The literature on banking crises emphasizes the importance of a prompt resolution to reduce adverse effects and limit overall costs.[17] A rapid and strict resolution reduces the likelihood that fragile institutions will gamble for resurrection and stop the flow of funds to loss-incurring borrowers.[18] It makes sense to grant liquidity support to financial institutions that do not present solvency problems, provided that liquidity and solvency problems can be disentangled. Some guarantees for depositors are desirable, but it is advisable that these not be generalized and that associated conditions be determined ex ante. (In Argentina, the blanket bailout offered by pesification was unnecessary, even considering that the authorities would assume part of the balance sheet effect resulting from the devaluation.) Limiting a bailout reduces both resolution costs and adverse signaling effects; unrestricted aid can create problems of moral hazard for the future.

With respect to transfers within the financial sector, it is again important to take measures before a crisis to increase transparency and minimize information asymmetry problems, for example through good accounting and information disclosure standards. Once a crisis is underway, the issue becomes how to intervene. Freezing or restructuring measures could discriminate across deposits by type and size (De la Torre, Levy Yeyati, and Schmukler 2003). For example, during the recent crisis in Uruguay, the authorities decided to concentrate central bank reserves on fully backed demand deposits at troubled banks in order to preserve the functioning of the payment system. By contrast, time deposits at troubled banks were restructured by decree.

Such a policy approach could be complemented by similar measures aimed at protecting small depositors. Since large, foreign investors tend to run first, ex ante stop-loss clauses on the use of liquidity could be imposed to ensure that something is left to share among small depositors. The government could also force the reprogramming of time deposits only for deposits larger than a certain threshold amount, thereby giving some form of priority of claim over available liquidity to small deposits.

Finally, the financing of restricted assistance to the financial sector is a question that deserves attention. Since increases in standard taxes, spending cuts, and inflation cause losses to individuals outside the financial system, governments could consider alternative financing schemes (such as a capital gains tax) that could potentially shift some of the burden to the financial system and its high-income participants.

Although policy tools with which to minimize financial transfers can be proposed, political economy factors also play an important role in regulatory and resolution-related policies. In the case of Mexico, for example, bank borrowers organized themselves and forced the government to reassign part of fiscal resources to support debt restructuring (see De Luna-Martinez 2000).[19] In Argentina, the late 2001 deposit freeze was driven in part by the liquidity problems of state banks, which helped the authorities to recirculate liquidity

from more liquid private banks. The legitimacy of the pesification—and thus the ultimate effects of the crisis—were subject to the influence over policymaking of different powers, such as Congress, the governors, the judiciary, and large debtors.[20] Although the specific impact of political economy factors on policy measures and financial transfers is difficult to predict, those parties with greater power and capacities to organize are often likely to exert greater influence.

8.4. Conclusions

To the extent that the causes and distributional consequences of macroeconomic crises are functions of weak and unequal institutions, the shift to a better equilibrium will not occur overnight. As a final comment, there are two corollaries of the policy conclusions sketched above.

First, one strand of thinking in the past two decades has focused on the need to give greater autonomy to macro-level and financial sector management in order to shield these policy domains from the fickle, myopic, or ill-informed pressures of public opinion and politicians. This is half correct. There is a large domain of technical analysis in macro and financial management. There is also a strong case to be made for creating institutions that provide incentives for behavior independent of electoral cycles, as occurs with independent central bankers with nonoverlapping terms.

However, there is also a case to be made for both greater transparency and public debate over the consequences of actions in the macro sphere, especially in the financial sector. In light of the technical and indirect nature of the relationships involved, there is a particular role for independent, technical analyses of fiscal and financial policy to play in the domain of fiscal management (as illustrated by the work of the Institute for Democracy in South Africa or the Institute of Fiscal Studies in the United Kingdom).

Second, there are implications for the rules-versus-discretion issue in macroeconomic policy, as already noted above. Support is increasing for rules as a means of ensuring greater prudence and credibility and in order to self-discipline the unruly child of policy management of "immature" states. This is illustrated by the range of fiscal rules (at national and local levels); by the Argentine currency choice of the 1990s (as well as the somewhat surreal layers of self-disciplining rules proposed in a desperate attempt to prevent crisis in the final year of the de la Rua administration); and in proposed rules to protect categories of social spending.

Rules can have a positive impact when they are well-designed and the surrounding incentives, including political incentives, are strong.[21] Italy's vigorous fiscal adjustment to join the European Union's Euro club is a case in point; this occurred in the context of strong domestic support for being at the core of the European project. Brazil's fiscal responsibility law has probably been a useful general instrument in the attempt by the political center to bring state finances under control. Chile's Copper Stabilization Fund and the recent structural surplus rule are good examples of how to incorporate the countercyclical elements emphasized here.

Badly designed rules, on the contrary, will have little value. Fiscal responsibility laws in Argentina and Peru that set rigid deficit and debt goals that were not cyclically adjusted became rapidly unviable in the recessionary environment of 2000–2001, and were therefore abandoned. Even more dramatic was the experience with the Argentine Currency Board: it worked well as long as the external environment was favorable, but once Argentina suffered major adverse external shocks after the Russian crisis and the Brazilian devaluation, it led to a significant real exchange overvaluation and a protracted recession, under which the required fiscal adjustment (that should have been made well before, during good times) proved to be not only difficult but even counterproductive. In the end, the rule became unsustainable but the costs of abandoning it were huge, as well as amplified by poor crisis management. This example shows that there are no short cuts to credibility, even less so when this is attempted through rigid rules that do not fit a given country's specific economic structure. A Currency Board pegged to the dollar can work well in a country that carries out most of its trade in dollars and is closely integrated in the U.S. economy, but it implies huge risks in a closed economy that conducts most of its trade with the European Union and neighboring Brazil (Perry and Serven 2002).

Further, rules work only in a context. Indonesia under Suharto formally had a balanced budget rule that was often cited as a source of its relative macroeconomic prudence from the 1970s to the mid-1990s. This situation was, in fact, an illusion, since the government's domestic borrowing and surpluses were hidden in the financial system. The budget rule was instead endogenous to the fear of hyperinflation and instability among the ruling elite in the wake of the macroeconomic and social conflagration of the mid-1960s. The political powers were willing to turn over policy to the technocrats when macro-level problems became a threat.

Well-designed rules have an important role to play, but are a complement rather than a substitute for the development of sound fiscal and monetary institutions and political behaviors that facilitate both greater prudence and fairer distributional resolutions.

Notes

1. For example, in the early 1990s the Financial Reform Index did not weight regulation and supervision sufficiently and then overstated the extent of reform.

2. This cross-country analysis has used a variety of measures of institutional performance and has paid particular attention to exploring the exogenous, or independent, influences of institutions, since it would be expected that the quality of institutions would improve with general economic development. See Acemoglu, Johnson, and Robinson (2001 and 2002); Easterly and Levine (2002); Rodrik, Subramanian, and Trebbi (2002); Dollar and Kraay (2002b), among other contributions to this debate. Kaufmann, Kraay, and Mastruzzi (2003) have argued that cross-country analysis indicates that although better institutions lead to better long-term economic performance, there is no evidence that growth is an independent source of institutional improvement.

3. See Sánchez-Páramo and Schady (2002) and de Ferranti and others (2003) for multiple country analyses and syntheses. There is a range of country-specific work in the region. Some examples are Cragg and Epelbaum (1996) for Mexico, Galiani and Sanguinetti (2000) for Argentina, Robbins (1994) for Chile, Robbins and Gindling (1999) for Costa Rica, Santamaría (2000) for Colombia, and Sanguinetti, Arim, and Pantano (2001) for Uruguay.

4. These arguments are based on models in the Hechsker-Ohlin tradition and, in particular, on the Stolper-Samuelson theorem. See Wood (1997) for arguments in this tradition.

5. It should be noted that Evans (1995) used the term "embedded" in a different but related way, also in the context of industrial development. He argued that East Asian governments managed a combination of some autonomy of action with embeddedness in societal structures, including connections with the business community. The line between embedded autonomy and state capture is possibly a fine one.

6. This section draws on the background paper by Cunningham and Santamaría (2003).

7. For a brief survey of the different generations of models of crises see Krugman (1999) and for selected references see Aghion, Bacchetta, and Banerjee (2001), Chang and Velasco (2001), Krugman (1979), Obstfeld (1996), and Velasco (1996).

8. While the measures used in Rodrik's analysis go some way in explaining Latin America's worst growth collapse, there remains an additional, negative "Latin American effect." This suggests that the

indicators can only partially serve as proxies for the patterns of weak and unequal institutions that this report has argued are so central to the region's performance.

9. See a range of authors, including Baldacci, de Melo, and Inchauste (2002), Ferreira, Prennushi, and Ravallion (1999), and Manuelyan Atinc and Walton (1998).

10. The surveys are repeated cross-sections; although representative of earnings in different parts of the distribution, they do not track changes of the same households, as is done in panel surveys.

11. This statement is based on official government statistics.

12. Inflation and devaluation are often mechanisms for effecting real wage adjustments; downward nominal wage flexibility is typically limited or sluggish.

13. This section draws in particular on Diwan (2001 and 2002).

14. See also Harrison (2002) and Ortega and Rodriguez (2002) for work on determinants of labor shares over the long term, within a somewhat similar overall framework as that presented here.

15. Household survey data in Argentina do not appear to be credible sources of financial income information because they show large pre-crisis declines in such income in the 1990s, which is inconsistent with the evidence provided by national accounts.

16. This is consistent with the cross-section finding that greater social insurance is associated with lower propensity for crisis. For more on this topic, see Rodrik (1999).

17. See, for example, Sheng (1996), Dziobec and Pazarbasioglu (1997), De Luna-Martinez (2000), and Honohan and Klingebiel (2000).

18. Honohan and Klingebiel (2000) provide empirical evidence that accommodating policies such as unlimited deposit guarantees, open-ended liquidity support, repeated recapitalization, debtor bailouts, and regulatory forbearance increases overall fiscal costs by a significant amount. Providing open-ended, extensive liquidity support, for example, adds to fiscal costs 6.3 percentage points of GDP.

19. Debtors also impeded reforms to the bankruptcy law that would have made it easier for banks to take possession of guarantees and for the government to rapidly sell the acquired impaired assets.

20. As part of a long dispute, the Supreme Court sponsored a resolution that declared pesification unconstitutional and mandated the redollarization of most pesified bank liabilities, significantly changing the allocation of the costs of the crisis. The government responded with a failed attempt to impeach all of its judges.

21. See Perry (2003) for a review of the issues and the case for rules that have a counter-cyclical element, with the objective of reducing political economy pressures for excessive fiscal expansion in good times.

CHAPTER 9

Taxation, Public Expenditures, and Transfers

A T THE BOTTOM OF THE SCHEMATIC REPRESENTATION OF HOW HOUSEHOLD INCOMES ARE determined (introduced in figure 1.1 in chapter 1 and further developed in box 6.1 in chapter 6), there is a clear link between the primary distribution of income, which is determined by market rewards to the private assets and efforts of individuals, and the secondary distribution, which refers to the income available for household consumption and savings. That link, which is described simply as "redistribution," refers to the fact that in virtually all modern societies, the state takes some income away from households through various types of taxes and gives some income back to households through various types of transfers. After considering policy options in the realms of institutional reform and asset redistribution in chapters 7 and 8, chapter 9 now focuses on inequality-reducing initiatives that are suitable for Latin America, in the areas of taxation, general public expenditures, and, in particular, income transfers.

States levy taxes in order to finance various responsibilities, of which—following Musgrave's (1959) classic taxonomy—there are three basic types: stabilization, allocation, and distribution. The first refers to the countercyclical role that government can play with respect to the business cycle, which leads to dampened fluctuation in economic activity and consumption. If households are risk-averse, this result improves welfare.

The second refers to the provision of public goods and the possible internalization of externalities. The third is derived from the long-held notion that societies need not necessarily accept the primary distribution of income as final and may, through a collective decisionmaking process, seek to redistribute income in order to reach a more desirable distribution of welfare.[1]

For a variety of reasons, tax revenues are used to finance a wide range of public actions across countries. Such reasons range from the historical to the political and include different levels of administrative capacity, the nature of public goods, and the quality of information about individual incomes available to the government. Basic roles, such as national defense and the enforcement of law and order, are financed by public revenues virtually everywhere. However, a number of private goods, such as education and health services, are also publicly provided in kind in most nations. This

may or may not be efficient, but it is generally not distributionally neutral. It is now widely accepted that even the universal public provision of goods and services in kind can have a progressive incidence, if quality is rationed and the richer members of society opt out of the public system and purchase higher-quality substitutes privately (Besley and Coate 1991).

To provide a benchmark of the potential for redistributive action by the state over the long run, table 9.1 provides estimates of income inequality before and after taxes and transfers for a set of industrialized societies. There are likely to be large standard errors around estimates such as these (see the discussion of tax incidence in section 9.1), and the capacity of the state in rich countries to pursue redistribution is much greater than in Latin America. Yet these differences are nonetheless significant, and show that very equal societies (for example in Scandinavia) are much less equal pretax than after tax.

TABLE 9.1

Income inequality before and after taxes and transfers in selected industrialized countries

	Gini coefficient for income inequality before taxes and transfers	Gini coefficient for income inequality after taxes and transfers
Australia	46.3	30.6
Belgium	52.7	27.2
Denmark	42.0	21.7
Finland	39.2	23.1
Germany	43.6	28.2
Italy	51.0	34.5
Japan	34.0	26.5
Netherlands	42.1	25.3
Sweden	48.7	23.0
United States	45.5	34.4

Source: OECD as reported in Burniaux and others 1998.

What is the evidence of the impact of taxation and social spending on inequality in Latin America? Has inequality, in terms of access to services, changed for the better? Are there specific programs and financing efforts that hold significant promise for redistribution, while at the same time enhancing growth opportunities or at least having low efficiency costs? This chapter attempts to answer these questions, using the information that is available. It is organized as follows. Section 9.1 looks at the level and composition of taxation; section 9.2 considers the structure and incidence of the social components of public spending; and section 9.3 focuses more narrowly on cash transfers as an element of those

expenditures, and on conditional cash transfers—a new and promising variety—in particular.

9.1. Taxes and distribution

In terms of the size of government (or aggregate fiscal position), as is the case with many other dimensions, there is considerable variation across Latin America. In table 9.2, countries are organized into a simplified typology along two dimensions, the aggregate engagement of the state in the economy (where spending shares equal to government revenues plus government deficit serve as a proxy) and the share of total public spending devoted to social sectors (including social security).

Large differences in social spending among countries are apparent. Argentina, Brazil, and Uruguay have high levels of social spending as a share of gross national product (GNP) because they have high spending levels overall and devote large shares to social programs. As a result, social spending accounts for more than 20 percent of national income. With somewhat different configurations of overall spending and social shares, Chile, Costa Rica, and Panama also have levels of social spending of 16 percent or more. So does Bolivia despite its low income, which is a notable result of both radical shifts in spending priorities during the 1990s and substantial donor support. At the other extreme are the Dominican Republic, El Salvador, and Peru, which have both low aggregate spending levels and low shares of social spending, at less than 7 percent of national income. Guatemala, Honduras, and Paraguay also have notably low social spending because of varying mixes of relatively low aggregate

TABLE 9.2

Typology of Latin American countries by fiscal position and social spending, 1998

Expenditures as share of GNP	Fiscal priority: Share of total public spending going to social sectors		
	Less than 40 percent	Between 40 and 60 percent	More than 60 percent
More than 30 percent	Nicaragua (12.7) Colombia (15.0) Panama (19.4)	Costa Rica (16.8)	Argentina (20.5) Brazil (21.0) Uruguay (22.8)
Between 20 and 30 percent	Honduras (7.4) Venezuela (8.6)	Bolivia (16.1)	Chile (16.0)
Less than 20 percent	El Salvador (4.3) Dominican Republic (6.6) Peru (6.8)	Guatemala (6.2) Mexico (9.1) Paraguay (7.4)	

Note: The numbers in parentheses correspond to the percentage share of social spending in a country's gross national product (GNP).
Source: ECLAC 2001.

spending and low shares of social spending. Although these patterns are influenced by the overall income level of the economy, this is only part of the story. For example, Mexico is an upper-middle-income country with unusually low taxes and spending, while Nicaragua is a low-income society with a high aggregate tax-spending position.

This variance in terms of both overall taxing and spending and of the composition of spending reflects different sociopolitical histories, tax collection capacities, and reactions to changes in thinking about tax and development policy across the continent. Ideas about the role of the state in the economy have changed considerably, even during the last half century, both in Latin America and elsewhere.

In the 1950s and 1960s, tax policy discussions in Latin America reflected the "developmentalist" views common in the postwar era and the emerging reformist approach of the largely U.S.-trained advisers and consultants financed by the Alliance for Progress and the United States Agency for International Development (USAID). The two main aims of taxation were to raise revenue—and lots of it—in order to finance the state as the "engine of development" and to redistribute income and wealth. Both goals could, it was generally thought, be achieved largely by imposing high effective tax rates on income. The depressing effects of taxes on investment and saving were judged to be small.

Indeed, it was sometimes argued that the extra bonus of high tax rates is that they make it easier to lead private investors by the very visible hand of well-designed fiscal incentives into those channels most needed for development purposes. Most analysts took it for granted that a highly progressive personal income tax (with marginal rates ranging as high as 60 percent) buttressed by a substantial corporate income tax (often at 40–50 percent) constituted something close to an "ideal" tax system. Consumption taxes—which at the time consisted mainly of excises, custom duties, and cascading manufacturer sales taxes—were grudgingly accepted as necessary for revenue purposes. No one talked about local taxes, since almost all the action took place at the central government level. In addition, no one seems to have worried much about the international context, and tax policy was almost invariably considered to be a largely domestic affair.

Views on the appropriate role and structure of taxation began to change in the 1970s and 1980s. Today, most economists and policymakers consider that high tax rates not only significantly discourage and distort economic activity but are largely ineffective in redistributing income and wealth. This view is the basis for the current preference for a broad-based consumption tax, with few exemptions and selected higher tax rates for items that either carry negative externalities or are considered "bads" by society (such as gasoline, tobacco, and alcohol). It is also now believed that income tax bases should be as broad as possible and treat all incomes, no matter from what source, as uniformly as possible.

Moreover, the decline of taxes on international trade due to unilateral liberalization and the multilateral rounds at the World Trade Organization (WTO), as well as increased competition for foreign investment, have moved international concerns from the bottom to the top of the tax policy action list in many countries. This in turn has led to reduced tax rates related to trade (which strengthens the trend toward the use of value added taxes, or VATs) and has put downward pressure on tax rates for internationally mobile factors of production, notably capital and highly skilled labor. At the same time, in many countries the fiscal implications of decentralization have become a major issue (IDB 1998, World Bank 2000b).

Reflecting this "new view," income tax rates on both people and corporations were cut sharply and are now almost universally in the 20–30 percent range throughout Latin America (down from around 50 and 40 percent for personal and corporate income tax, respectively, in the mid-1980s), as is the case elsewhere in the world (Shome 1999). Figure 9.1 shows the decline in the highest personal and corporate income tax rates between the 1980s and the present. This decline was accompanied by an increase in the personal exemption rate and reductions in the income bracket to which top rates applied. Trade tariffs were also drastically cut, from an average of about 40 percent to around 11 percent between the mid-1980s and the mid-1990s, and export taxes were eliminated altogether.[2] On the other hand, the VAT is now seen as the mainstay of the revenue system in the region, reflecting—or even anticipating—global trends (Ebrill and others 2001). Figure 9.2 details the pattern of VAT rates, which rose on average from 10 percent when first introduced (in various years) to about 15 percent in 2001.

This combination of falling income tax rates and trade tariffs and rising indirect domestic taxes yielded modest increases in overall tax revenues across the region. Between the 1970s and 2000, the unweighted average of aggregate tax effort rose by about 2 percentage points of gross domestic product (GDP) to 14 percent of national income (figure 9.3). Taxes on goods and services (mostly VATs) were the primary source of this increase, more than offsetting

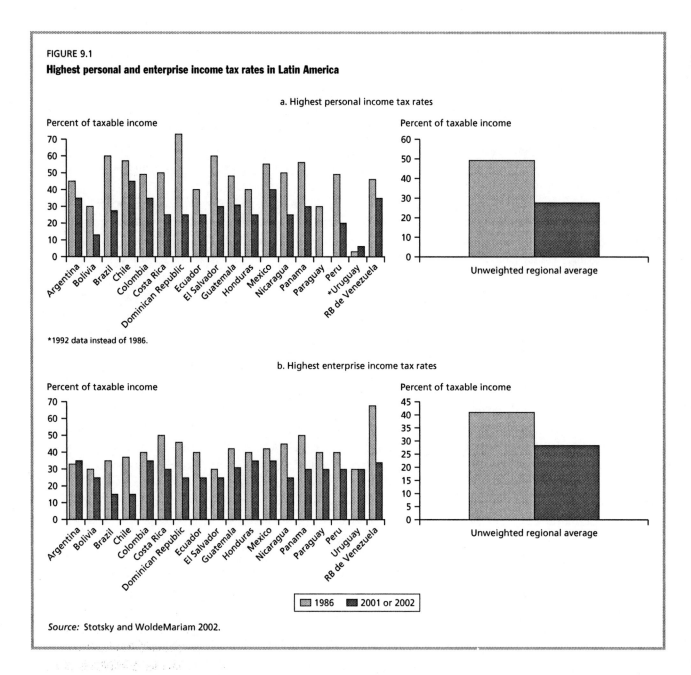

FIGURE 9.1

Highest personal and enterprise income tax rates in Latin America

a. Highest personal income tax rates

Percent of taxable income

Percent of taxable income

*1992 data instead of 1986.

b. Highest enterprise income tax rates

Percent of taxable income

Percent of taxable income

Unweighted regional average

Unweighted regional average

□ 1986   ■ 2001 or 2002

Source: Stotsky and WoldeMariam 2002.

declines in taxes on trade. Income tax collections rose slightly, in spite of the reduction in rates.

Despite this increase in the overall level of taxation, Latin America still taxes a considerably smaller share of total output than do richer countries. Table 9.3 compares the total revenue and its composition in Latin America at two points in time, with the relevant averages for developed countries. The most striking feature of the comparison with richer societies is the much lower take from income taxes. This is especially due to low levels of personal (as opposed to corporate) incomes taxes, which account for less than 1 percent of GDP in Latin America compared with more than 7 percent in developed countries. The other significant difference

is the much higher take from social security taxes in richer countries, which is associated with much more developed welfare states. Developed societies also tax trade less and get more from VAT and sales taxes. Property taxes are low in developed countries and even lower in Latin America, although these results are probably particularly biased by the exclusion of local government revenues.

The differences in the levels of taxation between Latin American and richer countries are in part due to what economists call Wagner's Law: the observation that government expenditures as a share of GDP tend to rise with per capita incomes. However, as figure 9.4 illustrates, Latin American tax efforts tend to lie below the average even in relation to

FIGURE 9.2

Value-added tax rate (in Latin America)

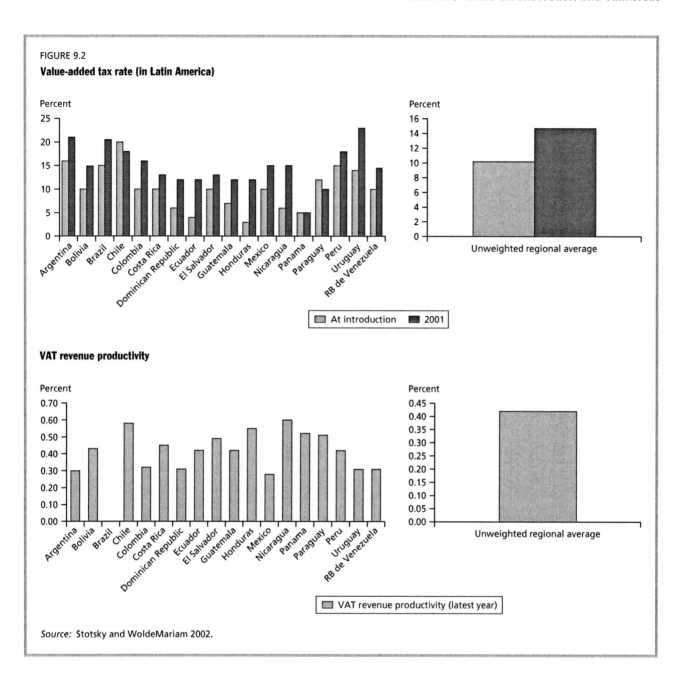

Source: Stotsky and WoldeMariam 2002.

income levels, with the exception of Nicaragua and Uruguay (Brazil is also close to the norm). This is particularly true with regard to personal income and property taxes collection, as well as social security contributions (the latter reflecting the low coverage of social security).

In terms of comparisons across Latin America, there is considerable diversity in tax efforts and tax composition, but also a relatively high degree of consistency over time. Countries that had relatively high tax ratios at the end of the 1970s were still above the regional average in the 1990s. Among relatively high tax countries, the major changes occurred in Nicaragua (in the early 1980s, following a regime

change) and in Brazil (in the early 1990s). There is no pattern among moderate-tax countries, and only modest increases in tax ratios in the low-tax countries.

Before turning to the possible policy alternatives which might be considered in the area of tax policy, it is important to understand the incidence of taxation in Latin America.

Who pays the taxes?

The question of who pays taxes is surprisingly hard to answer, despite decades of economic work on taxation. This is essentially because there can be major gaps between the

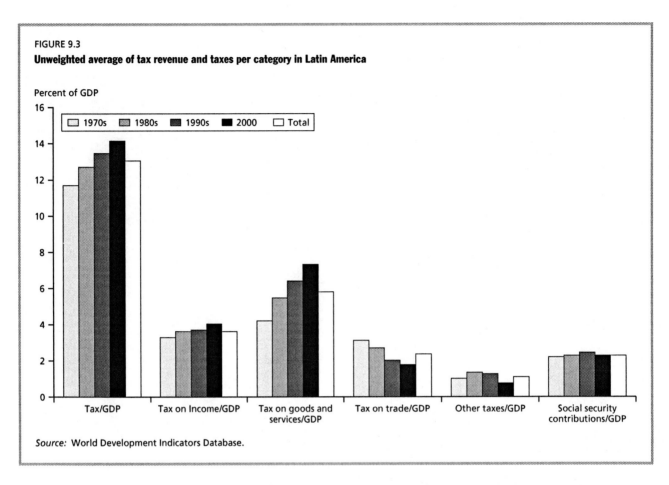

FIGURE 9.3

Unweighted average of tax revenue and taxes per category in Latin America

Percent of GDP

Source: World Development Indicators Database.

TABLE 9.3

Tax structure in the 1990s, Latin America and developed countries (in percent of GDP, consolidated central government)

Tax category	Latin America and the Caribbean		Developed countries
	1990–94	1995–99	1991–2000
Income taxes	3.6	3.4	9.7
Individual	0.5	0.9	7.1
Corporate	1.9	1.7	2.3
Social security	2.5	2.9	7.8
Taxes on goods and services	5.6	7.4	9.5
VAT and sales	3.2	4.8	6.5
Excises	2.1	2.3	3.0
Trade taxes	2.2	1.8	0.3
Imports	1.9	1.8	0.3
Exports	0.1	0.0	0.0
Property taxes	0.4	0.3	0.8
All taxes	14.2	16.1	28.7

Source: Stotsky and WoldeMariam 2002 and Government Finance Statistics database.

intention of tax systems embodied in statutory tax structures and actual payments. Firms and individuals respond to taxes, adjusting wages and prices when they can, to reduce taxes on themselves and shift the burden on to others. Most tax incidence studies resort to highly simplified assumptions about such responses (see box 9.1), so their results must be taken with due caution.

A recent review of quantitative studies of tax incidence in developing countries (Chu, Davoodi, and Gupta 2000) finds that taxes generally have little redistributive effect in Latin America, largely because of heavy dependence on indirect taxes in most countries.[3] The authors of the study find that tax structure is the most important factor in determining this outcome, since personal income taxes are assumed to be basically progressive and consumption taxes are not. Most studies assume that personal income taxes and specific taxes on "luxury" items are progressive, property taxes marginally progressive, and the rest usually regressive (although exemptions of basic foodstuffs and other items that have high weights in the consumption baskets of the poor may render sales or VAT taxes close to neutral or even mildly progressive).

FIGURE 9.4

A simple cross-country regression of total tax revenues against log GDP per capita

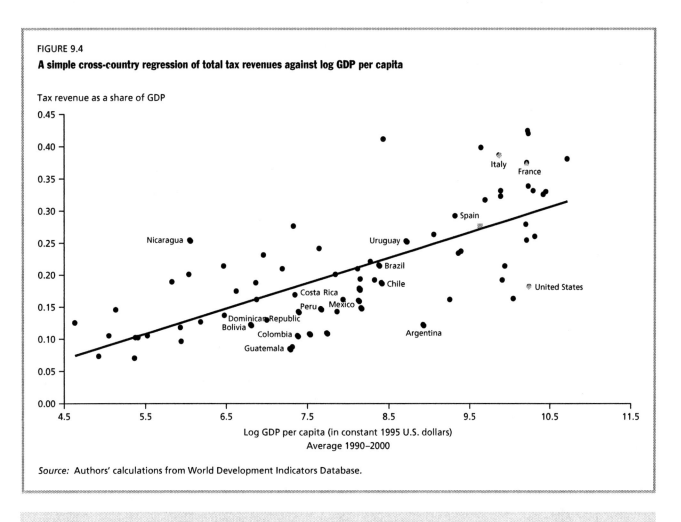

Tax revenue as a share of GDP

Source: Authors' calculations from World Development Indicators Database.

BOX 9.1

Do tax incidence numbers mean much?

It is not clear that the "evidence" provided even by such careful incidence studies as that by Engel, Galetovic, and Raddatz (1998) is of much value. Statements such as "most of the burden of the tax system falls on the bottom two income quintiles" are based on a series of assumptions about the incidence of different taxes that are invariably subject to considerable dispute (Whalley 1984).[4] In addition, in practice—though not in most analyses—these statements depend upon many factors specific to a particular country at a particular time, for instance with respect to market structures and macroeconomic conditions.[5]

What really matters is of course the economic and not the legal incidence of taxation. As a general rule, the economic incidence of a tax (at least in the long run) is determined by market conditions and not by whether the tax is legally imposed on the buyer or the seller. Businesses

attempt to pass on (shift) taxes to someone else whenever they can, including to consumers through higher product prices, to workers through lower wages, and to owners of land through lower land prices. Most tax incidence analyses apply a partial equilibrium approach based on assumptions of demand and supply elasticities (actual measures of such elasticities are rare in tax incidence analysis).

Depending on these assumptions, taxes are thus assumed to be shifted predominantly forward (if demand is assumed to be less elastic than supply) or backward. In some cases, assumptions are even cruder: personal income taxes are not thought to be shifted at all (hence most studies estimate a progressive effect) and sales tax and VAT are assumed to be shifted wholly to consumers. As a result, most studies estimate a slightly regressive effect that is normally tempered by the exemption of basic foodstuffs and other consumption items (such as clothing, transportation, and housing) that weigh heavily in the consumption baskets of the poor.

Some studies attempt to go beyond this by using computable general equilibrium models (CGEs). It would be expected that relative prices, output composition and level, and technological change would be altered with a different tax system. One result is that most of the time the exercise of comparing the incidence of a real tax structure with an imaginary counterfactual is fundamentally flawed, since doing so holds constant what simply cannot be held constant (Meerman 1980). However, tax incidence analysis with CGEs is still plagued by a variety of assumptions. (These include the model "closure" and the choice of counterfactual, both of which are normally critical to the end result; most exercises use static CGE models, in which effects on investment and technological change are either dismissed or extremely simplified, and many parameters, including elasticities, are not measured but assumed.)

To illustrate the difficulties inherent in incidence analysis, consider the incidence of corporate income taxes (which make up the bulk of income taxes in most Latin American countries). Incidence will depend on such factors as the openness of the overall economy; inflows and outflows of capital investment and the extent to which capital moves between the corporate and unincorporated sectors; the relative capital-intensity of corporations; the elasticity of demand for goods produced by corporations and other businesses; and the elasticity of supply of inputs (most importantly, labor). None of these factors is easy to measure, and thus neither is the incidence of the corporate income tax. Furthermore, since differing economic conditions in different countries mean that taxes that have the same legal incidence may have a quite different economic incidence (Shah and Whalley 1990), the specific characteristics of each country need to be taken into account when evaluating the economic incidence of each tax. Thus, one might attribute all taxes on corporations to owners in the highest income deciles if low capital mobility is assumed, or to unskilled workers if perfect international capital mobility is assumed.

This argument may seem unduly nihilistic. The key point about such incidence studies is simply that they do not matter much. Policy questions in taxation are almost never related to the question "who pays how much?" under the present system; rather, the relevant policy question is almost always "who will pay more (or less) if this or that particular change is made?" If the change is small enough, it will be possible to assume that relative prices will not change and to carry out a simple partial-equilibrium analysis. Usually, however, some form of general equilibrium analysis, with all the attendant sensitivity to parameter choices, clearing mechanisms, and the like will be necessary. (For an excellent recent example, see the study of Colombia by Rutherford, Light, and Barrera 2002.)

Whichever method is used, it is always and everywhere both more meaningful and more policy-relevant to analyze the incidence of taxation "at the margin," rather than "on the average." This is essentially the same point as made by for example, Ahmad and Stern (1991) with respect to the greater ease and meaningfulness of analyzing "optimal tax reform" rather than "optimal tax policy" per se. The assumptions needed to do so are less heroic, more testable, and more believable, and the results may help answer the critical question of the distributional impact of proposed policy reforms. Despite all the problems of incidence analysis, it remains important to do the best one can, and at the same time not to overstate what is possible to accomplish.

Given the low importance of personal income taxes and property taxes in Latin American countries, the direct redistributive leverage of the tax system in most countries should be expected to be very small or even negative. It is therefore not surprising that the Chu, Davoodi, and Gupta (2000) study, like the much earlier work of Bird and De Wulf (1973), found little evidence of much fiscal redistribution through taxes in Latin America, despite the sometimes wrenching tax changes undergone by many countries in the last three decades. A comparative recent study by Gemmel and Morrissey (2002) also found that tax systems in the region ranged from slightly progressive to slightly regressive. Their review of recent individual studies shows similar conclusions (see table 9.4).

In one of the more careful studies conducted, Engel, Galetovic, and Raddatz (1998) find Chile's taxes to be slightly regressive (with a pretax Gini coefficient of 0.488 rising to 0.496 after taxes). This was the case despite the fact that

TABLE 9.4

Tax incidence studies for Latin American countries, 1975–98

Author/s	Country	Period	Income Concept	Households, individuals covered	Taxes Included	Measures of progressivity	Author's conclusions
Foxley (1979)	Chile	1969	Household income and expenditure	All	Direct & indirect	Not indicated	Semi-proportional
Engel, Galetovic, Raddatz (1998)	Chile	1996	Household income and expenditure	All	Direct & indirect	Gini coeff.	Slightly regressive
Gillis, McLure (1978)	Colombia	1974	National income	High inc.	Direct & indirect	Not indicated	Progressive
Berry, Soligo (1980)	Colombia	1970	Household income and expenditure	All	Direct & indirect	Not indicated	Substantial progressivity
Santana, Rathe (1993)	Dominican Rep.	1989	Household income	All	Direct & indirect	Not indicated	A degree of progressivity
Galper, Ramos (1993)	Guatemala	1992	Household income	All	Overall tax system	Not indicated	Progressive
Bahl, Martinez-Vazquez, Wallace (1996)	Guatemala	1994 (est.)	Household income	All	Overall tax system	Not indicated	Progressive
Hicks, Lee (1997)	Guatemala	1992	Household income and expenditure	All	Direct & indirect	Not indicated	Mildly progressive
Gil-Diaz (1984)	Mexico	1972, 1980	Permanent household income	All	Direct, indirect, and inflation	Not indicated	Progressive, but uneven in 1972, smoother in 1990
Escobal et al. (1993)	Peru	1985–90	Household expenditure	All	Fuel taxes	Not indicated	Gasoline tax is progressive; kerosene tax is regressive

Source: Chu, Davoodi, and Gupta 2000.

Chile's tax system is the most effective in Latin America,[6] collects the most from the personal income tax, and has the highest marginal rates (up to 45 percent, compared to 25–30 percent in most countries). The authors of that study also find that if the income tax were made much more progressive by eliminating all tax allowances and all (estimated) underreporting of income, the Gini coefficient would fall to only 0.484 and the ratio of incomes between the top and bottom deciles would remain virtually unchanged at 13.4. Engel, Galetovic, and Raddatz (1998) also argue that the more unequal the pretax distribution, the greater the distortion costs and the less the redistributive effect of progressive taxation. They conclude that the most important factor affecting the distributional impact of the tax system is how much revenue it generates for potential redistribution by the public sector. Estimates from developed countries find diverse results. While the figures given in table 9.1 were not broken down between taxes and transfers, in individual country studies the estimates of this division range from income taxes accounting for the bulk of redistribution in Denmark to very little in the United Kingdom; Canada falls in between, with a third of redistribution being attributable to taxes.[7]

The empirical difficulties that plague average tax incidence studies (highlighted in box 9.1) may seem somewhat dispiriting. However, there is also a somewhat more optimistic message contained in those arguments: in designing tax reforms, there is less concern with levels than with changes, since it is possible to be more confident about the marginal effects of such changes. Although the dominant influence of taxes on distribution is probably their contribution to the overall redistributive capacities of a government, there is almost certainly some potential to make tax systems somewhat more progressive, although the extent to which this is possible will depend on issues of overall political and social consensus as much as on the details of tax instruments.

Implications for tax policy

So how can taxes be made somewhat more progressive in Latin America, without excessively compromising the gains in economic efficiency that have been attained over the last 30 years through the reduction in tax rates, broadening of tax bases, and other reforms? It should first be recognized that tax design is a policy realm in which efficiency-equity tradeoffs are unlikely to disappear. In this regard, there really is no such thing as a free lunch, and it is likely that efforts to make taxes more equitable will, in most cases, have some efficiency costs. The principles outlined below are therefore intended only as suggestions of aspects of tax policy through which it may be possible to make taxes marginally more progressive at a relatively low cost. They are only general principles; in every case a concrete recommendation can only be made after the country-specific context has been properly evaluated. Bearing these caveats in mind, the authors propose six broad principles for equity-enhancing tax reforms in Latin America, as follows.

(1) *Tax bases should be as broad as possible.* A broad-based consumption tax, for example, will still discourage work effort, but choices between tradable and nontradable goods and services will not be altered if all are taxed.[8] A few items (such as gasoline, tobacco products, and alcohol) may be chosen for differentially higher taxation rates for regulatory reasons or because the demand for these products is relatively unresponsive to taxation. As a result, at any given tax rate, efficiency costs will be relatively low and revenues relatively high. Income tax bases should also be as broad as possible and treat all incomes, no matter from what source, as uniformly as possible.

(2) *Tax rates should be as low as possible*, provided they raise sufficient revenue to finance the appropriate expenditures of government. Of course, the broader the base, the lower the rate needed to generate a given revenue level. However, lower rates are worthwhile in their own right because the efficiency cost of taxes arises from their effect on relative prices, and the size of this effect is directly related to the tax rate. In fact, the general rule is that the distorting effect of taxes increases proportionally to the square of the tax rate, so that doubling the rate of a tax implies a four-fold increase in its efficiency costs. From an efficiency perspective, it is therefore always better to raise revenue by imposing a single rate on a broad base of taxpayers, rather than dividing that base into segments and imposing differential rates on each one. In practice, of course, this consideration needs to be balanced against the equity argument for imposing graduated rate schedules.

(3) *Indirect taxes need not be regressive.* In particular, VATs— which are generally preferable to excise or import taxes—can often be made less regressive with a few key exemptions.[9] Similarly, reducing or removing obviously regressive excise taxes (as well as import duties), for example on food items or kerosene, is another obvious measure. It should also be remembered that the incidence of taxes on alcohol and tobacco is very variable, and in some instances a case can be made on equity grounds for moderating efficiency-driven rate increases. To make up for lost revenue from any of these measures, there are often good reasons for considering higher levels of taxation on private transport. Export taxes, on the other hand, are generally best avoided both on efficiency and on equity grounds.

(4) *There is scope for raising personal income tax collections.* Collections from personal income taxes are low in Latin America, even when compared with countries with the same level of income (figure 9.5). This suggests that there is scope for increasing such revenues, of course provided that increased revenues finance socially useful, and hopefully progressive, expenditures. The experience of Chile shows that this is indeed possible when there is political will and good administration. In light of point (2) above, higher revenues should be sought first by closing loopholes and enforcing greater compliance, and only later through higher marginal rates. Income taxes need to apply both to persons and to corporations. To keep tax avoidance in check, it would be wise to keep the top marginal rate of the personal income tax fairly close to the rate of the corporate income tax, which means that it is not likely to be all that high.

(5) *Property taxes are currently underutilized and should be made to generate more revenue.* Property taxes at present account for only about 0.3 percent of GDP for the region as a whole (Stotsky and WoldeMariam 2002). Collections from property taxes are low in Latin America even when compared with countries with the same level of income. Coverage of property taxes is not comprehensive and both assessments and collection rates are often low. Although nominal rates are also low, governments usually find rate increases in this very visible tax difficult to sell politically. Simply raising the legal tax rate would in any case usually burden only the few from whom taxes are actually collected. Increased nominal rates are likely to be acceptable only along with improvements in tax administration, such as more comprehensive coverage, better and more frequently evaluated assessments, and enforced penalties for late payment. (For a recent detailed discussion of land and property tax policy, see Bird and Slack 2002.)

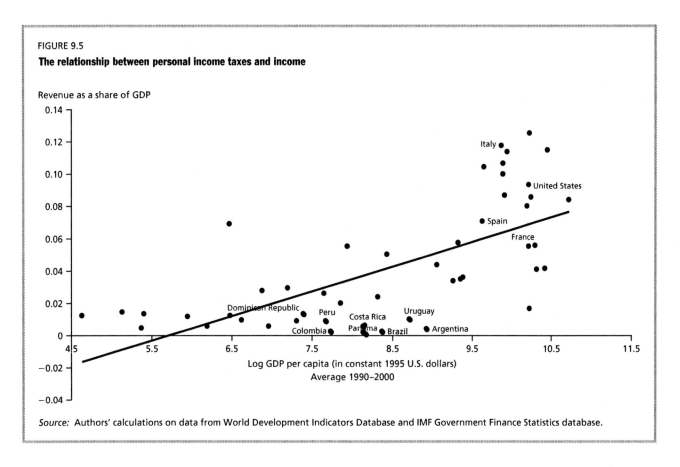

FIGURE 9.5

The relationship between personal income taxes and income

Revenue as a share of GDP

Source: Authors' calculations on data from World Development Indicators Database and IMF Government Finance Statistics database.

(6) In many instances, the most important taxes affecting the poor are not formal ones levied in the government budget, but rather *implicit taxes,* which include bribes and exactions of various kinds (see Prud'homme 1990), as well as the inflation tax. As explored at length in Bird (1991), implicit taxes also include many instances of "regulation as taxation" such as quasi-taxes imposed through controls on trade, prices, credit, foreign exchange, or capital markets.

The authors recognize, of course, that raising income and property tax revenues, as well as rebalancing the composition of indirect taxes so that they shift away from goods consumed relatively more intensively by the poor and toward, say, private transport, are highly charged political issues. Ultimately, just how much the rich are taxed remains a domestic political choice. The opening of capital markets, combined with weak international tax enforcement capabilities, does make it harder to tax the rich heavily. However, there is no doubt that if they wanted to, most Latin American countries could do more in this respect, as Chile's experience with personal income taxes shows. Similarly, most countries could make a greater effort to tax the poor

less and to tax the middle class both more fairly and more efficiently.

9.2. Public social spending and distribution

The point of taxing, as indicated above, is to raise resources that can be spent well. This chapter now turns to the evolution, composition, and incidence of public spending in Latin America, focusing on what is known as "social spending." Although the exact definitions of this spending category vary from country to country, the term generally includes expenditures on social security, education, health, social protection, social assistance, and active labor market programs. In some cases, housing subsidies and expenditures on basic urban services and infrastructure (for example, water and sanitation) are also included. First considered are overall trends in social spending, followed by the distributional aspects of access to various programs. The section concludes with a brief examination of the effects of economic cycles.

Changes in public social spending in the 1990s
According to an analysis of 17 Latin American countries conducted by the United Nations Economic Commission for

FIGURE 9.6

Public social spending in Latin America: expenditures per capita, as share of public spending and GNP, 1990s

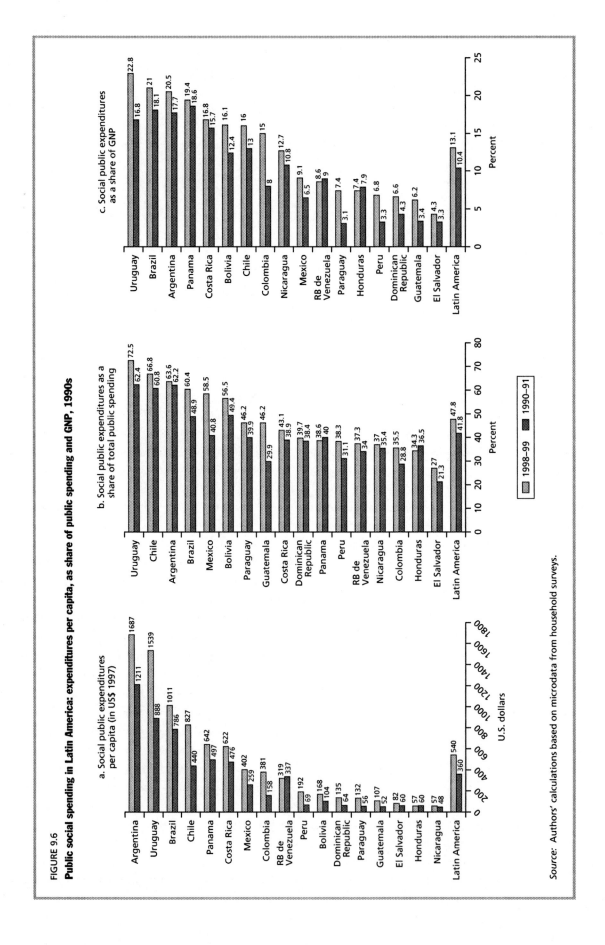

Source: Authors' calculations based on microdata from household surveys.

258

TABLE 9.5

Increase in social spending with and without social security, from ECLAC and IMF databases

	Social spending per capita (US$1995)	Social spending as share of total spending (%)	Social spending as share of GDP (%)
With social security			
ECLAC 1990–91	360	41.8	10.4
ECLAC 1998–99	540	47.8	13.1
IMF GFS 1991	369	48.7	8.5
IMF GFS 1998	549	54.8	11.0
Without social security			
ECLAC 1990–91	212	30.5	6.5
ECLAC 1998–99	304	33.1	8.0
IMF GFS 1991	218	27.4	4.7
IMF GFS 1998	289	28.7	5.7

Source: ECLAC 2001 and authors' own estimates from the IMF Government Finance Statistics database for eight countries for which data are available.

Latin America and the Caribbean (ECLAC) (2001), annual social public spending per capita increased on average by 50 percent between 1990–1991 and 1998–1999, from the equivalent of US$360 to US$540 per capita at 1997 prices (figure 9.6).[10] Although the exact magnitude of the increase in public social spending differed among the 17 countries, the increase was fairly general. It was greatest in the countries with initially low and medium levels of per capita social expenditure, notably Colombia, the Dominican Republic, Guatemala, Paraguay, and Peru, where spending per capita more than doubled. In countries with relatively high initial levels of spending, specifically Argentina, Brazil, Costa Rica, and Panama, the increase was approximately 30 percent over the course of the decade.

Three factors explain the increase in social public spending per capita during the 1990s: economic growth in GDP per capita (which accounted for some 40 percent of the gain); increased total spending as a share of GDP; and shifts in the composition of spending to benefit the social sector (the share of which grew from 42 to 48 percent). While the growth effect was particularly important in the first half of the decade, the impact of shifts in spending toward the social sector mattered more during the second half. This change allowed most countries to increase social spending per capita, even though economies were not doing well.

Social spending as a percent of GDP grew from 10.4 in 1991–1992 to 13.1 in 1998–1999. However, a disproportionate portion of the increase in the ratio of social expenditures to GDP and in the share of social spending in total expenditures was due to rapidly increasing pension outlays

(table 9.5). According to the ECLAC (2001) study, when social security is excluded from social spending, the increase as a share of GDP is only 1.5 percentage points, versus 2.7 percentage points when social security is included. Estimates made for this report, based on the International Monetary Fund's (IMF) Government Finance Statistics (GFS) database, provide results which are fairly close to those in the ECLAC study, with an even smaller gain in social spending during the 1990s when social security (and welfare spending according to the IMF classification) is excluded from the analysis (see http://www1.worldbank.org/publicsector/pe/crosscountrydata.htm).

Despite a common trend toward higher public spending on social sectors over time, there are still large differences in spending levels among countries. Countries with high levels of GDP per capita tend to have higher levels of social spending as a share of GDP (in part due to higher social security outlays). In addition, in many countries the increased share of social spending has taken place at the expense of public infrastructure investment, with the likelihood of adverse effects on long-term growth and inequality (see chapter 7). While in some countries this shift was a deliberate consequence of higher private sector involvement in infrastructure, in others a "crowding out" effect of infrastructure investment by higher pensions and other social expenditures occurred during the 1990s (see various chapters in Easterly and Servén 2003).

Why didn't large increases in social spending translate into falling income inequality? There are two reasons. First, social spending is not necessarily progressive (and can be quite regressive in the case of social security spending). Second, much social spending is in-kind, so that even if it affects the distribution of services (and indeed capabilities), it doesn't have a short-term impact on incomes.

Who uses public services?

While much social spending—for example, that related to better education and child health—affects incomes only with long lags, it may be of both direct value for well-being and can expand the capabilities of different groups. To properly assess the incidence of public expenditures, it is necessary first to establish who benefits from access to public services and then to value this access in equivalent income terms. Conceptually, it is critical to distinguish between average and marginal benefit incidence. Average benefit incidence refers to access to (and valuation of) services at a given time. Marginal benefit incidence refers to who benefits from increases in access that are related to increases in expenditures at the margin or over a period of time. There are difficulties involved in both stages (see box 9.2).

Most of the reduction in inequality measures adjusted for in-kind transfers is due to spending on education and health. With regard to *education,* Wodon (2003) estimated levels of usage of various education levels by income quintile in 11 Latin American countries: Bolivia (1999), Brazil (1998), Chile (1998), Colombia (1999), El Salvador (1997), Guatemala (1998–1999), Honduras (1999), Mexico (1996), Nicaragua (1998), Peru (1997), and Venezuela (1998). Net and gross enrollment rates were calculated by income quintile and by schooling cycle (that is, preschool, primary school, and secondary school).[11]

Although these estimates were conducted nationally, in urban and rural areas, and for both the male and female populations, only the national results are discussed here. In addition, because for many surveys information on publicly versus privately provided education was not available, the analysis does not make that differentiation; as a result, the progressivity of public expenditure benefits may often be understated (since the rich most likely opt for private services). Finally, the results obtained for the various countries were

---

BOX 9.2

Issues in the valuation of public services

Strong assumptions are used to value the distribution of the benefits of public spending. In theory it would be best to base valuations on estimates of underlying demand functions for public services. However, in practice benefit incidence analysis typically proceeds with valuations based on government unit costs, which are implicitly assumed to be equivalent to the benefits of the spending. This assumption begets entirely the problems of efficiency in public spending and differences in quality of services (see below).

Other problems are related to limits in the available household survey data to match the unit costs to households. With regard to education, for example, it is common practice to multiply enrollment rates by level (that is, primary, secondary, or tertiary) among various income groups, or within geographic areas, by an average estimate of the cost to the state of providing education services by level. However, if schools in rural areas—where a higher proportion of the population is poor—tend to be less well staffed and equipped than urban schools, inequality in the distribution of the benefits of public spending on education will be underestimated. The same will be true if

schools attended by the poor receive less funding. On the other hand, if the rich go to private school and this factor is not taken into account in the analysis, then some of the inequality in the distribution of public education benefits may be overestimated.

Demery (2003) highlights two other problems involved in benefit incidence analysis. First (as observed in the analysis of who benefits from health care services), requesting care is conditional on an illness or injury occurring in the household. In surveys, illnesses and injuries are often self-reported only when those who declare an illness or injury are asked questions on the use of health facilities. If some among the poor fail to report illnesses or injuries because they consider such events to be a common occurrence, a downward bias in the estimate of the benefits of the health care system for the poor may result. Second, household surveys, while representative at the national level, may not be representative of selected population subgroups, such as those attending a university. Small sample sizes may then also lead to a bias in the estimate of benefit incidence.

aggregated into overall measures of net and gross enrollment for a typical country in Latin America (each country was given an equal weight in the analysis.)

The analysis found that even if present average access to all levels of education is generally regressive (that is, it benefits the rich more), marginal increases in enrollment of children ages 6–11 have been strictly progressive, benefiting the poorest quintiles more than those above them. Marginal increases in enrollment up to 17 years of age were also progressive, although households in quintiles 2 and 3 benefited more than the poorest (which nonetheless benefited more than quintiles 4 and 5). Marginal enrollments were not progressive, however, for ages 18–24 or under 5 (see also discussion in chapter 2).

The story line is clear enough. When overall enrollment rates are low (as they are for preschool and tertiary education), increased access benefits the rich more than the poor. When overall enrollment rates are already high, on the contrary, increased access benefits the poor more, since children from rich families are already overwhelmingly enrolled in school.

The implication of this cross-country analysis is that the progressivity of an expansion in education services varies significantly among countries, depending on current levels of enrollment. In most cases, increased access to primary school is highly progressive, since average enrollment rates are already high. Increased access to secondary school is highly progressive in countries with high average enrollment rates, such as Argentina, Chile, and Uruguay. In most other countries, access to secondary school is just slightly progressive or regressive. However, once average enrollment rates are pushed up (as they should be), further increases in coverage will become progressive in most countries after a few years. Increased access to tertiary education is, in contrast, highly regressive and will remain so for many years in most countries. Together with evidence of much higher private returns on tertiary than on secondary or primary education (de Ferranti and others 2003), these results indicate that present patterns of allocation of public resources in most countries in Latin America—which is much higher for students in tertiary than in primary or secondary education—may well lead to overall regressive outcomes with regard to public spending in education.

Similar results were obtained with regard to *health, nutrition, and population services*. This conclusion is based on an analysis of data from Demographic and Health Surveys (DHS), combined with a measure of assets used to rank households into income quintiles. As for education, most average benefits tend to accrue to the rich at a higher rate than to the poor. For example, immunization rates among children ages 12–23 months increase along with assets.[12] On average, about 50.6 percent of all households obtain all vaccines for their children, while 5.6 percent do not get any immunizations. However, the rate of immunization for the poorest households is only 78 percent of the mean for all vaccines (a value of 0.8 in figure 4.6), while it is 112 percent for the richest households.

Antenatal care and delivery services are also used disproportionately by better-off households. For example, households in the first (lowest) income quintile are 50 percent less likely than the average to have a doctor preside over a birth, while households in quintile five are 45 percent more likely. As expected, the use of private facilities is even more strongly associated with household assets, with the poorest households capturing about 14 percent and the richest households capturing 254 percent of the overall mean. While there is less inequality in the use of public facilities, the benefits are still higher for better-off households.

This trend notwithstanding, expansions in the use of health services are much more likely to be progressive, as in the case of basic education. Figure 9.7 illustrates this through scatter plots of the ratio of average and marginal benefit incidence of 15 health services for the first and fourth quintiles, in terms of the distribution of assets of the 9 Latin American countries (as an unweighted average) for which the analysis has been conducted. A ratio of 1 means that the first quintile has the same access indicator as the fourth quintile.

In the figure on the left, apart from a few indicators such as treatment for diarrhea, most observations are well below 1, meaning that the access to health services for the first quintile is well below that for the fourth quintile. In the figure on the right, for marginal benefit incidence, the ratios tend to be much larger than 1, suggesting that at the margin the first quintile benefits more from increases in access than does the fourth quintile. The figure also shows that the higher the level of access to the service (the horizontal axis in both figures), the more progressive the marginal benefit incidence.

The overall pattern for most publicly provided services (including education, health, water, and infrastructure) is for access to be expanded from the top of the distribution down. Where service coverage is initially high, marginal incidence is often quite progressive. Figure 9.8 illustrates this in terms

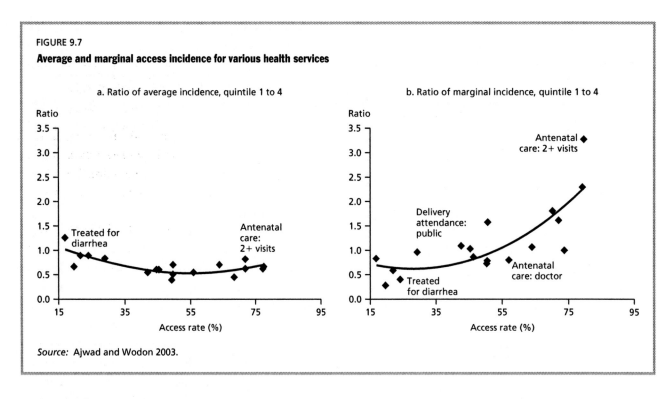

FIGURE 9.7

Average and marginal access incidence for various health services

Source: Ajwad and Wodon 2003.

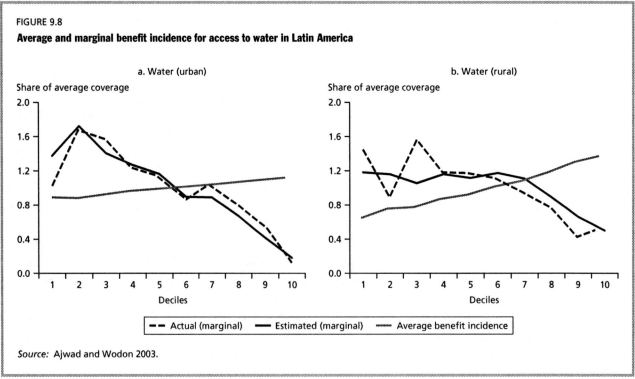

FIGURE 9.8

Average and marginal benefit incidence for access to water in Latin America

Source: Ajwad and Wodon 2003.

of access to water, and shows that although average incidence is regressive for both rural and urban access to water, marginal incidence is quite progressive in both cases. The redistributional effect of increasing the coverage of services that already enjoy high access rates can be quite significant, as shown by the progressive impact of the expansion of basic education and health services in Latin America during the 1990s. This is encouraging, but it must also be recognized that at best it brings poorer households up to service coverage levels routinely enjoyed by better-off households; in other words, this trend should *not* be interpreted as evidence that policy is sufficiently propoor. Moreover, since coverage of many services (for example, secondary and tertiary education, sewerage, and telecommunications) is not yet high in most Latin American countries, their initial expansion may not benefit the poor and may in fact have a regressive effect, unless deliberate, targeted efforts are made to improve access levels at the bottom of the income distribution.

Valuing the distribution of public spending

Following the analysis of *access* to services, it is natural to ask how much such access is worth to receiving households. This leads us to the difficult question of *valuing* the benefits of public spending across the income distribution. The valuation of public goods, and indeed also of publicly provided private goods, is still in its infancy. Box 9.2 summarizes the main difficulties faced when conducting studies on this topic. Although it is beyond the scope of this chapter to cover this complex issue in depth, and despite the serious methodological caveats, there is enough evidence from existing case studies to make three essential points.

The first point is that the (average) incidence of the benefits of public social expenditures varies enormously across programs. This is well-illustrated by a Mexican example, drawing on the work by Scott (2003). Using household survey data from 2000 and unit-level administrative cost figures, Scott considers public spending on education (primary, lower secondary, higher secondary, tertiary, and postgraduate levels); health (using data on social security institutions serving formal sector and state workers, as well as data on the services provided by the Ministry of Health to the uninsured population); social security pensions and other nonhealth benefits; and other subsidies and transfers, including programs targeted toward the poor (such as Oportunidades, previously known as Progresa, a grant program that is conditional on participation in education, nutrition, and health programs) and farmers (such as Procampo, a capacity-building project). Subsidies for residential electricity were also included, and measured by comparing the cost for households to the production costs published by the government.

An index of the inequality in incidence of benefits, the concentration coefficient, can be calculated using the same formula as the Gini coefficient, but with individuals ranked according to their incomes. Unlike the Gini coefficient, this can be negative, when poorer people receive absolutely more benefits than richer people. The concentration coefficients for the various categories of spending in Mexico are presented in figure 9.9. Their values range from 0.66 to 0.73, indicating widely different redistributive effects. Programs such as Oportunidades, health services for the uninsured provided by the Ministry of Health, basic education (primary and lower secondary levels), school breakfasts, and Procampo all have negative concentration coefficients that indicate high to mild absolute progressive incidence. Most other programs show a positive concentration coefficient that implies that public outlays are regressive. Values between zero and the value of the Gini for income inequality are still regressive in absolute terms, but are less unequally distributed than income. Public expenditures on higher secondary education and electricity subsidies, for example, are regressive, but not as badly distributed as income itself. Expenditures on tertiary education and pensions are almost as badly distributed as income, and thus highly regressive, or worse, as is the case of pensions from ISSSTE (for public sector workers).

Although incidence characteristics vary across countries—in addition to across programs within a country—some common patterns do emerge (see table 9.6). Basic education, for instance, tends to be progressive everywhere, with a higher share of total spending going to the lower part of the income distribution. Gini income elasticities (GIEs) (defined in box 9.3) are negative with regard to total spending for public education in Argentina (−0.28), Chile (−0.44), Mexico (−0.06), and Uruguay (−0.30). As expected, spending on primary education is highly redistributive, with GIEs ranging from –0.91 to –0.34, while spending for tertiary education is regressive, with GIEs ranging from 0.54 to 1.25 (the highest value is observed for Brazil). On average, the benefits from spending on secondary education tend to be distributed in a neutral way on average, with GIEs ranging from –0.33 to 0.32, depending on the initial rate of coverage; this distribution is more progressive in countries with higher levels of coverage.

Data on health are weaker than data on education, but there are indications that total health spending is distributed in a neutral way overall, with large variations between countries. The GIE is negative (that is, propoor) for programs in Chile and Colombia, zero in Brazil and Uruguay, and positive in Mexico. However, intercountry comparisons should be treated with caution. In general, spending by

FIGURE 9.9

Concentration coefficients for public social spending, Mexico 2000

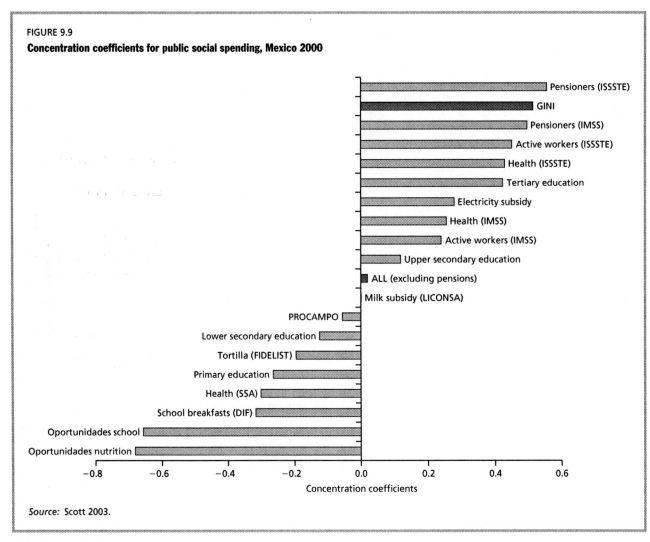

Source: Scott 2003.

TABLE 9.6

Synthesis of case studies using estimates of the Gini income elasticity (GIE)

GIE (Gini income elasticities)

	Argentina	Brazil	Chile	Colombia	Mexico	Uruguay
Education	−0.28	0.39	−0.44	−0.05	−0.06	−0.3
Primary	−0.52	−0.34	—	−0.58	−0.5	−0.91
Secondary	−0.19	0.32	—	−0.29	−0.005	−0.33
Tertiary	0.54	1.25	—	0.67	0.81	1.13
Health	−0.25	0.06	−1.05	−0.5	0.25	0.00
Pensions	—	0.7	0.91/−0.58*	—	1.0	1.15
Child care (or child development services)	—	−0.6	−0.6	−0.44	—	−1.79
Family allowances	—	—	−1.03	—	—	−1.17
Cash transfers	—	—	−0.78	—	−1.12 **	−0.1
Unemployment benefits (insurance or assistance)	—	0.17	—	—	—	−0.02
Nutrition	−1.06	−0.47	—	—	—	−1.56
Housing programs	−0.08	0.59	−0.56	—	—	−0.29
Infrastructure and transport	—	0.35	—	—	—	—
Subsidies	—	—	−0.35	—	0.49	—
Water			−0.35	—	—	—
Electricity			—	—	0.53	—

*Noncontributory pensions
**PROGRESA food transfers (−0.99) and PROGRESA scholarships (−1. 25)
Source: Wodon and others 2000.

BOX 9.3.

Summarizing benefit incidence using Gini income elasticities (GIE)

The GIE is a parameter that indicates the impact on inequality of a marginal percentage increase in spending for any given income source or public transfer (in cash or the monetary value of an in-kind transfer). A GIE less than zero means that income and spending are negatively correlated, implying that people in the lower part of the distribution benefit more than those in the higher part from the increase in spending. At zero, everybody benefits equally. A GIE between zero and one means that the distribution of the increase in spending is correlated with income, and therefore is regressive in absolute terms but progressive relative to income. A GIE of one means that public expenditures are distributed in the same way as the distribution of total per capita income, and a GIE greater than one implies an even more unequal distribution than that associated with income.

Ministries—which tend to cater to the uninsured—are often redistributive, while spending on the health plans linked to social security tend to favor better-off households.

Pensions are closely correlated with income, with benefits typically as unequally distributed as other sources of income. Related GIEs vary from 0.70 in Brazil to 1.15 in Uruguay. However, noncontributory pension schemes can reach the poor. In the case of Chile, the GIE for pensions (known as PASIS) is –0.58. In Mexico City, a new program of transfers to the elderly was recently implemented, which also had a negative GIE (MNPTSG 2002).

Existing programs that provide childcare or early child development services tend to be redistributive, with negative GIEs ranging from –1.79 in Uruguay to –0.16 in Colombia. Family allowances also tend to be redistributive (at least when they are means tested, as is the case in Chile and Uruguay). Targeted nutrition programs also tend to be highly redistributive, for example in Argentina, Chile, Mexico, and Uruguay. However, school breakfast and lunch programs, as well as food subsidies, appear to be much less effective in reaching the poor and contributing to a reduction in inequality.

In some other cases, there are no common patterns across countries. The impact of housing programs on inequality, for instance, varies greatly. Uruguay's rural housing program is highly redistributive, with a GIE of –1.61, and both Chile's programs and Brazil's favela upgrading programs have negative GIEs. However, benefits from several other programs are positively correlated with income and are therefore regressive. Utility subsidies for water and electricity are in most cases positively correlated with income. These subsidies tend to be allocated according to a "lifeline" threshold of consumption, below which water or electricity is sold at a discount. However this "lifeline" is typically set at a relatively high level. Evidence on unemployment benefits (via insurance or assistance) is also mixed. Some programs do reach the poor, but with low coverage rates (unemployment assistance in Chile, for example), while other programs are limited to formal sector workers with benefits that are positively correlated with income. Households that benefit from job training tend to be in the middle of the income distribution.

Overall, this comparison reinforces the enormous variability in the redistributive impact of different social programs. This is true both for individual programs within the same country and for similar programs across countries. Several factors explain such disparities. Programs that are intended to eventually have universal coverage are redistributive (and marginal increases are especially progressive) when the present access rate is already high, but are regressive (even marginally so) when access rates are low. Thus, the expansion of programs with relatively low access rates should be accompanied by targeting mechanisms to ensure that the poor share in the benefits of expansion.

This leads to the second essential point of this section: in many countries, a tradeoff seems to exist between *coverage of* the poor and *targeting to* the poor. In other words, those programs that effectively approach universal coverage explain most of the current redistributive effects of social public expenditures (that is, basic education in most countries and basic health in many). Meanwhile, several well-targeted programs that are highly cost-efficient in redistributing income or other benefits are generally small and cover only a small share of the poor. This apparent

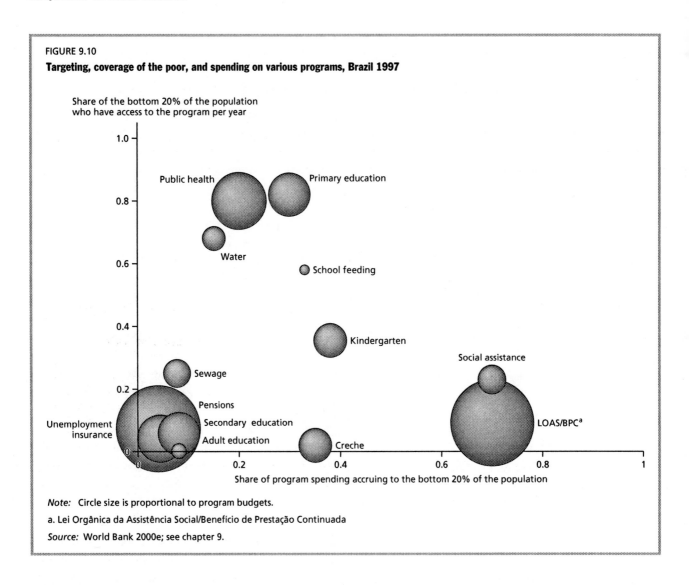

FIGURE 9.10

Targeting, coverage of the poor, and spending on various programs, Brazil 1997

Share of the bottom 20% of the population
who have access to the program per year

Note: Circle size is proportional to program budgets.

a. Lei Orgânica da Assistência Social/Benefício de Prestação Continuada

Source: World Bank 2000e; see chapter 9.

dilemma between targeting and coverage probably reflects both administrative and political economy constraints, which must be taken into account in the design and "packaging" of programs.

An excellent example of this tradeoff is the case of Brazil, as documented by von Amsberg, Lanjouw, and Nead (2003). These authors consider public social spending for education and health services, urban services, infrastructure (clean water, sanitation, transportation, and housing), and social protection (pensions and unemployment insurance). For each type of spending or service, three aspects were calculated: (1) the amount of government spending; (2) the share of spending accruing to the urban poor (that is, the targeting or benefit incidence for the poor); and (3) coverage among the urban poor for the service. The authors also present a ranking of programs according to effectiveness in transferring resources to the poor.

In figure 9.10, each bubble is proportional to the size of an expenditure category or program. The horizontal axis measures the share of benefits accruing to the bottom quintile, while the vertical axis measures coverage of the program within this group (that is, the share of households in the bottom quintile benefiting from the program). Programs in the lower left corner (pensions, unemployment insurance, sewage system provision, and secondary education) are poorly targeted and do not reach many of the poor. Programs in the bottom right corner (for example, social assistance programs) are well targeted but have low coverage among the poor. Programs near the top left (water, public health, public prepri-mary and primary education) tend to be universal. There are no programs near the top right, that is, programs that are both well-targeted and reach most of the poor. These patterns clearly illustrate the tradeoff between targeting and coverage in Brazil. The higher the coverage among the poor, the more difficult it is to avoid leakage to the nonpoor; in contrast, tightly targeted programs are small and tend to have low coverage even among the poor.

The third main point of this section is that, despite large variance in the incidence of the benefits of public social expenditures across both program types and countries, the evidence suggests that social public expenditure tends, on balance, to reduce inequality. This is generally true, as discussed above, with regard to childcare, primary education, and basic health care. In many cases, it is also true of secondary education and well-targeted housing programs.

More generally, however, the overall impact of social expenditures tends to be less unequally distributed than are incomes (as indicated in figure 9.9 in the case of Mexico), and would therefore contribute to a reduction of overall inequality, if only values for all public programs could be imputed into household incomes. However, such an exercise is fraught with difficulties (as partly summarized in box 9.2). Nevertheless, in the few cases where it has been (bravely) attempted, the results do suggest that the overall effect of public expenditures on social sectors is inequality-reducing.

Such is the case, for example, of Bravo, Contreras, and Millan (2002), who estimated the value of government transfers in cash and in kind in Chile and compared the distribution of these transfers to the distribution of monetary income. Public cash transfers include family allowances, noncontributory pensions, utility and other subsidies, and unemployment benefits. In-kind transfers arise from public expenditures on education, health, and housing. To estimate the value of in-kind benefits provided by government expenditures, Bravo, Contreras, and Millan (2002) conducted a detailed analysis of the various subcomponents of each type of expenditure program and developed valuation criteria. For example, 17 health categories were identified (such as surgery, dental services, laboratory tests, preventive checkups, X-rays, emergency services, and hospital expenses) and, for each of these categories, average monthly values were estimated. More than 25 subcomponents were identified for education and 6 for housing.

The main conclusion of this analysis is that rising, progressive public social expenditures more than offset the observed increase in income inequality during the 1990s (figure 9.11). The authors argue that including in-cash and in-kind transfers in the welfare aggregate reduces the Gini inequality index by 6 percentage points, from 0.56 to 0.50. In the first income quintile, for example, the value of the

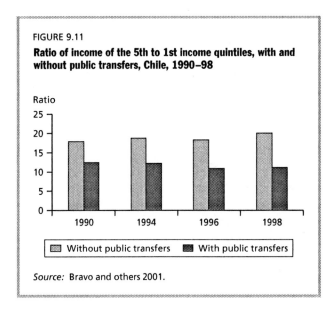

FIGURE 9.11

Ratio of income of the 5th to 1st income quintiles, with and without public transfers, Chile, 1990–98

Source: Bravo and others 2001.

transfers (17,000 pesos per month per person) was almost as large as the monetary income of households (19,000 pesos per month per person). In-kind subsidies for education were the main contributors to the reduction in inequality (59.9 percent of total transfers), followed by health (25.5 percent), monetary transfers (11.1 percent), and housing (6.5 percent).

Although a reduction of 6 percentage points in the Gini is not revolutionary, it is quite substantial. There is no evidence that this order of magnitude is representative of other countries in the continent, since Chile has one of the most progressive incidence patterns for social spending in Latin America. In the case of Colombia, for instance, Vélez and Foster (2003) found a concentration coefficient[13] for total public social spending of –0.06, implying that in absolute terms the subsidies were distributed in a marginally progressive way across quintiles and amounted to a substantial redistribution relative to the unequal pattern of income distribution. Given the valuation assumptions made, social spending contributed to a reduction in the Gini index of close to 3 percentage points.

Once again, there were large differences in the extent to which programs were redistributive. The patterns by program type conform to those identified above. Some nursery schools, primary education, and subsidized health insurance were the most redistributive programs. Housing subsidies, tertiary education, and family subsidies were the least redistributive.

Finally, it is important to note that the incidence patterns considered in this section—whether average or marginal and related to access or value—have all referred, in some sense, to a temporal average. They have been discussed without reference to whether they were observed in good times or in bad times, or whether the economy was in a boom or in a recession. However, macroeconomic volatility is an unfortunate but ubiquitous fact of Latin American life, and the manner in which social spending behaves throughout the economic cycle is a key attribute to consider. Does it provide some measure of insurance against increased risks in downturns? Or does it aggravate the volatility of the cycle?

The lack of countercyclical targeted spending during downturns

Macroeconomic shocks have plagued Latin American countries since the 1980s. The poor are particularly vulnerable to these shocks, as they are typically more exposed to risk and have little access to appropriate risk management instruments.[14] Social protection systems, including safety nets, should help the poor to deal with the risks brought about by economic shocks, as well as with idiosyncratic risks. According to the risk management framework spelled out in de Ferranti and others (2000), social public expenditures designed to manage risks should go up during economic crises.

Yet the opposite appears to be true. It is difficult to protect the poor during recessions because several forces combine to put downward pressures on the amount of public transfers that can be allocated per poor person. First, due to the highly procyclical nature of fiscal policy in most Latin American countries,[15] the share of GDP devoted to overall public spending tends to decrease in bad times. Second, GDP itself declines in a crisis, so that even if the share of GDP devoted to social public spending remains constant, there will still be fewer resources available. These two factors tend to make aggregate targeted public spending for the poor procyclical rather than countercyclical. Third, poverty increases during a crisis, so that the available aggregate resources targeted toward the poor have to be distributed among a larger pool of applicants, resulting in lower spending per poor person.

On average, in Latin America during the 1990s, a decrease of GDP by 1 percentage point led to a reduction of at least 2 percentage points in targeted public spending per poor person (Wodon and others 2003). About half of the impact was due to the reduction in per capita GDP and half to the increase in the number of poor people; the share of the GDP in targeted spending remained relatively stable. During economic expansions, social spending as a share of total spending increases, but it is better to save at least some public funds during expansions in order to better protect the poor during recessions. Although governments try to be propoor (or at least prosocial) whenever they can, they often do so in a shortsighted way that does not support good safety nets during crises.

In a deeper sense, procyclicality in public expenditures is the combined result of three factors (Perry 2003). First is the procyclicality of tax revenues: tax-to-GDP ratios are higher during economic booms because of high dependency on consumption taxes and commodity exports. Second are political economy factors that lead to the spending of any potential surpluses in good times (that is, to procyclical spending during economic booms). Third are procyclicality and informational asymmetry problems in financial markets, in particular with regard to the "true" nature of fiscal policy. In other words, markets can not distinguish between responsible counter-cyclical policies and relaxation of the intertemporal fiscal stance, especially when the track record in booms has been bad.

These three factors combine to force major expenditure restraints during recessions due to a lack of financing. In countries with no access to private financial markets, procyclicality might be partially attributed to deficiencies in official adjustment programs. Hence, overcoming the problems associated with the procyclicality of social expenditures requires building appropriate institutions (including fiscal rules) to overcome structural problems (see discussion in chapter 8). Equally important is creating some automaticity in the expansion of propoor programs in bad times, for example through the earmarking of funds, especially in light of the substantial pressures to spend regressively that are associated with financial crises (see chapter 8 and de Ferranti and others 2000).

9.3. Cash transfers and distribution

Following the discussion of the trends and incidence patterns of social public spending as a whole, this section turns to a specific subcomponent of public expenditures, namely *direct cash transfers* to households. Whereas governments might choose to spend money on education, labor market programs, or even housing purely for efficiency reasons (having to do with internalizing externalities, for instance), cash transfers appear, at first glance at least, to be more likely driven by equity concerns.

TABLE 9.7

Social security expenditures around the world, as percentage of GDP

	Pensions[1]	Health care[2]	Others[3]	Total social security expenditure[4]
Africa	1.4	1.7	1.2	4.3
Asia	3.0	2.7	0.7	6.4
Europe	12.1	6.3	6.4	24.8
Latin America and Caribbean	2.1	2.8	3.9	8.8
North America	7.1	7.5	2.0	16.6
Oceania	4.9	5.6	5.6	16.1

Notes: [1]Pension expenditures cover old age, disability, and survivors' pensions. [2]Health care expenditures cover health care services. [3]Other expenditures cover employment injury, sickness, family, housing, and social assistance benefits in cash and in kind, including administrative expenditures. [4]Total social security expenditures cover pensions, health care, and other aspects.
Source: Table originally published in ILO 2000, Statistical Annex, table 14. Regional averages are weighted by gross national product evaluated at Pricing and Purchasing Parities (PPP) prices. See http://www.ilo.org/public/english/protection/socsec/publ/css/table14.htm.

Indeed, in most developed countries the bulk of cash transfers are part of what is known as "social security systems" which have historically been associated with distributional concerns. As they developed over the course of the latter half of the last century, it became evident that social security systems were fundamentally more about *risk* (that is, inequality across states of nature) than about inequality per se (that is, a cross-section of inequality). Three principal risks seem to draw most public resources: the risk of having undersaved for and, in particular, falling into poverty in old age; the risk of disability; the risk of unemployment; and the risk of income loss through poor health. In developed countries, all social security payments typically account for almost half of total public spending, or roughly one-fifth of GDP. Old-age, disability, and survivor pensions account for just under half of those shares in Organisation for Economic Co-operation and Development (OECD) countries.

However, it would clearly be incorrect, or at least incomplete, to characterize these social security transfers simply as "insurance." Whereas the incidence of unemployment, disability, and illness do indeed have random components (though different income groups may be faced by different probabilities), old age is reasonably (if not perfectly) foreseeable. In addition, transfer levels are not identical among people faced with identical concerns, since benefits are generally means tested in order to achieve progressive incidence. In other words, transfers depend not only on the realization of the random variable of interest, but also on private incomes. Some benefit types are indeed explicitly designed

as social assistance to the poor and are formally intended to be redistributive. Examples include the Working Families Tax Credit (WFTC) in the United Kingdom or the Temporary Assistance for Needy Families (TANF) in the United States. The key point is that all public transfers of cash to households are to some extent a mix of social insurance and social assistance, since all such transfers can help mitigate the effects of negative shocks on the consumption stream and virtually all incorporate some element of progressive redistribution.

With this in mind, how do cash transfers—and indeed social security—in Latin America compare with those in other countries? Are they effective risk-management systems? Do they also enhance equity? Table 9.7 compares official social security expenditures (as a percentage of GDP) across regions of the world. Social security expenditures are broken down into pensions, health care, and other (mostly social assistance) according to the official definitions of the International Labour Organisation (ILO). The regional averages indicate that rich countries (in Europe, North America, and Oceania) allocate a much greater output share to overall social expenditures than do developing countries.

At 8.8 percent, the share of Latin America's GDP that is accounted for by social security is only one-third of the European share and roughly half that of North America and Oceania, but it is still substantially higher than in Africa or Asia. Indeed, overall social security expenditures in many Latin American countries are around what would be expected for their level of income per capita (See figure 9.12.) In addition, a large share of the total, corresponding to 3.9%

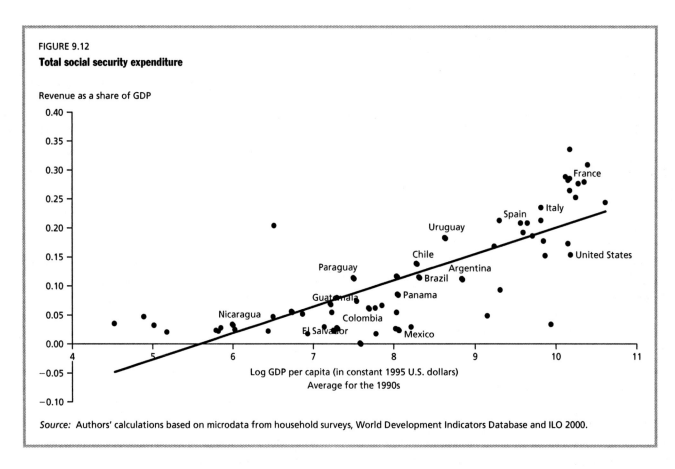

FIGURE 9.12

Total social security expenditure

Revenue as a share of GDP

Log GDP per capita (in constant 1995 U.S. dollars)
Average for the 1990s

Source: Authors' calculations based on microdata from household surveys, World Development Indicators Database and ILO 2000.

of GDP, is allocated to "other" expenditures, which include social assistance. If used well, these resources would hold real potential for redistribution in Latin America.

Table 9.8 presents some summary information on social security expenditures for 24 countries in Latin America. This information should be treated with some circumspection, as it is generally harder to aggregate across social security and social protection programs in developing countries than it is in industrial nations. The reason for this is that a wide variety of programs are seldom integrated and not all programs are well documented. Even basic data on program size and eligibility criteria are not always available. In addition, cash transfers appear to have traditionally been used less extensively in less developed countries than in developed countries; instead, a number of safety net programs in poor countries distribute food or other commodities. Although food stamps, for example, are also common in developed countries—indeed, they are prominent in the United States—these countries tend to rely more on cash transfers than do developing countries.

Social security as a share of total public expenditures in Latin America ranges from 14 percent in Belize to 68 per-

cent in Uruguay, with equally impressive heterogeneity among areas within individual countries. As is the case with other public expenditures, the effectiveness and incidence of social security expenditures vary considerably both across and within countries. Cash transfers under the general heading of "social security" include very disparate programs, with widely different incidence patterns. In the case of Mexico, for instance, cash transfers include both some of the most progressive of all public programs (such as Oportunidades), and some of the most regressive (such as the pensions paid by the ISSSTE, and the generalized electricity subsidies) (see figure 9.9). The same is true in Brazil (see chapter 6 for a discussion on the regressivity of the subsidies to civil servant retirement pensions), but where other components, such as rural pensions and the payments made under the BPC/LOAS scheme, are actually quite progressive.

Unfortunately, the evidence suggests that in most countries, the regressive components of the "welfare state" in present-day Latin America quantitatively dominate progressive elements. Table 9.9, drawn from Paes de Barros and Foguel (2000), illustrates this point through figures on retirement pensions and unemployment insurance in Brazil.

TABLE 9.8

Social security expenditures in Latin America and the Caribbean, as percentage of GDP

	Pensions[a]	Health care[b]	Others[c]	Total social security expenditure	
				Percentage of GDP[d]	Percentage of total public expenditure
Argentina	4.1	4.3	4.0	12.4	41.2
Bahamas	—	2.5	—	—	—
Barbados	4.1	4.4	1.5	9.0	—
Belize	—	2.1	—	3.5	14.2
Bolivia	—	2.3	—	7.0	29.3
Brazil	2.4	2.1	7.7	12.2	36.7
Chile	5.9	2.3	3.1	11.3	45.6
Colombia	0.9	5.1	0.1	6.1	—
Costa Rica	—	6.8	—	13.0	42.6
Cuba	—	—	—	—	—
Dominica	1.4	0.4	3.0	4.8	—
Dominican Republic	—	1.8	—	2.5	15.7
Ecuador	1.2	0.3	0.5	2.0	—
El Salvador	1.3	1.3	1.0	3.6	—
Grenada	—	2.8	—	—	—
Guatemala	—	1.7	—	—	—
Guyana	0.9	4.3	0.6	5.8	—
Jamaica	0.3	2.5	1.7	4.5	—
Mexico	0.4	2.8	0.5	3.7	22.6
Nicaragua	1.4	4.3	3.4	9.1	28.1
Panama	4.3	5.6	1.4	11.3	41.3
Peru	—	2.2	—	—	—
Trinidad and Tobago	0.6	2.5	3.5	6.6	22.7
Uruguay	8.7	2.0	11.7	22.4	67.8
Simple average	2.5	2.9	2.9	8.0	34.0

— Not available.

Notes: a. Pension expenditures cover old-age, disability, and survivors' pensions. b. Health care expenditures cover health care services. c. Other expenditures cover employment injury, sickness, family, housing, and social assistance benefits in cash and in kind, including administrative expenditures. d. Total social security expenditures cover pensions, health care, and other aspects.
Source: Table originally published in ILO 2000, Statistical Annex, table 14. See http://www.ilo.org/public/english/protection/socsec/publ/css/table14.htm.

TABLE 9.9

Distribution of government expenditures on pensions and unemployment insurance in Brazil by quintile (percent)

Income quintiles	Pensions	Unemployment insurance
First	2.4	3.0
Second	6.4	21.0
Third	9.7	20.2
Fourth	16.5	36.3
Fifth	65.1	19.5

Source: Paes de Barros and Foguel 2000.

The bottom 20 percent of the Brazilian income distribution receives a mere 3 percent of total disbursements in unemployment insurance, and an even smaller share of pension payouts. In the case of old-age pensions, this low share in part reflects different past levels of contributions during the working years. However, as indicated in chapter 6, those differences are actually magnified, rather than dampened, by a pension system that rewards well-off civil servants at the expense of poorer taxpayers.

The case of unemployment insurance is even more surprising, at least at first glance. One might have expected that the unemployed would be overrepresented in the bottom fifth of the income distribution, and it is thus disappointing to see that this group receives by far the lowest share of total disbursements and more than six times less than the richest quintile. Upon further analysis, however, the reason is clear: only workers in the formal sector qualify for unemployment insurance, and the poorest of the poor in Brazil do not work in the formal sector. More than half of the labor force has no signed labor documentation and are overrepresented among the poorest 20 percent of the population.

Table 9.9 serves as a reminder of the truncated and elitist nature of the social security systems that developed in Latin America over the course of the 20th century. Nevertheless, the existence of some social assistance and social protection programs (such as Oportunidades in Mexico, Famílias en Acción in Colombia, Trabajar in Argentina, and Bolsa Família in Brazil) which make cash transfers that actually reach some of the poorest citizens in their respective countries, and thereby attain highly progressive incidence measures, holds out the possibility of serious reform of the historically truncated "welfare state." Also noteworthy are initiatives in some countries that consolidate eligible beneficiaries for social assistance programs into one system. Examples are the ficha CAS in Chile and SISBEN (Sistema de Selección de Beneficiarios para Programas Sociales) in Colombia. Such efforts lead to significant savings on administrative costs and are associated with a set of highly progressive programs.

Some of these programs (such as Trabajar and its successor Jefes y Jefas de Hogar in Argentina) are essentially public employment schemes. Jefes y Jefas entails additional conditions and complexities, but the essence of the program remains self selection by the urban poor into a program that provides a transfer corresponding to a low wage, in exchange for community or other work. Although these programs run the risk of being used for clientelistic purposes, Trabajar has been evaluated as being highly effective in targeting the poorest citizens (Jalan and Ravallion 1999, 2003). Although they are no panacea, and do suffer from some leakage to the nonpoor and incomplete coverage of the poor, this family of programs has a long history and a number of features that deserve praise. (See Galasso and Ravallion 2003 for a discussion of the impact of Jefes y Jefas during Argentina's 2002 crisis.) Following is a brief discussion on a related family of programs known as conditional cash transfers (CCTs).

Smart transfers: A new breed of social assistance programs

In recent years, many developing countries, particularly in Latin America, have taken a relatively innovative approach to social safety nets, now known generically as conditional cash transfers.[16] One of the key defining features of CCTs is that the continued receipt of transfers is conditional on households investing in the education and health status of their members, in particular children. With some exceptions (discussed below), these programs are typically designed and implemented by the federal or central government. Participating communities and households are selected by program officials situated in the central government and transfers go directly to eligible households without passing through state budgets.

It has been hoped that this arrangement would eliminate the unnecessary bureaucracy inherent in many existing programs, as well as the potential for corruption. The programs use a range of targeting methods (for example, geographic and community targeting or household proxy-means) to ensure that program benefits reach the poorest households. It is often argued that such "fine" targeting can result in a loss of support from the excluded middle classes, and thus adversely affect the political sustainability of programs. However, in many cases the argument that programs reach only those who are very needy, with little leakage to the nonpoor, is used to generate political support domestically, as well as external support from international development institutions and donors.

Despite an increased supply of education and health services (see section 9.2 above), empirical evidence clearly shows that poor households have substantially lower utilization rates, a fact that reflects the high opportunity cost of access (for example, forgone earnings and the cost of travel, uniforms, and educational materials). Supply-side interventions in isolation are therefore not very effective at enticing poor households to access these services. Conditioning targeted cash transfers on access to services and facilities—which effectively transforms pure transfers into human capital subsidies—is an attractive policy response to this problem.[17] Yet access, although a necessary condition for capital accumulation, is in and of itself insufficient. Human capital accumulation requires that such access be complemented with quality services. For this reason, many transfer programs include a supply-side component in order to reinforce the impact of demand-side subsidies.

One of the main attractions of demand-side transfers is that they can help generate a sustained decrease in poverty independent of the transfers themselves, in addition to the obvious immediate decrease in poverty. This characteristic of program design can also be used to generate political support for larger transfers, since it can be argued that the transfers constitute investments in needy households (that is, a "hand up" as opposed to a handout) and that they are a required complement or component of universal coverage programs (for example, in basic education and health) that benefit the whole population. The requirement that households undertake such investments simultaneously recognizes the right of individuals to a basic living standard and their responsibility to achieve this goal.

Another innovative feature of the new CCT programs is the fact that in many cases, special emphasis has been placed on the need for a built-in, comprehensive evaluation of the program from its early stages. Some of the features identified above are discussed below in more detail with regard to a subset of these programs, that is, those for which sufficient information on their design, implementation, and impact is currently available. For this purpose, we focus in detail on the programs that have been implemented in Brazil (Programa Nacional de Bolsa Escola, henceforth denoted as BE, and Programa Bolsa Alimentação, henceforth denoted as BA);[18] in Honduras (Programa de Asignacion Familiar, henceforth denoted as PRAF); Nicaragua (Red de Protección Social, henceforth denoted as RPS); and Mexico (Programa de Educación, Salud, y Alimentación, henceforth denoted as Progresa and now known as Oportunidades).[19]

Table 9.10 summarizes information on the size of these transfer programs, including Chile's Subsidio Único Familiar (SUF) and Bangladesh's *Food for Education* (FFE) for comparison purposes, but excluding BA, for which data were not available. Column 1 presents information on the coverage of the programs, while column 2 describes the size of their budgets. Columns 3, 4, and 5 show the annual budget as a share of a country's GDP, total public expenditure (TPE), and total government expenditure on education, respectively.

Program implementation and selection of beneficiaries

As indicated above, a distinctive element of many of the transfer programs is the direct relationship between the federal or central government and the beneficiaries. In the case of Progresa, for example, once the program identifies which communities and households are eligible to receive program benefits, a general assembly is held in the community to inform households of their eligibility, to explain the workings of the program with regard to household entitlements and responsibilities, and to answer any questions on program operations or objectives.

Although the Progresa, PRAF, and RPS programs are heavily centralized in terms of both design and implementation, their structures also allow for direct community involvement. For example, at Progresa's general assemblies, participants select a woman beneficiary to act as the "community promoter." This person plays the role of a liaison officer, arranging regular community meetings with beneficiaries, informing them of their rights and responsibilities under the program, and communicating beneficiary concerns to program officials. It is this person who informs beneficiaries when and where to collect their transfers and answers any questions regarding the amounts they receive. Community promoters are volunteers who do not receive payment for their services, except for a small amount to cover expenses (for example, for travel to promoter meetings).

TABLE 9.10

Conditional cash transfers: comparison of program sizes

Program	Coverage	Total annual budget (U.S. dollars)	Budget as % GDP	Budget as percentage of total public expenditure	Budget as percentage of public expenditure on education
Progresa (Mexico, introduced August 1997)	2.6 million households in 1999	998 million in 2000	0.2	1.6	4.1
PRAF (Honduras, introduced late 2000)	47.8 thousand households	12.5 million in 2001	0.2	2.0	5.0
RPS (Nicaragua, pilot introduced October 2000)	10 thousand households in 2001	10 million in 2001–2002	0.2		
FFE (Bangladesh, introduced 1993)	2.1 million students in 2000	77 million in 1999	0.2	4.2	7.9
SUF (Chile 1998)	954,000 students	70 million	0.1	0.9	3.5
BE (Brazil 2001)	5 million families	680 million	0.15	0.7	2.5

Source: Morley and Coady 2003.

Once Progresa beneficiaries have been informed of program operations and their rights and responsibilities, they must register at schools and clinics. Proof of registration must be presented in order to receive the initial cash payment. Registration forms are then logged into electronic databases, which are then transmitted from Progresa's state office to the organization's central office. Attendance at school and health clinics is monitored and recorded by service providers, and this information is transmitted every two months to the central office. Household transfer levels are calculated based on this information and communicated to households at local distribution points via the national telegraphic system.

One of the issues that arose during the program implementation and evaluation process was the importance of ensuring that the effectiveness and integrity of the monitoring process was continuously evaluated. The validity of beneficiary compliance cannot be confirmed based solely on impact evaluations, since these rely on reporting by households, which obviously have an incentive to report attendance. Similarly, service providers may have incentives to falsely report attendance, for example because of community pressure, the consequences of withdrawing benefits from poor households, and the need to avoid congestion at schools and clinics.

Although a preliminary evaluation of the monitoring process indicated that incentives for truthful reporting also existed (for example, monitoring by beneficiaries who do comply with the rules, a commitment by service providers to improve human capital status, and the fact that there is a provision for noncompliance for health-related reasons), this process needs to be looked at systematically.

All of the programs considered here have paid particular attention to the need to ensure that benefits actually reach their intended populations. This has been achieved by using a combination of targeting methods to select beneficiaries. Most programs use a two-step process to determine the eligibility of households, combining some form of geographic targeting with proxy-means, categorical, or community-targeting methods.

In Progresa, the first stage of geographic targeting involves choosing the poorest or most marginal communities. Information from the national census on the demographic, housing, infrastructure, occupation, and education characteristics of communities is used to construct a "marginality index" (or score) for each community in the country, which is in turn used to identify the most marginal communities to be included in the program. In addition, communities must have access to education and health facilities within a certain radius and to have 50–2,500 inhabitants.

In PRAF, information from a 1999 height-for-age school census of first graders is used to identify the 70 rural municipalities (out of a total of 297) in which malnourishment is greatest. Geographic targeting in the RPS pilot program was based on poverty rates and on access to social infrastructure and organizational capacity. Using these criteria, two departments were initially chosen. Within these two departments, 6 (out of 20) municipalities were chosen using similar poverty and operational criteria. All of the 59 rural comarcas (localities) within these municipalities were eligible for the program.

Once the participating localities are identified, each program undertakes further targeting using proxy-means, categorical, or community-targeting methods. In Progresa, a community census is conducted in all localities. The resulting socioeconomic data on households is then used to calculate a proxy-means score for each household (using discriminant analysis, with income as the left-hand-side variable) and then to classify households as "poor" (that is, eligible for the program) and "nonpoor" (that is, not eligible).[20]

In the 70 participating municipalities selected by PRAF, only households with pregnant or lactating women or with children under the age of 12 are eligible for the program. For both the BE and BA programs in Brazil, only households classified as poor based on a monetary income cutoff level of 90 reais per month (equivalent to one half the official minimum wage in 2001) are eligible.

The process of household selection is a bit more complex in the RPS. To determine which households are eligible for the program, a marginality index is calculated for all of the 59 comarcas in the six participating municipalities. The index was based on the following variables from the 1995 National Population and Housing Census: family size, access to potable water, access to latrines, and illiteracy rates. These 59 localities were then divided into four groups on the basis of this index. In principle, all the households in the "poorest" two groups, which contained the 42 most marginal localities, were eligible. However, during implementation it was decided to exclude around 2 percent of the households that were deemed to be nonpoor because of ownership of a vehicle or large landholdings. In the remaining localities that were considered to be least marginal, 20 percent of households were excluded based on predicted consumption levels.

Benefit structure

A defining feature of CCT programs is that in order for beneficiaries to receive transfers, they must undertake a series of actions that are intended to enhance the human capital status of household members. In some programs, participating households receive two sets of demand-side transfers. One is the education subsidy, which is conditioned on regular attendance at school. The other set—often referred to as the food or nutrition transfer—is conditioned on regular attendance by household members (particularly children) at health and information clinics at which the importance of practicing specific nutrition and hygiene behaviors in the home is discussed. In other programs, such as Brazil's Bolsa Família, a single transfer is conditioned on both sets of actions.

In Progresa, only children aged 7 or older are eligible for education transfers, starting when they are in grade 3. This guideline is partly motivated by a desire to prevent incentives for higher fertility, as well as by the fact that school enrollment rates for the first two grades are very high even in the targeted "poor" populations. The benefit structure has a number of important features. Transfers increase by grade (primarily because of the higher opportunity costs for older children) and are higher for girls in middle school (grades 7–9). Higher subsidies for girls in middle school reflect a desire to reduce gender bias in education, as well as to internalize the widely documented social externalities that accrue from female education. Each eligible child also receives a stipend for school materials, fixed at 160 pesos annually for primary school children and at 205 pesos annually for secondary school. This information is summarized in table 9.11.

Education subsidies in the other programs have a simpler structure. In the RPS, only households with children ages 7–13 who have not yet completed grade 4 of primary school are eligible to receive transfers, which in 2000 were fixed at a monthly rate of 120 cordobas per household and an annual transfer of 275 cordobas to finance additional education expenses. All such children in the family are required to maintain an 85 percent school attendance rate. Unlike in Progresa, transfers through RPS are not inflation-indexed.

In PRAF, all households with children ages 6–12 who have not yet completed grade 4 are eligible for transfers. Each participating child receives a monthly transfer of US$58/12 reais, with a maximum of three such transfers per household.

TABLE 9.11

Benefit structure of Progresa, July–December 1999 (pesos/month)

Education scholarships	Boys	Girls
Primary		
Grade 3		80
Grade 4		95
Grade 5		125
Grade 6		165
Materials (annual)		160
Secondary		
Grade 7	240	250
Grade 8	250	285
Grade 9	265	305
Materials (annual)	205	205
Food transfer	125 per family	
Benefit cap	750 per family	

Note: The cap on the total benefits a household can receive is applied only to the sum of the education scholarships and food transfer (that is, excluding transfers for materials).
Source: Skoufias 2001 and Morley and Coady 2003.

All children in this age group must attain an 85 percent attendance rate. Under BE, households with children ages 6–15 receive a monthly transfer of 15 reais per child, up to a maximum of three such transfers and conditional on 85 percent attendance.

With regard to food transfers (that is, health subsidies), in Progresa this was fixed for each family at 250 pesos per month in the second half of 1999 and was conditioned on households making regular trips to health clinics for a range of preventive health checks and on attendance at monthly nutrition and hygiene information sessions. In addition to the cash transfer, beneficiary households with children under the age of 3 receive a monthly nutritional supplement (usually a box of 30 sachets per month) that contains essential micronutrients. The monthly nutrition and hygiene information sessions focus on such issues as the importance of consuming nutritional foods, preparing food properly, and following simple hygiene and preventive health care practices at home. Food transfers were similarly conditioned in the other programs.

In all of the programs considered here, a capping system is in place that puts a ceiling on the total amount of transfers a household can receive. This is usually motivated by a desire to not create dependency on the part of recipients, to not erode the incentive for self-help, and to avoid incentives for higher fertility. In Progresa, this ceiling is set at 750 pesos for education and health transfers combined. On average, the transfer to beneficiary households is substantial, constituting around 20 percent of total household consumption. In PRAF, households can receive at most three education transfers and two health transfers. On average, total transfers are less than 5 percent of total household expenditures for beneficiaries.

In RPS, the transfer is fixed at the household level and is not dependent on the number of eligible children. On average, the total transfers received by beneficiaries are just over 20 percent of total household expenditures. In both BE and BA, households can receive transfers for at most three children, equivalent to a transfer ceiling of 45 reais per family. With regard to BE, it has been estimated that the total transfers received by beneficiary households make up less than 5 percent of total income for households in the bottom two national income deciles.

One of the key differences among the programs is how they coordinate with the supply-side provision of education and health services. Although Progresa, BE, and BA do not have an explicit supply-side component in their education or health interventions, program personnel coordinate with national education and health ministries to plan for increased supply-side investments in areas where the programs operate, with demand for services therefore expected to expand.

However, both RPS and PRAF have explicit supply-side components. In RPS, each beneficiary student receives a monthly transfer of 5 cordobas, which is handed over to the school at the time of enrollment registration. It is expected that this transfer will be split evenly between teachers' salaries and school resources. On the health side, information clinics and health services are provided by nongovernmental organizations (NGOs).

In PRAF, schools directly receive transfers linked to the number of students and teachers, ranging from US$1,600 to US$23,000 annually, with an average of US$4,000. These funds are also channeled through school coordinating bodies, which include NGOs and parents and are intended to have discretion over how monies are spent. However, in practice it appears that for legal reasons, schools have not received the funds directly but have had to place orders for materials through conventional school channels. On the nutrition and health side, resources are distributed to both clinics and community health promotion groups. The size of these transfers depends on the size of the population covered and range from US$3,318 to US$15,000, with a ceiling of US$15,000 and an average of US$6,020. As with the education supply side—and possibly to an even greater degree—the nutrition and health program has encountered many unanticipated problems in implementing supply-side measures.

Do conditional cash transfers work?

One of the most innovative aspects of many CCT programs is the emphasis placed from the beginning on having a built-in, credible evaluation process. The evaluation of Progresa was perhaps the most extensive such evaluation. Although the decision to evaluate the program was "homegrown," the Inter-American Development Bank (IDB) also played a key role in facilitating and encouraging discussions on design, implementation, and evaluation issues.

Focus is placed here on the evaluation of Progresa, a discussion that is occasionally complemented with results for RPS. For both these programs, experimental evaluation designs were built into their structure from the start and the results of evaluations are now publicly available. Some estimates for BE that were obtained using an alternative methodology are also reported.

In Progresa, 506 communities were identified by the geographic targeting method as being the most marginal and thus eligible for the program (Behrman and Todd 1999b, Skoufias 2001). Out of these, 320 were randomly chosen as treatment communities (that is, those that would receive the program's services), and 186 as control communities for comparison purposes. The justification for withholding program benefits from the control group was that there were budgetary and operational constraints that would be relaxed over time and that a phased introduction of the program was therefore necessary.

With this in mind, the sequential expansion of Progresa due to such constraints presented the opportunity for a rigorous evaluation of the impact of the program by comparing the outcomes in participating communities with those of control communities that were to be incorporated into the program at a later stage. The control group was eventually incorporated in late November 1999, two years after the program was first launched. The decision to maintain a control group predictably generated heated public debate, but program officials were determined to defend this decision since it was seen to be crucial to maintaining the integrity of the program evaluation process.

Another defining feature of the Progresa evaluation was its extensiveness in terms of the use of both quantitative and qualitative evaluation techniques and the wide range of issues addressed. At the core of the quantitative evaluation was the collection of both "baseline" and "follow-up" household surveys during the period November 1997–November 1999. These surveys collected detailed socioeconomic information from all 24,000 households in the 506 evaluation communities. Altogether, five rounds of data were collected, one in 1997 and two each in 1998 and 1999. These data provided the opportunity to undertake a scientific evaluation that could provide a clean estimate of program impacts, since the presence of a control group enabled evaluators to "wash out" confounding factors, for example inherent time trends and exogenous shocks. As it turned out, having such a control group was crucial because the program area went through an economic shock in the form of a drought—which caused much distress and adversely affected many of the outcomes considered in the evaluation—that was exogenous to the program itself. As a final note, the design of the evaluation of RPS was very similar to that of Progresa (IFPRI 2002).

Targeting outcomes

The targeting performance of the CCT programs has been quite impressive. Table 9.12 presents the distribution of program beneficiaries across consumption deciles for four programs. The percentage of program beneficiaries in the bottom 40 percent of the national consumption distribution varies from more than 62 percent for Progresa to almost 89 percent for SUF. In other words, households classified as poor receive between 1.55 and 2.22 times their population shares.

Human capital impacts

The *education* impacts of the CCTs that have been evaluated are very impressive. Prior to the Progresa program, primary enrollments in the evaluated communities were about 93 percent in all primary grades. Enrollment rates dipped substantially after the final primary school level (grade 6), with enrollments rates in middle school (that is, grades 7–9) falling to 67 percent for girls and 73 percent for boys. Enrollment rates in high school showed another dip, with only 58 percent of those who successfully completed middle school enrolling in high school. This is the main motivation to increase grants by around 50 percent for children in middle school, compared to the level available to primary school students.

As expected, enrollment impacts in primary school were small, with the program increasing enrollment rates by 0.74–1.07 percentage points for boys and 0.96–1.45 percentage points for girls (Schultz 2000a–d, Behrman, Sengupta, and Todd 2000a–b). This relatively small change reflects high initial enrollment rates and captures a range of impacts, including improvements in starting dates, progression rates, and primary completion rates. In countries with lower primary enrollment, larger impacts would be expected.

The largest impact was on enrollments in middle school, with enrollment rates for girls increasing by 7.2–9.3 percentage points (that is, from 67 percent to around 75 percent) and for boys by 3.5–5.8 percentage points (that

TABLE 9.12

Cumulative distribution of beneficiaries across national consumption deciles, in percent

Decile	PRAF (Honduras)	RPS (Nicaragua)	Progresa (Mexico)	SUF (Chile)
1	22.1	32.6	22	
2	42.5	55	39.5	67
3	66.9	70.2	51.9	
4	79.5	80.9	62.4	88.8
5	88.6	89.6	70.9	
6	93.5	94.3	80.5	97.2
7	97	97.1	87.8	
8	97.3	99.1	93	99.8
9	97.7	99.8	98	
10	100	100	100	100

Sources: For Chile, MIDEPLAN 1998; for Honduras, Nicaragua, and Mexico, MNPTSG 2002.

is, from 73 percent to around 78 percent). Most of this increase came during the transition year from primary to middle school (that is, from grade 6 to 7). Among those students who successfully completed primary school, Progresa increased enrollment rates in the first year of middle school by 14.8 percentage points for girls and 6.5 percentage points for boys. There is also evidence that much of this overall increase in education rates is due to an increase in continuation rates (that is, continued enrollment by those already enrolled), as opposed to encouraging those who had dropped out prior to the program to return to school.

The accumulated effect of increased schooling in grades 1–9 is consistent with an average increase in educational attainment of 0.66 years by grade 9, or from an average of 6.2 to 6.9 years of schooling. The impact on girls is higher, at 0.72 extra years of schooling compared to 0.64 years for boys. It has been estimated that these educational gains are consistent with an increase of 8 percent in the earnings of these children when they reach adulthood. The use of conditional transfers also seems to be a much more cost-effective instrument for generating educational improvements than the increase in the building of schools that accompanied the Progresa program (Coady and Parker 2002). However, one study explores whether the program could be more effective with respect to the objective of getting kids into school, and finds scope for substantial improvements (de Janvry and Sadoulet 2003). This is because many transfers go to children in very poor households who would have attended school in any case, especially at primary levels, while some children in nonpoor households who do not attend school are excluded from the program. Whether programs such as these should be designed to maximize impacts on changes in school attendance or on reducing extreme poverty is an assessment that has to be made in a country-specific context. Both objectives matter—and in this report significant weight is given to the second objective of extending the current social protection system to the poor—but there will be trade-offs between them.

Evaluations of both Progresa and RPS also find that the programs have reduced child labor. The results for Progresa indicate that the program led to a substantial reduction in the incidence of child labor among boys and girls in both salaried and nonsalaried activities. For example, labor force participation rates for boys decreased by 15–25 percent due to the program. Nonetheless, a substantial number of children continue to combine work with school.

With regard to RPS, Maluccio (2003) reports a decrease in the incidence of child labor by 8.8 percentage points (from 27 percent) for 10- to 13-year-olds. For those children who work, the number of hours worked also decreased by 9 hours "in the previous week" (from an initial level of around 24 hours). The levels of children who only attend school increased substantially, from 59 percent to 84 percent, with this impact attributed primarily to those children who were neither in school nor working prior to the onset of the RPS program.

Comparable results are not available for BE in Brazil due to the nonexperimental design of the program. There was no random element in the assignment of treatment to communities. An alternative approach, adopted by Bourguignon, Ferreira, and Leite (2003), is to simulate the impact of the conditional transfer on occupational decisions by the families of the children who would qualify for the program. Using a model estimated econometrically on household survey data from Brazil in 1999 and then simulating the program parameters, those authors find that BE had as substantial an impact on enrollment as did Progresa and RPS. Some 8.9 percent of children ages 10–15 in households classified as poor were not enrolled in school in 1999. Simulation results suggest that this number would be reduced by almost 60 percent to 3.7 percent under the transfer rules and amounts stipulated in BE.

Results for child labor are somewhat less clear in the BE case, however. The share of children enrolled in school and not working would rise by only 4 percentage points, from 68 percent to 72 percent. The greatest incidence of child labor would remain in the category of children who both study and work, which would account for approximately one-quarter of all children ages 10–15 who live in poor households.

Impacts on *health and nutrition* have also been substantial. Prior to the Progresa program, stunting levels (that is, low height-for-age) among children ages 12–36 months were very high, at 44 percent. The program had a substantial effect on reducing the probability of stunting, increasing the annual mean growth rate by 16 percent (or 1 centimeter per year) for children receiving treatment in this critical age range.

The potential for increases in the health and nutrition status of households as a whole can also be seen from the fact that median food expenditures in 1999 were 11 percent higher than in 1998. Since this increase is mainly due to higher expenditures on fruits, vegetables, and meat and other animal products, it is consistent with substantial improvements in the availability of crucial micronutrients.

By November 1999, the median calorific value of household diets had also risen by 7.1 percent, accompanied by a clear sense among households that they were eating better. Even controlling for the amount of the program transfer, there is evidence that the acquisition of calories from fruits, vegetables, and animal products increased consistently with a change in consumption behavior, which is one of the objectives of the nutrition information meetings. There is also evidence that this dimension of the program has had positive spillover effects on nonbeneficiaries in the same community. Finally, there is no evidence to support the view that nutritional supplementation would "crowd out" calorie consumption from other foods.

Progresa has also substantially increased preventive health care visits, including an increase of 8 percent in visits by women in their first trimester of pregnancy. This has in turn led to substantial improvements in the health of babies and pregnant women. There has also been a substantial decrease in the incidence of illness, ranging from a 25 percent decrease among newborns, a 19 percent decrease for children ages 0–2 years, and a 22 percent decrease among children ages 3–5 years. Child height has increased by between 1 and 4 percent and children are on average 3.5 percent heavier. The prevalence of anemia among children 24–48 months has decreased by 19 percent. Health status appears to have improved among adults as well, with this group reporting on average 19 percent fewer days with difficulties undertaking daily activities due to illness, 17 percent fewer days of being incapacitated due to illness, 18 percent fewer days in bed due to illness, and being able to walk 7.5 percent further without getting tired.

Impacts on current poverty levels

In both Progresa and RPS, transfers represent a substantial increase in the total incomes of beneficiary households, corresponding on average to around 20 percent. However, beneficiaries of these programs are required to forgo any existing transfers from other programs. Due to the potential for household responses that reduce income and consumption (for example, reduced income from child labor, changes in the adult labor supply, or reductions in private transfers), this means that the effect of the programs on consumption and welfare may in fact be somewhat lower. (For more on child labor and labor supply responses, see Skoufias and Parker 2001; for more on private transfers, see Teruel and Davis 2000.)

For example, there is evidence that the percentage of households receiving transfers from other government programs decreased due to Progresa, as did the income received by children ages 8–17 (Skoufias 2001). Simulations that ignore such responses suggest that, in these communities, the program decreases the poverty gap index by 30 percent and the severity of the poverty index by 45 percent (Skoufias, Davis, and de la Vega 2001). Regression estimates using actual outcomes (which incorporate responses) find that the poverty gap and poverty indices decline by 36 percent and 46 percent, respectively, suggesting that adverse indirect income effects are negligible (Handa and others 2000, Skoufias 2001). This interpretation is supported by results that find that the labor force participation rates of men and women have not decreased as a result of participation in Progresa (Skoufias and Parker 2001). In addition, one analysis did not find any evidence that program transfers crowd out previously existing public transfers (Teruel and Davis 2000).

Similar results were found for the RPS. That program increased household per capita expenditures by 19 percent, which is almost identical to the average magnitude of the other transfers (IFPRI 2001). These analyses of the impact of the program on consumption also help to highlight the importance of including a control group in studies. For example, over the course of the year in which the analysis was conducted, per capita consumption in RPS control households decreased by 16 percent due to the ongoing crisis in the coffee industry, while per capita consumption increased by around 4 percent among the households participating in the program. Thus, the consumption impact of the program arose from its ability to protect household incomes in the presence of an adverse economic shock.

As in the case of child labor, simulated results for the BE program suggest a less pronounced impact on current poverty levels. Bourguignon, Ferreira, and Leite (2003) find that, under the assumptions in their model, the incidence of poverty in Brazil would fall by 1.3 percentage points (from 30.1 percent) and that the FGT(2) measure of the severity of poverty would fall from 7.9 to 6.8 percent due to the BE program. Since targeting is assumed perfect in the simulation, these modest impacts are evidently due to the small size of the transfers. Larger poverty declines were obtained for larger (simulated) program budgets.

As a final word, one should also consider the costs of conditional cash transfer programs. The available evidence suggests that despite their various successes, these programs are not particularly expensive. Coady, Perez, and Vera-Llamas (2002) found that the administrative costs of Progresa accounted for less than 9 percent of total program costs, implying that it cost less than a peso for every ten pesos transferred to households. This number is relatively low compared to those calculated for other programs such the LICONSA (subsidized milk) and TORTIVALES (subsidized tortilla) programs, which cost 40 and 14 pesos per 100 transferred to beneficiaries, respectively. In addition, since Progresa has large up-front, establishment costs, this number should decrease over time. For example, if the costs associated with the geographic and household proxy-means targeting methods are removed, it costs less than 6 pesos to transfer 100 pesos to beneficiaries.

9.4. Conclusions

As discussed in chapters 7 and 8, deep reforms in economic institutions and policies and a broader, more egalitarian pattern of asset ownership are two fundamental components in the process of breaking with a long history of persistent inequalities in Latin America. This chapter has considered a third key element: a reform in the redistributive role of the state itself through both taxes and public expenditures. In all areas, this reform process should be complemented by changes in political institutions, as discussed in chapter 5.

Throughout this report, the authors' analysis has been guided by an understanding that existing taxation and expenditure patterns reflect complex political equilibria, which in turn are the result of a long social and economic history. From a normative viewpoint, however, the justification for taxation in any country is that taxes need to be raised in order either to pay for goods or services which, because of market failure, require subsidies or are better produced by the government, or to make transfers to other households because of equity-related motives.

From this normative point of view, it is probably true that most countries in the region raise inadequate levels of taxes. There have been modest gains in tax effort over the past few decades, including as recently as the 1990s. However, many countries in Latin America still have levels of taxes significantly below what is needed to support rapid social and economic development and efficient redistribution, and less than prevailing levels in countries in other regions with similar levels of income per capita. There is also substantial variation among the countries. For example, among the upper-middle-income countries, Brazil stands out for its high

tax effort and Mexico for its low tax receipts; among lower-income countries, Nicaragua is a case of a high and Guatemala of a low tax effort.

Can taxes be raised in a more progressive fashion? The authors have been very cautious about *average* incidence studies, while also recognizing that it is important to pay attention to the distributional dimensions of tax *reform*. The analysis in this report suggests that in most countries there is scope to both reduce the tax burden on the poorest members of society and raise more of the required additional revenue from higher income groups. This process is likely to involve eliminating or reducing informal quasi-taxes, such as the inflation tax and local corruption. It involves revisiting the detail of indirect taxes in order to reduce rates on particularly regressive excises and to keep or consider exemptions of basic food items from VATs. The process also involves enforcing the collection of property and income taxes and eliminating most exemptions and loopholes, without necessarily increasing the marginal rates of the latter.

On the spending side, there is wide variation across countries and even greater variation across programs. Much spending is regressive, but most is less regressive than income patterns. Pension systems stand out for their regressivity, as do tertiary education and health programs associated with social security systems. Overall, however, social spending tends to dampen inequality. The biggest redistributive impact generally comes from large-scale, near-universal programs, including in basic education and health. The highest level of targeting toward the poor comes from an impressively large range of social assistance and focused propoor programs. However, these contributions tend to be relatively small in the overall spending picture.

During the 1990s, there was a large increase in social spending per capita in most Latin American countries due to the combined effect of economic growth and an increase in both the ratio of total expenditures to GDP and the share of social spending in total expenditures. Although a significant part of these trends was related to large increases in pension outlays—which in Latin America are on average as badly distributed as incomes—there were also major increases in programs such as basic education and health and targeted social assistance. Indeed, significant increases in the largest social programs (that is, basic education and health) were highly redistributive, since access by high- and medium-income families was already significant and most of the increase in access benefited the bottom two quintiles in particular.

Latin America has experimented with a variety of targeted programs and mechanisms. Some of these have been highly successful in reaching the poor, while in others the leakage of subsidies to the nonpoor is quite large. Unfortunately, the better targeted programs tend to be small, and thus have limited coverage even among the poor (with some encouraging exceptions such as the Oportunidades program in Mexico). There thus seems to be a tradeoff between the degree of effective targeting and the degree of coverage of the poor. This may be partially explained by administrative limitations, but mostly by political economy considerations: although better, more progressive programs have been proposed, the beneficiaries of the older, larger, regressive expenditures are well-organized and resist reductions in their budgets. Under tight overall budget constraints, the tradeoff between large programs and well-targeted ones persists.

It is difficult to achieve support to enlarge highly targeted programs, precisely because they do not benefit middle-income groups. Obviously (as discussed in chapter 5), such limitations can be overcome through political leadership and the adequate "bundling" of programs to include both those with universal coverage and those that are highly targeted. In particular, the expansion of programs that attempt universal coverage can be successfully coupled with conditional, targeted transfers (such as those in Oportunidades in Mexico or Bolsa Família in Brazil) that provide cash transfers to the poor with the stipulation that families keep kids in school and attend maternal, child, and other health-related programs.

The third part of this chapter focused on CCT programs. A review of the evidence suggests that these programs rank among the most progressive in Latin America, and indeed in the developing world as a whole. They also tend to have a substantial impact on current income levels among beneficiaries, thus contributing to measurable reductions in current poverty levels. In addition, by their very nature they contribute to greater investments by the poor in their own human capital. The evidence suggests that these impacts are real in terms of both educational attainment and health outcome indicators, particularly in Mexico and Nicaragua.

Conditional cash transfers (CCTs) are not a new panacea. They are likely to be most successful when combined with supply-side interventions that improve the availability and quality of the public services in which beneficiaries have to participate. Such combined supply- and demand-side inter-ventions are expensive and require considerable administrative capacity. In addition, existing CCTs are relatively small (in comparison to national populations) and categorical in selection. Because participation is usually linked to school year cycles and other structures, beneficiary selection is not usually very flexible, which may impair their effectiveness as social insurance (or risk management) programs. Nevertheless, given their various attractive features, effort is being made to expand the coverage of and refine CCTs so that they provide better coverage against risk, whether aggregate or idiosyncratic.[21]

CCT programs have been proven to reach the poorest parts of the population in a way that other programs could not. They complement efforts aimed at improving the underlying distribution of assets because they enhance the supply of health and education services to poor people. CCTs also present fewer incentive problems than do traditional, unconditional transfers. If they can be expanded to provide universal social insurance coverage—a process that is currently being tested in Brazil—they may well deserve a place as one of the pillars of a new, more inclusive, social security system in Latin America. Such a system would, together with open and more democratic institutions, deeper markets, and more egalitarian asset distributions, represent a real break with the region's history of inequality.

Notes

1. The phrase "need not necessarily" deliberately glosses over centuries of debate, in both political philosophy and economics, over what constitutes social justice and what is the optimal role of the state in redistribution. Opinions have ranged from the view that the state should redistribute only in order to correct some past injustice or coercive expropriation (Nozick 1974), to the view that equality is a goal in its own right that should be given weight independently of the level involved. In between, a variety of utilitarian views indicate that social welfare depends on the distribution of outcome levels, with positive value placed on individual levels but at a nonincreasing rate. Within this school, the two extremes are Jeremy Bentham's view that social utility is simply the unweighted sum of individual utilities and John Rawls's argument that the entire weight should be placed on the welfare of the worst-off individual. These arguments are revised in greater detail in a number of places, including Sen 2000. While this is not the place to discuss them further, it should be acknowledged that readers' degree of sympathy with these different schools of thought is likely to affect the resonance of some of the arguments presented in this chapter, which is written largely from a utilitarian viewpoint.

2. There has, however, been some resurgence in export taxes in cases of recent crises (for example, in Argentina and the Dominican Republic).

3. For other recent reviews, see Martínez-Vázquez (2001) and Gemmell and Morrissey (2002). For an earlier, detailed examination of tax incidence in Latin America, see Bird and De Wulf (1973).

4. To illustrate, Harberger (2003) suggests that Engel, Galetovic, and Raddatz (1998) underestimate the regressivity of the Chilean system because they overestimate the progressivity of the corporate income tax in an open economy.

5. Engel, Galetovic, and Raddatz (1998) recognize this argument, but suggest that it is not relevant in the case of Chile, which is viewed essentially more like a European (that is, developed) than a Latin American country.

6. As one small illustration of this effectiveness, note that the VAT evasion rate in Chile is estimated to be about 20 percent, compared to the range of 30 percent (Uruguay) to 68 percent (Peru) that is estimated for other large Latin American countries (Sour 2003). Similarly, Lledo, Schneider, and Moore (2003) note that the shadow economy in Chile is 20 percent of GDP, compared to the Latin American average of 41 percent.

7. Results for Denmark come from a Danish study (as reported in translation in a comment on a draft of this report by Andreas Blom), while studies for the United Kingdom and Canada are reported in Bird (2003).

8. In theory, in order to minimize efficiency losses, different tax rates should be imposed on each commodity, with higher rates imposed on those goods and services for which changes in behavior are the smallest. To do so, however, requires much more information about how taxes alter behavior than is available in most countries. Moreover, this approach does not take administrative and equity concerns into account. For these reasons, in practice it seems generally advisable to impose a uniform tax rate to the greatest extent possible.

9. To illustrate, as Bird and Miller (1989) show in the case of Jamaica, exempting just five specific items from VAT reduces the burden imposed on the poorest 40 percent of the population by half.

10. The analysis by ECLAC is especially interesting because in several of the larger, more decentralized countries (including Argentina, Brazil, and Colombia, but not Mexico), the authors were able to include spending by local governments in the estimates of total social spending.

11. Net enrollment rates are the ratio of children attending school at a particular level and at the age appropriate for the level in relation to all children of that age; gross enrollment rates include children of all ages attending school at a particular level.

12. The immunization variables considered here are the percentage of children in the appropriate age bracket who receive the measles vaccine, three doses of Diptheria, Pertussis, and Tetanus (DPT), or all vaccines (that is, Bacillus Calmette-Guérin (BCG), three doses each of DPT and oral polio, and measles).

13. The concentration coefficient is an index of inequality along some dimension—in this case public spending—that is calculated in the same way as the Gini coefficient, but with individuals or household ranked according to their income.

14. For more on this point, see de Ferranti and others (2000), Glewwe and Hall (1998), Lustig (1995 and 1999), and Ganuza, Taylor, and Morley (1998).

15. For more on this point, see Perry (2003), Gavin and Perotti (1997), and Talvi and Vegh (2000). See also World Bank (2003e) on the nature and extent of the procyclicality of fiscal policy in Caribbean nations.

16. For reviews of these types of programs, see Patrinos (2002); Coady, Grosh, and Hoddinott (2003); Rawlings and Rubio (2003); and Morley and Coady (2003). In this chapter, focus is placed solely on programs in Latin America.

17. Although the transfers are paid in cash, the fact that they are conditional on the "consumption" of certain public services (such as attending public schools or visiting health care facilities) turns them into subsidies. Since those services are usually already provided free of charge, what is being subsidized are the indirect (for example, travel) costs involved or the opportunity costs of consumption. Key among the latter is the opportunity cost of a child's school attendance time, in terms of forgone earnings from child labor or the forgone value of domestic work. Since the transfers are subsidies, there must be a market failure that makes them preferable to unconditional cash transfers; otherwise, families could be trusted to make the optimal decisions for themselves with the additional resources. Three reasons are thought to justify the paternalism implicit in these conditions: (1) externalities are generated from keeping kids healthy and in school; (2) child health and education decisions are the outcome of an intrafamily bargain, and thus not necessarily optimal from the social viewpoint; and (3) discount rates among very poor families may be myopically high.

18. Bolsa Escola and Bolsa Alimentação—together with two other, smaller programs—were integrated into a single initiative, known as Bolsa Família, in late 2003. The discussion here is based on data from when the individual programs were still run separately.

19. Although similar programs exist in other countries in Latin America (for example, Subsidio Unico Familiar in Chile, Familias en Acción in Colombia, Bono Solidario in Ecuador, and the Program for Advancement through Health and Education in Jamaica), much less detail is available on their design, implementation, and impact. For more details on the programs detailed in this chapter, see Skoufias

(2001) and Coady (2000) on Progresa; Maluccio (2003) and IFPRI (2002) on RPS; IFPRI (2001) on PRAF; Bourguignon, Ferreira, and Leite (2003) on BE; and IFPRI (2003) on BA.

20. Initially, around 50 percent of households concentrated in the most marginal communities were deemed eligible. However, after discussions with community leaders, it was decided that the proportion of households being classified as poor was too low. This reflected the crudeness of the statistical procedures employed and the fact that having children was weighted too heavily in the classification outcome, which in effect disproportionately excluded very poor elderly couples and households without children. It was thus decided that the eligibility rate for Progresa would be increased to around 80 percent, with the result that many previously excluded households were now included.

21. See, for example, Camargo and Ferreira (2001), which partly inspired the consolidation of Brazil's cash transfer programs under Bolsa Família in 2003.

Statistical Appendix

These statistics and other results of the current study are periodically updated with new information. See http://www.depeco.econo.unlp.edu.ar/cedlas/wb/.

TABLE A.1

Household surveys in Latin America: coverage and characteristics

Country	Year (i)	Name of survey (ii)	Coverage (iii)	Sample size individuals (iv)	Population (in millions) (v)	Does the survey report			
						Expenditures? (vi)	Nonlabor income? (vii)	Nonmonetary income? (viii)	Implicit rent own housing? (ix)
Argentina	1992	EPH	Urban	67,776	33.4	No	Yes	No	No
	1996	EPH	Urban	63,387	35.2	No	Yes	No	No
	2001	EPH	Urban	48,048	37.5	No	Yes	No	No
Bolivia	1992	EIH	Urban	28,502	6.9	Yes	Yes	No	No
	1996	ENE	National	35,648	7.6	No	Yes	No	No
	1999	ECH	National	13,031	8.1	Yes	Yes	Yes	Yes
Brazil	1990	PNAD	National	306,493	144.7	No	Yes	No	No
	1995	PNAD	National	334,106	155.8	No	Yes	No	No
	2001	PNAD	National	378,837	172.6	No	Yes	No	No
Chile	1990	CASEN	National	105,189	13.1	No	Yes	Yes	Yes
	1996	CASEN	National	134,262	14.4	No	Yes	Yes	Yes
	2000	CASEN	National	252,748	15.2	No	Yes	Yes	Yes
Colombia	1992	ENH-FT	Urban	13,936	36.4	No	Yes	Yes	No
	1996	ENH-FT	National	137,423	39.3	No	Yes	Yes	No
	1999	ENH-FT	National	152,298	41.6	No	Yes	Yes	No
Costa Rica	1990	EHPM	National	36,272	3.0	No	Yes	No	No
	1995	EHPM	National	40,613	3.3	No	Yes	No	No
	2000	EHPM	National	40,509	3.6	No	Yes	No	No
Dominican Republic	1995	ENFT	National	23,730	7.7	No	No	No	No
	1997	ENFT	National	15,842	8.0	No	Yes	Yes	No
Ecuador	1994	ECV	National	20,873	11.2	Yes	Yes	Yes	Yes
	1998	ECV	National	26,129	12.2	Yes	Yes	Yes	Yes
El Salvador	1991	EHPM	National	90,624	5.4	No	Yes	No	Yes
	1995	EHPM	National	40,004	5.7	No	Yes	No	Yes
	2000	EHPM	National	71,665	6.3	No	Yes	Yes	No
Guatemala	2000	ENCOVI	National	37,771	11.4	Yes	Yes	Yes	Yes
Honduras	1990	EPHPM	National	47,056	4.8	No	No	No	No
	1995	EPHPM	National	29,804	5.6	No	No	No	No
	1999	EPHPM	National	33,772	6.4	No	Yes	Yes	No
Jamaica	1990	JSLC/LFS	National	8,269	2.4	Yes	Yes	No	No
	1996	JSLC/LFS	National	8,280	2.5	Yes	Yes	No	No
	1999	JSLC/LFS	National	8,921	2.6	Yes	Yes	No	No
Mexico	1992	ENIGH	National	50,862	86.4	Yes	Yes	Yes	Yes
	1996	ENIGH	National	64,916	92.7	Yes	Yes	Yes	Yes
	2000	ENIGH	National	42,535	98.0	Yes	Yes	Yes	Yes
Nicaragua	1993	EMNV	National	25,162	4.3	Yes	Yes	Yes	No
	1998	EMNV	National	22,423	4.8	Yes	Yes	Yes	No
Panamá	1991	EH-MO	National	38,000	2.4	No	Yes	No	No
	1995	EH-MO	National	40,320	2.6	No	Yes	No	No
	2000	EH-MO	National	39,562	2.9	No	Yes	No	No
Paraguay	1990	EH-MO	Urban	4,795	4.2	No	Yes	Yes	No
	1995	EH-MO	National	21,910	4.8	No	Yes	Yes	No
	1999	EPH	National	24,193	5.4	No	Yes	Yes	No
Perú	1991	ENNIV	National	11,845	22.0	Yes	Yes	Yes	Yes
	1994	ENNIV	National	18,662	23.1	Yes	Yes	Yes	Yes
	2000	ENNIV	National	19,961	25.7	Yes	Yes	Yes	Yes
Trinidad & Tobago	1992	ECV	National	6,220	1.2	Yes	No	No	No
Uruguay	1989	ECH	Urban	31,766	3.1	No	Yes	Yes	Yes
	1995	ECH	Urban	64,930	3.2	No	Yes	Yes	Yes
	2000	ECH	Urban	57,984	3.3	No	Yes	Yes	Yes
RB de Venezuela	1989	EHM	National	224,172	18.9	No	No	No	No
	1995	EHM	National	92,450	21.8	No	Yes	Yes	Yes
	1998	EHM	National	80,311	23.4	No	Yes	Yes	Yes

Note: EPH = Encuesta Permanente de Hogares; EIH = Encuesta Integrada de Hogares; ENE = Encuesta Nacional de Empleo; ECH = Encuesta Continua de Hogares; PNAD = Pesquisa Nacional por Amostra de Domicilios; CASEN = Encuesta de Caracterización Socioeconómica Nacional; ENH-FT = Encuesta Nacional de Hogares-Fuerza de Trabajo; EHPM = Encuesta de Hogares de Propositos Multiples; ENCOVI = Encuesta Nacional sobre Condiciones de Vida; ENFT = Encuesta Nacional de Fuerza de Trabajo; ECV = Encuesta de Condiciones de Vida; EPHPM = Encuesta Permanente de Hogares de Propositos Multiples; JSLC = Jamaica Survey of Living Conditions; LFS = Labor Force Survey; ENIGH = Encuesta Nacional de Ingresos y Gastos de los Hogares; EMNV and ENNIV = Encuesta Nacional de Hogares Sobre Medicion de Niveles de Vida; EH-MO = Encuesta de Hogares-Mano de Obra; EHM = Encuesta de Hogares por Muestreo.

TABLE A.2

Distribution of household per capita income: share of deciles and income ratios

Country	Share of deciles										Income ratios		
	1 (i)	2 (ii)	3 (iii)	4 (iv)	5 (v)	6 (vi)	7 (vii)	8 (viii)	9 (ix)	10 (x)	10/1 (xi)	90/10 (xii)	95/80 (xiii)
Argentina													
1992	1.8	3.1	4.1	5.2	6.3	7.7	9.4	12.1	16.6	33.8	18.5	7.8	2.0
1996	1.4	2.7	3.7	4.7	5.9	7.3	9.2	11.9	16.8	36.4	25.4	9.6	2.2
1998	1.3	2.6	3.6	4.6	5.7	7.0	9.0	11.8	16.6	37.8	29.0	10.3	2.4
2001	1.0	2.1	3.1	4.1	5.4	6.9	9.0	12.0	17.5	38.9	39.1	13.8	2.4
Bolivia													
Urban													
1992	1.7	2.8	3.7	4.6	5.6	6.8	8.5	11.1	15.6	39.5	23.1	8.4	2.3
1996	1.7	2.7	3.5	4.4	5.4	6.6	8.2	10.9	15.9	40.8	24.5	9.3	2.4
National													
1996	0.5	1.5	2.6	3.7	5.0	6.4	8.4	11.1	16.4	44.4	81.2	20.8	2.5
1999	0.3	1.0	2.3	3.6	5.1	6.8	8.9	11.9	17.8	42.3	143.5	38.6	2.4
Brazil													
1990	0.8	1.5	2.2	3.0	4.1	5.4	7.3	10.4	16.5	48.7	63.2	19.2	3.0
1995	0.8	1.6	2.4	3.3	4.3	5.5	7.4	10.3	16.3	48.1	58.0	17.6	3.0
2001	0.9	1.7	2.5	3.4	4.5	5.8	7.5	10.4	16.1	47.2	54.4	16.1	2.9
Chile													
1990	1.3	2.3	3.0	3.8	4.8	6.0	7.6	10.1	15.4	45.8	36.2	11.1	2.9
1996	1.2	2.2	3.0	3.8	4.7	5.9	7.6	10.3	15.7	45.5	36.4	11.5	2.7
2000	1.2	2.2	2.9	3.7	4.7	5.8	7.4	10.0	15.2	47.0	40.6	11.4	2.9
Colombia													
Bogotá													
1992	1.0	2.2	3.0	3.9	4.9	6.3	8.1	11.0	16.8	42.7	42.0	12.9	2.8
1996	1.7	2.6	3.4	4.2	5.2	6.4	7.8	10.2	16.1	42.5	25.6	10.1	2.7
National													
1996	0.9	2.1	3.0	3.9	5.0	6.2	7.9	10.4	15.1	45.4	50.3	12.3	2.7
1999	0.8	1.9	2.8	3.7	4.8	6.1	7.7	10.3	15.4	46.5	57.8	14.5	2.8
Costa Rica													
1990	1.3	2.9	4.1	5.1	6.3	7.8	9.7	12.3	16.4	34.0	25.5	9.1	2.1
1995	1.4	2.9	4.0	5.1	6.3	7.7	9.6	12.2	16.5	34.2	24.1	9.0	2.0
2000	1.4	2.8	3.9	5.0	6.1	7.6	9.5	12.2	16.7	34.8	25.1	9.5	2.2
Dominican Rep.													
1995	1.5	2.6	3.5	4.4	5.4	6.7	8.3	10.9	15.6	41.2	26.8	9.4	2.5
1997	1.4	2.6	3.6	4.6	5.8	7.1	8.9	11.5	15.8	38.6	28.4	9.5	2.3
Ecuador													
1994	0.9	2.2	3.1	4.1	5.2	6.6	8.2	10.6	15.5	43.7	51.2	12.9	2.6
1998	0.7	1.9	2.9	3.9	5.0	6.4	8.3	10.8	15.9	44.2	63.6	15.2	2.6
El Salvador													
1991	1.1	2.3	3.3	4.3	5.4	6.7	8.5	11.1	15.7	41.5	37.4	10.8	2.4
1995	1.0	2.4	3.4	4.5	5.7	7.1	8.9	11.4	16.1	39.6	38.3	11.1	2.3
2000	0.9	2.0	3.1	4.2	5.5	6.9	8.8	11.4	16.5	40.6	47.4	14.1	2.3
Guatemala													
2000	0.7	1.7	2.6	3.6	4.7	6.1	7.8	10.4	15.6	46.8	63.3	16.6	2.9
Honduras													
1990	0.9	1.8	2.7	3.6	4.7	6.0	7.9	10.5	15.7	46.1	52.6	14.7	2.6
1995	1.0	2.0	2.8	3.8	4.9	6.3	8.0	10.8	16.2	44.2	44.9	13.4	2.5
1999	0.9	1.9	2.8	3.9	5.1	6.7	8.5	11.4	16.7	42.2	49.1	15.1	2.5
Jamaica													
1990	1.2	2.3	3.3	4.2	5.4	7.1	9.1	11.5	15.7	40.1	32.7	10.8	2.3
1996	0.9	2.1	3.1	4.0	5.3	6.7	8.2	10.9	16.2	42.7	46.9	13.7	2.6
1999	1.1	2.3	3.3	4.3	5.5	7.0	8.9	11.5	16.1	40.1	35.5	11.2	2.3
Mexico													
1992	1.0	2.1	3.0	4.0	5.0	6.3	7.9	10.4	15.6	44.8	47.1	13.2	2.5
1996	1.0	2.2	3.2	4.1	5.2	6.5	8.2	10.8	15.6	43.3	41.9	11.7	2.6
2000	1.0	2.1	3.1	4.1	5.2	6.5	8.2	10.7	16.0	43.1	45.0	12.9	2.5
Nicaragua													
1993	0.8	1.8	2.8	3.8	4.9	6.5	8.6	11.4	16.5	43.0	55.3	15.5	2.4
1998	0.8	1.9	2.9	4.0	5.2	6.6	8.3	11.0	15.6	43.9	56.2	14.6	2.3
Panama													
1991	0.5	1.5	2.7	3.8	5.0	6.4	8.6	11.9	17.7	42.0	80.5	22.7	2.4
1995	0.6	1.7	2.7	3.8	5.0	6.5	8.5	11.6	17.0	42.5	69.4	17.7	2.5
2000	0.7	1.7	2.7	3.8	4.9	6.3	8.3	11.3	17.0	43.3	62.3	18.2	2.6
Paraguay													
1995	0.7	1.5	2.4	3.4	4.5	6.0	7.8	10.5	15.6	47.5	67.9	18.0	2.8
1999	0.6	1.6	2.7	3.8	5.0	6.5	8.4	11.2	16.5	43.8	70.4	19.0	2.4
Peru													
Regions													
1991	1.1	2.5	3.8	5.1	6.5	8.1	9.9	12.6	16.8	33.7	30.9	11.3	2.0
1994	1.0	2.5	3.7	4.9	6.1	7.8	9.7	12.2	16.4	35.6	34.1	11.0	2.0
National													
1994	1.0	2.4	3.6	4.9	6.1	7.6	9.7	12.2	16.6	35.9	36.5	11.3	2.0
2000	0.8	2.3	3.6	4.8	6.3	7.8	9.5	12.0	16.0	36.9	46.2	12.2	2.1
Trinidad & Tobago													
1992	0.9	2.3	3.6	4.9	6.0	7.4	9.2	11.9	17.2	36.6	40.6	12.7	2.1
Uruguay													
1989	2.0	3.4	4.5	5.6	6.8	8.0	9.7	11.9	15.7	32.4	16.0	6.5	1.9
1995	1.8	3.2	4.4	5.5	6.7	8.0	9.7	12.2	16.4	32.1	17.6	7.6	2.0
2000	1.8	3.0	4.1	5.2	6.4	7.8	9.5	12.1	16.6	33.5	18.9	8.1	2.1
RB de Venezuela													
1989	1.7	3.1	4.2	5.3	6.5	7.9	9.7	12.2	16.3	33.2	19.5	7.9	2.0
1995	1.5	2.8	3.8	4.9	6.2	7.6	9.4	11.9	16.3	35.6	23.6	8.7	2.1
1998	1.3	2.7	3.7	4.9	6.1	7.6	9.4	12.0	16.7	35.6	28.2	9.5	2.2

Notes: Column (xi) = income ratio between deciles 10 and 1; column (xii) = income ratio between percentiles 90 and 10; column (xiii) = income ratio between percentiles 95 and 80. Data for Dominican Republic (1995) and for Honduras, Trinidad and Tobago, and RB de Venezuela (1989) include only monetary income from labor sources.
Source: Authors' calculations based on microdata from household surveys.

TABLE A.3

Distribution of household per capita income: inequality indices

Country	Gini (i)	Theil (ii)	CV (iii)	A(.5) (iv)	A(1) (v)	A(2) (vi)	E(0) (vii)	E(2) (viii)
Argentina								
1992	44.7	0.362	1.074	0.162	0.295	0.503	0.349	0.576
1996	48.2	0.435	1.249	0.191	0.343	0.588	0.419	0.780
1998	49.5	0.451	1.208	0.200	0.359	0.599	0.444	0.730
2001	52.2	0.497	1.276	0.223	0.405	0.677	0.517	0.814
Bolivia								
Urban								
1992	49.5	0.490	1.408	0.203	0.346	0.541	0.425	0.991
1996	51.1	0.532	1.539	0.216	0.363	0.551	0.450	1.185
National								
1996	57.6	0.675	1.846	0.282	0.493	0.790	0.679	1.704
1999	57.8	0.633	1.643	0.287	0.532	0.851	0.760	1.349
Brazil								
1990	61.2	0.767	2.062	0.310	0.511	0.739	0.716	2.125
1995	60.0	0.735	1.875	0.299	0.494	0.722	0.681	1.759
2001	59.0	0.713	1.866	0.289	0.481	0.714	0.655	1.740
Chile								
1990	55.9	0.668	1.944	0.262	0.430	0.655	0.562	1.889
1996	56.1	0.652	1.803	0.261	0.431	0.651	0.564	1.626
2000	57.1	0.703	2.022	0.274	0.447	0.674	0.592	2.043
Colombia								
Bogotá								
1992	54.6	0.569	1.440	0.246	0.434	0.778	0.569	1.037
1996	52.4	0.540	1.422	0.224	0.374	0.551	0.469	1.010
National								
1996	56.1	0.707	2.811	0.270	0.447	0.701	0.593	3.951
1999	57.6	0.721	2.191	0.282	0.469	0.728	0.633	2.399
Costa Rica								
1990	45.6	0.381	1.111	0.173	0.321	0.581	0.387	0.617
1995	45.7	0.383	1.111	0.173	0.319	0.573	0.384	0.617
2000	46.5	0.389	1.083	0.177	0.326	0.581	0.396	0.586
Dominican Rep.								
1995	51.5	0.542	1.578	0.221	0.371	0.563	0.462	1.244
1997	49.7	0.498	1.520	0.207	0.359	0.580	0.444	1.155
Ecuador								
1994	54.8	0.627	1.758	0.255	0.436	0.706	0.573	1.546
1998	56.2	0.658	1.866	0.269	0.463	0.755	0.623	1.741
El Salvador								
1991	52.7	0.585	1.867	0.236	0.402	0.655	0.514	1.742
1995	51.3	0.526	1.511	0.223	0.393	0.669	0.499	1.141
2000	53.2	0.582	1.914	0.241	0.422	0.699	0.548	1.831
Guatemala								
2000	58.3	0.697	1.823	0.285	0.482	0.739	0.656	1.662
Honduras								
1990	57.8	0.733	2.295	0.283	0.466	0.696	0.627	2.633
1995	56.1	0.653	1.793	0.264	0.444	0.678	0.586	1.608
1999	55.0	0.586	1.525	0.251	0.440	0.705	0.580	1.163
Jamaica								
1990	51.7	0.520	1.406	0.222	0.388	0.637	0.491	0.988
1996	54.4	0.583	1.535	0.247	0.427	0.685	0.558	1.178
1999	52.0	0.585	1.954	0.232	0.394	0.627	0.501	1.909
Mexico								
1992	55.9	0.667	1.935	0.264	0.441	0.685	0.582	1.872
1996	54.4	0.616	1.864	0.249	0.424	0.683	0.551	1.738
2000	54.6	0.609	1.692	0.251	0.429	0.693	0.561	1.431
Nicaragua								
1993	55.9	0.629	1.711	0.263	0.454	0.719	0.605	1.463
1998	55.9	0.693	2.202	0.270	0.455	0.719	0.606	2.424
Panama								
1991	56.4	0.603	1.518	0.267	0.483	0.784	0.659	1.153
1995	55.9	0.593	1.465	0.261	0.469	0.771	0.632	1.073
2000	56.4	0.613	1.531	0.265	0.466	0.748	0.626	1.172
Paraguay								
1995	59.5	0.728	1.830	0.297	0.497	0.742	0.688	1.675
1999	56.8	0.690	2.370	0.277	0.477	0.760	0.649	2.808
Peru								
Regions								
1991	46.5	0.394	1.131	0.182	0.344	0.642	0.422	0.640
1994	47.9	0.444	1.338	0.196	0.362	0.666	0.449	0.895
National								
1994	48.6	0.453	1.344	0.200	0.371	0.676	0.463	0.903
2000	49.4	0.477	1.358	0.211	0.392	0.721	0.497	0.923
Trinidad & Tobago								
1992	49.5	0.472	1.480	0.208	0.383	0.687	0.482	1.095
Uruguay								
1989	42.2	0.364	1.383	0.151	0.268	0.457	0.311	0.956
1995	42.7	0.326	0.982	0.149	0.275	0.487	0.321	0.482
2000	44.6	0.357	1.040	0.161	0.293	0.497	0.347	0.541
RB de Venezuela								
1989	44.2	0.360	1.087	0.161	0.294	0.521	0.348	0.591
1995	46.9	0.418	1.230	0.183	0.327	0.571	0.398	0.757
1998	47.6	0.420	1.216	0.188	0.345	0.626	0.424	0.740

Notes: CV = coefficient of variation. A(ε) refers to the Atkinson index with a CES function with parameter ε. E(ε) refers to the generalized entropy index with parameter ε. E(1) = Theil. Data for Dominican Republic (1995) and Honduras, Trinidad and Tobago, and Venezuela (1989) include only monetary income from labor sources.
Source: Authors' calculations based on microdata from household surveys.

TABLE A.4

Distribution of equalized household income: share of deciles and income ratios

Country	Share of deciles										Income ratios		
	1 (i)	2 (ii)	3 (iii)	4 (iv)	5 (v)	6 (vi)	7 (vii)	8 (viii)	9 (ix)	10 (x)	10/1 (xi)	90/10 (xii)	95/80 (xiii)
Argentina													
1992	2.0	3.4	4.4	5.4	6.5	7.9	9.5	12.0	16.5	32.4	15.9	7.0	2.0
1996	1.7	3.0	4.0	5.0	6.2	7.6	9.3	11.9	16.6	34.7	20.9	8.4	2.1
2001	1.1	2.4	3.4	4.4	5.6	7.1	9.0	11.9	17.2	37.8	32.9	11.8	2.4
Bolivia													
Urban													
1992	1.9	3.0	3.9	4.8	5.9	7.0	8.6	11.1	15.4	38.2	20.5	7.5	2.3
1996	1.8	2.9	3.8	4.6	5.6	6.8	8.4	10.9	15.7	39.6	21.6	8.1	2.3
National													
1996	0.6	1.6	2.8	4.0	5.3	6.7	8.7	11.3	16.3	42.8	72.9	18.6	2.5
1999	0.3	1.1	2.5	3.9	5.5	7.2	9.1	12.1	17.6	40.7	126.5	33.8	2.4
Brazil													
1990	0.9	1.7	2.4	3.2	4.3	5.7	7.5	10.5	16.6	47.3	53.4	17.1	2.9
1995	1.0	1.8	2.6	3.5	4.5	5.7	7.6	10.4	16.3	46.6	48.1	15.3	2.9
2001	1.0	1.9	2.8	3.7	4.7	5.9	7.7	10.5	16.1	45.7	45.4	14.0	2.8
Chile													
1990	1.4	2.5	3.2	4.0	4.9	6.0	7.6	10.1	15.3	45.0	32.5	10.1	2.9
1996	1.4	2.4	3.1	4.0	4.9	6.0	7.7	10.3	15.5	44.7	32.7	10.5	2.7
2000	1.3	2.3	3.1	3.9	4.8	5.9	7.4	10.0	15.0	46.3	37.0	10.4	2.8
Colombia													
Bogotá													
1992	1.1	2.4	3.3	4.1	5.2	6.7	8.4	11.2	17.0	40.5	36.1	11.7	2.7
1996	1.8	2.8	3.6	4.5	5.4	6.5	7.9	10.2	15.9	41.4	23.1	9.1	2.7
National													
1996	1.0	2.3	3.3	4.2	5.3	6.5	8.1	10.5	14.9	43.9	44.1	11.1	2.7
1999	0.9	2.1	3.1	4.0	5.0	6.3	7.9	10.4	15.3	45.0	51.3	13.0	2.8
Costa Rica													
1990	1.4	3.1	4.4	5.5	6.6	8.0	9.8	12.2	16.2	32.9	22.9	8.3	2.1
1995	1.5	3.1	4.3	5.4	6.6	7.9	9.7	12.1	16.2	33.1	21.5	8.0	2.0
2000	1.5	3.0	4.2	5.3	6.4	7.8	9.7	12.2	16.4	33.5	22.4	8.7	2.2
Dominican Rep.													
1995	1.6	2.7	3.6	4.6	5.5	6.8	8.5	10.8	15.6	40.2	24.5	8.9	2.4
1997	1.5	2.8	3.8	4.9	6.0	7.3	9.1	11.6	15.8	37.3	25.3	8.9	2.2
Ecuador													
1994	0.9	2.3	3.4	4.3	5.5	6.8	8.4	10.7	15.2	42.3	45.4	11.2	2.6
1998	0.7	2.1	3.2	4.2	5.3	6.7	8.5	10.9	15.8	42.6	57.5	13.7	2.5
El Salvador													
1991	1.2	2.6	3.6	4.7	5.7	7.0	8.7	11.2	15.5	39.7	32.6	9.4	2.3
1995	1.1	2.6	3.7	4.8	6.0	7.3	9.0	11.4	15.9	38.1	33.7	9.9	2.3
2000	0.9	2.2	3.3	4.4	5.7	7.2	9.0	11.5	16.2	39.6	43.0	12.8	2.2
Guatemala													
2000	0.8	1.9	2.9	4.0	5.1	6.4	8.2	10.6	15.6	44.6	54.2	14.6	2.8
Honduras													
1990	1.0	2.0	3.0	3.9	5.0	6.4	8.2	10.9	15.9	43.9	45.7	13.2	2.5
1995	1.1	2.1	3.1	4.1	5.2	6.6	8.4	11.0	16.0	42.5	39.3	11.9	2.4
1999	1.0	2.0	3.0	4.2	5.4	7.0	8.8	11.6	16.7	40.3	42.4	13.5	2.4
Jamaica													
1990	1.4	2.6	3.5	4.5	5.7	7.4	9.3	11.6	15.5	38.4	28.3	8.9	2.4
1996	1.1	2.3	3.3	4.4	5.7	7.2	8.9	11.0	16.0	40.1	37.5	11.7	2.5
1999	1.3	2.5	3.6	4.7	5.9	7.4	9.4	11.9	16.1	37.1	28.4	10.1	2.0
Mexico													
1992	1.1	2.3	3.3	4.2	5.3	6.5	8.1	10.5	15.5	43.2	40.7	11.7	2.5
1996	1.2	2.4	3.4	4.3	5.4	6.7	8.3	10.8	15.6	41.8	36.1	10.6	2.6
2000	1.1	2.3	3.3	4.3	5.4	6.7	8.5	10.9	15.9	41.5	39.0	11.8	2.6
Nicaragua													
1993	0.9	2.0	3.0	4.0	5.2	6.8	8.8	11.6	16.4	41.4	48.1	14.9	2.4
1998	0.8	2.0	3.1	4.2	5.5	6.8	8.6	11.1	15.5	42.3	50.0	13.5	2.2
Panama													
1991	0.6	1.6	2.9	4.0	5.3	6.8	8.8	11.9	17.5	40.5	71.6	21.1	2.4
1995	0.7	1.9	3.0	4.1	5.3	6.8	8.7	11.7	16.8	41.0	60.2	16.3	2.5
2000	0.8	1.9	3.0	4.1	5.2	6.6	8.5	11.4	16.9	41.5	53.5	15.7	2.5
Paraguay													
1995	0.8	1.7	2.6	3.6	4.8	6.3	8.1	10.6	15.4	46.1	58.6	15.7	2.7
1999	0.7	1.7	2.9	4.2	5.3	6.8	8.6	11.3	16.4	42.1	60.3	17.0	2.4
Peru													
Regions													
1991	1.1	2.6	4.0	5.3	6.7	8.2	10.1	12.6	16.6	32.7	28.6	10.5	1.9
1994	1.2	2.7	4.0	5.3	6.4	8.0	9.9	12.3	16.3	33.9	29.4	9.6	1.9
National													
1994	1.1	2.6	4.0	5.2	6.4	7.9	9.8	12.3	16.5	34.2	31.4	10.0	1.9
2000	0.9	2.4	3.8	5.1	6.5	8.1	9.7	12.0	15.9	35.6	41.0	11.0	2.0
Trinidad & Tobago													
1992	1.0	2.6	3.9	5.2	6.3	7.7	9.4	12.1	17.0	34.8	35.5	11.6	2.1
Uruguay													
1989	2.3	3.7	4.7	5.7	6.8	8.1	9.7	11.8	15.5	31.7	14.0	5.8	1.9
1995	2.1	3.5	4.7	5.7	6.8	8.1	9.8	12.2	16.2	31.0	15.0	6.7	2.0
2000	2.0	3.4	4.4	5.5	6.6	7.9	9.6	11.9	16.4	32.3	15.8	7.1	2.0
RB de Venezuela													
1989	1.9	3.4	4.5	5.6	6.8	8.2	9.9	12.3	16.0	31.4	16.6	6.9	1.9
1995	1.7	3.1	4.2	5.3	6.5	7.9	9.6	12.0	16.0	33.8	20.2	7.6	2.0
1998	1.4	2.9	4.0	5.2	6.4	7.9	9.6	12.1	16.5	34.0	24.6	8.4	2.1

Notes: Column (xi) = income ratio between deciles 10 and 1; column (xii) = income ratio between percentiles 90 and 10, and column (xiii) = income ratio between percentiles 95 and 80. Data for Dominican Republic (1995) and Honduras, Trinidad and Tobago, and Venezuela (1989) include only monetary income from labor sources.
Source: Authors' calculations based on microdata from household surveys.

289

TABLE A.5

Distribution of equivalized household income: inequality indices

Country	Gini (i)	Theil (ii)	CV (iii)	A(.5) (iv)	A(1) (v)	A(2) (vi)	E(0) (vii)	E(2) (viii)
Argentina								
1992	42.6	0.327	0.996	0.147	0.269	0.463	0.313	0.496
1996	45.8	0.391	1.155	0.173	0.311	0.541	0.373	0.667
2001	50.4	0.461	1.210	0.207	0.376	0.639	0.471	0.732
Bolivia								
Urban								
1992	47.7	0.457	1.349	0.190	0.324	0.515	0.392	0.910
1996	49.3	0.496	1.473	0.202	0.340	0.522	0.416	1.085
National								
1996	55.8	0.630	1.727	0.267	0.473	0.777	0.640	1.492
1999	55.9	0.587	1.487	0.271	0.511	0.836	0.715	1.105
Brazil								
1990	59.5	0.717	1.916	0.293	0.486	0.710	0.666	1.836
1995	58.3	0.684	1.752	0.280	0.466	0.690	0.628	1.535
2001	57.2	0.665	1.780	0.271	0.453	0.681	0.603	1.584
Chile								
1990	54.7	0.635	1.837	0.251	0.412	0.632	0.531	1.687
1996	54.9	0.624	1.722	0.251	0.414	0.631	0.535	1.483
2000	56.1	0.681	1.955	0.265	0.432	0.655	0.565	1.911
Colombia								
Bogotá								
1992	52.4	0.510	1.295	0.226	0.407	0.761	0.522	0.838
1996	50.8	0.508	1.374	0.211	0.354	0.525	0.437	0.944
National								
1996	54.3	0.662	2.735	0.253	0.423	0.677	0.551	3.740
1999	55.8	0.676	2.102	0.266	0.446	0.706	0.591	2.209
Costa Rica								
1990	43.9	0.350	1.039	0.160	0.300	0.559	0.357	0.540
1995	44.0	0.352	1.043	0.160	0.298	0.545	0.353	0.544
2000	44.6	0.354	1.008	0.163	0.304	0.553	0.363	0.508
Dominican Rep.								
1995	50.2	0.516	1.524	0.210	0.354	0.543	0.437	1.161
1997	48.1	0.462	1.438	0.194	0.339	0.557	0.413	1.033
Ecuador								
1994	53.0	0.585	1.670	0.240	0.415	0.688	0.535	1.395
1998	54.3	0.606	1.709	0.252	0.441	0.740	0.581	1.460
El Salvador								
1991	50.5	0.536	1.726	0.218	0.375	0.626	0.470	1.490
1995	49.4	0.490	1.462	0.207	0.368	0.641	0.459	1.068
2000	51.8	0.558	1.839	0.230	0.404	0.681	0.518	1.690
Guatemala								
2000	56.0	0.632	1.659	0.263	0.450	0.713	0.599	1.376
Honduras								
1990	55.6	0.664	2.083	0.262	0.438	0.672	0.577	2.169
1995	54.1	0.598	1.657	0.245	0.417	0.653	0.540	1.373
1999	53.0	0.537	1.414	0.234	0.415	0.680	0.535	1.000
Jamaica								
1990	49.6	0.484	1.362	0.206	0.362	0.611	0.449	0.927
1996	51.5	0.518	1.406	0.222	0.391	0.648	0.496	0.989
1999	49.0	0.513	1.756	0.206	0.357	0.584	0.441	1.541
Mexico								
1992	53.9	0.612	1.773	0.246	0.415	0.659	0.536	1.571
1996	52.5	0.571	1.770	0.233	0.398	0.655	0.508	1.566
2000	52.7	0.558	1.568	0.233	0.404	0.665	0.518	1.229
Nicaragua								
1993	54.2	0.583	1.602	0.246	0.431	0.697	0.564	1.283
1998	54.1	0.639	2.008	0.253	0.432	0.699	0.565	2.017
Panama								
1991	54.7	0.561	1.423	0.252	0.460	0.766	0.616	1.012
1995	54.0	0.549	1.378	0.244	0.443	0.749	0.585	0.949
2000	54.4	0.565	1.440	0.246	0.437	0.721	0.575	1.037
Paraguay								
1995	57.8	0.693	1.808	0.282	0.473	0.717	0.640	1.635
1999	54.9	0.640	2.314	0.259	0.451	0.735	0.599	2.677
Peru								
Regions								
1991	45.2	0.369	1.061	0.172	0.329	0.625	0.399	0.563
1994	45.9	0.399	1.207	0.179	0.335	0.635	0.409	0.729
National								
1994	46.4	0.406	1.213	0.183	0.344	0.647	0.421	0.735
2000	47.7	0.443	1.284	0.198	0.371	0.700	0.464	0.825
Trinidad & Tobago								
1992	47.2	0.415	1.277	0.188	0.355	0.661	0.438	0.815
Uruguay								
1989	40.8	0.344	1.359	0.142	0.250	0.425	0.287	0.923
1995	40.9	0.297	0.923	0.136	0.252	0.448	0.290	0.426
2000	42.5	0.324	0.980	0.146	0.266	0.454	0.309	0.480
RB de Venezuela								
1989	41.7	0.317	0.989	0.144	0.266	0.484	0.309	0.489
1995	44.5	0.374	1.138	0.165	0.300	0.539	0.356	0.647
1998	45.5	0.382	1.133	0.173	0.321	0.598	0.387	0.642

Notes: CV = coefficient of variation. A(ε) refers to the Atkinson index with a CES function with parameter ε. E(ε) refers to the generalized entropy index with parameter ε. E(1) = Theil. Data for Dominican Republic (1995) and Honduras, Trinidad and Tobago, and Venezuela (1989) include only monetary income from labor sources.
Source: Author's calculations based on microdata from household surveys.

TABLE A.6

Distribution of equivalized household income: Gini coefficients

Countries	Early 90s (i)	Mid-90s (ii)	Early 00s (iii)	Change (iv)
Argentina	42.6	45.8	50.4	7.7
Bolivia	54.3	55.8	55.9	1.6
Brazil	59.5	58.3	57.2	−2.3
Chile	54.7	54.9	56.1	1.4
Colombia	55.9	54.3	55.8	−0.1
Costa Rica	43.9	44.0	44.6	0.8
El Salvador	50.5	49.4	51.8	1.3
Honduras	55.6	54.1	53.0	−2.6
Jamaica	49.6	51.5	49.0	−0.6
Mexico	53.9	52.5	52.7	−1.2
Nicaragua	54.2		54.1	−0.1
Panama	54.7	54.0	54.4	−0.3
Peru	45.7	46.4	47.7	2.0
Uruguay	40.8	40.9	42.5	1.7
RB de Venezuela	41.7	44.5	45.5	3.8
Average (nonweighted)	50.5	50.7	51.4	0.9
Average (weighted)	51.9	51.2	51.5	−0.4
Dominican Rep.		50.2	48.1	
Ecuador		53.0	54.3	
Guatemala			56.0	
Paraguay		57.8	54.9	
Trinidad & Tobago	47.2			

Notes: The Gini coefficients for Bolivia and Colombia for the early 1990s were estimated by extrapolating the changes in the Gini for urban areas (see table 3.5). A similar procedure was applied for Peru using the areas covered in 1991. To compute the Latin American average for the mid-1990s, a Gini of 54.1 was assumed for Nicaragua.
Source: Authors' calculations based on microdata from household surveys.

TABLE A.7

Distribution of different concepts of household income among individuals, Gini coefficients

Country	Per capita income (i)	Equivalized income A (ii)	Equivalized income B (iii)	Equivalized income C (iv)	Equivalized income D (v)	Equivalized income E (vi)	Per capita income Only Urban (vii)	Per capita income Only rural (viii)	Per capita income Only labor (ix)	Per capita income Only monetary (x)	Per capita income Only labor monetary (xi)	Per capita income Urban labor monetary (xii)	Total household income (xiii)	Equivalized income A Age 0-10 (xiv)	Equivalized income A Age 20-30 (xv)	Equivalized income A Age 40-50 (xvi)	Equivalized income A Age 60-70 (xvii)
Argentina																	
1992	44.7	42.6	41.9	41.9	41.3	43.0	44.7		44.5	44.7	44.5	44.5	44.2	42.9	40.0	44.1	41.8
1996	48.2	45.8	44.8	45.0	44.1	46.3	48.2		47.9	48.2	47.9	47.9	45.3	45.0	43.8	48.0	42.7
2001	52.2	50.4	49.4	49.6	48.8	50.8	52.2		53.3	52.2	53.3	53.3	47.9	51.9	46.5	50.7	47.2
Bolivia																	
Urban																	
1992	49.5	47.7	47.2	47.1	46.6	47.9	49.5		49.3	49.5	49.3	49.3	48.7	47.1	46.6	49.7	48.9
1996	51.1	49.3	48.7	48.5	48.1	49.3	51.0		51.3	51.1	51.3	51.3	51.0	49.2	47.8	48.7	49.5
National																	
1996	57.6	55.8	55.4	55.1	54.8	55.8	50.7	59.1	57.4	57.6	57.4	51.1	58.0	54.9	52.4	57.5	61.7
1999	57.8	55.9	55.3	55.2	54.8	56.1	48.2	63.0	58.3	57.7	58.4	48.9	56.8	57.0	50.3	55.6	60.9
Brazil																	
1990	61.2	59.5	58.7	58.9	58.2	59.9	58.6	53.9	61.0	61.2	61.0	58.5	58.3	59.6	56.0	59.9	82.0
1995	60.0	58.3	57.5	57.6	56.9	58.6	58.0	54.2	60.6	60.0	60.5	58.2	56.9	57.8	55.7	58.8	57.4
2001	59.0	57.2	66.4	56.5	55.8	57.5	57.7	53.1	59.9	59.0	60.0	58.3	55.8	56.7	54.2	56.9	56.4
Chile																	
1990	55.9	54.7	54.1	54.3	53.8	54.9	54.9	58.2	56.8		57.1	55.5	55.4	55.7	52.7	54.4	55.1
1996	56.1	54.9	54.4	54.6	54.1	55.2	55.2	49.9	58.0		57.6	56.4	55.3	56.1	52.9	54.9	53.7
2000	57.1	56.1	55.5	55.9	55.3	56.4	56.5	52.4	58.5		57.8	56.9	55.5	57.9	52.6	59.4	52.7
Colombia																	
Bogotá																	
1992	54.6	52.4	51.6	52.2	51.3	52.9	54.6		55.4	56.0	55.5	55.5	51.7	52.5	50.7	52.2	55.0
1996	52.4	50.8	50.3	50.1	49.8	51.0	52.4		52.6	53.1	52.9	52.9	51.8	49.7	48.0	53.0	49.5
National																	
1996	56.1	54.3	53.5	53.4	52.9	54.5	53.6	50.2	55.0	56.9	55.3	52.9	54.4	53.1	51.2	55.4	57.7
1999	57.6	55.8	55.0	55.2	54.4	56.3	55.1	55.0	57.2	58.6	57.7	55.9	55.1	55.1	52.0	58.9	58.2
Costa Rica																	
1990	45.6	43.9	43.3	43.2	42.7	44.0	42.9	43.2	45.5	45.6	45.5	43.2	45.0	43.8	41.2	42.9	46.8
1995	45.7	44.0	43.3	43.3	42.8	44.1	42.9	43.7	45.5	45.7	45.5	43.1	44.9	44.8	40.1	45.1	45.1
2000	46.5	44.6	44.1	43.8	43.4	44.8	44.2	44.0	46.4	46.5	46.4	44.7	46.4	44.0	42.7	43.4	48.6
Dominican Rep.																	
1995	51.5	50.2	49.6	49.7	49.2	50.5	53.5	44.4	51.5	51.5	51.4	53.4	50.3	49.0	48.0	53.2	52.4
1997	49.7	48.1	47.5	47.3	46.9	48.3	48.0	47.5	48.8	50.0	49.0	47.5	49.7	46.5	45.1	47.3	52.2
Ecuador																	
1994	54.8	53.0	52.2	52.3	51.6	53.3	51.8	51.5	54.0	55.3	55.3	52.2	52.8	53.8	50.4	55.3	53.7
1998	56.2	54.3	53.5	53.6	52.9	54.8	52.2	54.1	55.1	57.3	56.6	52.1	54.4	52.6	50.8	55.1	60.8
El Salvador																	
1991	52.7	50.5	49.7	49.5	48.9	50.7	49.5	47.8	54.9	52.7	54.9	50.0	50.8	49.4	48.6	51.1	54.3
1995	51.3	49.4	48.6	48.5	47.9	49.6	47.4	44.1	51.5	51.3	51.5	47.4	49.7	49.6	46.6	50.2	50.8
2000	53.2	51.8	51.0	51.0	50.4	52.2	50.3	46.8	52.8	53.2	52.8	50.8	51.3	48.2	49.0	50.6	59.2
Guatemala																	
2000	58.3	56.0	55.3	54.8	54.3	56.2	54.2	50.7	57.5	59.0	58.0	54.0	55.8	54.1	53.7	56.3	61.6

Country / Year																
Honduras																
1990	57.8	55.6	54.8	54.8	54.1	55.9	55.3	49.4	57.8	57.8	57.8	55.3	55.2	52.6	54.9	57.6	64.1
1995	56.1	54.1	53.3	53.2	52.6	54.4	52.2	55.5	56.1	56.1	56.1	52.2	53.6	51.9	50.4	57.3	54.3
1999	55.0	53.0	52.3	52.2	51.6	53.3	50.2	53.2	55.0	55.0	55.0	50.2	52.9	52.9	50.3	53.5	54.8
Jamaica																	
1990	51.7	49.6	48.7	48.8	48.1	49.9	49.4	52.6	51.7	52.6	50.3	48.8	49.5	48.9	49.1	45.9
1996	54.4	51.5	50.3	50.4	49.4	51.7	55.5	58.0	54.4	58.0	61.5	50.4	45.3	50.4	52.6	52.4
1999	52.0	49.0	47.4	47.9	46.5	49.7	53.2	55.4	52.0	55.4	57.3	48.2	46.5	46.8	54.8	49.1
Mexico																	
1992	55.9	53.9	53.0	53.1	52.3	54.2	52.4	56.3	55.2	55.5	52.4	52.8	52.6	52.5	56.8	59.5
1996	54.4	52.5	51.5	51.8	50.9	52.9	50.8	55.7	53.8	55.0	51.8	50.3	51.8	50.9	53.4	52.4
2000	54.6	52.7	51.8	52.0	51.3	53.0	52.1	55.0	54.6	54.9	50.8	51.3	51.2	49.9	53.6	57.6
Nicaragua																	
1993	55.9	54.2	53.3	53.6	52.9	54.6	53.9	56.3	57.7	57.6	54.4	53.4	54.1	52.2	53.4	53.1
1998	55.9	54.0	53.5	53.4	52.9	54.2	54.3	55.5	58.4	57.8	54.8	55.4	52.4	49.3	62.4	53.9
Panama																	
1991	56.4	54.7	53.8	54.0	53.3	55.1		54.4	56.4	54.4		54.0	54.9	51.0	55.5	57.0
1995	55.9	54.0	53.2	53.3	52.6	54.4	52.7	55.1	55.9	55.1	52.5	53.5	54.8	49.9	53.3	55.5
2000	56.4	54.4	53.6	53.5	52.9	54.7	54.2	56.9	56.4	56.9	53.2	54.4	53.6	50.6	52.5	59.0
Paraguay																	
1995	59.5	57.8	57.3	57.0	56.6	57.8	56.7	59.9		50.7	48.7	56.7	57.2	53.5	58.4	58.2
1999	56.8	54.9	54.3	53.9	53.5	54.8	59.9	57.2		65.7	65.2	54.3	53.2	51.4	56.8	52.9
Peru																	
Regions																	
1991	46.5	45.2	44.9	44.8	44.5	45.4	48.7	46.5	47.1	47.0	43.4	47.5	46.5	42.8	46.0	51.2
1994	47.9	45.9	45.2	44.9	44.5	46.0	49.8	48.4	48.3	48.7	45.3	46.9	45.2	43.1	46.7	46.2
National																	
1994	48.6	46.4	45.8	45.5	45.0	46.6	49.3	48.8	48.9	49.2	45.4	47.2	45.9	43.7	47.4	46.2
2000	49.4	47.7	47.4	46.9	46.7	47.8	45.7	49.5	49.5	49.6	44.4	49.9	48.5	45.8	46.6	49.2
Trinidad & Tobago																	
1992	49.5	47.2	45.7	46.5	45.2	47.8	47.8	49.5	49.5	49.5	51.4	43.7	46.4	44.6	44.2	81.8
Uruguay																	
1989	42.2	40.8	40.2	40.3	39.9	41.0		45.0	43.3	46.1	46.1	43.2	41.5	37.6	40.2	41.8
1995	42.7	40.9	40.2	40.3	39.8	41.3	45.3	46.2	44.0	47.8	47.8	42.3	42.0	38.7	40.7	39.7
2000	44.6	42.5	41.5	41.8	41.0	43.1	45.4	47.9	45.8	49.5	49.5	42.0	43.0	40.9	41.6	40.6
RB de Venezuela																	
1989	44.2	41.7	40.6	40.7	39.7	42.1	42.6	44.2	44.2	44.2	42.3	40.7	40.7	39.0	43.5	44.2
1995	46.9	44.5	43.7	43.4	42.8	44.7	45.3	46.7	46.9	46.7	45.1	45.1	42.7	42.4	43.8	46.2
1998	47.6	45.5	44.7	44.7	44.0	45.9	45.4	47.9	47.6	47.9	46.9	46.0	45.1	43.5	44.9	47.4

Notes: Equivalized income A: θ = 0.9, α₁ = 0.5 and α₂ = 0.75; B: θ = 0.75, α₁ = 0.5 and α₂ = 0.75; C: θ = 0.9, α₁ = 0.3 and α₂ = 0.5; D: θ = 0.75, α₁ = 0.3 and α₂ = 0.5; E: Amsterdam scale. Adult equivalent equal to 0.98 for men aged 14–17, 0.9 for women over 14, 0.52 for children under 14, and 1 for all others.

Source: Author's calculations based on microdata from household surveys.

TABLE A.8

Distribution of household per capita income: signs of change in Gini coefficients

| Country | 1970s | | 1980s | | 1990s | |
	Londoño & Székely (i)	Morley/ Altimir (ii)	Londoño & Székely (iii)	Morley/ Altimir (iv)	Székely (v)	This study (vi)
Argentina		+		+		+
Bahamas	−	=	+	=		
Bolivia					+	+
Brazil	=	− or =	+	+	=	−
Chile	+	+ or =	+	+	=	+
Colombia	−	− or =	=	+ or −	=	=
Costa Rica		− or =	=	=	=	= or +
Dominican Rep.	=		+	+		
Ecuador					=	+
El Salvador					+	= or +
Guatemala	=		+			
Honduras	=		=		+	−
Jamaica	=	=	−	−	−	=
Mexico	−	−	+	+	=	= or −
Nicaragua					+	=
Panama	−		+	+	=	=
Paraguay					+	
Peru	−	+ or =	=		+	+
Uruguay		+ or =		−	=	+
RB de Venezuela	−	−	=	+	+	+

Note: Signs refer to changes in the Gini coefficient of the distribution of household per capita income.
Source: Altimir 1994 and 1996b, Morley 2001, Londoño and Székely 2000, and Székely 2001.

TABLE A.9

Perceptions about unfairness of the income distribution: Latinobarómetro survey for 2002

	Do you think the income distribution is ..?					Gini coefficient	
	Very Fair (i)	Fair (ii)	Unfair (iii)	Very unfair (iv)	Total (v)	Level around 2000 (vi)	Change in the 90s (vii)
Argentina	1.0	2.3	42.4	54.3	100.0	50.4	7.7
Bolivia	1.6	6.3	57.3	34.8	100.0	55.9	1.6
Brazil	0.8	12.8	50.7	35.7	100.0	57.2	−2.3
Chile	1.7	9.4	52.3	36.5	100.0	56.1	1.4
Colombia	0.6	3.5	41.4	54.5	100.0	55.8	−0.1
Costa Rica	1.3	14.2	51.9	32.7	100.0	44.6	0.8
Ecuador	3.2	6.6	57.9	32.3	100.0	54.3	
El Salvador	1.8	13.5	49.1	35.7	100.0	51.8	1.3
Guatemala	0.7	13.1	57.9	28.2	100.0	56.0	
Honduras	1.5	6.6	61.8	30.1	100.0	53.0	−2.6
Mexico	1.3	14.4	51.2	33.1	100.0	52.7	−1.2
Nicaragua	2.1	13.3	54.7	29.9	100.0	54.1	−0.1
Panama	0.4	4.7	40.8	54.0	100.0	54.4	−0.3
Paraguay	0.8	4.1	40.0	55.1	100.0	54.9	
Peru	1.3	4.0	57.7	36.9	100.0	47.7	2.0
Uruguay	1.1	6.8	60.5	31.6	100.0	42.5	1.7
RB de Venezuela	6.3	21.1	48.1	24.5	100.0	45.5	3.8
Average	1.7	9.4	51.7	37.3	100.0		

Source: Latinobarómetro (2002) and table 3.5.

TABLE A.10

Indices of bipolarization and inequality (Gini coefficient)

Country	Household per capita income			Equalized income		
	EGR	Wolfson	Gini	EGR	Wolfson	Gini
	(i)	(ii)	(iii)	(iv)	(v)	(vi)
Argentina						
1992	0.149	0.427	44.7	0.140	0.397	42.6
1996	0.158	0.454	48.2	0.147	0.419	45.8
2001	0.175	0.519	52.2	0.164	0.472	50.4
Bolivia						
Urban						
1992	0.171	0.442	49.5	0.162	0.413	47.7
1996	0.179	0.462	51.1	0.171	0.429	49.3
National						
1996	0.192	0.543	57.6	0.178	0.502	55.8
1999	0.200	0.630	57.8	0.188	0.587	55.9
Brazil						
1990	0.245	0.634	61.2	0.236	0.611	59.5
1995	0.239	0.629	60.0	0.230	0.593	58.3
2001	0.229	0.460	59.0	0.221	0.429	57.2
Chile						
1990	0.208	0.478	55.9	0.202	0.452	54.7
1996	0.195	0.482	56.1	0.189	0.454	54.9
2000	0.190	0.458	57.1	0.183	0.431	56.1
Colombia						
Bogotá						
1992	0.200	0.504	54.6	0.189	0.467	52.4
1996	0.190	0.425	52.4	0.183	0.393	50.8
National						
1996	0.183	0.422	56.1	0.172	0.391	54.3
1999	0.195	0.462	57.6	0.185	0.434	55.8
Costa Rica						
1990	0.146	0.430	45.6	0.137	0.396	43.9
1995	0.147	0.414	45.7	0.137	0.384	44.0
2000	0.155	0.442	46.5	0.145	0.412	44.6
Dominican Rep.						
1995	0.187	0.475	51.5	0.181	0.459	50.2
1997	0.163	0.446	49.7	0.156	0.428	48.1
Ecuador						
1994	0.196	0.496	54.8	0.185	0.466	53.0
1998	0.197	0.547	56.2	0.185	0.509	54.3
El Salvador						
1991	0.175	0.455	52.7	0.162	0.422	50.5
1995	0.163	0.446	51.3	0.151	0.414	49.4
2000	0.166	0.485	53.2	0.156	0.460	51.8
Guatemala						
2000	0.209	0.567	58.3	0.193	0.520	56.0
Honduras						
1990	0.209	0.519	57.8	0.196	0.483	55.6
1995	0.190	0.483	56.1	0.178	0.446	54.1
1999	0.189	0.496	55.0	0.177	0.461	53.0
Jamaica						
1990	0.168	0.492	51.7	0.155	0.447	49.6
1996	0.185	0.448	54.4	0.163	0.432	51.5
1999	0.171	0.473	52.0	0.155	0.440	49.0
Mexico						
1992	0.190	0.489	55.9	0.178	0.464	53.9
1996	0.185	0.490	54.4	0.176	0.460	52.5
2000	0.178	0.480	54.6	0.170	0.457	52.7
Nicaragua						
1993	0.204	0.569	55.9	0.194	0.537	54.2
1998	0.194	0.532	55.9	0.183	0.497	54.1
Panama						
1991	0.207	0.587	56.4	0.195	0.545	54.7
1995	0.199	0.537	55.9	0.186	0.499	54.0
2000	0.202	0.566	56.4	0.189	0.528	54.4
Paraguay						
1995	0.213	0.590	59.5	0.201	0.544	57.8
1999	0.225	0.609	56.8	0.214	0.564	54.9
Peru						
Regions						
1991	0.144	0.409	46.5	0.137	0.398	45.2
1994	0.151	0.461	47.9	0.143	0.430	45.9
National						
1994	0.158	0.471	48.6	0.148	0.436	46.4
2000	0.146	0.423	49.4	0.136	0.400	47.7
Trinidad & Tobago						
1992	0.161	0.445	49.5	0.151	0.414	47.2
Uruguay						
1989	0.130	0.352	42.2	0.126	0.343	40.8
1995	0.136	0.385	42.7	0.130	0.365	40.9
2000	0.151	0.426	44.6	0.144	0.398	42.5
RB de Venezuela						
1989	0.135	0.392	44.2	0.125	0.364	41.7
1995	0.144	0.418	46.9	0.132	0.381	44.5
1998	0.149	0.440	47.6	0.139	0.404	45.5

Note: EGR = Esteban, Gradín, and Ray 1999.
Source: Authors' calculations based on microdata from household surveys.

TABLE A.11

Class structure in Latin America: relative occupational income and share in working population

	Relative occupational incomes					Shares in working population				
	Employers (i)	Professional executives (ii)	Petty entrepreneurs (iii)	Formal workers (iv)	Informal workers (v)	Capitalists (vi)	Professional executives (vii)	Petty entrepreneurs (viii)	Formal workers (ix)	Informal workers (x)
Argentina (Greater Buenos Aires)										
1980	280	226	267	96	71	2.1	3.3	4.3	44.2	46.2
1990	322	147	288	70	91	1.6	6.9	6.4	44.8	40.3
1997	336		321			1.4	6.9	5.6	46.1	40.1
Bolivia										
1989	386	183	281	86	77	1.1	4.3	3.9	31.4	59.1
1994	294	209	231	77	57	1.4	6.8	7.8	28.3	55.8
1997	281	244	197	89	59	2.0	6.7	6.9	24.8	59.5
Brazil										
1979	389	168	296	86	72	1.5	7.5	3.8	49.7	37.5
1990	343	174	240	81	62	2.2	4.6	3.3	45.9	43.1
1996	382	214	280	78	63	2.5	4.9	3.9	44.6	44.1
Chile										
1990	528	157	404	74	83	1.6	12.9	2.7	45.7	37.0
1994	544	155	290	65	79	1.5	15.4	6.2	44.9	32.1
1998	457	158	331	58	86	1.6	17.0	7.2	43.4	30.8
Colombia										
1980	428	208		55	64					
1994	345	208		68	55					
1997	287	182		71	53					
Costa Rica										
1981	198	173	195	73	82	1.5	2.7	3.4	60.1	32.2
1994	208	162	177	85	69	1.1	6.1	6.5	54.5	31.7
1997	150	161	132	86	58	1.6	8.8	8.9	49.9	30.8
Ecuador										
1990	171	214	143	104	67	1.4	4.5	4.2	39.3	50.3
1994	228	179	210	90	63	1.4	5.6	8.5	35.5	49.0
1997	220	190	217	97	63	1.9	6.0	7.5	34.0	50.6
Mexico										
1984	308	183	277	92	33	0.2	6.2	3.3		
1994	416	216	314	68	36	0.5	9.0	4.4		
1998	444	168	285	76	39	0.9	6.6	5.8		
Panama										
1979	116	243		89	35	2.1	4.6		69.9	23.4
1991	236	188	154	82	45	0.8	7.4	3.6	53.6	34.6
1997	275	179	207	73	53	1.0	10.8	3.6	53.4	31.2
Paraguay (Asunción)										
1986	290	223	245	84	61	1.7	6.1	7.8	35.3	49.1
1990	303	138	241	76	86	2.1	5.5	8.3	36.8	47.3
1996	294	181	200	86	69	1.4	4.8	8.5	33.0	52.2
Uruguay										
1981	347	147	293	60	42	1.6	3.9	4.6	55.8	34.0
1990	279	177	207	86	51	1.9	5.1	5.0	51.9	36.2
1997	235	200	200	94	47	1.7	6.5	5.9	48.3	37.7
RB de Venezuela										
1981	153	196	145	91	69	1.5	5.2	6.4	43.5	44.3
1990	264	147	211	80	79	2.6	5.8	6.0	51.4	34.2
1997	311	161	261	67	84	1.9	6.1	6.1	45.2	40.6

Note: In panel 1, income is relative to the mean occupational income.
Source: Authors' calculations based on ECLAC 2000.

TABLE A.12

Class structure in Argentina and Brazil: percentage of working population and relative income

	Argentina		Brazil	
	1992 (i)	2001 (ii)	1995 (iii)	2001 (iv)
1. Share in working population				
Capitalists	1.6	1.1	1.2	1.3
Professionals/executives	4.4	5.8	4.1	4.5
Petty entrepreneurs	4.9	5.4	3.7	3.7
Formal workers	46.5	45.9	33.8	31.7
Informal workers	42.6	41.8	57.1	58.8
2. Relative individual income				
Capitalists	144	173	145	149
Professionals/executives	108	127	105	110
Petty entrepreneurs	100	100	100	100
Formal workers	41	46	26	29
Informal workers	38	28	17	19
3. Relative equivalized household income				
Capitalists	136	140	127	129
Professionals/executives	113	140	122	120
Petty entrepreneurs	100	100	100	100
Formal workers	51	50	32	33
Informal workers	48	35	21	22
4. Income share				
Capitalists	4.8	4.1	6.2	6.1
Professionals/executives	10.0	15.5	15.1	16.2
Petty entrepreneurs	10.5	11.3	13.0	12.1
Formal workers	40.4	44.2	31.1	29.6
Informal workers	34.2	24.9	34.6	36.0
5. Within Gini coefficient for individual income				
Capitalists	37.1	53.1	54.9	57.1
Professionals/executives	34.1	34.2	45.7	45.7
Petty entrepreneurs	40.9	40.9	48.7	49.4
Formal workers	33.1	36.3	45.0	41.8
Informal workers	39.9	43.1	51.8	49.6

Source: Authors' calculations based on microdata from Encuesta Permanente de Hogares (EPH) and Pesquisa Nacional por Amostra de Domicilios (PNAD).

TABLE A.13

Individual income and class structure in Argentina (1992, 2001) and Brazil (1995, 2001): decile distribution

Argentina, 1992

Deciles	Capitalists	Professional executives	Petty entrepreneurs	Formal workers	Informal workers
			Classes		
1	0.3	1.0	5.3	5.8	16.9
2	1.2	0.5	1.1	11.0	11.1
3	0.7	0.6	3.2	10.8	11.1
4	1.3	1.2	3.0	11.8	9.8
5	0.2	4.0	1.7	11.1	10.5
6	5.7	3.9	8.1	10.6	10.2
7	2.2	6.6	8.0	12.0	8.3
8	7.1	11.2	8.9	11.2	8.6
9	27.0	22.3	20.6	9.6	7.5
10	54.4	48.7	40.0	6.0	6.0
Total	100.0	100.0	100.0	100.0	100.0

Argentina, 2001

Deciles	Capitalists	Professional executives	Petty entrepreneurs	Formal workers	Informal workers
			Classes		
1	0.3	0.7	2.1	4.5	19.0
2	0.0	0.8	4.1	5.7	17.2
3	5.7	1.4	2.4	8.1	14.5
4	0.1	1.0	3.4	11.9	10.1
5	0.3	2.1	6.3	10.9	10.7
6	3.2	3.1	6.9	12.8	8.3
7	6.7	7.0	6.5	13.4	7.0
8	9.6	6.1	12.3	14.3	5.2
9	20.7	21.4	18.0	11.6	5.3
10	53.4	56.6	38.0	7.0	2.7
Total	100.0	100.0	100.0	100.0	100.0

Brazil, 1995

Deciles	Capitalists	Professional executives	Petty entrepreneurs	Formal workers	Informal workers
			Classes		
1	1.0	0.1	0.4	3.2	16.8
2	1.1	0.4	0.6	6.1	14.6
3	1.9	0.5	0.7	8.4	12.9
4	2.8	0.7	1.3	10.2	11.5
5	3.6	1.5	3.1	10.9	10.8
6	3.0	2.8	2.7	13.7	8.7
7	5.9	5.2	6.8	14.2	7.7
8	7.5	10.4	12.3	13.4	7.4
9	14.1	23.6	21.1	12.7	5.9
10	59.1	54.8	50.9	7.0	3.8
Total	100.0	100.0	100.0	100.0	100.0

Brazil, 2001

Deciles	Capitalists	Professional executives	Petty entrepreneurs	Formal workers	Informal workers
			Classes		
1	1.6	0.1	0.6	5.0	17.3
2	2.2	0.4	0.8	7.9	14.3
3	1.5	0.6	1.1	9.7	12.5
4	2.5	0.8	1.8	11.2	10.9
5	3.5	1.7	2.8	11.9	9.9
6	3.0	2.2	3.7	12.8	8.9
7	5.8	5.2	8.6	12.1	8.7
8	6.1	10.1	9.8	12.8	7.3
9	17.0	24.5	22.7	10.6	6.3
10	56.9	54.6	48.1	5.8	4.0
Total	100.0	100.0	100.0	100.0	100.0

Source: Authors' calculations based on microdata from Encuesta Permanente de Hogares (EPH) and Pesquisa Nacional por Amostra de Domicilios (PNAD).

TABLE A.14

Aggregate welfare: mean income

Country	Mean income from national accounts				Mean income from household surveys			
	Mean income (i)	Sen (ii)	Atk(1) (iii)	Atk(2) (iv)	Mean income (v)	Sen (vi)	Atk(1) (vii)	Atk(2) (viii)
Argentina								
1992	100	100	100	100	100	100	100	100
1996	109	102	102	90	91	86	85	76
1998	119	109	108	96	101	92	92	82
2001	111	96	94	72	89	77	75	58
Bolivia								
1996	100	100	100	100	100	100	100	100
1999	104	104	96	74	122	122	112	87
Brazil								
1990	100	100	100	100	100	100	100	100
1995	108	111	112	115	137	141	142	145
2001	113	120	120	124	133	140	141	145
Chile								
1990	100	100	100	100	100	100	100	100
1996	148	147	148	150	142	142	142	144
2000	161	157	157	153	153	149	148	144
Costa Rica								
1990	100	100	100	100	100	100	100	100
1995	116	116	116	118	119	118	119	121
2000	123	121	122	123	125	123	124	125
Dominican Rep.								
1995	100	100	100	100	100	100	100	100
1997	112	116	114	108	119	123	121	114
Ecuador								
1994	100	100	100	100	100	100	100	100
1998	100	97	95	83	96	93	91	80
El Salvador								
1991	100	100	100	100				
1995	120	123	122	115				
2000	126	125	122	110				
Honduras								
1990	100	100	100	100				
1995	103	107	107	109				
1999	101	108	106	98				
Mexico								
1992	100	100	100	100	100	100	100	100
1996	98	101	101	99	78	80	80	78
2000	116	120	119	114	104	107	107	102
Nicaragua								
1993	100	100	100	100	100	100	100	100
1998	108	108	108	108	111	111	111	111
Panama								
1991	100	100	100	100	100	100	100	100
1995	111	112	114	118	128	129	131	135
2000	123	123	127	143	130	130	134	151
Paraguay								
1995	100	100	100	100	100	100	100	100
1999	92	99	96	86	90	96	94	84
Peru								
1991	100	100	100	100	100	100	100	100
1994	112	107	107	101				
2000	124	118	115	97	114	108	106	89
Uruguay								
1989	100	100	100	100	100	100	100	100
1995	116	115	115	110	100	99	99	94
2000	123	118	118	114	112	107	108	104
RB de Venezuela								
1989	100	100	100	100	100	100	100	100
1995	109	104	104	98	90	86	86	81
1998	109	102	101	85	94	88	87	73

Notes: See Lambert 1993 for details on the aggregate welfare functions. Atk(ε) refers to the function proposed by Atkinson 1970, that is, a CES function with parameter equal to ε. First observation for each country = 100.
Source: Authors' calculations based on microdata from household surveys and per capita GDP from World Bank 2000b and World Development Indicators Database.

TABLE A.15

Poverty in Latin American countries: headcount ratio (share of population below the poverty line)

Country	Székely (1997) (i)	Székely (2001) (ii)	Wodon (2001) (iii)	Sala-i-Martin (2002) (iv)	Country	Székely (1997) (i)	Székely (2001) (ii)	Wodon (2001) (iii)	Sala-i-Martin (2002) (iv)
Argentina					Honduras				
Early 90s			14.6		Early 90s	67.8	77.2	60.1	36.7
Mid-90s		18.4	15.2		Mid-90s	65.6	76.3	63.0	
Late 90s		17.9			Late 90s		75.3		47.2
Bolivia					Jamaica				
Early 90s		63.4	73.4	26.5	Early 90s	27.4			8.1
Mid 90s		62.1	64.5		Mid 90s	25.1			
Late 90s		61.4		40.1	Late 90s				6.1
Brazil					Mexico				
Early 90s	46.3	48.3	46.7	16.5	Early 90s	19.3	16.2	26.9	4.5
Mid 90s	43.5	44.7	36.7		Mid 90s	19.7	21.2	32.1	
Late 90s		41.3		12.9	Late 90s		21.2		1.8
Chile					Nicaragua				
Early 90s	31.0	32.4	46.1	10.1	Early 90s		70.7		28.8
Mid 90s		18.3	28.0		Late 90s		72.7		47.3
Late 90s		16.1		2.2	Panama				
Colombia					Early 90s	48.4	47.8		17.9
Early 90s	23.8	42.4	53.6	17.2	Mid 90s		47.8		
Mid 90s		38.8	52.2		Late 90s		36.6		10.0
Late 90s		37.8		17.0	Paraguay				
Costa Rica					Early 90s			39.7	22.8
Early 90s	24.7	34.2		11.2	Mid 90s		52.1	39.5	
Mid 90s	22.1	28.7			Late 90s		61.1		22.3
Late 90s		30.5		9.2	Peru				
Dominican Rep.					Early 90s		41.9		15.3
Early 90s		49.5		22.6	Mid 90s	35.0	44.0		
Mid 90s		38.1	47.4		Late 90s		42.4		12.5
Late 90s		34.5		8.4	Trinidad & Tobago				
Ecuador					Early 90s				0.4
Early 90s		49.2		13.9	Late 90s				0.1
Mid 90s		49.5	55.2		Uruguay				
Late 90s		48.0		13.6	Early 90s		23.2	18.0	0.9
El Salvador					Mid 90s		16.6	19.4	
Early 90s				21.6	Late 90s		13.6		0.1
Mid 90s		58.6			RB de Venezuela				
Late 90s		64.0		16.8	Early 90s	14.3	12.6	30.2	4.2
Guatemala					Mid 90s	13.4	15.2	41.2	
Early 90s				28.5	Late 90s		20.6		4.8
Late 90s				25.1					
Guyana									
Early 90s				27.2					
Late 90s				12.8					

Notes: The poverty lines in Londono and Székely 1997, Székely 2001, and Sala-i-Martin 2002 is US$2 per day. In Wodon and others 2001, poverty line equals twice the food poverty lines, which is based on the cost of country-specific food baskets providing 2,200 kcal per day per person.
Source: Sala-i-Martin 2002, Londono and Székely 1997, Székely 2001, Wodon and others 2001.

TABLE A.16

Distribution of household per capita income: Gini coefficient (value, standard error, coefficient of variation, and 95% confidence interval)

Country	Value (i)	Standard error (ii)	Coefficient of variation (iii)	95% interval (iv)	Country	Value (i)	Standard error (ii)	Coefficient of variation (iii)	95% interval (iv)
Argentina					Guatemala				
1992	44.7	0.326	0.7	(44.1, 45.4)	2000	58.3	0.437	0.7	(57.4, 59.1)
1996	48.2	0.431	0.9	(47.8, 48.8)	Honduras				
1998	49.5	0.354	0.7	(49.0, 50.2)	1990	57.8	0.487	0.8	(56.8, 58.8)
2001	52.2	0.304	0.6	(51.7, 52.9)	1995	56.1	0.548	1.0	(55.1, 57.2)
Bolivia					1999	55.0	0.448	0.8	(54.1, 55.9)
Urban					Jamaica				
1992	49.5	0.406	0.8	(48.8, 50.4)	1990	51.7	0.691	1.3	(50.3, 52.9)
1996	51.1	0.529	1.0	(50.3, 52.1)	1996	54.4	1.216	2.2	(52.0, 56.8)
National					1999	52.0	1.245	2.4	(49.6, 54.5)
1996	57.6	0.360	0.6	(56.9, 58.4)	Mexico				
1999	57.8	0.573	1.0	(56.8, 59.1)	1992	55.9	0.493	0.9	(55.0, 57.1)
Brazil					1996	54.4	0.383	0.7	(53.6, 55.0)
1990	61.2	0.134	0.2	(60.9, 61.5)	2000	54.6	0.508	0.9	(53.7, 55.6)
1995	60.0	0.119	0.2	(59.8, 60.3)	Nicaragua				
2001	59.0	0.113	0.2	(58.8, 59.2)	1993	55.9	0.4	0.8	(54.9, 56.6)
Chile					1998	55.9	0.9	1.5	(54.4, 57.6)
1990	55.9	0.281	0.5	(55.3, 56.4)	Panama				
1996	56.1	0.360	0.6	(55.4, 56.7)	1991	56.4	0.294	0.5	(55.7, 56.9)
2000	57.1	0.435	0.8	(56.4, 58.1)	1995	55.9	0.293	0.5	(55.3, 56.5)
Colombia					2000	56.4	0.283	0.5	(55.9, 56.9)
Bogotá					Paraguay				
1992	54.6	0.451	0.8	(53.7, 55.4)	1995	59.5	0.401	0.7	(58.8, 60.3)
1996	52.4	0.496	0.9	(51.4, 53.3)	1999	56.8	0.516	0.9	(55.9, 58.0)
National					Peru				
1996	56.1	0.377	0.7	(55.3, 56.8)	1991	46.5	0.416	0.9	(45.7, 47.2)
1999	57.6	0.375	0.7	(56.9, 58.3)	1994	48.6	0.475	1.0	(47.7, 49.2)
Costa Rica					2000	49.4	0.387	0.8	(48.5, 50.1)
1990	45.6	0.297	0.7	(45.0, 46.2)	Trinidad & Tobago				
1995	45.7	0.250	0.5	(45.3, 46.2)	1992	49.5	0.950	1.9	(47.6, 51.4)
2000	46.5	0.234	0.5	(46.1, 47.0)	Uruguay				
Dominican Rep.					1989	42.2	0.391	0.9	(41.5, 43.0)
1995	51.5	0.407	0.8	(50.6, 52.2)	1995	42.7	0.137	0.3	(42.5, 43.0)
1997	49.7	0.497	1.0	(48.7, 50.6)	2000	44.6	0.147	0.3	(44.3, 44.9)
Ecuador					RB de Venezuela				
1994	54.8	0.545	1.0	(53.8, 55.9)	1989	44.2	0.137	0.3	(43.8, 44.4)
1998	56.2	0.494	0.9	(55.2, 57.2)	1995	46.9	0.237	0.5	(46.4, 47.4)
El Salvador					1998	47.6	0.213	0.4	(47.2, 48.0)
1991	52.7	0.272	0.5	(52.1, 53.1)					
1995	51.3	0.331	0.6	(50.7, 51.9)					
2000	53.2	0.664	1.2	(52.1, 54.7)					

Note: Estimation made using bootstrap technique with 200 replications.
Source: Authors' calculations based on microdata from household surveys.

TABLE A.17

Distribution of household income or expenditures, averages by decade, by region: Gini coefficients

Region	1960s	1970s	1980s	1990s	Overall average
Gini coefficients					
Latin America and the Caribbean	*53.2*	*49.1*	*49.8*	*49.3*	*49.8*
Sub-Saharan Africa	49.9	48.2	43.5	47.0	46.1
Middle East and North Africa	41.4	41.9	40.5	38.0	40.5
East Asia and Pacific	37.4	39.9	38.7	38.1	38.8
South Asia	36.2	34.0	35.0	31.9	35.1
Industrial countries and high-income developing countries	35.0	34.8	33.2	33.8	34.3
Eastern Europe	25.1	24.6	25.0	28.9	26.6
Difference in Gini points: LAC vs.					
Sub-Saharan Africa	3.3	0.9	6.3	2.4	3.7
Middle East and North Africa	11.9	7.1	9.3	11.3	9.3
East Asia and Pacific	15.8	9.2	11.1	11.2	11.0
South Asia	17.0	15.1	14.7	17.4	14.7
Industrial countries and high-income developing countries	18.2	14.3	16.5	15.6	15.5
Eastern Europe	28.2	24.4	24.7	20.4	23.2

Source: Deininger and Squire 1996.

TABLE A.18

Distribution of household per capita income, selected years by region: Gini coefficients

	Nonweighted statistics					Population-weighted statistics				
	1950	1960	1970	1980	1992	1950	1960	1970	1980	1992
Share bottom quintile										
Africa	5.4	5.4	5.3	5.3	5.1	6.8	6.8	6.6	6.6	6.5
Asia	6.0	6.1	6.1	6.0	6.1	6.3	6.5	6.4	6.3	6.2
Latin America	**4.3**	**4.2**	**4.2**	**4.0**	**4.0**	**4.2**	**4.1**	**4.1**	**4.0**	**4.0**
Eastern Europe	6.8	6.8	6.8	6.8	6.8	7.0	6.9	6.9	6.8	6.7
Developed countries	5.0	5.0	5.2	5.3	5.4	4.7	4.7	4.8	4.9	4.8
Share top quintile										
Africa	54.2	54.2	55.0	55.3	55.5	49.1	49.2	50.1	50.5	50.7
Asia	50.0	48.8	49.0	49.7	49.8	48.7	48.0	48.1	50.5	51.0
Latin America	**59.2**	**59.6**	**61.2**	**62.0**	**62.0**	**59.7**	**60.1**	**62.1**	**62.6**	**62.6**
Eastern Europe	45.7	45.7	45.7	45.7	45.7	44.4	44.6	44.7	44.9	45.2
Developed countries	45.9	45.7	44.6	44.3	44.5	45.8	45.8	44.8	44.5	45.4
Gini coefficient										
Africa	46.5	46.5	47.3	47.6	48.0	40.8	41.0	41.8	42.2	42.5
Asia	41.7	40.7	40.9	41.5	41.6	40.3	39.5	39.7	41.7	42.3
Latin America	**51.9**	**52.3**	**53.4**	**54.2**	**54.2**	**52.4**	**52.8**	**54.2**	**54.7**	**54.8**
Eastern Europe	37.2	37.2	37.2	37.2	37.2	35.8	36.1	36.3	36.5	36.9
Developed countries	39.5	39.3	38.2	37.8	37.8	39.8	39.8	38.9	38.6	39.2
Difference in Gini points: Latin America vs.										
Africa	5.4	5.8	6.1	6.6	6.3	11.6	11.8	12.4	12.5	12.3
Asia	10.1	11.7	12.5	12.8	12.7	12.1	13.3	14.4	13.0	12.4
Eastern Europe	14.7	15.1	16.2	17.1	17.1	16.6	16.8	17.9	18.2	17.9
Developed countries	12.4	13.0	15.1	16.5	16.5	12.6	13.0	15.2	16.1	15.5

LAC   Latin America and the Caribbean
Source: Authors' calculations based on Bourguignon and Morrison 2002.

TABLE A.19

Distribution of $PPP income/expenditures per capita, 1988 and 1993: regional Gini coefficients

Regions	1988	1993
Gini coefficients		
Africa	42.7	48.7
Asia	55.9	61.8
Latin America and the Caribbean	**57.1**	**55.6**
Eastern Europe, FSU	25.6	46.4
Western Europe, North America, Oceania	37.1	36.6
Difference in Gini points: LAC vs.		
Africa	14.4	6.9
Asia	1.2	−6.2
Eastern Europe, FSU	31.5	9.2
Western Europe, North America, Oceania	20.0	19.0

LAC   Latin America and the Caribbean
Note: Coefficients calculated on distributions of individuals for countries that were in the sample in both years.
Source: Milanovic 2002.

TABLE A.20

Poverty in different regions of the world: headcount ratio

According to Chen and Ravallion (2001)

	1987	1998	Change 1987–98
East Asia	67.0	48.7	−18.3
Eastern Europe and Central Asia	3.6	20.7	17.1
Latin America and the Caribbean	**35.5**	**31.7**	**−3.8**
Middle East and North Africa	30.0	20.9	−9.2
South Asia	86.3	83.9	−2.4
Sub-Saharan Africa	76.5	78.0	1.4
Total	61.0	57.9	−3.1

According to Sala-i-Martin (2002)

	1970	1980	1990	1998	Change 1970–98
Asia	60.3	48.3	29.7	15.6	−44.7
Latin America	**22.2**	**10.5**	**14.0**	**10.5**	**−11.7**
Africa	53.0	55.2	57.9	63.6	10.6
Total	41.0	34.6	25.8	18.6	−22.4

Source: Chen and Ravallion 2001 and Sala-i-Martin 2002.

TABLE A.21

Share of income sources in percent and Gini coefficients of individual income

Country	Share in total individual income					Gini coefficient				
	Labor (i)	Nonlabor (ii)	Capital & profits (iii)	Transfers (iv)	Pensions (v)	Individual income (vi)	Labor income (vii)	Labor income monetary (viii)	Labor income monetary & urban (ix)	Nonlabor income (x)
Argentina										
1992	82.2	17.8	2.3	15.5	13.4	43.1	39.2	39.2	39.2	42.4
1996	78.0	22.0	2.7	19.4	16.5	44.1	41.6	41.6	41.6	44.3
2001	77.8	22.2	3.0	19.3	14.9	46.6	45.7	45.7	45.7	44.1
Bolivia										
Urban										
1992	89.3	10.7		10.7	4.9	50.8	50.2	50.2	50.2	56.7
1996	89.6	10.4		6.6	2.6	53.5	52.8	52.8	52.8	60.7
National										
1996	89.6	10.4	4.0	6.4	2.3	55.7	55.7	55.7	52.5	65.7
1999	87.9	12.1	2.0	10.1	4.1	56.4	56.3	56.7	51.0	66.0
Brazil										
1990	85.4	14.6	3.9	10.7	10.7	62.0	60.2	60.2	59.1	85.7
1995	82.8	17.2	3.1	14.1	13.6	59.2	58.6	58.5	57.5	60.5
2001	78.7	21.3	2.8	18.5	17.8	57.1	56.4	56.4	55.6	58.2
Chile										
1990	78.4	21.6	11.2	10.3	9.5	57.7	53.0	53.0	51.9	61.5
1996	82.6	17.4	9.5	7.9	7.0	60.9	54.5	53.7	53.2	68.8
2000	80.0	20.0	11.5	8.5	7.5	61.8	55.0	53.8	53.4	70.3
Colombia										
Bogotá										
1992	86.9	13.1				51.9	49.7	50.2	50.2	55.0
1996	83.7	16.3				51.7	50.1	50.3	50.3	59.3
National										
1996	82.8	17.2	0.9	16.3		52.5	50.0	50.3	48.4	64.2
1999	82.9	17.1	5.4	11.7	6.7	53.9	52.1	52.7	50.4	58.7
Costa Rica										
1990	91.1	8.9		8.9		44.4	41.4	41.4	41.2	56.9
1995	89.8	10.2		10.2	5.7	46.1	43.0	43.0	42.6	55.9
2000	89.6	10.4		10.4	5.6	45.8	41.8	41.8	41.6	56.5
Dominican Rep.										
1995	100.0					48.9	48.9		52.2	
1997	85.5	14.5	1.8	12.7	2.9	48.8	43.9	44.0	44.5	62.5
Ecuador										
1994	96.0	4.0	1.4	2.6		55.6	53.8	55.9	53.4	71.9
1998	92.8	7.2	3.3	3.9		58.7	54.5	56.8	53.7	78.0
El Salvador										
1991	79.3	20.7	9.8	10.9	2.0	51.3	48.6	48.6	46.6	63.2
1995	84.8	15.2				49.5	47.4	47.4	46.4	56.3
2000	85.0	15.0	3.3	11.7	5.4	52.2	49.1	49.1	49.0	58.7
Guatemala										
2000	86.9	13.1	2.7	10.4	3.2	57.3	55.8	56.5	54.9	71.2
Honduras										
1990	100.0					55.0	55.0	55.0	54.1	
1995	100.0					53.3	53.3	53.3	50.7	
1999	100.0					53.9	53.9	53.9	49.9	
Jamaica										
1990	98.6	1.4				42.0	42.1	42.1	40.6	39.8
1996	97.0	3.0				44.9	45.2	45.2	49.5	61.4
1999	98.3	1.7				41.9	42.4	42.4	44.6	42.4
Mexico										
1992	93.9	6.1	1.6	4.5	2.8	54.3	54.3	53.3	51.3	52.6
1996	91.4	8.6	1.6	7.0	2.9	53.4	53.7	52.5	50.1	53.9
2000	89.9	10.1	1.6	8.5	5.2	54.5	52.7	52.2	49.5	65.5
Nicaragua										
1993	96.2	3.8	0.5	3.3	1.3	51.9	51.3	52.9	50.3	59.4
1998	89.3	10.7	2.5	8.3	0.9	55.4	53.8	56.4	55.4	68.4
Panama										
1991	78.9	21.1	1.9	19.2	13.2	54.1	47.9	47.9		63.3
1995	78.7	21.3	1.6	19.7	9.4	55.2	49.5	49.5	48.3	65.8
2000	78.7	21.3	1.6	19.6	13.7	53.7	47.9	47.9	46.5	62.3
Paraguay										
1995	89.2	10.8	2.7	8.1	4.0	56.6	55.5	43.9	43.1	64.3
1999	87.0	13.0	2.4	10.6	5.4	51.6	50.5	43.8	40.8	55.5
Peru										
Regions										
1991	89.6	10.4	2.4	8.0	6.0	48.1	47.4	48.4	46.4	61.5
1994	84.2	15.8	2.2	13.7	6.5	48.3	47.6	48.3	46.4	62.8
National										
1994	84.6	15.4	2.1	13.3	6.1	48.5	47.9	48.6	46.5	64.2
2000	85.6	14.4	2.0	12.4	7.0	50.0	48.9	49.1	46.5	61.0
Trinidad & Tobago										
1992	100.0					42.6	42.6	42.6	43.3	
Uruguay										
1989	75.8	24.2	4.2	20.0	19.6	48.1	44.5	45.9	45.9	50.7
1995	71.5	28.5	3.3	25.1	21.7	47.0	46.1	47.8	47.8	46.9
2000	68.4	31.6	3.4	28.2	23.7	46.3	45.9	47.6	47.6	47.6
RB de Venezuela										
1989	100.0					36.9	36.9	36.9	36.0	
1995	92.9	7.1	2.1	5.0		45.3	41.9	41.9	39.8	61.4
1998	92.8	7.2	1.8	5.4		46.3	44.4	44.4	44.6	54.7

Note: Nonlabor income = capital and profits + transfers. Transfers = pensions + other public and private transfers.
Source: Authors' calculations based on microdata from household surveys.

TABLE A.22

Years of education of adults ages 25–65, by equivalized income quintile, age, and gender

Country	By equivalized income quintiles						By age and gender													
	1	2	3	4	5	Average	(25–65)		(10–20)		(21–30)		(31–40)		(41–50)		(51–60)		(61+)	
							Female	Male	Female	Male	Female	Male	Female	Male	Female	Male	Female	Male	Female	Male
Argentina																				
1992	7.5	8.0	8.7	9.8	12.2	9.5	9.4	9.6	7.9	7.6	11.0	10.9	10.2	10.0	9.3	9.4	8.2	8.9	7.2	7.9
1996	7.3	8.1	9.0	10.0	12.8	9.8	9.8	9.9	7.7	7.4	11.3	10.8	10.5	10.3	9.7	9.8	8.7	8.9	7.3	8.2
2001	7.3	8.3	9.2	10.6	13.4	10.1	10.3	10.2	7.9	7.5	11.7	11.0	11.0	10.6	10.2	9.9	9.1	9.6	7.3	8.2
Bolivia																				
Urban																				
1992	6.3	7.3	8.2	9.3	11.5	8.7	7.8	9.7	7.6	7.7	9.7	10.9	8.3	9.9	6.8	9.3	6.1	8.2	4.3	7.1
1996	6.5	7.6	8.1	9.7	12.4	9.1	8.1	10.3	7.6	7.7	9.7	11.2	8.7	10.5	7.6	10.3	5.8	9.1	4.6	7.3
National																				
1996	2.8	4.7	6.3	7.6	10.7	6.7	5.6	7.6	6.3	6.6	7.8	9.2	6.3	8.2	5.0	7.2	3.1	5.8	2.4	4.1
1999	2.8	4.9	6.6	8.9	11.4	7.3	6.2	8.3	6.8	7.1	8.9	10.4	7.2	8.9	5.4	7.7	4.0	6.6	2.4	4.1
Brazil																				
1990	1.9	2.9	4.1	5.5	8.9	5.1	5.1	5.2	4.4	3.8	6.8	6.3	5.8	5.8	4.2	4.5	3.1	3.7	2.2	2.5
1995	2.3	3.4	4.5	6.1	9.7	5.6	5.6	5.6	4.9	4.2	7.0	6.4	6.5	6.3	5.3	5.3	3.7	4.1	2.5	3.0
2001	3.0	4.2	5.3	6.9	10.4	6.4	6.5	6.3	6.0	5.4	8.0	7.3	7.2	6.7	6.3	6.3	4.8	5.0	3.0	3.4
Chile																				
1990	6.6	7.2	7.9	9.2	11.8	8.8	8.6	9.0	8.3	8.0	10.4	10.2	9.4	9.8	7.9	8.5	6.7	7.3	5.4	6.0
1996	6.7	7.7	8.8	10.0	12.3	9.3	9.2	9.5	8.3	8.0	11.1	11.1	10.1	10.1	8.6	9.3	7.0	7.5	5.7	6.2
2000	7.4	8.3	9.2	10.6	13.2	10.0	9.8	10.1	8.4	8.2	11.6	11.5	10.6	10.7	9.8	10.2	7.7	8.3	6.0	6.5
Colombia																				
Bogotá																				
1992	6.8	7.1	7.9	9.4	12.4	9.0	8.7	9.4	7.0	6.5	10.0	10.3	9.4	9.9	7.5	8.7	6.4	7.7	5.4	6.6
1996	6.3	7.2	7.8	9.1	12.2	8.8	8.6	9.1	7.6	7.1	10.1	9.8	9.2	9.7	8.1	8.9	6.7	7.6	4.9	6.1
National																				
1996	3.7	4.8	5.8	6.9	10.1	6.6	6.6	6.7	6.2	5.6	8.2	7.8	7.4	7.4	5.9	6.4	4.6	4.9	3.5	3.9
1999	4.4	5.2	6.1	7.3	10.5	7.0	7.1	7.1	6.6	6.1	8.7	8.3	7.8	7.7	6.7	7.0	5.0	5.7	3.8	4.3
Costa Rica																				
1990	5.0	6.2	6.8	7.8	11.1	7.6	7.6	7.8	6.8	6.6	9.2	8.9	8.4	8.6	6.6	7.1	5.0	5.8	4.1	4.1
1995	5.6	6.5	7.3	8.4	11.6	8.2	8.2	8.3	7.1	6.8	9.3	9.2	9.1	9.1	7.8	8.0	6.2	6.5	4.5	4.7
2000	5.4	6.6	7.4	8.4	11.6	8.2	8.2	8.3	7.1	6.7	9.2	8.8	9.0	9.0	8.4	8.5	6.2	7.0	4.5	4.5
Dominican Rep.																				
1995	5.2	6.1	7.0	8.0	10.3	7.5	7.3	7.5	7.1	6.5	9.2	8.4	8.1	8.3	6.5	7.1	4.6	5.6	3.3	4.1
Ecuador																				
1994	4.2	5.2	6.7	7.5	10.6	7.1	6.8	7.3	6.7	5.3	8.9	8.9	7.6	7.9	5.9	6.8	4.3	4.8	3.2	4.2
1998	4.8	6.1	7.1	8.2	11.4	7.8	7.5	7.9	6.9	5.7	9.3	9.3	8.6	8.7	6.8	7.7	4.8	5.9	3.4	3.9
El Salvador																				
1991	2.4	3.0	4.1	5.4	8.5	5.0	4.6	5.5	5.7	5.6	6.7	7.2	5.2	6.4	3.8	4.9	2.8	3.4	1.8	2.5
1995	2.1	2.8	4.1	5.8	9.4	5.3	4.9	5.8	5.3	4.9	7.0	7.3	5.7	6.6	3.9	5.3	3.2	3.9	1.9	2.3
2000	3.8	4.4	5.3	6.5	9.0	6.1	5.8	6.7	5.7	5.6	8.0	8.2	6.6	7.4	5.1	6.5	3.8	4.9	2.3	2.9

Country / Year																				
Guatemala																				
2000	1.4	2.2	2.8	4.1	8.5	4.2	3.4	4.7	3.9	4.2	4.6	5.9	3.8	5.3	3.2	4.5	2.0	3.0	1.7	2.2
Honduras																				
1990	1.8	2.1	2.8	4.0	7.5	4.0	3.9	4.1	4.5	4.1	5.5	5.4	4.5	4.7	3.1	3.5	2.0	2.6	1.8	2.1
1995	2.5	3.1	4.1	5.4	8.0	4.9	4.7	5.0	5.1	4.7	6.4	6.2	5.4	5.7	4.0	4.7	2.6	3.1	1.9	2.3
1999	2.8	3.4	4.5	5.9	9.1	5.5	5.1	5.2	5.1	4.7	6.6	6.1	5.9	5.7	4.7	5.1	3.3	3.6	1.8	2.2
Jamaica																				
1990	7.2	7.3	7.7	8.1	9.4	8.1	8.2	8.2	8.3	8.1	10.2	9.9	9.0	8.6	7.2	7.3	6.4	6.6	5.6	5.8
1996	8.5	9.0	9.0	8.9	10.5	9.3	9.5	9.2	8.4	8.2	10.8	10.6	10.1	9.8	9.4	8.9	8.0	7.3	6.5	5.6
1999	8.5	8.5	8.7	9.0	9.7	9.0	9.2	9.1	8.1	7.9	10.3	9.9	9.9	9.6	9.1	9.0	7.3	8.2	6.7	5.6
Mexico																				
1992	2.7	4.1	5.1	6.6	10.0	6.1	5.6	6.5	6.5	6.3	7.6	8.3	6.1	7.2	4.5	5.7	3.9	4.6	2.5	3.1
1996	3.4	4.6	5.8	7.2	10.7	6.7	6.3	7.2	6.6	6.6	8.4	8.8	6.9	8.0	5.2	6.4	3.8	4.7	2.7	3.2
2000	3.5	5.3	6.8	8.1	11.6	7.4	6.9	8.0	7.0	6.9	9.0	9.5	7.5	8.6	6.5	7.8	4.7	6.2	3.0	3.5
Nicaragua																				
1993	2.3	3.5	4.5	5.6	7.3	4.9	4.4	4.8	4.3	4.0	5.9	5.7	4.9	5.5	3.3	4.0	2.4	2.6	1.8	1.9
1998	2.7	3.6	4.7	5.6	6.1	5.2	4.9	5.2	5.0	4.4	6.5	5.8	5.4	6.0	4.4	5.0	2.7	3.4	2.1	2.0
Panama																				
1991	4.7	6.5	7.8	9.2	12.0	8.5	8.4	8.2	7.2	6.8	10.2	9.5	9.3	9.0	7.7	7.7	6.3	6.4	4.9	4.8
1995	5.3	7.1	8.3	9.8	12.6	9.1	9.0	8.7	7.2	6.7	10.2	9.6	9.9	9.6	8.4	8.4	7.1	6.8	5.0	5.2
2000	6.6	7.9	9.0	10.0	13.1	9.7	9.9	9.5	7.5	7.1	10.9	10.1	10.7	9.9	9.7	9.7	8.3	8.5	7.2	7.2
Paraguay																				
1995	3.7	4.6	5.5	6.8	9.8	6.4	6.2	6.6	5.5	5.2	7.6	7.6	6.8	7.2	5.8	6.3	4.3	5.1	3.2	4.0
1999	4.0	5.1	6.2	7.7	10.1	7.0	6.6	7.0	6.1	5.8	8.1	8.3	7.2	7.6	6.0	6.6	5.0	5.4	3.5	4.2
Peru																				
Regions																				
1991	7.6	9.0	9.5	10.3	11.5	9.8	9.2	10.2	7.6	7.8	10.8	11.2	9.8	10.8	8.3	10.1	7.4	8.3	6.8	7.5
1994	6.8	8.5	9.3	10.7	12.5	9.9	9.6	10.1	7.8	7.8	11.0	11.4	10.5	10.9	8.7	9.9	7.7	8.1	6.8	7.7
National																				
1994	6.4	8.0	9.2	10.2	12.2	9.6	9.3	9.8	7.5	7.6	10.6	11.1	10.0	10.6	8.4	9.5	7.4	7.8	6.6	7.4
2000	5.9	7.5	9.1	10.4	12.5	9.4	8.7	10.0	7.5	7.4	10.8	11.2	9.6	10.5	7.9	9.7	6.5	8.8	4.9	6.7
Trinidad & Tobago																				
1992	6.6	6.8	7.6	8.3	10.3	8.2	8.1	7.9	7.7	7.3	9.8	9.2	8.8	8.3	7.2	7.6	6.1	6.3	5.1	6.3
Uruguay																				
1989	5.9	6.7	7.6	8.6	10.4	8.1	7.9	8.3	7.3	7.2	9.8	10.0	9.1	9.3	7.9	8.3	6.5	6.9	5.1	5.4
1995	6.5	7.1	8.0	9.2	11.6	8.7	8.7	8.7	7.7	7.4	10.5	10.1	9.8	9.5	8.8	8.8	7.4	7.6	5.5	5.7
2000	7.0	7.8	8.6	9.8	12.1	9.3	9.3	9.2	9.2	8.7	10.8	10.2	10.1	9.9	9.5	9.3	8.3	8.2	6.3	6.5
RB de Venezuela																				
1989	4.6	5.6	6.4	7.4	10.0	7.2	6.9	7.4	6.5	5.9	8.6	8.2	7.7	7.8	6.2	7.1	4.4	5.9	2.7	4.0
1995	5.2	5.9	6.7	7.7	9.9	7.4	7.3	7.4	7.1	6.3	9.0	8.4	8.2	7.9	6.9	7.2	5.2	6.2	3.2	4.1
1998	6.0	6.5	7.1	8.4	11.1	8.1	8.1	8.0	7.3	6.5	9.7	8.7	8.9	8.4	7.8	7.9	5.7	6.9	3.5	4.6

Source: Authors' calculations based on microdata from household surveys.

TABLE A.23

Years of education of adults ages 25–60, by equivalized income quintile and age

Age Country	(10–20) 1	2	3	4	5	Mean	(21–30) 1	2	3	4	5	Mean	(31–40) 1	2	3	4	5	Mean
Argentina																		
1992	6.9	7.4	7.7	8.3	8.5	7.7	8.5	9.3	10.4	11.4	13.1	10.9	7.8	8.5	9.5	10.8	12.9	10.2
1996	6.6	7.2	7.9	8.1	8.5	7.5	8.6	9.6	10.7	11.6	13.2	11.0	7.7	8.6	9.6	11.2	13.5	10.3
2001	6.8	7.4	7.8	8.4	8.6	7.6	8.6	9.6	10.7	12.1	13.7	11.3	7.7	9.0	9.9	11.4	14.3	10.8
Bolivia																		
Urban																		
1992	7.2	7.5	7.8	8.2	8.3	7.7	9.1	9.1	10.1	10.7	12.0	10.4	6.7	7.6	8.5	9.8	12.0	9.0
1996	7.1	7.4	7.6	7.9	8.5	7.7	9.2	9.4	10.1	10.3	12.8	10.5	6.9	7.7	9.0	10.4	13.1	9.6
National																		
1996	5.0	6.2	6.7	7.2	8.0	6.5	4.6	7.2	8.2	9.2	11.3	8.6	3.4	5.2	6.8	8.6	11.7	7.4
1999	5.0	6.5	7.4	7.9	8.4	7.0	5.2	7.7	9.0	10.8	12.6	9.7	3.2	5.6	7.3	9.7	12.3	8.0
Brazil																		
1990	2.3	3.4	4.3	5.3	6.0	4.1	3.0	4.4	5.7	7.3	10.1	6.6	2.2	3.4	4.6	6.2	10.1	5.8
1995	2.7	3.8	4.8	5.7	6.6	4.5	3.4	4.8	6.1	7.6	10.3	6.7	2.7	4.1	5.5	7.0	10.7	6.4
2001	4.0	5.1	6.1	6.9	7.6	5.7	4.3	5.7	7.2	8.8	11.2	7.6	3.4	4.8	6.2	7.8	11.3	7.0
Chile																		
1990	7.3	7.8	8.2	8.8	9.0	8.1	8.1	9.0	10.0	11.0	12.9	10.3	7.2	8.0	8.9	10.3	12.7	9.6
1996	7.3	7.8	8.4	8.8	8.9	8.2	8.4	9.7	10.8	11.9	13.7	11.1	7.4	8.7	9.7	11.1	13.2	10.1
2000	7.6	8.0	8.5	8.8	8.9	8.3	9.2	10.2	11.3	12.4	14.2	11.6	8.0	9.1	10.2	11.6	13.9	10.6
Colombia																		
Bogotá																		
1992	6.0	6.6	6.7	7.5	7.3	6.8	8.3	8.9	9.4	10.4	12.4	10.1	7.1	7.5	8.6	9.9	13.2	9.7
1996	6.5	6.8	7.8	7.9	8.2	7.4	7.9	8.5	9.2	10.5	12.5	10.0	6.7	7.8	8.4	10.1	13.2	9.4
National																		
1996	4.6	5.3	6.0	6.8	7.3	5.9	5.2	6.3	7.4	8.6	10.8	8.1	4.2	5.4	6.6	7.7	11.0	7.4
1999	5.2	5.8	6.4	7.1	7.7	6.4	6.1	6.9	7.8	8.9	11.1	8.5	4.9	5.9	6.9	8.2	11.3	7.7
Costa Rica																		
1990	5.7	6.1	6.5	7.3	7.9	6.6	6.8	7.5	8.3	9.3	11.7	9.0	5.7	6.6	7.4	8.9	12.2	8.4
1995	5.9	6.3	6.8	7.4	8.1	6.8	6.6	7.3	8.1	9.7	11.9	9.1	6.3	7.3	8.2	9.3	12.6	9.0
2000	5.8	6.5	6.9	7.3	8.1	6.9	6.0	7.2	8.0	9.3	12.0	8.8	6.3	7.3	8.2	9.4	12.4	8.9
Dominican Rep.																		
1995	6.0	6.3	6.7	7.3	8.1	6.8	7.1	7.6	8.6	9.1	10.9	8.8	6.0	7.0	7.6	9.1	11.0	8.3
Ecuador																		
1994	5.5	6.1	6.6	6.9	7.8	6.5	6.2	7.2	8.8	9.5	11.2	8.9	4.4	5.9	7.5	8.4	11.7	7.8
1998	5.6	6.5	6.8	7.3	8.2	6.8	6.9	7.9	8.7	9.8	12.1	9.4	5.6	6.8	7.9	9.4	12.1	8.7
El Salvador																		
1991	4.5	4.9	5.5	6.4	7.3	5.7	3.9	4.4	6.0	7.8	10.4	7.0	2.8	3.6	4.7	6.3	9.6	5.7
1995	3.7	4.1	5.1	6.2	7.0	5.1	3.5	4.4	5.8	8.0	11.0	7.2	2.4	3.3	4.9	6.5	10.6	6.1
2000	4.7	5.1	5.6	6.4	7.3	5.7	5.8	6.4	7.2	8.5	10.8	8.1	4.4	5.2	6.2	7.2	9.6	5.7
Guatemala																		
2000	2.61	3.1	3.84	4.95	6.57	4.18	2.27	3.17	4.09	6.15	9.44	5.49	1.56	2.33	3.52	5.29	9.31	4.69
Honduras																		
1990	3.2	3.6	3.9	4.7	5.8	4.2	3.0	3.6	3.9	5.5	8.4	5.4	2.1	2.4	3.2	4.5	8.1	4.5
1995	4.0	4.2	4.6	5.3	6.2	4.9	3.8	4.5	5.7	6.8	8.7	6.3	3.0	3.6	4.6	6.1	8.9	5.6
1999	4.0	4.4	5.0	5.6	6.5	5.1	3.6	4.7	5.8	6.8	9.6	6.7	3.3	4.1	5.1	6.8	9.9	6.1
Jamaica																		
1990	8.0	8.0	8.1	8.6	8.8	8.2	9.7	9.0	10.0	9.7	10.8	10.0	7.5	7.3	8.1	8.8	9.7	8.5
1996	8.2	8.0	8.3	8.7	8.4	8.3	10.3	10.0	9.9	10.3	11.5	10.6	9.0	9.6	9.8	9.7	10.7	9.9
1999	7.7	7.8	8.3	8.5	8.5	8.1	9.3	9.5	10.0	10.2	10.5	10.0	9.0	9.3	9.3	9.9	10.6	9.7
Mexico																		
1992	4.9	6.0	6.7	7.2	7.7	6.4	4.5	6.2	7.2	8.7	11.1	8.0	3.0	4.5	5.6	7.5	10.8	6.6
1996	5.1	6.2	7.0	7.4	7.6	6.6	5.4	6.7	8.0	9.3	11.4	8.6	3.9	5.2	6.4	8.0	11.7	7.4
2000	5.6	6.6	7.2	7.7	8.3	7.0	5.6	7.6	8.7	9.7	12.5	9.2	4.2	6.1	7.6	9.2	12.0	8.0
Nicaragua																		
1993	3.0	4.2	4.4	4.9	5.5	4.4	3.3	4.8	6.1	6.7	8.2	6.1	2.4	4.0	4.6	6.6	8.2	5.6
1998	3.2	4.0	5.2	5.4	6.4	4.8	3.6	4.9	6.0	7.3	8.8	6.3	3.1	4.2	5.4	6.5	8.7	5.8
Panama																		
1991	5.8	6.7	7.4	7.7	8.2	7.0	6.9	8.7	9.7	10.9	12.4	10.0	5.6	7.1	8.4	10.3	12.8	9.3
1995	5.7	6.7	7.2	8.0	8.2	7.1	7.0	8.4	9.7	11.1	12.5	10.1	6.2	8.0	9.2	10.9	13.4	10.1
2000	6.2	6.9	7.6	8.1	8.3	7.3	7.6	8.8	10.2	11.2	13.5	10.6	7.3	8.7	9.7	11.0	14.0	10.3
Paraguay																		
1995	4.3	4.7	5.4	5.9	6.9	5.4	4.8	5.7	6.5	8.2	10.2	7.6	3.9	5.0	6.4	7.6	10.6	7.0
1999	4.8	5.4	6.1	6.7	7.7	6.1	5.4	6.3	7.5	9.2	11.3	8.5	4.5	5.8	7.1	8.4	10.9	7.7
Peru																		
Regions																		
1991	6.9	7.6	8.0	8.1	8.2	7.7	9.2	10.3	11.1	11.8	12.1	11.1	7.8	9.6	10.2	10.9	12.8	10.5
1994	6.8	7.5	7.8	8.4	8.9	7.8	8.8	10.2	11.0	11.9	13.2	11.2	7.4	9.2	10.4	11.6	13.4	10.8
National																		
1994	6.5	7.2	7.5	8.2	8.7	7.6	8.0	10.0	10.6	11.6	12.9	10.9	6.9	8.5	10.4	11.1	13.1	10.4
2000	6.5	7.0	7.9	8.1	8.4	7.5	8.2	9.5	10.9	11.9	13.3	11.0	6.5	8.4	9.9	11.5	13.7	10.2
Trinidad & Tobago																		
1992	7.1	7.3	7.5	7.8	8.0	7.5	8.1	8.7	9.1	10.2	11.3	9.5	6.6	7.0	8.4	8.8	11.4	8.8
Uruguay																		
1989	6.3	7.1	7.6	7.8	8.2	7.3	7.6	8.5	9.7	10.7	11.7	9.9	6.7	7.9	9.0	10.0	11.7	9.2
1995	6.8	7.3	7.8	8.1	8.4	7.6	8.0	9.1	10.1	11.0	12.5	10.3	7.4	8.2	9.2	10.5	12.7	9.7
2000	7.9	8.8	9.1	9.8	10.1	8.9	8.1	9.3	10.4	11.2	13.1	10.5	7.5	8.3	9.5	10.8	13.1	10.0
RB de Venezuela																		
1989	5.2	5.8	6.2	6.8	7.5	6.2	6.5	7.2	7.7	8.6	10.5	8.4	5.0	6.1	7.1	8.2	10.7	7.8
1995	5.9	6.2	6.6	7.3	8.0	6.7	6.9	7.3	8.1	9.2	10.8	8.7	5.8	6.5	7.5	8.5	10.7	8.1
1998	6.0	6.4	6.9	7.3	8.2	6.9	7.2	7.9	8.6	9.7	11.8	9.2	6.6	7.3	7.7	9.2	11.7	8.7

Source: Authors' calculations based on microdata from household surveys.

		(41–50)						(51–60)			
1	2	3	4	5	Mean	1	2	3	4	5	Mean
7.4	7.7	8.2	9.4	12.0	9.3	6.5	7.1	7.8	8.4	10.9	8.5
7.2	7.8	8.7	9.8	13.2	9.7	6.5	7.0	7.6	8.7	11.5	8.6
7.2	8.1	8.9	10.7	13.6	10.0	6.1	7.1	8.2	9.1	12.3	9.1
5.4	6.9	7.0	8.9	11.0	8.0	4.1	5.2	6.2	7.3	10.4	7.1
6.0	7.7	6.9	9.5	11.8	8.8	4.3	4.7	5.7	8.4	11.5	7.4
2.4	3.9	6.3	6.9	10.3	6.3	1.5	2.6	3.8	5.3	9.5	4.5
2.3	4.9	6.1	8.5	10.8	6.7	1.8	3.1	4.2	5.9	9.6	5.3
1.4	2.1	3.3	4.5	8.2	4.4	1.0	1.5	2.4	3.5	6.6	3.4
1.8	2.8	3.9	5.6	9.6	5.3	1.2	1.8	2.8	3.9	7.8	3.9
2.6	3.9	4.9	6.6	10.5	6.3	1.6	2.3	3.2	4.7	8.9	4.8
5.7	6.4	7.1	8.5	11.5	8.2	4.7	5.0	5.7	7.3	10.2	7.0
6.0	7.0	8.5	9.6	12.0	9.0	4.4	5.2	6.3	7.6	10.5	7.3
7.2	8.2	8.9	10.7	13.4	10.0	5.0	5.9	6.7	8.2	11.6	8.0
5.4	6.0	7.0	8.8	12.0	8.1	5.4	5.3	5.7	7.6	10.1	7.0
5.7	6.6	7.4	8.6	12.1	8.5	4.4	5.2	5.7	6.4	10.6	7.0
3.1	4.2	5.1	6.4	9.7	6.1	2.5	3.2	3.8	4.6	8.0	4.7
4.0	4.7	5.4	6.9	10.5	6.7	3.1	3.5	4.1	5.1	8.9	5.2
4.4	5.5	5.8	6.5	10.4	6.8	2.9	4.2	4.1	5.1	8.9	5.3
5.2	6.1	6.9	7.8	11.4	7.8	4.2	4.4	5.1	6.0	9.8	6.2
5.8	6.9	7.4	8.4	11.5	8.4	3.7	4.4	5.3	6.5	10.1	6.4
4.5	5.3	6.2	6.9	10.1	6.8	3.4	3.9	4.2	5.5	8.3	5.2
3.8	4.5	5.1	6.5	10.1	6.4	3.1	3.0	4.3	4.3	7.7	4.6
4.2	5.4	6.2	7.2	11.4	7.3	3.1	3.8	4.3	5.5	9.2	5.4
1.9	2.6	3.5	4.4	7.7	4.3	1.3	1.5	2.2	3.2	6.0	3.1
1.7	2.4	3.6	4.9	8.3	4.5	1.2	1.5	2.2	4.1	7.0	3.5
3.6	3.8	4.8	5.7	8.2	5.5	2.3	3.0	3.4	4.1	7.6	4.4
1.07	2.36	2.32	3.15	8.19	3.94	0.56	0.69	1.12	1.95	6.7	2.54
1.5	1.6	2.2	3.0	7.1	3.2	0.9	1.2	1.5	2.0	5.2	2.2
2.3	2.4	3.3	4.8	7.6	4.4	1.3	1.6	2.0	3.0	5.8	2.9
2.6	2.9	4.0	5.3	8.8	5.2	1.3	2.1	2.7	4.1	7.5	3.8
5.8	7.0	6.6	7.1	8.3	7.1	6.3	5.7	6.7	6.8	7.4	6.7
8.0	8.4	8.0	8.6	10.2	8.9	6.9	7.6	8.2	7.4	9.3	8.0
8.2	8.2	8.6	8.4	9.5	8.7	7.9	7.1	7.2	7.2	7.4	7.3
2.2	3.3	4.0	5.3	9.3	5.1	1.4	2.6	3.3	4.2	8.2	4.3
2.7	3.8	5.0	6.2	10.1	5.8	1.8	2.3	3.4	4.4	7.9	4.2
3.3	4.3	6.2	7.5	11.6	7.2	1.7	3.0	4.5	5.3	10.5	5.5
1.7	3.0	3.6	4.7	5.9	3.9	1.5	1.7	2.3	2.7	4.7	2.7
2.3	3.2	4.2	5.1	8.1	4.9	1.7	1.9	2.6	2.8	6.1	3.2
4.1	5.6	7.1	8.1	11.7	7.9	3.2	4.4	5.7	7.0	10.4	6.5
4.6	6.2	7.2	9.2	12.4	8.7	3.3	4.8	6.1	7.6	11.6	7.0
6.1	7.5	8.5	9.8	13.1	9.7	5.0	6.3	6.9	7.8	12.0	8.4
3.4	4.1	5.2	6.4	9.6	6.1	2.6	3.4	3.7	4.5	8.4	4.7
3.5	4.6	5.6	6.9	10.3	6.5	2.9	3.4	4.9	5.6	8.2	5.4
6.7	8.8	9.0	10.1	10.4	9.2	7.1	7.1	7.4	7.8	9.2	7.8
5.7	7.7	8.8	10.2	12.1	9.3	5.3	6.3	7.2	8.2	10.5	8.0
5.6	7.0	8.5	10.0	11.9	9.0	5.3	5.8	7.0	7.7	10.3	7.8
5.4	6.7	8.9	10.1	12.0	8.9	4.0	5.6	7.1	8.2	10.7	7.7
5.8	6.0	6.7	7.6	9.7	7.5	6.2	5.3	5.1	5.7	7.8	6.2
5.7	7.0	7.6	8.7	10.3	8.1	4.4	5.3	6.1	6.9	8.9	6.7
6.4	7.2	8.2	9.6	12.0	8.8	5.1	5.8	6.7	7.8	10.3	7.5
7.1	8.0	8.7	10.1	12.3	9.4	5.7	6.8	7.2	8.5	11.1	8.3
3.9	5.0	5.6	6.9	9.7	6.6	2.7	3.6	4.2	5.1	8.1	5.1
4.8	5.4	6.4	7.5	9.5	7.1	3.3	4.0	4.6	5.6	8.5	5.7
5.7	6.1	6.6	8.0	11.0	7.9	4.2	4.1	5.3	6.3	9.4	6.3

Schooling in Latin American countries: share of population over age 25, by education level and average years of schooling

	% of no schooling					% of primary school completed					% of high school completed					Average schooling years				
	1960	1970	1980	1990	2000	1960	1970	1980	1990	2000	1960	1970	1980	1990	2000	1960	1970	1980	1990	2000
Argentina	12.0	8.3	7.1	5.7	5.8	19.9	30.6	33.0	34.6	30.1	1.8	2.4	3.7	7.2	11.9	5.0	5.9	6.6	7.8	8.5
Barbados	0.0	1.1	0.8	1.9	2.6	22.5	9.3	17.6	13.4	10.7	0.7	0.8	2.2	5.4	8.1	5.2	9.1	6.8	8.2	9.1
Bolivia	50.2	51.2	44.8	36.8	30.9	5.1	6.8	8.9	10.0	11.0	2.5	2.6	4.2	6.7	9.8	4.2	3.7	4.0	4.7	5.5
Brazil	43.2	42.6	32.9	22.4	21.2	11.8	19.4	4.9	12.4	11.5	1.4	1.4	3.4	4.9	5.7	2.8	2.9	3.0	3.8	4.6
Chile	20.2	12.4	9.4	5.8	5.3	22.1	14.2	12.8	10.7	9.6	1.4	2.6	4.9	8.4	10.7	5.0	5.5	6.0	7.1	7.9
Colombia	35.1	39.2	24.5	24.5	19.8	10.9	10.8	12.0	11.0	10.8	1.3	1.4	2.9	4.7	6.7	3.0	2.7	3.9	4.4	5.0
Costa Rica	17.7	20.6	14.5	10.8	9.4	21.0	12.1	16.0	14.0	13.6	1.8	2.1	5.7	9.4	12.7	3.9	3.6	4.7	5.6	6.0
Dominican Rep.	43.4	40.1	35.7	28.8	25.7	13.8	4.3	10.2	11.2	10.3	0.5	1.3	2.9	6.1	9.8	2.4	2.9	3.4	4.3	5.2
Ecuador	37.8	37.6	25.4	20.0	17.7	13.6	18.0	34.1	14.3	13.1	1.0	1.3	5.2	11.9	12.7	3.0	3.2	5.4	5.9	6.5
El Salvador	61.8	54.2	36.0	37.1	35.0	5.1	8.0	11.5	10.2	10.1	0.3	1.3	2.2	4.3	7.2	1.7	2.3	3.3	3.6	4.5
Guatemala	69.2	68.4	54.7	52.9	47.1	7.2	6.2	8.0	8.0	8.3	0.3	0.7	1.5	3.0	4.0	1.4	1.5	2.3	2.6	3.1
Guyana	13.7	12.2	8.1	9.6	7.3	23.0	21.5	20.2	16.0	14.6	0.4	0.7	1.2	1.4	2.7	3.5	4.0	4.7	5.4	6.0
Haiti	90.2	83.5	77.0	57.0	54.4	1.4	1.8	3.2	7.2	7.1	0.2	0.2	0.5	0.6	0.8	0.7	0.9	1.5	2.4	2.7
Honduras	60.9	61.9	49.0	31.9	25.9	6.9	7.9	8.6	11.5	12.4	0.4	0.6	1.2	3.1	4.4	1.7	1.7	2.3	3.7	4.1
Jamaica	18.8	5.1	3.2	3.5	3.3	20.8	24.0	22.1	17.7	15.1	0.3	0.7	1.4	1.8	2.8	2.5	3.0	3.6	4.6	5.2
Mexico	46.0	35.0	34.2	18.8	12.4	10.4	15.3	17.2	19.9	19.4	0.8	1.5	3.2	5.4	6.6	2.4	3.3	4.0	5.9	6.7
Nicaragua	59.0	53.9	48.9	41.3	31.7	9.1	7.9	8.7	9.0	9.5	1.7	3.1	3.8	5.4	6.0	2.1	2.6	2.9	3.6	4.4
Panama	28.0	24.9	18.3	12.9	11.4	24.4	16.4	23.2	21.6	21.0	1.8	2.9	5.7	11.4	13.5	4.3	4.6	5.9	7.3	7.9
Paraguay	26.4	19.6	14.2	8.7	9.8	16.8	10.3	15.4	20.7	20.7	1.0	1.7	2.7	6.0	6.6	3.4	3.7	4.6	5.8	5.7
Peru	42.8	35.0	24.0	20.5	13.8	11.7	16.1	17.2	10.3	8.8	1.8	3.1	6.9	9.6	15.3	3.0	3.9	5.4	5.9	7.3
Trinidad & Tobago	14.7	11.6	1.3	4.5	5.1	18.6	21.9	42.6	16.3	12.8	0.7	0.8	2.0	2.3	3.1	4.2	4.5	6.6	6.7	7.6
Uruguay	14.1	13.9	7.3	5.5	3.2	18.4	22.8	20.5	13.2	12.3	3.5	3.9	5.1	7.9	8.5	5.0	5.2	5.8	6.7	7.2
RB de Venezuela	49.1	47.1	23.5	21.2	15.7	15.7	9.5	10.6	12.2	12.6	1.0	1.8	4.8	8.0	12.2	2.5	2.9	4.9	4.9	5.6
Total	**37.1**	**33.9**	**25.9**	**21.0**	**18.0**	**14.4**	**13.7**	**16.5**	**14.1**	**13.3**	**1.2**	**1.7**	**3.4**	**5.9**	**7.9**	**3.2**	**3.6**	**4.4**	**5.2**	**5.9**
Middle East and North Africa	65.9	60.8	52.6	39.2	28.7	10.2	9.2	9.5	11.0	11.2	1.3	1.7	3.7	6.2	7.9	2.3	2.7	3.8	5.2	6.3
Sub-Saharan Africa	76.3	73.4	63.0	53.5	46.0	5.5	5.1	6.9	7.8	8.4	0.2	0.4	0.5	1.2	1.7	1.2	1.4	2.0	2.7	3.4
Latin America and the Caribbean	37.1	33.9	25.9	21.0	18.0	14.4	13.7	16.5	14.1	13.3	1.2	1.7	3.4	5.9	7.9	3.2	3.6	4.4	5.2	5.9
East Asia and the Pacific	51.5	41.7	31.4	26.0	18.1	15.7	16.2	18.9	19.4	19.0	1.7	2.2	3.4	5.2	8.5	3.1	3.7	4.8	6.1	7.3
South Asia	78.1	76.6	69.8	62.7	54.5	3.0	6.7	5.3	6.5	8.3	0.5	1.0	1.2	1.7	2.2	1.2	1.5	2.0	2.5	3.0
Advanced countries	5.8	5.1	4.5	3.1	3.3	34.8	32.3	23.4	19.9	17.1	3.1	4.2	6.9	9.4	12.5	6.6	7.2	8.2	8.8	9.5
World average	**46.3**	**43.0**	**36.0**	**29.8**	**24.8**	**15.7**	**15.1**	**14.3**	**13.5**	**12.9**	**1.4**	**2.0**	**3.4**	**5.2**	**7.1**	**3.2**	**3.6**	**4.5**	**5.3**	**6.1**

Source: Updated version of Barro and Lee 2000.

TABLE A.25

Distribution of years of education, Gini coefficients

	1960	1965	1970	1975	1980	1985	1990
Latin America and the Caribbean	50.1	50.2	47.0	46.0	43.1	42.6	41.8
Africa	78.5	77.7	74.7	70.2	66.3	63.8	61.8
Asia	67.0	64.5	61.4	58.4	54.3	51.5	47.9
Eastern Europe	29.6	29.8	27.6	28.0	25.3	26.1	22.8
Developed countries	29.3	29.2	28.2	29.2	27.1	27.2	27.5
Average	54.2	53.4	50.8	49.1	45.9	44.6	42.8
LAC countries							
Argentina	34.4	34.9	31.1	32.5	29.4	31.8	27.3
Barbados	25.3	27.9	18.0	19.1	29.6	29.9	30.0
Bolivia	51.9	54.6	55.7	56.4	55.9	54.7	53.7
Brazil	60.0	56.4	50.8	42.9	44.5	44.4	39.3
Chile	36.5	36.6	33.0	33.2	31.5	31.2	31.3
Colombia	53.4	49.3	50.9	46.0	47.2	47.5	48.6
Costa Rica	39.9	40.5	41.0	39.2	40.6	41.6	42.6
Cuba	44.6	46.0	31.7	34.0	32.2	33.1	33.5
Ecuador	51.3	51.5	51.1	47.0	39.3	44.0	44.9
Guatemala	75.8	75.2	74.3	73.2	63.8	63.6	62.6
Guyana	32.3	34.9	32.7	35.0	32.5	33.5	34.0
Haiti	92.7	91.7	85.1	84.6	78.0	63.9	65.0
Honduras	67.2	65.3	62.3	59.0	56.9	48.4	46.8
Jamaica	35.2	38.6	28.9	31.3	31.7	32.6	33.0
Mexico	56.0	56.9	51.0	49.8	49.7	46.9	38.4
Nicaragua	70.0	67.9	66.1	64.1	63.0	60.8	58.7
Panama	43.7	46.2	47.4	46.4	38.0	39.6	33.9
Paraguay	41.6	41.5	39.6	38.9	38.0	39.1	39.8
Peru	56.8	58.0	50.4	50.3	42.5	43.7	43.1
Trinidad & Tobago	35.7	36.0	33.7	33.9	23.9	29.7	31.2
Uruguay	38.8	38.1	39.2	34.9	35.8	33.5	34.2
RB de Venezuela	58.3	55.9	61.2	59.4	44.0	44.6	47.2

LAC   Latin America and the Caribbean
Source: Authors' calculations based on Thomas and others 2002.

TABLE A.26

Distribution of years of education by age group, Gini coefficients

Country	Age brackets						
	(25–65)	(10–20)	(21–30)	(31–40)	(41–50)	(51–60)	(61+)
Argentina							
1992	22.7	21.1	18.8	20.9	23.3	23.6	24.5
1996	22.5	21.4	17.6	20.3	23.1	24.5	26.3
2001	22.2	22.2	17.2	20.1	22.5	25.1	28.3
Bolivia							
Urban							
1992	31.7	22.8	19.7	29.3	36.6	42.9	51.4
1996	33.6	22.6	23.8	30.9	35.8	44.6	51.2
National							
1996	46.4	27.4	32.6	42.1	49.7	60.1	69.2
1999	43.4	26.2	28.1	38.2	45.7	55.9	69.6
Brazil							
1990	47.6	39.3	36.3	43.3	51.6	56.1	66.6
1995	45.2	36.4	34.7	40.0	48.1	55.6	65.2
2001	41.1	30.2	30.4	36.5	42.1	51.5	62.3
Chile							
1990	29.5	21.6	20.7	25.4	32.3	37.0	45.4
1996	27.1	21.0	18.4	22.2	28.9	35.6	43.2
2000	24.2	20.2	16.1	20.1	24.0	32.2	40.3
Colombia							
Bogotá							
1992	29.3	24.4	21.8	26.7	32.9	36.2	42.9
1996	28.1	22.4	20.5	25.2	30.8	34.9	39.3
National							
1996	38.3	29.2	28.9	34.5	41.4	45.9	50.3
1999	37.3	27.8	27.7	32.8	39.5	46.1	52.6
Costa Rica							
1990	32.3	23.3	23.3	27.9	35.2	41.7	46.1
1995	30.0	22.4	23.8	25.4	31.2	38.5	44.0
2000	29.7	22.8	25.7	25.7	28.6	37.5	46.0
Dominican Rep.							
1995	36.7	26.6	27.4	32.5	39.3	46.6	55.5
Ecuador							
1994	38.4	25.3	26.2	35.0	42.1	46.4	54.8
1998	35.3	23.5	24.2	30.5	38.4	45.5	53.3
El Salvador							
1991	52.3	32.5	40.9	46.8	54.7	63.3	71.2
1995	52.4	37.9	39.2	47.0	55.5	63.2	73.5
2000	47.3	33.9	34.1	42.7	49.5	57.6	69.4
Guatemala							
2000	61.8	42.9	48.7	57.7	65.2	74.6	78.5
Honduras							
1990	55.8	36.1	42.5	50.2	61.0	70.8	72.9
1995	48.5	31.0	35.3	43.3	51.9	65.3	69.0
1999	47.7	30.6	36.7	42.6	50.0	61.4	71.7
Jamaica							
1990	20.3	17.5	11.7	17.6	19.2	20.2	25.8
1996	16.8	17.6	11.0	12.0	17.7	21.3	23.4
1999	16.2	17.0	10.6	12.7	16.5	20.0	18.4
Mexico							
1992	42.8	25.5	30.3	39.1	46.1	52.0	61.5
1996	40.0	25.0	26.6	35.6	44.3	52.6	62.8
2000	36.6	23.1	24.7	31.4	38.7	49.8	60.2
Nicaragua							
1993	53.0	41.2	41.0	50.3	58.4	66.3	72.8
1998	48.3	37.6	37.4	42.9	53.7	63.4	69.5
Panama							
1991	32.2	24.3	22.7	27.8	34.4	40.3	47.7
1995	29.6	23.7	22.1	25.2	31.9	38.4	45.9
2000	24.7	22.7	20.3	21.8	25.5	29.0	31.5
Paraguay							
1995	35.8	28.8	28.0	33.1	37.2	42.2	49.6
1999	34.5	26.9	27.8	30.8	35.6	40.5	47.7
Peru							
Regions							
1991	25.361	20.235	17.009	22.905	28.471	29.332	29.563
1994	26.433	20.512	18.318	23.037	29.272	31.815	31.237
National							
1994	27.342	21.218	19.51	24.248	30	32.744	31.744
2000	30.049	22.158	19.816	25.939	31.782	39.161	44.779
Trinidad & Tobago							
1992	26.9	22.0	19.7	25.1	28.0	29.4	33.4
Uruguay							
1989	29.0	23.4	21.4	25.0	28.1	31.1	37.9
1995	26.3	20.7	18.3	21.5	25.5	29.6	36.0
2000	24.2	27.5	19.2	21.4	23.0	26.7	33.9
RB de Venezuela							
1989	33.4	26.1	24.6	29.2	35.9	44.7	59.9
1995	31.4	24.3	23.0	27.1	32.1	42.4	57.6
1998	30.9	24.1	24.0	27.0	31.7	39.9	55.4

Source: Authors' calculations based on microdata from household surveys.

TABLE A.27

Adult self-reported literacy rate by quintile

Country	1	2	3	4	5	Average	Country	1	2	3	4	5	Average
Argentina							Honduras						
1992	0.96	0.98	0.98	0.99	1.00	0.98	1990	0.51	0.55	0.66	0.76	0.90	0.70
1996	0.96	0.98	0.99	1.00	1.00	0.99	1995	0.61	0.65	0.77	0.84	0.92	0.77
2001	0.98	0.98	0.99	1.00	1.00	0.99	1999	0.65	0.72	0.81	0.89	0.95	0.82
Bolivia							Jamaica						
Urban							1990	0.91	0.94	0.95	0.98	0.99	0.96
1992	0.85	0.90	0.92	0.94	0.97	0.92	1996	0.98	0.98	0.96	0.97	0.99	0.98
1996	0.88	0.89	0.92	0.95	0.98	0.93	1999	0.96	0.97	0.97	0.96	0.97	0.97
National							Mexico						
1996	0.60	0.76	0.85	0.90	0.96	0.82	1992	0.66	0.83	0.88	0.93	0.98	0.87
1999	0.58	0.77	0.88	0.91	0.97	0.83	1996	0.70	0.82	0.91	0.94	0.98	0.89
Brazil							2000	0.70	0.87	0.93	0.95	0.99	0.90
1990	0.51	0.68	0.82	0.91	0.97	0.81	Nicaragua						
1995	0.59	0.73	0.85	0.93	0.98	0.84	1993	0.38	0.52	0.64	0.76	0.80	0.64
2001	0.67	0.79	0.87	0.95	0.99	0.87	1998 (a)	0.46	0.57	0.69	0.76	0.87	0.69
Chile							1998 (b)	0.60	0.67	0.78	0.83	0.91	0.77
1990	0.91	0.92	0.94	0.97	0.99	0.95	Panama						
1996	0.90	0.93	0.96	0.98	0.99	0.96	1991	0.74	0.85	0.91	0.94	0.97	0.90
2000	0.92	0.94	0.96	0.98	1.00	0.96	1995	0.78	0.89	0.93	0.96	0.98	0.92
Colombia							2000	0.94	0.96	0.98	0.98	1.00	0.98
Bogotá							Paraguay						
1992	0.96	0.98	0.98	0.99	0.99	0.98	1995	0.68	0.79	0.83	0.89	0.95	0.84
1996	0.96	0.98	0.99	0.99	0.99	0.98	1999	0.79	0.86	0.92	0.96	0.98	0.91
National							Peru						
1996	0.90	0.94	0.95	0.97	0.99	0.96	Regions						
1999	0.91	0.93	0.96	0.96	0.99	0.96	1991	0.81	0.90	0.94	0.97	0.98	0.92
Costa Rica							1994	0.74	0.88	0.92	0.95	0.98	0.90
1990	0.70	0.83	0.83	0.88	0.96	0.85	National						
1995	0.76	0.84	0.88	0.91	0.97	0.88	1994	0.74	0.87	0.90	0.94	0.97	0.90
2000	0.76	0.86	0.88	0.92	0.97	0.89	2000	0.82	0.89	0.94	0.96	0.99	0.93
Dominican Rep.							Trinidad & Tobago						
1995	0.83	0.88	0.90	0.93	0.97	0.91	1992	0.71	0.74	0.81	0.83	0.88	0.81
Ecuador							Uruguay						
1994	0.74	0.85	0.86	0.91	0.96	0.87	1989	0.88	0.91	0.95	0.96	0.96	0.94
1998	0.78	0.86	0.90	0.93	0.98	0.90	1995	0.91	0.93	0.96	0.97	0.99	0.95
El Salvador							2000	0.93	0.96	0.97	0.98	0.99	0.97
1991	0.49	0.57	0.68	0.76	0.88	0.69	RB de Venezuela						
1995	0.52	0.60	0.72	0.84	0.93	0.75	1989	0.78	0.86	0.90	0.94	0.98	0.90
2000	0.64	0.71	0.79	0.86	0.93	0.80	1995	0.82	0.88	0.92	0.94	0.98	0.92
Guatemala							1998	0.86	0.90	0.93	0.95	0.99	0.93
2000	0.40	0.52	0.59	0.72	0.91	0.65							

Note: Data for Nicaragua 1993 and 1998 (a): share of adults with less than three years of formal education; for Nicaragua 1998 (b): self-reported literacy rate.
Source: Authors' calculations based on microdata from household surveys.

TABLE A.28

Educational structure of the adult population by age and gender (population shares)

Country	Population, 18–65			Population, 25–55			Males, 25–55			Females, 25–55			Working males, 25–55		
	Low (i)	Medium (ii)	High (iii)	Low (iv)	Medium (v)	High (vi)	Low (vii)	Medium (viii)	High (ix)	Low (x)	Medium (xi)	High (xii)	Low (xiii)	Medium (xiv)	High (xv)
Argentina															
1992	42.2	38.8	18.9	42.5	37.3	20.2	42.1	37.5	20.4	42.9	37.2	19.9	41.7	38.5	19.8
1996	42.0	39.4	18.6	41.2	37.8	21.0	41.2	38.4	20.4	41.2	37.3	21.6	42.3	38.1	19.6
2001	37.8	39.8	22.4	38.0	36.7	25.3	39.3	38.2	22.6	36.9	35.4	27.7	37.7	39.4	22.9
Bolivia															
Urban															
1992	40.1	45.1	14.8	43.3	37.6	19.1	35.1	44.8	20.2	50.8	31.1	18.2	35.9	43.5	20.6
1996	41.4	37.2	21.5	42.7	30.6	26.7	34.2	33.6	32.2	50.0	28.1	21.9	35.3	34.3	30.4
National															
1996	62.2	25.3	12.6	65.1	20.8	14.2	59.1	23.8	17.1	70.5	18.0	11.5	58.0	24.7	17.3
1999	54.1	30.0	15.8	59.0	22.6	18.4	52.7	25.9	21.5	64.8	19.6	15.6	52.1	26.9	21.0
Brazil															
1990	76.4	17.6	6.0	75.8	16.5	7.8	76.1	16.1	7.7	75.4	16.8	7.8	76.1	16.1	7.7
1995	73.8	19.9	6.4	73.1	18.8	8.1	74.3	17.8	7.9	72.0	19.7	8.3	74.2	17.9	7.9
2001	64.6	27.9	7.5	66.1	24.7	9.1	67.9	23.6	8.5	64.5	25.8	9.8	67.8	23.8	8.4
Chile															
1990	43.7	42.7	13.6	50.0	37.6	12.4	43.7	40.2	16.1	46.2	40.0	13.8	43.6	40.2	16.2
1996	37.7	45.9	16.4	38.5	44.7	16.9	37.6	44.0	18.3	39.3	45.2	15.5	37.5	44.2	18.4
2000	33.1	48.3	18.6	33.0	47.0	20.0	32.5	46.2	21.3	33.5	47.7	18.9	32.3	46.2	21.5
Colombia															
Bogotá															
1992	42.6	39.0	18.3	43.2	34.7	22.1	40.5	33.8	25.8	45.6	35.4	19.0	40.3	34.3	25.4
1996	43.5	41.1	15.5	45.0	36.9	18.1	44.1	36.6	19.3	45.8	37.2	17.0	43.5	37.6	19.0
National															
1996	62.8	28.9	8.2	63.8	26.1	10.0	63.8	25.3	10.9	63.8	26.9	9.3	64.1	25.4	10.6
1999	57.8	31.9	10.4	59.6	28.1	12.4	60.0	26.7	13.3	59.1	29.3	11.6	61.5	26.1	12.3
Costa Rica															
1990	59.4	29.4	11.2	59.7	27.5	12.8	59.3	27.5	13.1	59.9	27.5	12.6	59.3	27.4	13.3
1995	55.4	30.6	14.0	54.9	29.5	15.6	55.2	28.7	16.1	54.6	30.3	15.1	56.2	28.0	15.8
2000	55.2	30.7	14.1	58.6	27.6	13.9	58.5	27.8	13.7	58.6	27.4	14.1	59.6	27.5	12.9
Dominican Rep.															
1995	57.9	30.6	11.5	59.7	26.8	13.5	60.3	25.7	14.0	59.1	27.8	13.0	60.2	25.7	14.1
Ecuador															
1994	61.4	27.1	11.5	64.1	21.9	14.0	63.3	21.8	14.9	64.9	22.1	13.1	63.1	21.9	15.0
1998	56.5	30.3	13.2	56.9	27.1	16.1	56.3	26.6	17.1	57.4	27.6	15.0	55.7	26.8	17.5
El Salvador															
1991	67.9	24.8	7.3	70.9	21.4	7.7	67.0	23.8	9.2	74.1	19.5	6.4	66.0	24.6	9.4
1995	67.0	26.0	7.1	69.1	22.4	8.5	65.0	24.9	10.1	72.4	20.5	7.2	60.5	28.2	11.4
2000	59.5	30.6	9.9	61.6	26.7	11.7	57.7	29.4	12.9	64.7	24.5	10.8	62.6	29.2	8.2
Guatemala															
2000	79.8	14.9	5.4	81.1	12.6	6.4	77.9	13.4	8.7	83.8	11.9	4.3	74.4	15.6	9.9
Honduras															
1990	84.0	12.8	3.2	80.2	14.9	5.0	80.0	13.5	6.5	80.4	16.1	3.6	80.0	13.3	6.6
1995	79.4	17.1	3.5	73.6	21.1	5.3	73.2	19.9	6.9	74.0	22.1	3.9	73.0	20.1	6.9
1999	77.8	17.7	4.6	73.1	20.5	6.5	73.5	18.5	8.1	72.7	22.1	5.2	72.7	22.1	5.2
Jamaica															
1990	38.7	56.1	5.2	41.1	52.8	6.1	42.6	52.3	5.1	39.7	53.3	7.0	40.3	55.4	4.4
1999	31.1	63.1	5.8	27.8	65.7	6.6	26.7	67.5	5.9	28.8	64.0	7.2	22.6	71.9	5.5
Mexico															
1992	62.5	28.1	9.4	67.6	22.1	10.4	64.3	22.0	13.8	70.6	22.2	7.2	64.4	22.0	13.6
1996	56.6	32.8	10.7	59.0	28.8	12.2	55.8	29.0	15.2	62.0	28.6	9.4	55.5	29.1	15.3
2000	50.3	35.8	14.0	51.6	33.9	14.5	48.1	33.5	18.4	54.8	34.1	11.1	47.1	34.0	19.0
Nicaragua															
1993	77.7	18.7	3.6	77.2	17.7	5.2	76.6	16.9	6.5	77.7	18.3	4.0	74.1	18.5	7.4
1998	74.9	20.8	4.3	74.9	19.8	5.3	73.9	19.9	6.2	75.7	19.8	4.5	71.4	21.6	7.1
Panama															
1991	49.0	37.5	13.5	49.3	34.2	16.4	51.4	32.9	15.7	47.4	35.4	17.1	51.5	32.9	15.6
1995	45.2	39.9	14.9	44.7	37.6	17.7	46.5	36.9	16.6	42.9	38.3	18.9	46.5	36.9	16.6
2000	39.0	43.0	18.0	38.5	40.7	20.7	40.7	40.8	18.5	36.5	40.6	22.9	37.2	43.0	19.8
Paraguay															
1995	71.0	22.0	7.0	71.7	20.1	8.2	70.1	21.7	8.2	73.3	18.5	8.2	69.1	22.5	8.5
1999	65.1	27.0	7.9	67.4	23.5	9.2	65.5	25.8	8.7	69.2	21.2	9.6	60.7	29.4	9.9
Peru															
Regions															
1991	34.2	48.2	17.6	36.8	41.5	21.8	32.2	42.8	25.1	41.1	40.2	18.6	29.6	44.2	26.2
1994	34.2	45.1	20.7	35.7	39.7	24.7	33.1	40.5	26.4	38.1	38.9	23.0	31.8	41.0	27.3
National															
1994	37.7	43.3	19.0	39.2	38.2	22.6	36.5	39.4	24.1	41.8	37.1	21.1	34.6	40.0	25.4
2000	37.5	42.7	19.8	37.9	39.4	22.8	32.1	43.8	24.1	43.2	35.3	21.6	30.3	45.1	24.6
Trinidad & Tobago															
1992	49.8	42.2	8.0	52.9	38.4	8.8	54.3	35.9	9.9	51.6	40.8	7.7	55.3	34.2	10.5
Uruguay															
1989	53.5	35.3	11.3	51.3	35.9	12.8	49.7	36.6	13.7	52.8	35.3	12.0	49.6	36.6	13.8
1995	45.4	41.4	13.2	43.4	40.8	15.8	43.7	41.6	14.7	43.1	40.2	16.7	43.8	41.6	14.6
2000	41.6	41.9	16.5	39.5	43.0	17.6	40.0	44.6	15.4	39.1	41.5	19.5	39.7	44.7	15.5
RB de Venezuela															
1989	61.0	30.4	8.6	61.9	27.5	10.6	61.2	27.3	11.6	62.6	27.7	9.7	61.6	27.7	10.7
1998	52.6	33.6	13.8	52.7	32.3	15.0	54.1	32.1	13.9	51.5	32.4	16.1	53.3	32.5	14.2

Note: Low education = less than 8 years of schooling; medium = between 9 and 13 years of schooling; high = more than 14 years of schooling.
Source: Authors' calculations based on microdata from household surveys.

TABLE A.29

Distribution of hourly wages, Gini coefficients

Country	All workers (i)	Urban workers (ii)	All workers Primary job (iii)	Urban workers Primary job (iv)	Men 16–65 Primary job (v)	Men 25–55 Primary job (vi)	Men 25–55 Urban salaried Primary job (vii)	Salaried workers (viii)	Urban salaried workers (ix)
Argentina									
1992	38.2	38.2	38.0	38.0	38.9	39.8	38.3	36.1	36.1
1996	40.4	40.4	40.1	40.1	40.5	40.4	38.9	37.9	37.9
2001	43.3	43.3	43.2	43.2	44.6	43.8	42.6	41.1	41.1
Bolivia									
Urban									
1992	56.9	56.9	57.0	57.0	54.2	50.9	48.2	56.1	56.1
1996	54.3	54.3	54.3	54.3	52.5	52.4	48.6	52.1	52.1
National									
1996	57.0	53.8	56.9	53.8	56.8	57.2	47.9	50.7	51.4
1999	60.9	55.9	61.7	56.7	57.2	57.5	50.8	52.3	52.4
Brazil									
1990	60.2	58.8	60.3	59.0	59.2	58.2	54.0	58.3	57.0
1995	58.8	57.7	59.1	58.0	59.1	58.2	53.9	55.9	55.1
2001	57.4	56.6	57.6	56.8	58.0	57.6	53.7	53.8	53.4
Chile									
1990	56.8	56.0	56.8	56.0	57.7	57.1	50.4		
1996	56.3	55.7	56.3	55.7	56.8	56.3	49.0		
2000	55.8	55.4	55.8	55.4	57.5	57.5	49.5		
Colombia									
Bogotá									
1992	51.5	51.5	51.5	51.5	51.5	50.3	48.5	48.0	48.0
1996	52.3	52.3	51.9	51.9	53.5	52.4	49.6	50.0	50.0
National									
1996	52.2	50.3	51.7	49.5	51.8	51.7	45.9	46.2	46.8
1999	54.1	51.3	54.1	51.3	55.0	55.0	48.2	48.9	46.9
Costa Rica									
1990	42.1	42.2	42.2	42.4	41.7	42.1	40.9	39.8	40.6
1995	42.6	41.7	42.8	41.8	41.6	42.3	39.4	40.1	39.9
2000	43.2	44.0	43.2	44.0	42.2	41.9	41.2	39.8	41.1
Dominican Rep.									
1995	49.1	52.2	49.1	52.2	48.1	47.2	42.8	43.3	45.9
1997	45.6	46.3	45.6	46.4	44.7	46.0	41.7	43.6	44.0
Ecuador									
1994	54.1	50.9	54.6	51.6	52.7	54.0	47.3	47.1	48.9
1998	54.3	53.0	53.3	52.2	50.9	51.7	44.1	47.5	47.6
El Salvador									
1991	54.0	49.6	50.6	48.4	49.5	49.8	41.8	49.5	43.5
1995	49.2	48.6	47.6	47.4	45.3	45.2	39.1	45.3	44.0
2000	48.4	48.9	48.0	48.9	45.1	45.4	38.6	38.5	39.3
Guatemala									
2000	56.9	55.3	56.6	56.1	54.7	56.3	51.6	56.9	55.3
Honduras									
1990	56.2	55.7	56.1	54.7	54.7	55.1	47.9	52.6	51.8
1995	54.7	52.6	55.5	52.7	56.1	55.9	41.3	44.3	44.0
1999	56.3	53.0	57.7	54.3	57.5	57.8	47.1	49.6	48.0
Jamaica									
1990	42.5	41.2	42.5	41.2	39.8	41.9	36.0	40.6	41.1
1999	43.0	45.5	43.0	45.5	39.6	41.9	45.5	42.9	45.8
Mexico									
1992	55.6	53.2	56.3	54.1	56.7	55.3	48.5	49.5	48.1
1996	54.9	52.4	55.5	53.3	55.4	55.1	49.4	51.3	49.4
2000	54.1	51.2	53.9	51.6	54.0	53.2	49.0	49.6	47.8
Nicaragua									
1993	53.2	50.4	53.1	50.3	55.7	56.1	47.1	46.6	45.2
1998	56.6	56.2	56.8	57.1	58.8	58.3	53.9	52.4	54.1
Panama									
1991	48.1		48.4		47.7	46.4		45.7	
1995	49.3	48.3	49.0	48.1	49.1	48.7	46.0	47.2	46.3
2000	50.0	48.8	50.8	49.6	51.7	51.0	46.2	45.6	44.7
Paraguay									
1995	59.0	56.7	57.2	54.8	57.3	57.8	45.1	48.1	48.4
1999	52.7	50.6	53.1	51.2	52.5	52.2	44.1	45.7	45.5
Peru									
Regions									
1991	50.9	48.3	50.5	48.4	47.6	45.5	39.4	44.3	43.8
1994	51.8	49.5	51.4	49.5	50.1	49.1	41.6	45.1	44.0
National									
1994	51.6	49.3	51.2	49.1	50.0	49.0	41.3	45.1	43.8
2000	52.5	50.0	52.4	50.2	50.2	50.0	42.8	46.7	45.5
Trinidad & Tobago									
1992	43.3	46.1	43.3	46.1	40.4	37.7	38.3	41.1	44.7
Uruguay									
1989	43.4	43.4	42.0	42.0	40.7	38.3	35.9	37.8	37.8
1995	44.4	44.4	45.2	45.2	44.6	42.9	40.8	41.3	41.3
2000	44.7	44.7	45.3	45.3	44.7	42.7	39.7	40.9	40.9
RB de Venezuela									
1989	37.1	36.5	37.1	36.5	36.5	35.9	33.7	33.4	32.2
1995	43.8	43.2	43.8	43.2	43.0	42.2	35.6	38.9	36.7
1998	46.6	44.9	46.6	44.9	46.2	46.3	43.2	42.5	41.3

Source: Authors' calculations based on microdata from household surveys.

TABLE A.30

Ratio of hourly wages by educational groups, men ages 25–55

Country	High/medium (i)	High/low (ii)	Medium/low (iii)	Country	High/medium (i)		
Argentina				Guatemala			
1992	1.9	2.5	1.4	2000	2.4		
1996	2.0	2.6	1.3	Honduras			
2001	2.1	2.8	1.4	1990	2.1		
Bolivia				1995	3.0		
Urban				1999	1.9		
1992	1.9	2.5	1.3	Jamaica			
1996	2.2	2.9	1.3	1990	1.7		
National				1999	1.9		
1996	2.1	3.8	1.7	Mexico			
1999	2.1	3.7	1.7	1992	2.2		
Brazil				1996	2.2		
1990	2.2	5.8	2.6	2000	2.7		
1995	2.6	6.2	2.4	Nicaragua			
2001	2.8	6.5	2.3	1993	1.7	3.2	1.9
Chile				1998	2.5	4.7	1.8
1990	2.8	3.8	1.4	Panama			
1996	2.8	4.6	1.7	1991	2.2	3.3	1.5
2000	3.1	5.2	1.7	1995	2.3	3.8	1.7
Colombia				2000	2.3	3.6	1.6
Bogotá				Paraguay			
1992	2.5	4.0	1.6	1995	2.0	3.6	1.8
1996	3.2	4.6	1.4	1999	2.1	2.9	1.4
National				Peru			
1996	2.6	4.8	1.8	Regions			
1999	2.5	4.7	1.9	1991	1.3	1.9	1.5
Costa Rica				1994	1.6	2.4	1.5
1990	2.1	3.2	1.5	National			
1995	2.1	3.0	1.4	1994	1.6	2.3	1.5
2000	2.0	2.9	1.5	2000	1.9	3.0	1.5
Dominican Rep.				Trinidad & Tobago			
1995	2.0	2.7	1.3	1992	2.0	2.6	1.3
1997	1.9	2.5	1.3	Uruguay			
Ecuador				1989	1.6	2.2	1.4
1994	2.0	2.6	1.3	1995	1.9	2.9	1.5
1998	1.8	3.0	1.7	2000	1.9	2.7	1.4
El Salvador				RB de Venezuela			
1991	2.0	3.4	1.6	1989	1.7	2.5	1.4
1995	2.1	3.4	1.6	1995	1.5	2.4	1.6
2000	2.0	3.1	1.6	1998	2.0	2.7	1.4

Source: Authors' calculations based on microdata from household surveys.

TABLE A.31

Marginal returns on completing a given educational level: Mincer equation coefficients on education

	All workers						Urban salaried workers					
	Men			Women			Men			Women		
Country	Primary (i)	Secondary (ii)	College (iii)	Primary (iv)	Secondary (v)	College (vi)	Primary (vii)	Secondary (viii)	College (ix)	Primary (x)	Secondary (xi)	College (xii)
Argentina												
1992	0.179	0.395	0.540	−0.037	0.385	0.403	0.155	0.437	0.526	0.017	0.387	0.223
1996	0.122	0.346	0.721	0.006	0.290	0.601	0.108	0.328	0.722	0.095	0.226	0.523
2001	0.217	0.402	0.758	0.138	0.404	0.630	0.262	0.353	0.745	0.130	0.390	0.580
Bolivia												
Urban												
1992	0.384	0.002	0.631	0.190	0.195	0.594	0.302	0.058	0.680	0.014	0.660	0.670
1996	0.077	0.138	0.908	0.050	0.247	0.991	−0.010	0.149	1.073	0.043	0.518	0.889
National												
1996	0.283	0.177	0.882	0.201	0.244	0.843	0.010	0.166	1.025	0.097	0.442	0.905
1999	0.129	0.413	0.766	0.184	0.664	0.782	0.264	0.073	0.800	0.114	0.621	0.753
Brazil												
1990	0.505	0.415	0.847	0.509	0.500	0.933	0.493	0.478	0.870	0.525	0.545	0.929
1995	0.459	0.412	0.885	0.459	0.594	1.030	0.458	0.426	0.941	0.399	0.485	0.818
2001	0.399	0.392	0.942	0.329	0.376	0.903	0.382	0.395	0.996	0.297	0.437	0.961
Chile												
1990	0.107	0.383	0.808	−0.007	0.716	0.952	0.109	0.380	0.835	−0.024	0.591	0.661
1996	0.057	0.425	0.966	0.099	0.652	1.091	0.040	0.445	0.934	0.005	0.510	0.747
2000	0.084	0.388	0.942	0.115	0.473	0.971	0.088	0.398	0.932	0.015	0.405	0.813
Colombia												
Bogotá												
1992	0.141	0.661	0.891	0.262	0.640	0.804	0.094	0.743	0.874	0.469	0.579	0.824
1996	0.088	0.453	0.990	0.169	0.576	0.966	0.096	0.473	1.020	0.098	0.446	0.911
National												
1996	0.204	0.478	0.840	0.255	0.598	0.777	0.134	0.400	0.943	0.128	0.471	0.793
1999	0.202	0.429	0.905	0.227	0.521	0.859	0.094	0.407	0.875	0.054	0.360	0.833
Costa Rica												
1990	0.142	0.440	0.694	0.211	0.505	0.668	0.130	0.523	0.670	0.014	0.536	0.583
1995	0.157	0.368	0.688	0.196	0.428	0.716	0.178	0.352	0.694	0.361	0.441	0.643
2000	0.077	0.380	0.665	0.023	0.461	0.694	0.055	0.440	0.748	0.155	0.327	0.694
Dominican Rep.												
1995	0.216	0.114	0.862	0.392	0.485	1.198	0.266	0.033	0.904	0.393	0.345	0.815
1997	0.246	0.107	0.711	0.280	0.553	0.955	0.169	0.181	0.746	0.129	0.570	0.611
Ecuador												
1994	0.212	0.399	0.558	0.008	0.641	0.721	0.144	0.529	0.515	0.196	0.571	0.496
1998	0.306	0.378	0.645	0.124	0.649	0.567	−0.050	0.470	0.691	−0.253	0.721	0.411
El Salvador												
1991	0.235	0.351	0.539	0.185	0.537	0.538	0.176	0.436	0.556	0.268	0.563	0.458
1995	0.156	0.433	0.668	0.159	0.737	0.729	0.196	0.382	0.622	0.333	0.762	0.667
2000	0.141	0.351	0.531	0.234	0.221	0.589	0.203	0.265	0.408	0.298	0.262	0.459
Guatemala												
2000	0.356	0.652	0.498	0.307	0.876	0.515	0.370	0.693	0.552	0.193	0.898	0.509
Honduras												
1990	0.368	0.622	0.714	0.349	1.177	0.655	0.376	0.580	0.738	0.342	1.248	0.630
1995	0.243	0.616	0.851	0.384	0.892	0.478	0.207	0.527	0.745	0.321	0.919	0.447
1999	0.330	0.655	0.659	0.409	0.797	0.587	0.331	0.626	0.765	0.391	0.789	0.732
Jamaica												
1990	0.762	0.116	1.000	−0.032	0.386	0.534	0.231	0.280	0.946	0.378	0.431	0.430
1999	0.000	0.296	0.943	0.005	0.478	1.385	0.431	0.090	0.983	0.071	0.490	1.226
Mexico												
1992	0.326	0.504	0.755	0.217	1.051	0.173	0.239	0.573	0.683	0.221	0.957	0.206
1996	0.303	0.686	0.575	0.283	0.858	0.389	0.306	0.641	0.649	0.285	0.898	0.383
2000	0.347	0.449	0.840	0.195	0.663	0.416	0.259	0.459	0.846	0.210	0.856	0.533
Nicaragua												
1993	0.190	0.296	0.435	0.098	0.288	0.379	0.236	0.219	0.576	0.043	0.345	0.502
1998	0.350	0.290	0.771	0.136	0.236	0.823	0.269	0.418	0.696	0.222	0.354	0.803
Panama												
1991	0.081	0.377	0.805	0.273	0.815	0.743	0.193	0.509	0.750	0.255	0.814	0.698
1995	0.232	0.424	0.851	0.223	0.799	0.797	0.271	0.472	0.841	0.193	0.752	0.804
2000	0.182	0.365	0.956	0.256	0.534	0.712	0.126	0.310	0.936	0.159	0.430	0.768
Paraguay												
1995	0.193	0.543	0.822	0.163	0.703	0.647	0.269	0.473	0.723	0.325	0.673	0.633
1999	0.250	0.425	0.837	0.335	0.439	0.983	0.333	0.349	0.821	0.401	0.502	0.706
Peru												
Regions												
1991	0.300	0.139	0.360	0.047	0.285	0.458	0.118	0.342	0.314	−0.167	0.217	0.407
1994	−0.005	0.332	0.513	0.151	0.299	0.410	0.125	0.400	0.510	−0.224	0.410	0.567
National												
1994	0.016	0.321	0.496	0.180	0.286	0.407	0.077	0.391	0.492	−0.096	0.397	0.554
2000	0.156	0.370	0.637	0.021	0.368	0.727	0.167	0.189	0.690	0.078	0.356	0.572
Trinidad & Tobago												
1992	0.208	0.252	0.601	−0.027	0.682	0.965	0.152	0.379	0.563	0.309	0.583	0.881
Uruguay												
1989	0.088	0.338	0.600	−0.010	0.433	0.544	0.088	0.336	0.599	−0.012	0.437	0.529
1995	0.140	0.426	0.626	0.088	0.608	0.627	0.129	0.462	0.593	0.054	0.604	0.520
2000	0.150	0.403	0.689	0.097	0.511	0.688	0.215	0.407	0.681	0.082	0.478	0.580
RB de Venezuela												
1989	0.257	0.338	0.504	0.327	0.521	0.480	0.095	0.322	0.522	0.151	0.422	0.498
1995	0.215	0.355	0.444	0.172	0.278	0.371	0.098	0.261	0.483	0.240	0.389	0.543
1998	0.192	0.347	0.510	0.092	0.246	0.408	−0.020	0.418	0.638	−0.018	0.638	0.524

Notes: Regressions are estimated by Heckman's two-stage procedure. Dependent variable: logarithm of hourly wage from primary job of individuals ages 25–55.
Explanatory variables: educational dummies, age, age squared, regional dummies, and urban/rural dummy. Selection equation: same variables plus number of children and school attendance.
Source: Authors' calculations based on microdata from household surveys.

TABLE A.32

Dispersion in unobservables and gender wage gap

Country	Dispersion in unobservables				Gender wage gap Urban salaried workers (v)	Country	Dispersion in unobservables				Gender wage gap Urban salaried workers (v)
	All workers		Urban salaried				All workers		Urban salaried		
	Men (i)	Women (ii)	Men (iii)	Women (iv)			Men (i)	Women (ii)	Men (iii)	Women (iv)	
Argentina						Guatemala					
1992	0.571	0.596	0.532	0.507	0.867	2000	0.804	0.942	0.753	0.921	0.757
1996	0.600	0.621	0.553	0.518	0.909	Honduras					
2001	0.659	0.652	0.601	0.543	0.874	1990	0.851	0.884	0.620	0.654	0.777
Bolivia						1995	0.862	0.813	0.549	0.590	0.817
Urban						1999	0.967	0.902	0.628	0.625	0.834
1992	0.764	0.915	0.676	0.695	0.765	Jamaica					
1996	0.736	1.013	0.663	0.686	0.801	1990	0.638	0.560	0.524	0.572	0.599
National						1999	0.615	0.803	0.608	0.689	0.817
1996	0.953	0.944	0.658	0.702	0.792	Mexico					
1999	1.009	1.131	0.689	0.764	0.778	1992	0.783	0.821	0.644	0.625	0.824
Brazil						1996	0.790	0.834	0.662	0.635	1.074
1990	0.806	0.784	0.735	0.702	0.636	2000	0.738	0.930	0.609	0.633	0.960
1995	0.770	0.927	0.689	0.665	0.625	Nicaragua					
2001	0.748	0.727	0.660	0.636	0.693	1993	0.930	0.795	0.684	0.633	0.828
Chile						1998	0.960	0.831	0.769	0.703	0.779
1990	0.780	0.914	0.662	0.618	0.699	Panama					
1996	0.735	1.010	0.624	0.625	0.754	1991	0.756	0.659	0.587	0.602	0.798
2000	0.727	0.802	0.577	0.574	0.777	1995	0.665	0.673	0.583	0.593	0.743
Colombia						2000	0.698	0.658	0.587	0.556	0.824
Bogotá						Paraguay					
1992	0.856	0.836	0.750	0.774	0.825	1995	0.898	0.929	0.603	0.657	0.812
1996	0.718	0.670	0.597	0.536	0.802	1999	0.815	0.831	0.585	0.585	0.853
National						Peru					
1996	0.795	0.742	0.553	0.519	0.822	Regions					
1999	0.875	0.809	0.608	0.574	0.887	1991	0.786	1.051	0.676	0.664	0.835
Costa Rica						1994	0.770	0.857	0.609	0.609	0.869
1990	0.634	0.671	0.562	0.514	0.770	National					
1995	0.634	0.678	0.525	0.535	0.789	1994	0.784	0.856	0.628	0.601	0.881
2000	0.629	0.689	0.553	0.554	0.845	2000	0.867	0.918	0.663	0.749	0.903
Dominican Rep.						Trinidad & Tobago					
1995	0.716	0.953	0.628	0.603	0.825	1992	0.637	0.700	0.573	0.566	0.858
1997	0.664	0.929	0.595	0.606	0.829	Uruguay					
Ecuador						1989	0.604	0.667	0.535	0.601	0.752
1994	0.853	0.940	0.683	0.752	0.754	1995	0.667	0.688	0.585	0.600	0.768
1998	0.838	0.947	0.661	0.700	0.798	2000	0.662	0.657	0.574	0.588	0.789
El Salvador						RB de Venezuela					
1991	0.849	0.806	0.601	0.597	0.806	1989	0.552	0.547	0.476	0.426	0.832
1995	0.606	0.716	0.539	0.627	0.782	1995	0.722	0.863	0.593	0.599	0.858
2000	0.691	0.830	0.628	0.596	0.815	1998	0.814	0.928	0.667	0.629	0.855

Notes: Dispersion in unobservables = standard deviation of error term in Mincer equations of table A.31. Gender wage gap = ratio of the mean of the counterfactual wage that men would earn if they were paid like women over the actual average wage for men. Higher values in column (v) mean a narrower gender gap in hourly wages.
Source: Authors' calculations based on microdata from household surveys.

TABLE A.33

Distribution of hourly wages by educational group, men ages 25–55, Gini coefficients

Country	Educational groups			Total (iv)	Country	Educational groups			Total (iv)
	Low (i)	Medium (ii)	High (iii)			Low (i)	Medium (ii)	High (iii)	
Argentina					Guatemala				
1992	31.1	34.0	41.5	39.8	2000	47.2	43.2	46.6	56.3
1996	32.2	33.8	40.6	40.4	Honduras				
2001	35.3	36.6	42.5	43.8	1990	51.0	40.9	39.8	55.1
Bolivia					1995	51.1	41.1	54.6	56.0
Urban					1999	55.3	47.6	42.5	57.8
1992	46.9	48.0	47.1	50.9	Jamaica				
1996	40.0	49.2	49.1	52.4	1990	44.2	40.7	19.9	41.9
National					1999	29.7	42.9	33.9	41.9
1996	53.3	48.9	48.8	57.2	Mexico				
1999	58.7	44.1	48.6	57.5	1992	48.4	48.6	45.9	55.3
Brazil					1996	45.6	49.8	47.0	55.1
1990	49.7	47.0	41.9	58.2	2000	45.0	42.2	45.2	53.2
1995	48.7	46.7	44.9	58.2	Nicaragua				
2001	45.6	47.6	48.0	57.6	1993	54.2	48.4	51.3	56.1
Chile					1998	53.1	49.0	58.9	58.3
1990	50.3	48.2	53.7	57.1	Panama				
1996	43.1	46.5	53.0	56.3	1991	38.2	39.0	42.3	46.4
2000	39.8	45.8	55.6	57.5	1995	37.4	41.2	44.2	48.7
Colombia					2000	39.7	44.9	46.4	51.0
Bogotá					Paraguay				
1992	39.0	42.5	39.7	50.3	1995	55.3	51.4	45.9	57.8
1996	39.0	40.1	44.7	52.4	1999	53.4	40.4	43.8	52.2
National					Peru				
1996	42.2	42.5	42.7	51.7	Regions				
1999	44.9	47.6	45.4	55.0	1991	43.0	46.0	40.9	45.5
Costa Rica					1994	44.0	47.3	45.9	49.1
1990	34.5	34.7	36.7	42.1	National				
1995	34.8	34.7	37.0	42.3	1994	46.0	46.7	45.5	49.0
2000	33.2	38.1	36.7	41.9	2000	48.7	43.1	46.6	50.0
Dominican Rep.					Trinidad & Tobago				
1995	41.2	44.5	45.5	47.2	1992	32.2	31.9	38.3	37.7
1997	42.6	41.7	43.3	46.0	Uruguay				
Ecuador					1989	31.8	36.1	41.3	38.3
1994	51.7	46.2	48.2	54.0	1995	34.0	38.7	43.4	42.9
1998	44.3	50.1	45.5	51.7	2000	34.9	38.3	43.3	42.7
El Salvador					RB de Venezuela				
1991	46.6	41.6	41.7	49.8	1989	30.8	32.1	33.2	35.9
1995	38.7	37.2	37.0	45.2	1995	39.1	39.5	36.5	42.2
2000	40.4	41.6	42.8	45.4	1998	40.7	40.8	44.2	46.3

Source: Authors' calculations based on microdata from household surveys.

TABLE A.34

Wages and hours worked, by education level

Country	Correlation between hours worked and hourly wages — All workers (i)	Urban salaried workers (ii)	Hours worked — Education — Low (iii)	Medium (iv)	High (v)	Total (vi)
Argentina						
1992	−0.1700*	−0.1617*	44.6	44.7	40.0	43.7
1996	−0.2131*	−0.1835*	42.2	45.6	41.5	43.3
2001	−0.1916*	−0.1758*	40.2	44.0	40.2	41.6
Bolivia						
Urban						
1992	−0.1355*	−0.1359*	50.8	48.7	41.1	48.3
1996	−0.1872*	−0.2472*	48.9	48.1	41.9	47.2
National						
1996	−0.1776*	−0.2479*	48.6	47.9	41.4	47.5
1999	−0.2094*	−0.2484*	49.6	50.0	42.2	48.4
Brazil						
1990	−0.0718*	−0.1368*	44.5	41.7	41.1	43.8
1995	−0.0915*	−0.1356*	44.7	42.5	42.1	44.0
2001	−0.1081*	−0.1276*	44.5	43.1	42.2	43.9
Chile						
1990	−0.1581*	−0.2322*	50.4	50.5	45.6	49.6
2000	−0.1507*	−0.1856*	48.0	49.0	46.0	48.0
Colombia						
Bogotá						
1992	−0.1986*	−0.2142*	49.1	46.8	44.8	47.4
1996	−0.1809*	−0.2157*	49.3	48.2	45.6	48.3
National						
1996	−0.1777*	−0.2390*	48.2	47.1	44.2	47.5
1999	−0.1280*	−0.2709*	47.5	46.9	44.1	46.9
Costa Rica						
1990	−0.1655*	−0.1853*	47.3	47.7	44.6	47.1
1995	−0.1653*	−0.1662*	45.8	47.7	45.3	46.3
2000	−0.1795*	−0.2255*	46.7	48.1	45.6	46.9
Dominican Rep.						
1995	−0.1144*	−0.1526*	44.1	43.2	42.8	43.7
1997	−0.1841*	−0.2221*	43.4	43.2	41.2	43.1
Ecuador						
1994	−0.1153*	−0.1359*	44.0	46.4	43.6	44.5
1998	−0.1057*	−0.1866*	44.7	49.3	45.9	46.1
El Salvador						
1991	−0.0582*	−0.2361*	48.1	48.2	43.2	47.7
1995	−0.1575*	−0.3035*	48.0	47.3	42.7	47.4
2000	−0.1551*	−0.1718*	44.3	46.6	42.7	44.8
Guatemala						
2000	−0.1603*	−0.2060*	51.0	50.3	46.7	50.7

Country	Correlation between hours worked and hourly wages — All workers (i)	Urban salaried workers (ii)	Hours worked — Education — Low (iii)	Medium (iv)	High (v)	Total (vi)
Honduras						
1990	−0.1451*	−0.2773*	46.7	45.0	43.2	46.4
1995	−0.1330*	−0.2341*	48.0	46.8	46.4	47.8
1999	−0.1336*	−0.2261*	47.0	47.1	48.7	47.1
Jamaica						
1990	−0.0872*	−0.1035*	38.7	40.1	38.7	39.6
1999	−0.0666*	−0.0525	41.0	42.9	41.5	42.4
Mexico						
1992	−0.1267*	−0.1787*	48.1	46.6	44.4	47.3
1996	−0.1290*	−0.1437*	47.0	47.0	44.7	46.8
2000	−0.1361*	−0.2006*	48.3	48.2	44.0	47.6
Nicaragua						
1993	−0.1563*	−0.1677*	49.1	46.3	46.2	48.4
1998	−0.1456*	−0.1756*	49.9	48.4	46.7	49.4
Panama						
1991	−0.1164*	−0.1713*	42.3	42.5	41.7	42.3
1995	−0.1078*	−0.1462*	43.1	43.7	43.3	43.4
2000	−0.1237*	−0.1705*	42.2	43.7	43.1	43.1
Paraguay						
1995	−0.1642*	−0.2746*	41.8	45.0	40.9	42.4
1999	−0.1591*	−0.1960*	45.9	47.6	43.5	46.2
Peru						
Regions						
1991	−0.2170*	−0.2321*	47.0	46.2	43.5	45.9
1994	−0.2417*	−0.2098*	47.6	48.4	44.0	47.1
National						
1994	−0.2371*	−0.2169*	47.2	48.3	44.1	46.9
2000	−0.2137*	−0.2085*	46.1	49.9	46.3	47.7
Trinidad & Tobago						
1992	−0.1493*	−0.1904*	38.7	40.8	41.1	39.9
Uruguay						
1989	−0.0583*	−0.1221*	46.3	47.0	44.3	46.3
1995	−0.1139*	−0.1101*	45.5	45.9	43.1	45.3
2000	−0.0927*	−0.1095*	43.2	45.2	41.7	43.8
RB de Venezuela						
1989	−0.1180*	−0.1835*	42.9	41.8	40.5	42.4
1995	−0.1344*	−0.2186*	42.6	42.2	40.8	42.3
1998	−0.1359*	−0.1832*	41.8	42.2	40.8	41.8

*Significant at 5%.
Source: Authors' calculations based on microdata from household surveys.

TABLE A.35

Between- and within-group inequality in the distribution of hourly wages, Theil decompositions

Country	Education		Gender		Age		Urban/rural	
	Between	Within	Between	Within	Between	Within	Between	Within
Argentina								
1992	18.3	81.7	0.3	99.7	0.2	99.8		
1996	22.6	77.4	0.0	100.0	0.5	99.5		
2001	24.4	75.6	0.0	100.0	0.7	99.3		
Bolivia								
Urban								
1992	9.8	90.2	0.7	99.3	0.2	99.8		
1996	16.4	83.6	1.5	98.5	1.7	98.3		
National								
1996	19.7	80.3	0.3	99.7	0.3	99.7	10.4	89.6
1999	15.9	84.1	0.0	100.0	0.3	99.7	11.0	89.0
Brazil								
1990	35.0	65.0	1.2	98.8	0.6	99.4	8.3	91.7
1995	33.6	66.4	1.2	98.8	1.4	98.6	5.7	94.3
2001	32.3	67.7	0.6	99.4	1.7	98.3	4.2	95.8
Chile								
1990	16.1	83.9	1.0	99.0	1.7	98.3	1.8	98.2
1996	24.1	75.9	0.4	99.6	2.1	97.9	3.7	96.3
2000	24.7	75.3	1.3	98.7	1.8	98.2	2.7	97.3
Colombia								
Bogotá								
1992	32.7	67.3	1.6	98.4	0.7	99.3		
1996	36.9	63.1	1.5	98.5	1.7	98.3		
National								
1996	32.2	67.8	0.1	99.9	0.5	99.5	8.4	91.6
1999	28.7	71.3	0.0	100.0	0.8	99.2	5.1	94.9
Costa Rica								
1990	28.0	72.0	0.1	99.9	0.9	99.1	9.8	90.2
1995	25.9	74.1	0.0	100.0	0.6	99.4	5.3	94.7
2000	24.2	75.8	0.3	99.7	0.8	99.2	7.2	92.8
Dominican Rep.								
1995	17.0	83.0	0.2	99.8	1.0	99.0	3.5	96.5
Ecuador								
1994	12.1	87.9	0.6	99.4	1.4	98.6	2.6	97.4
1998	17.5	82.5	0.7	99.3	0.5	99.5	6.9	93.1
El Salvador								
1991	16.9	83.1	0.3	99.7	0.3	99.7	8.5	91.5
1995	29.6	70.4	3.1	96.9	0.3	99.7	8.9	91.1
2000	14.9	85.1	1.5	98.5	0.6	99.4	5.7	94.3
Guatemala								
2000	32.8	67.2	1.4	98.6	0.9	99.1	9.6	90.4
Honduras								
1990	26.6	73.4	0.1	99.9	0.4	99.6	11.1	88.9
1995	22.6	77.4	1.0	99.0	1.6	98.4	3.7	96.3
1999	16.6	83.4	0.4	99.6	0.6	99.4	4.4	95.6
Jamaica								
1990	4.8	95.2	6.5	93.5	1.1	98.9	0.6	99.4
1999	12.4	87.6	0.3	99.7	1.4	98.6	5.0	95.0
Mexico								
1992	24.2	75.8	0.5	99.5	1.2	98.8	5.5	94.5
1996	25.0	75.0	0.5	99.5	0.3	99.7	5.5	94.5
2000	31.0	69.0	1.2	98.8	2.6	97.4	6.0	94.0
Nicaragua								
1993	11.1	88.9	0.3	99.7	1.9	98.1	5.6	94.4
1998	19.7	80.3	1.1	98.9	0.4	99.6	5.2	94.8
Panama								
1991	27.6	72.4	0.2	99.8	2.2	97.8		
1995	25.0	75.0	0.4	99.6	3.0	97.0	6.9	93.1
2000	18.9	81.1	0.0	100.0	1.4	98.6	5.6	94.4
Paraguay								
1995	15.0	85.0	0.3	99.7	1.2	98.8	5.3	94.7
1999	16.2	83.8	0.4	99.6	0.4	99.6	5.6	94.4
Peru								
1991	5.7	94.3	0.0	100.0	0.1	99.9	4.7	95.3
1994	13.9	86.1	0.8	99.2	1.2	98.8	5.3	94.7
2000	14.7	85.3	0.1	99.9	0.7	99.3	8.0	92.0
Trinidad & Tobago								
1992	27.0	73.0	1.0	99.0	1.8	98.2	0.6	99.4
Uruguay								
1989	14.5	85.5	3.0	97.0	0.9	99.1		
1995	20.2	79.8	0.7	99.3	0.8	99.2		
2000	17.3	82.7	0.3	99.7	1.5	98.5		
RB de Venezuela								
1989	21.7	78.3	0.9	99.1	1.4	98.6	4.0	96.0
1995	10.7	89.3	0.3	99.7	0.6	99.4	2.2	97.8
1998	14.1	85.9	0.8	99.2	0.8	99.2	2.0	98.0

Source: Authors' calculations based on microdata from household surveys.

TABLE A.36

Employment and unemployment, by education level

| | % adults employed | | | | | | % adults unemployed | | | | | | Duration of unemployment (months) | | | |
| | Education | | | Gender | | | Education | | | Gender | | | Education | | | |
Country	Low (i)	Medium (ii)	High (iii)	Female (iv)	Male (v)	Total (vi)	Low (vii)	Medium (viii)	High (ix)	Female (x)	Male (xi)	Total (xii)	Low (xiii)	Medium (xiv)	High (xv)	Total (xvi)
Argentina																
1992	57.1	63.0	74.3	45.0	81.5	62.7	4.1	4.6	3.5	3.2	5.3	4.2	3.1	4.4	4.7	3.9
1996	52.6	57.7	70.9	41.6	74.4	57.3	12.1	12.1	8.6	10.5	12.7	11.6	6.7	8.7	10.0	8.0
2001	52.2	54.7	72.5	45.0	70.0	57.7	13.9	14.0	8.0	9.6	16.2	12.6	6.2	7.2	8.8	7.0
Bolivia																
Urban																
1992	65.0	54.7	79.8	48.7	78.0	62.8	2.9	4.3	2.6	2.9	4.0	3.4	5.7	6.7	7.4	6.4
1996	74.3	62.2	68.8	58.6	80.2	68.6	1.9	3.9	3.8	2.9	3.3	3.1	3.7	3.3	5.1	3.9
National																
1996	82.4	65.9	72.0	67.5	87.6	76.9	1.0	3.4	3.4	1.7	2.1	1.9	3.1	3.1	5.1	3.6
1999	79.1	62.3	71.1	62.5	84.1	72.8	1.5	5.3	3.0	2.9	2.8	2.9	4.1	3.3	10.1	4.7
Brazil																
1990	63.9	71.4	85.0	46.6	87.6	66.5	2.2	3.4	1.4	1.5	3.3	2.4	3.6	4.5	5.0	3.9
1995	68.4	72.1	85.1	55.2	86.2	70.2	3.8	5.5	2.3	3.9	4.3	4.1	0.6	0.7	1.0	0.6
2001	64.9	69.1	82.8	53.8	82.1	67.4	5.9	8.8	3.7	6.9	6.2	6.6	0.7	0.7	0.7	0.7
Chile																
1990	50.5	55.0	69.5	34.1	78.0	55.0	4.4	5.6	3.7	3.6	6.2	4.8				
1996	54.9	60.6	69.0	39.7	81.2	59.8	3.0	4.3	2.6	3.1	4.0	3.5	1.9	2.7	2.6	2.4
2000	52.2	57.7	68.4	41.0	76.0	57.9	6.2	7.6	4.5	5.4	7.8	6.6	3.6	3.7	4.6	3.8
Colombia																
Bogotá																
1992	64.1	64.2	81.9	53.4	84.2	67.4	4.8	6.4	4.2	5.9	4.6	5.3	6.5	8.5	8.3	7.7
1996	62.2	65.4	76.2	52.1	81.4	65.7	7.1	7.5	5.6	7.2	6.8	7.0	5.6	6.6	8.7	6.4
National																
1996	60.2	61.7	80.3	43.2	83.6	62.3	4.7	8.5	5.2	6.0	5.6	5.8	5.9	7.5	8.2	6.7
1999	59.1	56.5	75.6	43.3	78.5	60.0	8.1	15.2	10.2	11.1	10.1	10.6	7.5	9.2	10.1	8.6
Costa Rica																
1990	57.0	62.6	72.2	34.3	87.5	60.3	2.0	3.2	2.0	1.7	2.9	2.3	3.3	4.8	5.6	4.1
1995	57.8	62.6	73.6	37.2	86.9	61.5	2.3	3.7	2.4	2.2	3.3	2.7	3.0	4.0	5.9	3.8
2000	57.6	64.2	76.1	39.5	86.1	62.2	3.3	3.1	1.8	2.6	3.5	3.0	3.9	5.1	6.8	4.6
Dominican Rep.																
1995	55.9	55.0	72.5	34.6	81.9	57.5	8.7	12.7	9.6	11.7	8.3	10.0	0.9	1.0	2.5	1.1
1997	57.8	58.6	72.4	36.3	83.6	59.5	8.9	13.6	12.6	12.9	8.0	10.5	1.1	1.4	1.5	1.3
Ecuador																
1994	73.7	69.9	81.3	56.6	90.3	73.4	0.9	2.8	2.5	1.4	1.7	1.6	1.2	2.3	3.4	2.1
1998	74.2	69.7	81.6	58.2	90.3	73.9	1.9	3.6	2.5	2.1	2.9	2.5	1.9	1.9	3.5	2.1
El Salvador																
1991	58.1	63.6	69.0	41.7	82.8	60.3	4.7	6.6	4.6	3.5	7.2	5.2	4.6	7.0	8.7	5.9
1995	60.7	63.5	76.3	45.2	83.4	62.5	3.9	6.3	3.2	2.6	6.8	4.5	3.3	5.6	7.8	4.3
2000	61.5	63.0	72.8	49.2	79.6	63.1	3.9	6.2	3.6	2.0	7.7	4.6	1.0	1.6	1.8	1.3
Guatemala																
2000	66.1	70.5	83.7	46.2	92.2	67.7	0.8	2.5	1.2	0.8	1.3	1.1	1.2	2.1	3.8	1.7
Honduras																
1990	61.6	63.2	66.8	36.5	89.6	62.0	2.5	8.3	7.3	2.9	4.0	3.4	4.3	8.1	7.7	5.7
1995	61.7	64.7	73.9	37.5	90.4	62.6	1.6	3.7	2.4	1.3	2.8	2.0	3.8	6.4	7.3	4.7
1999	66.4	69.9	75.0	47.6	90.5	67.4	2.1	3.2	2.8	1.6	3.1	2.3	2.2	4.7	3.9	2.9
Jamaica																
1990	68.3	63.4	79.7	53.4	78.9	65.9	7.2	13.6	3.7	14.9	6.4	10.7	9.7	9.6	9.5	9.6
1999	69.2	72.4	86.8	59.2	82.9	70.6	5.4	8.5	1.9	9.4	5.0	7.3	8.6	8.6	9.6	8.6
Mexico																
1992	52.4	60.1	69.6	32.7	81.5	56.2	1.5	2.7	2.7	1.0	3.0	2.0				
1996	59.6	64.0	73.8	42.2	85.1	62.5	1.8	3.7	3.7	1.5	3.8	2.6				
2000	61.9	65.7	73.1	43.2	86.7	63.8	0.8	1.7	1.6	0.6	1.9	1.2				
Nicaragua																
1993	50.3	54.1	70.9	35.2	70.3	51.7	12.8	16.2	15.2	9.3	18.1	13.5	5.2	6.5	7.6	5.7
1998	56.1	54.7	63.0	35.8	76.4	56.1	5.9	9.4	9.6	5.6	7.9	6.8	2.0	2.0	2.0	2.0
Panama																
1991	53.4	51.9	67.5	34.5	76.0	54.8	6.6	15.4	11.4	9.9	11.2	10.5	10.5	14.2	19.4	13.8
1995	56.9	58.8	74.0	39.5	81.1	60.2	7.0	13.2	9.1	10.0	9.6	9.8	8.7	10.4	13.2	10.2
2000	56.9	57.1	75.2	40.3	79.8	60.3	5.9	9.5	5.6	5.6	9.0	7.4	6.4	8.0	11.1	7.9
Paraguay																
1995	79.2	76.9	88.8	66.1	92.9	79.4	1.5	3.7	2.0	1.8	2.2	2.0	5.3	5.0	7.1	5.3
1999	66.7	68.7	83.4	50.9	86.5	68.6	2.9	5.3	2.6	3.1	4.0	3.5	5.1	6.8	6.7	5.9
Peru																
Regions																
1991	68.4	61.0	73.6	52.5	80.2	65.6	1.5	4.0	3.3	2.4	3.2	2.8				
1994	69.3	59.7	71.2	51.3	81.3	65.4	1.6	4.1	4.1	2.3	3.9	3.0				
National																
1994	71.0	61.2	71.8	52.5	82.9	66.9	1.4	3.9	4.1	2.1	3.6	2.8				
2000	75.1	67.4	73.6	60.0	84.1	71.6	1.7	4.5	4.8	3.1	3.9	3.5	1.4	2.3	2.3	2.2
Trinidad & Tobago																
1992	47.0	53.9	77.1	36.2	69.1	52.4	13.3	14.7	4.7	10.1	16.3	13.2				
Uruguay																
1989	60.3	70.7	79.1	49.9	85.2	66.1	3.4	6.5	4.6	4.9	4.3	4.6	5.8	7.1	9.3	6.8
1995	59.9	70.8	80.9	53.0	83.3	67.2	5.5	8.2	3.5	6.9	5.8	6.3	5.9	6.5	8.2	6.4
2000	59.3	70.1	74.0	54.0	80.0	66.3	9.7	10.3	8.8	10.6	8.8	9.8	7.0	7.7	7.1	7.3
RB de Venezuela																
1989	56.4	58.8	73.4	36.7	80.3	58.5	6.3	6.1	4.4	3.0	9.0	6.0	7.0	8.0	6.9	7.3
1995	60.0	62.7	75.5	41.1	82.4	61.8	6.0	7.6	6.4	6.0	7.3	6.6	9.5	12.3	17.2	11.0
1998	62.7	65.0	72.7	47.5	82.2	64.9	7.2	8.8	6.9	6.6	8.8	7.7	8.6	10.6	13.7	9.9

Note: Data for Brazil, 1995 and 2001: duration refers to average months since workers left their last jobs.
Source: Authors' calculations based on microdata from household surveys.

TABLE A.37

Distributions of income sources, by equivalized household income quintile

Country	Capital income, rents, and profits					Pensions					Transfers excluding pensions				
	1	2	3	4	5	1	2	3	4	5	1	2	3	4	5
Argentina															
1992	0.9	1.3	2.3	11.9	83.6	9.0	18.1	19.0	21.2	32.6	3.3	6.7	14.4	28.1	47.5
1996	1.0	0.6	5.1	9.1	84.2	5.0	11.2	17.1	21.4	45.4	5.8	8.7	12.5	29.7	43.4
2001	1.5	4.6	7.4	16.3	70.3	2.7	9.0	17.0	26.5	44.8	8.1	9.3	12.3	23.4	46.9
Bolivia															
Urban															
1992						4.9	8.0	14.5	19.0	53.8	3.7	4.8	6.7	15.7	69.0
1996	4.1	6.7	6.1	11.5	71.7	5.1	6.6	8.7	25.9	53.6	7.7	11.3	14.6	19.2	47.1
National															
1996	0.4	2.6	7.2	9.4	80.4	0.4	4.9	10.1	20.1	64.6	2.1	8.6	14.5	21.0	53.8
1999	0.5	2.0	5.9	15.7	75.8	0.0	1.9	5.8	14.4	77.9	1.7	6.4	14.2	22.0	55.7
Brazil															
1990	1.4	3.2	5.8	10.9	78.7	3.4	6.1	8.4	15.5	66.6	0.0	3.8	2.9	15.9	77.5
1995	0.5	1.5	3.8	9.6	84.6	2.6	7.3	11.4	16.2	62.6	7.6	10.6	13.4	19.9	48.5
2001	3.2	3.4	4.5	10.5	78.4	2.0	6.0	11.6	17.4	62.9	9.7	10.9	10.8	18.0	50.5
Chile															
1990	0.0	0.0	1.1	9.7	89.1	4.7	9.3	15.3	25.2	45.5	23.4	22.5	20.9	18.0	15.2
1996						2.8	8.1	16.6	25.8	46.7	28.7	26.6	22.2	16.7	5.8
2000						2.4	7.1	14.6	23.8	52.1	33.0	29.0	20.8	12.3	4.9
Colombia															
1999	2.0	3.2	5.5	13.5	75.7	0.4	3.4	7.8	16.6	71.9	5.4	8.5	10.3	15.9	59.9
Costa Rica															
1995						5.4	8.6	13.0	19.8	53.2	10.7	10.4	10.7	17.3	51.0
2000						6.6	8.7	10.3	18.2	56.2	11.0	10.5	10.6	16.2	51.7
Dominican Rep.															
1997	4.4	6.4	8.8	16.4	63.9	3.6	6.5	6.0	9.8	74.1	6.2	9.7	12.3	23.3	48.5
Ecuador															
1994	2.4	4.1	11.5	17.1	64.9										
1998	1.2	3.1	4.5	8.7	82.5										
El Salvador															
1991	1.1	2.5	5.3	9.9	81.2	1.6	4.2	9.4	21.9	62.8	4.7	8.7	13.3	20.7	52.5
2000	2.1	3.2	4.0	9.9	80.8	1.4	6.3	11.4	17.9	63.0	11.1	13.8	14.6	17.1	43.4
Guatemala															
2000	0.1	0.2	1.4	2.3	95.9	0.7	2.3	5.9	12.9	78.2	2.1	5.4	11.4	16.0	65.0
Mexico															
1992	1.8	3.8	5.8	17.2	71.4	1.5	11.6	13.4	21.0	52.5	5.0	11.4	14.5	15.3	53.8
1996	1.4	4.0	5.3	9.1	80.2	1.8	8.5	14.8	24.0	50.9	3.4	11.5	13.1	22.6	49.4
2000	1.6	1.8	6.0	7.1	83.4	1.3	5.9	9.9	12.3	70.5	10.5	11.0	14.5	18.9	45.0
Nicaragua															
1993	1.8	13.3	4.5	6.0	74.4	8.9	12.9	17.2	19.5	41.4	3.1	4.9	9.5	15.3	67.2
1998	0.2	0.8	1.3	4.1	93.6	3.9	3.2	10.7	19.0	63.2	3.7	7.8	10.4	16.5	61.5
Panama															
1991	4.7	5.4	7.3	13.2	69.4	0.7	4.6	9.5	21.1	64.1	18.4	20.7	17.7	17.4	25.9
1995	2.3	3.4	7.3	12.7	74.3	0.8	4.4	9.5	20.5	64.8	8.2	10.6	13.3	21.5	46.4
2000	0.7	2.4	8.4	9.1	79.3	0.7	3.6	7.8	19.0	69.0	12.1	13.7	15.3	19.9	38.9
Paraguay															
1995	0.1	0.9	2.7	8.2	88.1	0.2	10.6	7.5	16.5	65.3	5.1	7.5	17.4	18.8	51.2
1999	1.1	1.8	3.9	11.4	81.7	0.5	1.9	12.0	19.2	66.4	6.2	14.4	17.8	17.0	44.7
Peru															
1994	0.8	1.8	5.8	5.8	85.8	1.8	5.8	15.7	22.1	54.6	5.4	10.8	16.2	22.3	45.4
2000	0.8	2.9	5.6	12.3	78.5	0.4	3.5	9.3	22.6	64.1	4.7	9.5	13.6	18.8	53.4
Uruguay															
1995	1.1	2.6	6.2	13.1	76.9	5.7	13.1	17.7	22.6	40.9	12.3	15.1	18.6	22.9	31.1
2000	0.6	2.2	5.2	10.8	81.2	3.7	9.6	15.5	23.3	47.9	13.7	16.3	20.1	23.0	26.8
RB de Venezuela															
1995	5.0	5.8	10.9	11.5	66.8						10.5	11.7	15.0	17.7	45.1
1998	3.6	7.4	8.9	12.1	68.1						8.7	10.8	15.8	22.4	42.3

Source: Authors' calculations based on microdata from household surveys.

TABLE A.38

Distribution of operational holdings of agricultural land worldwide: Gini coefficients

Region	Deininger & Olinto (i)	UNDP (ii)
Latin America	**0.81**	**0.74**
Middle East and North Africa	0.67	0.56
North America	0.64	
Sub-Saharan Africa	0.61	0.51
Western Europe	0.57	
East Asia & South Asia	0.56	0.52

Note: Column (i) shows averages for the 1950–1994 period; Column (ii) shows values around 1981.
Source: Deininger and Olinto 2000 and UNDP 1993.

TABLE A.39

Distribution of operational holdings of agricultural land in Latin America: Gini coefficients

	Deininger & Olinto		UNDP
	1950–1979 (i)	1980–1994 (ii)	1981 (iii)
Antigua	0.74		
Argentina	0.86	0.85	
Bahamas	0.90	0.87	
Barbados	0.90	0.93	
Belize	0.72	0.71	
Bolivia		0.77	
Brazil	0.83	0.85	0.86
Colombia	0.85	0.77	0.70
Costa Rica	0.81		
Chile			0.64
Dominican Rep.	0.80		0.70
Ecuador	0.86		0.69
El Salvador	0.83		
Grenada	0.78	0.74	0.69
Guatemala	0.86		
Guyana		0.68	
Honduras	0.75		0.64
Jamaica	0.81	0.81	
Mexico	0.59		
Nicaragua	0.80		
Panama	0.71	0.87	0.84
Paraguay	0.86	0.78	0.94
Peru	0.94		0.61
Puerto Rico	0.73	0.77	
Suriname	0.73		
Trinidad & Tobago	0.68		
Uruguay	0.82	0.80	0.84
RB de Venezuela	0.92		

Note: The values for each country correspond in column (i) to the first value in the 1950–1979 period and in column (ii) to the most recent observation in the 1980–1994 period.
Source: Authors' calculations based on Deininger and Olinto 2002 and UNDP 1993.

TABLE A.40

Housing ownership, number of rooms, and persons per room, by quintile

Country	Ownership of housing						Number of rooms						Persons per room					
	1	2	3	4	5	Mean	1	2	3	4	5	Mean	1	2	3	4	5	Mean
Argentina																		
1992	0.67	0.72	0.74	0.73	0.71	0.72	2.6	2.6	2.8	3.0	3.2	2.9	2.0	1.4	1.4	1.2	1.0	1.4
1996	0.65	0.71	0.71	0.71	0.74	0.71	2.7	2.7	2.8	3.0	3.2	2.9	2.1	1.6	1.4	1.2	0.9	1.4
2001	0.65	0.71	0.70	0.73	0.75	0.72	2.5	2.6	2.7	2.9	3.3	2.9	2.3	1.7	1.4	1.1	0.9	1.4
Bolivia																		
Urban																		
1992							1.6	1.8	1.8	2.0	2.2	1.9	3.9	3.6	3.3	2.8	2.1	3.0
1996	0.50	0.50	0.47	0.50	0.56	0.51	1.6	1.8	1.8	2.0	2.3	2.0	3.8	3.4	3.1	2.6	1.9	2.8
National																		
1996	0.89	0.71	0.60	0.53	0.57	0.66	1.3	1.4	1.7	1.7	2.1	1.7	3.8	3.8	3.4	2.9	2.2	3.1
1999	0.88	0.70	0.55	0.54	0.61	0.65	1.4	1.6	1.7	1.8	2.0	1.7	3.5	3.3	3.2	2.7	2.0	2.9
Brazil																		
1990	0.69	0.68	0.66	0.68	0.70	0.68	2.1	2.0	2.0	2.1	2.1	2.1	2.6	2.4	2.3	2.1	1.8	2.2
1995	0.62	0.65	0.67	0.68	0.71	0.67	2.1	2.0	2.0	2.0	2.1	2.0	2.7	2.3	2.1	2.0	1.7	2.1
2001	0.62	0.65	0.68	0.69	0.73	0.68	2.0	2.0	1.8	1.9	2.0	1.9	2.6	2.2	1.9	1.8	1.6	2.0
Chile																		
1996	0.53	0.56	0.60	0.64	0.56	0.58	2.1	2.3	2.5	2.6	3.0	2.5	2.4	2.1	1.8	1.6	1.2	1.8
2000	0.61	0.63	0.67	0.68	0.65	0.65	2.3	2.4	2.5	2.7	3.0	2.6	2.2	2.0	1.7	1.5	1.1	1.7
Colombia																		
1996	0.73	0.63	0.58	0.58	0.63	0.63	2.8	2.9	3.1	3.2	3.8	3.2	2.1	2.0	1.7	1.5	1.1	1.6
1999	0.71	0.60	0.55	0.57	0.60	0.60	2.8	2.9	3.0	3.3	3.8	3.2	2.1	2.0	1.7	1.5	1.0	1.6
Dominican Rep.																		
1995	0.82	0.79	0.75	0.75	0.68	0.76												
1997	0.89	0.83	0.79	0.71	0.65	0.76	2.9	3.2	3.2	3.4	3.9	3.4	1.8	1.6	1.5	1.3	1.0	1.4
Ecuador																		
1994	0.77	0.73	0.66	0.66	0.63	0.68	1.6	1.8	2.0	2.0	2.4	2.0	3.6	3.6	3.2	2.7	1.9	2.9
1998	0.79	0.68	0.64	0.62	0.59	0.66	1.7	1.9	1.9	2.1	2.4	2.0	3.2	3.3	3.0	2.6	1.8	2.7
El Salvador																		
1991	0.61	0.55	0.58	0.60	0.67	0.61	1.2	1.3	1.4	1.6	2.1	1.6	5.0	4.6	4.1	3.3	2.2	3.7
1995	0.65	0.60	0.62	0.64	0.71	0.65	1.3	1.3	1.5	1.7	2.2	1.6	4.6	4.4	3.7	3.0	2.1	3.4
2000	0.69	0.65	0.65	0.63	0.70	0.66	1.8	1.8	1.9	2.0	2.3	2.0	3.7	3.3	3.1	2.8	1.9	2.8
Guatemala																		
2000	0.82	0.72	0.69	0.64	0.66	0.70	1.4	1.4	1.6	1.7	2.2	1.7	4.8	4.5	4.0	3.4	2.3	3.7
Honduras																		
1990	0.84	0.76	0.71	0.64	0.62	0.71	1.2	1.2	1.3	1.5	2.0	1.5	5.7	5.4	4.9	4.2	2.7	4.4
1995	0.83	0.74	0.69	0.69	0.69	0.72	1.3	1.4	1.5	1.6	2.1	1.6	5.3	4.8	4.2	3.7	2.4	4.0
1999	0.80	0.76	0.65	0.62	0.63	0.69	1.4	1.6	1.7	1.8	2.2	1.8	4.8	4.2	3.8	3.3	2.2	3.6
Jamaica																		
1990	0.80	0.76	0.73	0.71	0.55	0.69												
1996	0.64	0.65	0.65	0.62	0.53	0.60	2.9	2.8	2.9	2.8	2.9	2.9	2.3	1.9	1.8	1.5	1.0	1.6
1999	0.64	0.54	0.64	0.57	0.49	0.56	2.6	2.7	2.9	2.8	2.6	2.7	2.4	1.8	1.6	1.5	1.1	1.6
Mexico																		
1992	0.51	0.56	0.57	0.60	0.68	0.59	1.5	1.7	1.8	2.0	2.1	1.9	4.2	3.6	3.1	2.6	2.0	3.0
1996	0.48	0.56	0.63	0.66	0.67	0.61	1.6	1.7	1.9	2.0	2.1	1.9	4.0	3.4	2.9	2.4	1.9	2.8
2000	0.48	0.63	0.63	0.66	0.69	0.62	1.7	1.8	1.9	2.0	2.2	1.9	3.5	2.9	2.5	2.2	1.7	2.5
Paraguay																		
1995	0.89	0.82	0.77	0.75	0.67	0.77	1.8	1.8	1.9	2.1	2.3	2.0	3.8	3.2	2.8	2.4	1.7	2.7
1999	0.89	0.84	0.78	0.81	0.75	0.81	2.0	1.9	2.1	2.2	2.4	2.1	3.4	2.9	2.5	2.2	1.6	2.4
Peru																		
Regions																		
1991	0.81	0.79	0.73	0.71	0.66	0.74	2.9	3.3	3.4	3.7	3.7	3.4	2.4	2.1	2.1	1.9	1.6	2.0
1994	0.78	0.71	0.68	0.70	0.70	0.71	2.8	3.1	3.4	3.7	4.5	3.6	2.7	2.2	1.9	1.6	1.2	1.9
National																		
1994	0.77	0.71	0.67	0.69	0.69	0.70	2.7	3.0	3.3	3.6	4.4	3.4	2.6	2.4	2.0	1.7	1.2	2.0
2000	0.84	0.74	0.73	0.72	0.73	0.75	2.7	3.0	3.2	3.7	4.4	3.5	2.4	2.2	2.0	1.7	1.2	1.9
Trinidad & Tobago																		
1992	0.26	0.34	0.38	0.39	0.51	0.39	2.4	2.5	2.6	2.7	2.7	2.6	2.6	2.3	2.0	1.7	1.2	1.9
Uruguay																		
1989	0.62	0.65	0.68	0.67	0.73	0.67	1.9	1.9	2.0	2.1	2.2	2.0	2.3	1.8	1.8	1.6	1.4	1.7
1995	0.64	0.68	0.70	0.71	0.75	0.70	2.0	2.0	2.0	2.0	2.0	2.0	2.2	1.8	1.7	1.6	1.4	1.7
2000	0.57	0.65	0.68	0.70	0.76	0.68	2.0	2.0	2.0	2.0	2.0	2.0	2.4	1.9	1.6	1.5	1.3	1.7
RB de Venezuela																		
1989	0.83	0.81	0.75	0.73	0.69	0.75	2.5	2.6	2.7	2.8	2.9	2.7	3.1	2.7	2.4	2.0	1.5	2.2
1995	0.86	0.85	0.82	0.80	0.79	0.82	2.3	2.3	2.4	2.4	2.4	2.4	2.8	2.7	2.3	2.0	1.7	2.3
1998	0.84	0.84	0.83	0.81	0.80	0.82	2.2	2.2	2.3	2.4	2.3	2.3	2.8	2.6	2.4	2.1	1.8	2.3

Note: In most cases, "rooms" refer to the number of rooms used only by the household, excluding the kitchen and bathrooms.
Source: Authors' calculations based on microdata from household surveys.

TABLE A.41

Number of children under age 12 per household, by parental income and education

	Parental income quintile						Parental education		
Country	1 (i)	2 (ii)	3 (iii)	4 (iv)	5 (v)	Mean	Low (vi)	Medium (vii)	High (viii)
Argentina									
1992	1.80	1.70	1.68	1.44	1.32	1.59	1.87	1.53	1.15
1996	1.80	1.76	1.55	1.28	1.20	1.52	1.90	1.34	1.09
2001	1.89	1.68	1.35	1.25	1.04	1.44	1.96	1.31	0.93
Bolivia									
Urban									
1992	2.11	2.27	2.18	2.10	1.94	2.12	2.37	2.08	1.65
1996	1.89	2.13	1.91	2.00	1.63	1.91	2.15	1.92	1.51
National									
1996	2.09	2.13	2.26	2.09	1.93	2.10	2.27	2.04	1.56
1999	2.61	2.18	2.03	1.86	1.61	2.06	2.47	1.76	1.39
Brazil									
1990	2.13	1.90	1.72	1.55	1.42	1.74	1.90	1.36	1.23
1995	1.89	1.66	1.47	1.32	1.18	1.50	1.65	1.18	0.99
2001	1.63	1.41	1.27	1.13	0.97	1.28	1.43	1.04	0.83
Chile									
1990	1.59	1.59	1.51	1.38	1.43	1.50	1.55	1.50	1.36
1996	1.55	1.52	1.46	1.35	1.32	1.44	1.48	1.48	1.28
2000	1.44	1.41	1.37	1.24	1.30	1.35	1.45	1.35	1.24
Colombia									
Bogotá									
1992	1.67	1.56	1.35	1.14	1.20	1.38	1.61	1.36	1.03
1996	1.28	1.29	1.36	1.19	1.11	1.25	1.43	1.20	0.94
National									
1996	1.97	1.67	1.61	1.50	1.29	1.61	1.76	1.40	1.14
1999	1.77	1.70	1.56	1.37	1.24	1.53	1.69	1.35	1.05
Costa Rica									
1990	2.06	2.00	1.94	1.72	1.88	1.92	2.02	1.75	1.64
1995	2.05	1.77	1.80	1.67	1.51	1.76	1.93	1.60	1.40
2000	1.86	1.68	1.64	1.57	1.30	1.61	1.75	1.49	1.23
Dominican Rep.									
1995	1.51	1.64	1.69	1.62	1.58	1.61	1.61	1.51	1.56
1997	1.54	1.61	1.57	1.68	1.53	1.59	1.64	1.52	1.40
Ecuador									
1994	2.30	2.05	2.12	1.86	1.56	1.98	2.29	1.56	1.39
1998	2.07	2.21	1.86	1.77	1.55	1.89	2.17	1.63	1.48
El Salvador									
1991	2.43	2.32	2.20	2.05	1.82	2.16	2.40	1.79	1.42
1995	2.28	2.15	1.86	1.82	1.64	1.95	2.17	1.60	1.47
2000	1.90	1.81	1.83	1.76	1.65	1.82	2.05	1.56	1.36
Guatemala									
2000	2.98	2.97	2.81	2.41	1.95	2.62	2.87	2.04	1.64
Honduras									
1990	3.00	2.85	2.68	2.53	2.28	2.67	2.85	1.90	1.77
1995	2.75	2.71	2.40	2.46	1.94	2.45	2.64	1.91	1.70
1999	2.70	2.47	2.19	2.08	1.80	2.25	2.50	1.72	1.46
Jamaica									
1990	1.62	1.24	1.10	1.41	1.53	1.38	1.36	1.40	1.15
1996	1.45	1.33	1.05	1.29	1.40	1.31	1.27	1.35	0.86
1999	1.18	1.24	1.10	1.19	1.04	1.15	1.20	1.17	0.86
Mexico									
1992	2.59	2.22	2.14	1.93	1.75	2.13	2.37	1.77	1.58
1996	2.32	2.14	1.85	1.67	1.51	1.90	2.19	1.69	1.35
2000	2.15	1.81	1.62	1.63	1.40	1.72	1.94	1.55	1.30
Nicaragua									
1993	3.11	2.60	2.66	2.39	2.16	2.58	2.85	1.93	1.71
1998	2.61	2.60	2.44	2.28	2.05	2.40	2.64	1.87	1.56
Panama									
1991	1.86	1.70	1.73	1.51	1.38	1.64	1.89	1.52	1.32
1995	1.84	1.65	1.61	1.30	1.24	1.53	1.81	1.46	1.20
2000	1.76	1.55	1.48	1.23	1.17	1.44	1.67	1.40	0.98
Paraguay									
1995	2.70	2.60	2.11	2.08	1.95	2.29	2.50	1.81	1.61
1999	2.48	2.27	2.16	2.04	1.72	2.14	2.41	1.86	1.52
Peru									
Regions									
1991	2.30	1.97	2.04	2.06	1.76	2.02	2.29	2.00	1.65
1994	2.57	2.34	2.10	1.94	1.65	2.12	2.68	1.99	1.49
National									
1994	2.59	2.43	2.15	2.09	1.71	2.19	2.70	2.06	1.54
2000	2.48	2.25	1.93	2.01	1.68	2.07	2.45	1.97	1.63
Trinidad & Tobago									
1992	1.96	1.52	1.59	1.62	1.67	1.67	1.84	1.63	1.42
Uruguay									
1989	1.48	1.47	1.46	1.26	1.42	1.42	1.53	1.33	1.32
1995	1.45	1.38	1.28	1.28	1.30	1.34	1.47	1.30	1.14
2000	1.33	1.33	1.26	1.11	1.11	1.23	1.46	1.15	0.92
RB de Venezuela									
1989	2.35	2.23	2.10	1.84	1.65	2.03	2.28	1.73	1.38
1995	2.13	2.22	1.96	1.72	1.47	1.90	2.16	1.63	1.08
1998	1.99	1.95	1.80	1.74	1.50	1.80	2.03	1.65	1.27

Source: Authors' calculations based on microdata from household surveys.

TABLE A.42

Household size, by income quintile and education of household head

Country	Equivalized income quintile						Education of household head		
	1 (i)	2 (ii)	3 (iii)	4 (iv)	5 (v)	Mean (vi)	Low (vii)	Medium (viii)	High (ix)
Argentina									
1992	4.39	3.36	3.64	3.37	2.89	3.46	3.50	3.58	3.12
1996	4.75	3.86	3.45	3.18	2.73	3.47	3.64	3.42	3.06
2001	5.00	3.89	3.46	2.96	2.63	3.42	3.63	3.35	2.97
Bolivia									
Urban									
1992	5.15	5.11	4.67	4.36	3.81	4.56	4.75	4.44	4.23
1996	4.74	4.67	4.42	4.07	3.61	4.26	4.42	4.17	3.99
National									
1996	4.38	4.43	4.53	4.15	3.61	4.19	4.22	4.19	3.96
1999	4.47	4.74	4.64	4.19	3.63	4.29	4.44	4.19	3.78
Brazil									
1990	4.95	4.43	4.13	3.96	3.44	4.11	4.25	3.56	3.41
1995	5.00	4.14	3.81	3.66	3.24	3.89	4.01	3.46	3.26
2001	4.80	4.07	3.41	3.33	3.00	3.62	3.74	3.33	3.06
Chile									
1990	4.66	4.37	4.03	3.89	3.53	4.06	4.17	3.99	3.71
1996	4.42	4.30	3.95	3.82	3.43	3.95	4.02	3.95	3.70
2000	4.52	4.28	3.90	3.65	3.24	3.86	3.96	3.87	3.57
Colombia									
Bogotá									
1992	4.79	4.33	4.29	3.74	3.36	4.04	4.34	3.83	3.45
1996	4.46	4.22	3.80	3.75	3.38	3.88	4.00	3.74	3.53
National									
1996	4.87	4.74	4.43	4.02	3.52	4.25	4.36	3.90	3.67
1999	4.87	4.82	4.39	4.09	3.37	4.23	4.39	3.83	3.47
Costa Rica									
1990	4.75	4.71	4.48	4.32	3.71	4.36	4.47	4.06	3.98
1995	4.56	4.52	4.31	4.02	3.51	4.15	4.25	3.94	3.78
2000	4.31	4.40	4.24	4.05	3.54	4.08	4.09	4.16	3.69
Dominican Rep.									
1995	5.07	4.64	4.43	4.17	3.76	4.38	4.31	3.89	4.10
1997	4.77	4.55	4.31	3.96	3.60	4.19	4.20	3.90	4.08
Ecuador									
1994	5.10	5.40	5.10	4.78	3.88	4.79	5.05	4.08	3.94
1998	4.72	5.23	4.80	4.47	3.71	4.53	4.75	4.09	4.01
El Salvador									
1991	5.60	5.33	5.03	4.54	3.88	4.79	4.95	4.24	3.92
1995	5.31	5.26	4.83	4.45	3.86	4.68	4.84	4.12	3.92
2000	5.11	4.77	4.62	4.27	3.53	4.39	4.53	3.93	3.85
Guatemala									
2000	5.90	5.76	5.44	5.02	4.17	5.18	5.36	4.27	4.18
Honduras									
1990	6.19	6.07	5.77	5.39	4.36	5.47	5.50	4.32	4.17
1995	6.20	5.95	5.57	5.12	4.34	5.35	5.36	4.45	4.19
1999	5.80	5.59	5.39	4.99	4.14	5.11	5.18	4.18	4.13
Jamaica									
1990	6.07	5.47	4.64	4.50	2.92	4.44	4.17	3.82	3.48
1996	5.67	4.58	4.56	3.85	2.58	3.97	3.59	3.79	2.95
1999	5.14	4.30	4.34	3.72	2.47	3.76	3.59	3.27	3.00
Mexico									
1992	5.75	5.38	4.93	4.54	3.83	4.79	5.04	4.06	3.99
1996	5.67	5.18	4.84	4.25	3.62	4.60	4.85	4.07	3.78
2000	5.11	4.68	4.27	4.07	3.43	4.24	4.37	3.91	3.67
Nicaragua									
1993	6.71	6.28	5.97	5.43	4.68	5.72	5.79	4.61	4.52
1998	5.97	5.75	5.64	5.10	4.71	5.39	5.56	4.74	4.38
Panama									
1991	4.62	4.82	4.74	4.06	3.42	4.26	4.42	4.06	3.74
1995	4.59	4.65	4.18	3.88	3.26	4.03	4.16	3.95	3.57
2000	4.36	4.34	4.10	3.63	3.11	3.84	4.03	3.79	3.37
Paraguay									
1995	5.82	5.11	4.75	4.41	3.76	4.68	4.83	4.18	4.02
1999	5.73	4.99	4.66	4.32	3.69	4.58	4.80	4.12	4.06
Peru									
Regions									
1991	5.42	5.48	5.50	5.35	4.73	5.28	5.39	4.91	4.74
1994	5.82	5.49	5.13	5.89	4.35	5.09	5.45	4.88	4.50
National									
1994	5.77	5.67	5.22	4.91	4.34	5.13	5.46	4.91	4.49
2000	5.24	5.21	5.17	5.04	4.38	4.98	5.09	4.93	4.69
Trinidad & Tobago									
1992	5.54	5.10	4.78	4.26	3.09	4.37	4.20	3.87	3.41
Uruguay									
1989	3.89	3.35	3.25	3.15	2.86	3.27	3.19	3.45	3.35
1995	4.11	3.41	3.18	3.03	2.72	3.23	3.13	3.46	3.20
2000	4.49	3.53	3.13	2.81	2.54	3.17	3.14	3.33	2.95
RB de Venezuela									
1989	6.45	5.87	5.36	4.96	3.95	5.16	5.30	4.43	4.07
1995	5.59	5.52	5.03	4.65	3.93	4.86	5.11	4.37	3.81
1998	5.37	5.22	4.88	4.61	3.86	4.72	4.98	4.43	3.83

Source: Authors' calculations based on microdata from household surveys.

TABLE A.43

Correlations between spouses: education, wages, and hours worked

Country	Years of education (i)	Hourly wages (ii)	Hours worked All (iii)	Hours worked Workers (iv)
Argentina				
1992	0.6427*	0.5061*	0.0648*	0.0562*
1996	0.6525*	0.4600*	0.0793*	0.0715*
2001	0.6623*	0.4709*	0.0815*	0.0946*
Bolivia				
Urban				
1992	0.7516*	0.2248*	0.0638*	0.2122*
1996	0.6749*	0.3529*	0.0805*	0.2027*
National				
1996	0.7584*	0.1698*	0.1264*	0.2265*
1999	0.8119*	0.1335*	0.1369*	0.2769*
Brazil				
1990	0.7452*	0.4493*	0.0985*	0.1594*
1995	0.7300*	0.5077*	0.1594*	0.1467*
2001	0.7151*	0.3466*	0.1386*	0.1485*
Chile				
1990	0.7390*	0.4770*	0.0970*	0.3341*
1996	0.7392*	0.4672*	0.0981*	0.3479*
2000	0.7388*	0.4579*	0.1081*	0.3130*
Colombia				
Bogotá				
1992	0.7783*	0.6230*	0.1713*	0.3009*
1996	0.7596*	0.5002*	0.1522*	0.1824*
National				
1996	0.7538*	0.4354*	0.0817*	0.2006*
1999	0.7384*	0.2066*	0.0763*	0.2034*
Costa Rica				
1990	0.6735*	0.3569*	0.0959*	0.1403*
1995	0.6436*	0.4362*	0.0862*	0.1793*
2000	0.6406*	0.3951*	0.0745*	0.1004*
Dominican Rep.				
1995	0.6938*	0.3940*	0.0597*	0.2368*
1997	0.6680*	0.4168*	0.0333	0.1432*
Ecuador				
1994	0.7710*	0.2378*	0.1356*	0.1883*
1998	0.7689*	0.2863*	0.1889*	0.2689*
El Salvador				
1991	0.6977*	0.2501*	0.0441*	0.1388*
1995	0.7169*	0.4435*	0.0581*	0.2261*
2000	0.7118*	0.2896*	0.0673*	0.1681*
Guatemala				
2000	0.7419*	0.3163*	0.0665*	0.1546*

Country	Years of education (i)	Hourly wages (ii)	Hours worked All (iii)	Hours worked Workers (iv)
Honduras				
1990	0.7355*	0.3095*	0.0001	0.1527*
1995	0.7184*	0.2364*	0.0198	0.1472*
1999	0.7298*	0.0787*	0.0303	0.1262*
Jamaica				
1990	0.7121*	0.7662*	0.0273	0.3356*
1996	0.6898*	0.5984*	0.1581*	0.0983
1999	0.7125*	0.4922*	0.1412*	0.1981*
Mexico				
1992	0.7017*	0.3234*	−0.0273*	0.1329*
1996	0.6985*	0.2268*	0.0325*	0.1201*
2000	0.7366*	0.3241*	0.0761*	0.0849*
Nicaragua				
1993	0.7239*	0.2155*	−0.0227	0.2060*
1998	0.6623*	0.6166*	0.0419*	0.1893*
Panama				
1991	0.7458*	0.4696*	0.2068*	0.2262*
1995	0.7262*	0.3263*	0.1739*	0.1734*
2000	0.6585*	0.5420*	0.1277*	0.1401*
Paraguay				
1995	0.7303*	0.2241*	0.0662*	0.2433*
1999	0.7280*	0.3111*	0.1100*	0.2183*
Peru				
Regions				
1991	0.7370*	0.2337*	0.1889*	0.2101*
1994	0.7162*	0.4383*	0.1571*	0.1938*
National				
1994	0.7073*	0.3079*	0.1260*	0.1770*
2000	0.7178*	0.3858*	0.1053*	0.1780*
Trinidad & Tobago				
1992	0.5856*	0.5178*	0.1514*	0.3559*
Uruguay				
1989	0.5287*	0.4347*	0.2316*	0.1469*
1995	0.6193*	0.3601*	0.2322*	0.1480*
2000	0.5953*	0.3073*	0.2377*	0.1677*
RB de Venezuela				
1989	0.7197*	0.3516*	0.0376*	0.1552*
1995	0.7036*	0.2386*	0.0147	0.1232*
1998	0.6921*	0.1353*	0.0291*	0.1267*

*Significant at 5%.

Source: Authors' calculations based on microdata from household surveys.

TABLE A.44

Share of children ages 10–14 who work (percent)

Country	Equivalized household income quintile						Country	Equivalized household income quintile					
	1	2	3	4	5	Average		1	2	3	4	5	Average
Argentina							Guatemala						
1992	1.6	1.5	3.5	1.9	0.3	1.8	2000	36.2	27.4	28.4	27.5	15.4	27.7
1996	0.9	1.6	0.9	2.1	0.1	1.1	Honduras						
2001	0.9	0.4	0.5	0.1	0.1	0.5	1990	16.1	14.9	13.1	9.9	11.2	13.2
Bolivia							1995	14.3	13.4	9.9	7.6	9.4	11.2
Urban							1999	16.2	15.7	17.3	14.8	12.5	15.5
1992	7.2	9.0	8.9	10.2	9.4	8.8	Jamaica						
1996	8.7	10.4	13.1	13.7	8.5	10.9	1990	0.7	2.3	1.8	2.3	1.3	1.7
National							1996	0.8	0.0	0.9	0.0	1.5	0.6
1996	61.7	26.8	18.6	17.5	12.1	29.3	1999	0.0	1.5	0.0	1.2	3.6	1.0
1999	60.3	32.0	16.9	20.2	10.0	29.1	Mexico						
Brazil							1992	9.0	5.9	4.1	4.2	2.5	5.6
1990	25.0	21.3	15.0	11.6	7.2	17.3	1996	14.6	10.2	7.5	4.7	2.9	8.9
1995	30.5	20.8	15.6	11.4	6.8	18.8	2000	9.3	7.1	4.5	4.7	4.8	6.5
2001	19.1	11.5	9.1	6.8	4.4	11.6	Nicaragua						
Chile							1993	9.2	10.5	8.4	7.5	9.4	9.0
1990	1.2	0.7	2.1	1.3	0.9	1.2	1998	18.1	11.1	10.8	10.3	9.4	12.2
1996	1.2	1.9	2.4	1.0	1.6	1.6	Panama						
2000	1.2	1.9	0.6	1.0	0.3	1.1	1995	5.2	2.0	1.8	1.5	3.1	2.9
Colombia							2000	2.9	2.0	0.6	0.8	1.5	1.8
Bogotá							Paraguay						
1992	6.3	4.2	3.5	0.8	6.1	4.4	1995	49.9	35.4	30.6	26.2	20.0	34.3
1996	4.0	2.7	5.1	1.2	7.0	4.0	1999	19.5	12.7	9.6	7.0	9.6	12.3
National							Peru						
1996	16.0	10.8	11.6	8.4	7.7	11.3	Regions						
1999	10.7	8.0	7.6	5.8	5.8	7.9	1991	24.2	13.0	9.2	7.7	6.9	12.8
Costa Rica							1994	36.4	18.2	9.1	8.7	6.4	17.5
1990	8.0	6.5	6.6	7.1	1.2	6.1	National						
1995	10.6	11.3	7.5	6.2	3.0	8.3	1994	38.8	21.1	12.5	9.7	8.5	20.0
2000	4.3	4.0	4.3	2.5	1.4	3.5	2000	52.7	26.1	19.2	14.5	9.0	26.8
Dominican Rep.							Uruguay						
1995	5.0	3.4	5.6	5.5	3.5	4.6	1989	9.2	9.8	4.3	5.9	2.0	6.7
1997	7.3	3.2	3.3	5.2	4.7	4.9	1995	9.7	12.4	7.8	5.5	2.2	8.3
Ecuador							2000	7.2	3.8	1.3	2.8	1.4	3.9
1994	35.1	26.1	31.9	30.0	21.3	29.4	RB de Venezuela						
1998	46.3	32.7	33.5	28.7	22.7	33.8	1989	5.5	3.8	3.4	2.9	1.2	3.7
El Salvador							1995	3.6	3.6	3.7	2.4	2.7	3.3
1991	14.3	16.8	16.6	15.7	12.5	15.3	1998	3.6	3.4	4.2	3.5	1.7	3.4
1995	12.7	11.3	11.4	9.6	6.4	10.7							
2000	10.5	8.6	8.9	7.3	5.0	8.4							

Source: Authors' calculations based on microdata from household surveys.

TABLE A.45

**Wages for prime-age men and household per capita income:
ratio of nonwhites to whites**

Country	Wages, prime-age men		Per capita income	
	Total (i)	Urban (ii)	Total (iii)	Urban (iv)
Bolivia				
1999	0.534	0.686	0.478	0.637
Brazil				
1990	0.515	0.540	0.454	0.480
1995	0.518	0.545	0.446	0.470
2001	0.511	0.527	0.457	0.474
Guatemala				
2000	0.524	0.530	0.448	0.512
Peru				
2000	0.438	0.485	0.415	0.497
Trinidad & Tobago				
1992	0.241	0.223	0.358	0.414

Source: Authors' calculations based on microdata from
household surveys.

TABLE A.46

Interpersonal and institutional trust in Latin America, by age, education, subjective income, and inequality perception, 1996–2001

		Interpersonal trust	Institutional trust
Age	18–30	0.423	0.196
	31–55	0.426	0.202
	56–65	0.446	0.207
	more than 65	0.466	0.225
Education	No school	0.436	0.221
	Some primary	0.437	0.210
	Some secondary	0.403	0.158
	Some tertiary	0.400	0.181
Subjective income	Great difficulties to finance living costs	0.394	0.168
	Not enough to finance living costs	0.417	0.183
	Finance living cost	0.444	0.217
	Finance living cost, and save	0.469	0.261
Income distribution perception	Very unfair	0.390	0.159
	Unfair	0.435	0.188
	Fair	0.510	0.362
	Very fair	0.508	0.422

Source: Authors' calculations based on microdata from Latinobarómetro.

TABLE A.47

School enrollment rates, by age and income quintile

Country	3 to 5 years old						6 to 12 years old						13 to 17 years old						18 to 23 years old					
	1	2	3	4	5	Mean	1	2	3	4	5	Mean	1	2	3	4	5	Mean	1	2	3	4	5	Mean
Argentina																								
1992	0.22	0.34	0.29	0.43	0.51	0.34	0.97	0.99	0.98	0.99	0.99	0.98	0.73	0.74	0.77	0.81	0.94	0.78	0.33	0.34	0.35	0.44	0.54	0.41
1996	0.22	0.26	0.35	0.42	0.48	0.32	0.98	0.98	0.99	1.00	1.00	0.99	0.67	0.76	0.85	0.80	0.97	0.79	0.26	0.29	0.41	0.49	0.62	0.42
2001	0.34	0.43	0.44	0.54	0.54	0.44	0.97	0.98	1.00	1.00	0.99	0.99	0.87	0.91	0.95	0.95	0.99	0.92	0.36	0.36	0.45	0.57	0.72	0.49
Bolivia																								
1996	0.40	0.38	0.60	0.53	0.74	0.50	0.89	0.96	0.96	0.97	0.99	0.95	0.39	0.59	0.65	0.66	0.77	0.61	0.08	0.28	0.35	0.36	0.49	0.33
1999							0.87	0.96	0.97	0.96	0.97	0.94	0.41	0.62	0.76	0.75	0.89	0.68	0.13	0.40	0.32	0.48	0.62	0.42
Brazil																								
1990	0.25	0.29	0.36	0.47	0.64	0.38	0.70	0.79	0.87	0.92	0.96	0.83	0.52	0.56	0.65	0.75	0.84	0.65	0.14	0.16	0.21	0.26	0.40	0.24
1995	0.24	0.28	0.32	0.39	0.60	0.34	0.81	0.89	0.93	0.96	0.98	0.90	0.64	0.68	0.74	0.82	0.91	0.74	0.20	0.23	0.24	0.30	0.48	0.29
2001	0.36	0.40	0.44	0.52	0.72	0.45	0.93	0.95	0.97	0.98	0.99	0.96	0.81	0.83	0.87	0.91	0.96	0.86	0.32	0.30	0.31	0.34	0.55	0.36
Chile																								
1990	0.24	0.23	0.29	0.35	0.48	0.31	0.96	0.96	0.98	0.97	0.99	0.97	0.79	0.81	0.81	0.88	0.94	0.83	0.25	0.22	0.25	0.32	0.52	0.31
1996	0.30	0.32	0.41	0.43	0.63	0.40	0.96	0.98	0.99	0.99	1.00	0.98	0.82	0.84	0.90	0.95	0.97	0.89	0.27	0.29	0.35	0.43	0.63	0.39
2000	0.37	0.39	0.45	0.50	0.65	0.46	0.98	0.98	0.99	0.99	1.00	0.99	0.87	0.89	0.93	0.96	0.98	0.92	0.26	0.31	0.38	0.45	0.64	0.40
Colombia																								
1996	0.16	0.18	0.23	0.26	0.26	0.21	0.86	0.90	0.93	0.96	0.98	0.91	0.64	0.73	0.74	0.81	0.83	0.75	0.20	0.25	0.26	0.29	0.47	0.31
1999	0.18	0.18	0.21	0.27	0.29	0.22	0.88	0.90	0.93	0.96	0.97	0.92	0.66	0.72	0.74	0.81	0.85	0.75	0.22	0.22	0.23	0.28	0.46	0.29
Costa Rica																								
1990	0.22	0.25	0.35	0.37	0.43	0.32	0.83	0.89	0.88	0.88	0.82	0.88	0.45	0.53	0.56	0.60	0.82	0.58	0.16	0.15	0.17	0.24	0.42	0.23
1995	0.28	0.38	0.41	0.36	0.56	0.38	0.93	0.95	0.96	0.98	0.99	0.96	0.58	0.61	0.62	0.69	0.89	0.67	0.22	0.17	0.22	0.28	0.46	0.28
2000							0.94	0.96	0.97	0.97	0.98	0.96	0.59	0.63	0.63	0.70	0.84	0.66	0.20	0.25	0.27	0.35	0.55	0.34
Dominican Rep.																								
1995	0.26	0.30	0.25	0.31	0.51	0.32	0.92	0.94	0.94	0.95	0.96	0.94	0.85	0.87	0.88	0.89	0.91	0.88	0.37	0.38	0.35	0.37	0.47	0.39
Ecuador																								
1994	0.22	0.23	0.30	0.32	0.48	0.30	0.78	0.82	0.91	0.91	0.95	0.86	0.47	0.57	0.60	0.68	0.77	0.61	0.22	0.26	0.24	0.30	0.39	0.29
1998	0.18	0.25	0.33	0.36	0.47	0.31	0.91	0.92	0.95	0.98	0.99	0.94	0.50	0.65	0.68	0.74	0.85	0.68	0.19	0.24	0.21	0.29	0.48	0.29
El Salvador																								
1991	0.12	0.14	0.20	0.35	0.54	0.24	0.64	0.69	0.76	0.86	0.92	0.75	0.47	0.51	0.59	0.66	0.74	0.59	0.14	0.14	0.19	0.26	0.39	0.24
1995	0.21	0.23	0.31	0.46	0.70	0.35	0.74	0.77	0.84	0.91	0.96	0.83	0.53	0.58	0.64	0.71	0.80	0.64	0.17	0.14	0.19	0.27	0.43	0.25
2000	0.22	0.21	0.26	0.33	0.47	0.29	0.79	0.83	0.86	0.92	0.97	0.86	0.61	0.68	0.71	0.77	0.81	0.70	0.24	0.21	0.22	0.23	0.42	0.27
Guatemala																								
2000	0.06	0.08	0.08	0.13	0.29	0.11	0.67	0.71	0.78	0.86	0.93	0.77	0.42	0.44	0.49	0.57	0.75	0.53	0.09	0.12	0.13	0.19	0.40	0.21
Honduras																								
1990							0.73	0.70	0.78	0.88	0.91	0.79	0.38	0.33	0.40	0.49	0.63	0.45	0.04	0.07	0.09	0.16	0.31	0.15
1995							0.83	0.84	0.89	0.91	0.96	0.88	0.40	0.41	0.45	0.53	0.64	0.49	0.06	0.10	0.08	0.19	0.31	0.16
1999							0.78	0.84	0.85	0.91	0.92	0.85	0.40	0.43	0.52	0.58	0.67	0.52	0.07	0.13	0.18	0.18	0.34	0.20

Country / Year	1	2	3	4	5	6	7	8	9	10	11	12	13	14	15	16	17	18	19	20	21	22	23	24
Jamaica																								
1990	0.79	0.72	0.75	0.75	0.84	0.77	0.98	0.99	0.98	0.96	1.00	0.98	0.81	0.77	0.85	0.81	0.79	0.80	0.05	0.02	0.03	0.04	0.03	0.04
1996	0.85	0.73	0.73	0.87	0.90	0.82	0.99	0.99	0.99	1.00	1.00	1.00	0.88	0.87	0.84	0.92	0.94	0.89	0.14	0.08	0.09	0.12	0.14	0.12
1999	0.96	1.00	0.96	0.97	0.98	0.97	1.00	0.99	1.00	1.00	1.00	0.99	0.87	0.86	0.88	0.95	0.96	0.90	0.13	0.14	0.29	0.18	0.18	0.19
Mexico																								
1992	0.39	0.53	0.66	0.78	0.83	0.62	0.86	0.94	0.96	0.96	0.97	0.93	0.48	0.54	0.65	0.63	0.84	0.61	0.12	0.15	0.19	0.24	0.40	0.23
1996	0.55	0.75	0.84	0.88	0.95	0.77	0.91	0.96	0.98	0.98	0.99	0.96	0.47	0.58	0.67	0.74	0.88	0.65	0.07	0.14	0.21	0.28	0.46	0.23
2000	0.67	0.84	0.94	0.92	0.92	0.85	0.93	0.95	0.98	0.98	1.00	0.96	0.57	0.63	0.70	0.78	0.90	0.70	0.16	0.15	0.29	0.28	0.52	0.29
Nicaragua																								
1993	0.11	0.19	0.26	0.33	0.54	0.28	0.93	0.95	0.98	0.98	0.99	0.97	0.54	0.70	0.74	0.78	0.86	0.72	0.21	0.23	0.20	0.29	0.41	0.28
1998	0.22	0.37	0.38	0.40	0.54	0.37	0.73	0.81	0.88	0.94	0.95	0.85	0.45	0.58	0.66	0.66	0.79	0.62	0.13	0.20	0.31	0.28	0.42	0.28
Panama																								
1991	0.30	0.43	0.43	0.58	0.76	0.47	0.93	0.95	0.98	0.97	0.98	0.96	0.56	0.76	0.83	0.87	0.88	0.76	0.14	0.24	0.32	0.38	0.53	0.33
1995	0.29	0.46	0.63	0.79	0.83	0.56	0.95	0.96	0.98	0.99	1.00	0.97	0.63	0.78	0.84	0.92	0.87	0.79	0.16	0.26	0.30	0.37	0.50	0.33
2000	0.52	0.58	0.79	0.88	0.91	0.69	0.96	0.97	0.99	0.99	1.00	0.98	0.70	0.82	0.85	0.91	0.96	0.83	0.22	0.29	0.34	0.44	0.65	0.39
Paraguay																								
1995	0.02	0.07	0.12	0.14	0.17	0.10	0.84	0.89	0.89	0.91	0.96	0.89	0.48	0.56	0.67	0.64	0.76	0.61	0.10	0.14	0.21	0.21	0.35	0.22
1999	0.11	0.17	0.16	0.17	0.17	0.15	0.90	0.93	0.97	0.98	0.99	0.95	0.60	0.69	0.75	0.83	0.84	0.73	0.13	0.27	0.21	0.31	0.49	0.30
Peru																								
Regions																								
1991							0.99	0.99	0.99	1.00	1.00	0.99	0.87	0.94	0.96	0.93	0.95	0.93	0.41	0.42	0.46	0.44	0.56	0.46
1994							0.99	0.99	1.00	1.00	1.00	0.99	0.88	0.91	0.94	0.93	0.96	0.92						
National																								
1994			0.59	0.71	0.80	0.67	0.98	0.99	0.99	0.99	0.99	0.99	0.84	0.88	0.90	0.92	0.95	0.89	0.35	0.37	0.45	0.41	0.56	0.43
2000			0.63				0.99	0.99	1.00	0.99	1.00	0.99	0.86	0.88	0.93	0.92	0.96	0.91	0.25	0.35	0.31	0.45	0.56	0.39
Trinidad & Tobago																								
1992	0.53	0.62	0.74	0.70	0.73	0.66	0.98	0.96	1.00	1.00	0.98	1.00	0.69	0.76	0.77	0.89	0.93	0.79	0.07	0.19	0.18	0.24	0.30	0.19
Uruguay																								
1989	0.24	0.39	0.56	0.67	0.85	0.50	0.96	0.98	0.98	0.98	0.99	0.98	0.68	0.78	0.82	0.89	0.92	0.78	0.17	0.23	0.29	0.36	0.50	0.32
1995	0.36	0.50	0.59	0.73	0.86	0.57	0.98	0.99	1.00	0.99	1.00	0.99	0.66	0.71	0.82	0.85	0.95	0.77	0.18	0.23	0.30	0.39	0.59	0.34
2000	0.51	0.60	0.70	0.80	0.91	0.65	0.98	0.99	0.99	1.00	0.99	0.99	0.68	0.78	0.86	0.92	0.98	0.81	0.17	0.24	0.36	0.42	0.68	0.36
RB de Venezuela																								
1989	0.25	0.32	0.34	0.42	0.55	0.36	0.86	0.91	0.93	0.96	0.97	0.92	0.65	0.72	0.74	0.75	0.84	0.73	0.24	0.24	0.24	0.30	0.43	0.29
1995	0.45	0.45	0.50	0.58	0.67	0.51	0.94	0.95	0.97	0.98	0.97	0.96	0.75	0.75	0.77	0.80	0.89	0.78	0.28	0.29	0.30	0.36	0.48	0.35
1998	0.45	0.46	0.50	0.59	0.68	0.52	0.94	0.96	0.96	0.97	0.99	0.96	0.72	0.76	0.76	0.80	0.91	0.78	0.27	0.28	0.30	0.37	0.54	0.35

Note: Some country statistics in the first panel refer to schooling for children age 5 and older, since no information is recorded for younger children.

See www.depeco.econo.unlp.edu.ar/cedlas/wb/ for details.

Source: Authors' calculations based on microdata from household surveys.

TABLE A.48

Distribution of conditional probabilities of school attendance, Gini coefficients

Country	Primary (i)	Secondary (ii)	College (iii)	College all (iv)	Country	Primary (i)	Secondary (ii)	College (iii)	College all (iv)
Argentina					Guatemala				
1992	0.6	12.4	15.0	37.3	2000	6.2	23.4	28.2	73.0
1996	0.7	12.7	16.9	38.9	Honduras				
2001	1.1	4.5	13.5	33.6	1990	3.4	29.2	26.4	77.1
Bolivia					1995	5.1	23.9	24.3	74.5
Urban					1999	5.2	24.9	27.1	74.7
1992	0.9	6.3	15.5	28.3	Mexico				
1996	0.5	11.6	23.0	33.0	1992	3.2	21.7	15.7	53.1
National					1996	3.0	19.3	20.3	56.3
1996	1.1	10.7	26.3	43.5	2000	2.3	18.6	18.7	48.8
1999	1.1	8.6	28.7	38.6	Nicaragua				
Brazil					1993	7.2	13.5	29.4	63.6
1990	15.2	20.4	38.1	65.2	1998	5.7	13.7	25.3	58.9
1995	3.2	24.6	40.1	69.8	Panama				
2001	1.0	26.2	50.1	69.7	1991	2.0	14.7	35.8	55.2
Chile					1995	1.7	14.0	32.0	50.1
1990	6.9	9.1	26.9	47.6	2000	0.9	10.3	26.7	44.3
1996	0.3	7.2	22.7	43.5	Paraguay				
2000	0.4	5.8	25.6	46.5	1995	1.6	15.6	27.7	47.9
Colombia					1999	1.0	11.4	32.3	54.8
Bogotá					Peru				
1992	2.8	3.5	17.8	34.1	Regions				
1996	1.9	7.0	23.1	38.5	1991	0.7	5.0	25.6	30.5
National					1994	1.0	5.1	27.5	35.6
1996	2.9	8.3	24.1	49.9	National				
1999	2.3	8.4	29.8	49.6	1994	1.0	7.1	25.1	33.8
Costa Rica					2000	0.9	5.5	30.5	40.1
1990	2.0	24.5	19.4	53.9	Trinidad & Tobago				
1995	1.3	22.1	18.2	51.9	1992	1.2	11.9	58.4	66.7
2000	1.5	19.2	20.8	51.8	Uruguay				
Dominican Rep.					1989	2.1	12.5	36.2	58.9
1995	0.8	8.6	20.4	46.9	1995	1.5	14.0	18.9	48.5
Ecuador					2000	1.4	12.8	17.4	49.1
1994	3.2	24.1	24.3	48.9	RB de Venezuela				
1998	7.5	17.2	30.6	54.6	1989	3.2	13.5	24.0	49.4
El Salvador					1995	3.7	11.8	17.7	41.8
1991	6.1	10.8	20.1	61.8	1998	3.3	11.9	19.8	41.5
1995	11.4	8.9	17.1	55.9					
2000	4.8	8.6	21.6	54.0					

Note: (i) children between 9 and 12; (ii) youth between 15 and 17 who finished primary school; (iii) youth between 19 and 21 who finished high school; (iv) all youth between 19 and 21.
Source: Authors' calculations based on microdata from household surveys.

TABLE A.49

Index of intergenerational educational mobility, by age groups

Country	13–19 (i)	20–25 (ii)	Country	13–19 (i)	20–25 (ii)
Argentina			Honduras		
1992	0.922	0.851	1990	0.841	0.727
1996	0.904	0.834	1995	0.853	0.746
2001	0.907	0.814	1999	0.840	0.728
Bolivia			Jamaica		
Urban			1990	0.990	0.929
1992	0.898	0.908	1996	0.990	0.941
1996	0.892	0.900	1999	0.984	0.973
National			Mexico		
1996	0.828	0.799	1992	0.905	0.842
1999	0.838	0.799	1996	0.905	0.846
Brazil			2000	0.868	0.768
1990	0.827	0.763	Nicaragua		
1995	0.808	0.762	1993	0.860	0.855
2001	0.844	0.795	1998	0.828	0.811
Chile			Panama		
1990	0.918	0.862	1991	0.867	0.822
1996	0.914	0.823	1995	0.850	0.798
2000	0.922	0.834	2000	0.893	0.856
Colombia			Paraguay		
Bogotá			1995	0.846	0.768
1992	0.911	0.829	1999	0.851	0.762
1996	0.930	0.838	Peru		
National			Regions		
1996	0.845	0.794	1991	0.938	0.905
1999	0.842	0.812	1994	0.923	0.900
Costa Rica			National		
1990	0.854	0.806	1994	0.917	0.912
1995	0.853	0.778	2000	0.898	0.874
2000	0.856	0.766	Trinidad & Tobago		
Dominican Rep.			1992	0.964	0.944
1995	0.885	0.871	Uruguay		
Ecuador			1989	0.923	0.880
1994	0.852	0.815	1995	0.907	0.842
1998	0.824	0.782	2000	0.900	0.820
El Salvador			RB de Venezuela		
1991	0.865	0.786	1989	0.831	0.799
1995	0.844	0.774	1995	0.857	0.816
2000	0.819	0.793	1998	0.843	0.788
Guatemala					
2000	0.799	0.735			

Source: Authors' calculations based on microdata from household surveys.

TABLE A.50

Health status measures and health services indicators, by quintiles of socioeconomic status

a. Under-5 mortality and children underweight

Country/region	Under-5 mortality rates (per thousand)							Children underweight rates						
	1	2	3	4	5	Average	CI	1	2	3	4	5	Average	CI
Bolivia	146.5	114.9	104.0	47.8	32.0	99.1	−0.22	16.9	9.8	6.3	3.9	3.1	9.0	−0.31
Brazil	98.9	56.0	39.2	26.7	33.3	56.7	−0.26	11.5	5.1	2.8	1.9	3.0	5.7	−0.21
Colombia	52.1	37.1	30.7	34.9	23.6	37.4	−0.13	14.7	9.4	6.7	3.2	3.0	8.4	−0.29
Dominican Rep.	89.9	73.0	60.1	37.3	26.6	61.0	−0.21	12.9	6.6	3.2	1.7	1.0	5.9	−0.42
Guatemala	89.1	102.9	82.0	60.7	37.9	79.2	−0.12	35.1	33.2	28.5	16.2	7.3	26.6	−0.19
Haiti	163.3	150.1	137.1	130.6	105.6	140.6	−0.07	38.9	29.8	26.8	22.2	10.2	27.5	−0.17
Nicaragua	68.8	66.6	52.5	48.5	29.7	56.0	−0.12	18.4	14.2	11.4	6.5	3.9	12.2	−0.23
Paraguay	57.2	50.0	59.0	39.4	20.1	46.6	−0.13	5.9	4.3	4.0	1.8	0.8	3.7	−0.28
Peru	110.0	76.2	48.0	44.1	22.1	68.4	−0.25	16.7	7.8	4.6	1.9	1.4	7.8	−0.40
Latin America and the Caribbean	97.3	80.8	68.1	52.2	36.8	71.7	−0.17	19.0	13.4	10.5	6.6	3.7	11.9	−0.28
East Asia, Pacific	84.0	62.9	53.7	41.1	27.1	57.1	−0.19							
Central Asia	82.5	64.5	69.8	57.5	40.2	64.9	−0.09	17.8	14.2	11.0	7.8	6.5	12.1	−0.19
Middle East, North Africa	140.6	117.8	92.2	80.1	50.4	100.3	−0.17	30.1	26.5	22.0	19.6	13.7	22.7	−0.19
South Asia	144.2	152.6	136.1	110.8	71.7	126.6	−0.11	56.8	52.9	49.5	42.2	29.2	46.7	−0.11
Sub-Saharan Africa	191.7	190.9	174.3	156.6	112.4	168.4	−0.09	36.2	32.9	29.5	26.2	18.1	28.9	−0.13
All countries	148.3	140.8	126.8	110.0	77.4	124.2	−0.12	32.2	28.3	24.9	21.2	14.6	24.8	−0.17

b. Complete immunization coverage rates and prevalence of diarrhea

Country/region	Complete immunization coverage rates							Prevalence of diarrhea (%)						
	1	2	3	4	5	Average	CI	1	2	3	4	5	Average	CI
Bolivia	21.8	24.9	21.0	33.4	30.6	25.5	0.08	21.8	19.8	20.5	17.9	11.7	19.2	−0.07
Brazil	56.6	74.0	84.9	83.1	73.8	72.5	0.07	18.3	12.9	12.7	9.3	7.4	13.1	−0.16
Colombia	53.8	66.9	68.1	70.6	74.1	65.5	0.06	18.4	19.8	16.8	14.9	10.0	16.7	−0.09
Dominican Rep.	28.0	30.2	46.9	42.6	51.7	38.7	0.12	17.9	16.4	17.8	14.1	10.1	15.7	−0.08
Guatemala	41.2	43.0	47.1	38.3	42.5	42.6	0.00	22.8	21.5	23.3	17.7	16.0	20.9	−0.06
Haiti	18.8	20.1	35.3	37.9	44.1	30.2	0.17	30.9	27.1	24.4	31.6	20.4	27.4	−0.04
Nicaragua	61.0	74.6	75.3	85.7	73.1	72.6	0.05	16.1	14.0	14.2	14.4	8.7	14.0	−0.07
Paraguay	20.2	30.8	36.4	40.7	53.0	34.2	0.18	9.8	8.5	9.2	7.4	4.6	8.1	−0.11
Peru	55.3	63.8	63.5	71.7	66.0	63.0	0.04	21.4	20.3	18.6	14.1	9.3	17.9	−0.11
Latin America and the Caribbean	39.6	47.6	53.2	56.0	56.5	49.4	0.09	19.7	17.8	17.5	15.7	10.9	17.0	−0.09
East Asia, Pacific	48.3	56.8	60.3	64.6	72.9	59.3	0.08	10.5	9.9	9.9	8.6	6.3	9.3	−0.08
Central Asia	64.2	67.9	71.8	75.7	77.4	70.9	0.04	19.0	15.6	15.0	14.6	13.7	15.8	−0.02
Middle East, North Africa	42.2	53.3	62.5	73.2	81.1	61.0	0.17	21.0	20.3	19.1	17.2	14.7	18.7	−0.06
South Asia	29.8	31.4	41.6	49.8	64.4	42.0	0.17	17.0	14.4	14.3	15.3	12.4	14.9	−0.04
Sub-Saharan Africa	33.6	42.0	44.4	53.1	66.9	47.3	0.17	24.5	23.3	22.5	22.6	18.2	22.3	−0.05
All countries	38.3	45.8	50.3	57.2	66.6	50.7	0.14	21.2	19.6	19.1	18.5	14.8	18.9	−0.05

c. Basic antenatal care and attended delivery

Country/region	Basic antenatal care rates (to a medically trained person)							Attended delivery rate (by a medically trained person)						
	1	2	3	4	5	Average	CI	1	2	3	4	5	Average	CI
Bolivia	38.8	57.8	70.4	88.6	95.3	65.1	0.17	19.8	44.8	67.7	87.9	97.9	56.7	0.28
Brazil	67.5	87.7	93.4	96.9	98.1	85.6	0.08	71.6	88.7	95.7	97.7	98.6	87.7	0.07
Colombia	62.3	81.1	89.8	95.4	95.9	82.5	0.09	60.6	85.2	92.8	98.9	98.1	34.5	0.09
Dominican Rep.	96.1	98.2	99.0	99.2	99.9	98.3	0.01	88.6	96.9	97.3	98.4	97.8	95.3	0.02
Guatemala	34.6	41.1	49.3	72.2	90.0	52.5	0.19	9.3	16.1	31.1	62.8	91.5	34.8	0.42
Haiti	44.3	60.0	72.3	83.7	91.0	67.7	0.14	24.0	37.3	47.4	60.7	78.2	46.3	0.21
Nicaragua	67.0	80.9	86.9	89.0	96.0	81.5	0.07	32.9	58.8	79.8	86.0	92.3	64.6	0.19
Paraguay	69.5	79.5	85.6	94.8	98.5	83.9	0.07	41.2	49.9	69.0	87.9	98.1	66.0	0.18
Peru	37.3	64.8	79.1	87.7	96.0	67.3	0.17	13.7	48.0	75.1	90.3	96.6	56.4	0.31
Latin America and the Caribbean	57.5	72.3	80.6	89.7	95.6	76.0	0.11	40.2	58.4	72.9	85.6	94.3	65.8	0.20
East Asia, Pacific	64.9	80.7	86.9	91.4	96.2	81.9	0.08	30.5	53.0	68.4	80.6	93.4	60.8	0.22
Central Asia	78.2	84.7	86.8	93.3	96.3	86.9	0.05	82.7	92.3	95.1	98.6	99.7	92.8	0.04
Middle East, North Africa	13.7	21.1	33.4	49.3	73.0	35.2	0.32	12.8	21.7	37.7	58.6	82.2	38.5	0.36
South Asia	16.8	23.2	28.8	43.0	70.9	34.6	0.30	5.3	8.1	11.7	21.9	49.3	17.7	0.46
Sub-Saharan Africa	61.1	69.5	74.9	84.2	93.6	75.7	0.10	24.6	32.9	41.2	59.2	82.1	46.2	0.26
All countries	55.0	64.8	71.1	80.6	91.0	70.8	0.13	31.2	42.1	51.6	66.2	84.0	52.5	0.25

CI   Concentration index
Source: Demographic and Health Surveys (DHS) 2002.

TABLE A.51

Disabled people as a share of population in Latin American and Caribbean countries

Country	Percent	Year	Data instrument
Belize	6.6	1991	Census
Brazil	16.0	2001	Census
Chile	4.3	1996	Census
Colombia	1.8	1993	Census
Costa Rica	9.3	1998	Survey
Ecuador	13.2	1996	Census
El Salvador	1.9	1992	Census
Jamaica	4.8	1991	Census
México	2.3	2000	Census
Nicaragua	12.3	1995	Census
Panama	1.5	1990	Census
Paraguay	1.0	1992	Census
Peru	13.1	1993	Census
St. Vincent and the Grenadines	7.2	1991	Census
Uruguay	16.0	1992	Survey

TABLE A.52

Overview of disability types, share of total disabled population

Country	Visual	Auditory and speech	Physical	Mental	Other	Source
Barbados	23.8	14.1	26.1	12.9	28.3	BARNOD
Chile	26.9	32.9	21.2	13.1	5.9	MIDEPLAN
Colombia	48.0	31.7	24.0	17.0	NA	Down Syndrome Corporation
Costa Rica	26.5	4.8	18.9	8.1	41.7	National Council of Rehabilitation and Special Education
El Salvador	22.2	21.0	29.4	16.2	NA	Salvadoran Institute of Disability Rehabilitation
Mexico	28.6	21.0	44.9	14.6	0.7	XII General Population and Housing Census
Nicaragua	63.1	14.1	8.5	4.0	9.6	National Autonomous University of Nicaragua
Paraguay	11.0	20.2	19.5	13.2	36.1	Ministry of Public Health and Social Well-being
Peru	9.0	20.0	49.0	22.0	NA	CONADIS
Uruguay	11.6	16.0	45.0	19.0	NA	National Commission of Disability

TABLE A.53

Malapportionment in Latin America, 1999

Country	Chamber	
	Lower	Upper
Argentina	0.14	0.49
Belize	0.08	n/a
Bolivia	0.17	0.38
Brazil	0.09	0.40
Chile	0.15	0.31
Colombia	0.13	0.00
Costa Rica	0.02	n/a
Dominican Rep.	0.08	0.38
Ecuador	0.20	n/a
El Salvador	0.07	n/a
Guatemala	0.06	n/a
Honduras	0.04	n/a
Mexico	0.06	0.23
Nicaragua	0.06	n/a
Panama	0.06	n/a
Paraguay	0.04	0.00
Peru	0.00	n/a
Uruguay	0.03	0.00
RB de Venezuela	0.07	0.33
Latin America	**0.08**	**0.25**
United States	0.01	0.36
Industrial democracies	0.04	0.18
World (without Latin America)	0.06	0.18

Note: Percentage of political seats allocated to districts that would not receive those seats in the case of perfect apportionment, 1999.
Source: Samuels and Snyder 2001.

TABLE A.54

Crime victimization across quintiles

	1	2	3	4	5
Argentina	34.1	37.7	34.5	40.4	41.2
Bolivia	33.0	32.9	37.8	37.7	30.7
Brazil	34.1	34.5	32.0	40.5	45.8
Colombia	29.4	34.3	34.9	39.4	42.2
Costa Rica	33.7	35.5	36.0	43.2	35.0
Chile	27.8	32.2	27.2	33.2	33.6
Ecuador	42.0	39.7	45.5	42.6	43.0
El Salvador	45.3	38.5	47.5	41.6	59.8
Guatemala	54.8	50.9	52.5	58.9	58.5
Honduras	28.4	27.8	39.7	44.3	41.4
México	40.3	39.1	44.5	48.2	47.6
Nicaragua	29.7	32.9	34.9	40.9	42.2
Panama	25.9	26.4	34.1	29.6	26.1
Paraguay	27.2	32.1	37.5	38.9	32.9
Peru	34.9	33.8	35.4	44.0	39.3
Uruguay	20.1	17.5	23.9	31.5	31.8
RB de Venezuela	37.9	42.3	47.0	45.8	53.8
Spain	9.4	13.3	15.2	17.3	18.0

Note: Percent answering yes to the question "Have you or any member of your family been assaulted, robbed, or victimized in any way during the past 12 months?"
   Quintiles of a socioeconomic index constructed from the ownership of durable goods and household characteristics.
Source: Gaviria and Pagés 1999.

TABLE A.55

Access to water, hygienic restrooms, electricity, and telephone

Country	Water						Hygienic restrooms						Electricity						Telephone					
	1	2	3	4	5	Mean	1	2	3	4	5	Mean	1	2	3	4	5	Mean	1	2	3	4	5	Mean
Argentina																								
1992	0.93	0.97	0.96	0.98	1.00	0.97	0.74	0.85	0.87	0.91	0.97	0.88												
1996	0.94	0.96	0.98	0.99	1.00	0.98	0.75	0.87	0.91	0.96	0.99	0.91												
2001	0.96	0.98	0.99	1.00	1.00	0.99	0.60	0.81	0.87	0.96	0.99	0.87	0.98	0.99	1.00	1.00	1.00	1.00						
Bolivia																								
Urban																								
1992	0.75	0.77	0.82	0.87	0.94	0.84	0.69	0.68	0.72	0.76	0.85	0.76	0.92	0.93	0.94	0.95	0.98	0.95						
1996	0.78	0.83	0.89	0.92	0.95	0.88	0.60	0.69	0.80	0.87	0.94	0.79	0.92	0.95	0.96	0.98	0.99	0.96						
National																								
1996	0.45	0.60	0.75	0.84	0.91	0.72	0.26	0.40	0.60	0.74	0.86	0.59	0.21	0.55	0.77	0.85	0.93	0.68						
1999	0.20	0.58	0.75	0.81	0.90	0.66	0.24	0.55	0.75	0.83	0.90	0.67	0.22	0.63	0.85	0.90	0.95	0.72						
Brazil																								
1990							0.17	0.35	0.56	0.73	0.87	0.56	0.60	0.82	0.93	0.98	0.99	0.88	0.01	0.08	0.18	0.31	0.58	0.25
1995							0.23	0.41	0.58	0.75	0.89	0.60	0.73	0.88	0.95	0.99	1.00	0.92	0.02	0.04	0.10	0.23	0.61	0.22
2001							0.33	0.52	0.64	0.79	0.90	0.67	0.86	0.95	0.97	0.99	1.00	0.96						
Chile																								
1996	0.79	0.88	0.92	0.96	0.98	0.91	0.55	0.70	0.81	0.90	0.97	0.80	0.89	0.95	0.96	0.98	0.99	0.96	0.17	0.37	0.52	0.76	0.93	0.59
2000	0.83	0.91	0.94	0.97	0.99	0.93	0.65	0.78	0.86	0.92	0.98	0.85	0.95	0.97	0.98	0.99	1.00	0.98	0.29	0.44	0.59	0.75	0.91	0.62
Colombia																								
Bogotá																								
1992	0.97	0.98	0.99	0.99	1.00	0.99	0.97	0.99	1.00	1.00	1.00	0.99	0.99	0.99	1.00	0.99	0.99	0.99	0.74	0.81	0.83	0.89	0.97	0.86
1996	0.98	0.99	1.00	1.00	1.00	0.99							1.00	0.99	0.99	1.00	1.00	0.99	0.88	0.89	0.92	0.93	0.94	0.91
National																								
1996	0.60	0.78	0.86	0.91	0.96	0.84	0.54	0.76	0.84	0.90	0.97	0.82	0.81	0.91	0.94	0.96	0.98	0.92	0.13	0.24	0.35	0.51	0.71	0.41
1999	0.70	0.80	0.86	0.92	0.96	0.86	0.65	0.77	0.85	0.91	0.96	0.84	0.87	0.93	0.95	0.96	0.98	0.94	0.24	0.37	0.50	0.63	0.80	0.53
Ecuador																								
1994	0.40	0.46	0.59	0.65	0.80	0.59	0.42	0.53	0.68	0.75	0.90	0.67	0.70	0.86	0.90	0.93	0.96	0.88	0.05	0.04	0.13	0.15	0.37	0.16
1998	0.55	0.62	0.68	0.78	0.86	0.71	0.55	0.68	0.76	0.83	0.96	0.77	0.81	0.92	0.95	0.97	0.99	0.93	0.06	0.11	0.16	0.26	0.56	0.25
El Salvador																								
1991	0.19	0.27	0.40	0.55	0.76	0.46	0.05	0.12	0.23	0.38	0.64	0.31	0.42	0.55	0.69	0.81	0.91	0.70	0.01	0.01	0.03	0.06	0.23	0.08
1995	0.22	0.29	0.38	0.56	0.77	0.47	0.08	0.13	0.25	0.43	0.71	0.35	0.51	0.64	0.76	0.88	0.96	0.77	0.02	0.03	0.07	0.16	0.41	0.16
2000							0.22	0.29	0.40	0.54	0.77	0.47	0.68	0.77	0.87	0.92	0.98	0.86	0.17	0.21	0.28	0.39	0.63	0.36

Country	Year	(1)	(2)	(3)	(4)	(5)	(6)	(7)	(8)	(9)	(10)	(11)	(12)	(13)	(14)	(15)	(16)	(17)	(18)	(19)	(20)	(21)	(22)	(23)	(24)
Guatemala	2000	0.57	0.60	0.68	0.75	0.92	0.72	0.08	0.17	0.23	0.38	0.74	0.35	0.49	0.64	0.76	0.84	0.93	0.75	0.01	0.04	0.07	0.15	0.48	0.18
Honduras	1990	0.43	0.50	0.59	0.69	0.85	0.63	0.05	0.09	0.16	0.30	0.62	0.27	0.15	0.22	0.35	0.59	0.80	0.45						
	1995	0.73	0.70	0.81	0.84	0.92	0.82	0.27	0.36	0.43	0.53	0.76	0.49	0.33	0.53	0.69	0.77	0.87	0.66						
	1999	0.79	0.83	0.89	0.93	0.97	0.89	0.26	0.31	0.48	0.59	0.82	0.51	0.41	0.60	0.75	0.90	0.94	0.74						
Jamaica	1990	0.33	0.38	0.49	0.54	0.65	0.50	0.27	0.36	0.45	0.42	0.60	0.45	0.52	0.50	0.62	0.67	0.76	0.64	0.03	0.04	0.05	0.08	0.14	0.08
	1996	0.46	0.47	0.50	0.57	0.71	0.57	0.32	0.34	0.46	0.40	0.65	0.47	0.70	0.64	0.69	0.70	0.87	0.74	0.19	0.18	0.16	0.21	0.40	0.25
	1999	0.54	0.44	0.65	0.62	0.72	0.61	0.32	0.40	0.52	0.50	0.68	0.51	0.74	0.69	0.80	0.83	0.84	0.79	0.26	0.28	0.34	0.40	0.48	0.37
Mexico	1992	0.63	0.81	0.88	0.93	0.96	0.86	0.28	0.54	0.70	0.80	0.91	0.68	0.76	0.93	0.96	0.98	0.99	0.93	0.03	0.08	0.14	0.27	0.54	0.24
	1996	0.80	0.90	0.93	0.96	0.98	0.92	0.32	0.53	0.71	0.84	0.93	0.70	0.85	0.95	0.98	0.99	1.00	0.96	0.05	0.10	0.21	0.35	0.60	0.29
	2000	0.74	0.88	0.95	0.96	0.98	0.91	0.35	0.70	0.85	0.90	0.96	0.78	0.92	0.98	1.00	1.00	1.00	0.98	0.06	0.20	0.33	0.51	0.74	0.40
Paraguay	1995	0.687	0.71	0.79	0.85	0.95	0.81	0.09	0.24	0.48	0.66	0.87	0.50	0.42	0.64	0.82	0.90	0.97	0.78	0.00	0.01	0.04	0.10	0.37	0.12
	1999	0.708	0.78	0.85	0.92	0.97	0.86	0.16	0.39	0.60	0.75	0.89	0.60	0.73	0.88	0.94	0.97	0.97	0.91	0.02	0.06	0.14	0.34	0.59	0.26
Peru Regions	1991	0.56	0.74	0.77	0.82	0.88	0.76	0.67	0.81	0.87	0.90	0.93	0.84	0.50	0.79	0.89	0.93	0.97	0.82	0.076	0.093	0.101	0.189	0.248	0.145
	1994	0.55	0.71	0.78	0.85	0.91	0.77	0.55	0.76	0.82	0.92	0.96	0.81	0.49	0.78	0.87	0.91	0.95	0.81	0.01	0.048	0.095	0.208	0.389	0.163
National	1994	0.43	0.63	0.71	0.80	0.87	0.70	0.50	0.71	0.77	0.89	0.94	0.78	0.39	0.68	0.80	0.88	0.92	0.75	0.008	0.026	0.085	0.176	0.36	0.145
	2000	0.51	0.64	0.79	0.85	0.93	0.75	0.60	0.72	0.85	0.90	0.97	0.82	0.53	0.66	0.84	0.89	0.96	0.78	0.033	0.072	0.199	0.358	0.623	0.271
Trinidad & Tobago	1992	0.60	0.62	0.61	0.81	0.88	0.73	0.43	0.48	0.56	0.68	0.83	0.63	0.86	0.93	0.98	0.95	0.96	0.94	0.261	0.227	0.359	0.508	0.6	0.42
Uruguay	1989	0.84	0.93	0.96	0.98	0.99	0.95	0.71	0.86	0.93	0.97	0.99	0.91	0.89	0.96	0.99	1.00	1.00	0.97						
	1995	0.99	0.99	1.00	1.00	1.00	1.00	0.76	0.89	0.95	0.99	1.00	0.93	0.96	0.99	1.00	1.00	1.00	0.99						
	2000	0.99	0.99	1.00	1.00	1.00	1.00							0.97	0.99	1.00	1.00	1.00	0.99						
RB de Venezuela	1989	0.82	0.88	0.92	0.95	0.97	0.92	0.70	0.80	0.86	0.91	0.96	0.86	0.92	0.95	0.97	0.98	0.99	0.97	0.15	0.17	0.24	0.33	0.52	0.30
	1995	0.88	0.90	0.92	0.96	0.98	0.93	0.75	0.80	0.87	0.92	0.97	0.87	0.98	0.98	0.99	0.99	1.00	0.99	0.19	0.23	0.31	0.39	0.61	0.36
	1998	0.87	0.91	0.93	0.96	0.97	0.93	0.759	0.822	0.885	0.936	0.969	0.882	0.97	0.98	0.99	0.99	0.99	0.98						

Notes: The variable water refers to the availability of a source of water in the house or lot. The variable restroom is equal to 1 when the household has a restroom with a toilet connected to the sewage system or to a septic tank. The variable electricity includes all sources of electricity. Telephone includes fixed and cellular phones.

Source: Authors' calculations based on microdata from household surveys.

Access to water, hygienic restrooms, electricity, and telephone: urban areas only

Country		Water 1	2	3	4	5	Mean	Hygienic restrooms 1	2	3	4	5	Mean	Electricity 1	2	3	4	5	Mean	Telephone 1	2	3	4	5	Mean
Argentina	1992	0.93	0.97	0.96	0.98	1.00	0.97	0.74	0.85	0.87	0.91	0.97	0.88												
	1996	0.94	0.96	0.98	0.99	1.00	0.98	0.75	0.87	0.91	0.96	0.99	0.91												
	2001	0.96	0.98	0.99	1.00	1.00	0.99	0.60	0.81	0.87	0.96	0.99	0.87	0.98	0.99	1.00	1.00	1.00	1.00						
Bolivia																									
Urban	1992	0.75	0.77	0.82	0.87	0.94	0.84	0.69	0.68	0.72	0.76	0.85	0.76	0.92	0.93	0.94	0.95	0.98	0.95						
	1996	0.78	0.83	0.89	0.92	0.95	0.88	0.60	0.69	0.80	0.87	0.94	0.79	0.92	0.95	0.96	0.98	0.99	0.96						
National	1996	0.79	0.78	0.85	0.90	0.94	0.88	0.62	0.59	0.70	0.84	0.92	0.79	0.86	0.93	0.94	0.96	0.98	0.96						
	1999	0.86	0.91	0.87	0.89	0.94	0.91	0.67	0.76	0.83	0.87	0.93	0.86	0.98	0.97	0.97	0.98	0.99	0.98						
Brazil	1990							0.32	0.49	0.65	0.79	0.90	0.70	0.89	0.95	0.98	1.00	1.00	0.98						
	1995							0.38	0.53	0.66	0.79	0.91	0.71	0.94	0.97	0.99	1.00	1.00	0.99						
	2001							0.48	0.62	0.72	0.83	0.92	0.76	0.97	0.99	0.99	1.00	1.00	0.99	0.12	0.17	0.22	0.35	0.63	0.39
Chile	1996	0.96	0.98	0.99	0.99	0.99	0.99	0.76	0.85	0.91	0.95	0.98	0.91	0.98	0.99	1.00	1.00	1.00	0.99	0.03	0.05	0.11	0.25	0.62	0.26
	2000	0.97	0.98	0.99	0.99	1.00	0.99	0.84	0.90	0.93	0.96	0.99	0.94	0.99	1.00	1.00	1.00	1.00	1.00	0.24	0.43	0.58	0.79	0.94	0.67
Colombia																									
Bogotá	1992	0.97	0.98	0.99	0.99	1.00	0.99							0.99	0.99	1.00	0.99	1.00	0.99						
	1996	0.98	0.99	1.00	1.00	1.00	0.99	0.97	0.99	1.00	1.00	1.00	0.99	1.00	0.99	0.99	1.00	0.99	0.99	0.36	0.51	0.65	0.78	0.93	0.69
National	1996	0.95	0.96	0.98	0.98	1.00	0.98	0.89	0.93	0.96	0.97	0.99	0.96	0.99	0.98	0.99	0.99	0.99	0.99	0.74	0.81	0.83	0.89	0.97	0.86
	1999	0.96	0.98	0.98	0.99	0.99	0.98	0.90	0.94	0.97	0.98	0.99	0.97	0.99	0.99	1.00	0.99	1.00	0.99	0.88	0.89	0.92	0.93	0.94	0.91
Ecuador	1994	0.62	0.62	0.67	0.75	0.85	0.74	0.79	0.78	0.84	0.89	0.97	0.88	0.98	0.99	1.00	1.00	1.00	0.99	0.38	0.42	0.50	0.63	0.78	0.61
	1998	0.77	0.77	0.78	0.87	0.90	0.84	0.86	0.85	0.86	0.90	0.98	0.91	0.99	0.99	1.00	1.00	1.00	1.00	0.56	0.62	0.69	0.76	0.88	0.74
El Salvador	1991	0.40	0.50	0.62	0.73	0.89	0.72	0.21	0.31	0.46	0.58	0.79	0.58	0.78	0.86	0.92	0.96	0.99	0.94	0.14	0.10	0.18	0.21	0.44	0.26
	1995	0.44	0.48	0.55	0.68	0.83	0.67	0.26	0.31	0.44	0.57	0.79	0.57	0.83	0.90	0.93	0.96	0.99	0.95	0.18	0.17	0.21	0.31	0.61	0.36
	2000							0.54	0.56	0.61	0.69	0.85	0.69	0.92	0.92	0.95	0.96	0.99	0.96						
Guatemala	2000	0.81	0.77	0.84	0.84	0.97	0.89	0.40	0.47	0.52	0.58	0.85	0.67	0.80	0.88	0.90	0.94	0.98	0.94	0.06	0.11	0.15	0.24	0.58	0.35
Honduras	1990	0.67	0.72	0.76	0.79	0.90	0.82	0.20	0.31	0.36	0.45	0.75	0.54	0.65	0.75	0.77	0.88	0.95	0.86	0.02	0.03	0.06	0.09	0.28	0.14
	1995	0.83	0.79	0.81	0.86	0.94	0.87	0.50	0.47	0.52	0.63	0.83	0.65	0.78	0.86	0.93	0.94	0.98	0.93	0.07	0.07	0.12	0.21	0.47	0.26
	1999	0.90	0.88	0.94	0.94	0.99	0.95	0.52	0.49	0.60	0.69	0.88	0.71	0.90	0.89	0.95	0.99	1.00	0.97	0.37	0.36	0.39	0.47	0.68	0.50

Jamaica																								
1990	0.60	0.79	0.80	0.83	0.81	0.79	0.50	0.62	0.72	0.62	0.74	0.67	0.64	0.68	0.76	0.79	0.82	0.77	0.10	0.10	0.06	0.10	0.20	0.13
1996	0.72	0.88	0.87	0.79	0.88	0.84	0.56	0.60	0.78	0.61	0.80	0.70	0.83	0.75	0.89	0.77	0.93	0.86	0.33	0.36	0.30	0.33	0.58	0.43
1999	0.83	0.77	0.80	0.87	0.93	0.87	0.55	0.65	0.67	0.72	0.83	0.73	0.83	0.78	0.80	0.86	0.88	0.85	0.42	0.51	0.49	0.59	0.65	0.57
Mexico																								
1992	0.85	0.89	0.91	0.95	0.97	0.93	0.54	0.70	0.79	0.86	0.95	0.82	0.96	0.98	0.99	0.99	0.99	0.99	0.09	0.11	0.17	0.30	0.57	0.31
1996	0.90	0.93	0.95	0.97	0.99	0.96	0.56	0.69	0.81	0.89	0.96	0.83	0.95	0.99	0.99	1.00	1.00	0.99	0.11	0.15	0.25	0.39	0.64	0.37
2000	0.86	0.92	0.97	0.97	0.99	0.96	0.67	0.83	0.92	0.93	0.97	0.91	0.95	1.00	1.00	1.00	1.00	0.99	0.12	0.26	0.37	0.53	0.76	0.49
Paraguay																								
1995	0.68	0.81	0.87	0.90	0.95	0.89	0.30	0.46	0.65	0.78	0.92	0.75	0.78	0.92	0.96	0.97	1.00	0.96	0.02	0.04	0.07	0.14	0.42	0.21
1999	0.89	0.87	0.88	0.95	0.99	0.93	0.49	0.62	0.72	0.87	0.94	0.81	0.95	0.97	0.96	1.00	0.98	0.98	0.09	0.11	0.19	0.42	0.65	0.39
Peru																								
Regions																								
1991	0.81	0.83	0.82	0.86	0.89	0.85	0.85	0.89	0.92	0.93	0.94	0.92	0.85	0.92	0.94	0.98	0.98	0.95	0.18	0.12	0.12	0.21	0.26	0.18
1994	0.80	0.81	0.86	0.88	0.94	0.87	0.84	0.85	0.89	0.95	0.98	0.92	0.83	0.92	0.96	0.97	0.98	0.95	0.03	0.06	0.11	0.23	0.41	0.21
National																								
1994	0.75	0.79	0.84	0.86	0.92	0.86	0.80	0.85	0.86	0.94	0.97	0.91	0.78	0.89	0.95	0.96	0.97	0.94	0.03	0.04	0.11	0.20	0.39	0.20
2000	0.87	0.83	0.88	0.92	0.96	0.91	0.86	0.90	0.97	0.97	0.98	0.96	0.86	0.89	0.97	0.97	0.99	0.96	0.12	0.13	0.27	0.42	0.66	0.40
Trinidad & Tobago																								
1992	0.64	0.76	0.83	0.96	0.96	0.81	0.59	0.65	0.70	0.74	0.91	0.75	0.86	0.93	0.98	0.95	0.96	0.94	0.37	0.35	0.50	0.54	0.71	0.53
Uruguay																								
1989	0.84	0.93	0.96	0.98	0.99	0.95							0.89	0.96	0.99	1.00	1.00	0.97						
1995	0.99	0.99	1.00	1.00	1.00	1.00	0.71	0.86	0.93	0.97	0.99	0.91	0.96	0.99	1.00	1.00	1.00	0.99						
2000	0.99	0.99	1.00	1.00	1.00	1.00	0.76	0.89	0.95	0.99	1.00	0.93	0.97	0.99	1.00	1.00	1.00	0.99						
RB de Venezuela																								
1989	0.98	0.99	1.00	1.00	1.00	1.00	0.97	0.98	0.99	0.99	1.00	0.99	0.99	1.00	1.00	1.00	1.00	1.00						
1995	0.96	0.99	1.00	1.00	1.00	1.00	0.92	0.98	0.99	0.99	1.00	0.99	1.00	0.99	1.00	0.99	1.00	1.00	0.34	0.25	0.31	0.39	0.67	0.49
1998	0.96	0.99	0.99	0.99	1.00	0.99	0.97	0.98	0.99	1.00	1.00	0.99	1.00	1.00	0.99	0.99	1.00	0.99	0.32	0.28	0.36	0.43	0.72	0.54

Notes: Water refers to the availability of a source of water in the house or lot. The variable restroom is equal to 1 when the household has a restroom with a toilet connected to the sewage system or to a septic tank. The variable electricity includes all sources of electricity. Telephone includes fixed and cellular phones.

Source: Authors' calculations based on microdata from household surveys.

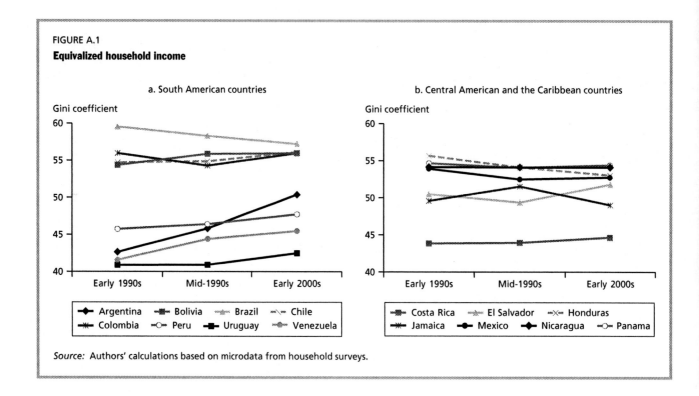

FIGURE A.1

Equivalized household income

a. South American countries

b. Central American and the Caribbean countries

Gini coefficient

Gini coefficient

Source: Authors' calculations based on microdata from household surveys.

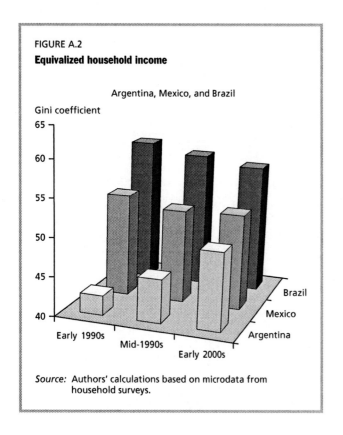

FIGURE A.2

Equivalized household income

Argentina, Mexico, and Brazil

Gini coefficient

Source: Authors' calculations based on microdata from household surveys.

FIGURE A.3

Aggregate welfare measures

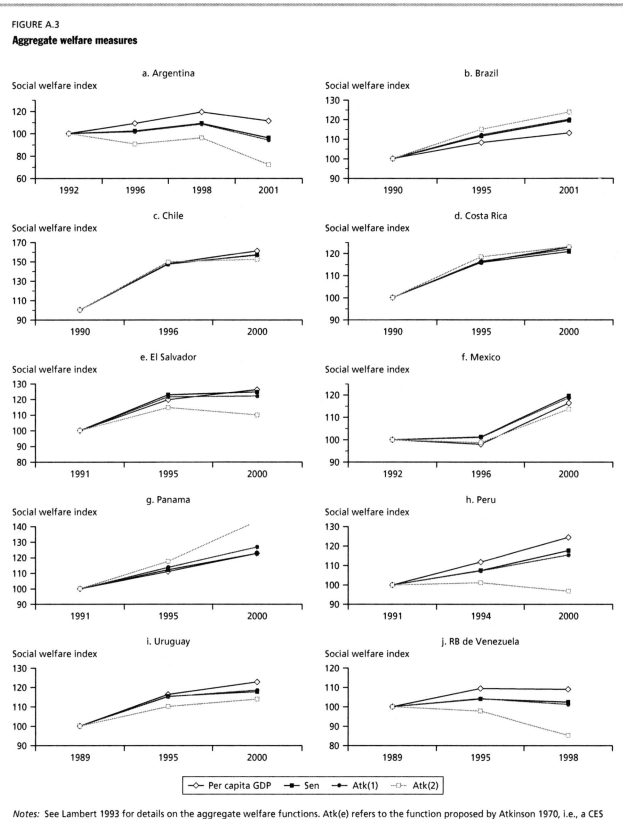

a. Argentina

b. Brazil

c. Chile

d. Costa Rica

e. El Salvador

f. Mexico

g. Panama

h. Peru

i. Uruguay

j. RB de Venezuela

—◇— Per capita GDP   —■— Sen   —●— Atk(1)   ⋯◻⋯ Atk(2)

Notes: See Lambert 1993 for details on the aggregate welfare functions. Atk(e) refers to the function proposed by Atkinson 1970, i.e., a CES function with parameter equal to e. First observation for each country = 100.

Source: Authors' calculations based on microdata from household surveys and per capita GDP from World Bank 2000b and World Development Indicators Database.

FIGURE A.4

Poverty headcount ratio: share of individuals who live on less than US$2 a day, late 1990s

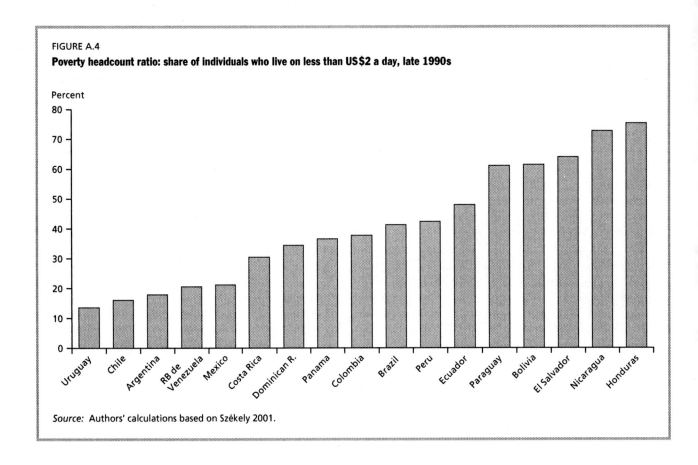

Source: Authors' calculations based on Székely 2001.

FIGURE A.5

Relative income of each percentile of within-class distributions

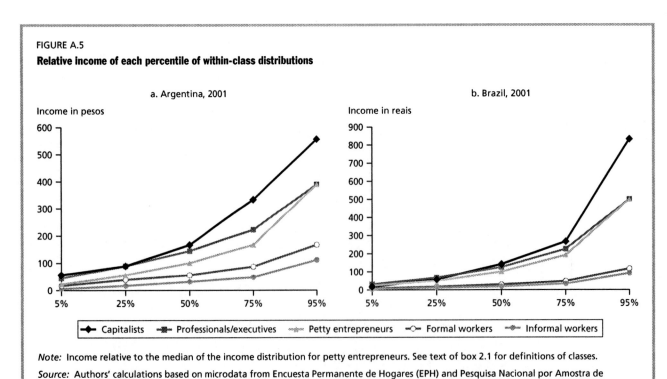

Note: Income relative to the median of the income distribution for petty entrepreneurs. See text of box 2.1 for definitions of classes.

Source: Authors' calculations based on microdata from Encuesta Permanente de Hogares (EPH) and Pesquisa Nacional por Amostra de Domicilios (PNAD).

FIGURE A.6

Difference in average hours of work between unskilled and skilled workers

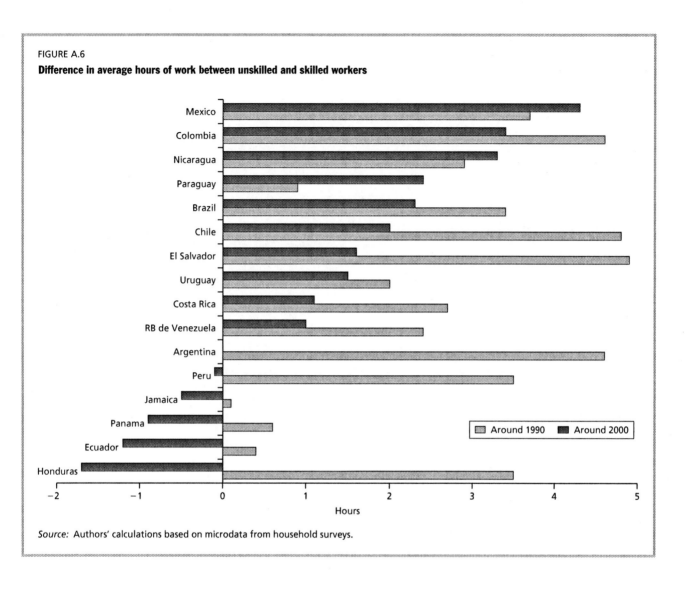

Source: Authors' calculations based on microdata from household surveys.

FIGURE A.7

Difference in unemployment rates between unskilled and skilled workers

Percentage points

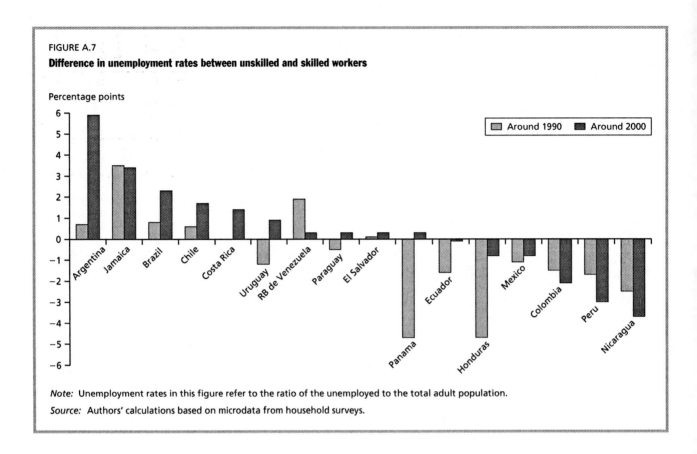

Note: Unemployment rates in this figure refer to the ratio of the unemployed to the total adult population.

Source: Authors' calculations based on microdata from household surveys.

FIGURE A.8

Difference in housing ownership between top and bottom quintiles, by percentage points

Percentage points

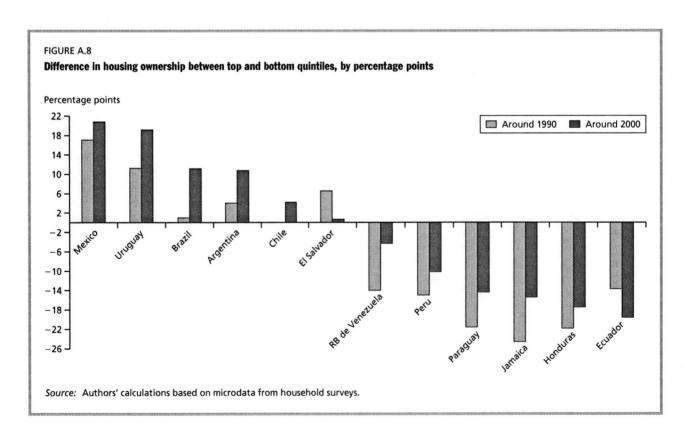

Source: Authors' calculations based on microdata from household surveys.

FIGURE A.9

Distribution of conditional probabilities of attending college for youths, ages 19–21

Gini coefficient

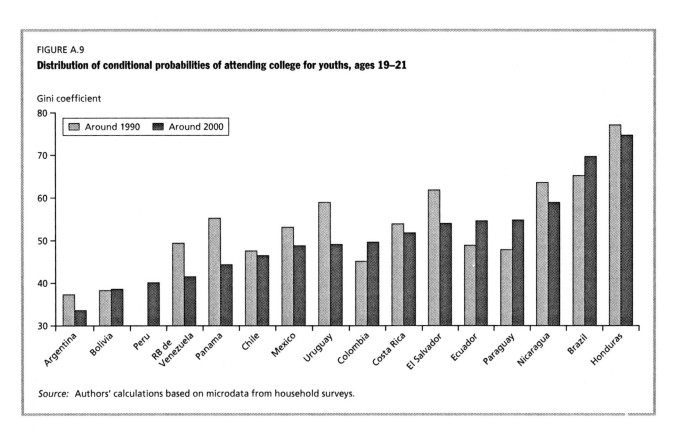

Source: Authors' calculations based on microdata from household surveys.

FIGURE A.10

Index of intergenerational educational mobility for youths, ages 13–19

Index

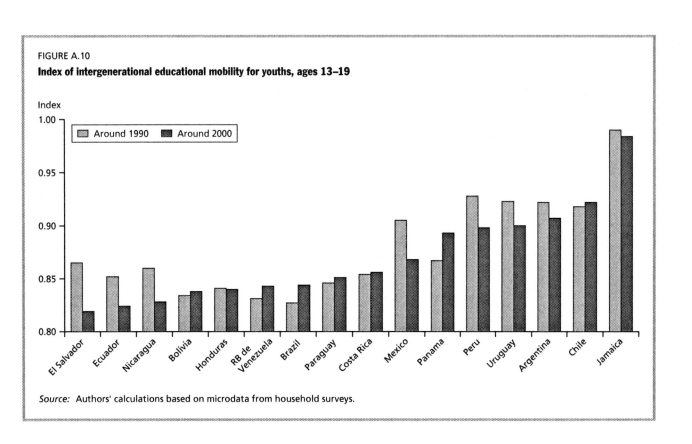

Source: Authors' calculations based on microdata from household surveys.

Bibliography

Background Papers

The following papers or notes were commissioned for this study, and are as yet unpublished manuscripts. Copies can be obtained by contacting the Office of the Chief Economist, Latin America and the Caribbean, The World Bank, or directly from the authors.

Ames, Barry. 2003. "The State, Civil Society, and Inequality."

Baiocchi, Gianpaolo. 2003. "After Dependency: New Approaches to (New) Inequalities in Latin America and the Caribbean in the Sociological Literature."

Bird, Richard. 2003. "Taxation in Latin America: The Balance between Equity, Efficiency, and Sustainability."

Cunningham, Wendy, and Joyce P. Jacobsen. 2003. "Income Inequality Within and Across Racial and Ethnic Groups in Latin America."

Cunningham, Wendy, and Mauricio Santamaría. 2003. "Labor Markets as a Source of Income Inequality."

Fiszbein, Ariel, and Sebastián Galiani. 2003a. "Does Inflation Increase Wage Inequality? Some Preliminary Evidence from Argentina."

Fiszbein, Ariel, and Sebastián Galiani. 2003b. "A Brief Note on the Evolution of the Income Distribution in Argentina: 1950–2000."

Halac, Marina, and Sergio Schmukler. 2003. "Distributional Effects of Crises: The Role of Financial Transfers."

Heller, Patrick, and James Mahoney. 2003. "The Resilience and Transformability of Social Inequality in Latin America."

Malone, Mary. 2002. "The State and Inequality in Latin America."

Maldonado, Alberto. 2003. "Nota sobre la Experiencia de la Ciudad Bogotá, Colombia."

Tendler, Judith. 2003. "The Fear of Education."

References

Note: The word *processed* describes informally reproduced works that may not be commonly available through libraries.

Abente, Diego. 1995. "A Party System in Transition: The Case of Paraguay." In Scott Mainwaring and Timothy R. Scully, eds., *Building Democratic Institutions: Party Systems in Latin America.* Stanford, CA: Stanford University Press.

Abers, Rebecca Naeara. 1996. "From Ideas to Practice: The Partido dos Trabalhadores and Participatory Governance in Brazil." *Latin American Perspectives* 23 (4): 35–53.

———. 1998. "From Clientelism to Cooperation: Local Government, Participatory Policy, and Civic Organizing in Porto Alegre, Brazil." *Politics and Society* 26 (4): 511–37.

———. 2000a. "Inventing Local Democracy: Neighborhood Organizing and Participatory Policymaking in Porto Alegre, Brazil." PhD diss. University of California, Los Angeles.

———. 2000b. *Inventing Local Democracy. Grassroots Politics in Brazil.* Boulder, CO: Lynne Rienner Publishers.

Acemoglu, Daron, and James Robinson. 2000. "Why did the West Extend the Franchise?" *Quarterly Journal of Economics* 115: 1167–99.

Acemoglu, Daron, Simon Johnson, and James Robinson. 2001. "Colonial Origins of Comparative Development: An Empirical Investigation." *American Economic Review* 91: 1369–401.

———. 2002. "Reversal of Fortune: Geography and Institutions in the Making of the Modern World Income Distribution." *Quarterly Journal of Economics* 118: 1231–94.

Acemoglu, Daron, Simon Johnson, James Robinson, and Yunyong Thaicharoen. 2002. "Institutional Causes,

Macroeconomic Symptoms: Volatility, Crises and Growth." National Bureau of Economic Research Working Paper 9124. Cambridge, MA.

Acosta, M. 1999. "Overcoming the Discrimination against Women in Mexico: A Task for Sisyphus." In J. Méndez, G. O'Donnell, and P. Pinheiro, eds., *The Rule of Law and the Underprivileged in Latin America.* Notre Dame, IN: University of Notre Dame Press.

Adato, M. 2000. "Final Report: The Impact of PROGRESA on Community Social Relationships." International Food Policy Research Institute, Washington, D.C.

Adato, M., D. Coady, and M. Ruel. 2000. "Final Report: An Operations Evaluation of PROGRESA from the Perspective of Beneficiaries, Promotors, School Directors, and Health Staff." International Food Policy Research Institute, Washington, D.C.

Adato, M., B. de la Brière, D. Mindek, and A. Quisumbing. 2000. "Final Report: The Impact of PROGRESA on Women's Status and Intra-household Relations." International Food Policy Research Institute, Washington, D.C.

Agarwal, Bina. 1994. *A Field of One's Own: Gender and Land Rights in South Asia.* Cambridge, U.K.: Cambridge University Press.

Aghion, Philippe, Philippe Bacchetta, and Abhijit Banerjee. 2001. "A Corporate Balance Sheet Approach to Currency Crises." Discussion Paper 3092. Centre for Economic Policy Research, London.

Aghion, Philppe, and Patrick Bolton. 1997. "A Theory of Trickle-Down Growth and Development." *Review of Economic Studies* 64: 151–72.

Aghion, Philippe, Eve Caroli, and Cecilia García-Peñalosa. 1999. "Inequality and Economic Growth: The Perspective of the New Growth Theories." *Journal of Economic Literature* 37: 1615–60.

Aghion, Philippe, and Simon Commander. 1999. "On the Dynamics of Inequality in the Transition." *Economics of Transition* 7 (2): 275–98.

Agier, Michel. 1995. "Racism, Culture, and Black Identity in Brazil." *Bulletin of Latin American Research* 14 (3): 245–64.

Agier, Michel, Olivier Barbary, Odile Hoffman, Pedro Quintin, Hector Fabio Ramírez, and Fernando Urrea. 2000. "Espacios Culturales, Movilidad, y Urbanización, Dinámicas Culturales e Identidades en las Poblaciones Afro-Colombianas del Pacífico Sur y Cali: Una Perspectiva Integrada." Cidse-IRD-COLCIENCIAS Project, Cali and Paris.

Ahmad, Ehtisham, and Nicholas Stern. 1991. *The Theory and Practice of Tax Reform in Developing Countries.* Cambridge: Cambridge University Press.

Ahuja, Vinod, Benu Bidani, Francisco Ferreira, and Michael Walton. 1997. *Everyone's Miracle? Revisiting poverty and inequality in East Asia.* Washington, D.C.: World Bank.

Ajwad, M. I., and Q. Wodon. 2002. "Who Benefits from Increased Access to Public Services at the Local Level? A Marginal Benefit Incidence Analysis for Education and Basic Infrastructure" (2: 155–75). In Devarajan, S. and F. H. Rogers, eds., *World Bank Economists' Forum.* Washington, D.C.: World Bank.

_____. 2003. "Benefit and Marginal Benefit Incidence Analysis for Education and Health Services in Latin America." World Bank, Washington, D.C. Processed.

_____. Forthcoming. "Marginal Benefit Incidence Analysis Using a Single Cross-section of Data." *Applied Economics Letters.*

Akerlof, George, and Rachel Kranton. 2000. "Economics and Identity." *Quarterly Journal of Economics* 115 (3): 715–53.

Alarcón, D., and T. McKinley. 1998. "Increasing Wage Inequality and Trade Liberalization in Mexico." In A. Berry, ed., *Poverty, Economic Reform, and Income Distribution in Latin America.* Boulder, CO: Lynne Rienner Publishers, Inc.

Albernaz, Ângela, Francisco Ferreira, and Creso Franco. 2002. "Qualidade e Eqüidade no Ensino Fundamental Brasileiro." *Pesquisa e Planejamento Econômico* 32 (3): 453–76.

Alesina, Alberto, and Dani Rodrik. 1994. "Distributive Politics and Economic Growth." *Quarterly Journal of Economics* 109: 465–89.

Alesina, Alberto, and G. Angeletos. 2003. "Fairness and Redistribution: US versus Europe." National Bureau of Economic Research Working Paper 9502. Cambridge, MA.

Alesina, Alberto, Reza Baqir, and William Easterly. 1999. "Public Goods and Ethnic Divisions." *Quarterly Journal of Economics* 114 (4): 1243–84.

Alesina, Alberto, Edward Glaeser, and Bruce Sacerdote. 2001. "Why Doesn't the US Have a European-Style Welfare System?" National Bureau of Economic Research Working Paper 8524. Cambridge, MA.

Alesina, Alberto, Arnaud Devleeschauwer, William Easterly, Sergio Kurlat, and Roumain Wacziag. 2002. "Fractionalization." National Bureau of Economic Research Working Paper 9411. Cambridge, MA.

Altimir, O. 1986. "Estimaciones de la distribución del ingreso en la Argentina, 1953–1980." *Desarrollo Económico* 25 (100).

———. 1994. "Income Distribution and Poverty Through Crisis and Adjustment." *ECLAC Review* 52: 7–31.

———. 1996a. "Economic Development and Social Equity: A Latin American Perspective." *Journal of Interamerican Studies and World Affairs* 38 (2/3): 47–71.

———. 1996b. "Cambios de la desigualdad y la pobreza en la América Latina." *El Trimestre Económico* 241 (61): 1.

———. 1998a. "Income Distribution and Poverty through Crisis and Adjustment." In A. Berry, ed., *Poverty, Economic Reform, and Income Distribution in Latin America*. Boulder, CO: Lynne Rienner Publishers, Inc.

———. 1998b. "Inequality, Employment, and Poverty in Latin America: An Overview." In V. Tokman and G. O'Donnell, eds. *Poverty and Inequality in Latin America: Issues and New Challenges*. Notre Dame, IN: University of Notre Dame Press.

Altimir, O., and L. Beccaria. 2001. "Persistent Deterioration of Income Distribution in Argentina." *Desarrollo Económico: Revista de Ciencias Sociales* 40 (160): 589–618.

Altonji, Joseph, and Rebecca Blank. 1999. "Race and Gender in the Labor Market." In O. Ashenfelter and David Card, eds., *Handbook of Labor Economics, Volume 3C*. Amsterdam: Elsevier.

Ames, Barry. 2001. *The Deadlock of Democracy in Brazil*. Ann Arbor, MI: University of Michigan Press.

———. 2003. "The State, Civil Society, and Inequality." Background Paper for the World Bank project on inequality in Latin America and the Caribbean. University of Pittsburgh, Pittsburgh, PA. Processed.

Amiel, Yoram and Frank Cowell. 1997. "The Measurement of Poverty: an Experimental Questionnaire Investigation." *Empirical Economics* 22 (4): 571–88.

Andersen, L. 2001. "Social Mobility in Latin America: Links with Adolescent Schooling." Working Paper R-433. Inter-American Development Bank Research Network, Washington, D.C.

Angell, Alan, Pamela Lowden, and Rosemary Thorp. 2001. *Decentralizing Development: The Political Economy of Institutional Change in Colombia and Chile*. New York: Oxford University Press.

Angel-Urdinola, Diego F. 2003. "Minimum Wage Increases Can Have an Adverse Impact on Wage Inequality: The Case of Colombia." World Bank, Washington, D.C. Processed.

Angrist, Joshua David, Eric Bettinger, Erik Bloom, Elizabeth King, and Michael Kremer. 2002. "Vouchers for Private Schooling in Colombia: Evidence from a Randomized Natural Experiment." *American Economic Review* 92 (5): 1535–58.

Appadurai, Arjun. 2004. "The Capacity to Aspire: Culture and the Terms of Recognition." In Vijayendra Rao and Michael Walton, eds. 2004. *Culture and Public Action*. Stanford, CA: Stanford University Press.

Arbache, Jorge S. 2002. "Do Unions Always Decrease Wage Dispersion? The Case of Brazilian Manufacturing." *Journal of Labor Research* 20 (3): 425–36.

Archer, Ronald P. 1990. "The Transition from Traditional to Broker Clientelism in Colombia: Political Stability and Social Unrest." Working Paper 140. Kellogg Institute for International Studies, University of Notre Dame.

Arellano, Manuel and Stephen R. Bond. 1991. "Some Tests of Specification for Panel Data: Monte Carlo Evidence and an Application to Employment Equations." *Review of Economic Studies* 58 (2): 277–97.

Arias, Omar, Gustavo Yamada, and Luis Tejerina. 2002. *Education, Family Background, and Racial Earnings Inequality in Brazil*. Washington, D.C.: Inter-American Development Bank.

Armingeon, K. 2002. "The Effects of Negotiation Democracy: A Comparative Analysis." *European Journal of Political Research* 41 (1): 81–105.

Arocha, Jaime. 1998. "Inclusion of Afro-Colombians: Unreachable National Goals?" *Latin American Perspectives* 25 (3): 70–88.

Atkinson, Anthony B. 1970. "On the Measurement of Inequality." *Journal of Economic Theory* 2: 244–63.

———. 1997. "Bringing Income Distribution in from the Cold." *Economic Journal* 107: 291–321.

———. 2000. "Countries and the Redistributive Impact of the Government Budget." World Institute for Development Economics Research Working Paper 202. Helsinki: WIDER.

———. 2003. "Income Inequality in OECD Countries: Data and Explanations." Working Paper 881. Munich: CESifo.

Atkinson, Anthony B. and A. Brandolini. 2001. "Promise and Pitfalls in the Use of 'Secondary' Data-sets." *Journal of Economic Literature* 39 (3).

Atkinson, Anthony B. and Joseph E. Stiglitz. 1980. *Lectures on Public Economics*. London: McGraw-Hill.

Atkinson, Anthony B., A. Brandolini, and T. Smeeding. 2002. "Producing Time Series Data for Income Distribution: Sources, Methods, and Techniques." Luxemborg Income Study Working Paper 295. Syracuse, NY: University of Syracuse.

Baer, Werner. 1986. "Growth with Inequality: The Cases of Brazil and Mexico." *Latin American Research Review* 21 (2): 197–207.

Baiocchi, Gianpaolo. 2001. "Participation, Activism, and Politics: the Porto Alegre Experiment and Deliberative Democratic Theory." *Politics and Society* 29 (1): 43–72.

Baker, J. L. 2003. "Protecting the Poor through Social Protection Programs." In Q. Wodon, ed., "Public Spending, Poverty, and Inequality in Latin America." World Bank, Washington, D.C.

Bakewell, Peter. 1997. *A History of Latin America*. New York: Blackwell Publishing.

Baland, Jean-Marie and James A. Robinson. 2003. "Land and Power." Centre for Economic Policy Research Discussion Paper 3800. CEPR, London.

Baldacci, Emanuele, Luiz de Melo, and Gabriela Inchauste. 2002. "Financial Crises, Poverty, and Income Distribution." Working Paper 02/04. International Monetary Fund, Washington, D.C.

Banco de España. 1999. Circular 9/1999. Madrid.

Banerjee, Abhijit V., and Andrew F. Newman. 1993. "Occupational Choice and the Process of Development." *Journal of Political Economy* 101 (2): 274–98.

Baron, James N., and Michael T. Hannan. 1994. "The Impact of Economics on Contemporary Sociology." *Journal of Economic Literature* 32 (3): 1111–46.

Barro, Robert J., and Jong-Wha Lee. 2001. "International Data on Educational Attainment: Updates and Implications." *Oxford Economic Papers* 53 (3): 541–63.

Barrett, P. 2001. "Labour Policy, Labour-Business Relations, and the Transition to Democracy in Chile." *Journal of Latin American Studies* 33: 561–97.

Bates, Robert H. 1981. *Markets and States in Tropical Africa*. Berkeley: University of California Press.

Becker, Gary. 1971. *The Economics of Discrimination* (second edition). Chicago: University of Chicago Press.

Behrman, J., and P. E. Todd. 1999a. "Randomness in the Experimental Samples of PROGRESA (Education, Health, and Nutrition Program)." International Food Policy Research Institute, Washington, D.C.

———. 1999b. "A Preliminary Evaluation of the Sample Sizes Used for the Evaluation of the Education, Health, and Nutrition Program (PROGRESA) of Mexico." International Food Policy Research Institute, Washington, D.C.

Behrman, J., and J. Hoddinott. 2000. "An Evaluation of the Impact of PROGRESA on Pre-school Child Height." International Food Policy Research Institute, Washington, D.C.

Behrman, J., Piyali Sengupta, and P. Todd. 2000a. "Final Report: The Impact of PROGRESA on Achievement Test Scores in the First Year." International Food Policy Research Institute, Washington, D.C.

———. 2000b. "Progressing Through PROGRESA: An Impact Assessment of a School Subsidy Experiment." International Food Policy Research Institute, Washington, D.C.

Behrman, J., A. Gaviria, and M. Székely. 2001. "Intergenerational Schooling Mobility in Latin America." *Economía* 2 (3): 1–44.

Behrman Jere, Nancy Birdsall, and Miguel Székely. 2001. "Economic Policy and Wage Differentials in Latin America." Inter-American Development Bank, Washington, D.C.

Behrman, J., B. Davis, D. Levy, and E. Skoufias. 1998. "A Preliminary Evaluation of the Selection of Beneficiary Households in the Education, Health, and Nutrition Program (PROGRESA) of Mexico." Report submitted to PROGRESA. International Food Policy Research Institute, Washington, D.C.

Bénabou, Roland. 2000. "Unequal Societies: Income Distribution and the Social Contract." *American Economic Review* 90 (1): 96–129.

Bernanke, Ben S., and Refet S. Gurkaynak. 2002. "Is Growth Exogenous? Taking Mankiw, Romer, and Weil Seriously." National Bureau of Economic Research Working Paper 8365. Cambridge, MA.

Berry, A. 1998. *Poverty, Economic Reform, and Income Distribution in Latin America*. Boulder, CO: Lynne Rienner Publishers, Inc.

Berry, A., and J. Tenjo. 1998. "Trade Liberalization, Labor Reform, and Income Distribution in Colombia." In A. Berry, ed., *Poverty, Economic Reform, and Income Distribution in Latin America*. Boulder, CO: Lynne Rienner Publishers, Inc.

Bértola, Luis, and Gabriel Porcile. 2002. *Rich and Impoverished Cousins: Economic Performance and Income Distribution in Southern Settler Societies.* Montevideo: Universidad de la República.

Besley, Timothy, and Stephen Coate. 1991. "Public Provision of Private Goods and the Redistribution of Income." *American Economic Review* 81 (4): 979–984.

Biewen, M. 2002. "Bootstrap Inference for Inequality, Mobility, and Poverty Measurement." *Journal of Econometrics* 108: 317–42.

Binder, A. 1991. *Reform of the Penal System in Latin America.* Arlington, VA: National Council of State Courts.

Binswanger, Hans P., and Klaus Deininger. 1995. "World Bank Land Policy: Evolution and Current Challenges." World Bank, Washington, D.C.

Binswanger, Hans P., Klaus Deininger, and Gershon Feder. 1995. "Power, Distortions, Revolt and Reform in Agricultural Land Relations." In *Handbook of Development Economics, Volume 3.* Amsterdam: North-Holland Publishing Company.

Bird, Richard 1992. "Tax Reform in Latin America: A Review of Some Recent Experiences." *Latin American Research Review* 27: 7–34.

Bird, Richard, ed. 1991. *More Taxing than Taxes? The Tax-like Effects of Non-Tax Policies in LDCs.* San Francisco: ICS Press.

Bird, Richard, and O. Oldman. 1968. "Tax Research and Tax Reform in Latin America: A Survey and Commentary." *Latin American Research Review* 3: 5–28.

Bird, R., and De Wulf, L. 1973. "Taxation and Income Distribution in Latin America: A Critical Review of Empirical studies." *International Monetary Fund Staff Papers* 20 (3): 639–82.

Bird, Richard, and Barbara Miller. 1989. "The Incidence of Indirect Taxes on Low-Income Households in Jamaica." *Economic Development and Cultural Change* 37 (2): 393–409.

Bird, Richard, and Enid Slack. 2002. "Land and Property Taxation: A Review." Paper prepared for World Bank Workshop, "Regional Workshop on Land Issues in Latin America and the Caribbean," Pachuca, México.

Birdsall, Nancy, and Juan L. Londoño. 1997. "Asset Inequality Matters: An Assessment of the World Bank's Approach to Poverty Reduction." *American Economic Review* 82 (2): 32–37.

Blau, Francine, and Lawrence Kahn. 1999. "Institutions and Laws in the Labor Market." In Orley Ashenfelter and David Card, eds., *Handbook of Labor Economics, Volume 3A.* Amsterdam: Elsevier.

Boix, Carles. 1998. *Political Parties, Growth and Equity: Conservative and Social Democratic Economic Strategies in the World Economy.* Cambridge, U.K.: Cambridge University Press.

Bordo, Michael, Barry Eichengreen, Daniela Klingebiel, and Maria Soledad Martínez Peria. 2001. "Financial Crises: Lessons from the Last 120 Years." *Economic Policy* 16 (32): 51–82.

Borjas, George J., and Stephen G. Bronars. 1989. "Consumer Discrimination and Self-employment." *Journal of Political Economy* 97 (3): 581–605.

Boschi, R. 1999. "Decentralization, Clientelism, and Social Capital in Urban Governing: Comparing Belo Horizonte and Salvador." *Dados: Revista de Ciencias Sociais* 42 (4): 655–90.

Bouloukos, A., and B. Dakin. 2001. "Toward a Universal Declaration of the Rule of Law: Implications for Criminal Justice and Sustainable Development." *International Journal of Comparative Sociology* 42 (1/2): 145–62.

Bourdieu, Pierre 1984. *Distinction: A Critique of the Judgement of Taste.* Cambridge, MA: Harvard University Press.

———. 1986. "The Forms of Capital." In John Richardson, ed., *Handbook of Theory and Research for the Sociology of Education.* New York: Greenwood Press.

———. 1990. *The Logic of Practice.* Stanford, CA: Stanford University Press.

———. 1998. *Practical Reason.* Stanford, CA: Stanford University Press.

Bourguignon, François. 2002. "The Growth Elasticity of Poverty Reduction: Explaining Heterogeneity across Countries and Time Periods." In T. Eichler and S. Turnovsky, eds., *Growth and Inequality.* Cambridge, MA: Massachusetts Institute of Technology Press.

Bourguignon, François, and Thierry Verdier. 2000. "Oligarchy, Democracy, Inequality and Growth." *Journal of Development Economics* 62 (2): 285–313.

Bourguignon, François, and Christian Morrison. 2002. "Inequality among World Citizens: 1820–1992." *American Economic Review* 92 (4): 727–44.

Bourguignon, François, and Satya Chakravarty. 2003. "The Measurement of Multidimensional Poverty." *Journal of Economic Inequality* 1 (1): 25–49.

Bourguignon, François, Francisco H. G. Ferreira, and Nora Lustig. 1998. "The Microeconomics of Income

Distribution Dynamics in East Asia and Latin America." Research Proposal 638-18. World Bank, Washington, D.C.

Bourguignon, François, Francisco H.G. Ferreira, and Phillippe Leite. 2003. "Beyond Oaxaca-Blinder: Accounting for Differences in Household Income Distributions across Countries." Policy Research Paper 2828. World Bank, Washington, D.C.

————. 2003. "Conditional Cash Transfers, Schooling, and Child Labor: Micro-Simulating Brazil's Bolsa Escola Program." *World Bank Economic Review* 17 (2): 229–54.

Bourguignon, François, Francisco H. G. Ferreira, and Marta Menéndez. 2003. "Inequality of Outcomes and Inequality of Opportunities in Brazil." Policy Research Paper 3174. World Bank, Washington, D.C.

Boyland, Delia. 1996. "Taxation and Transition: The Politics of the 1990 Chilean Tax Reform." *Latin American Research Review* 31 (1).

Bravo, D., D. Contreras, and I. Millan. 2001. "The Distributional Impact of Social Expenditure: Chile 1990–1998." In World Bank, *Chile's High Growth Economy: Poverty and Income Distribution 1987–1998*. World Bank Country Study 73–114. Washington, D.C.: World Bank.

Bresser Pereira, Luiz Carlos. 1998. *Reforma do Estado para a Cidadania: A Reforma Gerencial Brasileira no Perspectiva Internacional*. Sao Paulo: Editora 34.

Bruhn, K. 1997. "The Seven-Month Itch? Neoliberal Politics, Popular Movements, and the Left in Mexico." In Chalmers, D., Carlos M. Vilas, Katherine Hite, Scott B. Martin, Kerianne Piester, and Monique Segarra, eds. *The New Politics of Inequality in Latin America: Rethinking Participation and Representation*. New York: Oxford University Press.

Buhmann, B., G. Rainwater, G. Schmaus, and T. Smeeding. 1988. "Equivalence Scales, Well-being, Inequality and Poverty: Sensitivity Estimates Across Ten Countries Using the Luxembourg Income Study Database." *Review of Income and Wealth* 34: 115–42.

Bunwaree, S. 2001. "The Marginal in the Miracle: Human Capital in Mauritius." *International Journal of Educational Development* 21 (3): 257–71.

Burki, Shahid Javed, and Guillermo Perry. 1998. *Beyond the Washington Consensus: Institutions Matter*. Washington D.C.: World Bank.

Burniaux, Jean-Michel, Thai-Thanh Dang, Douglas Fore, Michael Förster, Marco Mira d'Ercole, and Howard Oxley. 1998. "Income Distribution and Poverty in Selected OECD Countries." OECD Economics Department Working Paper 189. Paris.

Buscaglia, E., and T. Ulen. 1997. "A Quantitative Assessment of the Efficiency of the Judicial Sector in Latin America." *International Review of Law and Economics* 17 (2).

Calderón, Fernando, and Alicia Szmukler. 2004. "Political Culture and Development." In Vijayendra Rao and Michael Walton, eds., *Culture and Public Action*. Stanford, CA: Stanford University Press.

Calderón, César, and Alberto Chong. 2004. "Volume and Quality of Infrastructure and the Distribution of Income: An Empirical Investigation." *Review of Income and Wealth* 50 (1): 87.

Calderón, César, and Luis Servén. 2003. "Macroeconomic Dimensions of Infrastructure in Latin America." World Bank, Washington, D.C., and the Central Bank of Chile, Santiago. Processed.

Calderón, César, William Easterly, and Luis Servén. 2002. "How did Latin America's Infrastructure Fare in the Era of Macroeconomic Crises?" Central Bank of Chile Working Paper 285. World Bank, Washington, D.C.

Calvo, Ernesto. 2001. "Transformation of Labor Markets in Latin America: Collective Bargaining and Industrial Wage Disparities." *Desarrollo Económico: Revista de Ciencias Sociales* 41 (163): 395–410.

Calvo, Ernesto, Juan-Carlos Torre, and Mariela Szwarcberg. 2002. *The New Welfare Alliance*. Buenos Aires: Universidad di Tella, Department of Political Science.

Calvo, Guillermo. 1998. "Capital Flows and Capital-Market Crises: The Simple Economics of a Sudden Stop." *Journal of Applied Economics* 1 (1): 35–54.

Calvo, Guillermo, and Carmen Reinhart. 2000. "When Capital Inflows Come to a Sudden Stop: Consequences and Policy Options." In P. Kenen and A. Swoboda, eds., *Key Issues in Reform of the International Monetary and Financial System*. Washington, D.C.: International Monetary Fund.

Camargo, José, and Ferreira, Francisco. 2001. "O Benefício Social Único: Una proposta de reforma da política social no Brasil." Discusión Paper 443, Departamento de Economía, Pontificia Universidad Católica, Rio de Janeiro.

Cameron, D. 1984. "Social Democracy, Corporatism, Labor Quiescence, and the Representation of Economic Interests in Advanced Capitalist Democracies." In John Goldthorpe, ed., *Order and Conflict in Contemporary Capitalism*. Oxford: Oxford University Press.

Campbell, Tim E. J. 2003. *The Quiet Revolution: Decentralization and the Rise of Political Participation in Latin American Cities*. Pittsburgh: University of Pittsburgh Press.

Caprio, Gerard, and Daniela Klingebiel. 1997. "Bank Insolvency: Bad Luck, Bad Policy, or Bad Banking?" In M. Bruno and B. Pleskovic, eds., *Annual World Bank Conference on Development Economics 1996.* Washington, D.C: World Bank.

Card, David, and John E. DiNardo. 2002. "Skill Biased Technological Change and Rising Wage Inequality: Some Problems and Puzzles." National Bureau of Economic Research Working Paper 8769. Cambridge, MA.

Cardoso, Eliana. 1992. "Inflation and Poverty." National Bureau of Economic Research Working Paper 4006. Cambridge, MA.

Cardoso, Eliana, and A. Helwege. 1992. *Latin America's Economy: Diversity, Trends and Conflicts.* Cambridge, MA: Massachusetts Institute of Technology Press.

Cardoso, Fernando Henrique. 1973. "Associated-Dependent Development: Theoretical and Practical Implications." In Alfred Stepan, ed. *Authoritarian Brazil: Origins, Policies, and Future.* New Haven: Yale University Press.

Carey, J., and M. Shugart. 1995. "Incentives to Cultivate a Personal Vote: A Rank Ordering of Electoral Formulas." *Electoral Studies* 14 (4): 417–39.

Carnoy, Martin, 2002. "Is Latin American Education Preparing its Workforce for 21st Century Economies?" Background paper for De Ferranti and others. 2003. *Closing the Gap in Education and Technology.* Washington, D.C.: World Bank.

Carter, Michael R., Bradford L. Barham, and Dina Mesbah. 1996. "Agricultural Export Booms and the Rural Poor in Chile, Guatemala, and Paraguay." *Latin American Research Review* 31 (1): 33–65.

Carvalho, José Murilo de. 1997. "Mandonismo, Coronelismo, Clientelismo: Uma Discussão Conceitual." *Dados: Revista de Ciências Sociais* 40 (2).

Castelló, Amparo, and Rafael Doménech. 2002. "Human Capital Inequality and Economic Growth: Some New Evidence." *Economic Journal* 112: C187–200.

Castells, Manuel. 1997. *The Power of Identity. The Information Age, Economy, Society, and Culture* (Volume 2). Malden, MA and Oxford: Blackwell Publishing.

CEDLAS. 2003. *Estadísticas distributivas de la Argentina.* La Plata, Argentina: Universidad Nacional de La Plata, Centro de Estudios Distributivos, Laborales y Sociales.

Chalmers, D., Carlos M. Vilas, Katherine Hite, Scott B. Martin, Kerianne Piester, and Monique Segarra, eds. 1997. *The New Politics of Inequality in Latin America:* *Rethinking Participation and Representation.* New York: Oxford University Press.

Chang, Roberto, and Andrés Velasco. 2001. "A Model of Financial Crises in Emerging Markets." *Quarterly Journal of Economics* 116 (2): 489–517.

Chavas, Jean-Paul. 2001. "Structural Change in Agricultural Production: Economics, Technology and Policy." In B. Gardner and G. Rausser, eds., *Handbook of Agricultural Economics, Volume 1.* Amsterdam and New York: Elsevier.

Chen, S., Datt, G., and Martin Ravallion. 1995. "Is Poverty Increasing in the Developing World?" World Bank Policy Research Paper 40 (updated version). Washington, D.C.

Chen, S., and M. Ravallion. 2001. "How Did the World's Poorest Fare in the 1990s?: Methodology." Global Poverty Monitoring Database. World Bank, Washington, D.C. Available at http://www.worldbank.org/research/povmonitor/method.htm.

Chevigny, P. 1999. "Defining the Role of the Police in Latin America." In Méndez, J., G. O'Donnell, and P. Pinheiro, eds. *The Rule of Law and the Underprivileged in Latin America.* Notre Dame, IN: University of Notre Dame Press.

Chong, Alberto, and Florencio López-de-Silanes. 2003. "Privatization in Latin America: What Is the True Record?" Inter-American Development Bank, Washington, D.C. Processed.

Chu, Ke-young, Hamid Davoodi, and Sanjeev Gupta. 2000. "Income Distribution and Tax and Government Social Spending Policies in Developing Countries." United Nations University and World Institute for Development Economics Research Working Paper 214. Helsinki.

Chubb, Judith. 1983. *Patronage, Power and Poverty in Southern Italy: A Tale of Two Cities.* Cambridge: Cambridge University Press.

Clert, C. 2000. "Social Exclusion, Gender, and the Chilean Government's Anti-Poverty Strategy: Priorities and Methods in Question." In E. Gacitua-Mario and C. Sojo, eds. *Social Exclusion and Poverty Reduction in Latin America.* Washington, D.C.: World Bank and FLACSO.

Clert, C. and Q. Wodon. 2002. "The Targeting of Government Programs in Chile: A Quantitative and Qualitative Assessment." In *Chile's High Growth Economy: Poverty and Income Distribution 1987–1998.* World Bank Country Study 141–66. Washington, D.C.: World Bank.

Coady, David. 2000. "Final Report: The Application of Social Cost-Benefit Analysis to the Evaluation of PROGRESA." International Food Policy Research Institute, Washington, D.C.

_____. 2001. "Evaluation of the Distributional Power of PROGRESA's Cash Transfers in Mexico." International Food Policy Research Institute, Food Consumption Nutrition Division Discussion Paper 117. Washington, D.C.

Coady, David, and R. L. Harris. 2000. "A General Equilibrium Analysis of the Welfare Impact of PROGRESA Transfers." International Food Policy Research Institute, Washington, D.C.

Coady, David P., and Susan Parker. 2002. "A Cost-Effectiveness Analysis of Demand and Supply-Side Education Interventions: the Case of PROGRESA in Mexico." International Food Policy Research Institute, Food Consumption Nutrition Division Discussion Paper 127. Washington, D.C.

Coady, David, R. Perez, and H. Vera-Llamas. 2002. "A Cost Analysis of PROGRESA." International Food Policy Research Institute. Washington, D.C. Processed.

Coady, David, Margaret Grosh, and John Hoddinott. 2003. "Targeting Outcomes Redux." International Food Policy Research Institute, Food Consumption Nutrition Division Discussion Paper 144. Washington, D.C.

Coatsworth, John H. 1981. *Growth against Development: The Economic Impact of Railroads in Porfirian Mexico*. De Kalb, IL: Northern Illinois University Press.

Cohen, Yousef. 1989. *The Manipulation of Consent: The State and Working-Class Consciousness in Brazil*. Pittsburgh: University of Pittsburgh Press.

Coleman, J. 1990. *Foundations of Social Theory*. Cambridge, MA: Harvard University Press.

Collier, David, and Ruth Berins Collier. 1991. *Shaping the Political Arena: Critical Junctures, the Labor Movement, and Regime Dynamics in Latin America*. Princeton, NJ: Princeton University Press.

Conaghan, Catherine M. 1995. "Politicians against Parties: Discord and Disconnection in Ecuador's Party System." In Scott Mainwaring and Timothy R. Scully, eds., *Building Democratic Institutions: Party Systems in Latin America*. Stanford, CA: Stanford University Press.

Conning, Jonathan, and James A. Robinson. 2002. "Land Reform and the Political Organization of Agriculture." Centre for Economic Policy Research Discussion Paper 3204. London.

Conning, J., and M. Kevane. 2002. "Community-based Targeting Mechanisms for Social Safety Nets: A Critical Review." *World Development* 30 (3): 375–94.

Conning, Jonathan, Pedro Olinto, and A. Trigueros. 2000. "Managing Economic Insecurity in Rural El Salvador." Williams College, Department of Economics, Williamstown, MA.

Contreras, Dante, and Andrés Gómez-Lobo. 2000. Privatization of Telecommunications and Electricity in Chile: How did the Poor Fare?" University of Chile, Department of Economics, Santiago. Processed.

Contreras, Dante, Oscar Larrañaga, Julie Litchfield, and Alberto Valdés. 2001. "Poverty and Income Distribution in Chile, 1987–1998: New Evidence." *Cuadernos de Economía* 38 (114): 191–208.

Coppedge, Michael. 1994. *Strong Parties and Lame Ducks: Presidential Partyarchy and Factionalism in Venezuela*. Stanford, CA: Stanford University Press.

Cornelius, Wayne A. 1977. "Leaders, Followers, and Official Patrons in Urban Mexico." In Steffen W. Schmidt, James C. Scott, Carl Landé, and Laura Guasti, eds., *Friends, Followers, and Factions: A Reader in Political Clientelism*. Berkeley: University of California Press.

Corrales, J., and I. Cisneros. 1999. "Corporatism, Trade Liberalization, and Sectoral Responses: The Case of Venezuela, 1989–1999." *World Development* 27 (12): 2099–122.

Cortez, W. 2001. "What Is Behind Increasing Wage Inequality in Mexico?" *World Development* 29 (11): 1905–22.

Cotler, Julio. 1978. *Clases, Estado y Nación en el Perú*. Lima: IEP.

Coudouel, A., J. Hentschel, and Q. Wodon. 2002. "Poverty Measurement and Analysis." In J. Klugman, ed., *A Sourcebook for Poverty Reduction Strategies. Volume 1: Core Techniques and Crosscutting Issues*. Washington, D.C.: World Bank.

Cowell, Frank. 1995. *Measuring Inequality*. Hemel Hempstead: Harvester Wheatsheaf.

_____. 2000. "Measurement of Inequality." In François Bourguignon and Anthony B. Atkinson, eds., *Handbook of Income Distribution*. Amsterdam: North-Holland Publishing Company.

Cox, G., and M. Shugart. 1991. "Proportionality, Disproportionality, and Electoral Systems: Comment." *Electoral Studies* 10 (4): 348–52.

_____. 1996. "In the Absence of Vote Pooling: Nomination and Vote Allocation Errors in Colombia." *Electoral Studies* 14 (4): 441–60.

Cragg, Michael Ian, and Mario Epelbaum. 1996. "Why Has Wage Dispersion Grown in Mexico? Is It the Incidence of Reforms of the Growing Demand for Skills?" *Journal of Development Economics* 51 (1): 99–116.

Criscuolo, Alberto. 2002 "Crafting Capitalism: Artisan Associations and Small Business Development in the Third Italy." Master's Thesis, Massachusetts Institute of Technology, Department of Urban Studies and Planning. Cambridge, MA.

Cubberley, Ellwood P. 1920. *The History of Education: Educational Practice and Progress Considered as a Phase of the Development and Spread of Western Civilization.* Boston: Houghton Mifflin.

Cunningham, Wendy. 2000. "Breadwinner versus Caregiver." In Elizabeth Katz and Maria Correia, eds., *The Economics of Gender in Mexico: Market, Family, State.* Washington, D.C.: World Bank.

_____. 2001. "Sectoral Allocation by Gender of Latin American Workers over the Liberalization Period of the 1990s." World Bank Policy Research Working Paper 2742. Washington, D.C.

Cunningham, Wendy, and William Maloney. 2000. "Measuring Vulnerability: Who Suffered in the 1995 Mexican Crisis?" World Bank, Washington, D.C. Processed.

_____. 2003. "Heterogeneity among Mexico's Microenterprises: An Application of Factor and Cluster Analysis." *Economic Development and Cultural Change* 50 (1): 131–56.

Cunningham, Wendy, and Joyce P. Jacobsen. 2003. "Income Inequality Within and Across Racial and Ethnic Groups in Latin America." World Bank, Washington, D.C. Processed.

Cunningham, Wendy, and Mauricio Santamaría. 2003. "Labor Markets as a Source of Income Inequality." World Bank, Washington, D.C. Processed.

Damiani, Octavio. 2003. "Effects on Employment, Wages, and Labor Standards of Nontraditional Export Crops in Northeast Brazil." *Latin American Research Review* 38 (1): 83–112.

David, M., M. Dirven, and F. Vogelgesang. 2000. "The Impact of the New Economic Model on Latin America's Agriculture." *World Development* 28 (9): 1673–88.

Davidson, R., and J. Y. Duclos. 2000. "Statistical Inference for Stochastic Dominance and for the Measurement of Poverty and Inequality." *Econometrica* 68 (6): 1435–64.

Davies, J. B., and Anthony F. Shorrocks. 2000. "The Distribution of Wealth." In A. B. Atkinson and F. Bourguignon, eds., *Handbook of Income Distribution.* Amsterdam: North-Holland Publishing Company.

Deaton, Angus. 1997. *The Analysis of Household Surveys: Microeconomic Analysis for Development Policy.* Washington, D.C.: World Bank.

Deaton, Angus, and S. Zaidi. 2002. "Guidelines for Constructing Consumption Aggregates for Welfare Analysis." World Bank Living Standards Measurement Study Working Paper 135. Washington, D.C.

Deere, C., and M. Leon. 2001a. *Empowering Women: Land and Property Rights in Latin America.* Pittsburgh, PA: University of Pittsburgh Press.

_____. 2001b. "Institutional Reform of Agriculture under Neoliberalism: The Impact of the Women's and Indigenous Movements." *Latin American Research Review* 36 (2): 31–64.

De Ferranti, David, Guillermo Perry, Indermit Gill, and Luis Servén. 2000. *Securing our Future in a Global Economy.* Washington, D.C.: World Bank.

De Ferranti, David, Guillermo E. Perry, Daniel Lederman, and William E. Maloney. 2002. *From Natural Resources to the Knowledge Economy: Trade and Job Quality.* Washington D.C.: World Bank.

De Ferranti, David, Guillermo Perry, Indermit Gill, José Luis Guasch, William F. Maloney, Carolina Sánchez-Páramo, and Norbert Schady. 2003. *Closing the Gap in Education and Technology.* Washington, D.C: World Bank.

Deininger, Klaus, and Pedro Olinto. 2000. "Asset Distribution, Inequality, and Growth." World Bank Policy Research Paper 2375. Washington, D.C.

Deininger, Klaus, and Lyn Squire. 1996. "A New Dataset: Measuring Income Inequality." *World Bank Economic Review* 10 (3): 565–91.

_____. 1998. "New Ways of Looking at Old Issues: Inequality and Growth." *Journal of Development Economics* 57 (2): 257–85.

De Janvry, Alain, and Elisabeth Sadoulet. 1989. "A Study in Resistance to Institutional Change: The Lost Game of Latin American Land Reform." *World Development* 17 (9): 1397–407.

_____. 2000. "Growth, Poverty and Inequality in Latin America: a Causal Analysis, 1970–1994." *Review of Income and Wealth* 46 (3): 267–87.

_____. 2002a. "Comments on Political and Equity Aspects of Land Rights." Paper presented at the Regional Workshop on Land Issues in Latin America and the Caribbean, Pachuca, Mexico (May 19–22).

_____. 2002b. "Land Reforms in Latin America: Ten Lessons toward a Contemporary Agenda." Paper presented at the Regional Workshop on Land Issues in Latin America and the Caribbean, Pachuca, Mexico (May 19–22).

———. 2003. "Targeting and Calibrating Educational Grants: Focus on Poverty or on Non-Enrollment Risk?" University of California, Berkeley. Processed.

De la Torre, Augusto, Eduardo Levy Yeyati, and Sergio Schmukler. 2003. "Living and Dying with Hard Pegs: The Rise and Fall of Argentina's Currency Board." *Economía* 3 (2): 43–102.

De Luca, M., M. Jones, and M. Tula. 2002. "Back Rooms or Ballot Boxes? Candidate Nomination in Argentina." *Comparative Political Studies* 35 (4): 413–36.

De Luna-Martinez, José. 2000. "Management and Resolution of Banking Crises: Lessons from the Republic of Korea and Mexico." World Bank Discussion Paper 413. Washington, D.C.: World Bank.

Demery, Lionel. 2003. "Analyzing the Incidence of Public Spending." In Bourguignon, François and L. Pereira da Silva, eds. *The Impact of Economic Policies on Poverty and Income Distribution: Evaluation Techniques and Tools.* Washington, D.C.: World Bank.

Deruyttere, Anne. 2001. *Pueblos indígenas, globalización y desarrollo con identidad: algunas reflexiones de estrategia.* Washington, D.C.: Inter-American Development Bank.

De Soto, Hernando. 1989. *The Other Path: The Invisible Revolution in the Third World.* New York: Harper and Row.
———. 2000. *The Mystery of Capital.* New York: Basic Books.

De Sousa, Santos B. 1998. "Participatory Budgeting in Porto Alegre: Toward a Redistributive Democracy." *Politics and Society* 26 (4).

Diaz-Alejandro, Carlos F. 1970. *Essays on the Economic History of the Argentine Republic.* New Haven, CT: Yale University Press.

Diaz-Cayeros, A. 1996. "Federal Resource Allocations Under a Dominant Party: Fiscal Transfers in Mexico." Paper prepared for the 92nd American Political Science Association Meeting, San Francisco.

Diaz-Cayeros, A., B. Magaloni, and B. Weingast. 2002. "Federalism and Democratization in Mexico." Paper prepared for the 2002 Annual Meeting of the American Political Science Association, Washington, D.C.

Di Gropello, Emanuela. 2003. "Background Paper on Decentralization in Education for the Latin America and Caribbean companion to the 2004 *World Development Report.*" World Bank, Washington, D.C. Processed.

DiNardo, John, Nicole Fortin, and Thomas Lemieux. 1996. "Labor Market Institutions and the Distribution of Wages 1973–1992: A Semiparametric Approach." *Econometrica* 64 (5): 1001–44.

Di Tella, R., S. Galiani, and E. Schargrodsky. 2002. "Crime Victimization and Income Distribution." Inter-American Development Bank, Washington, D.C.

Diwan, Ishac. 2001. "Debt as Sweat: Labor, Financial Crises, and the Globalization of Capital." World Bank, Washington, D.C. Processed.
———. 2002. "The Labor Share During Financial Crises: New Results." World Bank, Washington, D.C. Processed.

Dollar, David, and Aart Kraay. 2002a. "Growth is Good for the Poor." *Journal of Economic Growth* 7: 195–225.
———. 2002b. "Institutions, Trade and Growth." Carnegie-Rochester Conference Series on Public Policy. University of Rochester Simon School of Business, Rochester, NY and Carnegie-Mellon University, Pittsburgh, PA.

Doner, R. 1992. "Limits of State Strength: Toward an Institutional View of Economic Development." *World Politics* 44 (3): 398–431.

Drèze, Jean, and Amartya Sen. 1996. *Indian Development: Selected Regional Perspectives.* New Delhi: Oxford University Press.

Dupor, Bill, and Wen-Fang Liu. 2003. "Jealousy and Equilibrium Overconsumption." *American Economic Review* 93 (1): 423–28.

Duryea, S., and C. Pagés. 2002. "Human Capital Policies: What They Can and Cannot Do for Productivity and Poverty Reduction in Latin America." Inter-American Development Bank Working Paper 468. Washington, D.C.

Dziobec, Claudia, and Ceyla Pazarbasioglu. 1997. "Lessons from Systemic Bank Restructuring: A Survey of 24 Countries." International Monetary Fund Working Paper 97/161. Washington, D.C.

Easterly, William, and Stanley Fischer. 2001. "Inflation and the Poor." *Journal of Money, Credit, and Banking* 33 (2): 160–78.

Easterly, William, and Ross Levine. 2002. "Tropics, Germs and Crops: How Institutions Influence Economic Development." Center for Global Development and Institute for International Economics, Washington, D.C. Processed.

Easterly, William, and L. Servén. 2003. *The Limits of Stabilization: Infrastructure, Public Deficits and Growth in Latin America.* Stanford, CA and Washington D.C.: Stanford University Press and World Bank.

Ebrill, Liam P., Michael Keen, Jean-Paul Bodin, and Victoria Summers. 2001. *The Modern VAT.* Washington, D.C: International Monetary Fund.

ECLAC (Economic Commission for Latin America and the Caribbean). 1996. *Anuario Estadístico para América Latina y el Caribe.* Santiago: ECLAC.

———. 2000. *Panorama Social, 1999–2000.* Santiago: ECLAC.

———. 2001. *Panorama Social 2000–2001.* Santiago: ECLAC.

Edwards, John, and Donald Winkler. 2002. "Education, Ethnicity, and Poverty: A Study with Applications to the Maya of Guatemala." Paper presented at the meeting on Etnicidad, Raza, Género en América Latina, Grupo de Análisis para el Desarrollo, Lima, Peru.

Elbers, Chris, Jean O. Lanjouw, Peter Lanjouw, and Phillippe G. Leite. 2003. "Poverty and Inequality in Brazil: New Evidence from combined PPV-PNAD data." World Bank, Washington, D.C. Processed.

Elwan, Ann. 1999. "Poverty and Disability: A Survey of the Literature," World Bank Social Protection Discussion paper 9932. Washington, D.C.

Engel, Eduard, Alexander Galetovic, and Claudio Raddatz. 1998. "Taxes and Income Distribution in Chile: Some Unpleasant Redistributive Arithmetic." National Bureau of Economic Research Working Paper 6828. Cambridge, MA.

Engerman, Stanley L., and Kenneth L. Sokoloff. 1997. "Factor Endowments, Institutions, and Differential Paths of Growth among New World Economies." In Stephen Haber, ed., *How Latin America Fell Behind.* Stanford, CA: Stanford University Press.

———. 2000. "Institutions, Factor Endowments, and Paths of Development in the New World." *Journal of Economic Perspectives* 3: 217–32.

———. 2002. "Factor Endowments, Inequality, and Paths of Development among New World Economies." *Economía* 3: 41–109.

Engerman, Stanley L., and Robert E. Gallman, eds. *The Cambridge Economic History of the United States. Volume I: The Colonial Era.* New York: Cambridge University Press.

Engerman, Stanley L., Stephen Haber, and Kenneth L. Sokoloff. 2000. "Inequality, Institutions, and Differential Paths of Growth among New World Economies." In Claude Menard, ed., *Institutions, Contracts, and Organization.* Cheltenham: Edward Elgar.

Ennis, Huberto, and Santiago Pinto. 2002. "Privatization and Income Distribution in Argentina." In John Nellis and Nancy Birdsall, eds., *A Glass Half Full: Assessing the Distributional Impact of Privatization.* Washington, D.C.: Center for Global Development.

Escobal, Javier, and Carmen Ponce. 2002. "The Benefits of Rural Roads: Enhancing Income Opportunities for the Poor." Paper presented at the fifth meeting of the LACEA/IDB/World Bank network on inequality and poverty, Madrid. Also available from the Grupo de Análisis para el Desarrollo (GRADE), Lima, Peru.

Eskeland, Gunnar S. and Filmer, Deon. 2000. "Does Decentralization Improve Learning? Autonomy and Parental Participation in Argentine Schools." World Bank, Washington, D.C. Processed.

———. 2002. "Autonomy, Participation and Learning in Argentine Schools: Findings and their Implications for Decentralization." World Bank, Washington, D.C. Processed.

Estache, Antonio. 2002. "Argentina's 1990s Utilities Privatization: A Cure or a Disease?" World Bank, Washington, D.C. Processed.

———. 2003. "On Latin America's Privatization and its Distributional Effects." World Bank, Washington, D.C. Processed.

Estache, Antonio, Vivien Foster, and Quentin T. Wodon. 2002. *Accounting for Poverty in Infrastructure Reform: Learning from Latin America's Experience.* World Bank Development Studies Series. Washington, D.C.: World Bank.

Esteban, J., and D. Ray. 1994. "On the Measurement of Polarization." *Econometrica* 62 (4): 819–51.

Esteban, J., C. Gradín, and D. Ray. 1999. "Extension of a Measure of Polarization, with an Application to the Income Distribution of Five OECD Countries." Working Paper Series 24. La Coruña, Spain: Instituto de Estudios Economicos de Galicia Pedro Barrie de la Maza.

Evans, P. 1979. *Dependent Development: The Alliance of Multinational, State, and Local Capital in Brazil.* Princeton, NJ: Princeton University Press.

———. 1995. *Embedded Autonomy: States and Industrial Transformation.* Princeton, NJ: Princeton University Press.

Evans, P., B. Rueschemeyer, and T. Skocpol, eds. 1985. *Bringing the State Back in.* Cambridge: Cambridge University Press.

Faguet, Jean-Paul. 2000. "Does Decentralization Increase Responsiveness to Local Needs? Evidence from Bolivia." World Bank Policy Research Working Paper 2516. Washington, D.C.

Fajnzylber, Pablo, Daniel Lederman, and Norman Loayza. 1998. *Determinants of Crime Rates in Latin America and the World: An Empirical Assessment.* World Bank Latin America and Caribbean Studies: Viewpoints. Washington, D.C.: World Bank.

———. 2000. "Crime and Victimization: An Economic Perspective." *Economía* 1 (1): 219–78.

Fay, Marianne, Danny Leipziger, Quentin Wodon, and Tito Yepes. 2003. "Achieving the Millennium Development Goals: The Role of Infrastructure." World Bank Policy Research Working Paper 3163. Washington, D.C.

Fay, Marianne, Tito Yepes, and Vivien Foster. 2002. "Asset Inequality in Developing Countries: The Case of Housing." World Bank, Washington, D.C. Processed.

Felix, D. 1982. "Income Distribution Trends in Mexico and the Kuznets Curves." In Hewlett and Weinert, eds., *Brazil and Mexico: Patterns in Recent Development.* Philadelphia: Institute for the Study of Human Issues.

Fernández, R., N. Gunerm, and J. Knowles. 2001. "Love and Money: A Theoretical and Empirical Analysis of Household Sorting and Inequality." New York University, New York. Processed.

Ferreira, Francisco H. G. 2001. "Education for the Masses? The Interaction Between Wealth, Educational, and Political Inequalities." *Economics of Transition* 9 (2): 533–52.

Ferreira, Francisco H. G., and Julie Litchfield. 1996. "Growing Apart: Inequality and Poverty Trends in Brazil in the 1980s." LSE STICERD, Distributional Analysis Research Programme Discussion Paper 23. London.

———. 1999. "Calm After the Storms: Income Distribution and Welfare in Chile, 1987–94." *The World Bank Economic Review* 13 (3): 509–38.

Ferreira, Francisco H. G., and Philippe George Leite. 2004. "Educational Expansion and Income Distribution. A Micro-Simulation for Ceará." In R. van der Hoven, and A. Shorrocks, eds. *Growth, Inequality and Poverty.* New York: Oxford University Press.

Ferreira, Francisco H. G., Giovanna Prennushi, and Martin Ravallion. 1999. "Protecting the Poor from Macroeconomic Shocks: An Agenda for Action in a Crisis and Beyond." World Bank Working Paper 2160. Washington, D.C.

Fields, G. 1989. "A compendium of data on inequality and poverty for the Developing World." Cornell University, Ithaca, NY.

Filgueira, F., and Papadópulos, J. 1997. "Putting Conservatism to Good Use? Long Crisis and Vetoed Alternatives in Uruguay." In D. Chalmers, Carlos M. Vilas, Katherine Hite, Scott B. Martin, Kerianne Piester, and Monique Segarra, eds., *The New Politics of Inequality in Latin America: Rethinking Participation and Representation.* New York: Oxford University Press.

Filmer, Deon, Jeffrey S. Hammer, and Lant Pritchett. 2000. "Health Policy in Poor Countries: Weak Links in the Chain." *World Bank Research Observer* 15 (2): 199–224.

———. 2002. "Weak Links in the Chain II: A Prescription for Health Policy in Poor Countries." *World Bank Research Observer* 17 (1): 47–66.

Finan, Frederico, Elisabeth Sadoulet, and Alain de Janvry. 2002. "Measuring the Poverty Reduction Potential of Land in Rural Mexico." University of California, Berkeley. Processed.

Fiszbein, A., P. Giovagnoli, and I. Aduriz. 2002. "Argentina's Crisis and Its Impact on Household Welfare." World Bank Working Paper. Washington, D.C.

Flórez, Carmen Elisa, Carlos Medina, and Fernando Urrea. 2001. "Understanding the Cost of Social Exclusion Due to Race or Ethnic Background in Latin American and Caribbean Countries." Inter-American Development Bank, Washington, D.C.

Food and Agriculture Organization and World Bank. 2003. *La Nueva Ruralidad en Europa y su Interés para América Latina.* Rome: FAO.

Forbes, Kristin J. 2000. "A Reassessment of the Relationship Between Inequality and Growth." *American Economic Review* 90 (4): 869–87.

Foster, James, and Amartya K. Sen. 1997. "On Economic Inequality after a Quarter of a Century." Annex to Amartya K. Sen, *On Economic Inequality* (expanded edition). Oxford, U.K.: Clarendon Press.

Foster, Vivien. 2002. "Ten Years of Water Service Reform in Latin America: Towards an Anglo-French Model." In Paul Seidenstat, David Haarmeyer, and Simon Hakim, eds., *Reinventing Water and Wastewater Systems: Global Lessons for Improving Management.* New York: John Wiley and Sons, Inc.

———. 2003. "Background Paper on Utilities for the Latin America and Caribbean Companion to the *2004 World Development Report*." World Bank, Washington, D.C. Processed.

Fox, J. 1993. *The Politics of Food in Mexico.* Ithaca and London: Cornell University Press.

———. 1994. "The Difficult Transition from Clientelism to Citizenship: Lessons from Mexico." *World Politics* 46: 151–84.

Foxley, Alejandro T., and Claudio Sapelli. 1999. "Chile's Political Economy in the 1990s: Some Governance Issues." In Guillermo Perry and Danny M. Leipziger, eds., *Chile: Recent Policy Lessons and Emerging Challenges.* World

Bank Institute Development Studies. Washington, D.C.: World Bank.

Frankel, Jeffrey, and Sergio Schmukler. 2000. "Country Funds and Asymmetric Information." *International Journal of Finance and Economics* 5 (3): 177–95.

Freije, Samuel, and Luis Rivas. 2002. "Privatization, Inequality, and Welfare: Evidence from Nicaragua. Instituto de Estudios Superiores Administración." Caracas: IESA.

Freire, Paulo. 1970. *Pedagogy of the Oppressed.* New York: The Continuum Publishing Company.

Friedman, Jed, and James Levinsohn. 2002. "The Distributional Impacts of Indonesia's Crisis on Household Welfare: A 'Rapid Response' Methodology." *World Bank Economic Review* 16 (3): 397–423.

Friedman, Milton. 1956. *Studies in the Quantity Theory of Money.* Chicago: University of Chicago Press.

Fry, P. 1999. "Color and the Rule of Law in Brazil." In J. Méndez, G. O'Donnell, and P. Pinheiro, eds., *The Rule of Law and the Underprivileged in Latin America.* Notre Dame, IN: University of Notre Dame Press.

Gacitúa-Marió, Estanislao, and Carlos Sojo, eds., with Shelton H. Davis. 2001. *Social Exclusion and Poverty Reduction in Latin America and the Caribbean.* Washington, D.C.: World Bank.

Gacitúa-Marió, Estanislao, and Quentin Wodon. Forthcoming. "Social Exclusion in Latin America and the Caribbean." World Bank, Washington, D.C.

Galal, Ahmed, and Mary Shirley, eds. 1994. *Does Privatization Deliver? Highlights from a World Bank Conference.* EDI Development Studies. Washington, D.C.: World Bank.

Galasso, Emanuela, and Martin Ravallion. 2003. "Decentralized Targeting of an Anti-Poverty Program." World Bank, Washington, D.C. Processed.

Galenson, David W. 1996. "The Settlement and Growth of the Colonies: Population, Labor and Economic Development." In Stanley L. Engerman and Robert E. Gallman, eds., *The Cambridge Economic History of the United States. Volume I: The Colonial Era.* New York: Cambridge University Press.

Galiani, Sebastián, and Pablo Sanguinetti. 2000. "Wage Inequality and Trade Liberalization: Evidence from Argentina." Buenos Aires: Universidad Torcuato Di Tella.

Galiani, Sebastián, Paul Gertler, and Ernesto Schargrodsky. 2002. "Water for Life: The Impact of the Privatization of Water Services on Child Mortality." Buenos Aires: Universidad Torcuato di Tella.

Galor, Oded, and Joseph Zeira. 1993. "Income Distribution and Macroeconomics." *Review of Economic Studies* 60: 35–52.

Ganuza E., L. Taylor, and S. Morley. 1998. *Politica macroeconomica y pobreza en America Latina y el Caribe.* PNUD-CEAPL-IDB. Madrid: Ediciones Mundi-Prensa.

García Aracil, Adela, and Donald Winkler. 2002. "Ethnicity, Gender, and Education in Ecuador." Paper presented at the meeting on Etnicidad, Raza, Género en América Latina, Grupo de Análisis para el Desarrollo, Lima, Peru.

Garretón, Antonio. 1989. *The Chilean Political System.* Boston, MA: Unwin Hyman.

Gasparini, Leonardo. 2002. "On the Measurement of Unfairness: An Application to High School Attendance in Argentina." *Social Choice and Welfare* 19 (4): 795–810.

Gasparini, L., and W. Sosa Escudero. 2001. "Assessing aggregate welfare: growth and inequality in Argentina." *Cuadernos de Economía* 38 (113).

Gasparini, Leonardo, M. Marchionni, and W. Sosa Escudero. 2001. *La distribución del ingreso en la Argentina.* Buenos Aires: Editorial Triunfar.

Gates, Paul W. 1968. *History of Public Land Law Development.* Washington, D.C.: Zenger Publishing Company, Inc.

Gauri, Varun, and Ayesha Vawda. 2003. "Vouchers for Basic Education in Developing Countries: A Principal-agent Perspective." World Bank Policy Research Working Paper 3005. Washington, D.C.

Gavin, M., and R. Perotti. 1997. *Fiscal Policy in Latin America.* Cambridge, MA: MIT Press for National Bureau of Economic Research.

Gaviria, A., and C. Pages. 1999. *Patterns of Crime Victimization in Latin America.* Washington, D.C.: Inter-American Development Bank.

Gelbach, Jonathan, and Lant H. Pritchett. 1997. "More for the Poor is Less for the Poor: The Politics of Targeting." World Bank Policy Research Working Paper 1799. Washington, D.C.

GenderStats database. http://devdata.worldbank.org/genderstats/. World Bank, Washington, D.C.

Gemmell, N., and O. Morrissey. 2002. "The Impact of Taxation on Inequality and Poverty: A Review of Empirical Methods and Evidence." Nottingham, U.K.: University of Nottingham.

Gertler, P. J. 2000. *Final report: The Impact of PROGRESA on Health.* Washington, D.C.: International Food Policy Research Institute.

Gillespie, S., and L. Haddad. 2001. "Attacking the Double Burden of Malnutrition in Asia and the Pacific." Asian Development Bank Nutrition and Development Series, Paper 4. Manila. Also available from the International Food Policy Research Institute, Washington, D.C.

Glaeser, Edward, José Scheinkman, and Andres Schleifer. 2002. "The Injustice of Inequality." *Journal of Monetary Economics* 50 (1): 199–224.

Glewwe, Paul W., Margaret Grosh, Hanan Jacoby, and Marlaine Lockheed. 1995. "An Eclectic Approach to Estimating the Determinants of Achievements in Jamaican Primary Education." *World Bank Economic Review* 9 (2): 231–58.

Glewwe, P., and G. Hall. 1998. "Are Some Groups More Vulnerable to Macroeconomic Shocks Than Others? Hypothesis Tests Based on Panel Data from Peru." *Journal of Development Economics* 56: 181–206.

Goldin, C. 1987. "Work and Ideology in the Maya Highlands of Guatemala: Economic Beliefs in the Context of Occupational Change." *Economic Development and Cultural Change* 41 (1): 103–23.

Goldin, Claudia. 1999. "Egalitarianism and the Returns to Education during the Great Transformation of American Education." *Journal of Political Economy* 107 (6): S65–94.

———. 2001. "The Human-Capital Century and American Leadership: Virtues of the Past." *Journal of Economic History* 61 (2): 263–92.

Goldin, Claudia, and Lawrence F. Katz. 1999. "The Returns to Skill across the Twentieth Century United States." National Bureau of Economic Research Working Paper 7126. Cambridge, MA.

Gollin, D. 2002. "Getting Income Shares Right." *Journal of Political Economy* 110 (2).

Gómez-Lobo, Andrés and Dante Contreras. 2000. "Subsidy Policies for the Utility Industries: A Comparison of the Chilean and Colombian Water Subsidy Schemes." University of Chile, Department of Economics, Santiago. Processed.

Gonzaga, Gustavo M., Naercio Menezes Filho, and Cristina Terra. 2002. "Trade Liberalization and Evolution of Skills Earnings Differentials in Brazil." Discussion Paper 463. Pontifícia Universidade Católica, Department of Economics. Rio de Janeiro.

Gonzáles-Vega, C., and V. Cespedes. 1993. "Costa Rica." In Rottemberg, ed., *The Political Economy of Poverty, Equity and Growth: Costa Rica and Uruguay.* Washington, D.C.: World Bank.

González, E. 2001. *Paraguay: determinantes regionales en la inequidad de ingresos. ¿Son desiguales las regiones del país?* Asunción: Centro de Análisis y Difusión de Economía Paraguaya.

González, Luis E. 1991. *Political Structures and Democracy in Uruguay.* Notre Dame, IN: Notre Dame University Press.

Gottschalk, Peter and Enrico Spolaore. 2002. "On the Evaluation of Economic Mobility." *Review of Economic Studies* 69: 191–208.

Gottschalk, P., and T. Smeeding. 2000. "Empirical Evidence on Income Inequality in Industrial Countries." In Anthony B. Atkinson and François Bourguignon, eds., *Handbook of Income Distribution.* Amsterdam: North-Holland Publishing Company.

Governance Indicators Database. http://www.worldbank.org/wbi/governance/govdata2002/. World Bank Institute, World Bank, Washington, D.C.

Government Finance Statistics database. Statistics Department, International Monetary Fund, Washington, D.C.

Graham, Carol, and Stefano Pettinato. 2002. *Happiness and Hardship: Opportunity and Insecurity in New Market Economies.* Washington, D.C.: Brookings Institution Press.

Graham, Richard, Thomas E. Skidmore, Aline Helg, and Alan Knight. 1990. *The Ideas of Race in Latin America 1870–1940.* Austin: University of Texas Press.

Graham, Richard. 1990. *Patronage and Politics in Nineteenth-Century Brazil.* Stanford, CA: Stanford University Press.

Grant, E. 2001. "Social Capital and Community Strategies: Neighborhood Development in Guatemala City." *Development and Change* 32 (5): 975–97.

Gray-Molina, George. 2002. "The Offspring of 1952: Poverty, Exclusion and the Promise of Popular Participation." Conference paper prepared for "The Bolivian Revolution at 50: Comparative Views on Social, Economic, and Political Change." Harvard University, Cambridge, MA.

Grindle, Merilee S. 1977. *Bureaucrats, Politicians, and Peasants in Mexico: A Case Study in Public Policy.* Berkeley: University of California Press.

———. 2002. "Despite the Odds: Contentious Politics and Education Reform." Harvard University, Cambridge, MA. Processed.

Grosh, Margaret. 1994. *Administering Targeted Social Programs in Latin America: From Platitudes to Practice.* Washington, D.C.: World Bank.

Haber, Stephen H. 2002a. *Political Institutions and Banking Systems: Lessons from the Economic Histories of Mexico and the*

United States, 1790–1914. Stanford, CA: Stanford University Department of Political Science.

———, ed. 2002b. *Crony Capitalism and Economic Growth in Latin America: Theory and Evidence.* Stanford, CA: University of California, Hoover Institution.

Haber, Stephen, Noel Maurer, and Armando Razo. 2003. *The Politics of Property Rights: Political Instability, Credible Commitments, and Economic Growth in Mexico: 1876–1929.* New York: Cambridge University Press.

Haddad, L., H. Alderman, S. Appleton, L. Song, and Y. Yohannes. 2002. "Reducing Child Undernutrition: How Far Does Income Growth Take Us?" International Food Policy Research Institute, Food Consumption Nutrition Division Discussion Paper. Washington, D.C.

Hager, B. 2000. *The Rule of Law: A Lexicon for Policy Makers.* Missoula, MT: Mansfield Center for Pacific Affairs.

Haggard, Stephan, and Robert Kaufman. 1990. "The Political Economy of Inflation and Stabilization in Middle-Income Countries." World Bank Policy Research Working Paper 444. Washington, D.C.

Haggard, Stephan, Chung H. Lee, and Sylvia Maxfield. 1993. *The Politics of Finance in Developing Countries.* Ithaca, NY: Cornell University Press.

Hagopian, F. 1996. *Traditional Politics and Regime Change in Brazil.* Cambridge: Cambridge University Press.

———. 2000. "Political Development, Revisited." *Comparative Political Studies* 33 (6/7): 800–911.

Halac, Marina, and Sergio L. Schmukler. 2003. "Distributional Effects of Crises: The Role of Financial Transfers." Working Paper 3173. World Bank, Washington, D.C.

Hamann, A. Javier, and Alessandro Prati. 2002. "Why Do Many Disinflations Fail? The Importance of Luck, Timing, and Political Institutions." International Monetary Fund Working Paper 02/228. Washington, D.C.

Handa, S., M.-C. Huerta, R. Perez, and B. Straffon. 2000. "Final Report: Poverty, Inequality, and 'Spill-over' in Mexico's Education, Health, and Nutrition Program." Report submitted to PROGRESA. Washington, D.C.: International Food Policy Research Institute.

Harberger, Arnold C. 2003. "Reflections on Distributional Considerations and the Public Finances." Prepared for Practical Issues of Tax Policy in Developing Countries (course), April 28–May 1, 2003. World Bank, Washington, D.C.

Harrison, A. 2002. "Has Globalization Eroded Labor's Share? Some Cross-Country Evidence." University of California, Berkeley, and National Bureau of Economic Research, Cambridge, MA.

Hartlyn, Jonathan. 1998. *The Struggle for Democratic Politics in the Dominican Republic.* Chapel Hill: University of North Carolina Press.

Hausman, R. and Rigobon, R., eds. 1993. *Government Spending and Income Distribution in Latin America.* Washington, D.C.: Inter-American Development Bank.

Heckman, James, and Carmen Pagés-Serra. 2000. "The Cost of Job Security Regulation: Evidence from Latin American Labor Markets." *Economía* 1 (1): 109–54.

Heller, Patrick. 2001. "Moving the State: the Politics of Democratic Decentralization in Kerala, South Africa, and Porto Alegre." *Politics & Society* 29 (1): 131–63.

Hellman, Joel, and Daniel Kaufmann. 2003. "The Inequality of Influence." World Bank, Washington, D.C. Processed.

Hentschel, J., J. O. Lanjouw, Peter Lanjouw, and J. Poggi. 2000. "Combining Census and Survey Data to Trace the Spatial Dimension of Poverty: A Case Study of Ecuador." *World Bank Economic Review* 14: 147–65.

Henriques, Ricardo. 2001. "Desigualdade Racial no Brasil: Evolução das Condições de Vida na Década de 90." Discussion paper 807. Instituto de Pesquisa Econômica Aplicada, Rio de Janeiro, Brasil.

Hicks, N., and Q. Wodon. 2001. "Social Protection for the Poor in Latin America." *ECLAC Review* 73: 93–113.

Hiskey, J. 1999. "Does Democracy Matter? Electoral Competition and Local Development in Mexico." PhD diss. University of Pittsburgh, Pittsburgh, PA.

Hoddinott, J., E. Skoufias, and R. Washburn. 2000. "The Impact of PROGRESA on Consumption: A Final Report." Report submitted to PROGRESA. International Food Policy Research Institute, Washington, D.C.

Hoggarth, Glenn, Ricardo Reis, and Victoria Saporta. 2002. "Costs of Banking System Instability: Some Empirical Evidence." *Journal of Banking and Finance* 26 (5): 825–55.

Holston, J., and T. Caldeira. 1998. "Democracy, Law, and Violence: Disjunctions of Brazilian Citizenship." In Felipe Aguero and J. Stark, eds., *Fault Lines of Democracy in Post-Transition Latin America.* Miami: North-South Center Press.

Holzer, Harry, and David Neumark. 2000. "What Does Affirmative Action Do?" *Industrial and Labor Relations Review* 53 (2), 240–70.

Honohan, Patrick, and Daniela Klingebiel. 2000. "Controlling the Fiscal Costs of Banking Crises." World Bank Policy Research Working Paper 2441. Washington, D.C.

Hsieh, Chang-Tai, and Miguel Urquiola. 2003. "When Schools Compete, How Do They Compete? An Assessment of Chile's Nationwide School Voucher Program." National Bureau of Economic Research Working Paper 10008. Cambridge, MA.

Hutchcroft, P. 1997. The Politics of Privilege: Assessing the Impact of Rents, Corruption, and Clientelism on Third World Development. *Political Studies* 45 (3): 639–58.

Inter-American Development Bank. 1998. *Facing Up to Inequality in Latin America.* Baltimore, MD: Johns Hopkins University Press.

———. 2002. "The Privatization Paradox." *Latin American Economic Policies Newsletter* 18.

ICRG (*International Country Risk Guide*). Various years. East Syracuse, NY: PRS Group, Inc.

IFPRI (International Food Policy Research Institute). 2001. "Evaluation System for the Pilot Phase of Nicaraguan 'Red de Protección,' Social Impact Evaluation." Report to the Red de Protección Social, International Food Policy Research Institute. Washington, D.C.

———. 2002. "Evaluation System for the Pilot Phase of the Nicaraguan Red de Protección Social: Impact Evaluation." International Food Policy Research Institute. Washington, D.C.

———. 2003. "An Evaluation of Geographic Targeting in Bolsa Alimentação in Brazil." International Food Policy Research Institute. Washington, D.C.

ILO (International Labour Organization). 2000. *World Labour Report 2000.* Geneva.

Itzigsohn, José. 2000. *Developing Poverty: The State, Labor Market Deregulation and the Informal Economy in Costa Rica and the Dominican Republic.* University Park, PA: Pennsylvania State University Press.

Jacobsen, Joyce. 2002. "What About Us? Men's Issues in Development." World Bank, Washington, D.C. Processed.

Jakee, K., and S. Turner. 2002. "The Welfare State as a Fiscal Commons: Problems of Incentives Versus Problems of Cognitions." *Public Finance Review* 30: 481–508.

Jalan, Jyotsna, and Martin Ravallion. 1999. "Income Gains to the Poor from Workfare: Estimates from Argentina's Trabajar Program." World Bank Working Paper 2149. Washington, D.C.

———. 2003. "Estimating the Benefit Incidence of an Antipoverty Program by Propensity Score Matching." *Journal of Business and Economic Statistics* 21 (1): 19–30.

Jayasuriya, R., and Q. Wodon. 2003. "Improving Health and Education Outcomes in Latin America: Spending More or Spending Better?" In Q. Wodon, ed., "Public Spending, Poverty, and Inequality in Latin America." World Bank, Washington, D.C. Processed.

Jimenez, Emmanuel. 2000. "Equity and the Decentralization of Social Services." In Shahid Javed Burki and Guillermo E. Perry, eds., *Decentralization and Accountability of the Public Sector.* Proceedings of the 1999 Annual World Bank Conference on Development in Latin America and the Caribbean. Washington, D.C.: World Bank.

Jimenez, Emmanuel, and Sawada, Y. 1998. "Do Community School Managed Schools Work? An Evaluation of El Salvador's EDUCO Program." *World Bank Economic Review* 13 (3): 415–41.

Jones, M. 1993. "The Political Consequences of Electoral Laws in Latin America and the Caribbean." *Electoral Studies* 12 (1): 59–75.

———. 1994. "Presidential Election Laws and Multipartism in Latin America." *Political Research Quarterly* 47 (1): 41–57.

———. 1995. *Electoral Laws and the Survival of Presidential Democracies.* Notre Dame, IN: University of Notre Dame Press.

———. 1997. "A Guide to the Electoral Systems of the Americas: An Update." *Electoral Studies* 16 (1): 13–15.

Jones M., P. Sanguinetti, and M. Tommasi. 2000. "Politics, Institutions, and Fiscal Performance in a Federal System: an Analysis of the Argentine Provinces." *Journal of Development Economics* 61 (2): 305–33.

Juhn, Chinhui, Kevin Murphy, and Brooks Pierce. 1993. "Wage Inequality and the Rise in Returns to Skill." *Journal of Political Economy* 101 (3): 410–42.

Kabeer, Naila. 1994. *Reversed Realities: Gender Hierarchies in Development Thought.* London and New York: Verso Press.

Kabeer, Naila, and R. Subrahmanian. 2000. *Institutions, Relations and Outcomes.* London: Zed Books.

Kanbur, Ravi. 2000. "Income Distribution and Development." In Anthony B. Atkinson and François Bourguignon, eds. *Handbook of Income Distribution.* Amsterdam: North-Holland Publishing Company.

Karl, Terry Lynn. 1995. *Paradox of Plenty: Oil Booms and Petro-States.* Berkeley: University of California Press.

Katzenstein, Peter J. 1984. *Corporatism and Change: Austria, Switzerland, and the Politics of Industry.* Ithaca, NY: Cornell University Press.

———. 1985. *Small States in World Markets: Industrial Policy in Europe.* Ithaca, NY: Cornell University Press.

Kaufman, R. 1974. "The Patron-Client Concept and Macro-Politics: Prospects and Problems." *Comparative Studies in Society and History* 16 (3): 284–308.

Kaufmann, Daniel, and Aart Kraay. 2002. "Growth without Governance." *Economía* 3 (1): 169–229.

Kaufmann, Daniel, Aart Kraay, and Massimo Mastruzzi. 2003. *Governance Matters III: Governance Indicators for 1996–2002.* Washington D.C.: World Bank Institute.

Kaufmann, Daniel, Francesca Recanatini, and Sergiy Biletsky. 2002. "Assessing Governance: Diagnostic Tools and Applied Methods for Capacity Building and Action Learning." Discussion draft. World Bank, Washington, D.C.

Keefer, Philip. 2002. "Clientelism, Credibility and Democracy." World Bank Development Research Group, Washington D.C. Processed.

Keefer, Philip, and Stephen Knack 2000. "Polarization, Politics, and Property Rights: Links Between Inequality and Growth." World Bank Policy Research Working Paper 2418. Washington, D.C.

Kelley, Jonathan, and Herbert Klein. 1981. *Revolution and the Rebirth of Inequality: A Theory Applied to the National Revolution in Bolivia.* Berkeley: University of California Press.

Kenworthy, L. 2002. "Corporatism and Unemployment in the 1980s and 1990s." *American Sociological Review* 67 (3): 367–88.

Key Indicators of the Labour Market database. http://www.ilo.org/public/english/employment/strat/kilm/. Employment Sector, International Labour Organization, Geneva.

Kim, Dae-Il, and Robert H. Topel. 1995. "Labor Markets and Economic Growth: Lessons from Korea's Industrialization, 1970–1990." In Richard B. Freeman and Lawrence F. Katz, eds., *Differences and Changes in Wage Structures.* Chicago: University of Chicago Press.

King, Elizabeth M., and Berk Ozler. 1998. "What's Decentralization Got to Do with Learning? The Case of Nicaragua's Autonomy Reform." Series on Impact Evaluation of Education Reforms. World Bank Development Economics Research Group Working Paper 9. Washington, D.C.

Kitschelt, H. 2000. "Linkages between Citizens and Politicians in Democratic Polities." *Comparative Political Studies* 33 (6/7): 845–79.

Klein, Hebert 1992. *Bolivia: The Evolution of a Multi-Ethnic Society.* Oxford: Oxford University Press.

Knack, S., and P. Keefer. 1997. "Does Social Capital Have an Economic Payoff? A Cross-country Investigation." *The Quarterly Journal of Economics* 112 (4): 1251–88.

Knaul, Felicia Marie. 2001. "The Impact of Child Labor and School Dropout on Human Capital: Gender Differences in Mexico." In Maria Correia and Elizabeth Katz, eds., *The Economics of Gender in Mexico.* Washington D.C.: World Bank.

Kohli, Atul. 1986. *The State and Development in the Third World.* Princeton, NJ: Princeton University Press.

Kohli, A., M. Altfeld, S. Lotfian, and R. Mardon. 1984. "Inequality in the Third World: An Assessment of Competing Explanations." *Comparative Political Studies* 17: 259–68.

Korpi, W. 1980. "Social Policy and Distributional Conflict in the Capitalist Democracies: A Preliminary Comparative Framework." *West European Politics*, 3 (3): 296–315.

Krueger, Alan. 2002. "Putting Development Dollars to Use South of the Border." *The New York Times* (May 2).

Krugman, Paul 1979. "A Model of Balance of Payments Crises." *Journal of Money, Credit, and Banking* 11 (3): 311–25.

———. 1999. "Balance Sheets, the Transfer Problem and Financial Crises." In P. Isard, A. Razin, and A.K. Rose, eds., *International Finance and Financial Crises: Essays in Honor of Robert P. Flood.* Dordrecht, The Netherlands: Kluwer Academic Publishers and Washington, D.C.: International Monetary Fund.

Kurer, O. 1993. "Clientelism, Corruption, and the Allocation of Resources." *Public Choice* 77 (2): 259–73.

———. 1996. "The Political Foundations of Economic Development Policies." *Journal of Development Studies* 32 (5): 645–68.

Kurtz, Marcus J. 1999. "Social Origins of Central American Democracy." *Journal of InterAmerican Studies and World Affairs* 41 (1): 87–96.

LABORSTA database. http://laborsta.ilo.org/. International Labour Office, Geneva, Switzerland.

Laeven, Luc, and Giovanni Majnoni. 2002. "Loan Loss Provisioning and Economic Slowdowns: Too Much, Too Late?" World Bank Policy Research Working Paper 2749. Washington, D.C.

Lam, David. 2001. "The Impact of Race on Earnings and Human Capital in Brazil, South Africa and the United States." Paper presented at the meeting of the Network on Inequality and Poverty in LACEA, Montevideo, Uruguay.

Lambert, P. 1993. *The Distribution and Redistribution of Income.* Manchester: Manchester University Press.

Lang, James. 1975. *Conquest and Commerce; Spain and England in the Americas.* New York: Academic Press.

Lanjouw, Peter, and Martin Ravallion. 1995. "Poverty and household size." *Economic Journal* 105: 1415–34.

———. 1999. "Benefit Incidence, Public Spending Reforms, and the Timing of Program Capture." *World Bank Economic Review* 13: 257–73.

La Porta, Rafael, and Florencio López-de-Silanes. 1999. "The Benefits of Privatization: Evidence from Mexico." *Quarterly Journal of Economics* 114 (4): 1193–242.

La Porta, Rafael, Florencio López-de-Silanes, Andres Schleifer, and Robert Vishny. 1997. "Trust in large organizations." *American Economic Review* 87 (2): 333–38.

Larrea, C. 1998. "Structural Adjustment, Income Distribution, and Employment in Ecuador." In A. Berry, ed., *Poverty, Economic Reform, and Income Distribution in Latin America.* Boulder, CO: Lynne Rienner Publishers.

Latinobarómetro. Various years. *Informe-Resumen: La Democracia y la Economía.* Santiago.

———. 2003. *Informe-Resumen: La Democracia y la Economía.* Santiago.

Laurell, A. 2001. "Health Reform in Mexico: The Promotion of Inequality." *International Journal of Health Services* 31 (2): 291–321.

Leal, Victor Nunes. 1948. "Coronelismo, Enxada e Voto." Rio de Janeiro: *Revista Forense.*

Leamer, Edward E., Hugo Maul, Sergio Rodríguez, and Peter K. Schott. 1999. "Does Natural Resource Abundance Increase Latin American Income Inequality?" *Journal of Development Economics* 59: 3–42.

Lederman Daniel, Norman Loayza, and Ana Maria Menéndez. 2002. "Violent Crime: Does Social Capital Matter?" *Economic Development and Cultural Change* 50 (3): 509–39.

Le Grand, J. 1991. *Equity and Choice: An Essay in Economics and Applied Philosophy.* New York: Harper Collins Academic.

Levenson, Alec R., and William F. Maloney. 1998. "The Informal Sector, Firm Dynamics, and Institutional Participation." World Bank Policy Research Working Paper 1988. Washington, D.C.

Levine, Daniel H. 1973. *Conflict and Political Change in Venezuela.* Princeton, NJ: Princeton University Press.

Levy, S. 1994. "La pobreza en Mexico." In F. Vélez, ed., *Causas y políticas para combatir la pobreza en Mexico.* Mexico City: ITAM and FCE.

Levy Yeyati, Eduardo, Sergio Schmukler, and Neeltje Van Horen. 2003. "The Price of Inconvertible Deposits: The Stock Market Boom during the Argentine Crisis." World Bank, Washington, D.C. Processed.

Li, H. 2000. "Political Economy of Income Distribution: A Comparative Study of Taiwan and Mexico." *Policy Studies Journal* 28 (2): 275–291.

Lindauer, David, and Lant Pritchett. 2002. "What's the Big Idea? Three Generations of Development Advice." *Economía* 3 (1): 1–39.

Lindert, P. 2002. "Why the Welfare State Looks Like a Free Lunch." Working Paper 02-7. University of California, Department of Economics. Davis, CA.

Linz, J., and A. Valenzuela. 1994. *The Failure of Presidential Democracy.* Baltimore: Johns Hopkins University Press.

Litchfield, Julie. 1999. "Inequality: Methods and Tools." Available online at <http://www.worldbank.org/poverty/inequal/index.htm.>

Lledo, V., A. Schneider, and M. Moore. 2003. *Pro-poor Tax Reform in Latin America: A Critical Survey and Policy Recommendations.* Sussex: University of Sussex, Institute of Development Studies.

Loayza, Norman, Pablo Fajnzylber, and César Calderón. 2002. "Economic Growth in Latin America and the Caribbean: Stylized Facts, Explanations, and Forecasts." World Bank, Washington, D.C. Processed.

Lokshin, Michael, and Martin Ravallion. 2000. "Welfare Impacts of the 1998 Financial Crisis in Russia and the Response of the Public Safety Net." *Economics of Transition* 8 (2): 269–95.

Londoño, Juan-Luis. 1995. *Distribución del Ingreso y Desarrollo Económico: Colombia en el Siglo XX.* Bogotá: TM Editores.

Londoño, Juan-Luis, and Miguel Székely. 1997. "Persistent Poverty and Excess Inequality: Latin America, 1970–1995." Office of the Chief Economist, Working Paper series 375, Inter-American Development Bank, Washington, D.C.

López, Humberto. 2003. "Macroeconomics and Inequality." World Bank, Washington D.C. Processed.

López, Ramón, and Alberto Valdés. 2000a. "Fighting Rural Poverty in Latin America: New Evidence of the Effects of Education, Demographics, and Access to Land." *Economic and Development and Cultural Change* 49 (1): 197–211.

———, eds. 2000b. *Rural Poverty in Latin America.* New York: St. Martin's Press.

López-Acevedo, Gladys, and Angel Salinas. 2000. "How Mexico's Financial Crisis Affected Income Distribution."

World Bank Policy Research Working Paper 2406. Washington, D.C.

_____. 2002. "The Distribution of Mexico's Public Spending on Education." World Bank, Washington, D.C. Processed.

López-Cálix, J., L. Alcázar, and E. Wachtenheim. 2003. "Improving the Efficiency of Public Spending in Peru." In Q. Wodon, ed., "Public Spending, Poverty, and Inequality in Latin America." World Bank, Washington, D.C. Processed.

López-Calva, Luis Felipe, and Juan Rosellón. 2002. "Privatization and Inequality: The Mexican Case." Puebla, Mexico: Universidad de las Américas.

López-Maya, M. 1997. "The Rise of Causa R in Venezuela." In D. Chalmers, Carlos M. Vilas, Katherine Hite, Scott B. Martin, Kerianne Piester, and Monique Segarra, eds. *The New Politics of Inequality in Latin America: Rethinking Participation and Representation.* New York: Oxford University Press.

Lora, Eduardo. 2001. "Structural Reforms in Latin America: What Has Been Reformed and How to Measure It." Inter-American Development Bank Working Paper 348. Washington, D.C.

Loury, Glenn C. 2002. *The Anatomy of Racial Inequality.* Cambridge, MA: Harvard University Press.

Lucas, Robert E. 1988. "On the Mechanics of Economic Development." *Journal of Monetary Economics* 22 (1): 3–42.

Lustig, Nora. 1994. "Solidarity as a Strategy of Poverty Alleviation." In Wayne Cornelius, Ann L. Craig, and Jonathan Fox, eds., *Transforming State-Society Relations in Mexico: The National Solidarity Strategy.* San Diego: Center for US-Mexican Studies.

_____, ed. 1995. *Coping with Austerity: Poverty and Inequality in Latin America.* Washington, D.C.: Brookings Institution.

_____. 1999. *Poverty and Inequality in Latin America.* Santafé de Bogotá: Tercer Mundo S.A.

_____. 2000. "Crises and the Poor: Socially Responsible Macroeconomics." *Economía* 1 (1): 1–30.

McAdam, D., S. Tarrow, and C. Tilly. 2001. *Dynamics of Contention.* Cambridge: Cambridge University Press.

McClintock, Cynthia. 1998. *Revolutionary Movements in Latin America. El Salvador's FMLN and Peru's Shining Path.* Washington D.C.: United States Institute of Peace Press.

Maceira, Daniel, and María Victoria Murillo 2001. "Social Sector Reform in Latin America and the Role of Unions." Inter-American Development Bank Working Paper 456. Washington D.C.

McEwan, Patrick and Wilson Jiménez. 2002. "Estudiantes Indígenas y Acceso a la Educación Primaria en Bolivia." Paper presented at the meeting on Etnicidad, Raza, Género en América Latina, Grupo de Análisis para el Desarrollo, Lima, Peru.

MacIsaac, Donna J. and Harry Anthony Patrinos. 1995. "Labor Market Discrimination against Indigenous People in Peru." *Journal of Development Studies* 32 (2): 218–33.

McKenzie, David, and Dilip Mookherjee. 2003. "The Distributive Impact of Privatization in Latin America: An Overview of Evidence from Four Countries." *Economía* 3 (2): 161–233.

Maddison, A. 1992. *The Political Economy of Poverty, Equity and Growth: Brazil and Mexico.* New York: Oxford University Press.

Mahoney, James. 2001. *The Legacies of Liberalism: Path Dependence and Political Regimes in Central America.* Baltimore: Johns Hopkins University Press.

Mahoney, James, and Vom Hau. 2002. "Indigenous People, Colonialism, and Social Development in Spanish America." Brown University, Providence, RI. Processed.

Mainwaring, S. 2000. *Rethinking Party Systems in the Third Wave of Democratization: The Case of Brazil.* Stanford, CA: Stanford University Press.

Mainwaring, S., and M. Shugart. 1995. *Building Democratic Institutions: Party Systems in Latin America.* Stanford, CA: Stanford University Press.

_____. 1997. "Juan Linz, Presidentialism, and Democracy: A Critical Appraisal." *Comparative Politics* 29 (4): 449–471.

Malloy, J. 1977. *Authoritarianism and Corporatism in Latin America.* Pittsburgh, PA: University of Pittsburgh Press.

_____. 1979. *The Politics of Social Security in Brazil.* Pittsburgh, PA: University of Pittsburgh Press.

Malloy, James M., and Eduardo Gamarra. 1988. *Revolution and Reaction: Bolivia, 1964–1985.* New Brunswick, NJ: Transaction Books.

Maloney, William F. 2003. "Informality Revisited." World Bank, Washington D.C. Processed.

Maloney, William, and Jairo Nuñez. 2000. "Measuring the Impact of Minimum Wages: Evidence from Latin America." Working Paper 2597. World Bank, Washington, D.C. Processed.

Maluccio, J. 2003. "Education and Child Labor: Experimental Evidence from a Nicaraguan Conditional Cash Transfer Program." International Food Policy Research Institute, Washington, D.C. Processed.

Manuelyan Atinc, Tamar, and Michael Walton. 1998. *Social Consequences of the East Asian Financial Crisis.* Washington, D.C.: World Bank.

Marcel, Mario. 1999. "Effectiveness of the State and Development Lessons from the Chilean Experience." In Guillermo Perry and Danny M. Leipziger, eds., *Chile: Recent Policy Lessons and Emerging Challenges.* World Bank Institute Development Studies. Washington, D.C.: World Bank.

Martínez-Vázquez, J. 2001. "The Impact of Budgets on the Poor: Tax and Benefit Incidence." Teaching Module 10, prepared for the World Bank Institute. Washington, D.C.: World Bank.

Martz, John D. 1983. "Populist Leadership and the Party Caudillo: Ecuador and the CFP, 1962–81." *Studies in Comparative International Development* 18 (3): 22–49.

Matthews, M. 2001. "Institutions, Interests, Energy, and the Environment: Policymaking in Corporatism, Pluralism, and Beyond." *Policy Studies Journal* 29 (3): 407–13.

Meerman, J. 1980. "The Incidence of Sales and Excise Taxes, or Where Do We Put the Transfers?" *Journal of Political Economy* 88 (6): 1242–48.

Melo, Marcus André. 1998. "When Institutions Matter: The Politics of Administrative, Social Security, and Tax Reforms in Brazil." Paper delivered at the Latin American Studies Association meeting, Chicago, Illinois.

Méndez, Juan E., Guillermo O'Donnell, and Paulo Sérgio Pinheiro, eds. 1999. *The (Un)Rule of Law and the Underprivileged in Latin America.* Notre Dame, IN: University of Notre Dame Press.

Menezes-Filho, Naercio. 2001. "Educação e desigualdade." In M. Lisboa and N. Menezes-Filho, eds., *Microeconomia e Sociedade no Brasil.* Sao Paolo: Editora Contracapa.

Menocal, A. R. 2001. "Old Habits Die Hard? A Statistical Exploration of the Politicisation of PROGRESA, Mexico's Latest Federal Poverty-Alleviation Programme Under the Zedillo Administration." *Journal of Latin American Studies* 33 (3): 513–38.

Middlebrook, Kevin. 1995. *The Paradox of Revolution: Labor, the State, and Authoritarianism in Mexico.* Baltimore: Johns Hopkins University Press.

MIDEPLAN (Ministerio de Planificación y Cooperación). 1998. "Resultados de la VII Encuesta de Caracterizacion Socioeconomica Nacional." Ministerio de Planificación y Cooperación. Santiago, Chile.

Milanovic, B. 2000. "The Median Voter Hypothesis, Income Inequality and Income Redistribution: An Empirical Test with the Required Data." *European Journal of Political Economy* 16 (3): 367–410.

———. 2002. "True World Income Distribution, 1988 and 1993: First Calculation Based on Household Surveys Alone." *Economic Journal* 112 (476): 51–92.

Milanovic, B., and S. Yitzhaki. 2002. "Decomposing World Income Distribution: Does the World Have a Middle Class?" *The Review of Income and Wealth* 48 (2): 155–78.

Mills, J., and S. Zandvakili. 1997. "Statistical Inference via Bootstrapping for Measures of Inequality." *Journal of Applied Econometrics* 12: 133–50.

Miraftab, F. 1997. "Flirting with the Enemy: Challenges Faced by NGOs in Development and Empowerment." *Habitat International* 21 (4): 361–75.

MNPTSG (Mesoamerica Nutrition Program Targeting Study Group). 2002. "Targeting Performance of Three Large-Scale Nutrition Oriented Social Programs in Central America and Mexico." *Food and Nutrition Bulletin* 23(2): 162–171. The United Nations University Press, Tokyo.

Molina, O., and M. Rhodes. 2002. "Corporatism: The Past, Present, and Future of a Concept." *Annual Review of Political Science* 5: 305–31.

Molinar Horcasitas, Juan, and Jeffrey Weldon. 1994. "Electoral Determinants and Consequences of National Solidarity." In Wayne Cornelius, Ann Craig, and Jonathan Fox, eds., *Transforming State-Society Relations in Mexico: The National Solidarity Strategy.* La Jolla: Center for US-Mexican Studies, University of California, San Diego.

Mondino, Guillermo, Esteban Fernández Medrano, and Luciano Laspina. 2002. "Argentina's Neopopulism Voyage." *Latin Source Monthly Report* (December).

Morgan, Edmund S. 1975. *American Slavery, American Freedom: The Ordeal of Colonial Virginia.* New York: W.W. Norton and Company.

Morley, S. 2001. *The Income Distribution Problem in Latin America and the Caribbean.* Santiago: Economic Commission for Latin America and the Caribbean.

Morley, S., and D. Coady. 2003. *From Social Assistance to Social Development: A Review of Targeted Education Subsidies in Developing Countries.* Washington, D.C.: International Food Policy Research Institute.

Morley, S., and R. Vos. 1997. *Poverty and Dualistic Growth in Paraguay.* Washington, D.C.: Inter-American Development Bank.

Morrison, Christian. 2000. "Inequality in Historical Perspective." In Anthony B. Atkinson and François Bourguignon, eds., *Handbook of Income Distribution.* Amsterdam: North-Holland Publishing Company.

Murillo, María Victoria. 1997. "Union Politics, Market-Oriented Reforms, and the Reshaping of Argentine Corporatism." In D. Chalmers, Carlos M. Vilas, Katherine Hite, Scott B. Martin, Kerianne Piester, and Monique Segarra, eds., *The New Politics of Inequality in Latin America: Rethinking Participation and Representation.* New York: Oxford University Press.

———. 2002. "Political Bias in Policy Convergence: Privatization Choices in Latin America." *World Politics* 54 (4): 462–93.

Murrugarra, E. 2003. "Targeted Social Assistance Programs in Uruguay." In Quentin Wodon, ed., *Public Spending, Poverty, and Inequality in Latin America.* Washington, D.C.: World Bank.

Musgrave, R. 1959. *The Theory of Public Finance.* New York: McGraw-Hill Book Company.

Neri, Marcelo, and José Márcio Camargo. 1999. "Structural Reforms, Macroeconomic Fluctuations and Income Distribution in Brazil." Reformas Económicas series 39. Economic Commission for Latin America and the Caribbean, Santiago.

Neri, Marcelo, Gustavo Gonzaga, and José Márcio Camargo. 2001. "Salário Mínimo, Efeito-Farol e Pobreza." *Revista de Economia Política* 21 (2): 78–90. São Paulo.

Nielson, D., and M. Shugart. 1999. "Constitutional Change in Colombia: Policy Adjustment through Institutional Reform." *Comparative Political Studies* 32 (3): 313–41.

North, Douglass C. 1990. *Institutions, Institutional Change, and Economic Performance.* Cambridge: Cambridge University Press.

Nozick, R. 1974. *Anarchy, State, and Utopia.* Oxford: Basil Blackwell Publishing.

Nylen, W. 1997. "Reconstructing the Workers' Party (PT): Lessons from Northeastern Brazil." In D. Chalmers, Carlos M. Vilas, Katherine Hite, Scott B. Martin, Kerianne Piester, and Monique Segarra, eds., *The New Politics of Inequality in Latin America: Rethinking Participation and Representation.* New York: Oxford University Press.

Oaxaca, R.L. 1973. "Male-Female Wage Differentials in Urban Labor Markets." *International Economic Review* 14 (3): 693–709.

Obstfeld, M. 1996. "Models of Currency Crises with Self-fulfilling Features." *European Economic Review* 40: 1037–47.

Ocampo, J. A., María José Pérez, Camilo Tovar, and Francisco Lasso. 1998. "Macroeconomía, ajuste estructural y equidad en Colombia: 1978–1996." In Ganuza, Taylor, and Morley, eds., *Política macroeconómica y pobreza en América Latina y el Caribe.* New York: United Nations Development Programme.

O'Donnell, Guillermo. 1973. *Modernization and Bureaucratic-Authoritarianism: Studies in South American Politics.* Berkeley: University of California Press.

———. 1998a. "Horizontal Accountability in New Democracies." *Journal of Democracy* 9 (3): 112–26.

———. 1998b. "Poverty and Inequality in Latin America: Some Political Reflections." In V. Tokman and G. O'Donnell, eds. *Poverty and Inequality in Latin America: Issues and New Challenges.* Notre Dame, IN: The University of Notre Dame Press.

———. 1999a. "Democratic Theory and Comparative Politics." University of Notre Dame, Kellogg Institute of International Studies. Notre Dame, IN.

———. 1999b. "Polyarchies and the (Un)Rule of Law in Latin America." In Juan E. Méndez, Guillermo O'Donnell, and Paulo Sérgio Pinheiro, eds., *The (Un)Rule of Law and the Underprivileged in Latin America.* Notre Dame, IN: University of Notre Dame Press.

Oliveira Barbosa, Maria Ligia de. 2002. "Gender and Color Differences at School in Brazil: Teachers and Students' Evaluations." (Unpublished manuscript.)

Olson, M. 1982. *The Rise and Decline of Nations: Economic Growth, Stagflation, and Social Rigidities.* New Haven, CT: Yale University Press.

OECD (Organisation for Economic Co-operation and Development). 2001. *Knowledge and Skills for Life: First Results from the OECD Programme for International Student Assessment (PISA) 2000.* Paris.

O'Rourke, Kevin H., and Jeffery G. Williamson. 2002. From Malthus to Ohlin: Trade, Growth and Distribution Since 1500. National Bureau of Economic Research Working Paper 8955. Cambridge, MA.

Ortega, Daniel, and Francisco Rodríguez. 2002. "Openness and Factor Shares." Office of Economic and Financial Advisors, National Assembly, Caracas, Venezuela.

Paes De Barros, Ricardo, and Rosane Mendonça. 1997. "A Absorção de Mão-de-Obra no Setor de Serviços." *Dados: Revista de Ciências Sociais* 40 (1).

———. 1998. "The Impact of Three Institutional Innovations in Brazilian Education." In W. D. Savedoff, ed., *Organization matters: Agency Problems in Health and Education.* Washington, D.C.: Inter-American Development Bank.

Paes de Barros, Ricardo, and M. Foguel. 2000. "Focalizaçao dos Gastos Públicos Sociais e erradicaçao da pobreza no Brasil." In Ricardo Henriques, ed., *Desigualdade e Pobreza no Brasil.* Rio de Janeiro: IPEA.

Paes de Barros, Ricardo, Rosane Mendonça, D. Santos, and G. Quintaes. 2001. "Determinantes do desempenho educacional no Brasil." *Pesquisa e Planejamento Econômico* 31 (1).

Page, B., and Simmons J. 2000. *What Government Can Do: Dealing with Poverty and Inequality.* Chicago: University of Chicago Press.

Paige, Jeffrey M. 1997. *Coffee and Power: Revolution and the Rise of Democracy in Central America.* Cambridge, MA: Harvard University Press.

Parker, S., and E. Skoufias. 2000. "The Impact of PROGRESA on Work, Leisure, and Time Allocation." International Food Policy Research Institute, Washington, D.C.

Patrinos, Harry Anthony. 1997. "Differences in Education and Earnings across Ethnic Groups in Guatemala." *Quarterly Review of Economics and Finance* 37 (4): 809–21.

———. 2002. *A Review of Demand-side Financing Initiatives in Education.* Washington, D.C.: World Bank.

Patrinos, Harry Anthony, and Eduardo Vélez. 1996. "Costs and Benefits of Bilingual Education in Guatemala: A Partial Analysis." World Bank Working Paper HCDWP 74. Washington, D.C.

Patrinos, Harry Anthony, Eduardo Vélez, and George Psacharopoulos. 1994. "Language, Education, and Earnings in Asunción, Paraguay." *Journal of Developing Areas* 29: 57–68.

Patroni, V. 2001. "The Decline and Fall of Corporatism? Labour Legislation Reform in Mexico and Argentina during the 1990s." *Canadian Journal of Political Science* 34 (2): 249–74.

Paxson, Christina, and Norbert Schady. 2002. "The Allocation and Impact of Social Funds: Spending on School Infrastructure in Peru." *World Bank Economic Review* 16 (2): 297–310.

Pero, Valéria. 2003. "Intergenerational Social Mobility in Brazil." Instituto de Economia-UFRJ, Rio de Janeiro.

Perotti, Roberto. 1996. "Growth, Income Distribution, and Democracy: What the Data Say." *Journal of Economic Growth* 1: 149–87.

Perry, Guillermo. 2003. "Can Fiscal Rules Help Reduce Macroeconomic Volatility in the Latin America and Caribbean Region?" World Bank Working Paper 3080. Washington, D.C.

Perry, Guillermo, and Luis Servén. 2002. "La anatomía de una crisis múltiple: qué tenia Argentina de especial y qué podemos aprender de ella." *Desarrollo Económico* 42 (167): 323–75.

Persson, Torsten, and Guido Tabellini. 1994. "Is Inequality Harmful for Growth? Theory and Evidence." *American Economic Review* 84 (3): 600–21.

Piketty, Thomas, and Emmanuel Saez. 2001. "Income Inequality in the United States, 1913–1988." National Bureau of Economic Research Working Paper 8467. Cambridge, MA.

Pinheiro, P. 1997. "Popular Responses to State-Sponsored Violence in Brazil." In D. Chalmers, Carlos M. Vilas, Katherine Hite, Scott B. Martin, Kerianne Piester, and Monique Segarra, eds., *The New Politics of Inequality in Latin America: Rethinking Participation and Representation.* New York: Oxford University Press.

———. 1999. "Introduction: The Rule of Law and the Underprivileged in Latin America." In J. Méndez, G. O'Donnell, and P. Pinheiro, eds., *The Rule of Law and the Underprivileged in Latin America.* Notre Dame, IN: University of Notre Dame Press.

Pirez, P. 2002. "Buenos Aires: Fragmentation and Privatization of the Metropolitan City." *Environment and Urbanization* 14 (1): 145–58.

Pissarides, Christopher A. 1990. *Equilibrium Unemployment Theory.* Oxford, U.K.: Basil Blackwell Publishing.

Political Risk Service Group, Inc. 2003. *International Country Risk Guide.* East Syracuse, NY: The PRS Group, Inc.

POLITY IV database. http://www.cidcm.umd.edu/inscr/polity/. Integrated Network for Societal Conflict Research (INSCR) program at the Center for International Development and Conflict Management (CIDCM), University of Maryland, College Park, MD.

Pontusson, J, D. Rueda, and C. Way. 2002. "Comparative Political Economy of Wage Distribution: The Role of Partisanship and Labour Market Institutions." *British Journal of Political Science* 32: 281–308.

Portes, Alejandro, and Ruben G. Rumbaut. 2001a. *Legacies: The Story of the Immigrant Second Generation.* Berkeley: University of California Press.

———. 2001b. *Ethnicities: Children of Immigrants in America.* Berkeley: University of California Press.

Portes, A., and K. Hoffman. 2003. "Latin American Class Structures: Their Composition and Change During the Neoliberal Era." *Latin American Research Review* 38 (1): 41–82.

Powell, John Duncan 1970. "Peasant Society and Clientelistic Practices." *American Political Science Review* 64 (2): 411–25.

———. 1977. "Peasant Society and Clientelist Politics." In Steffen W. Schmidt, James C. Scott, Carl Landé, and Laura Guasti, eds., *Friends, Followers, and Factions: A Reader in Political Clientelism.* Berkeley: University of California Press.

Powers, Nancy R. 2001. *Grassroots Expectations of Democracy and Economy: Argentina in Comparative Perspective.* Pittsburgh, PA: University of Pittsburgh Press.

Prillaman, W. 2000. *The Judiciary and Democratic Decay in Latin America: Declining Confidence in the Rule of Law.* Westport, CT: Praeger Press.

Pritchett, Lant. 2001. "Where Has All the Education Gone?" *World Bank Economic Review* 15 (3): 367–91.

Prud'homme, R. 1990. "Decentralization of Expenditures or Taxes: The Case of France." In R. J. Bennett, ed., *Decentralization, Local Governments, and Markets.* Oxford, U.K.: Clarendon Press.

Psacharopoulos, George, and Zafiris Tzannatos. 1992. *Women's Employment and Pay in Latin America.* Washington, D.C.: World Bank.

Psacharopoulos, George, and Harry Patrinos. 1994. *Indigenous People and Poverty in Latin America: An Empirical Analysis.* Washington, D.C.: World Bank.

Psacharopoulos, George, Samuel Morley, Ariel Fiszbein, Haeduck Lee, and William C. Wood. 1995. "Poverty and Income Inequality in Latin America during the 1980s." *Review of Income and Wealth* 41 (3): 245–64.

———. 1997. *Poverty and Income Distribution in Latin America: The Story of the 1980s.* Technical Paper 351. Washington, D.C.: World Bank.

Putnam, R. 1993. *Making Democracy Work: Civic Traditions in Modern Italy.* Princeton, NJ: Princeton University Press.

Putnam, R. D., S. J. Pharr, and R. J. Dalton. 2000. "Introduction: What's Troubling the Trilateral Democracies?" In R. D. Putnam and S. Pharr, eds., *Disaffected Democracies.* Princeton, NJ: Princeton University Press.

Quintero, Rafael. 1980. *El Mito del Populismo en el Ecuador.* Quito: Editorial Universitaria.

Randall, Laura J. 1978. *An Economic History of Argentina in the Twentieth Century.* New York: Columbia University Press.

Rao, Vijayendra, and Michael Walton. 2004. "Introduction." In Rao, Vijayendra and Michael Walton, eds. *Culture and Public Action.* Stanford, CA: Stanford University Press.

Ratliff, W., and E. Buscaglia. 1997. "Judicial Reform: The Neglected Priority in Latin America." *Annals of the American Academy of Political Science* 550: 59–71.

Ravallion, Martin. 1997. "Can High-inequality Developing Countries Escape Absolute Poverty?" Policy Research Working Paper 1775. World Bank, Washington, D.C.

———. 2000. "Are the Poor Protected from Budget Cuts? Theory and Evidence from Argentina." Policy Research Working Paper 2391. World Bank, Washington, D.C. (Also forthcoming in the *Journal of Applied Economics.*)

———. 2002. "Who Is Protected? On the Incidence of Fiscal Adjustment." World Bank, Washington, D.C. Processed.

Ravallion, Martin, and Shaohua Chen. 1997. "What Can New Survey Data Tell Us about Recent Changes in Distribution and Poverty?" *World Bank Economic Review* 11 (2): 357–82.

Rawlings, Laura, and Gloria M. Rubio. 2003. "Evaluating the Impact of Conditional Cash Transfer Programs: Lessons from Latin America." World Bank Policy Research Working Paper 3119. Washington, D.C.

Rees, H., and Shah, A. 1986: "An Empirical Analysis of Self-employment in the UK." *Journal of Applied Econometrics* 1 (1): 95–108.

Rehren, A. 1996. "Corruption and Local Politics in Chile." *Crime Law and Social Change* 25 (4): 323–34.

Reich, G. M. 1998. "The 1988 Constitution a Decade Later: Ugly Compromises Reconsidered." *Journal of Inter-American Studies and World Affairs* 40 (4): 5–24.

Reis, Elisa. 1999. "Elite Perceptions of Poverty: Brazil." *IDS Bulletin* 30 (2).

Reis, E. J., P. Tafner, and L. O. Reiff. 2001. "Distribuição de Riqueza Imobiliária e de Renda no Brasil: 1992–1999." Seminários DIMAC N 75. IPEA, Rio de Janeiro.

Remmer, K., and E. Wibbels. 2000. "The Subnational Politics of Economic Adjustment: Provincial Politics and Fiscal Performance in Argentina." *Comparative Political Studies* 33 (4): 419–51.

Rey, Juan Carlos. 1990. "El Papel de los Partidos en la Instauración y el Mantenimiento de la Democracia en Venezuela." Fundación IDEA, Caracas. Processed.

Reynolds, Clark W. 1970. *The Mexican Economy: Twentieth-Century Structure and Growth.* New Haven, CT: Yale University Press.

Rinne, Jeffrey James. 2001. "Redesigning the State in Latin America: Pundits, Policymakers, and Organized Labor in Argentina and Brazil." PhD diss. Princeton University. Princeton, NJ.

Rivera, J.A., G. Rodríguez, T. Shamah, J. L. Rosado, E. Casanueva, I. Maulén, G. Toussaint, and A. García-Aranda. 2000. "Implementation, Monitoring, and Evaluation of the Nutrition Component of the Mexican Social Programme (PROGRESA)." *Food and Nutrition Bulletin* 21 (1): 35–42.

Riveros, Luis 1998. "Chile's Structural Adjustment: Relevant Policy Lessons for Latin America." In A. Berry, ed., *Poverty, Economic Reform, and Income Distribution in Latin America.* Boulder, CO: Lynne Rienner Publishers.

Robbins, Donald. 1994. "Relative Wage Structure in Chile, 1957–1992: Changes in the Structure of Demand for Schooling." *Estudios de Económica* 21: 49–78

Robbins, Donald, and T. H. Gindling. 1999. "Trade Liberalization and the Relative Wages for More Skilled Workers in Costa Rica." *Review of Development Economics* 3 (2): 140–54.

Roberts, K. 1995. "Neoliberalism and the Transformation of Populism in Latin America: The Peruvian Case." *World Politics* 48 (1): 82–116.

———. 1997. "Rethinking Economic Alternatives: Left Parties and the Articulation of Popular Demands in Chile and Peru." In D. Chalmers, Carlos M. Vilas, Katherine Hite, Scott B. Martin, Kerianne Piester, and Monique Segarra, eds., *The New Politics of Inequality in Latin America: Rethinking Participation and Representation.* New York: Oxford University Press.

Robinson, James. 2002. "Politician-Proof Policy?" Background paper for the 2004 *World Development Report.* Washington, D.C.: World Bank.

Robinson, James, and Thierry Verdier. 2002. "The Political Economy of Clientelism." Centre for Economic Policy Research Working Paper 3205. London.

Robles, M. 1999. "Pobreza y distribución del ingreso en Paraguay." Asunción: Programa MECOVI-DGEEC.

Rodley, N. 1999. "Torture and Conditions of Detention in Latin America." In J. Méndez, G. O'Donnell, and P. Pinheiro, eds., *The Rule of Law and the Underprivileged in Latin America.* Notre Dame, IN: University of Notre Dame Press.

Rodrik, Dani. 1999. "Where Did All the Growth Go? External Shocks, Social Conflict and Growth Collapses." *Journal of Economic Growth* 4 (4): 385–412.

———. 2003. "Growth Strategies." Paper prepared for the *Handbook on Economic Growth.* Cambridge, MA: Harvard University Press.

Rodrik, Dani, Arvind Subramanian, and Francesco Trebbi. 2002. "Institutions Rule: The Primacy of Institutions over Geography and Integration in Economic Development." Harvard University, Cambridge, MA. Processed.

Roemer, John E. 1996. *Theories of Distributive Justice.* Cambridge, MA: Harvard University Press.

———. 1998. *Equality of Opportunity.* Cambridge, MA: Harvard University Press.

Rojas, F. 2000. "The Political Context of Decentralization in Latin America." In Shahid Javed Burki and Guillermo E. Perry, eds., *Decentralization and Accountability of the Public Sector.* Washington, D.C.: World Bank.

Rosado, J. L., J. Rivera, G. Lopez, and L. Solano. 2000. "Development, Production, and Quality Control of Nutritional Supplements for a National Supplementation Program in Mexico." *Food and Nutrition Bulletin* 21 (1): 30–34.

Rose, R., and D. Shin. 2001. "Democratization Backwards: The Problem of Third-Wave Democracies." *British Journal of Political Science* 31 (2): 331–54.

Rothschild, Emma. 2001. *Economic Sentiments: Adam Smith, Condorcet, and the Enlightenment.* Cambridge, MA, and London: Harvard University Press.

Rueschemeyer, Dietrich, Evelyne Huber Stephens, and John D. Stephens. 1992. *Capitalist Development and Democracy.* Chicago: University of Chicago Press.

Rutherford, T., M. Light, and F. Barrera. 2002. *Equity and Efficiency Costs of Raising Tax Revenue in Colombia.* Bogotá: Fedesarrollo.

Saavedra, Jaime, and María de los Ángeles Cárdenas. 2002. "Access, Efficiency, and Equity of the Peruvian Educational System: An Analysis of Indicators Using the LSMS and the School Census." Paper presented at the meeting on Etnicidad, Raza, Género en América Latina, Grupo de Análisis para el Desarrollo, Lima, Peru.

Sabate, R., and A. Schneider. 2003. "Taxation, Accountability, and the Poor." University of Sussex, Institute of Development Studies Seminar Report. Sussex.

Sahn, David, and D. Stifel. 2003. "Progress Towards the Millennium Development Goals in Africa." *World Development* 31 (1): 23–52.

Sahn, E. David, Paul Dorosh, and Stephen Younger. 1997. *Structural Adjustment Reconsidered: Economic Policy and Poverty in Africa.* Cambridge, U.K., and New York: Cambridge University Press.

Safa, Helen. 1998. "Introduction." *Latin American Perspectives* 100 (25): 3–20.

Sala-i-Martin, X. 2002. "The World Distribution of Income (Estimated from Individual Country Distributions)." National Bureau of Economic Research Working Paper 8933. Cambridge, MA.

Salinas de Gortari, C. 1978. "Political Participation, Public Investment, and System Support: A Study of Three Rural Communities in Central Mexico." PhD diss. Harvard University, Cambridge, MA.

Samuels, D. 2002. "Pork Barreling is not Credit Claiming or Advertising: Campaign Finance and the Sources of the Personal Vote in Brazil." *Journal of Politics* 64 (3): 845–63.

Samuels, David, and Richard Snyder. 2001. "Devaluing the vote in Latin America." *Journal of Democracy* 12(1): 146–59.

———. 2002. "The Value of a Vote: Malapportionment in Comparative Perspective." *British Journal of Political Science* 31 (4): 651–71.

Sánchez-Páramo, Carolina, and Norbert R. Schady. 2002. "Off and Running? The Rising Demand for Skilled Workers in Latin America." World Bank Policy Research Working Paper 3015. Washington, D.C.

Sanguinetti, Pablo, Rodrigo Arim, and Juan Pantano. 2001. "Changes in Production Structure and Employment Structure and Relative Wages in Argentina and Uruguay." Universidad Torcuato Di Tella, Buenos Aires.

Santamaría, Mauricio. 2000. "External Trade, Skill, Technology and the Recent Increase of Income Inequality in Colombia." PhD diss. Georgetown University, Washington, D.C.

Scalon, M. C., and C.A.C. Ribeiro. 2001. "Mobilidade de classe em perspectiva comparada." *Dados: Revista de Ciências Sociais* 44 (1).

Schady, N. 2000. "The Political Economy of Expenditures by the Peruvian Social Fund (FONDCODES) 1991–1995." *American Political Science Review* 94 (2): 289–304.

Schamis, Hector E. 2002. *Re-Forming the State: The Politics of Privatization in Latin America and Europe (Interests, Identities,*

and Institutions in Comparative Politics). Ann Arbor: University of Michigan Press.

Scheper-Hughes, Nancy. 1992. *Death Without Weeping: The Violence of Everyday Life in Brazil.* Berkeley: University of California Press.

Schiff, Maurice. 2003. "The Inefficiency of Inequality, with Implications for Development Institutions." World Bank, Washington, D.C. Processed.

Schiff, Maurice and Alberto Valdés. 1992. *The Plundering of Agriculture in Developing Countries.* Washington D.C.: World Bank.

Schmidt, Steffen W. 1977. "The Transformation of Clientelism in Rural Colombia." In Steffen W. Schmidt, James C. Scott, Carl Landé, and Laura Guasti, eds., *Friends, Followers, and Factions: A Reader in Political Clientelism.* Berkeley: University of California Press.

Schmitter, Philippe C., and Wolfgang Streeck, eds. 1971. *Interest Conflict and Political Change in Brazil.* Stanford, CA: Stanford University Press.

———. 1974. "Still the Century of Corporatism?" *Review of Politics* 36 (1): 85–131.

———. 1985. *Private Interest Government and Public Policy.* Beverly Hills and London: Sage Publications.

Schneider, B. 1991. *Politics within the State: Elite Bureaucrats and Industrial Policy in Authoritarian Brazil.* Pittsburgh, PA: University of Pittsburgh Press.

———. 2002. "Why is Mexican business so organized?" *Latin American Research Review* 37 (1): 77–118.

Schultz, T. P. 2000a. "School Subsidies for the Poor: Evaluating a Mexican Strategy for Reducing Poverty." International Food Policy Research Institute, Food Consumption Nutrition Division Discussion Paper 102. Washington, D.C.

———. 2000b. "Final Report: The Impact of PROGRESA on School Enrollments." International Food Policy Research Institute, Washington, D.C.

———. 2000c. "Impact of PROGRESA on School Attendance Rates in the Sampled Population." International Food Policy Research Institute, Washington, D.C.

———. 2000d. "Preliminary Evidence of PROGRESA's Impact on School Enrollments from 1997/98 to 1998/99." International Food Policy Research Institute, Washington, D.C.

Scobie, James. 1964. *Revolution on the Pampas: A Social History of Argentine Wheat.* Austin, TX: Texas University Press.

Scott, John. 2003. "Public Spending and Inequality of Opportunities in Mexico: 1970–2000." In Q. Wodon, ed., "Public Spending, Poverty, and Inequality in Latin America." World Bank, Washington, D.C. Processed.

Scott, James. 1998. *Seeing Like a State: How Certain Schemes to Improve the Human Condition Have Failed*. New Haven, CT: Yale University Press.

SDStats (Social Development Indicators) database. http://esd. worldbank.org/sdstats/. World Bank, Washington, D.C.

Segarra, M. "Redefining the Public/Private Mix: NGOs and the Emergency Social Investment Fund in Ecuador." In D. Chalmers, Carlos M. Vilas, Katherine Hite, Scott B. Martin, Kerianne Piester, and Monique Segarra, eds. *The New Politics of Inequality in Latin America: Rethinking Participation and Representation*. New York: Oxford University Press.

Seligmann, Linda. 1995. *Between Reform and Revolution: Political Struggles in the Peruvian Andes, 1969–1991*. Stanford, CA: Stanford University Press.

Sen, Amartya. 1973. (Expanded edition 1997.) *On Economic Inequality*. Oxford: Clarendon Press.

———. 1985a. *Commodities and Capabilities*. Amsterdam: Elsevier.

———. 1985b. "Well-being, Agency and Freedom. The Dewey Lectures, 1984." *Journal of Philosophy* 82 (4): 169–221.

———. 1992. *Inequality Reexamined*. Cambridge, MA: Harvard University Press.

———. 1999. *Development as Freedom*. New York: Knopf Press.

———. 2000. "Social Justice and the Distribution of Income." In François Bourguignon and Anthony B. Atkinson, eds. *Handbook of Income Distribution*. Amsterdam: North-Holland Publishing Company.

Shadlen, K. 2000. "Neoliberalism, Corporatism, and Small Business Political Activism in Contemporary Mexico." *Latin American Research Review* 35 (2): 73–106.

Shah, A., and J. Whalley. 1990. "An Alternative View of Tax Incidence Analysis for Developing Countries." World Bank Working Paper 462. Washington, D.C.

Shefner, J. 2001. "Coalitions and Clientelism in Mexico." *Theory and Society* 30 (5): 593–628.

Shefter, Martin. 1994. *Political Parties and the State: The American Historical Experience*. Princeton, NJ: Princeton University Press.

Sheng, Andrew, ed. 1996. *Bank Restructuring: Lessons from the 1980s*. Washington, D.C.: World Bank.

Shome, Parthasarathi. 1999. "Taxation in Latin America: Structural Trends and Impact of Administration." International Monetary Fund Working Paper 99/19. Washington, D.C.

Shrader, E. 2001. "Methodologies to Measure the Gender Dimensions of Crime and Violence." World Bank, Washington, D.C.

Shugart, M. 2001. "Electoral 'Efficiency' and the Move to Mixed-Member Systems." *Electoral Studies* 20 (2): 173–93.

Shugart, M. 1992. "Leaders, Rank-and-File, and Constituents: Electoral Reform in Colombia and Venezuela." *Electoral Studies* 11 (1): 21–45.

———. 1995. "The Electoral Cycle and Institutional Sources of Divided Presidential Government." *American Political Science Review* 89 (2): 327–43.

———. 1998. "The Inverse Relationship between Party Strength and Executive Strength: A Theory of Politicians' Constitutional Choices." *British Journal of Political Science* 28: 1–29.

Shugart, M., and R. Taagepera. 1994. "Plurality Versus Majority Election of Presidents: A Proposal for a Double Complement Rule." *Comparative Political Studies* 27 (3): 323–48.

Siaens, Corinne, and Quentin Wodon. 2003. "Public Social Spending and Inequality in Latin America: Gini Income Elasticities." World Bank, Washington, D.C. Processed.

Silva, Nelson do V., and D. Roditi. 1988. "Et plus ça change.Tendências históricas da fluidez social no Brasil." *Dados: Revista de Ciências Sociais* 29 (3).

Skoufias, Emmanuel. 2001. "PROGRESA and its Impacts on the Human Capital and Welfare of Households in Rural Mexico: A Synthesis of the Results of an Evaluation by IFPRI." International Food Policy Research Institute, Washington, D.C.

Skoufias, Emmanuel, and B. McClafferty. 2001. "Is PROGRESA Working? Summary of the Results of an Evaluation by IFPRI." International Food Policy Research Institute, Washington, D.C.

Skoufias, Emmanuel, and S. W. Parker. 2001. "Conditional cash Transfers and their Impact on Child Work and Schooling: Evidence from the PROGRESA program in Mexico." *Economía* 2 (1): 45–96.

Skoufias, Emmanuel, B. Davis, and J. Behrman. 1999. "Final Report: An Evaluation of the Selection of Beneficiary Households in the Education, Health, and Nutrition Program (PROGRESA) of Mexico." International Food Policy Research Institute, Washington, D.C.

Skoufias, Emmanuel, B. Davis, and S. de la Vega. 2001. "Targeting the Poor in Mexico: An Evaluation of the Selection of Beneficiary Households into PROGRESA." *World Development* 29 (10): 1769–84.

Smeeding, T., and Grodner, A. 2000. "Changing Income Inequality in OECD Countries: Updated Results from the Luxembourg Income Study (LIS)." Luxemborg Income Study Working Paper 252. Syracuse University, Maxwell School of Citizenship and Public Affairs, Syracuse, NY.

Smith, J., and K. Subbarao. 2000. "What Role for Safety Net Transfers in Very Low-income Countries?" World Bank Discussion Paper. Washington, D.C.

Smith, W., and R. Korzeniewicz. 1997. *Politics, Social Change, and Economic Restructuring in Latin America.* Miami: North-South Center Press.

Snow, Peter G., and Gary Wynia. 1990. "Argentina." In Howard J. Wiarda and Harvey F. Kline, eds., *Latin American Politics and Development.* 3rd ed. Boulder, CO: Westview Press.

Soares, Sergei. 2000. "O Perfil da Discriminação no Mercado de Trabalho: Homens Negros, Mulheres Brancas e Mulheres Negras." Discussion Paper 769. Instituto de Pesquisa Econômica Aplicada, Brasília, Brazil.

Sosa Escudero, W., and L. Gasparini. 2000. "A Note on the Statistical Significance of Changes in Inequality." *Económica* 46 (1): 111–22.

Sosa Escudero, W., and M. Marchionni. 2000. "Household Structure, Gender, and Economic Determinants of School Attendance in Argentina." In *Argentina: Poor People in a Rich Country, Vol. II.* Washington, D.C.: World Bank.

Sour, Laura. 2003. "Return of the Enforcement Spending on VAT Revenues in Mexico." Mexico City: CIDE.

Stame, N. 1999. "Small and Medium Enterprise Aid Programs: Intangible Effects and Evaluation Practice." *Evaluation and Program Planning* 22 (1): 105–11.

Steinmo, S. 1993. *Taxation and Democracy: Swedish, British, and American Approaches to Financing the Modern State.* New Haven, CT: Yale University Press.

———. 2002. *The Evolution of Policy Ideas: Tax Policy in the 20th Century.* Boulder, CO: University of Colorado.

Stepan, A. 1978. *The State and Society: Peru in Comparative Perspective.* Princeton, NJ: Princeton University Press.

———. 2000. "Brazil's Decentralized Federalism: Bringing Government Closer to Citizens?" *Daedalus* 129 (2): 145–69.

Stephan, Cookie White, and Walter G. Stephan. 2000. "The Measurement of Racial and Ethnic Identity." *International Journal of Intercultural Relations* 24: 541–52.

Stern, Nicholas H. Forthcoming. *Poor People and Economic Opportunity.* Cambridge, MA: Massachusetts Institute of Technology Press.

Stokes, Susan C. 1995. *Cultures in Conflict: Social Movements and the State in Peru.* Berkeley: University of California Press.

Stotsky, Janet, and Asegedech WoldeMariam. 2002. "Central American Tax Reform: Trends and Possibilities." International Monetary Fund Working Paper 02/227. Washington, D.C.

Sumarto, Sudarno, Asep Suryahadi, and Lant Pritchett. 2003. "Safety Nets or Safety Ropes? Dynamic Benefit Incidence Analysis of Two Crisis Programs in Indonesia." *World Development* 31 (7): 1257–77.

Sutil, J. 1999. "Judicial Reforms in Latin America: Good News for the Underprivileged?" In J. Méndez, G. O'Donnell, and P. Pinheiro, eds., *The Rule of Law and the Underprivileged in Latin America.* Notre Dame, IN: University of Notre Dame Press.

Székely, M. 2001. "The 1990s in Latin America: Another Decade of Persistent Inequality, but with Somewhat Lower Poverty." Inter-American Development Bank Working Paper 454. Washington, D.C.

Székely, M., and M. Hilgert. 1999. "What's Behind the Inequality We Measure: An Investigation Using Latin American Data." Inter-American Development Bank Working Paper 409. Washington, D.C.

———. 2001. "What Drives Differences in Inequality Across Countries?" Inter-American Development Bank Working Paper 439. Washington, D.C.

Székely, M., Nora Lustig, M. Cumpa, and J. Mejía. 2000. "Do We Know How Much Poverty There Is?" Inter-American Development Bank Working Paper 437. Washington, D.C.

Tabatabai, H. 1996. *Statistics on Poverty and Income Distribution: An ILO Compendium of Data.* Geneva: International Labour Office.

Talvi, Ernesto, and Vegh, Carlos. 2000. "Tax Base Variability and Procyclical Fiscal Policy." National Bureau of Economic Research Working Paper 7499. Cambridge, MA.

Tavares, J., and Wacziarg, R. 2001. "How Democracy Affects Growth." *European Economic Review* 45 (8): 1341–78.

Telles, Edward, and Nelson Lim. 1999. "Interessa Quem Reponde a Questão Sobre Classificacão Racial e Desigualdade de Renda no Brasil?" *Estudio Afro-Asiaticos* 35: 7–27.

Tendler, Judith. 1997. *Good Government in the Tropics.* Baltimore: Johns Hopkins University Press.

———. 2001. "Transforming Local Economies: Lessons from the Northeast Brazilian Experience." Massachusetts Institute of Technology, Department of Urban Studies and Planning, Cambridge, MA. Processed.

———. 2002. "Small Firms, the Informal Sector and the Devil's Deal." *IDS Bulletin* 33 (3).

Teranishi, Juro. 1997. "Sectoral Resource Transfers, Conflict and Macrostability in Economic Development: A Comparative Analysis." In Masahiko Aoki, Hyung-Ki Kim, and Masahiro Okuno-Fujiwara, eds. *The Role of Government in East Asian Economic Development.* Oxford and New York: Oxford University Press.

Teruel, G., and B. Davis. 2000. "Final Report: An Evaluation of the Impact of PROGRESA Cash Payments on Private Inter-household Transfers." International Food Policy Research Institute, Washington, D.C.

Teulings, C., J. Hartog, and S. Bazen. "Corporatism or Competition? Labour Contracts, Institutions, and Wage Structures in International Comparison." *Economic Journal* 111 (475): F802–04.

Thiesenhusen, W. 1995. *Broken Promises: Agrarian Reform and the Latin American Campesino.* Boulder, CO: Westview Press.

Thomas, D. 1999. "Comments on Acosta." In J. Méndez, G. O'Donnell, and P. Pinheiro, eds., *The Rule of Law and the Underprivileged in Latin America.* Notre Dame, IN: University of Notre Dame Press.

Thomas, Vinod, Yan Wang, and Xibo Fan. 2002. "A New Dataset on Inequality and Education: Gini and Theil Indices of Schooling for 140 countries: 1960–2000." Washington, D.C. World Bank.

Tilly, Charles. 1999. *Durable Inequality.* Berkeley: University of California Press.

Tobin, J. 1970. "On Limiting the Domain of Inequality." *Journal of Law and Economics* 13: 263–77.

Tokman, V., and G. O'Donnell. 1998. *Poverty and Inequality in Latin America: Issues and New Challenges.* Notre Dame, IN: The University of Notre Dame Press.

Torres-Saillant, Silvia. 1998. "The Tribulations of Blackness: Stages in Dominican Racial Identity." *Latin American Perspectives* 25 (3): 126–46.

Trejos, J. 1999. "Reformas Económicas y Distribución del Ingreso en Costa Rica." Reformas Económicas series 37. Economic Commision for Latin America and the Caribbean, Santiago.

Tsebelis, George. 1995. "Decision Making in Political Systems: Veto Players in Presidentialism, Parliamentarism, Multicameralism, and Multipartyism." *British Journal of Political Science* 25 (3): 289–325.

———. 1999. "Veto Players and Law Production in Parliamentary Democracies: An Empirical Analysis." *American Political Science Review* 93 (3): 591–609.

———. Forthcoming. *Veto Players: How Political Institutions Work.* Princeton, NJ: Princeton University Press.

Ungar, M. 2002. *Elusive Reform: Democracy and the Rule of Law in Latin America.* Boulder, CO: Lynne Rienner Publishers, Inc.

United Nations Development Programme, Population Division. 1993. *Human Development Report 1993.* New York: United Nations Development Programme and Oxford University Press.

———. 2000. *World Population Prospects: The 2000 Revision, Volume I.* New York: United Nations.

United Nations Statistics Division. 2002. *Population and Vital Statistics Report*, Statistical papers, Series A, 54 (4). http://unstats.un.org/unsd/seriesa

Valenzuela, Arturo. 1977. *Political Brokers in Chile.* Durham, NC: Duke University Press.

Valle Silva, Nelson do. 2001. "Race, Poverty, and Social Exclusion in Brazil." In Estanislao Gacitúa-Marió and Carlos Sojo, eds., *Social Exclusion and Poverty Reduction in Latin America and the Caribbean.* Washington, D.C: World Bank.

Van Cott, D. 2000. "Party System Development and Indigenous Populations in Latin America: The Bolivian Case." *Party Politics* 6 (2): 155–74.

Velasco, Andrés. 1996. "Fixed Exchange Rates: Credibility, Flexibility and Multiplicity." *European Economic Review* 40: 1023–35.

Velázquez, Ernesto. 1982. "Los Mecanismos del Subdesarrollo en una Región Marginada de Colombia: Estudio de la Evolución de las Condiciones de Vida de la Población Nariñense-1982." Bogotá, Cámara de Representantes. Mimeo.

Vélez, C. E. 1995. *Gasto Social y Desigualdad: Logros y Extravíos.* Santa Fé de Bogotá: Misión Social, Departamento Nacional de Planeación.

Vélez, C. E., and V. Foster. 2003. "Public Social Spending in Colombia: Incidence and Sector Priorities in the 1990s." In Q. Wodon, ed., "Public Spending, Poverty, and Inequality in Latin America." World Bank, Washington, D.C. Processed.

Vianna, M. L. 1998. *Americanização (Perversa) da Seguridade Social no Brasil: Estratégias de Bem-estar e Políticas Públicas.* Rio de Janeiro: Editora Revan.

Vicepresidencia de la República de Colombia. 2002. "Observatory on Human Rights in Colombia." Bulletin 22. Presidential Program on Human Rights, Bogotá.

von Amsberg, J., Peter Lanjouw, and K. Nead. 2003. "The Poverty Targeting of Social Spending in Brazil." In Q. Wodon, ed., "Public Spending, Poverty, and Inequality in Latin America." World Bank, Washington, D.C. Processed.

Wagstaff, A. 2000. "Socioeconomic Inequality in Child Mortality: Comparisons Across Nine Developing Countries." *Bulletin of the World Health Organization* 78 (1): 19–29.

———. 2001. "Inequalities in Health in Developing Countries: Swimming Against the Tide?" World Bank Working Paper 2795. Washington, D.C.

Wagstaff, A., and N. Watanabe. 2000. *Socioeconomic Inequalities in Child Malnutrition in the Developing World.* World Bank Working Paper 2434. Washington, D.C.

Weisman, S. 2002. *The Great Tax Wars.* New York: Simon and Schuster.

Weyland, Kurt. 1995. "Social Movements and the State: the Politics of Health Reform in Brazil." *World Development* 23 (10): 1699–712.

———. 1996a. "Neopopulism and Neoliberalism in Latin America: Unexpected Affinities." *Studies in Comparative International Development.* 31 (3): 3–31.

———. 1996b. *Democracy without Equity: Failures of Reform in Brazil.* Pittsburgh, PA.: University of Pittsburgh Press.

———. 1997. "Growth with Equity in Chile's New Democracy?" *Latin American Research Review* 32 (1).

Whalley, J. 1984. "Regression or Progression: The Taxing Question of Incidence Analysis." *Canadian Journal of Economics* 17 (4): 654–82.

Williamson, Jeffery G. 1999. "Real Wages, Inequality and Globalization in Latin America before 1940." *Revista de Historia Economica* 17: 101–42.

Willis E., C. Garman, and S. Haggard. 1999. "The Politics of Decentralization in Latin America." *Latin American Research Review* 34 (1): 7–56.

Wodon, Quentin, ed. 2003. "Public Spending, Poverty, and Inequality in Latin America." World Bank, Washington, D.C. Processed.

Wodon, Quentin T., Robert Ayres, Matias Barenstein, Norman Hicks, Kihoon Lee, William F. Maloney, Pia Peeters, Corinne Siaens, and Shlomo Yitzhaki. 2000. *Poverty and Policy in Latin America and the Caribbean.* Washington, D.C.: World Bank.

Wodon, Quentin, Rodrigo Castro-Fernández, Kihoon Lee, Gladys López-Acevedo, Corinne Siaens, Carlos Sobrado, Jean-Philippe Tre. 2001. "Poverty in Latin America: Trends (1986–1998) and Determinants." *Cuadernos de Economía* 38 (114): 127–53.

Wodon, Quentin, N. Hicks, B. Ryan, and G. González. 2003. "Are Governments Pro-Poor but Short-Sighted? Targeted and Social Spending for the Poor during Booms and Busts." In Quentin Wodon, ed., "Public Spending, Poverty, and Inequality in Latin America." World Bank, Washington, D.C. Processed.

Wodon, Quentin, and William Maloney. 2000. "Self-employment as an Explanation for High Inequality in Latin America." World Bank, Washington, D.C. Processed.

Wolfson, M. 1994. "When Inequalities Diverge." *The American Economic Review.* 84 (2): 353–58.

Wood, Adrian. 1997. "Openness and Wage Inequality in Developing Countries: The Latin American Challenge to East Asia Conventional Wisdom." *The World Bank Economic Review* 11 (1): 33–57.

Woodward, Ralph L. 1966. *Class Privilege and Economic Development: The Consulado de Comercio of Guatemala 1793–1871.* Chapel Hill: University of North Carolina Press.

World Bank. 1990. *World Development Report 1990: Poverty.* New York: Oxford University Press.

———. 1993. *The East Asian Miracle.* New York: Oxford University Press.

———. 1995. *World Development Report 1995: Workers in an Integrating World.* New York: Oxford University Press.

———. 1997. *World Development Report 1997: The State in a Changing World.* New York: Oxford University Press.

———. 1999. *World Development Report: Entering the 21st Century: The Changing Development Landscape.* New York: Oxford University Press.

———. 2000a. *Argentina: Poor People in a Rich Country.* Washington, D.C.: World Bank.

———. 2000b. *World Development Report 2000/01: Attacking Poverty.* New York: Oxford University Press.

———. 2000c. *Bolivia: From Patronage to a Professional State, Institutional and Governance Review.* Washington D.C.: World Bank.

———. 2000d. *Making Transition Work for Everyone: Poverty and Inequality in Europe and Central Asia.* Washington D.C.: World Bank.

———. 2000e. *Reforming Public Institutions and Strengthening Governance: A World Bank Strategy.* Washington, D.C.: World Bank, Public Sector Group, Poverty Reduction and Economic Management (PREM) Network.

———. 2000f. *Ecuador Gender Review: Issues and Recommendations.* Washington D.C.: World Bank.

———. 2001a. *Household Risk, Self-Insurance, and Coping Strategies in Urban Argentina.* Report 22426-AR. Washington D.C.: World Bank.

———. 2001b. *Mexico: Land Policy: A Decade after the Ejido Reform.* Washington D.C.: World Bank.

———. 2001c. *Peru—Institutional and Governance Review.* Washington D.C.: World Bank.

———. 2002a. *A Review of Gender Issues in the Dominican Republic, Haiti, and Jamaica.* Report 21866. Washington D.C.: World Bank.

———. 2002b. *Guatemala Poverty Assessment.* Washington D.C.: World Bank.

———. 2002c. *Brazil Gender Review: Issues and Recommendations.* Washington D.C.: World Bank.

———. 2003a. *World Development Report 2004: Making Services Work for Poor People.* New York: Oxford University Press.

———. 2003b. *Colombia: The Economic Foundation of Peace.* Washington D.C.: World Bank.

———. 2003c. *Land Policy for Growth and Poverty Reduction.* Washington D.C.: World Bank.

———. 2003d. *Brazil: Strategies for Poverty Reduction in Ceará.* Washington D.C.: World Bank.

———. 2003e. *Caribbean Economic Overview 2002: Macroeconomic Volatility, Household Vulnerability and Institutional and Policy Responses.* Washington D.C.: World Bank.

———. 2003f. *Jamaica: The Road to Sustained Growth and Poverty Reduction, Country Economic Memorandum 2003.* Washington D.C.: World Bank.

———. 2003g. *Country Assistance Strategy for the Dominican Republic.* Washington D.C.: World Bank.

———. 2003h. *Colombia: Land Policy in Transition.* Washington D.C: World Bank.

———. 2004 "Minimum Wages in Latin America: The Impact on Employment, Inequality and Poverty." Latin America and Caribbean Region, Washington, D.C., World Bank. Mimeographed.

———. Forthcoming. *El Salvador: Poverty Assessment.* Washington D.C.: World Bank.

World Development Indicators Database. http://www.worldbank.org/data/wdi2003/. World Bank, Washington, D.C.

World Economic Forum. 2003. *Global Competitiveness Report 2002–2003.* Peter Cornelius, Klaus Schwab, and Michael E. Porter, eds. New York: Oxford University Press.

WIDER (World Institute for Development Economics Research). 2000. UNU/WIDER-UNDP World Income Database, Version 1.0 (September).

Wossmann, L. 2000. "Schooling Resources, Educational Institutions and Student Performance: The International Evidence." Kiel Institute of World Economics Working Paper 983, Kiel, Germany.

Yaschine, Iliana. 1999. "The Changing Anti-poverty Agenda: What can the Mexican Case Tell Us?" *IDS Bulletin* 30 (2): 47–60.

Printed in the United States
56028LVS00005B/23-56

9 780821 356654